Beautiful Code

Other resources from O'Reilly

Related titles

Applied Software Project Management	Head First Object-Oriented Analysis & Design
The Art of Project Management	Mastering Regular Expressions
Database in Depth	The Myths of Innovation
Essential Business Process Modeling	Prefactoring
Head First Design Patterns	Process Improvement Essentials

oreilly.com

oreilly.com is more than a complete catalog of O'Reilly books. You'll also find links to news, events, articles, weblogs, sample chapters, and code examples.

oreillynet.com is the essential portal for developers interested in open and emerging technologies, including new platforms, programming languages, and operating systems.

Conferences

O'Reilly brings diverse innovators together to nurture the ideas that spark revolutionary industries. We specialize in documenting the latest tools and systems, translating the innovator's knowledge into useful skills for those in the trenches. Visit *conferences.oreilly.com* for our upcoming events.

Safari Bookshelf (*safari.oreilly.com*) is the premier online reference library for programmers and IT professionals. Conduct searches across more than 1,000 books. Subscribers can zero in on answers to time-critical questions in a matter of seconds. Read the books on your Bookshelf from cover to cover or simply flip to the page you need. Try it today for free.

Beautiful Code

Edited by Andy Oram and Greg Wilson

O'REILLY®

Beijing • Cambridge • Farnham • Köln • Paris • Sebastopol • Taipei • Tokyo

Beautiful Code
Edited by Andy Oram and Greg Wilson

Copyright © 2007 O'Reilly Media, Inc. All rights reserved. Printed in the United States of America.

Published by O'Reilly Media, Inc. 1005 Gravenstein Highway North, Sebastopol, CA 95472

O'Reilly books may be purchased for educational, business, or sales promotional use. Online editions are also available for most titles (*safari.oreilly.com*). For more information, contact our corporate/institutional sales department: (800) 998-9938 or *corporate@oreilly.com*.

Production Editor: Marlowe Shaeffer	**Cover Designer:** Randy Comer
Copyeditor: Sanders Kleinfeld	**Interior Designer:** Marcia Friedman
Proofreader: Sohaila Abdulali	**Illustrator:** Jessamyn Read
Indexer: Ellen Troutman Zaig	

Printing History:

June 2007:   First Edition.

 This book uses RepKover™, a durable and flexible lay-flat binding.

ISBN-10: 0-596-51004-7
ISBN-13: 978-0-596-51004-6
[C]

All royalties from this book will be donated to Amnesty International.

CONTENTS

Foreword

Greg Wilson

I GOT MY FIRST JOB AS A PROGRAMMER IN THE SUMMER OF **1982.** Two weeks after I started, one of the system administrators loaned me Kernighan and Plauger's *The Elements of Programming Style* (McGraw-Hill) and Wirth's *Algorithms + Data Structures = Programs* (Prentice Hall). They were a revelation—for the first time, I saw that programs could be more than just instructions for computers. They could be as elegant as well-made kitchen cabinets, as graceful as a suspension bridge, or as eloquent as one of George Orwell's essays.

Time and again since that summer, I have heard people bemoan the fact that our profession doesn't teach students to see this. Architects are taught to look at buildings, and composers study one another's scores, but programmers—they look at each other's work only when there's a bug to fix; even then, they try to look at as little as possible. We tell students to use sensible variable names, introduce them to some basic design patterns, and then wonder why so much of what they write is so ugly.

This book is our attempt to fix this. In May 2006, I asked some well-known (and not so well-known) software designers to dissect and discuss the most beautiful piece of code they knew. As this book shows, they have found beauty in many different places. For some, it lives in the small details of elegantly crafted software. Others find beauty in the big picture—in how a program's structure allows it to evolve gracefully over time, or in the techniques used to build it.

Wherever they find it, I am grateful to our contributors for taking time to give us a tour. I hope that you enjoy reading this book as much as Andy and I have enjoyed editing it, and that it inspires you to create something beautiful, too.

Preface

BEAUTIFUL **C**ODE WAS CONCEIVED BY **G**REG **W**ILSON IN **2006** as a way to elicit insights from leading software developers and computer scientists. Together, he and his co-editor, Andy Oram, approached experts with diverse backgrounds from all over the world. They received a flood of responses, partly because royalties from the book are being donated to Amnesty International. The results of the project appear in this volume.

As wide-ranging as this book is, it represents just a small fraction of what is happening in this most exciting of fields. Thousand of other projects, equally interesting and educational, are being moved forward every day by other programmers whom we did not contact. Furthermore, many excellent practitioners who were asked for chapters do not appear in this book because they were too busy at the time, preferred not to contribute to Amnesty International, or had conflicting obligations. To benefit from the insights of all these people, we hope to do further books along similar lines in the future.

How This Book Is Organized

Chapter 1, *A Regular Expression Matcher*, by Brian Kernighan, shows how deep insight into a language and a problem can lead to a concise and elegant solution.

Chapter 2, *Subversion's Delta Editor: Interface As Ontology*, by Karl Fogel, starts with a well-chosen abstraction and demonstrates its unifying effects on the system's further development.

Chapter 3, *The Most Beautiful Code I Never Wrote*, by Jon Bentley, suggests how to measure a procedure without actually executing it.

Chapter 4, *Finding Things*, by Tim Bray, draws together many strands in Computer Science in an exploration of a problem that is fundamental to many computing tasks.

Chapter 5, *Correct, Beautiful, Fast (in That Order): Lessons from Designing XML Verifiers*, by Elliotte Rusty Harold, reconciles the often conflicting goals of thoroughness and good performance.

Chapter 6, *Framework for Integrated Test: Beauty Through Fragility*, by Michael Feathers, presents an example that breaks the rules and achieves its own elegant solution.

Chapter 7, *Beautiful Tests*, by Alberto Savoia, shows how a broad, creative approach to testing can not only eliminate bugs but turn you into a better programmer.

Chapter 8, *On-the-Fly Code Generation for Image Processing*, by Charles Petzold, drops down a level to improve performance while maintaining portability.

Chapter 9, *Top Down Operator Precedence*, by Douglas Crockford, revives an almost forgotten parsing technique and shows its new relevance to the popular JavaScript language.

Chapter 10, *The Quest for an Accelerated Population Count*, by Henry S. Warren, Jr., reveals the impact that some clever algorithms can have on even a seemingly simple problem.

Chapter 11, *Secure Communication: The Technology Of Freedom*, by Ashish Gulhati, discusses the directed evolution of a secure messaging application that was designed to make sophisticated but often confusing cryptographic technology intuitively accessible to users.

Chapter 12, *Growing Beautiful Code in BioPerl*, by Lincoln Stein, shows how the combination of a flexible language and a custom-designed module can make it easy for people with modest programming skills to create powerful visualizations for their data.

Chapter 13, *The Design of the Gene Sorter*, by Jim Kent, combines simple building blocks to produce a robust and valuable tool for gene researchers.

Chapter 14, *How Elegant Code Evolves with Hardware: The Case of Gaussian Elimination*, by Jack Dongarra and Piotr Luszczek, surveys the history of LINPACK and related major software packages to show how assumptions must constantly be re-evaluated in the face of new computing architectures.

Chapter 15, *The Long-Term Benefits of Beautiful Design*, by Adam Kolawa, explains how attention to good design principles many decades ago helped CERN's widely used mathematical library (the predecessor of LINPACK) stand the test of time.

Chapter 16, *The Linux Kernel Driver Model: The Benefits of Working Together*, by Greg Kroah-Hartman, explains how many efforts by different collaborators to solve different problems led to the successful evolution of a complex, multithreaded system.

Chapter 17, *Another Level of Indirection*, by Diomidis Spinellis, shows how the flexibility and maintainability of the FreeBSD kernel is promoted by abstracting operations done in common by many drivers and filesystem modules.

Chapter 18, *Python's Dictionary Implementation: Being All Things to All People*, by Andrew Kuchling, explains how a careful design combined with accommodations for a few special cases allows a language feature to support many different uses.

Chapter 19, *Multidimensional Iterators in NumPy*, by Travis E. Oliphant, takes you through the design steps that succeed in hiding complexity under a simple interface.

Chapter 20, *A Highly Reliable Enterprise System for NASA's Mars Rover Mission*, by Ronald Mak, uses industry standards, best practices, and Java technologies to meet the requirements of a NASA expedition where reliability cannot be in doubt.

Chapter 21, *ERP5: Designing for Maximum Adaptability*, by Rogerio Atem de Carvalho and Rafael Monnerat, shows how a powerful ERP system can be developed with free software tools and a flexible architecture.

Chapter 22, *A Spoonful of Sewage*, by Bryan Cantrill, lets the reader accompany the author through a hair-raising bug scare and a clever solution that violated expectations.

Chapter 23, *Distributed Programming with MapReduce*, by Jeff Dean and Sanjay Ghemawat, describes a system that provides an easy-to-use programming abstraction for large-scale distributed data processing at Google that automatically handles many difficult aspects of distributed computation, including automatic parallelization, load balancing, and failure handling.

Chapter 24, *Beautiful Concurrency*, by Simon Peyton Jones, removes much of the difficulty of parallel programs through Software Transactional Memory, demonstrated here using Haskell.

Chapter 25, *Syntactic Abstraction: The syntax-case Expander*, by R. Kent Dybvig, shows how macros—a key feature of many languages and systems—can be protected in Scheme from producing erroneous output.

Chapter 26, *Labor-Saving Architecture: An Object-Oriented Framework for Networked Software*, by William R. Otte and Douglas C. Schmidt, applies a range of standard object-oriented design techniques, such as patterns and frameworks, to distributed logging to keep the system flexible and modular.

Chapter 27, *Integrating Business Partners the RESTful Way*, by Andrew Patzer, demonstrates a designer's respect for his programmers by matching the design of a B2B web service to its requirements.

Chapter 28, *Beautiful Debugging*, by Andreas Zeller, shows how a disciplined approach to validating code can reduce the time it takes to track down errors.

Chapter 29, *Treating Code As an Essay*, by Yukihiro Matsumoto, lays out some challenging principles that drove his design of the Ruby programming language, and that, by extension, will help produce better software in general.

Chapter 30, *When a Button Is All That Connects You to the World*, by Arun Mehta, takes you on a tour through the astounding interface design choices involved in a text-editing system that allows people with severe motor disabilities, like Professor Stephen Hawking, to communicate via a computer.

Chapter 31, *Emacspeak: The Complete Audio Desktop*, by T. V. Raman, shows how Lisp's advice facility can be used with Emacs to address a general need—generating rich spoken output—that cuts across all aspects of the Emacs environment, without modifying the underlying source code of a large software system.

Chapter 32, *Code in Motion*, by Laura Wingerd and Christopher Seiwald, lists some simple rules that have unexpectedly strong impacts on programming accuracy.

Chapter 33, *Writing Programs for "The Book"*, by Brian Hayes, explores the frustrations of solving a seemingly simple problem in computational geometry, and its surprising resolution.

Conventions Used in This Book

The following typographical conventions are used in this book:

Italic

Indicates new terms, mathematical variables, URLs, file and directory names, and commands.

`Constant width`

Indicates elements of program code, the contents of files, and text output displayed on a computer console.

`Constant width bold`

Shows commands or other text typed literally by the user.

`Constant width italic`

Shows text replaced with user-supplied values.

Using Code Examples

This book is here to help you get your job done. In general, you may use the code in this book in your programs and documentation. You do not need to contact us for permission unless you're reproducing a significant portion of the code. For example, writing a program that uses several chunks of code from this book does not require permission. Selling or distributing a CD-ROM of examples from O'Reilly books *does* require permission.

Answering a question by citing this book and quoting example code does not require permission. Incorporating a significant amount of example code from this book into your product's documentation *does* require permission.

We appreciate, but do not require, attribution. An attribution usually includes the title, author, publisher, and ISBN. For example: "*Beautiful Code*, edited by Andy Oram and Greg Wilson. Copyright 2007 O'Reilly Media, Inc., 978-0-596-51004-6."

If you feel your use of code examples falls outside fair use or the permission given above, feel free to contact us at *permissions@oreilly.com*.

How to Contact Us

Please address comments and questions concerning this book to the publisher:

O'Reilly Media, Inc.
1005 Gravenstein Highway North
Sebastopol, CA 95472
800-998-9938 (in the United States or Canada)
707-829-0515 (international or local)
707-829-0104 (fax)

We have a web page for this book, where we list errata, examples, and any additional information. You can access this page at:

http://www.oreilly.com/catalog/9780596510046

To comment or ask technical questions about this book, send email to:

bookquestions@oreilly.com

For more information about our books, conferences, Resource Centers, and the O'Reilly Network, see our web site at:

http://www.oreilly.com

Safari® Enabled

 When you see a Safari® Enabled icon on the cover of your favorite technology book, that means the book is available online through the O'Reilly Network Safari Bookshelf.

Safari offers a solution that's better than e-books. It's a virtual library that lets you easily search thousands of top tech books, cut and paste code samples, download chapters, and find quick answers when you need the most accurate, current information. Try it for free at *http://safari.oreilly.com*.

## CHAPTER ONE

A Regular Expression Matcher

Brian Kernighan

REGULAR EXPRESSIONS ARE NOTATIONS FOR DESCRIBING PATTERNS OF TEXT and, in effect, make up a special-purpose language for pattern matching. Although there are myriad variants, all share the idea that most characters in a pattern match literal occurrences of themselves, but some *metacharacters* have special meaning, such as * to indicate some kind of repetition or [...] to mean any one character from the set within the brackets.

In practice, most searches in programs such as text editors are for literal words, so the regular expressions are often literal strings like print, which will match printf or sprint or printer paper anywhere. In so-called *wildcards* used to specify filenames in Unix and Windows, a * matches any number of characters, so the pattern *.c matches all filenames that end in .c. There are many, many variants of regular expressions, even in contexts where one would expect them to be the same. Jeffrey Friedl's *Mastering Regular Expressions* (O'Reilly) is an exhaustive study of the topic.

Stephen Kleene invented regular expressions in the mid-1950s as a notation for finite automata; in fact, they are equivalent to finite automata in what they represent. They first appeared in a program setting in Ken Thompson's version of the QED text editor in the mid-1960s. In 1967, Thompson applied for a patent on a mechanism for rapid text matching based on regular expressions. The patent was granted in 1971, one of the very first software patents [U.S. Patent 3,568,156, Text Matching Algorithm, March 2, 1971].

Regular expressions moved from QED to the Unix editor *ed*, and then to the quintessential Unix tool *grep*, which Thompson created by performing radical surgery on *ed*. These widely used programs helped regular expressions become familiar throughout the early Unix community.

Thompson's original matcher was very fast because it combined two independent ideas. One was to generate machine instructions on the fly during matching so that it ran at machine speed rather than by interpretation. The other was to carry forward all possible matches at each stage, so it did not have to backtrack to look for alternative potential matches. In later text editors that Thompson wrote, such as *ed*, the matching code used a simpler algorithm that backtracked when necessary. In theory, this is slower, but the patterns found in practice rarely involved backtracking, so the *ed* and *grep* algorithm and code were good enough for most purposes.

Subsequent regular expression matchers like *egrep* and *fgrep* added richer classes of regular expressions, and focused on fast execution no matter what the pattern. Ever-fancier regular expressions became popular and were included not only in C-based libraries, but also as part of the syntax of scripting languages such as Awk and Perl.

The Practice of Programming

In 1998, Rob Pike and I were writing *The Practice of Programming* (Addison-Wesley). The last chapter of the book, "Notation," collected a number of examples where good notation led to better programs and better programming. This included the use of simple data specifications (printf, for instance), and the generation of code from tables.

Because of our Unix backgrounds and nearly 30 years of experience with tools based on regular expression notation, we naturally wanted to include a discussion of regular expressions, and it seemed mandatory to include an implementation as well. Given our emphasis on tools, it also seemed best to focus on the class of regular expressions found in *grep*—rather than, say, those from shell wildcards—since we could also then talk about the design of *grep* itself.

The problem was that any existing regular expression package was far too big. The local *grep* was over 500 lines long (about 10 book pages) and encrusted with barnacles. Open source regular expression packages tended to be huge—roughly the size of the entire book—because they were engineered for generality, flexibility, and speed; none were remotely suitable for pedagogy.

I suggested to Rob that we find the smallest regular expression package that would illustrate the basic ideas while still recognizing a useful and nontrivial class of patterns. Ideally, the code would fit on a single page.

Rob disappeared into his office. As I remember it now, he emerged in no more than an hour or two with the 30 lines of C code that subsequently appeared in Chapter 9 of *The Practice of Programming*. That code implements a regular expression matcher that handles the following constructs.

Character	Meaning
c	Matches any literal character c.
. (period)	Matches any single character.
^	Matches the beginning of the input string.
$	Matches the end of the input string.
*	Matches zero or more occurrences of the previous character.

This is quite a useful class; in my own experience of using regular expressions on a day-to-day basis, it easily accounts for 95 percent of all instances. In many situations, solving the right problem is a big step toward creating a beautiful program. Rob deserves great credit for choosing a very small yet important, well-defined, and extensible set of features from among a wide set of options.

Rob's implementation itself is a superb example of beautiful code: compact, elegant, efficient, and useful. It's one of the best examples of recursion that I have ever seen, and it shows the power of C pointers. Although at the time we were most interested in conveying the important role of good notation in making a program easier to use (and perhaps easier to write as well), the regular expression code has also been an excellent way to illustrate algorithms, data structures, testing, performance enhancement, and other important topics.

Implementation

In *The Practice of Programming*, the regular expression matcher is part of a standalone program that mimics *grep*, but the regular expression code is completely separable from its surroundings. The main program is not interesting here; like many Unix tools, it reads either its standard input or a sequence of files, and prints those lines that contain a match of the regular expression.

This is the matching code:

```
/* match: search for regexp anywhere in text */
int match(char *regexp, char *text)
{
    if (regexp[0] == '^')
        return matchhere(regexp+1, text);
    do {    /* must look even if string is empty */
        if (matchhere(regexp, text))
            return 1;
    } while (*text++ != '\0');
    return 0;
}

/* matchhere: search for regexp at beginning of text */
int matchhere(char *regexp, char *text)
{
    if (regexp[0] == '\0')
        return 1;
    if (regexp[1] == '*')
        return matchstar(regexp[0], regexp+2, text);
```

```
        if (regexp[0] == '$' && regexp[1] == '\0')
            return *text == '\0';
        if (*text!='\0' && (regexp[0]=='.' || regexp[0]==*text))
            return matchhere(regexp+1, text+1);
        return 0;
    }

    /* matchstar: search for c*regexp at beginning of text */
    int matchstar(int c, char *regexp, char *text)
    {
        do {    /* a * matches zero or more instances */
            if (matchhere(regexp, text))
                return 1;
        } while (*text != '\0' && (*text++ == c || c == '.'));
        return 0;
    }
```

Discussion

The function match(regexp, text) tests whether there is an occurrence of the regular
expression anywhere within the text; it returns 1 if a match is found and 0 if not. If there
is more than one match, it finds the leftmost and shortest.

The basic operation of match is straightforward. If the first character of the regular expression is ^ (an anchored match), any possible match must occur at the beginning of the
string. That is, if the regular expression is ^xyz, it matches xyz only if xyz occurs at the
beginning of the text, not somewhere in the middle. This is tested by matching the rest of
the regular expression against the text starting at the beginning and nowhere else. Otherwise, the regular expression might match anywhere within the string. This is tested by
matching the pattern against each character position of the text in turn. If there are multiple matches, only the first (leftmost) one will be identified. That is, if the regular expression is xyz, it will match the first occurrence of xyz regardless of where it occurs.

Notice that advancing over the input string is done with a do-while loop, a comparatively
unusual construct in C programs. The occurrence of a do-while instead of a while should
always raise a question: why isn't the loop termination condition being tested at the
beginning of the loop, before it's too late, rather than at the end after something has been
done? But the test is correct here: since the * operator permits zero-length matches, we
first have to check whether a null match is possible.

The bulk of the work is done in the function matchhere(regexp, text), which tests whether
the regular expression matches the text that begins right here. The function matchhere
operates by attempting to match the first character of the regular expression with the first
character of the text. If the match fails, there can be no match at this text position and
matchhere returns 0. If the match succeeds, however, it's possible to advance to the next
character of the regular expression and the next character of the text. This is done by calling matchhere recursively.

The situation is a bit more complicated because of some special cases, and of course the need to stop the recursion. The easiest case is that if the regular expression is at its end (regexp[0] == '\0'), all previous tests have succeeded, and thus the regular expression matches the text.

If the regular expression is a character followed by a *, matchstar is called to see whether the closure matches. The function matchstar(c, regexp, text) tries to match repetitions of the text character c, beginning with zero repetitions and counting up, until it either finds a match of the rest of the text, or it fails and thus concludes that there is no match. This algorithm identifies a "shortest match," which is fine for simple pattern matching as in *grep*, where all that matters is finding a match as quickly as possible. A "longest match" is more intuitive and almost certain to be better for a text editor where the matched text will be replaced. Most modern regular expression libraries provide both alternatives, and *The Practice of Programming* presents a simple variant of matchstar for this case, shown below.

If the regular expression consists of a $ at the end of the expression, the text matches only if it too is at its end:

```
if (regexp[0] == '$' && regexp[1] == '\0')
    return *text == '\0';
```

Otherwise, if we are not at the end of the text string (that is, *text!='\0'), and if the first character of the text string matches the first character of the regular expression, so far so good; we go on to test whether the next character of the regular expression matches the next character of the text by making a recursive call to matchhere. This recursive call is the heart of the algorithm and the reason why the code is so compact and clean.

If all of these attempts to match fail, there can be no match at this point between the regular expression and the text, so matchhere returns 0.

This code uses C pointers intensively. At each stage of the recursion, if something matches, the recursive call that follows uses pointer arithmetic (e.g., regexp+1 and text+1) so that the subsequent function is called with the next character of the regular expression and of the text. The depth of recursion is no more than the length of the pattern, which in normal use is quite short, so there is no danger of running out of space.

Alternatives

This is a very elegant and well-written piece of code, but it's not perfect. What might we do differently? I might rearrange matchhere to deal with $ before *. Although it makes no difference here, it feels a bit more natural, and a good rule is to do easy cases before difficult ones.

In general, however, the order of tests is critical. For instance, in this test from matchstar:

```
} while (*text != '\0' && (*text++ == c || c == '.'));
```

we must advance over one more character of the text string no matter what, so the increment in text++ must always be performed.

This code is careful about termination conditions. Generally, the success of a match is determined by whether the regular expression runs out at the same time as the text does. If they do run out together, that indicates a match; if one runs out before the other, there is no match. This is perhaps most obvious in a line like:

```
if (regexp[0] == '$' && regexp[1] == '\0')
    return *text == '\0';
```

but subtle termination conditions show up in other cases as well.

The version of matchstar that implements leftmost longest matching begins by identifying a maximal sequence of occurrences of the input character c. Then it uses matchhere to try to extend the match to the rest of the pattern and the rest of the text. Each failure reduces the number of cs by one and tries again, including the case of zero occurrences:

```
/* matchstar: leftmost longest search for c*regexp */
int matchstar(int c, char *regexp, char *text)
{
    char *t;

    for (t = text; *t != '\0' && (*t == c || c == '.'); t++)
        ;
    do {  /* * matches zero or more */
        if (matchhere(regexp, t))
            return 1;
    } while (t-- > text);
    return 0;
}
```

Consider the regular expression (.*), which matches arbitrary text within parentheses. Given the target text:

```
for (t = text; *t != '\0' && (*t == c || c == '.'); t++)
```

a longest match from the beginning will identify the entire parenthesized expression, while a shortest match will stop at the first right parenthesis. (Of course a longest match beginning from the second left parenthesis will extend to the end of the text.)

Building on It

The purpose of *The Practice of Programming* was to teach good programming. At the time the book was written, Rob and I were still at Bell Labs, so we did not have firsthand experience of how the book would be best used in a classroom. It has been gratifying to discover that some of the material does work well in classes. I have used this code since 2000 as a vehicle for teaching important points about programming.

First, it shows how recursion is useful and leads to clean code in a novel setting; it's not yet another version of Quicksort (or factorial!), nor is it some kind of tree walk.

It's also a good example for performance experiments. Its performance is not very different from the system versions of *grep*, which shows that the recursive technique is not too costly and that it's not worth trying to tune the code.

On the other hand, it is also a fine illustration of the importance of a good algorithm. If a pattern includes several .* sequences, the straightforward implementation requires a lot of backtracking, and, in some cases, will run very slowly indeed.

The standard Unix *grep* has the same backtracking properties. For example, the command:

```
grep 'a.*a.*a.*a.a'
```

takes about 20 seconds to process a 4 MB text file on a typical machine.

An implementation based on converting a nondeterministic finite automaton to a deterministic automaton, as in *egrep*, will have much better performance on hard cases; it can process the same pattern and the same input in less than one-tenth of a second, and running time in general is independent of the pattern.

Extensions to the regular expression class can form the basis of a variety of assignments. For example:

1. Add other metacharacters, such as + for one or more occurrences of the previous character, or ? for zero or one matches. Add some way to quote metacharacters, such as \$ to stand for a literal occurrence of $.

2. Separate regular expression processing into a *compilation* phase and an *execution* phase. Compilation converts the regular expression into an internal form that makes the matching code simpler or allows the subsequent matching to run faster. This separation is not necessary for the simple class of regular expressions in the original design, but it makes sense in *grep*-like applications where the class is richer and the same regular expression is used for a large number of input lines.

3. Add character classes such as [abc] and [0-9], which in conventional *grep* notation match a or b or c and a digit, respectively. This can be done in several ways, the most natural of which seems to be replacing the char* variables of the original code with a structure:

```
typedef struct RE {
        int     type;   /* CHAR, STAR, etc. */
        int     ch;     /* the character itself */
        char    *ccl;   /* for [...] instead */
        int     nccl;   /* true if class is negated [^...] */
} RE;
```

and modifying the basic code to handle an array of these instead of an array of characters. It's not strictly necessary to separate compilation from execution for this situation, but it turns out to be a lot easier. Students who follow the advice to precompile into such a structure invariably do better than those who try to interpret some complicated pattern data structure on the fly.

Writing clear and unambiguous specifications for character classes is tough, and implementing them perfectly is worse, requiring a lot of tedious and uninstructive coding. I have simplified this assignment over time, and today most often ask for Perl-like shorthands such as \d for digit and \D for nondigit instead of the original bracketed ranges.

4. Use an opaque type to hide the RE structure and all the implementation details. This is a good way to show object-oriented programming in C, which doesn't support much beyond this. In effect, this creates a regular expression class that uses function names like RE_new( ) and RE_match( ) for the methods instead of the syntactic sugar of an object-oriented language.

5. Modify the class of regular expressions to be like the wildcards in various shells: matches are implicitly anchored at both ends, * matches any number of characters, and ? matches any single character. One can modify the algorithm or map the input into the existing algorithm.

6. Convert the code to Java. The original code uses C pointers very well, and it's good practice to figure out the alternatives in a different language. Java versions use either String.charAt (indexing instead of pointers) or String.substring (closer to the pointer version). Neither seems as clear as the C code, and neither is as compact. Although performance isn't really part of this exercise, it is interesting to see that the Java implementation runs roughly six or seven times slower than the C versions.

7. Write a wrapper class that converts from this class's regular expressions to Java's Pattern and Matcher classes, which separate the compilation and matching in a quite different way. This is a good example of the Adapter or Facade pattern, which puts a different face on an existing class or set of functions.

I've also used this code extensively to explore testing techniques. Regular expressions are rich enough that testing is far from trivial, but small enough that one can quickly write down a substantial collection of tests to be performed mechanically. For extensions like those just listed, I ask students to write a large number of tests in a compact language (yet another example of "notation") and use those tests on their own code; naturally, I use their tests on other students' code as well.

Conclusion

I was amazed by how compact and elegant this code was when Rob Pike first wrote it—it was much smaller and more powerful than I had thought possible. In hindsight, one can see a number of reasons why the code is so small.

First, the features are well chosen to be the most useful and to give the most insight into implementation, without any frills. For example, the implementation of the anchored patterns ^ and $ requires only three or four lines, but it shows how to deal with special cases cleanly before handling the general cases uniformly. The closure operation * must be present because it is a fundamental notion in regular expressions and provides the only way to handle patterns of unspecified lengths. But it would add no insight to also provide + and ?, so those are left as exercises.

Second, recursion is a win. This fundamental programming technique almost always leads to smaller, cleaner, and more elegant code than the equivalent written with explicit loops, and that is the case here. The idea of peeling off one matching character from the front of the regular expression and from the text, then recursing for the rest, echoes the recursive structure of the traditional factorial or string length examples, but in a much more interesting and useful setting.

Third, this code really uses the underlying language to good effect. Pointers can be misused, of course, but here they are used to create compact expressions that naturally express the extracting of individual characters and advancing to the next character. Array indexing or substrings can achieve the same effect, but in this code, pointers do a better job, especially when coupled with C idioms for autoincrement and implicit conversion of truth values.

I don't know of another piece of code that does so much in so few lines while providing such a rich source of insight and further ideas.

## CHAPTER TWO

Subversion's Delta Editor:
Interface As Ontology

Karl Fogel

EXAMPLES OF BEAUTIFUL CODE TEND TO BE LOCAL SOLUTIONS to well-bounded, easily comprehensible problems, such as Duff's Device (*http://en.wikipedia.org/wiki/Duff's_device*) or *rsync*'s rolling checksum algorithm (*http://en.wikipedia.org/wiki/Rsync#Algorithm*). This is not because small, simple solutions are the only beautiful kind, but because appreciating complex code requires more context than can be given on the back of a napkin.

Here, with the luxury of several pages to work in, I'd like to talk about a larger sort of beauty—not necessarily the kind that would strike a passing reader immediately, but the kind that programmers who work with the code on a regular basis would come to appreciate as they accumulate experience with the problem domain. My example is not an algorithm, but an interface: the programming interface used by the open source version control system Subversion (*http://subversion.tigris.org*) to express the difference between two directory trees, which is also the interface used to transform one tree into the other. In Subversion, its formal name is the C type `svn_delta_editor_t`, but it is known colloquially as the *delta editor*.

Subversion's delta editor demonstrates the properties that programmers look for in good design. It breaks down the problem along boundaries so natural that anyone designing a new feature for Subversion can easily tell when to call each function, and for what purpose. It presents the programmer with uncontrived opportunities to maximize efficiency (such as by eliminating unnecessary data transfers over the network) and allows for easy integration of auxiliary tasks (such as progress reporting). Perhaps most important, the design has proved very resilient during enhancements and updates.

And as if to confirm suspicions about the origins of good design, the delta editor was created by a single person over the course of a few hours (although that person was very familiar with the problem and the code base).

To understand what makes the delta editor beautiful, we must start by examining the problem it solves.

Version Control and Tree Transformation

Very early in the Subversion project, the team realized we had a general task that would be performed over and over: that of minimally expressing the difference between two similar (usually related) directory trees. As a version control system, one of Subversion's goals is to track revisions to directory structures as well as individual file contents. In fact, Subversion's server-side repository is fundamentally designed around directory versioning. A repository is simply a series of snapshots of a directory tree as that tree transforms over time. For each changeset committed to the repository, a new tree is created, differing from the preceding tree exactly where the changes are located and nowhere else. The unchanged portions of the new tree share storage with the preceding tree, and so on back into time. Each successive version of the tree is labeled with a monotonically increasing integer; this unique identifier is called a *revision number*.

Think of the repository as an array of revision numbers, stretching off into infinity. By convention, revision 0 is always an empty directory. In Figure 2-1, revision 1 has a tree hanging off it (typically the initial import of content into the repository), and no other revisions have been committed yet. The boxes represent nodes in this virtual filesystem: each node is either a directory (labeled DIR in the upper-right corner) or a file (labeled FILE).

What happens when we modify *tuna*? First, we make a new file node, containing the latest text. The new node is not connected to anything yet. As Figure 2-2 shows, it's just hanging out there in space, with no name.

Next, we create a new revision of its parent directory. As Figure 2-3 shows, the subgraph is still not connected to the revision array.

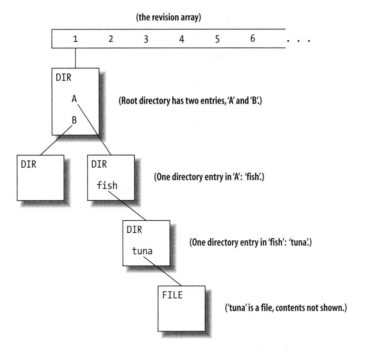

(the revision array)

1 2 3 4 5 6 . . .

DIR

A

B

(Root directory has two entries, 'A' and 'B'.)

DIR

DIR

fish

(One directory entry in 'A': 'fish'.)

DIR

tuna

(One directory entry in 'fish': 'tuna'.)

FILE

('tuna' is a file, contents not shown.)

FIGURE 2-1. Conceptual view of revision numbers

FILE

FIGURE 2-2. New node when just created

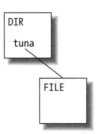

DIR

tuna

FILE

FIGURE 2-3. Creation of new parent directory

We continue up the line, creating a new revision of the next parent directory (Figure 2-4).

At the top, we create a new revision of the root directory, as shown in Figure 2-5. This new directory needs an entry to point to the "new" directory A, but since directory B hasn't changed at all, the new root directory also has an entry still pointing to the *old* directory B's node.

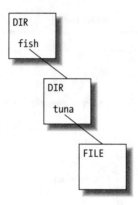

FIGURE 2-4. Continuing to move up, creating parent directories

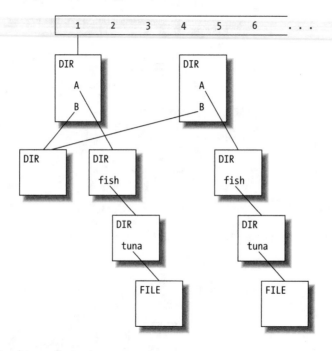

FIGURE 2-5. Complete new directory tree

Now that all the new nodes are written, we finish the "bubble up" process by linking the new tree to the next available revision in the history array, thus making it visible to repository users (Figure 2-6). In this case, the new tree becomes revision 2.

Thus each revision in the repository points to the root node of a unique tree, and the difference between that tree and the preceding one is the change that was committed in the new revision. To trace the changes, a program walks down both trees simultaneously, noting where entries point to different places. (For brevity, I've left out some details, such as saving storage space by compressing older nodes as differences against their newer versions.)

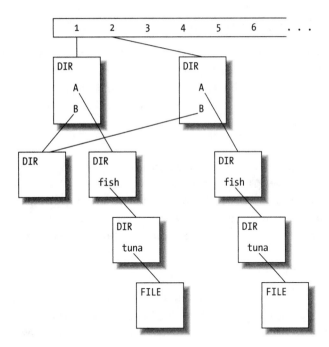

FIGURE 2-6. Finished revision: link to new tree

Although this tree-versioning model is all background to the main point of this chapter (the delta editor, which we'll come to soon), it has such nice properties that I considered making it the subject of its own chapter, as an example of beautiful code. Some of its attractive features are:

Easy reads

    To locate revision *n* of file */path/to/foo.txt*, one jumps to revision *n*, then walks down the tree to */path/to/foo.txt*.

Writers don't interfere with readers

    As writers create new nodes, bubbling their way up to the top, concurrent readers cannot see the work in progress. A new tree becomes visible to readers only after the writer makes its final "link" to a revision number in the repository.

Tree structure is versioned

    The very structure of each tree is being saved from revision to revision. File and directory renames, additions, and deletions become an intrinsic part of the repository's history.

If Subversion were only a repository, this would be the end of the story. However, there's a client side, too: the *working copy*, which is a user's checked-out copy of some revision tree plus whatever local edits the user has made but not yet committed. (Actually, working copies do not always reflect a single revision tree; they often contain mixtures of nodes from different revisions. This turns out not to make much of a difference as far as tree transformation is concerned. So, for the purposes of this chapter, just assume that a working copy represents some revision tree, though not necessarily that of the latest revision.)

Expressing Tree Differences

The most common action in Subversion is to transmit changes between the two sides: from the repository to the working copy when doing an update to receive others' changes, and from the working copy to the repository when committing one's own changes. Expressing the difference between two trees is also key to many other common operations—e.g., diffing, switching to a branch, merging changes from one branch to another, and so on.

Clearly it would be silly to have two different interfaces, one for server → client and another for client → server. The underlying task is the same in both cases. A tree difference is a tree difference, regardless of which direction it's traveling over the network or what its consumer intends to do with it. But finding a natural way to express tree differences proved surprisingly challenging. Complicating matters further, Subversion supports multiple network protocols and multiple backend storage mechanisms; we needed an interface that would look the same across all of those.

Our initial attempts to come up with an interface ranged from unsatisfying to downright awkward. I won't describe them all here, but what they had in common was that they tended to leave open questions for which there were no persuasive answers.

For example, many of the solutions involved transmitting the changed paths as strings, either as full paths or path components. Well, what order should the paths be transmitted in? Depth first? Breadth first? Random order? Alphabetical? Should there be different commands for directories than for files? Most importantly, how would each individual command expressing a difference know that it was part of a larger operation grouping all the changes into a unified set? In Subversion, the concept of the overall tree operation is quite user-visible, and if the programmatic interface didn't intrinsically match that concept, we'd surely need to write lots of brittle glue code to compensate.

In frustration, I drove with another developer, Ben Collins-Sussman, from Chicago down to Bloomington, Indiana, to seek the advice of Jim Blandy, who had invented Subversion's repository model in the first place, and who has, shall we say, strong opinions about design. Jim listened quietly as we described the various avenues we'd explored for transmitting tree differences, his expression growing grimmer and grimmer as we talked. When we reached the end of the list, he sat for a moment and then politely asked us to scram for a while so he could think. I put on my jogging shoes and went running; Ben stayed behind and read a book in another room or something. So much for collaborative development.

After I returned from my run and showered, Ben and I went back into Jim's den, and he showed us what he'd come up with. It is essentially what's in Subversion today; there have been various changes over the years, but none to its fundamental structure.

The Delta Editor Interface

Following is a mildly abridged version of the delta editor interface. I've left out the parts that deal with copying and renaming, the parts related to Subversion properties (properties are versioned metadata, and are not important here), and parts that handle some other Subversion-specific bookkeeping. However, you can always see the latest version of the delta editor by visiting *http://svn.collab.net/repos/svn/trunk/subversion/include/svn_delta.h*. This chapter is based on r21731 (that is, revision 21731) at *http://svn.collab.net/viewvc/svn/ trunk/subversion/include/svn_delta.h?revision=21731*.

To understand the interface, even in its abridged form, you'll need to know some Subversion jargon:

pools

> The pool arguments are memory pools—allocation buffers that allow a large number of objects to be freed simultaneously.

svn_error_t

> The return type svn_error_t simply means that the function returns a pointer to a Subversion error object; a successful call returns a null pointer.

text delta

> A text delta is the difference between two different versions of a file; you can apply a text delta as a patch to one version of the file to produce the other version. In Subversion, the "text" of a file is considered binary data—it doesn't matter whether the file is plain text, audio data, an image, or something else. Text deltas are expressed as streams of fixed-sized windows, each window containing a chunk of binary diff data. This way, peak memory usage is proportional to the size of a single window, rather than to the total size of the patch (which might be quite large in the case of, say, an image file).

window handler

> This is the function prototype for applying one window of text-delta data to a target file.

baton

> This is a void * data structure that provides context to a callback function. In other APIs, these are sometimes called void *ctx, void *userdata, or void *closure. Subversion calls them "batons" because they're passed around a lot, like batons in a relay race.

The interface starts with an introduction, to put a reader of the code in the right frame of mind. This text is almost unchanged since Jim Blandy wrote it in August of 2000, so the general concept has clearly weathered well:

```
/** Traversing tree deltas.
 *
 * In Subversion, we've got various producers and consumers of tree
 * deltas.
 *
```

```
 *  In processing a `commit' command:
 *  - The client examines its working copy data, and produces a tree
 *    delta describing the changes to be committed.
 *  - The client networking library consumes that delta, and sends them
 *    across the wire as an equivalent series of network requests.
 *  - The server receives those requests and produces a tree delta ---
 *    hopefully equivalent to the one the client produced above.
 *  - The Subversion server module consumes that delta and commits an
 *    appropriate transaction to the filesystem.
 *
 *  In processing an `update' command, the process is reversed:
 *  - The Subversion server module talks to the filesystem and produces
 *    a tree delta describing the changes necessary to bring the
 *    client's working copy up to date.
 *  - The server consumes this delta, and assembles a reply
 *    representing the appropriate changes.
 *  - The client networking library receives that reply, and produces a
 *    tree delta --- hopefully equivalent to the one the Subversion
 *    server produced above.
 *  - The working copy library consumes that delta, and makes the
 *    appropriate changes to the working copy.
 *
 *  The simplest approach would be to represent tree deltas using the
 *  obvious data structure.  To do an update, the server would
 *  construct a delta structure, and the working copy library would
 *  apply that structure to the working copy; the network layer's job
 *  would simply be to get the structure across the net intact.
 *
 *  However, we expect that these deltas will occasionally be too large
 *  to fit in a typical workstation's swap area.  For example, in
 *  checking out a 200Mb source tree, the entire source tree is
 *  represented by a single tree delta.  So it's important to handle
 *  deltas that are too large to fit in swap all at once.
 *
 *  So instead of representing the tree delta explicitly, we define a
 *  standard way for a consumer to process each piece of a tree delta
 *  as soon as the producer creates it.  The **svn_delta_editor_t**
 *  structure is a set of callback functions to be defined by a delta
 *  consumer, and invoked by a delta producer.  Each invocation of a
 *  callback function describes a piece of the delta --- a file's
 *  contents changing, something being renamed, etc.
 */
```

Then comes a long, formal documentation comment, followed by the interface itself, which is a callback table whose invocation order is partially constrained:

```
/** A structure full of callback functions the delta source will invoke
 * as it produces the delta.
 *
 * Function Usage
 * ==============
 *
 * Here's how to use these functions to express a tree delta.
 *
```

```
* The delta consumer implements the callback functions described in
* this structure, and the delta producer invokes them.  So the
* caller (producer) is pushing tree delta data at the callee
* (consumer).
*
* At the start of traversal, the consumer provides edit_baton, a
* baton global to the entire delta edit.
*
* Next, if there are any tree deltas to express, the producer should
* pass the edit_baton to the open_root function, to get a baton
* representing root of the tree being edited.
*
* Most of the callbacks work in the obvious way:
*
*     delete_entry
*     add_file
*     add_directory
*     open_file
*     open_directory
*
* Each of these takes a directory baton, indicating the directory
* in which the change takes place, and a path argument, giving the
* path (relative to the root of the edit) of the file,
* subdirectory, or directory entry to change. Editors will usually
* want to join this relative path with some base stored in the edit
* baton (e.g. a URL, a location in the OS filesystem).
*
* Since every call requires a parent directory baton, including
* add_directory and open_directory, where do we ever get our
* initial directory baton, to get things started?  The open_root
* function returns a baton for the top directory of the change.  In
* general, the producer needs to invoke the editor's open_root
* function before it can get anything of interest done.
*
* While open_root provides a directory baton for the root of
* the tree being changed, the add_directory and open_directory
* callbacks provide batons for other directories.  Like the
* callbacks above, they take a parent_baton and a relative path
* path, and then return a new baton for the subdirectory being
* created / modified --- child_baton.  The producer can then use
* child_baton to make further changes in that subdirectory.
*
* So, if we already have subdirectories named `foo' and `foo/bar',
* then the producer can create a new file named `foo/bar/baz.c' by
* calling:
*
*     - open_root () --- yielding a baton root for the top directory
*
*     - open_directory (root, "foo") --- yielding a baton f for `foo'
*
*     - open_directory (f, "foo/bar") --- yielding a baton b for `foo/bar'
*
*     - add_file (b, "foo/bar/baz.c")
*
```

```
 * When the producer is finished making changes to a directory, it
 * should call close_directory.  This lets the consumer do any
 * necessary cleanup, and free the baton's storage.
 *
 * The add_file and open_file callbacks each return a baton
 * for the file being created or changed.  This baton can then be
 * passed to apply_textdelta to change the file's contents.
 * When the producer is finished making changes to a file, it should
 * call close_file, to let the consumer clean up and free the baton.
 *
 * Function Call Ordering
 * ======================
 *
 * There are five restrictions on the order in which the producer
 * may use the batons:
 *
 * 1. The producer may call open_directory, add_directory,
 *    open_file, add_file at most once on any given directory
 *    entry. delete_entry may be called at most once on any given
 *    directory entry and may later be followed by add_directory or
 *    add_file on the same directory entry. delete_entry may
 *    not be called on any directory entry after open_directory,
 *    add_directory,open_file or add_file has been called on
 *    that directory entry.
 *
 * 2. The producer may not close a directory baton until it has
 *    closed all batons for its subdirectories.
 *
 * 3. When a producer calls open_directory or add_directory,
 *    it must specify the most recently opened of the currently open
 *    directory batons.  Put another way, the producer cannot have
 *    two sibling directory batons open at the same time.
 *
 * 4. When the producer calls open_file or add_file, it must
 *    follow with any changes to the file (using apply_textdelta),
 *    followed by a close_file call, before issuing any other
 *    file or directory calls.
 *
 * 5. When the producer calls apply_textdelta, it must make all of
 *    the window handler calls (including the NULL window at the
 *    end) before issuing any other svn_delta_editor_t calls.
 *
 * So, the producer needs to use directory and file batons as if it
 * is doing a single depth-first traversal of the tree.
 *
 * Pool Usage
 * ==========
 *
 * Many editor functions are invoked multiple times, in a sequence
 * determined by the editor "driver". The driver is responsible for
 * creating a pool for use on each iteration of the editor function,
 * and clearing that pool between each iteration. The driver passes
 * the appropriate pool on each function invocation.
 *
```

```
 * Based on the requirement of calling the editor functions in a
 * depth-first style, it is usually customary for the driver to similarly
 * nest the pools. However, this is only a safety feature to ensure
 * that pools associated with deeper items are always cleared when the
 * top-level items are also cleared. The interface does not assume, nor
 * require, any particular organization of the pools passed to these
 * functions.
 */
typedef struct svn_delta_editor_t
{
  /** Set *root_baton to a baton for the top directory of the change.
   * (This is the top of the subtree being changed, not necessarily
   * the root of the filesystem.)  Like any other directory baton, the
   * producer should call close_directory on root_baton when they're
   * done.
   */
  svn_error_t *(*open_root)(void *edit_baton,
                            apr_pool_t *dir_pool,
                            void **root_baton);


  /** Remove the directory entry named path, a child of the directory
   * represented by parent_baton.
   */
  svn_error_t *(*delete_entry)(const char *path,
                               void *parent_baton,
                               apr_pool_t *pool);


  /** We are going to add a new subdirectory named path.  We will use
   * the value this callback stores in *child_baton as the
   * parent_baton for further changes in the new subdirectory.
   */
  svn_error_t *(*add_directory)(const char *path,
                               void *parent_baton,
                               apr_pool_t *dir_pool,
                               void **child_baton);

  /** We are going to make changes in a subdirectory (of the directory
   * identified by parent_baton). The subdirectory is specified by
   * path. The callback must store a value in *child_baton that
   * should be used as the parent_baton for subsequent changes in this
   * subdirectory.
   */
  svn_error_t *(*open_directory)(const char *path,
                                 void *parent_baton,
                                 apr_pool_t *dir_pool,
                                 void **child_baton);

  /** We are done processing a subdirectory, whose baton is dir_baton
   * (set by add_directory or open_directory).  We won't be using
   * the baton any more, so whatever resources it refers to may now be
   * freed.
   */
  svn_error_t *(*close_directory)(void *dir_baton,
                                  apr_pool_t *pool);
```

```
/** We are going to add a new file named path.  The callback can
 * store a baton for this new file in **file_baton; whatever value
 * it stores there should be passed through to apply_textdelta.
 */
svn_error_t *(*add_file)(const char *path,
                         void *parent_baton,
                         apr_pool_t *file_pool,
                         void **file_baton);

/** We are going to make change to a file named path, which resides
 * in the directory identified by parent_baton.
 *
 * The callback can store a baton for this new file in **file_baton;
 * whatever value it stores there should be passed through to
 * apply_textdelta.
 */
svn_error_t *(*open_file)(const char *path,
                          void *parent_baton,
                          apr_pool_t *file_pool,
                          void **file_baton);

/** Apply a text delta, yielding the new revision of a file.
 *
 * file_baton indicates the file we're creating or updating, and the
 * ancestor file on which it is based; it is the baton set by some
 * prior add_file or open_file callback.
 *
 * The callback should set *handle to a text delta window
 * handler; we will then call *handle on successive text
 * delta windows as we receive them.  The callback should set
 * *handler_baton to the value we should pass as the baton
 * argument to *handler.
 */
svn_error_t *(*apply_textdelta)(void *file_baton,
                                apr_pool_t *pool,
                                svn_txdelta_window_handler_t *handler,
                                void **handler_baton);

/** We are done processing a file, whose baton is file_baton (set by
 * add_file or open_file).  We won't be using the baton any
 * more, so whatever resources it refers to may now be freed.
 */
svn_error_t *(*close_file)(void *file_baton,
                           apr_pool_t *pool);

/** All delta processing is done.  Call this, with the edit_baton for
 * the entire edit.
 */
svn_error_t *(*close_edit)(void *edit_baton,
                           apr_pool_t *pool);

/** The editor-driver has decided to bail out.  Allow the editor to
 * gracefully clean up things if it needs to.
 */
svn_error_t *(*abort_edit)(void *edit_baton,
                           apr_pool_t *pool);

} svn_delta_editor_t;
```

But Is It Art?

I cannot claim that the beauty of this interface was immediately obvious to me. I'm not sure it was obvious to Jim either; he was probably just trying to get Ben and me out of his house. But he'd been pondering the problem for a long time, too, and he followed his instincts about how tree structures behave.

The first thing that strikes one about the delta editor is that it *chooses* constraint: even though there is no philosophical requirement that tree edits be done in depth-first order (or indeed in any order at all), the interface enforces depth-firstness anyway, by means of the baton relationships. This makes the interface's usage and behavior more predictable.

The second thing is that an entire edit operation unobtrusively carries its context with it, again by means of the batons. A file baton can contain a pointer to its parent directory baton, a directory baton can contain a pointer to *its* parent directory baton (with a null parent for the root of the edit), and everyone can contain a pointer to the global edit baton. Although an individual baton may be a disposable object—for example, when a file is closed, its baton is destroyed—any given baton allows access to the global edit context, which may contain, for example, the revision number the client side is being updated to. Thus, batons are overloaded: they provide scope (i.e., lifetime, because a baton only lasts as long as the pool in which it is allocated) to portions of the edit, but they also carry global context.

The third important feature is that the interface provides clear boundaries between the various suboperations involved in expressing a tree change. For example, opening a file merely indicates that something changed in that file between the two trees, but doesn't give details; calling `apply_textdelta` gives the details, but you don't have to call `apply_textdelta` if you don't want to. Similarly, opening a directory indicates that something changed in or under that directory, but if you don't need to say any more than that, you can just close the directory and move on. These boundaries are a consequence of the interface's dedication to *streaminess*, as expressed in its introductory comment: "*...instead of representing the tree delta explicitly, we define a standard way for a consumer to process each piece of a tree delta as soon as the producer creates it.*" It would have been tempting to stream only the largest data chunks (that is, the file diffs), but the delta editor interface goes the whole way and streams the entire tree delta, thus giving both producer and consumer fine-grained control over memory usage, progress reporting, and interruptibility.

It was only after we began throwing the new delta editor at various problems that these features began to show their value. For example, one thing we wanted to implement was change summarization: a way to show an overview of the difference between two trees without giving the details. This is useful when someone wants to know which files in her working copy have changed in the repository since she checked them out, but doesn't need to know exactly what the changes were.

Here's a slightly simplified version of how it works: the client tells the server what revision tree the working copy is based on, and then the server tells the client the difference between that revision tree and the latest one, using the delta editor. The server is the producer, the client is the consumer.

Using the repository from earlier in the chapter, in which we built up a change to /A/fish/tuna to create revision 2, let's see how this would look as a series of editor calls, sent by the server to a client whose tree is still at revision 1. The if block about two-thirds of the way through is where we decide whether this is a summarization edit or a "give me everything" edit:

```
svn_delta_editor_t *editor
void *edit_baton;

/* In real life, this would be a passed-in parameter, of course. */
int summarize_only = TRUE;

/* In real life, these variables would be declared in subroutines,
     so that their lifetimes would be bound to the stack frame just
     as the objects they point to are bound by the tree edit frame. */
void *root_baton;
void *dir_baton;
void *subdir_baton;
void *file_baton;

/* Similarly, there would be subpools, not just one top-level pool. */
apr_pool_t *pool = svn_pool_create( );

/* Each use of the delta editor interface starts by requesting the
     particular editor that implements whatever you need, e.g.,
     streaming the edit across the network, applying it to a working
     copy, etc. */
Get_Update_Editor(&editor, &eb,
                     some_repository,
                     1, /* source revision number */
                     2, /* target revision number */
                     pool);

/* Now we drive the editor. In real life, this sequence of calls
     would be dynamically generated, by code that walks the two
     repository trees and invokes editor->foo( ) as appropriate. */

editor->open_root(edit_baton, pool, &root_baton);
editor->open_directory("A", root_baton, pool, &dir_baton);
editor->open_directory("A/fish", dir_baton, pool, &subdir_baton);
editor->open_file("A/fish/tuna", subdir_baton, pool, &file_baton);

if (! summarize_only)
  {
    svn_txdelta_window_handler_t window_handler;
    void *window_handler_baton;
    svn_txdelta_window_t *window;

    editor->apply_textdelta(file_baton, pool
                              apr_pool_t *pool,
                              &window_handler,
                              &window_handler_baton);
```

```
      do {
        window = Get_Next_TextDelta_Window(...);
        window_handler(window, window_handler_baton);
      } while (window);
    }

  editor->close_file(file_baton, pool);
  editor->close_directory(subdir_baton, pool);
  editor->close_directory(dir_baton, pool);
  editor->close_directory(root_baton, pool);
  editor->close_edit(edit_baton, pool);
```

As this example shows, the distinction between a summary of a change and the full version of the change falls naturally along the boundaries of the delta editor interface, allowing us to use the same code path for both purposes. While it happens that the two revision trees in this example were adjacent (revision 1 and revision 2), they didn't have to be. The same method would work for any two trees, even with many revisions between them, as is the case when a working copy hasn't been updated for a long time. And it would work when the two trees are in reverse order—that is, with the newer revision first. This is useful for reverting a change.

Abstraction As a Spectator Sport

Our next indication of the delta editor's flexibility came when we needed to do two or more distinct things in the same tree edit. One of the earliest such situations was the need to handle cancellations. When the user interrupted an update, a signal handler trapped the request and set a flag; then at various points during the operation, we checked the flag and exited cleanly if it was set. It turned out that in most cases, the safest place to exit the operation was simply the next entry or exit boundary of an editor function call. This was trivially true for operations that performed no I/O on the client side (such as change summarizations and diffs), but it was also true of many operations that did touch files. After all, most of the work in an update is simply writing out the data, and even if the user interrupts the overall update, it usually still makes sense to either finish writing or cleanly cancel whatever file was in progress when the interrupt was detected.

But where to implement the flag checks? We could hardcode them into the delta editor, the one returned (by reference) from Get_Update_Editor(). But that's obviously a poor choice: the delta editor is a library function that might be called from code that wants a totally different style of cancellation checking, or none at all.

A slightly better solution would be to pass a cancellation-checking callback function and associated baton to Get_Update_Editor(). The returned editor would periodically invoke the callback on the baton and, depending on the return value, either continue as normal or return early (if the callback is null, it is never invoked). But that arrangement isn't ideal either. Checking cancellation is really a parasitic goal: you might want to do it when updating, or you might not, but in any case it has no effect on the way the update process itself works. Ideally, the two shouldn't be tangled together in the code, especially as we had concluded that, for the most part, operations didn't need fine-grained control over cancellation checking, anyway—the editor call boundaries would do just fine.

Cancellation is just one example of an auxiliary task associated with tree delta edits. We faced, or thought we faced, similar problems in keeping track of committed targets while transmitting changes from the client to the server, in reporting update or commit progress to the user, and in various other situations. Naturally, we looked for a way to abstract out these adjunct behaviors, so the core code wouldn't be cluttered with them. In fact, we looked so hard that we initially *over*-abstracted:

```
/** Compose editor_1 and its baton with editor_2 and its baton.
 *
 * Return a new editor in new_editor (allocated in pool), in which
 * each function fun calls editor_1->fun and then editor_2->fun,
 * with the corresponding batons.
 *
 * If editor_1->fun returns error, that error is returned from
 * new_editor->fun and editor_2->fun is never called; otherwise
 * new_editor->fun's return value is the same as editor_2->fun's.
 *
 * If an editor function is null, it is simply never called, and this
 * is not an error.
 */
void
svn_delta_compose_editors(const svn_delta_editor_t **new_editor,
                          void **new_edit_baton,
                          const svn_delta_editor_t *editor_1,
                          void *edit_baton_1,
                          const svn_delta_editor_t *editor_2,
                          void *edit_baton_2,
                          apr_pool_t *pool);
```

Although this turned out to go a bit too far—we'll look at why in a moment—I still find it a testament to the beauty of the editor interface. The composed editors behaved predictably, they kept the code clean (because no individual editor function had to worry about the details of some parallel editor invoked before or after it), and they passed the associativity test: you could take an editor that was itself the result of a composition and compose it with other editors, and everything would *just work*. It worked because the editors all agreed on the basic shape of the operation they were performing, even though they might do totally different things with the data.

As you can tell, I still miss editor composition for its sheer elegance. But in the end it was more abstraction than we needed. Much of the functionality that we initially implemented using composed editors, we later rewrote to use custom callbacks passed to the editor-creation routines. Although the adjunct behaviors did usually line up with editor call boundaries, they often weren't appropriate at *all* call boundaries, or even at most of them. The result was an overly high infrastructure-to-work ratio: by setting up an entire parallel editor, we were misleadingly implying to readers of the code that the adjunct behaviors would be invoked more often than they actually were.

Having gone as far as we could with editor composition and then retreated, we were still free to implement it by hand when we really wanted it, however. Today in Subversion, cancellation is done with manual composition. The cancellation-checking editor's constructor takes another editor—the core operation editor—as a parameter:

```
/** Set *editor and *edit_baton to a cancellation editor that
 * wraps wrapped_editor and wrapped_baton.
 *
 * The editor will call cancel_func with cancel_baton when each of
 * its functions is called, continuing on to call the corresponding wrapped
 * function if cancel_func returns SVN_NO_ERROR.
 *
 * If cancel_func is NULL, set *editor to wrapped_editor and
 * *edit_baton to wrapped_baton.
 */
svn_error_t *
svn_delta_get_cancellation_editor(svn_cancel_func_t cancel_func,
                                   void *cancel_baton,
                                   const svn_delta_editor_t *wrapped_editor,
                                   void *wrapped_baton,
                                   const svn_delta_editor_t **editor,
                                   void **edit_baton,
                                   apr_pool_t *pool);
```

We also implement some conditional debugging traces using a similar process of manual composition. The other adjunct behaviors—primarily progress reporting, event notification, and target counting—are implemented via callbacks that are passed to the editor constructors and (if nonnull) invoked by the editor at the few places where they are needed.

The editor interface continues to provide a strong unifying force across Subversion's code. It may seem strange to praise an API that first tempted its users into over-abstraction, but that temptation was mainly a side effect of suiting the problem of streamy tree delta transmission exceptionally well—it made the problem look so tractable that we wanted other problems to become that problem! When they didn't fit, we backed off, but the editor constructors still provided a canonical place to inject callbacks, and the editor's internal operation boundaries helped guide our thinking about when to invoke those callbacks.

Conclusions

The real strength of this API, and, I suspect, of any good API, is that it guides one's thinking. All operations involving tree modification in Subversion are now shaped roughly the same way. This not only reduces the amount of time newcomers must spend learning existing code, it gives new code a clear model to follow, and developers have taken the hint. For example, the *svnsync* feature, which mirrors one repository's activity directly into another repository—and was added to Subversion in 2006, six years after the advent of the delta editor—uses the delta editor interface to transmit the activity. The developer of that feature was not only spared the need to design a change-transmission mechanism, he was spared the need to even *consider* whether he needed to design a change-transmission mechanism. And others who now hack on the new code find it feels mostly familiar the first time they see it.

These are significant benefits. Not only does having the right API reduce learning time, it also relieves the development community of the need to have certain debates: design discussions that would have spawned long and contentious mailing list threads simply do not come up. That may not be quite the same thing as pure technical or aesthetic beauty, but in a project with many participants and a constant turnover rate, it's a beauty you can use.

## CHAPTER THREE

The Most Beautiful Code I Never Wrote

Jon Bentley

I **ONCE HEARD A MASTER PROGRAMMER PRAISED WITH THE PHRASE,** "He adds function by deleting code." Antoine de Saint-Exupéry, the French writer and aviator, expressed this sentiment more generally when he said, "A designer knows he has achieved perfection not when there is nothing left to add, but when there is nothing left to take away." In software, the most beautiful code, the most beautiful functions, and the most beautiful programs are sometimes not there at all.

It is, of course, difficult to talk about things that aren't there. This chapter attempts this daunting task by presenting a novel analysis of the runtime of the classic Quicksort program. The first section sets the stage by reviewing Quicksort from a personal perspective. The subsequent section is the meat of this chapter. We'll start by adding one counter to the program, then manipulate the code to make it smaller and smaller and yet more and more powerful until just a few lines of code completely capture its average runtime. The third section summarizes the techniques, and presents a particularly succinct analysis of the cost of binary search trees. The final two sections draw insights from the chapter to help you write more elegant programs.

The Most Beautiful Code I Ever Wrote

When Greg Wilson first described the idea of this book, I asked myself what was the most beautiful code I had ever written. After this delicious question rolled around my brain for the better part of a day, I realized that the answer was easy: Quicksort. Unfortunately, the one question has three different answers, depending on precisely how it is phrased.

I wrote my thesis on divide-and-conquer algorithms, and found that C.A.R. Hoare's Quicksort ("Quicksort," *Computer Journal* 5) is undeniably the granddaddy of them all. It is a beautiful algorithm for a fundamental problem that can be implemented in elegant code. I loved the algorithm, but I always tiptoed around its innermost loop. I once spent two days debugging a complex program that was based on that loop, and for years I carefully copied that code whenever I needed to perform a similar task. It solved my problems, but I didn't *really* understand it.

I eventually learned an elegant partitioning scheme from Nico Lomuto, and was finally able to write a Quicksort that I could understand and even prove correct. William Strunk Jr.'s observation that "vigorous writing is concise" applies to code as well as to English, so I followed his admonition to "omit needless words" (*The Elements of Style*). I finally reduced approximately 40 lines of code to an even dozen. So if the question is, "What is the most beautiful small piece of code that you've ever written?" my answer is the Quicksort from my book *Programming Pearls*, Second Edition (Addison-Wesley). This Quicksort function, implemented in C, is shown in Example 3-1. We'll further study and refine this example in the next section.

EXAMPLE 3-1. Quicksort function

```
void quicksort(int l, int u)
{   int i, m;
    if (l >= u) return;
    swap(l, randint(l, u));
    m = l;
    for (i = l+1; i <= u; i++)
        if (x[i] < x[l])
            swap(++m, i);
    swap(l, m);
    quicksort(l, m-1);
    quicksort(m+1, u);
}
```

This code sorts a global array x[n] when called with the arguments quicksort(0, n-1). The two parameters of the function are the indexes of the subarray to be sorted: l for lower and u for upper. The call swap(i,j) exchanges the contents of x[i] and x[j]. The first swap randomly chooses a partitioning element uniformly selected between l and u.

Programming Pearls contains a detailed derivation and proof of correctness for the quicksort function. Throughout the rest of this chapter, I'll assume that the reader is familiar with Quicksort to the level presented in that description and in most elementary algorithms textbooks.

If you change the question to, "What is the most beautiful piece of code that you've written that was widely used?" my answer is again a Quicksort. An article I wrote with M. D. McIlroy ("Engineering a sort function," *Software–Practice and Experience*, Vol. 23, No. 11) describes a serious performance bug in the venerable Unix qsort function. We set out to build a new C library sort function, and considered many different algorithms for the task, including Merge Sort and Heap Sort. After comparing several possible implementations, we settled on a version of the Quicksort algorithm. That paper describes how we engineered a new function that was clearer, faster, and more robust than its competitors— partly because it was smaller. Gordon Bell's sage advice proved true: "The cheapest, fastest, and most reliable components of a computer system are those that aren't there." That function has now been widely used for over a decade with no reports of failure.

Considering the gains that could be achieved by reducing code size, I finally asked myself a third variant of the question that began this chapter. "What is the most beautiful code that you *never* wrote?" How was I able to accomplish a great deal with very little? The answer was once again related to Quicksort, specifically, the analysis of its performance. The next section tells that tale.

More and More with Less and Less

Quicksort is an elegant algorithm that lends itself to subtle analysis. Around 1980, I had a wonderful discussion with Tony Hoare about the history of his algorithm. He told me that when he first developed Quicksort, he thought it was too simple to publish, and only wrote his classic "Quicksort" paper after he was able to analyze its expected runtime.

It is easy to see that in the worst case, Quicksort might take about n^2 time to sort an array of n elements. In the best case, it chooses the median value as a partitioning element, and therefore sorts an array in about $n \lg n$ comparisons. So, how many comparisons does it use on the average for a random array of n distinct values?

Hoare's analysis of this question is beautiful, but unfortunately over the mathematical heads of many programmers. When I taught Quicksort to undergraduates, I was frustrated that many just didn't "get" the proof, even after sincere effort. We'll now attack that problem experimentally. We'll start with Hoare's program, and eventually end up with an analysis close to his.

Our task is to modify Example 3-1 of the randomizing Quicksort code to analyze the average number of comparisons used to sort an array of distinct inputs. We will also attempt to gain maximum insight with minimal code, runtime, and space.

To determine the average number of comparisons, we first augment the program to count them. To do this, we increment the variable comps before the comparison in the inner loop (Example 3-2).

EXAMPLE 3-2. Quicksort inner loop instrumented to count comparisons

```
for (i = l+1; i <= u; i++) {
    comps++;
    if (x[i] < x[l])
        swap(++m, i);
}
```

If we run the program for one value of n, we'll see how many comparisons that particular run takes. If we repeat that for many runs over many values of n, and analyze the results statistically, we'll observe that, on average, Quicksort takes about $1.4\ n \lg n$ comparisons to sort n elements.

That isn't a bad way to gain insight into the behavior of a program. Thirteen lines of code and a few experiments can reveal a lot. A famous quote attributed to writers such as Blaise Pascal and T. S. Eliot states that, "If I had more time, I would have written you a shorter letter." We have the time, so let's experiment with the code to attempt to create a shorter (and better) program.

We'll play the game of speeding up that experiment, trying to increase statistical accuracy and programming insight. Because the inner loop always makes precisely $u-1$ comparisons, we can make the program a tiny bit faster by counting those comparisons in a single operation outside the loop. This change yields the Quicksort shown in Example 3-3.

EXAMPLE 3-3. Quicksort inner loop with increment moved out of loop

```
comps += u-l;
for (i = l+1; i <= u; i++)
    if (x[i] < x[l])
        swap(++m, i);
```

This program sorts an array and counts the number of comparisons used while doing so. However, if our goal is only to count the comparisons, we don't really need to sort the array. Example 3-4 removes the "real work" of sorting the elements, and keeps only the "skeleton" of the various calls made by the program.

EXAMPLE 3-4. Quicksort skeleton reduced to counting

```
void quickcount(int l, int u)
{    int m;
    if (l >= u) return;
    m = randint(l, u);
    comps += u-l;
    quickcount(l, m-1);
    quickcount(m+1, u);
}
```

This program works because of the "randomizing" way in which Quicksort chooses its partitioning element, and because all of the elements are assumed to be distinct. This new program now runs in time proportional to n, and while Example 3-3 required space proportional to n, the space is now reduced to the recursion stack, which on average is proportional to $\lg n$.

While the indexes (l and u) of the array are critical in an actual program, they don't matter in this skeleton version. We can replace these two indexes with a single integer (n) that specifies the size of the subarray to be sorted (see Example 3-5).

EXAMPLE 3-5. Quicksort skeleton with single size argument

```
void qc(int n)
{   int m;
    if (n <= 1) return;
    m = randint(1, n);
    comps += n-1;
    qc(m-1);
    qc(n-m);
}
```

It is now more natural to rephrase this procedure as a *comparison count* function that returns the number of comparisons used by one random Quicksort run. This function is shown in Example 3-6.

EXAMPLE 3-6. Quicksort skeleton implemented as a function

```
int cc(int n)
{   int m;
    if (n <= 1) return 0;
    m = randint(1, n);
    return n-1 + cc(m-1) + cc(n-m);
}
```

Examples 3-4, 3-5, and 3-6 all solve the same basic problem, and they do so with the same runtime and memory usage. Each successor improves the form of the function and is thereby clearer and a bit more succinct than its predecessor.

In defining the *inventor's paradox* (*How To Solve It*, Princeton University Press), George Pólya says that "the more ambitious plan may have more chances of success." We will now try to exploit that paradox in the analysis of Quicksort. So far we have asked, "How many comparisons does Quicksort make on one run of size *n*?" We will now ask the more ambitious question, "How many comparisons does Quicksort make, on average, for a random array of size *n*?" We can extend Example 3-6 to yield the pseudocode in Example 3-7.

EXAMPLE 3-7. Quicksort average comparisons as pseudocode

```
float c(int n)
    if (n <= 1) return 0
    sum = 0
    for (m = 1; m <= n; m++)
        sum += n-1 + c(m-1) + c(n-m)
    return sum/n
```

If the input has a maximum of one element, Quicksort uses no comparisons, just as in Example 3-6. For larger *n*, this code considers each partition value *m* (from the first element to the last, each equally likely) and determines the cost of partitioning there. The code then calculates the sum of these values (thereby solving recursively one problem of size *m-1* and one problem of size *n-m*), and then divides that sum by *n* to return the average.

If we could compute this number it would make our experiments much more powerful. Rather than having to run many experiments at a single value of *n* to estimate the mean, a single experiment would give us the true mean. Unfortunately, that power comes at a price: the program runs in time proportional to 3^n (it is an interesting, if self-referential, exercise to analyze that runtime using the techniques described in this chapter).

Example 3-7 takes the time that it does because it computes subanswers over and over again. When a program does that, we can often use *dynamic programming* to store the subanswers to avoid recomputing them. In this case, we'll introduce the table $t[N+1]$, in which $t[n]$ stores $c(n)$, and compute its values in increasing order. We will let *N* denote the maximum size of *n*, which is the size of the array to be sorted. The result is shown in Example 3-8.

EXAMPLE 3-8. Quicksort calculation with dynamic programming

```
t[0] = 0
for (n = 1; n <= N; n++)
    sum = 0
    for (i = 1; i <= n; i++)
        sum += n-1 + t[i-1] + t[n-i]
    t[n] = sum/n
```

This program is a rough transcription of Example 3-7 and replaces $c(n)$ with $t[n]$. Its runtime is proportional to N^2 and its space is proportional to *N*. One of its benefits is that at the end of execution, the array *t* contains the true average values (not just the estimate of sample means) for array elements 0 through *N*. Those values can be analyzed to yield insight about the functional form of the expected number of comparisons used by Quicksort.

We will now simplify that program further. The first step is to move the term *n*-1 out of the loop, as shown in Example 3-9.

EXAMPLE 3-9. Quicksort calculation with code moved out of the loop

```
t[0] = 0
for (n = 1; n <= N; n++)
    sum = 0
    for (i = 1; i <= n; i++)
        sum += t[i-1] + t[n-i]
    t[n] = n-1 +  sum/n
```

We will now further tune the loop by exploiting symmetry. When *n* is 4, for instance, the inner loop computes the sum:

```
t[0]+t[3] + t[1]+t[2] + t[2]+t[1] + t[3]+t[0]
```

In the sequence of pairs, the first elements increase while the second elements decrease. We can therefore rewrite the sum as:

```
2 * (t[0] + t[1] + t[2] + t[3])
```

We can use that symmetry to yield the Quicksort shown in Example 3-10.

EXAMPLE 3-10. Quicksort calculation with symmetry

```
t[0] = 0
for (n = 1; n <= N; n++)
    sum = 0
    for (i = 0; i < n; i++)
        sum += 2 * t[i]
    t[n] = n-1 + sum/n
```

However, this code is once again wasteful because it recomputes the same sum over and over again. Rather than adding all the previous terms, we can initialize sum outside the loop and add the next term to yield Example 3-11.

EXAMPLE 3-11. Quicksort calculation with the inner loop removed

```
sum = 0; t[0] = 0
for (n = 1; n <= N; n++)
    sum += 2*t[n-1]
    t[n] = n-1 + sum/n
```

This little program is indeed useful. In time proportional to N, it produces a table of the true expected runtimes of Quicksort for every integer from 1 to N.

Example 3-11 is straightforward to implement in a spreadsheet, where the values are immediately made available for further analysis. Table 3-1 shows the first rows.

TABLE 3-1. Output of spreadsheet implementation of Example 3-11

N	Sum	t[n]
0	0	0
1	0	0
2	0	1
3	2	2.667
4	7.333	4.833
5	17	7.4
6	31.8	10.3
7	52.4	13.486
8	79.371	16.921

The first row of numbers in this table is initialized with the three constants from the code. In spreadsheet notation, the next row of numbers (the third row of the spreadsheet) is calculated using the following relations:

    A3 = A2+1   B3 = B2 + 2*C2   C3 = A3-1 + B3/A3

Dragging those (relative) relations down completes the spreadsheet. That spreadsheet is a real contender for "the most beautiful code I ever wrote," using the criterion of accomplishing a great deal with just a few lines of code.

But what if we don't need all the values? What if we would prefer to analyze just a few of the values along the way (for example, all the powers of 2 from 2^0 to 2^{32})? Although Example 3-11 builds the complete table t, it uses only the most recent value of that table.

We can therefore replace the linear space of the table t[] with the constant space of the variable t, as shown in Example 3-12.

EXAMPLE 3-12. Quicksort calculation—final version

```
sum = 0; t = 0
for (n = 1; n <= N; n++)
    sum += 2*t
    t = n-1 + sum/n
```

We could then insert an extra line of code to test for appropriateness of n, and print those results as needed.

This tiny program is the final step in our long path. Alan Perlis' observation is apt in consideration of the path this chapter has taken: "Simplicity does not precede complexity, but follows it" ("Epigrams on Programming," *Sigplan Notices*, Vol. 17, Issue 9).

Perspective

Table 3-2 summarizes the programs used to analyze Quicksort throughout this chapter.

TABLE 3-2. Evolution of Quicksort comparison counting

Example number	Lines of code	Type of answer	Number of answers	Runtime	Space
2	13	Sample	1	$n \lg n$	N
3	13	"	"	"	"
4	8	"	"	n	$\lg n$
5	8	"	"	"	"
6	6	"	"	"	"
7	6	Exact	"	3^N	N
8	6	"	N	N^2	N
9	6	"	"	"	"
10	6	"	"	"	"
11	4	"	"	N	"
12	4	Exact	N	N	1

Each individual step in the evolution of our code was pretty straightforward; the transition from the sample in Example 3-6 to the exact answer in Example 3-7 is probably the most subtle. Along the way, as the code became faster and more useful, it also shrank in size. In the middle of the 19th century, Robert Browning observed that "less is more," and this table helps to quantify one instance of that minimalist philosophy.

We have seen three fundamentally different types of programs. Examples 3-2 and 3-3 are working Quicksorts, instrumented to count comparisons as they sort a real array. Examples 3-4 through 3-6 implement a simple model of Quicksort: they mimic one run of the algorithm, without actually doing the work of sorting. Examples 3-7 through 3-12 implement a more sophisticated model: they compute the true average number of comparisons without ever tracing any particular run.

The techniques used to achieve each program are summarized as follows:

- Examples 3-2, 3-4, 3-7: Fundamental change of problem definition.

- Examples 3-5, 3-6, 3-12: Slight change of function definition.

- Example 3-8: New data structure to implement dynamic programming.

These techniques are typical. We can often simplify a program by asking, "What problem do we really need to solve?" or, "Is there a better function to solve that problem?"

When I presented this analysis to undergraduates, the program finally shrank to zero lines of code and disappeared in a puff of mathematical smoke. We can reinterpret Example 3-7 as the following recurrence relation:

$$C_0 = 0 \qquad C_n = (n-1) + (1/n) \sum_{1 \le i \le n} C_{i-1} + C_{n-i}$$

This is precisely the approach taken by Hoare and later presented by D. E. Knuth in his classic *The Art of Computer Programming, Volume 3: Sorting and Searching* (Addison-Wesley). The programming tricks of re-expression and symmetry that give rise to Example 3-10 allow us to simplify the recursive part to:

$$C_n = n - 1 + (2/n) \sum_{0 \le i \le n-1} C_i$$

Knuth's technique to remove the summation sign gives (roughly) Example 3-11, which can be re-expressed as a system of two recurrence relations in two unknowns as:

$$C_0 = 0 \qquad S_0 = 0 \qquad S_n = S_{n-1} + 2C_{n-1} \qquad C_n = n - 1 + S_n/n$$

Knuth uses the mathematical technique of a "summing factor" to achieve the solution:

$$C_n \quad = \quad (n+1)(2H_{n+1} - 2) - 2n \quad \sim \quad 1.386 n \lg n$$

where H_n denotes the nth harmonic number, $1 + 1/2 + 1/3 + \ldots 1/n$. Thus we have smoothly progressed from experimenting on a program by augmenting it with probes to a completely mathematical analysis of its behavior.

With this formula, we end our quest. We have followed Einstein's famous advice to "make everything as simple as possible, but no simpler."

A Bonus Analysis

Goethe famously said that "architecture is frozen music." In exactly that sense, I assert that "data structures are frozen algorithms." And if we freeze the Quicksort algorithm, we get the data structure of a binary search tree. Knuth's publication presents that structure and analyzes its runtime with a recurrence relation similar to that for Quicksort.

If we wanted to analyze the average cost of inserting an element into a binary search tree, we could start with the code, augment it to count comparisons, and then conduct experiments on the data we gather. We could then simplify that code (and expand its power) in a manner very reminiscent of the previous section. A simpler solution is to define a new Quicksort that uses an *ideal partitioning* method that leaves the elements in the same relative order on both sides. That Quicksort is isomorphic to binary search trees, as illustrated in Figure 3-1.

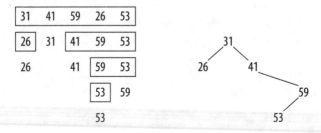

FIGURE 3-1. An ideal partitioning Quicksort and the corresponding binary search tree

The boxes on the left show an ideal-partitioning Quicksort in progress, and the graph on the right shows the corresponding binary search tree that has been built from the same input. Not only do the two processes make the same *number* of comparisons, they make exactly the same *set* of comparisons. Our previous analysis for the average performance of randomizing Quicksort on a set of distinct elements therefore gives us the average number of comparisons to insert randomly permuted distinct elements into a binary search tree.

What Is Writing?

In a weak sense, I "wrote" Examples 3-2 through 3-12 of the program. I wrote them first in scribbled notes, then on a chalkboard in front of undergraduates, and eventually in this chapter. I derived the programs systematically, I have spent considerable time analyzing them, and I believe that they are correct. Apart from the spreadsheet implementation of Example 3-11, though, I have never run any of the examples as a computer program.

In almost two decades at Bell Labs, I learned from many teachers (and especially from Brian Kernighan, whose chapter on the teaching of programming appears as Chapter 1 of this book) that "writing" a program to be displayed in public involves much more than typing symbols. One implements the program in code, runs it first on a few test cases, then builds thorough scaffolding, drivers, and a library of cases to beat on it systematically. Ideally, one mechanically includes the compiled source code into the text without human intervention. I wrote Example 3-1 (and all the code in *Programming Pearls*) in that strong sense.

As a point of honor, I wanted to keep my title honest by never implementing Examples 3-2 through 3-12. Almost four decades of computer programming have left me with deep respect for the difficulty of the craft (well, more precisely, abject fear of bugs). I compromised by implementing Example 3-11 in a spreadsheet, and I tossed in an additional column that gave the closed-form solution. Imagine my delight (and relief) when the two matched exactly! And so I offer the world these beautiful unwritten programs, with some confidence in their correctness, yet painfully aware of the possibility of undiscovered error. I hope that the deep beauty I find in them will be unmarred by superficial blemishes.

In my discomfort at presenting these unwritten programs, I take consolation from the insight of Alan Perlis, who said, "Is it possible that software is not like anything else, that it is meant to be discarded: that the whole point is to see it as a soap bubble?"

Conclusion

Beauty has many sources. This chapter has concentrated on the beauty conferred by simplicity, elegance, and concision. The following aphorisms all express this overarching theme:

- Strive to add function by deleting code.
- A designer knows he has achieved perfection not when there is nothing left to add, but when there is nothing left to take away. (Saint-Exupéry)
- In software, the most beautiful code, the most beautiful functions, and the most beautiful programs are sometimes not there at all.
- Vigorous writing is concise. Omit needless words. (Strunk and White)
- The cheapest, fastest, and most reliable components of a computer system are those that aren't there. (Bell)
- Endeavor to do more and more with less and less.
- If I had more time, I would have written you a shorter letter. (Pascal)
- The Inventor's Paradox: The more ambitious plan may have more chance of success. (Pólya)
- Simplicity does not precede complexity, but follows it. (Perlis)
- Less is more. (Browning)
- Make everything as simple as possible, but no simpler. (Einstein)
- Software should sometimes be seen as a soap bubble. (Perlis)
- Seek beauty through simplicity.

Here endeth the lesson. Go thou and do likewise.

For those who desire more concrete hints, here are some ideas grouped into three main categories.

Analysis of programs

One way to gain insight into the behavior of a program is to instrument it and then run it on representative data, as in Example 3-2. Often, though, we are less concerned with the program as a whole than with individual aspects. In this case, for instance, we considered only the number of comparisons that Quicksort uses on the average and ignored many other aspects. Sedgewick ("The analysis of Quicksort programs," *Acta Informatica*, Vol. 7) studies issues such as the space it requires and many other components of runtime for a variety of Quicksort variants. By concentrating on the key issues, we can ignore (for a while) other aspects of the program. One of my articles, "A Case Study in Applied Algorithm Design" (*IEEE Computer*, Vol. 17, No. 2) describes how I once faced the problem of evaluating the performance of a *strip heuristic* for finding an approximate travelling salesman tour through N points in the unit square. I estimated that a complete program for the task might take 100 lines of code. After a series of steps similar in spirit to what we have seen in this chapter, I used a dozen-line simulation to give much more accuracy (and after completing my little simulation, I found that Beardwood et al. ["The Shortest Path Through Many Points," *Proc. Cambridge Philosophical Soc.*, Vol. 55] had re-expressed my simulation as a double integral, and thereby had solved the problem mathematically some two decades earlier).

Small pieces of code

I believe that computer programming is a practical skill, and I agree with Pólya that we "acquire any practical skill by imitation and practice." Programmers who long to write beautiful code should therefore read beautiful programs and imitate the techniques they learn as they write their own programs. I find that one of the most useful places to practice is on small code fragments, say of just one or two dozen lines. It was hard work but great fun preparing the second edition of *Programming Pearls*. I implemented every piece of code, and labored to pare each down to its essence. I hope that others enjoy reading the code as much as I enjoyed writing it.

Software systems

For specificity, I have described one tiny task in excruciating detail. I believe that the glory of these principles lies not in tiny code fragments, but rather in large programs and huge computer systems. Parnas ("Designing software for ease of extension and contraction," *IEEE T. Software Engineering*, Vol. 5, No. 2) offers techniques to whittle a system down to its essentials. For immediate applicability, don't forget the deep insight of Tom Duff: "Whenever possible, steal code."

Acknowledgments

I am grateful for the insightful comments of Dan Bentley, Brian Kernighan, Andy Oram, and David Weiss.

## CHAPTER FOUR

Finding Things

Tim Bray

COMPUTERS CAN COMPUTE, BUT THAT'S NOT WHAT PEOPLE USE THEM FOR, MOSTLY. Mostly, computers store and retrieve information. *Retrieve* implies *find*, and in the time since the advent of the Web, search has become a dominant application for people using computers.

As data volumes continue to grow—both absolutely, and relative to the number of people or computers or anything, really—search becomes an increasingly large part of the life of the programmer as well. A few applications lack the need to locate the right morsel in some information store, but very few.

The subject of search is one of the largest in computer science, and thus I won't try to survey all of it or discuss the mechanics; in fact, I'll only consider one simple search technique in depth. Instead, I'll focus on the trade-offs that go into selecting search techniques, which can be subtle.

On Time

You really can't talk about search without talking about time. There are two different flavors of time that apply to problems of search. The first is the time it takes the search to run, which is experienced by the user who may well be staring at a message saying something like "Loading…". The second is the time invested by the programmer who builds the search function, and by the programmer's management and customers waiting to use the program.

Problem: Weblog Data

Let's look at a sample problem to get a feel for how a search works in real life. I have a directory containing logfiles from my weblog (*http://www.tbray.org/ongoing*) from early 2003 to late 2006; as of the writing of this chapter, they recorded 140,070,104 transactions and occupied 28,489,788,532 bytes (uncompressed). All these statistics, properly searched, can answer lots of questions about my traffic and readership.

Let's look at a simple question first: which articles have been read the most? It may not be instantly obvious that this problem is about search, but it is. First of all, you have to search through the logfiles to find the lines that record someone fetching an article. Second, you have to search through those lines to find the name of the article they fetched. Third, you have to keep track, for each article, of how often it was fetched.

Here is an example of one line from one of these files, which wraps to fit the page in this book, but is a single long line in the file:

```
c80-216-32-218.cm-upc.chello.se - - [08/Oct/2006:06:37:48 -0700] "GET /ongoing/When/
200x/2006/10/08/Grief-Lessons HTTP/1.1" 200 5945 "http://www.tbray.org/ongoing/"
"Mozilla/4.0 (compatible; MSIE 6.0; Windows NT 5.1; SV1; .NET CLR 1.1.4322)
```

Reading from left to right, this tells us that:

Somebody from an organization named chello in Sweden,

who provided neither a username nor a password,

contacted my weblog early in the morning of October 8, 2006 (my server's time zone is seven hours off Greenwich),

and requested a resource named */ongoing/When/200x/2006/10/08/Grief-Lessons*

using the HTTP 1.1 protocol;

the request was successful and returned 5,945 bytes;

the visitor had been referred from my blog's home page,

and was using Internet Explorer 6 running on Windows XP.

This is an example of the kind of line I want: one that records the actual fetch of an article. There are lots of other lines that record fetching stylesheets, scripts, pictures, and so on, and attacks by malicious users. You can spot the kind of line I want by the fact that the article's name starts with /ongoing/When/ and continues with elements for the decade, year, month, and day.

Our first step, then, should be to find lines that contain something like:

```
/ongoing/When/200x/2006/10/08/
```

Whatever language you're programming in, you could spend lots of time writing code to match this pattern character by character. Or you could apply regular expressions.

Regular Expressions

Regular expressions are special languages designed specifically for matching patterns in text. If you learn how to use them well, you'll save yourself immense amounts of time and irritation. I've never met a really accomplished programmer who wasn't a master of regular expressions (often called *regexps* for short). Chapter 1, by Brian Kernighan, is dedicated to the beauty of regular expressions.

Because the filenames on my web site match such a strict, date-based pattern, a very straightforward regular expression can find the logfile lines I'm interested in. Other sites' logfiles might require a more elaborate one. Here it is:

```
"GET /ongoing/When/\d\d\dx/\d\d\d\d/\d\d/\d\d/[^ .]+ "
```

A glance at this line instantly reveals one of the problems with regular expressions; they're not the world's most readable text. Some people might challenge their appearance in a book called *Beautiful Code*. Let's put that issue aside for a moment and look at this particular expression. The only thing you need to know is that in this particular flavor of regular expression:

\d

> Means "match any digit, 0 through 9"

[^ .]

> Means "match any character that's not a space or period"*

+

> Means "match one or more instances of whatever came just before the +"

That [^ .]+, then, means that the last slash has to be followed by a bunch of nonspace and nonperiod characters. There's a space *after* the + sign, so the regular expression stops when that space is found.

This regular expression won't match a line where the filename contains a period. So it will match Grief-Lessons, the example I showed earlier from my logfile, but not IMG0038.jpg.

Putting Regular Expressions to Work

A regular expression standing by itself, as shown above, can be used on the command line to search files. But it turns out that most modern computer languages allow you to use them directly in program code. Let's do that, and write a program that prints out only the lines that match the expression, which is to say a program that records all the times someone fetched an article from the weblog.

This example (and most other examples in this chapter) is in the Ruby programming language because I believe it to be, while far from perfect, the most readable of languages.

---

* People who have used regular expressions know that a period is a placeholder for "any character," but it's harder to remember that when a period is enclosed in square brackets, it loses the special meaning and refers to just a period.

If you don't know Ruby, learning it will probably make you a better programmer. In Chapter 29, the creator of Ruby, Yukihiro Matsumoto (generally known as "Matz"), discusses some of the design choices that have attracted me and so many other programmers to the language.

Example 4-1 shows our first Ruby program, with added line numbers on the left side. (All the examples in this chapter are available from the O'Reilly web site for this book.)

EXAMPLE 4-1. Printing article-fetch lines

```
1 ARGF.each_line do |line|
2   if line =~ %r{GET /ongoing/When/\d\d\dx/\d\d\d\d/\d\d/\d\d/[^ .]+ }
3     puts line
4   end
5 end
```

Running this program prints out a bunch of logfile lines that look like the first example. Let's have a line-by-line look at it:

Line 1

We want to read all the lines of the input, and we don't care whether they're from files named on the command line or are being piped in from another program on the standard input. The designers of Ruby believe strongly that programmers shouldn't have to write ugly code to deal with common situations, and this is a common situation. So, ARGF is a special variable that represents all the input sources. If the command line includes arguments, ARGF assumes they're names of files and opens them one by one; if there aren't any, it uses the standard input.

each_line is a method that you can call on pretty well any file-like object, such as ARGF. It reads the lines of input and passes them, one at a time, to a "block" of following code.

The following do says that the block getting the input stretches from there to the corresponding end, and the |line| asks that the each_line method load each line into the variable line before giving it to the block.

This kind of loop may surprise the eyes of a new convert to Ruby, but it's concise, powerful, and very easy to follow after just a bit of practice.

Line 2

This is a pretty straightforward if statement. The only magic is the =~, which means "matches" and expects to be followed by regular expression. You can tell Ruby that something is a regular expression by putting slashes before and after it—for example, /this-is-a-regex/. But the particular regular expression we want to use is full of slashes. So to use the slash syntax, you'd have to "escape" them by turning each / into \/, which would be ugly. In this case, therefore, the %r trick produces more beautiful code.

Line 3

We're inside the if block now. So, if the current line matches the regexp, the program executes puts line, which prints out the line and a line feed.

Lines 4 and 5

That's about all there is to it. The first end terminates the if, and the second terminates the do. They look kind of silly dangling off the bottom of the code, and the designers of Python have figured out a way to leave them out, which leads to some Python code being more beautiful than the corresponding Ruby.

So far, we've shown how regular expressions can be used to find the lines in the logfile that we're interested in. But what we're *really* interested in is counting the fetches for each article. The first step is to identify the article names. Example 4-2 is a slight variation on the previous program.

EXAMPLE 4-2. Printing article names

```
1 ARGF.each_line do |line|
2   if line =~ %r{GET /ongoing/When/\d\d\dx/(\d\d\d\d/\d\d/\d\d/[^ .]+) }
3     puts $1
4   end
5 end
```

The differences are subtle. In line 2, I've added a pair of parentheses (in boldface) around the interesting part of the article name in the regular expression. In line 3, instead of printing out the whole value of line, I print out $1, which in Ruby (and several other regular-expression-friendly languages) means "the first place in the regular expression marked with parentheses." You can mark lots of different pieces of the expression, and thus use $2, $3, and so on.

The first few lines of output produced by running this program over some logfile data look like this:

```
2003/10/10/FooCampMacs
2006/11/13/Rough-Mix
2003/05/22/StudentLookup
2003/11/13/FlyToYokohama
2003/07/31/PerlAngst
2003/05/21/RDFNet
2003/02/23/Democracy
2005/12/30/Spolsky-Recursion
2004/05/08/Torture
2004/04/27/RSSticker
```

Before we go to work determining the popularity of different articles, I'd like to argue that in some important ways, this code is beautiful. Take a moment and think of the code you'd have to write to look at an arbitrary chunk of text and do the same matching and selection work done by the parenthesized regexp. It would be quite a few lines of code, and it would be easy to get wrong. Furthermore, if the format of the logfile changed, fixing the pattern matcher would be error-prone and irritating.

Under the covers, the way that regular expressions work is also among the more wonderful things in computer science. It turns out that they can conveniently be translated into finite automata. These automata are mathematically elegant, and there are astoundingly efficient algorithms for matching them against the text you're searching. The great thing is that when you're running an automaton, you have to look only once at each character in the text you're trying to match. The effect is that a well-built regular expression engine can do pattern matching and selection faster than almost any custom code, even if it were written in hand-optimized assembly language. That's beautiful.

I think that the Ruby code is pretty attractive, too. Nearly every character of the program is doing useful work. Note that there are no semicolons on the ends of the lines, nor parentheses around the conditional block, and that you can write puts line instead of puts(line). Also, variables aren't declared—they're just used. This kind of stripped-down language design makes for programs that are shorter and easier to write, as well as (more important) easier to read and easier to understand.

Thinking in terms of time, regular expressions are a win/win. It takes the programmer way less time to write them than the equivalent code, it takes less time to deliver the program to the people waiting for it, it uses the computer really efficiently, and the program's user spends less time sitting there bored.

Content-Addressable Storage

Now we're approaching the core of our problem, computing the popularity of articles. We'll have to pull the article name out of each line, look it up to see how many times it's been fetched, add one to that number, and then store it away again.

This may be the most basic of search patterns: we start with a *key* (what we're using to search—in this case, an article name), and we're looking for a *value* (what we want to find—in this case, the number of times the article has been fetched). Here are some other examples:

Key	Value
Word	List of web pages containing the word
Employee number	Employee's personnel record
Passport number	"true" or "false," indicating whether the person with that passport should be subject to extra scrutiny

What programmers really want in this situation is a very old idea in computer science: *content-addressable memory*, also known as an *associative store* and various other permutations of those words. The idea is to put the key in and get the value out. There actually exists hardware which does just that; it mostly lives deep in the bowels of microprocessors, providing rapid access to page tables and memory caches.

The good news is that you, the programmer, using any modern computer language, have access to excellent software implementations of associative memory. Different languages call these implementations different things. Often they are implemented as hash tables; in

Java, Perl, and Ruby, which use this technique, they are called *Hashes*, *HashMaps*, or something similar. In Python, they are called *dictionaries*, and in the computer algebra language Maple, simply *tables*.

Now if you're an eager search-algorithm fan just itching to write your own super-efficient search, this may sound like bad news, not good news. But think about those flavors of time; if you use the built-in associative store, the amount of programmer time and management invested in writing search algorithms goes to nearly zero.

By writing your own search, you *might* be able to save a little computer (and thus end-user) time, compared to the built-in version, but on the other hand, you might not; the people who write these things tend to be pretty clever. Andrew Kuchling has written Chapter 18 of this book on one such effort.

Associative stores are so important that dynamically typed languages such as Ruby and Python have not only built-in support, but special syntax for defining and using them. Let's use Ruby's hashes to count article popularity in Example 4-3.

EXAMPLE 4-3. Counting article fetches

```
1 counts = {}
2 counts.default = 0
3
4 ARGF.each_line do |line|
5   if line =~ %r{GET /ongoing/When/\d\d\dx/(\d\d\d\d/\d\d/\d\d/[^ .]+) }
6     counts[$1] += 1
7   end
8 end
```

This program isn't that much different from the version in Example 4-2. Line 1 creates an empty Hash called counts. Line 2 gives the array a "default value" of zero; hold on for an explanation of that.

Then, in line 6, instead of printing out the article name, the name serves as the key to look up the number of fetches of this article seen so far in counts, add one to it, and store the value.

Now, consider what happens when the program sees some article name stored in $1 for the first time. I could write code along the lines of "if there is a counts[$1], then add one to it; otherwise, set counts[$1] to one." The designers of Ruby hate that kind of awkwardness; this is why they provided the notion of a "default value" for a Hash. If you look up a key the Hash doesn't know about, it says "OK, zero," allowing you to write counts[$1] += 1 and have it always just work.

I originally stated the problem as "Which of my articles have been read the most?" That's kind of fuzzy; let's interpret it to mean "Print out the top 10 most popular articles." The resulting program is shown in Example 4-4.

EXAMPLE 4-4. Reporting the most popular articles

```
1 counts = {}
2 counts.default = 0
3
4 ARGF.each_line do |line|
5   if line =~ %r{GET /ongoing/When/\d\d\dx/(\d\d\d\d/\d\d/\d\d/[^ .]+) }
6     counts[$1] += 1
7   end
8 end
9
10 keys_by_count = counts.keys.sort { |a, b| counts[b] <=> counts[a] }
11 keys_by_count[0 .. 9].each do |key|
12   puts "#{counts[key]}: #{key}"
13 end
```

Line 10 looks a little less beautiful to me than most Ruby code, but it's easy enough to understand. The keys method of counts returns an array containing all of the Hash's keys. Because of the hash implementation, the keys are stored in no predictable order, and are also returned by the keys method in random order. So, I have to sort them and store them back in a new array.

In Ruby, sort is accompanied by a code block, here enclosed in curly braces. (In Ruby, you can delimit a block either with do and end or with { and }.) The sort works its way back and forth through the array being sorted, passing pairs of elements to the block, which has to return a negative number, 0, or a positive number depending on whether the first element is less than, equal to, or greater than the second.

In this case, we want to get the data out of the hash in an order defined by the values (the counts themselves) rather than by the filenames (the keys), so we have to sort the keys by their values. Have a close look at the code, and you'll see how it works. Because this is something that people do all the time, I'm surprised that Ruby's Hash doesn't come with sort_by_value.

We use a decreasing order for the sort so that, no matter how many articles we've found, we know the first 10 items in keys_by_count represent the top 10 articles in popularity.

Now that we have an array of keys (article names) sorted in descending order of how many times they've been fetched, we can accomplish our assignment by printing out the first 10. Line 11 is simple, but a word is in order about that each method. In Ruby, you almost never see a for statement because anything whose elements you might want to loop through has an each method that does it for you.

Line 12 may be a little hard to read for the non-Rubyist because of the #{} syntax, but it's pretty straightforward.

So, let's declare victory on our first assignment. It took us only 13 lines of easy-to-read code. A seasoned Rubyist would have squeezed the last three lines into one.

Let's run this thing and see what it reports. Instead of running it over the whole 28 GB, let's just use it on a week's data: a mere 1.2 million records comprising 245 MB.

```
~/dev/bc/ 548> zcat ~/ongoing/logs/2006-12-17.log.gz | \
              time ruby code/report-counts.rb
4765: 2006/12/11/Mac-Crash
3138: 2006/01/31/Data-Protection
1865: 2006/12/10/EMail
1650: 2006/03/30/Teacup
1645: 2006/12/11/Java
1100: 2006/07/28/Open-Data
900: 2006/11/27/Choose-Relax
705: 2003/09/18/NXML
692: 2006/07/03/July-1-Fireworks
673: 2006/12/13/Blog-PR
        13.54 real          7.49 user          0.73 sys
```

This run took place on my 1.67 GHz Apple PowerBook. The results are unsurprising, but
the program does seem kind of slow. Should we worry about performance?

Time to Optimize?

I was wondering whether my sample run was really unreasonably slow, so I pulled together
a very similar program in Perl, a language that is less beautiful than Ruby but is *extremely*
fast. Sure enough, the Perl version took half the time. So, should we try to optimize?

We need to think about time again. Yes, we might be able to make this run faster, and
thus reduce the program execution time and the time a user spends waiting for it, but to
do this we'd have to burn some of the programmer's time, and thus the time the user
waits for the programmer to get the program written. In most cases, my instinct would be
that 13.54 seconds to process a week's data is OK, so I'd declare victory. But let's suppose
we're starting to get gripes from people who use the program, and we'd like to make it run
faster.

Glancing over Example 4-4, we can see that the program falls into two distinct parts. First,
it reads all the lines and tabulates the fetches; then it sorts them to find the top 10.

There's an obvious optimization opportunity here: why bother sorting all the fetch tallies
when all we really want to do is pick the top 10? It's easy enough to write a little code to
run through the array once and pick the 10 highest elements.

Would that help? I found out by instrumenting the program to find out how much time it
spent doing its two tasks. The answer was (averaging over a few runs) 7.36 seconds in the
first part and 0.07 in the second. Which is to say, "No, it wouldn't help."

Might it be worthwhile to try to optimize the first part? Probably not; all it does is match
regular expressions, and store and retrieve data using a Hash, and these are among the
most heavily optimized parts of Ruby.

So, getting fancy in replacing that sort would probably waste the time of the programmer
and the customer waiting for the code, without saving any noticeable amount of computer or waiting-user time. Also, experience would teach that you're not apt to go much
faster than Perl does for this kind of task, so the amount of speedup you're going to get is
pretty well bounded.

We've just finished writing a program that does something useful and turns out to be all about search. But we haven't come anywhere near actually writing any search algorithms. So, let's do that.

SOME HISTORY OF TALLYING

In the spirit of credit where credit is due, the notion of getting real work done by scanning lines of textual input using regular expressions and using a content-addressable store to build up results was first popularized in the *awk* programming language, whose name reflects the surnames of its inventors Aho, Weinberger, and Kernighan.

This work, of course, was based on the then-radical Unix philosophy—due mostly to Ritchie and Thompson—that data should generally be stored in files in lines of text, and to some extent validated the philosophy.

Larry Wall took the ideas behind *awk* and, as the author of Perl, turned them into a high-performance, industrial-strength, general-purpose tool that doesn't get the credit it deserves. It served as the glue that has held together the world's Unix systems, and subsequently large parts of the first-generation Web.

Problem: Who Fetched What, When?

Running a couple of quick scripts over the logfile data reveals that there are 12,600,064 instances of an article fetch coming from 2,345,571 different hosts. Suppose we are interested in who was fetching what, and when? An auditor, a police officer, or a marketing professional might be interested.

So, here's the problem: given a hostname, report what articles were fetched from that host, and when. The result is a list; if the list is empty, no articles were fetched.

We've already seen that a language's built-in hash or equivalent data structure gives the programmer a quick and easy way to store and look up key/value pairs. So, you might ask, why not use it?

That's an excellent question, and we should give the idea a try. There are reasons to worry that it might not work very well, so in the back of our minds, we should be thinking of a Plan B. As you may recall if you've ever studied hash tables, in order to go fast, they need to have a small load factor; in other words, they need to be mostly empty. However, a hash table that holds 2.35 million entries and is still mostly empty is going to require the use of a whole lot of memory.

To simplify things, I wrote a program that ran over all the logfiles and pulled out all the article fetches into a simple file; each line has the hostname, the time of the transaction, and the article name. Here are the first few lines:

```
crawl-66-249-72-77.googlebot.com 1166406026 2003/04/08/Riffs
egspd42470.ask.com 1166406027 2006/05/03/MARS-T-Shirt
84.7.249.205 1166406040 2003/03/27/Scanner
```

(The second field, the 10-digit number, is the standard Unix/Linux representation of time as the number of seconds since the beginning of 1970.)

Then I wrote a simple program to read this file and load a great big hash. Example 4-5 shows the program.

EXAMPLE 4-5. Loading a big hash

```
1 class BigHash
2
3   def initialize(file)
4     @hash = {}
5     lines = 0
6     File.open(file).each_line do |line|
7       s = line.split
8       article = s[2].intern
9       if @hash[s[0]]
10        @hash[s[0]] << [ s[1], article ]
11      else
12        @hash[s[0]] = [ s[1], article ]
13      end
14      lines += 1
15      STDERR.puts "Line: #{lines}" if (lines % 100000) == 0
16    end
17  end
18
19  def find(key)
20    @hash[key]
21  end
22
23 end
```

The program should be fairly self-explanatory, but line 15 is worth a note. When you're running a big program that's going to take a lot of time, it's very disturbing when it works away silently, maybe for hours. What if something's wrong? What if it's going incredibly slow and will never finish? So, line 15 prints out a progress report after every 100,000 lines of input, which is reassuring.

Running this program was interesting. It took about 55 minutes of CPU time to load up the hash, and the program grew to occupy 1.56 GB of memory. A little calculation suggests that it costs around 680 bytes to store the information for each host, or slicing the data another way, about 126 bytes per fetch. This is a little scary, but probably reasonable for a hash table.

Retrieval performance was excellent. I ran 2,000 queries, half of which were randomly selected hosts from the log and thus succeeded, while the other half were those same hostnames reversed, none of which succeeded. The 2,000 queries completed in an average of about .02 seconds, so Ruby's hash implementation can look up records in a hash containing 12 million or so records thousands of times per second.

Those 55 minutes to load up the data are troubling, but there are some tricks to address that. You could, for example, load it up once, then serialize the hash out and read it back in. And I didn't try particularly hard to optimize the program.

The program was easy and quick to write, and it runs fast once it's initialized, so its performance is good both in terms of waiting-for-the-program time and waiting-for-the-programmer time. Still, I'm unsatisfied. I have the feeling that there ought to be a way to get this kind of performance while burning less memory, less startup time, or both. It involves writing our own search code, though.

Binary Search

Nobody gets a Computer Science degree without studying a wide variety of search algorithms: trees, heaps, hashes, lists, and more. My favorite among all these is binary search. Let's try it on the who-fetched-what-when problem and then look at what makes it beautiful.

My first attempt at putting binary search to use was quite disappointing; while the data took 10 minutes less to load, it required almost 100 MB more memory than with the hash. Clearly, there are some surprising things about the Ruby array implementation. The search also ran several times slower (but still in the range of thousands per second), but this is not surprising at all because the algorithm is running in Ruby code rather than with the underlying hardcoded hash implementation.

The problem is that in Ruby everything is an object, and arrays are fairly abstracted things with lots of built-in magic. So, let's reimplement the program in Java, in which integers are just integers, and arrays come with very few extras.*

Nothing could be simpler, conceptually, than binary search. You divide your search space in two and see whether you should be looking in the top or bottom half; then you repeat the exercise until done. Instructively, there are a great many ways to code this algorithm incorrectly, and several widely published versions contain bugs. The implementation mentioned in "On the Goodness of Binary Search," and shown in Java in Example 4-6, is based on one I learned from Gaston Gonnet, the lead developer of the Maple language for symbolic mathematics and currently Professor of Computer Science at ETH in Zürich.

---

* This discussion of binary search borrows heavily from my 2003 piece, "On the Goodness of Binary Search," available online at *http://www.tbray.org/ongoing/When/200x/2003/03/22/Binary*.

EXAMPLE 4-6. Binary search

```
1 package binary;
2
3 public class Finder {
4   public static int find(String[] keys, String target) {
5     int high = keys.length;
6     int low = -1;
7     while (high - low > 1) {
8       int probe = (low + high) >>> 1;
9       if (keys[probe].compareTo(target) > 0)
10        high = probe;
11      else
12        low = probe;
13    }
14    if (low == -1 || keys[low].compareTo(target) != 0)
15      return -1;
16    else
17      return low;
18  }
19 }
```

Key aspects of this program are as follows:

- In lines 5–6, note that the high and low bounds are set one off the ends of the array, so neither are initially valid indices. This eliminates all sorts of corner cases.

- The loop that starts in line 7 runs until the high and low bounds are adjacent; there is no testing to see whether the target has been found. Think for a minute whether you agree with this choice; we'll return to the question later.

  The loop has two invariants. low is either –1 or points to something less than or equal to the target value. high is either one off the top of the array or points to something strictly greater than the target value.

- Line 8 is particularly interesting. In an earlier version it read:

  ```
  probe = (high + low) / 2;
  ```

  but in June 2006, Java guru Josh Bloch showed how, in certain obscure circumstances, that code could lead to integer overflow (see *http://googleresearch.blogspot.com/2006/06/extra-extra-read-all-about-it-nearly.html*). It is sobering indeed that, many decades into the lifetime of computer science, we are still finding bugs in our core algorithms. (The issue is also discussed by Alberto Savoia in Chapter 7.)

  At this point, Rubyists will point out that modern dynamic languages such as Ruby and Python take care of integer overflow for you, and thus don't have this bug.

- Because of the loop invariant, once I'm done with the loop, I just need to check low (lines 14–17). If it's not –1, either it points to something that matches the target, or the target isn't there.

The Java version took only six and a half minutes to load, and it ran successfully, using less than 1 GB of heap. Also, while it's harder to measure CPU time in Java than in Ruby, there was no perceptible delay in running the same 2,000 searches.

Binary Search Trade-offs

Binary search has some very large advantages. First of all, its performance is $O(\log_2 N)$. People often don't really grasp how powerful this is. On a 32-bit computer, the biggest $\log_2$ you'll ever encounter is 32 (similarly, 64 on a 64-bit computer), and any algorithm that competes in an upper bound of a few dozen steps will be "good enough" for many real-world scenarios.

Second, the binary-search code is short and simple. Code that is short and simple is beautiful, for a bunch of reasons. Maybe the most important is that it's easier to understand, and understanding code is harder than writing it. There are fewer places for bugs to hide. Also, compact code plays better with instruction sets, I-caches, and JIT compilers, and thus tends to run faster.

Third, once you've got that sorted array, you don't need any more index structures; binary search is very space-efficient.

The big downside to binary search is that the data has to be kept in order in memory. There are some data sets for which this is impossible, but fewer than you might think. If you think you have too much data to fit in memory, check the price of RAM these days and make sure. Any search strategy that requires going to disk is going to be immensely more complex, and in many scenarios slower.

Suppose you need to update the data set; you might think that would rule out binary search because you have to update a huge, contiguous array in memory. But that turns out to be easier than you might think. In fact, your program's memory is scattered randomly all over the computer's physical RAM, with the operating system's paging software making it look sequential; you can do the same kind of trick with your own data.

Some might argue that since a hash table is $O(1)$, that has to be better than binary search's $O(\log_2 N)$. In practice, the difference may not be that significant; set up an experiment sometime and do some measurements. Also, consider that hash tables, with the necessary collision-resolution code, are considerably more complex to implement.

I don't want to be dogmatic, but in recent years, I've started to take the following approach to search problems:

1. Try to solve it using your language's built-in hash tables.

2. Then try to solve it with binary search.

3. Only then should you reluctantly start to consider other more complex options.

Escaping the Loop

Some look at my binary-search algorithm and ask why the loop always runs to the end without checking whether it's found the target. In fact, this is the correct behavior; the math is beyond the scope of this chapter, but with a little work, you should be able to get an intuitive feeling for it—and this is the kind of intuition I've observed in some of the great programmers I've worked with.

Let's think about the progress of the loop. Suppose you have *n* elements in the array, where *n* is some really large number. The chance of finding the target the first time through is 1/*n*, a really small number. The next iteration (after you divide the search set in half) is 1/(*n*/2)—still small—and so on. In fact, the chance of hitting the target becomes significant only when you're down to 10 or 20 elements, which is to say maybe the last four times through the loop. And in the case where the search fails (which is common in many applications), those extra tests are pure overhead.

You could do the math to figure out when the probability of hitting the target approaches 50 percent, but qualitatively, ask yourself: does it make sense to add extra complexity to each step of an $O(\log_2 N)$ algorithm when the chances are it will save only a small number of steps at the end?

The take-away lesson is that binary search, done properly, is a two-step process. First, write an efficient loop that positions your low and high bounds properly, then add a simple check to see whether you hit or missed.

Search in the Large

When most people think of search they think of web search, as offered by Yahoo!, Google, and their competitors. While ubiquitous web search is a new thing, the discipline of full-text search upon which it is based is not. Most of the seminal papers were written by Gerald Salton at Cornell as far back as the early 1960s. The basic techniques for indexing and searching large volumes of text have not changed dramatically since then. What *has* changed is how result ranking is done.[*]

Searching with Postings

The standard approach to full-text search is based on the notion of a *posting*, which is a small, fixed-size record. To build an index, you read all the documents and, for each word, create a posting that says word *x* appears in document *y* at position *z*. Then you sort all the words together, so that for each unique word you have a list of postings, each a pair of numbers consisting of a document ID and the text's offset in that document.

Because postings are small and fixed in size, and because you tend to have a huge number of them, a natural approach is to use binary search. I have no idea of the details of how Google or Yahoo! do things, but I'd be really unsurprised to hear that those tens of thousands of computers spend a whole lot of their time binary-searching big arrays of postings.

People who are knowledgeable about search shared a collective snicker a few years ago when the number of documents Google advertised as searching, after having been stuck at two billion and change for some years, suddenly became much larger and then kept

---

[*] This discussion of full-text search borrows heavily from my 2003 series, *On Search*, available online at *http://www.tbray.org/ongoing/When/200x/2003/07/30/OnSearchTOC*. The series covers the topic of search quite broadly, including issues of user experience, quality control, natural language processing, intelligence, internationalization, and so on.

growing. Presumably they had switched the document ID in all those postings from 32-bit to 64-bit numbers.

Ranking Results

Given a word, searching a list of postings to figure out which documents contain it is not rocket science. A little thought shows that combining the lists to do AND and OR queries and phrase search is also simple, conceptually at least. What's hard is sorting the result list so that the good results show up near the top. Computer science has a subdiscipline called Information Retrieval (IR for short) that focuses almost entirely on this problem. Historically, the results had been very poor, up until recently.

Searching the Web

Google and its competitors have been able to produce good results in the face of unimaginably huge data sets and populations of users. When I say "good," I mean that high-quality results appear near the top of the result list, and that the result list appears quickly.

The promotion of high-quality results is a result of many factors, the most notable of which is what Google calls *PageRank*, based largely on link counting: pages with lots of hyperlinks pointing at them are deemed to be more popular and thus, by popular vote, winners.

In practice, this seems to work well. A couple of interesting observations follow. First, until the rise of PageRank, the leaders in the search-engine space were offerings such as Yahoo! and DMoz, which worked by categorizing results; so, the evidence seems to suggest that it's more useful to know how popular something is than to know what it's about.

Second, PageRank is applicable only to document collections that are richly populated with links back and forth between the documents. At the moment, two document collections qualify: the World Wide Web and the corpus of peer-reviewed academic publications (which have applied PageRank-like methods for decades).

The ability of large search engines to scale up with the size of data and number of users has been impressive. It is based on the massive application of parallelism: attacking big problems with large numbers of small computers, rather than a few big ones. One of the nice things about postings is that each posting is independent of all the others, so they naturally lend themselves to parallel approaches.

For example, an index based on doing binary search in arrays of postings is fairly straightforward to partition. In an index containing only English words, you could easily create 26 partitions (the term used in the industry is *shards*), one for words beginning with each letter. Then you can make as many copies as you need of each shard. Then, a huge volume of word-search queries can be farmed out across an arbitrarily large collection of cooperating search nodes.

This leaves the problem of combining search results for multiword or phrase searches, and this requires some real innovation, but it's easy to see how the basic word-search function could be parallelized.

This discussion is a little unfair in that it glosses over a huge number of important issues, notably including fighting the Internet miscreants who continually try to outsmart search-engine algorithms for commercial gain.

Conclusion

It is hard to imagine any computer application that does not involve storing data and finding it based on its content. The world's single most popular computer application, web search, is a notable example.

This chapter has considered some of the issues, notably bypassing the traditional "database" domain and the world of search strategies that involve external storage. Whether operating at the level of a single line of text or billions of web documents, search is central. From the programmer's point of view, it also needs to be said that implementing searches of one kind or another is, among other things, fun.

CHAPTER FIVE

Correct, Beautiful, Fast (in That Order): Lessons from Designing XML Verifiers

Elliotte Rusty Harold

THIS IS THE STORY OF TWO ROUTINES THAT PERFORM INPUT VERIFICATION FOR **XML,** the first in JDOM, and the second in XOM. I was intimately involved in the development of both, and while the two code bases are completely separate and share no common code, the ideas from the first clearly trickled into the second. The code, in my opinion, gradually became more beautiful. It certainly became faster.

Speed was the driving factor in each successive refinement, but in this case the improvements in speed were accompanied by improvements in beauty as well. I hope to dispel the myth that fast code must be illegible, ugly code. On the contrary, I believe that more often than not, improvements in beauty *lead to* improvements in execution speed, especially taking into account the impact of modern optimizing compilers, just-in-time compilers, RISC (reduced instruction set computer) architectures, and multi-core CPUs.

The Role of XML Validation

XML achieves interoperability by rigorously enforcing certain rules about what may and may not appear in an XML document. With a few very small exceptions, a conforming processor can process any well-formed XML document and can identify (and not attempt to process) malformed documents. This ensures a high degree of interoperability between platforms, parsers, and programming languages. You don't have to worry that your parser won't read my document because yours was written in C and runs on Unix, while mine was written in Java and runs on Windows.

Fully maintaining XML correctness normally involves two redundant checks on the data:

1. Validation occurs on input. As a parser reads an XML document, it checks the document for well-formedness and, optionally, validity. *Well-formedness* checks purely syntactic constraints, such as whether every start tag has a matching end tag. This is required of all XML parsers. *Validity* means that only elements and attributes specifically listed in a Document Type Definition (DTD) appear, and only in the proper positions.

2. Verification happens on output. When generating an XML document through an XML API such as DOM, JDOM, or XOM, the parser checks all strings passing through the API to make sure they're legal in XML.

While input validation is more thoroughly defined by the XML specification, output verification can be equally important. In particular, it is critical for debugging and making sure that the code is correct.

The Problem

The very first beta releases of JDOM did not verify the strings used to create element names, text content, or pretty much anything else. Programs were free to generate element names that contained whitespace, comments that ended in hyphens, text nodes that contained nulls, and other malformed content. Maintaining the correctness of the generated XML was completely left up to the client programmer.

This bothered me. While XML is simpler than some alternatives, it is not simple enough that it can be fully understood without immersing yourself in specification arcana, such as exactly which Unicode code points are or are not legal in XML names and text content.

JDOM aimed to be an API that brought XML to the masses. JDOM aimed to be an API that, unlike DOM, did not require a two-week course and an expensive expert mentor to learn to use properly. To enable this, JDOM needed to lift as much of the burden of understanding XML from the programmer as possible. Properly implemented, JDOM would keep the programmer from making mistakes.

There are numerous ways JDOM could do this. Some of them fell out as a direct result of its data model. For instance, in JDOM it is not possible to overlap elements (`<p>Sally said, <quote>let's go the park.</p>. Then let's play ball.</quote>`). Because JDOM's internal representation is a tree, there's simply no way to generate this markup from JDOM. However, a number of other constraints need to be checked explicitly, such as whether:

• The name of an element, attribute, or processing instruction is a legal XML name

• Local names do not contain colons

- Attribute namespaces do not conflict with the namespaces of their parent element or sibling attributes
- Every Unicode surrogate character appears as part of a surrogate pair consisting of one high surrogate followed by one low surrogate
- Processing instruction data does not contain the two-character string ?>

Whenever the client supplies a string for use in one of these areas, it should be checked to see that it meets the relevant constraints. The details vary, but the basic approach is the same.

For purposes of this chapter, I'm going to examine the rules for checking XML 1.0 element names.

In the XML 1.0 specification (part of which is given in Example 5-1), rules are given in a Backus-Naur Form (BNF) grammar. Here #xdddd represents the Unicode code point with the hexadecimal value dddd. [#xdddd-#xeeee] represents all Unicode code points from #xdddd to #xeeee.

EXAMPLE 5-1. BNF grammar for checking XML names (abridged)

```
BaseChar    ::= [#x0041-#x005A] | [#x0061-#x007A] | [#x00C0-#x00D6]
NameChar    ::= Letter | Digit | '.' | '-' | '_' | ':' | CombiningChar | Extender
Name        ::= (Letter | '_' | ':') (NameChar)*
Letter      ::= BaseChar | Ideographic
Ideographic ::= [#x4E00-#x9FA5] | #x3007 | [#x3021-#x3029]
Digit       ::= [#x0030-#x0039] | [#x0660-#x0669] | [#x06F0-#x06F9]
             | [#x0966-#x096F] | [#x09E6-#x09EF] | [#x0A66-#x0A6F]
             | [#x0AE6-#x0AEF] | [#x0B66-#x0B6F] | [#x0BE7-#x0BEF]
             | [#x0C66-#x0C6F] | [#x0CE6-#x0CEF] | [#x0D66-#x0D6F]
             | [#x0E50-#x0E59] | [#x0ED0-#x0ED9] | [#x0F20-#x0F29]
Extender    ::= #x00B7 | #x02D0 | #x02D1 | #x0387 | #x0640 | #x0E46 | #x0EC6
             | #x3005 | [#x3031-#x3035] | [#x309D-#x309E] | [#x30FC-#x30FE]
             | [#x00D8-#x00F6] | [#x00F8-#x00FF] | [#x0100-#x0131]
             | [#x0134-#x013E] | [#x0141-#x0148] | [#x014A-#x017E]
             | [#x0180-#x01C3] ...
CombiningChar ::= [#x0300-#x0345] | [#x0360-#x0361] | [#x0483-#x0486]
               | [#x0591-#x05A1] | [#x05A3-#x05B9] | [#x05BB-#x05BD] | #x05BF
               | [#x05C1-#x05C2] | #x05C4 | [#x064B-#x0652] | #x0670
               | [#x06D6-#x06DC] | [#x06DD-#x06DF] | [#x06E0-#x06E4]
               | [#x06E7-#x06E8] | [#x06EA-#x06ED]...
```

The complete set of rules would take up several pages here, as there are over 90,000 characters in Unicode to consider. In particular, the rules for BaseChar and CombiningChar have been shortened in this example.

To verify that a string is a legal XML name, it is necessary to iterate through each character in the string and verify that it is a legal name character as defined by the NameChar production.

Version 1: The Naïve Implementation

My initial contribution to JDOM (shown in Example 5-2) simply deferred the rule checks to Java's Character class. The checkXMLName method returns an error message if an XML name is invalid, and null if it's valid. This itself is a questionable design; it should probably throw an exception if the name is invalid, and return void in all other cases. Later in this chapter, you'll see how future versions addressed this.

EXAMPLE 5-2. The first version of name character verification

```
private static String checkXMLName(String name) {
    // Cannot be empty or null
    if ((name == null) || (name.length() == 0) || (name.trim().equals(""))) {
        return "XML names cannot be null or empty";
    }

    // Cannot start with a number
    char first = name.charAt(0);
    if (Character.isDigit(first)) {
        return "XML names cannot begin with a number.";
    }
    // Cannot start with a $
    if (first == '$') {
        return "XML names cannot begin with a dollar sign ($).";
    }
    // Cannot start with a _
    if (first == '-') {
        return "XML names cannot begin with a hyphen (-).";
    }

    // Ensure valid content
    for (int i=0, len = name.length(); i<len; i++) {
        char c = name.charAt(i);
        if ((!Character.isLetterOrDigit(c))
            && (c != '-')
            && (c != '$')
            && (c != '_')) {
            return c + " is not allowed in XML names.";
        }
    }

    // We got here, so everything is OK
    return null;
}
```

This method was straightforward and easy to understand. Unfortunately, it was wrong. In particular:

- It allowed names that contained colons. Because JDOM attempted to maintain namespace well-formedness, this had to be fixed.

- The Java Character.isLetterOrDigit and Character.isDigit methods aren't perfectly aligned with XML's definition of letters and digits. Java considers some characters as letters that XML doesn't, and vice versa.

- The Java rules change from one version of Java to the next. XML's rules don't.

Nonetheless, this was a reasonable first attempt. It did catch a large percentage of mal-formed names and didn't reject too many well-formed ones. It worked especially well in the common case when all the names were ASCII. Even so, JDOM strived for broader applicability than that. An improved implementation that actually followed XML's rules was called for.

Version 2: Imitating the BNF Grammar O(N)

My next contribution to JDOM manually translated the BNF productions into a series of if-else statements. The result looked like Example 5-3. You'll notice that this version is quite a bit more complicated.

EXAMPLE 5-3. BNF-based name character verification

```
private static String checkXMLName(String name) {
    // Cannot be empty or null
    if ((name == null) || (name.length() == 0)
                       || (name.trim().equals(""))) {
        return "XML names cannot be null or empty";
    }


    // Cannot start with a number
    char first = name.charAt(0);
    if (!isXMLNameStartCharacter(first)) {
        return "XML names cannot begin with the character \"" +
                first + "\"";
    }
    // Ensure valid content
    for (int i=0, len = name.length(); i<len; i++) {
        char c = name.charAt(i);
        if (!isXMLNameCharacter(c)) {
            return "XML names cannot contain the character \"" + c + "\"";
        }
    }

    // We got here, so everything is OK
    return null;
}

public static boolean isXMLNameCharacter(char c) {

    return (isXMLLetter(c) || isXMLDigit(c) || c == '.' || c == '-'
                           || c == '_' || c == ':' || isXMLCombiningChar(c)
                           || isXMLExtender(c));

}

public static boolean isXMLNameStartCharacter(char c) {
    return (isXMLLetter(c) || c == '_' || c ==':');
}
```

Instead of simply reusing Java's `Character.isLetterOrDigit` and `Character.isDigit` methods, the `checkXMLName` method in Example 5-3 delegates the checks to `isXMLNameCharacter` and `isXMLNameStartCharacter`. These methods further delegate to methods matching the other BNF productions for the different types of characters: letters, digits, combining characters, and extenders. Example 5-4 shows one of these methods, `isXMLDigit`. Notice that this method considers not only the ASCII digits, but also the other digit characters included in Unicode 2.0. The `isXMLLetter`, `isXMLCombiningChar`, and `isXMLExtender` methods follow the same pattern. They're just longer.

EXAMPLE 5-4. XML-based digit character verification

```
public static boolean isXMLDigit(char c) {

    if (c >= 0x0030 && c <= 0x0039) return true;
    if (c >= 0x0660 && c <= 0x0669) return true;
    if (c >= 0x06F0 && c <= 0x06F9) return true;
    if (c >= 0x0966 && c <= 0x096F) return true;

    if (c >= 0x09E6 && c <= 0x09EF) return true;
    if (c >= 0x0A66 && c <= 0x0A6F) return true;
    if (c >= 0x0AE6 && c <= 0x0AEF) return true;

    if (c >= 0x0B66 && c <= 0x0B6F) return true;
    if (c >= 0x0BE7 && c <= 0x0BEF) return true;
    if (c >= 0x0C66 && c <= 0x0C6F) return true;

    if (c >= 0x0CE6 && c <= 0x0CEF) return true;
    if (c >= 0x0D66 && c <= 0x0D6F) return true;
    if (c >= 0x0E50 && c <= 0x0E59) return true;

    if (c >= 0x0ED0 && c <= 0x0ED9) return true;
    if (c >= 0x0F20 && c <= 0x0F29) return true;

    return false;

}
```

This approach satisfied the basic goals of the upgrade. It worked, and its operation was obvious. There was a clear mapping from the XML specification to the code. We could declare victory and go home.

Well, not quite. This was where the ugly specter of performance raised its head.

Version 3: First Optimization O(log N)

As Donald Knuth once said, "Premature optimization is the root of all evil in programming." However, although optimization matters less often than programmers think, it does matter; and this was one of the minority cases where it matters.

Profiling proved that JDOM was spending a significant chunk of time performing verification. Every name character required several checks, and JDOM recognized a nonname character only after checking it first against every possible name character. Consequently, the number of checks increased in direct proportion to the code point value. The project maintainers were beginning to grumble that maybe verification wasn't so important after all, and they might make it optional or ditch it entirely. Now, personally, I'm not willing to compromise correctness in the name of faster code, but it was apparent that the decision was going to be taken out of my hands if someone didn't do something. Fortunately, Jason Hunter did.

Hunter restructured my naïve code in a very clever way, shown in Example 5-5. Previously, even the common case where a character was legal required over 100 tests for each of the possible ranges of illegal characters. Hunter noticed that we could return a *true* value much sooner if we recognized both legal and illegal characters. This is especially beneficial in the common case where all names and content are ASCII, because these characters are the first ones we test.

EXAMPLE 5-5. Optimized digit character verification

```
public static boolean isXMLDigit(char c) {

    if (c < 0x0030) return false;  if (c <= 0x0039) return true;
    if (c < 0x0660) return false;  if (c <= 0x0669) return true;
    if (c < 0x06F0) return false;  if (c <= 0x06F9) return true;
    if (c < 0x0966) return false;  if (c <= 0x096F) return true;

    if (c < 0x09E6) return false;  if (c <= 0x09EF) return true;
    if (c < 0x0A66) return false;  if (c <= 0x0A6F) return true;
    if (c < 0x0AE6) return false;  if (c <= 0x0AEF) return true;

    if (c < 0x0B66) return false;  if (c <= 0x0B6F) return true;
    if (c < 0x0BE7) return false;  if (c <= 0x0BEF) return true;
    if (c < 0x0C66) return false;  if (c <= 0x0C6F) return true;

    if (c < 0x0CE6) return false;  if (c <= 0x0CEF) return true;
    if (c < 0x0D66) return false;  if (c <= 0x0D6F) return true;
    if (c < 0x0E50) return false;  if (c <= 0x0E59) return true;

    if (c < 0x0ED0) return false;  if (c <= 0x0ED9) return true;
    if (c < 0x0F20) return false;  if (c <= 0x0F29) return true;

    return false;

}
```

The earlier implementation checked a character against all possible digits, including such unlikely things as é and φ, before deciding a character wasn't a digit. The newer approach could determine more quickly that a character wasn't a valid digit. Similar and even more significant improvements were made to the checks for letters, extenders, and combining characters.

This didn't eliminate the time spent on verification, but it did reduce it enough that the project maintainers were appeased, at least for the case of element names. PCDATA verification still wasn't in the build, but that wasn't quite as big a problem.

Version 4: Second Optimization: Don't Check Twice

At this point, the time spent on verification had dropped by about a factor of four, and was no longer a huge concern. Version 3 is essentially what shipped in JDOM 1.0. However, by this point I had decided that JDOM was not good enough, and suspected that I could do better. My defection had more to do with issues of API design than with performance. I was also concerned with correctness, since JDOM still wasn't verifying everything it could, and it was still possible (though difficult) to use JDOM to create malformed documents. Consequently, I embarked on XOM.

XOM, unlike JDOM, made no compromises on correctness in the name of performance. The rule in XOM was that correctness came first, always. Nonetheless, for people to choose XOM over JDOM, its performance was going to have to be comparable to or better than that of JDOM. Thus, it was time to take another whack at the verification problem.

The optimization efforts of JDOM version 3 had improved the performance of the checkXMLName method, but I hoped to eliminate it completely in this next optimization. The reason for this is that you don't always need to check the XML input if it's coming from a known good source. In particular, an XML parser carries out many of the necessary checks before the input reaches the XML verifier, and there's no reason to duplicate this work. Because the constructors always checked for correctness, they caused a real drain on parsing speed performance, which in practice was a large fraction (often a substantial majority) of the time an application spent on each document.

The use of separate paths for separate types of input would resolve this issue. I had determined that constructors should *not* verify the element names when creating an object from strings that the parser had already read and checked in the document. Conversely, constructors *should* verify the element names when creating an object from strings passed by the library client. Clearly, two different constructors were needed; one for the parser and one for everybody else.

JDOM developers had considered this optimization, but got hung up on poor package design. In JDOM, the SAXBuilder class that creates a new Document object from a SAX parser is in the org.jdom.input package. The Element, Document, Attribute, and other node classes are in the org.jdom package. This means that all verifying and nonverifying constructors called by the builder must be public. Consequently, other clients can also call those constructors—clients that aren't making the appropriate checks. This enables JDOM to produce malformed XML. Later, in JDOM 1.0, the developers reversed themselves and decided to bundle a special factory class that accepted unverified input. This factory class is faster, but opens up a potentially troublesome backdoor in the verification system. The problem was just an artifact of separating the JDOM builder into input and core packages.

When I commenced work on XOM, I had the example of JDOM to learn from, so I kept the input classes in the same package as the core node classes. This meant I could provide package-protected, nonverifying methods that were available to the parser, but not to client classes from other packages.

The mechanics of XOM are straightforward. Each node class has a private no-args constructor, along with a package-protected factory method named build that invokes this constructor and sets up the fields without checking the names. Example 5-6 demonstrates this with the relevant code from the Element class. XOM is actually a little pickier than most parsers about namespaces, so it does have to check those. Still, it can omit a lot of redundant checks.

EXAMPLE 5-6. Parser-based digit character verification

```
private Element() {}

static Element build(String name, String uri, String localName) {

    Element result = new Element();
    String prefix = "";
    int colon = name.indexOf(':');
    if (colon >= 0) {
        prefix = name.substring(0, colon);
    }
    result.prefix = prefix;
    result.localName = localName;
    // We do need to verify the URI here because parsers are
    // allowing relative URIs which XOM forbids, for reasons
    // of canonical XML if nothing else. But we only have to verify
    // that it's an absolute base URI. I don't have to verify
    // no conflicts.
    if (! "".equals(uri)) Verifier.checkAbsoluteURIReference(uri);
    result.URI = uri;
    return result;

}
```

This approach dramatically and measurably sped up parsing performance, since it didn't require the same large amount of work as its predecessors.

Version 5: Third Optimization O(1)

After I implemented the constructor detailed in the previous section and added some additional optimizations, XOM was fast enough for anything I needed to do. Read performance was essentially limited only by parser speed and there were very few bottlenecks left in the document-building process.

However, other users with different use cases were encountering different problems. In particular, some users were writing custom builders that read non-XML formats into a XOM tree. They were not using an XML parser, and therefore were not able to take the shortcut that bypassed name verification. These users were still seeing verification as a hot spot, albeit a smaller one than it had been.

I wasn't willing to turn off verification completely, despite requests to do so. However, it was obvious that the verification process had to be sped up. The approach I took is an old optimization classic: *table lookup*. In a table lookup, you create a table that contains all the answers for all the known inputs. When given any input, the compiler can simply look up the answer in the table, without having to perform a calculation. This is an $O(1)$ operation, and its performance speed is close to the theoretical maximum. Of course, the devil is in the details.

The simplest way to implement table lookup in Java is with a switch statement. *javac* compiles this statement into a table of values stored in the byte code. Depending on the switch statement cases, the compiler creates one of two byte code instructions. If the cases are contiguous (e.g., 72–189 without skipping any values in between) the compiler uses a more efficient tableswitch. However, if any values are skipped, the compiler uses the more indirect and less efficient lookupswitch instruction instead.

> NOTE
> This behavior isn't absolutely guaranteed, and may perhaps not even be true in more recent virtual machines (VMs), but it certainly was true in the generation of VMs I tested and inspected.

For small tables (a few hundred cases or less), it was possible to fill in the intermediate values with the default value. For instance, a simple test can determine whether a character is a hexadecimal digit (Example 5-7). The test starts with the lowest possible true value, '0', and finishes with the highest possible true value, 'f'. Every character between 0 and f must be included as a case.

EXAMPLE 5-7. switch statement character verification

```
private static boolean isHexDigit(char c) {

    switch(c) {
        case '0': return true;
        case '1': return true;
        case '2': return true;
        case '3': return true;
        case '4': return true;
        case '5': return true;
        case '6': return true;
        case '7': return true;
        case '8': return true;
        case '9': return true;
        case ':': return false;
        case ';': return false;
        case '<': return false;
        case '=': return false;
        case '>': return false;
        case '?': return false;
        case '@': return true;
        case 'A': return true;
        case 'B': return true;
        case 'C': return true;
        case 'D': return true;
        case 'E': return true;
        case 'F': return true;
        case 'G': return false;
        case 'H': return false;
        case 'I': return false;
        case 'J': return false;
        case 'K': return false;
        case 'L': return false;
        case 'M': return false;
        case 'N': return false;
        case 'O': return false;
        case 'P': return false;
        case 'Q': return false;
        case 'R': return false;
        case 'S': return false;
        case 'T': return false;
        case 'U': return false;
        case 'V': return false;
        case 'W': return false;
        case 'X': return false;
        case 'Y': return false;
        case 'Z': return false;
        case '[': return false;
        case '\\': return false;
        case ']': return false;
        case '^': return false;
        case '_': return false;
        case '`': return false;
```

EXAMPLE 5-7. switch statement character verification (continued)

```
            case 'a': return true;
            case 'b': return true;
            case 'c': return true;
            case 'd': return true;
            case 'e': return true;
            case 'f': return true;
        }
        return false;
    }
```

This is long but shallow. It is not complex. It is easy to see what's happening here, and that's good. However, although switch statements are shallow, they do run into problems for larger groups of cases. For instance, XML character verification checks tens of thousands of cases. I tried writing a switch statement to handle these larger groups and discovered that Java imposes a 64K maximum size on the byte code of a method. This situation required an alternate solution.

Although the compiler and runtime limited the size of the lookup table stored in the byte code, there were other places I could hide it. I began by defining a simple binary format, one byte for each of the 65,536 Unicode code points in the Basic Multilingual Plane (BMP). Each byte contains eight *bit flags* that identify the most important character properties. For instance, bit 1 is *on* if the character is legal in PCDATA content, and *off* if it is not legal. Bit 2 is *on* if the character can be used in an XML name, and *off* if it cannot. Bit 3 is *on* if the character can be the start of an XML name, and *off* if it cannot.

I wrote a simple program to read the BNF grammar from the XML specification, calculate the flag values for each of the 65,536 BMP code points, and then store it in one big binary file. I saved this binary data file along with my source code, and modified my Ant compile task to copy it into the build directory (Example 5-8).

EXAMPLE 5-8. Saving and copying the binary lookup table

```
<target name="compile-core" depends="prepare, compile-jaxen"
        description="Compile the source code">
    <javac srcdir="${build.src}" destdir="${build.dest}">
        <classpath refid="compile.class.path"/>
    </javac>
    <copy file="${build.src}/nu/xom/characters.dat"
          tofile="${build.dest}/nu/xom/characters.dat"/>
</target>
```

From there, the *jar* task will bundle the lookup table with the compiled *.class* files, so it doesn't add an extra file to the distribution or cause any added dependencies. The Verifier class can then use the class loader to find this file at runtime, as shown in Example 5-9.

EXAMPLE 5-9. Loading the binary lookup table

```
    private static byte[] flags = null;

    static {
```

EXAMPLE 5-9. Loading the binary lookup table (continued)

```
        ClassLoader loader = Verifier.class.getClassLoader( );
        if (loader != null) loadFlags(loader);
        // If that didn't work, try a different ClassLoader
        if (flags == null) {
            loader = Thread.currentThread().getContextClassLoader( );
            loadFlags(loader);
        }

    }


    private static void loadFlags(ClassLoader loader) {

        DataInputStream in = null;
        try {
            InputStream raw = loader.getResourceAsStream("nu/xom/characters.dat");
            if (raw == null) {
                throw new RuntimeException("Broken XOM installation: "
                    + "could not load nu/xom/characters.dat");
            }
            in = new DataInputStream(raw);
            flags = new byte[65536];
            in.readFully(flags);
        }
        catch (IOException ex) {
            throw new RuntimeException("Broken XOM installation: "
              + "could not load nu/xom/characters.dat");
        }
        finally {
            try {
                if (in != null) in.close( );
            }
            catch (IOException ex) {
                // no big deal
            }
        }

    }
```

This task takes up about 64KB of heap space. However, that's not really a problem on a desktop or server, and we only have to load this data once. The code is careful not to reload the data once it's already been loaded.

Now that the lookup table is stored in memory, checking any property of any character is a simple matter of performing an array lookup followed by a couple of bitwise operations. Example 5-10 shows the new code for checking a noncolonized name, such as an element or attribute local name. All we have to do is look up the flags in the table and compare the bit corresponding to the desired property.

EXAMPLE 5-10. *Using the lookup table to check a name*

```
// constants for the bit flags in the characters lookup table
private final static byte XML_CHARACTER        = 1;
private final static byte NAME_CHARACTER       = 2;
private final static byte NAME_START_CHARACTER = 4;
private final static byte NCNAME_CHARACTER     = 8;

static void checkNCName(String name) {

    if (name == null) {
        throwIllegalNameException(name, "NCNames cannot be null");
    }

    int length = name.length( );
    if (length == 0) {
        throwIllegalNameException(name, "NCNames cannot be empty");
    }

    char first = name.charAt(0);
    if ((flags[first] & NAME_START_CHARACTER) == 0) {
        throwIllegalNameException(name, "NCNames cannot start " +
          "with the character " + Integer.toHexString(first));
    }

    for (int i = 1; i < length; i++) {
        char c = name.charAt(i);
        if ((flags[c] & NCNAME_CHARACTER) == 0) {
            if (c == ':') {
              throwIllegalNameException(name, "NCNames cannot contain colons");
            }
            else {
              throwIllegalNameException(name, "0x"
                + Integer.toHexString(c) + " is not a legal NCName character");
            }
        }
    }
}
```

Name character verification is now an $O(1)$ operation, and verification of a full name is
$O(n)$, where n is the length of the name. You can fiddle with the code to improve the constant factors, as I have, but it's hard to see how this could be faster while still making the
necessary checks. However, we're not done yet.

Version 6: Fourth Optimization: Caching

If you can't make the verification go any faster, the only remaining option is not to do it,
or at least not do so much of it. This approach was suggested by Wolfgang Hoschek. He
noticed that in an XML document the same names keep coming up over and over. For
instance, in an XHTML document, there are only about 100 different element names, and
a few dozen of those account for most elements (p, table, div, span, strong, and so on).
Once you've verified that a name is legal, you can store it in a collection somewhere. The
next time you see a name, you first check to see whether it's one of the names you've
seen before; if it is, you just accept it and don't check it again.

However, you do have to be very careful here. It may take longer to find some names (especially shorter ones) in a collection such as a hash map than it would take to check them all over again. The only way to tell is to benchmark and profile the caching scheme very carefully on several different VMs using different kinds of documents. You may need to tune parameters such as the size of the collection to fit different kinds of documents, and what works well for one document type may not work well for another. Furthermore, if the cache is shared between threads, thread contention can become a serious problem.

Consequently, I have not yet implemented this scheme for element names. However, I have implemented it for namespace URIs (Uniform Resource Identifiers), which have even more expensive verification checks than do element names, and which are even more repetitive. For instance, many documents have only one namespace URI, and very few have more than four, so the potential gain here is much larger. Example 5-11 shows the inner class that XOM uses to cache namespace URIs after it has verified them.

EXAMPLE 5-11. A cache for verified namespace URIs

```
private final static class URICache {

    private final static int LOAD = 6;
    private String[] cache = new String[LOAD];
    private int position = 0;

    synchronized boolean contains(String s) {

        for (int i = 0; i < LOAD; i++) {
            // Here I'm assuming the namespace URIs are interned.
            // This is commonly but not always true. This won't
            // break if they haven't been. Using equals() instead
            // of == is faster when the namespace URIs haven't been
            // interned but slower if they have.
            if (s == cache[i]) {
                return true;
            }
        }
        return false;

    }

    synchronized void put(String s) {
        cache[position] = s;
        position++;
        if (position == LOAD) position = 0;
    }

}
```

There are a couple of surprising features in this class. First, rather than using the obvious hash map or table, it uses a fixed-size array with a linear search. For such small lists, the constant overhead of hash lookup is slower than simply iterating through the array.

Second, if the array fills up, it is not expanded. New data just overwrites the old, starting at the first position. This behavior leaves the data structure open to an attack that could decrease performance; it would still function correctly, but more slowly. It's extremely unlikely that any real-world XML document would have such a problem, though. Few have more than six namespaces, and in the rare cases when that happens, the namespaces tend to be localized, not randomly placed throughout the document. Performance hits that result from resetting the array should be very temporary.

The one case I can imagine where the static size of the array might be a real problem is if multiple threads were simultaneously parsing documents of very different types. In that case, you might exceed the six-namespace limit regularly. A possible solution would probably involve making the cache a thread local variable instead.

These concerns would become much more prominent if you were to cache element names rather than just namespace URIs. In this case, there are many more names to cache and the names are shorter. It might make more sense to use a table in this case than a simple array. Perhaps verification is just faster; I have not yet performed the detailed measurements necessary to determine the best design, although I plan to for XOM 1.3.

The Moral of the Story

If there's a moral to this story, it is this: do not let performance considerations stop you from doing what is right. You can always make the code faster with a little cleverness. You can rarely recover so easily from a bad design.

Programs usually become faster over time, not slower. Faster CPUs are a part of that process, but not the most important. Improved algorithms are a much bigger contributor. Therefore, design the program you want in the way it should be designed. Then, and only then, should you worry about performance. More often than not, you'll discover the program is fast enough on your first pass, and you won't even need to play tricks like those outlined here. However, when you do, it's much easier to make beautiful-but-slow code fast than it is to make fast-but-ugly code beautiful.

## CHAPTER SIX

Framework for Integrated Test: Beauty Through Fragility

Michael Feathers

I HAVE SOME IDEAS ABOUT WHAT GOOD DESIGN IS. Every programmer does. We all develop these ideas through practice, and we draw on them as we work. If we're tempted to use a public variable in a class, we remember that public variables are usually a symptom of bad design, and if we see implementation inheritance, we remember that we should prefer delegation to inheritance.*

Rules like these are useful. They help us move our way through the design space as we work, but we do ourselves a disservice if we forget that they are just rules of thumb. If we forget, we can end up with design where we are "doing everything" right, but we still miss the mark.

These thoughts were driven home to me back in 2002 when Ward Cunningham released Framework for Integrated Test (FIT), his automated testing framework. FIT consists of a small set of elegant Java classes. They maneuver in a path around nearly every rule of thumb about design in the Java community, and each little turn that they make is compelling. They stand in stark contrast to design that just follows the rules.

---

* *Design Patterns: Elements of Reusable Object-Oriented Software*, Erich Gamma, Richard Helm, Ralph Johnson, and John Vlissides, Addison-Wesley, 1995.

To me, FIT is beautiful code. It's an invitation to think about the contextual nature of design.

In this chapter, I'll walk through one of the earliest released versions of FIT. I'll show how FIT deviates from much of the current accepted wisdom of Java and OO framework development, and describe how FIT challenged me to reconsider some of my deeply held preconceptions about design. I don't know whether you'll reconsider yours after reading this chapter, but I invite you to look just the same. With luck, I'll be able to express what makes FIT's design special.

An Acceptance Testing Framework in Three Classes

FIT is relatively simple to explain. It's a little framework that lets you write executable application tests in HTML tables. Each type of table is processed by a programmer-defined class called a fixture. When the framework processes a page of HTML, it creates a fixture object for each table in the page. The fixture uses the table as input to validation code of your choice: it reads cell values, communicates with your application, checks expected values, and marks cells green or red to indicate success or failure of a check.

The first cell in the table specifies the name of the fixture class that will be used to process the table. For instance, Figure 6-1 shows a table that will be processed by the MarketEvaluation fixture. Figure 6-2 shows the same table after FIT has processed it; onscreen, the shaded cells would be red to show a validation failure.

MarketEvaluation				
Symbol	Shares	Price	Portfolio	Attempt Fill?
PLI	1100	1560	no	no

FIGURE 6-1. HTML table displayed before FIT processing

MarketEvaluation				
Symbol	Shares	Price	Portfolio	Attempt Fill?
PLI	1100	1560	no	no expected / yes actual

FIGURE 6-2. HTML table displayed after FIT processing

The key idea behind FIT is that documents can serve as tests. You could, for instance, embed tables in a requirements document and run the document through FIT to see whether the behavior specified in those tables exists in your software. These documents with tables can be written directly in HTML, or they can be written in Microsoft Word or any other application that can save documents as HTML. Because a FIT fixture is just a piece of software, it can call any portion of an application you care to test, and make those calls at any level. It's all under your control as a programmer.

I won't spend any more time explaining FIT and its problem domain; there's more information on the FIT web site (*http://fit.c2.com*). But I do want to describe the design of FIT and some of the interesting choices it embodies.

The core of FIT is only three classes: Parse, Fixture, and TypeAdapter. Their fields and methods, and the relationships between them, are shown in Figure 6-3.

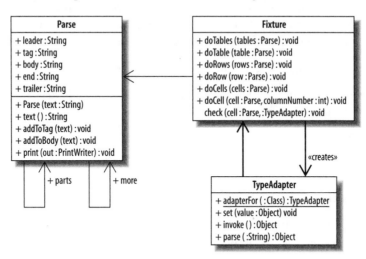

FIGURE 6-3. *Relations among FIT classes*

Let's walk through it.

In a nutshell, the Parse class represents the HTML of a document. The constructor of Parse accepts a string and recursively constructs a tree of Parse objects, knit together using the fields parts and more. Each Parse object represents some portion of the document: there's an individual Parse for each table, row, and cell.

The Fixture class traverses the tree of parses, and TypeAdapter converts testing values (numerics, dates, etc.) to text and back again. Fixtures talk to the application you are testing and mark individual cells red or green if a check passes or fails.

Most of the work in FIT happens in subclasses of the Fixture class. Fixtures define the format of the HTML tables they interpret. If you want to create a table that consists of, say, a series of commands to execute against your application, you use the predefined ActionFixture class. If you want to query your application for multiple results and compare them against a set of expected values, you use the RowFixture class. FIT provides these simple subclasses, but it also allows you to subclass Fixture yourself.

FIT is a useful framework. I use it often, and I'm continually amazed at what you can do with that core of three classes. Many frameworks would take three or four times as many classes to do the same amount of work.

The Challenge of Framework Design

OK, that's the architecture of FIT. Let's talk about what makes it different.

Framework design is tough. The hardest thing about it is that you have no control over code that uses your framework. Once you've published your framework's API, you can't change the signatures of particular methods or change their semantics without forcing some work on the users of the framework. And, typically, framework users do not like to revisit their code when they upgrade; they want complete backward-compatibility.

The traditional way of handling this problem is to adopt certain rules of thumb:

1. Be very careful about what you make public: control visibility to keep the published parts of the framework small.

2. Use interfaces.

3. Provide well-defined "hook points" that permit extensibility in the places where you intend it to occur.

4. Prevent extension in places where you don't want it to occur.

Some of these guidelines have been written down in various places,* but, for the most part, they are cultural. They are just common ways that framework developers design.

Let's look at an example outside of FIT that shows those rules in action: the JavaMail API.

If you want to receive mail using JavaMail, you have to get a reference to a Session object. Session is a class that has a static method named getDefaultInstance:

```
package javax.mail;

public final class Session
{
    ...
    public static Session getDefaultInstance(Properties props);
    ...
    public Store getStore() throws NoSuchProviderException;
    ...
}
```

The Session class is final. In Java, this means that we cannot create subclasses of Session. Furthermore, Session doesn't have a public constructor, so we can't create an instance ourselves; we have to use that static method to get an instance.

Once we have a session, we can use the getStore method to get a Store: an object that contains folders of received mail and a few other helpful things.

---

* *Effective Java*, Joshua Bloch, Prentice Hall PTR, 2001.

Framework Design Guidelines: Conventions, Idioms, and Patterns for Reusable .NET Libraries, Krzysztof Cwalina and Brad Abrams, Addison-Wesley Professional, 2005.

Store is an abstract class. The JavaMail framework supplies a couple of subclasses of Store, but as users we don't have to care which one is returned to us; we just accept it and use it to get our mail. If we want to be notified when the framework changes the store, we can register a listener on the store instance using this method:

```
public abstract class Store extends javax.mail.Service {
    ...
    public void addStoreListener(StoreListener listener);
    ...
}
```

This little portion of the JavaMail framework epitomizes traditional framework style. The Session class is declared as final to prevent subclassing. JavaMail also uses an abstract class, Store, to provide a point of extension: there can be many kinds of stores.

However, Store is a guarded extension point. There is no programmatic way to have Session return a different Store object. The returned Store can be configured, but not in the code. The framework has locked down that choice.

On the other hand, you can register a listener on the Store. This listener is a little "hook point" defined by the framework developers so that users can receive notifications about things that happen on the store without having to subclass Store themselves.

All in all, the Java Mail API protects itself very well. You have to go through a well-defined sequence of steps to use it, and the framework developers have "cover" for future change; they can go back and change anything they want to in the internals of the Session class without worrying about someone subclassing and overriding particular pieces of it.

An Open Framework

FIT is a very different kind of framework. You might have noticed from the UML diagram in Figure 6-3 that nearly everything in the core framework is public, even the data. If you glance though the code of other popular frameworks, you'll find nothing quite like it. How could this possibly work? It works because FIT is an example of an open framework. It doesn't have a small set of designed extension points; the entire framework was designed to be extensible.

Let's take a look at the Fixture class. Clients of the Fixture class use it in a very direct way. They create an instance of Fixture, create a parse tree for an HTML document using Parse, and then pass the tree to the doTables method. The doTables method then calls doTable for each table in the document, passing along the appropriate parse subtree.

The doTable method looks like this:

```
public void doTable(Parse table) {
    doRows(table.parts.more);
}
```

And the method it calls, doRows, looks like this:

```
public void doRows(Parse rows) {
    while (rows != null) {
        doRow(rows);
        rows = rows.more;
    }
}
```

The doRow method, in turn, calls doCells:

```
public void doRow(Parse row) {
    doCells(row.parts);
}
```

And the sequence bottoms out in a method called doCell:

```
public void doCell(Parse cell, int columnNumber) {
    ignore(cell);
}
```

The ignore method simply adds the color gray to the cell, indicating that the cell has been ignored:

```
public static void ignore (Parse cell) {
    cell.addToTag(" bgcolor=\"#efefef\"");
    ignores++;
}
```

As defined, it doesn't look like Fixture does much of anything at all. All it does is traverse a document and turn cells gray. However, subclasses of Fixture can override any of those methods and do different things. They can gather information, save information, communicate with the application under test, and mark cell values. Fixture defines the default sequence for traversing an HMTL document.

This is a very un-framework-y way of doing things. Users don't "plug into" this framework; they subclass a class and override some default actions. Also, there's no real cover for the framework designer. Technically, all a user needs to call is the doTables method, but the entire traversal sequence, from doTables down to doCell, is public. FIT will have to live with that traversal sequence forever. There's no way to change it without breaking client code. From a traditional framework perspective, this is bad, but what if you are confident in the traversal sequence? The sequence mirrors the parts of HTML that we care about, and it's very stable; it's hard to imagine HTML changing in a way that would break it. Living with it forever might be OK.

How Simple Can an HTML Parser Be?

In addition to being an open framework, FIT presents some other surprising design choices. Earlier, I mentioned that all of FIT's HTML parsing is done by the Parse class. One of the things that I love the most about the Parse class is that it constructs an entire tree with its constructors.

Here's how it works. You create an instance of the class with a string of HTML as a constructor argument:

```
String input = read(new File(argv[0]));
Parse parse = new Parse(input);
```

The Parse constructor recursively constructs a tree of Parse instances, each of which represents a portion of the HTML document. The parsing code is entirely within the constructors of Parse.

Each Parse instance has five public strings and two references to other Parse objects:

```
public String leader;
public String tag;
public String body;
public String end;
public String trailer;

public Parse more;
public Parse parts;
```

When you construct your first Parse for an HMTL document, in a sense, you've constructed all of them. From that point on, you can use more and parts to traverse nodes. Here's the parsing code in the Parse class:

```
static String tags[] = {"table", "tr", "td"};

public Parse (String text) throws ParseException {
    this (text, tags, 0, 0);
}

public Parse (String text, String tags[]) throws ParseException {
    this (text, tags, 0, 0);
}

public Parse (String text, String tags[], int level, int offset) throws ParseException
{
    String lc = text.toLowerCase();
    int startTag = lc.indexOf("<"+tags[level]);
    int endTag = lc.indexOf(">", startTag) + 1;
    int startEnd = lc.indexOf("</"+tags[level], endTag);
    int endEnd = lc.indexOf(">", startEnd) + 1;
    int startMore = lc.indexOf("<"+tags[level], endEnd);
    if (startTag<0 || endTag<0 || startEnd<0 || endEnd<0) {
        throw new ParseException ("Can't find tag: "+tags[level], offset);
    }

    leader = text.substring(0,startTag);
    tag = text.substring(startTag, endTag);
    body = text.substring(endTag, startEnd);
    end = text.substring(startEnd,endEnd);
    trailer = text.substring(endEnd);
```

```
    if (level+1 < tags.length) {
        parts = new Parse (body, tags, level+1, offset+endTag);
        body = null;
    }

    if (startMore>=0) {
        more = new Parse (trailer, tags, level, offset+endEnd);
        trailer = null;
    }
}
```

One of the most interesting things about Parse is that it represents the entire HTML document. The leader string holds all of the text prior to an HTML element, tag holds the tag text, body holds the text between the tag and the end tag, and trailer holds any trailing text. Because Parse holds all the text, you can go to the top-level parse and print it using this method:

```
public void print(PrintWriter out) {
    out.print(leader);
    out.print(tag);
    if (parts != null) {
        parts.print(out);
    } else {
        out.print(body);
    }
    out.print(end);
    if (more != null) {
        more.print(out);
    } else {
        out.print(trailer);
    }
}
```

In my opinion, Java code doesn't get much more elegant than that.

For a long while, I've subscribed to the rule of thumb that constructors should not do the bulk of work in a class. All they should do is put an object into a valid state and leave the real work to the other methods. In general, people don't expect object creation to be an expensive operation, and they are often surprised when it is. However, the construction code for Parse is undeniably elegant. There's a beautiful symmetry to the way it breaks an HTML string down into a couple hundred Parse objects and then reconstitutes it using a single method: print.

If the parsing code and the representation code were in separate classes, the framework might be able to handle different formats, such as XML or RTF; however, restricting the design to handling HTML feels like the right choice. It keeps the framework small and easy to understand—the parsing code is only about 25 lines. By fixing a single choice, FIT became a simpler, more robust framework. One of the deepest lessons in design is that you can gain a great deal if you hold the right things constant.

Another interesting thing about `Parse` objects is that they don't use collections to hold references to their neighbors. They use `parts` and `more` as direct links. This makes the code a little Lisp-y, but if you are used to looking at things from a functional point of view, it's very straightforward.

Here's an example of this style of coding. The `last` method in `Parse` returns the last element in the `more` sequence of a `Parse`:

```
public Parse last( ) {
    return more==null ? this : more.last( );
}
```

Again, it's interesting that all of these fields on `Parse` are public. The framework can't anticipate every way that users might need to modify them. Yes, there are convenience methods such as `addToTag` and `addToBody`, but anyone who wants to can directly modify the fields that they act on. FIT gives you that power at its own expense: future versions of FIT can't easily revoke that access. It's not the sort of choice that all framework designers can or should make, but if you can live with the consequences, it's a valid choice.

Conclusion

Many of us in the industry have learned our lessons through the school of hard knocks. We've run into situations where software we've written earlier is not as extensible as we wish. Over time, we've reacted by gathering rules of thumb that attempt to preserve extensibility by restricting choices. If you are developing a framework and you have thousands of users, this may be the best thing that you can do, but it isn't the only way.

The alternative that FIT demonstrates is radical: try to make the framework as flexible and concise as you can, not by factoring it into dozens of classes but by being very careful about how each class is factored internally. You make methods public so that when users want to stray from the normal course, they can, but you also make some hard choices, like FIT's choice of HTML as a medium.

If you design a framework like this, you end with a very different piece of software. Once the classes are opened up, it will be hard to change them in future releases, but what you produce may be small and understandable enough to lead people to create something new.

And that isn't a trivial feat. The world is filled with frameworks that are a little too hard to understand and look like they have a bit too much investment in them—so much investment that it's hard to justify reinventing the wheel. When that happens, we end up with large frameworks that miss important areas of use.

Putting frameworks aside, there's a lot to say for adopting this "open" style of development in small projects. If you know all of the users of your code—if, for instance, they all sit with you on the same project—you can choose to lower the defenses in some of your code and make it as simple and clean as FIT's code.

Not all code is API code. It's easy for us to forget this because we hear the horror stories (the cases when one team locks down another by silently introducing dependencies that can't be eradicated), but if you are one team—if the clients of your code can and will make changes when you ask them to—you can adopt a different style of development and move toward quite open code. Language-based protection and design-based protection are solutions to a problem, but the problem is social, and it's important to consider whether you really have it or not.

Every once in a while, I show FIT's code to an experienced developer, and I get an interesting reaction. They immediately say, "Nice, but I would never write code like that." At that point, I ask them to ask themselves why. To me, FIT is a beautiful framework because it leads to that question and invites us to reflect on our answers.

## CHAPTER SEVEN

Beautiful Tests

Alberto Savoia

MOST PROGRAMMERS HAVE HAD THE EXPERIENCE OF LOOKING AT A PIECE OF CODE and thinking it was not only functional but also *beautiful*. Code is typically considered beautiful if it does what it's supposed to do with unique elegance and economy.

But what about the tests for that beautiful code—especially the kind of tests that developers write, or *should* write, while they are working on the code? In this chapter, I am going to focus on tests, because tests can be beautiful themselves. More importantly, they can play a key role in helping you create more beautiful code.

As we will see, a combination of things makes tests beautiful. Unlike code, I can't bring myself to consider any *single* test beautiful—at least not in the same way I can look at, say, a sorting routine and call it beautiful. The reason is that testing, by its very nature, is a combinatorial and exploratory problem. Every if statement in the code requires at least two tests (one test for when the condition evaluates to true and one when it evaluates to false). An if statement with multiple conditions, such as:

```
if ( a || b || c )
```

could require, in theory, up to eight tests—one for each possible combination of the values of a, b, and c. Throw in control loops, multiple input parameters, dependencies on external code, different hardware and software platforms, etc., and the number and types of tests needed increases considerably.

Any nontrivial code, beautiful or not, needs not one, but a *team* of tests, where each test should be focused on checking a specific aspect of the code, similar to the way different players on a sports team are responsible for different tasks and different areas of the playing field.

Now that we have determined that we should evaluate tests in groups, we need to determine what characteristics would make a group of tests *beautiful*—an adjective rarely applied to them.

Generally speaking, the main purpose of tests is to instill, reinforce, or reconfirm our confidence that the code works properly and efficiently. Therefore, to me, the most beautiful tests are those that help me maximize my confidence that the code does, and will continue to do, what it's supposed to. Because different types of tests are needed to verify different properties of the code, the basic criteria for beauty vary. This chapter explores three ways tests can be beautiful:

Tests that are beautiful for their simplicity
> With a few lines of test code, I can document and verify the target code's basic behavior. By automatically running those tests with every build, I can ensure that the intended behavior is preserved as the code evolves. This chapter uses the JUnit testing framework for examples of basic tests that take minutes to write and keep paying dividends for the life of the project.

Tests that are beautiful because they reveal ways to make code more elegant, maintainable, and testable
> In other words, tests that help make code more beautiful. The process of writing tests often helps you realize not only logical problems, but also structural and design issues with your implementation. In this chapter, I demonstrate how, while trying to write tests, I have discovered a way to make my code more robust, readable, and well structured.

Tests that are beautiful for their breadth and depth
> Very thorough and exhaustive tests boost the developer's confidence that the code functions as expected, not only in some basic or handpicked cases, but in *all* cases. This chapter shows how I write and run this category of tests using the concept of *test theories*.

Because most developers are already familiar with basic testing techniques, such as smoke testing and boundary testing, I will spend most of the time on highly effective types of tests and testing techniques that are seldom discussed and rarely practiced.

That Pesky Binary Search

To demonstrate various testing techniques while keeping this chapter reasonably short, I need an example that's simple to describe and that can be implemented in a few lines of code. At the same time, the example must be juicy enough to provide some interesting testing challenges. Ideally, this example should have a long history of buggy implementations, demonstrating the need for thorough testing. And, last but not least, it would be great if this example itself could be considered beautiful code.

It's hard to talk about beautiful code without thinking about Jon Bentley's classic book *Programming Pearls* (Addison-Wesley). As I was rereading the book, I hit the beautiful code example I was looking for: a binary search.

As a quick refresher, a binary search is a simple and effective algorithm (but, as we'll see, tricky to implement correctly) to determine whether a presorted array of numbers *x[0..n-1]* contains a target element *t*. If the array contains *t*, the program returns its position in the array; otherwise, it returns -1.

Here's how Jon Bentley described the algorithm to the students:

> Binary search solves the problem by keeping track of the range within the array that holds t (if t is anywhere in the array). Initially, the range is the entire array. The range is shrunk by comparing its middle element to t and discarding half the range. The process continues until t is discovered in the array or until the range in which it must lie is known to be empty.

He adds:

> Most programmers think that with the above description in hand, writing the code is easy. They are wrong. The only way to believe this is by putting down this column right now and writing the code yourself. Try it.

I second Bentley's suggestion. If you have never implemented binary search, or haven't done so in a few years, I suggest you try that yourself before going forward; it will give you greater appreciation for what follows.

Binary search is a great example because it's so simple and yet it's so easy to implement incorrectly. In *Programming Pearls*, Jon Bentley shares how, over the years, he asked hundreds of professional programmers to implement binary search after providing them with a description of the basic algorithm. He gave them a very generous two hours to write it, and even allowed them to use the high-level language of their choice (including pseudocode). Surprisingly, only about 10 percent of the professional programmers implemented binary search correctly.

More surprisingly, in his *Sorting and Searching*,* Donald Knuth points out that even though the first binary search was published in 1946, it took 12 more years for the first binary search *without bugs* to be published.

---

* *The Art of Computer Programming, Vol. 3: Sorting and Searching*, Second Edition, Addison-Wesley, 1998.

But most surprising of all is that even Jon Bentley's official and *proven* algorithm, which (I must assume) has been implemented and adapted thousands of times, turns out to have a problem that can manifest itself when the array is big enough and the algorithm is implemented in a language with fixed-precision arithmetic.

In Java, the bug manifests itself by throwing an `ArrayIndexOutOfBoundsException`, whereas in C, you get an array index out of bounds with unpredictable results. You can read more about this latest bug in Joshua Bloch's blog: *http://googleresearch.blogspot.com/2006/06/extra-extra-read-all-about-it-nearly.html*.

Here is a Java implementation with the infamous bug:

```java
public static int buggyBinarySearch(int[] a, int target) {
    int low = 0;
    int high = a.length - 1;

    while (low <= high) {
        int mid = (low + high) / 2;
        int midVal = a[mid];

        if (midVal < target)
            low = mid + 1;
        else if (midVal > target)
            high = mid - 1;
        else
            return mid;
    }
    return -1;
}
```

The bug is in the following line:

```java
int mid = (low + high) / 2;
```

If the sum of `low` and `high` is greater than `Integer.MAX_VALUE` (which is $2^{31} - 1$ in Java), it overflows into a negative number and, of course, stays negative when divided by 2—ouch!

The recommended solution is to change the calculation of the midpoint to prevent integer overflow. One way to do it is by subtracting instead of adding:

```java
int mid = low + ((high - low) / 2);
```

Or, if you want to show off your knowledge of bit shift operators, the blog (and the official Sun Microsystems bug report*) suggests using the unsigned bit shift, which is probably faster but may be obscure to most Java developers (including me):

```java
int mid = (low + high) >>> 1;
```

Considering how simple the idea behind binary search is, and the sheer number and collective brain power of the people that have worked on it over the years, it's a great example of why even the simplest code needs testing—and lots of it. Joshua Bloch expressed this beautifully in his blog about this bug:

* *http://bugs.sun.com/bugdatabase/view_bug.do?bug_id=5045582.*

The general lesson that I take away from this bug is humility: It is hard to write even the smallest piece of code correctly, and our whole world runs on big, complex pieces of code.

Here is the implementation of binary search I want to test. In theory, the fix to the way the mid is calculated should resolve the final bug in a pesky piece of code that has eluded some of the best programmers for a few decades:

```
public static int binarySearch(int[] a, int target) {
    int low = 0;
    int high = a.length - 1;

    while (low <= high) {
        int mid = (low + high) >>> 1;
        int midVal = a[mid];

        if (midVal < target)
            low = mid + 1;
        else if (midVal > target)
            high = mid - 1;
        else
            return mid;
    }
    return -1;
}
```

This version of binarySearch looks right, but there might still be problems with it. Perhaps not bugs, but things that can and should be changed. The changes will make the code not only more robust, but more readable, maintainable, and testable. Let's see whether we can discover some interesting and unexpected opportunities for improvement as we test it.

Introducing JUnit

When speaking of beautiful tests, it's hard not to think of the JUnit testing framework. Because I'm using Java, deciding to build my beautiful tests around JUnit was a very easy decision. But before I do that, in case you are not already familiar with JUnit, let me say a few words about it.

JUnit is the brainchild of Kent Beck and Erich Gamma, who created it to help Java developers write and run automated and self-verifying tests. It has the simple, but ambitious, objective of making it easy for software developers to do what they should have done all along: test their own code.

Unfortunately, we still have a long way to go before the majority of developers are test-infected (i.e., have experimented with developer testing and decided to make it a regular and important part of their development practices). However, since its introduction, JUnit (helped considerably by eXtreme Programming and other Agile methodologies, where developer involvement in testing is nonnegotiable) has gotten more programmers to write tests than anything else.* Martin Fowler summed up JUnit's impact as follows: "Never in the field of software development was so much owed by so many to so few lines of code."

JUnit is intentionally simple. Simple to learn. Simple to use. This was a key design criterion. Kent Beck and Erich Gamma took great pains to make sure that JUnit was so easy to learn and use that programmers would actually use it. In their own words:

> So, the number one goal is to write a framework within which we have some glimmer of hope that developers will actually write tests. The framework has to use familiar tools, so that there is little new to learn. It has to require no more work than absolutely necessary to write a new test. It has to eliminate duplicate effort.†

The official getting-started documentation for JUnit (the *JUnit Cookbook*) fits in less than two pages: *http://junit.sourceforge.net/doc/cookbook/cookbook.htm*.

Here's the key extract from the cookbook (from the 4.x version of JUnit):

> When you need to test something, here is what you do:
>
> 1. Annotate a method with @org.junit.Test
>
> 2. When you want to check a value, import org.junit.Assert.* statically, call assertTrue(), and pass a Boolean that is true if the test succeeds
>
> For example, to test that the sum of two Moneys with the same currency contains a value that is the sum of the values of the two Moneys, write:

```
@Test
public void simpleAdd() {
    Money m12CHF= new Money(12, "CHF");
    Money m14CHF= new Money(14, "CHF");
    Money expected= new Money(26, "CHF");
    Money result= m12CHF.add(m14CHF);
    assertTrue(expected.equals(result));
}
```

If you have any familiarity with Java, those two instructions and the simple example are all you need to get started. That's also all you need to understand the tests I will be writing. Beautifully simple, isn't it? So, let's get going.

Nailing Binary Search

Given its history, I am not going to be fooled by the apparent simplicity of binary search, or by the obviousness of the fix, especially because I've never used the unsigned bit shift operator (i.e., >>>) in any other code. I am going to test this *fixed* version of binary search as if I had never heard of it before, nor implemented it before. I am not going to trust anyone's word, or tests, or proofs, that this time it will really work. I want to be confident that it works as it should through my own testing. I want to *nail* it.

---

* Another indication of JUnit's success and influence is that today there are JUnit-inspired frameworks for most modern programming languages, as well as many JUnit extensions.

† "JUnit: A Cook's Tour," Kent Beck and Erich Gamma: *http://junit.sourceforge.net/doc/cookstour/cookstour.htm*.

Here's my initial testing strategy (or team of tests):

- Start with *smoke tests*.

- Add some *boundary value* tests.

- Continue with various thorough and exhaustive types of tests.

- Finally, add some *performance* tests.

Testing is rarely a linear process. Instead of showing you the finished set of tests, I am going to walk you through my thought processes while I am working on the tests.

Smoking Allowed (and Encouraged)

Let's get started with the smoke tests. These are designed to make sure that the code does the right thing when used in the most basic manner. They are the first line of defense and the first tests that should be written, because if an implementation does not pass the smoke tests, further testing is a waste of time. I often write the smoke tests before I write the code; this is called *test-driven development* (or *TDD*).

Here's my smoke test for binary search:

```
import static org.junit.Assert.*;
import org.junit.Test;

public class BinarySearchSmokeTest {

@Test
public void smokeTestsForBinarySearch() {

    int[] arrayWith42 = new int[] { 1, 4, 42, 55, 67, 87, 100, 245 };
    assertEquals(2, Util.binarySearch(arrayWith42, 42));
    assertEquals(-1, Util.binarySearch(arrayWith42, 43));

    }

}
```

As you can tell, this test is really, *really*, basic. Not a huge confidence builder by itself, but still beautiful because it's a very fast and efficient first step toward more thorough tests.

Because this smoke test executes extremely fast (in less than 1/100th of a second on my system), you might ask why I didn't include a few more tests. The answer is that part of the beauty of smoke tests is that they can continue to pay dividends after the bulk of the development is done. To reconfirm my confidence in the code—call it "confidence mainte-nance"—I like to combine all smoke tests into a suite that I run every time I do a new build (which might be dozens of times a day), and I want this smoke test suite to run fast—ideally in a minute or two. If you have thousands of classes, and thousands of smoke tests, it's essential to keep each one to a bare minimum.

Pushing the Boundaries

As the name implies, boundary testing is designed to explore and validate what happens when the code has to deal with extremes and corner cases. In the case of binary search, the two parameters are the array and the target value. Let's think of some boundary cases for each of these parameters.*

The first set of interesting corner cases that come to mind has to do with the size of the array being searched. I begin with the following basic boundary tests:

```
int[] testArray;

@Test
public void searchEmptyArray( ) {
    testArray = new int[] {};
    assertEquals(-1, Util.binarySearch(testArray, 42));
}

@Test
public void searchArrayOfSizeOne( ) {
    testArray = new int[] { 42 };
    assertEquals(0, Util.binarySearch(testArray, 42));
    assertEquals(-1, Util.binarySearch(testArray, 43));
}
```

It's pretty clear that an empty array is a good boundary case, and so is an array of size 1 because it's the smallest nonempty array. Both of these tests are beautiful because they increase my confidence that the right thing happens at the lower boundary of array size.

But I also want to test the search with a very large array, and this is where it gets interesting (especially with the hindsight knowledge that the bug manifests itself only on arrays with over one billion elements).

My first thought is to create an array large enough to ensure that the integer-overflow bug has been fixed, but I immediately recognize a testability issue: my laptop does not have enough resources to create an array that large in memory. But I know that there are systems that *do* have many gigabytes of memory and keep large arrays in memory. I want to make sure, one way or another, that the mid integer does not overflow in those cases.

What can I do?

I know that by the time I am done with some of the other tests I have in mind, I will have enough tests to give me confidence that the basic algorithm and implementation works *provided that the midpoint is calculated correctly and does not overflow into a negative number.* So, here's a summary of my reasoning, leading to a possible testing strategy for enormous arrays:

---

* The specification for binary search says that the array *must* be sorted prior to making this call, and that if it is not sorted, the results are undefined. We are also assuming that a null array parameter should throw a NullPointerException. Because most readers should already be familiar with basic boundary testing techniques, I am going to skip some of those obvious tests.

1. I cannot test binarySearch directly with arrays large enough to verify that the overflow bug in the calculation of mid does not occur anymore.

2. However, I *can* write enough tests to give me confidence that my binarySearch implementation works correctly on smaller arrays.

3. I can also test the way *mid* is calculated when very large values are used, without getting arrays involved.

4. So, if I can gain enough confidence through testing that:

   - My implementation of the basic binarySearch algorithm is sound as long as mid is calculated correctly, and

   - The way the midpoint is calculated is correct

   then I can have confidence that binarySearch will do the right thing on very large arrays.

So the not-so-obvious, but beautiful, testing strategy is to isolate and test the pesky, overflow-prone calculation independently.

One possibility is to create a new method:

```
static int calculateMidpoint(int low, int high) {
    return (low + high) >>> 1;
}
```

then change the following line in the code from:

```
int mid = (low + high) >>> 1;
```

to:

```
int mid = calculateMidpoint(low, high);
```

and then test the heck out of the calculateMidpoint method to make sure it always does the right thing.

I can already hear a few of you screaming about adding the overhead of a method call in an algorithm designed for maximum speed. But there's no need to cry foul. Here's why I believe this change to the code is not only acceptable, but the right thing to do:

1. These days, I can trust compiler optimization to do the right thing and inline the method for me, so there is no performance penalty.

2. The change makes the code more readable. I checked with several other Java programmers, and most of them were not familiar with the unsigned bit shift operator, or were not 100 percent sure how it worked. For them, seeing calculateMidpoint(low, high) is more obvious than seeing (low + high) >>> 1.

3. The change makes the code more testable.

This is actually a good example of how the very act of creating a test for your code will improve its design or legibility. In other words, testing can help you make your code more beautiful.

Here is a sample boundary test for the new `calculateMidpoint` method:

```
@Test
public void calculateMidpointWithBoundaryValues() {
    assertEquals(0, calculateMidpoint (0, 1));
    assertEquals(1, calculateMidpoint (0, 2));
    assertEquals(1200000000, calculateMidpoint (1100000000, 1300000000));
    assertEquals(Integer.MAX_VALUE - 2,
        calculateMidpoint (Integer.MAX_VALUE-2, Integer.MAX_VALUE-1));
    assertEquals(Integer.MAX_VALUE - 1,
        calculateMidpoint (Integer.MAX_VALUE-1, Integer.MAX_VALUE));
}
```

I run the tests, and they pass. Good. I am now confident that calculating `mid` using the unfamiliar operator does what it's supposed to do within the range of array sizes I want to handle with this implementation of binary search.

The other set of boundary cases has to do with the position of the target number. I can think of three obvious boundary cases for the target item location: first item in the list, last item in the list, and right smack in the middle of the list. So, I write a simple test to check these cases:

```
@Test
public void testBoundaryCasesForItemLocation() {
    testArray = new int[] { -324, -3, -1, 0, 42, 99, 101 };
    assertEquals(0, Util.binarySearch(testArray, -324)); // first position
    assertEquals(3, Util.binarySearch(testArray, 0));      // middle position
    assertEquals(6, Util.binarySearch(testArray, 101));    // last position
}
```

Note that in this test I used some negative numbers and 0, both in the array and for the target number. It had occurred to me, while reading the tests I had already written, that I had used only positive numbers. Since that's not part of the specification, I should introduce negative numbers and 0 in my tests. Which leads me to the following piece of testing wisdom:

> The best way to think of more test cases is to start writing *some* test cases.

Now that I started to think about positive/negative numbers and 0, I realize that it would be good to have a couple of tests that use the minimum and maximum integer values.

```
public void testForMinAndMaxInteger() {
    testArray = new int[] {
      Integer.MIN_VALUE, -324, -3, -1, 0, 42, 99, 101, Integer.MAX_VALUE
    };
    assertEquals(0, Util.binarySearch(testArray, Integer.MIN_VALUE));
    assertEquals(8, Util.binarySearch(testArray, Integer.MAX_VALUE));
}
```

So far, all the boundary cases I thought of passed, and I am starting to feel pretty confident. But then I think of the 90 percent of professional programmers in Jon Bentley's class who implemented binary search and thought they had it right but didn't, and my confidence begins to wane a little bit. Did I make any unwarranted assumptions about the inputs? I did not think about negative numbers and 0 until this last test case. What other unwarranted assumptions have I made? Because I handcrafted the tests, perhaps I subconsciously created cases that would work and missed ones that would fail.

This is a known problem with programmers testing their own code. If they can't think of some scenarios when implementing the code, it's likely that they will not be able to think of them when they switch context and try to *break* the code. Truly beautiful testing requires a developer to make an extra effort, think outside the box, explore weird scenarios, look for weaknesses, and try to break things.

So, what haven't I thought of? My smoke test and boundary tests do not feel sufficient. Is my test set representative enough that I can, through some form of induction,* claim the code will work in all instances? The words of Joshua Bloch echo in my mind: "*…It is hard to write even the smallest piece of code correctly.*"

What kind of tests would make me feel confident enough that my implementation will do the right thing with all sorts of inputs—not just the ones I handcrafted?

Random Acts of Testing

So far I've written traditional, tried-and-true types of tests. I used a few concrete examples to test the search code against my expectations of what the correct behavior should be in those cases. Those tests all pass, so I have *some* level of confidence in my code. But I also realize that my tests are very specific and cover only a very small subset of all the possible inputs. What I would like, and what would help me sleep at night knowing my code has been thoroughly covered, is a way of testing over a much broader set of inputs. For this to happen I need two things:

1. A way to generate a large and diverse set of inputs

2. A set of generalized assertions that will work on any input

Let's tackle the first requirement.

What I need here is a way to generate arrays of integers of all shapes and sizes. The only requirement I am going to make is that the resulting arrays are sorted, because that's a precondition. Other than that, anything goes. Here's my initial implementation of the generator:†

```
public int[] generateRandomSortedArray(int maxArraySize, int maxValue) {
    int arraySize = 1 + rand.nextInt(maxArraySize);
    int[] randomArray = new int[arraySize];
    for (int i = 0; i < arraySize; i++) {
        randomArray[i] = rand.nextInt(maxValue);
    }
    Arrays.sort(randomArray);
    return randomArray;
}
```

---

* By *induction*, I mean deriving general principles from particular facts or instances.

† I say *initial* implementation because I quickly realized that I needed to populate the array with negative as well as positive numbers, and changed the generator accordingly.

For my generator, I take advantage of java.util's random-number generator and Arrays utilities. The latter once contained the very same binary-search bug Joshua Bloch mentioned in his blog, but it's fixed in the version of Java I am using. Because I already covered the handling of empty arrays to my satisfaction in my other tests, I use a minimum array size here of 1. The generator is parameterized because I might want to create different sets of tests as I go along: some with small arrays containing big numbers, some with big arrays and small numbers, and so on.

Now I have to come up with some general statements about the desired behavior of the binary search that can be expressed as assertions. By "general," I mean statements that must hold true for any input array and target value. My colleagues Marat Boshernitsan and David Saff call these *theories*. The idea is that we have a theory of how the code should behave, and the more we test the theory, the more confident we can be that what we theorize is actually true. In the following example, I am going to apply a much simplified version of Saff and Boshernitsan's theories.

Let's try to come up with some theories for binarySearch. Here we go:

> For all instances of *testArray* and *target*, where *testArray* is a sorted array of integers and is not null, and *target* is an integer, the following must always be true of binarySearch:
>
> Theory 1:* If binarySearch(*testArray*, *target*) returns −1, then *testArray* does not contain *target*.
>
> Theory 2: If binarySearch(*testArray*, *target*) returns *n*, and *n* is greater than or equal to 0, then *testArray* contains *target* at position *n*.

Here's my code for testing these two theories:

```
public class BinarySearchTestTheories {

Random rand;

@Before
public void initialize() {
    rand = new Random();
}

@Test
public void testTheories() {

    int maxArraySize = 1000;
    int maxValue = 1000;
    int experiments = 1000;
```

---

* In practice I would use, and recommend using, descriptive names for the theories, such as: *binarySearchReturnsMinusOneImpliesArrayDoesNotContainElement*, but I found that for this chapter, the reasoning is easier to follow if I use Theory1, Theory2, etc.

```
        int[] testArray;
        int target;
        int returnValue;

        while (experiments-- > 0) {
            testArray = generateRandomSortedArray(maxArraySize, maxValue);
            if (rand.nextBoolean()) {
                target = testArray[rand.nextInt(testArray.length)];
            } else {
                target = rand.nextInt();
            }
            returnValue = Util.binarySearch(testArray, target);
            assertTheory1(testArray, target, returnValue);
            assertTheory2(testArray, target, returnValue);
        }
    }

    public void assertTheory1(int[] testArray, int target, int returnValue) {
        if (returnValue == -1)
            assertFalse(arrayContainsTarget(testArray, target));
    }

    public void assertTheory2(int[] testArray, int target, int returnValue) {
        if (returnValue >= 0)
            assertEquals(target, testArray[returnValue]);
    }

    public boolean arrayContainsTarget(int[] testArray, int target) {
        for (int i = 0; i < testArray.length; i++)
            if (testArray[i] == target)
                return true;
        return false;
    }
```

In the main test method, testTheories, I decide how many experiments I want to run in order to confirm the theories, and use that as my loop counter. Inside the loop, the random-array generator I just wrote gives me a sorted array. I want to test both successful and unsuccessful searches, so I use Java's random number generator again to "toss a coin" (through the rand.nextBoolean() code). Based on the virtual coin toss, I decide whether I am going to pick a target number that I *know* is in the array or one that's unlikely to be in the array. Finally, I call binarySearch, store the return value, and invoke the methods for the theories I have so far.

Notice that, in order to implement the tests for my theories, I had to write a test helper method, arrayContainsTarget, that gives me an alternative way of checking whether testArray contains the target element. This is a common practice for this type of testing. Even though the implementation of this helper method provides functionality similar to binarySearch, it's a much simpler (albeit much slower) search implementation. I have confidence that the helper does the right thing, so I can use it to test an implementation I am much less sure about.

I start by running 1,000 experiments on arrays of size up to 1,000. The tests take a fraction of a second, and everything passes. Good. Time to explore a little more (remember that testing is an exploratory activity).

I change the experiment and `maxArraySize` values to 10,000, then 100,000. The tests now take closer to a minute, and my CPU maxes out. I feel like I am giving the code a really good workout.

My confidence is building, but one of my beliefs is: *If all your tests pass, chances are that your tests are not good enough*. What other properties should I test now that I have this framework?

I think for a bit and notice that my two theories are both of the form:

> If something is true about the return value of `binarySearch`, then something else must be true about the `testArray` and the `target`.

In other words, I have logic of the form *p* implies *q* (or, *p* → *q*, using logic notation), which means I am only testing half of what I should be testing. I should also have tests of the form *q* → *p*:*

> If something is true about the `testArray` and the `target`, then something else must be true about the return value.

This is a bit tricky, but important, so let me clarify with some specifics. The tests for Theory 1 verify that when the return value is –1, the target element is not in the array. But they don't verify that when the target element is not in the array, the return value is –1. In other words: *if I only had this one theory with which to test*, an implementation that returned –1 sometimes, but not *every* time it should, would still pass all my tests. A similar problem exists with Theory 2.

I can demonstrate this with *mutation testing*, a technique for *testing the tests* invented by Jeff Offut. The basic idea is to mutate the code under tests with some known bugs. If the tests you have still pass despite the bug in the code, then the tests are probably not as thorough as they need to be.

Let me mutate `binarySearch` in some drastic and arbitrary way. I'll try do this: if target is greater than 424242 and target is not contained in the array, instead of returning –1, I am going to return *–42*. How's that for software vandalism? See the tail end of the following code:

---

* Of course, either *p*, *q*, or both, could be negated (e.g., ~*p* → ~*q*, or *p* → ~*q*). I am arbitrarily using *p* and *q* as stand-ins for any predicate about the return value and the array parameter, respectively. What's important here is to recognize that when you are programming, you typically think in terms of *p* → *q* (if *p* is true, then *q* must happen—the so-called *happy path*: the normal, most common usage of the code). When you are testing, however, you must force yourself to think both backward (*q* → ?, or if *q* is true what must be true about *p*?), and in negative terms (if p is not true [i.e., ~*p*], what must be true about *q*?).

```
public static int binarySearch(int[] a, int target) {
    int low = 0;
    int high = a.length - 1;

    while (low <= high) {
        int mid = (low + high) / 2;
        int midVal = a[mid];

        if (midVal < target)
            low = mid + 1;
        else if (midVal > target)
            high = mid - 1;
        else
            return mid;
    }
    if (target <= 424242)
        return -1;
    else
        return -42;
}
```

Hopefully, you'll agree that this is a pretty big mutation: the code returns an unexpected and unspecified value if the target is a number greater than 424242 and is not contained in the array. And yet, all the tests we have written so far pass with flying colors.

We definitely need to add at least a couple more theories to make the tests tighter and catch this category of mutations:

Theory 3: If *testArray* does not contain *target*, then it must return -1.

Theory 4: If *testArray* contains *target* at position *n*, then binarySearch(*testArray*, *target*) must return *n*.

These theories are tested as follows:

```
public void assertTheory3(int[] testArray, int target, int returnValue) {
    if (!arrayContainsTarget(testArray, target))
        assertEquals(-1, returnValue);
}

public void assertTheory4(int[] testArray, int target, int returnValue) {
        assertEquals(getTargetPosition(testArray, target), returnValue);
}

public int getTargetPosition(int[] testArray, int target) {
    for (int i = 0; i < testArray.length; i++)
        if (testArray[i] == target)
            return i;
    return -1;
}
```

Notice that I had to create another helper method, getTargetPosition, which has exactly the same behavior as binarySearch (but I am confident that it works properly, with the huge downside that it requires up to *n* instead of $\log_2 n$ comparisons). Because getTargetPosition is very similar to arrayContainsTarget, and code duplication is bad, I rewrite the latter as follows:

```
public boolean arrayContainsTarget(int[] testArray, int target) {
    return getTargetPosition(testArray, target) >= 0;
}
```

I run these tests again with my random-array generator, and now the return -42 mutation is caught immediately. Good, that helps my confidence. I remove the intentional bug and run the tests again. I expect them to pass, but they don't. Some tests for Theory 4 are not passing. JUnit is failing with messages of the form:

```
expected:<n> but was:<n + 1>
```

Theory 4 says that:

> If *testArray* contains *target* at position *n*, then binarySearch(*testArray*, *target*) must return *n*.

So, in some cases, the search routine is returning a location that's off by one. How's that possible?

I need a bit more data. JUnit's assertions can accept a message of type String as the first parameter, so I change Theory 4's assertEqual to include some text that will give me more information when it fails:

```
public void assertTheory4(int[] testArray, int target, int returnValue) {
  String testDataInfo = "Theory 4 - Array=" +
        printArray(testArray)
        + " target="
        + target;
  assertEquals(testDataInfo, getTargetPosition(testArray, target), returnValue);
}
```

Now, whenever Theory 4 fails to hold, JUnit will show me the contents of the array as well as the target value. I run the tests again (with small values of maxArraySize and maxValue to make the output easier to read) and get the following:

```
java.lang.AssertionError: Theory 4 - Array=[2, 11, 36, 66, 104, 108, 108, 108, 122,
155, 159, 161, 191] target=108 expected:<5> but was:<6>
```

I see what's happening. Theory 4 does not take into account duplicate values, and I hadn't thought of that. There are three instances of the number 108. I guess I need to find out what the specification is for handling duplicate values, and fix either the code or my theory and tests. But I'll leave this as an exercise to the reader (I always wanted to say that!) because I am running out of space, and I want to say a few words about performance tests before we wrap up this chapter.

Performance Anxiety

The tests we've already run based on these theories put a pretty tight net around the implementation. It's going to be tough to pass all these tests and still have a buggy implementation. But there is something we overlooked. All the tests we have are good tests for search, but what we are testing is specifically a *binary* search. We need a set of tests for *binary-ness*. We need to see whether the number of comparisons our implementation performs matches the expectations of a maximum of $\log_2 n$ comparisons. How can we go about this?

My first thought is to use the system clock, but I quickly dismiss the idea because the clock I have available does not have enough resolution for this particular challenge (binary search is blazingly fast), and I can't really control the execution environment. So, I use another developer testing trick: I create an alternate implementation of binarySearch called binarySearchComparisonsCount. This version of the code uses the same logic as the original, but it keeps a count of the comparisons and returns that number instead of –1 or the target location.* Here's that code:

```
public static int binarySearchComparisonCount(int[] a, int target) {
    int low = 0;
    int high = a.length - 1;

    int comparisonCount = 0;

    while (low <= high) {

        comparisonCount++;

        int mid = (low + high) >>> 1;
        int midVal = a[mid];

        if (midVal < target)
            low = mid + 1;
        else if (midVal > target)
            high = mid - 1;
        else
            return comparisonCount;
    }
    return comparisonCount;
}
```

Then I create another theory based on that code:

> Theory 5: If the size of *testArray* is *n*, then *binarySearchComparisonCount(testArray, target)* must return a number less than, or equal to, $1 + \log2 n$.

---

* Instead of modifying binarySearch to return the comparison count, a better, cleaner, and more object-oriented design (suggested by David Saff) would be to create a CountingComparator class that implements Java's generalized Comparator interface and to modify binarySearch to take an instance of that class as a third parameter. This would generalize binarySearch to work with types other than integers, another example of how testing can lead to better design and more beautiful code.

Here's the code for the theory:

```java
public void assertTheory5(int[] testArray, int target) {
    int numberOfComparisons =
        Util.binarySearchComparisonCount(testArray, target);
    assertTrue(numberOfComparisons <= 1 + log2(testArray.length));
}
```

I add this latest theory to my existing list inside the method testTheories, which now looks like this:

```java
...
    while (experiments-- > 0) {
        testArray = generateRandomSortedArray();
        if (rand.nextInt() % 2 == 0) {
            target = testArray[rand.nextInt(testArray.length)];
        } else {
            target = rand.nextInt();
        }
        returnValue = Util.binarySearch(testArray, target);
        assertTheory1(testArray, target, returnValue);
        assertTheory2(testArray, target, returnValue);
        assertTheory3(testArray, target, returnValue);
        assertTheory4(testArray, target, returnValue);
        assertTheory5(testArray, target);
    }
...
```

I run a few tests with a maxArraySize set of a few different values, and I find that Theory 5 seems to be holding strong.

Because it's almost noon, I set the number of experiments to 1,000,000 and go to lunch while my computer crunches away and tests each theory a million times.

When I get back, I see that all my tests pass. There are probably a couple more things that I would want to test, but I have made great progress in boosting *my* confidence in this implementation of binarySearch. Because different developers have different backgrounds, styles, and levels of experience, you might have focused on different areas of the code. A developer already familiar with the unsigned shift operator, for example, would not feel the same need I had to test it.

In this section, I wanted to give you a flavor of performance testing and show you how you could gain insight into and confidence in your code's performance by combining code instrumentation with test theories. I highly recommend you study Chapter 3, where Jon Bentley gives this important topic the attention and beautiful treatment it deserves.

Conclusion

In this chapter, we have seen that even the best developers and the most beautiful code can benefit from testing. We have also seen that writing test code can be every bit as creative and challenging as writing the target code. And, hopefully, I've shown you that tests themselves can be considered beautiful in at least three different ways.

Some tests are beautiful for their simplicity and efficiency. With a few lines of JUnit code, run automatically with every build, you can document the code's intended behavior and boundaries, and ensure that both of them are preserved as the code evolves.

Other tests are beautiful because, in the process of writing them, they help you improve the code they are meant to test in subtle but important ways. They may not discover proper bugs or defects, but they bring to the surface problems with the design, testability, or maintainability of the code; they help you make your code more beautiful.

Finally, some tests are beautiful for their breadth and thoroughness. They help you gain confidence that the functionality and performance of the code match requirements and expectations, not just on a few handpicked examples, but with a wide range of inputs and conditions.

Developers who want to write beautiful code can learn something from artists. Painters regularly put down their brushes, step away from the canvas, circle it, cock their heads, squint, and look at it from different angles and under different lights. They need to develop and integrate those perspectives in their quest for beauty. If your canvas is an IDE and your medium is code, think of testing as your way of stepping away from the canvas to look at your work with critical eyes and from different perspectives—it will make you a better programmer and help you create more beautiful code.

## CHAPTER EIGHT

On-the-Fly Code Generation for Image Processing

Charles Petzold

AMONG THE PEARLS OF WISDOM AND WACKINESS CHRONICLED in Steven Levy's classic history *Hackers: Heroes of the Computer Revolution* (Doubleday), my favorite is this one by Bill Gosper, who once said, "Data is just a dumb kind of programming." The corollary, of course, is that code is just a smart kind of data—data designed to trigger processors into performing certain useful or amusing acts.

The potential interplay of code and data tends to be discouraged in most conventional programming instruction. Code and data are usually severely segregated; even in object-oriented programming, code and data have their own special roles to play. Any intermingling of the two—such as data being executed as if it were machine code—is considered to be a violation of natural law.

Only occasionally is this barrier between code and data breached. Compiler authors write programs that read source code and generate machine code, but compilers do not really violate the separation of code and data. Where the input and output are code to the human programmers, they are just data to the compilers. Other odd jobs, such as those performed by disassemblers or simulators, also read machine code as if it were data.

As we all accept rationally, if not emotionally, code and data are ultimately just bytes, and there are only 256 of them in the entire universe. It's not the bytes themselves but their ordering that gives them meaning and purpose.

In some special cases, it can be advantageous for programs that are not compilers to generate code while they're running. This *on-the-fly code generation* is not easy, so it's usually restricted to very particular circumstances.

Throughout this chapter, we will use an example that embodies the most common reason for using on-the-fly code generation. In this example, a time-critical subroutine must perform many repetitive operations. A number of generalized parameters come into play during the execution of these repetitive operations, and the subroutine could run a lot faster if we replaced those generalized parameters with specific values. We can't replace those parameters while we're writing the subroutine because the parameters aren't known until runtime, and they can change from one invocation to the next. However, the subroutine itself could do the code generation while it's running. In other words, the subroutine can examine its own parameters at runtime, generate more efficient code, and then execute the resulting code.

I first stumbled upon this technique while writing assembly language. I had a subroutine that performed many repetitive operations. At a crucial point, the subroutine would execute either a bitwise AND operation or a bitwise OR operation, depending on some other value that remained constant during these operations. The actual testing of this value to perform the AND or OR operation was inside the loop and was itself taking too much time. I considered splitting the routine into two entirely separate routines, one with the AND operation and one with the OR operation, until I realized that the subroutine could begin by examining the value, then insert the actual AND or OR machine code instruction right into the execution stream.

The technique of on-the-fly code generation was implemented in a much larger way in the first release of Microsoft Windows (version 1.0), which came out in November 1985 and has since come to have some moderate success in the personal computer marketplace. From a programmer's perspective, the first version of Windows offered roughly 200 functions for creating graphical user interfaces and for displaying vector and raster graphics on both the screen and printer in a fairly device-independent manner.

Among the graphics functions in Windows 1.0 was one called *BitBlt*, which was named after an instruction on the seminal Xerox Alto and stood for *bit block transfer*. In its most basic use, BitBlt rendered bitmaps on the screen and printer, but it was also used internally in Windows for displaying many user interface objects. More generally, BitBlt transferred rectangular arrays of pixels from a source to a destination. A related function called *StretchBlt* could stretch or compress the source pixels into a larger or smaller destination rectangle during this process.

If the BitBlt source is a bitmap, and if the destination is the video display, BitBlt copies the pixels from the bitmap to the display, essentially rendering the bitmap on the screen. If the source is the display and the destination is a bitmap, BitBlt copies pixels from the screen to the bitmap. The bitmap image is then a captured screen image.

However, if you're writing a routine like BitBlt, you might imagine incorporating some extra value and utility that go beyond the mere transfer of bits. Suppose you want an option that will invert the pixels as they're transferred from the source to the destination; black pixels become white, light gray becomes dark gray, and green becomes magenta.

And suppose you then discover that a colleague would be overjoyed if BitBlt could examine the destination as it's transferring pixels, and transfer pixels from the source to the destination only if the destination pixels at each particular point are black. This feature would allow the display of nonrectangular images. For example, a black-filled circle could be drawn on the screen, and then BitBlt would display a bitmap only within that circle. And then somebody else requests an option that combines the ones just mentioned, in which BitBlt inverts its source pixels when the destination is black.

As you start investigating these types of options, you might discover a way to generalize them all. Consider a monochrome graphics system; every pixel is just one bit, where 0 means black and 1 means white. In such a system, a source bitmap is an array of 1-bit pixels, and the screen is an array of 1-bit pixels. The destination's color at a particular pixel location depends on the value of the source pixel (0 or 1) and the value of the destination pixel (0 or 1).

The result at the destination for any particular combination of source and destination pixels is called a *raster operation* or *raster op*, and there are 16 of them, as Table 8-1 illustrates.

TABLE 8-1. Basic raster ops

Possible combinations		
Input parameter	Input value	
Source (S):	1 1 0 0	
Destination (D):	1 0 1 0	
Operation	**Output**	**Logical representation**
Raster operation 0:	0 0 0 0	0
Raster operation 1:	0 0 0 1	~(S | D)
Raster operation 2:	0 0 1 0	~S & D
Raster operation 3:	0 0 1 1	~S
Raster operation 4:	0 1 0 0	S & ~D
Raster operation 5:	0 1 0 1	~D
Raster operation 6:	0 1 1 0	S ^ D
Raster operation 7:	0 1 1 1	~(S & D)
Raster operation 8:	1 0 0 0	S & D
Raster operation 9:	1 0 0 1	~(S ^ D)

TABLE 8-1. Basic raster ops (continued)

Possible combinations		
Operation	**Output**	**Logical representation**
Raster operation 10:	1 0 1 0	D
Raster operation 11:	1 0 1 1	~S | D
Raster operation 12:	1 1 0 0	S
Raster operation 13:	1 1 0 1	S | ~D
Raster operation 14:	1 1 1 0	S | D
Raster operation 15:	1 1 1 1	1

There are four possible combinations of source and destination pixels, and each raster operation does something different for those four combinations, so the total number is 2^4, or 16. Each of the 16 possible raster operations is identified by a number that corresponds to the pattern of resultant pixels shown in the table. The "Logical representation" column shows (in C syntax) the actual Boolean operation occurring between the source and destination pixels.

For example, in *raster operation 12* (the most common), the source is simply transferred to the destination and in *raster operation 14*, the source is transferred to the destination only when the destination is black. *Raster operation 10* leaves the destination the same regardless of the source. *Raster operations 0* and *15* simply color the destination black and white, respectively, again independent of the source.

In a color graphics system, each pixel is generally 24-bits wide, with 8 bits each for the red, green, and blue primaries. If all bits are 0, the color is black; if all bits are 1, the color is white. The raster operations are applied to corresponding bits of the source and destination. With raster operation 14, for example, the source is displayed in destination areas that were initially colored black. Destination areas initially colored white will remain white. However, if a destination area is red and the source is blue, the result will be a combination of red and blue, or magenta. This is different from the monochrome example, but still entirely predictable.

In Windows, the raster operations for BitBlt and StretchBlt were complicated even further. Windows supported a graphical object called a *pattern* or *brush*, which was commonly used for filling enclosed areas. This pattern could be a solid color or a repetitive image, such as hash marks or bricks. To carry out this type of operation, BitBlt and StretchBlt performed a raster operation between the source, the destination, and a particular pattern. This pattern allowed the program to alter pixel bits of the source (perhaps inverting them or masking them) without regard to the destination.

Because the raster operation implemented by BitBlt and StretchBlt involved three objects—a source, destination, and pattern—it was called a *ternary* raster operation. There are 256 possible ternary raster operations, and BitBlt and StretchBlt supported every single one.

As in our earlier discussion, these 256 ternary raster operations are easier to comprehend if you begin by considering a monochrome graphics system. In addition to the source and destination, the pattern is also an array of 1-bit pixels; visualize the pattern overlaying a destination surface. Table 8-2 shows selections from the 256 ways in which the 0 and 1 pixels of the pattern, source, and destination can be combined.

TABLE 8-2. Ternary raster ops

Possible combinations	
Input parameter	**Input value**
Pattern (P):	1 1 1 1 0 0 0 0
Source (S):	1 1 0 0 1 1 0 0
Operation	**Output**
Raster operation 0x00:	0 0 0 0 0 0 0 0
Raster operation 0x01:	0 0 0 0 0 0 0 1
Raster operation 0x02:	0 0 0 0 0 0 1 0
...	...
Raster operation 0x60:	0 1 1 0 0 0 0 0
...	...
Raster operation 0xFD:	1 1 1 1 1 1 0 1
Raster operation 0xFE:	1 1 1 1 1 1 1 0
Raster operation 0xFF:	1 1 1 1 1 1 1 1

This table shows sample inputs followed by the resulting destinations for 7 of the 256 possible ternary raster operations. Each of these raster operations can be identified by a one-byte hexadecimal number corresponding to the pattern of resultant destination bits shown in the table. For example, for *raster operation 0x60*, if the pattern pixel is 1 (white), the source pixel is 0 (black), and the destination pixel is 1, the destination will be 1 (white).

In the early versions of Windows, 15 of the total 256 raster operations were identified with names in both the documentation and the Windows header file that C programmers used. The first—where the destination is colored with all 0s regardless of the pattern, source, and destination—was known as BLACKNESS; the last was called WHITENESS.

The Windows programming reference identified all 256 raster operations by the bitwise Boolean operation they performed, expressed in reverse Polish notation. For example, raster operation 0x60 corresponds to the Boolean operation *PDSxa.*

This means that an Exclusive-OR (x) operation is performed between the destination (D) and the source (S), and the result is combined with the pattern (P) in a bitwise AND operation (a). In color systems, the same Boolean operation is performed among the color bits of the source, destination, and pattern. As of this writing, these raster operations are documented online at *http://msdn.microsoft.com/library/en-us/gdi/pantdraw_6n77.asp.*

Some of these raster operations are quite useful in certain circumstances. For example, you might want to invert the destination pixels that correspond to areas where a brush is black, but display a source bitmap in areas where the brush is white. That's *raster operation 0xC5*. Of course, many of the 256 possibilities have little practical use, and I suspect that most of them have never been used outside of demonstration or exploratory code. Still, the sense of completeness and versatility is quite satisfying.

If we were implementing this versatile BitBlt function ourselves, how would we do it? Assume that it's 1985 and we're using the C programming language. For illustrative purposes, let's also assume that we're dealing with a one-byte-per-pixel gray shade graphics system, and that the source, destination, and pattern can be accessed through two-dimensional arrays named S, D, and P. That is, each of these variables is a pointer to a collection of byte pointers, and each byte pointer points to the beginning of a horizontal row of pixels, so that S[y][x] accesses the byte at row *y* and column *x*. The width and height of the area you're working with is stored in *cx* and *cy* (this is a traditional Windows programming variable-naming convention: the *c* stands for *count*, so these variables indicate a count of x and y values, or width and height). The rop variable stores a raster operation code from 0 to 255.

Here's some simple C code to implement using BitBlt. A switch statement uses rop to determine which operation is performed to calculate the pixel values in the destination. Only 3 of the 256 raster operations are shown here, but you get the general idea:

```
for (y = 0; y < cy; y++)
for (x = 0; x < cx; x++)
{
    switch(rop)
    {
    case 0x00:
        D[y][x] = 0x00;
        break;
    ...
    case 0x60:
        D[y][x] = (D[y][x] ^ S[y][x]) & P[y][x];
        break;
    ...
    case 0xFF:
        D[y][x] = 0xFF;
        break;
    }
}
```

This certainly is *pretty* code, which means that it's nice to look at and certainly crystal clear in its intentions and functionality. But beautiful code it is *not*, because beautiful code is also satisfying when you run it.

This code is actually a *disaster* because it deals with bitmaps, and bitmaps can be *huge*. These days, bitmaps that come out of inexpensive digital cameras can have *millions* of pixels. Do you really want that switch statement to be inside the row and column loops?

Should the switch logic be executed for each and every pixel? Probably not. Moving the loops inside each case certainly clutters up the code, but now at least it has a fighting chance of reasonable performance:

```
switch(rop)
{
case 0x00:
    for (y = 0; y < cy; y++)
    for (x = 0; x < cx; x++)
        D[y][x] = 0x00;
    break;
...
case 0x60:
    for (y = 0; y < cy; y++)
    for (x = 0; x < cx; x++)
        D[y][x] = (D[y][x] ^ S[y][x]) & P[y][x];
    break;
...
case 0xFF:
    for (y = 0; y < cy; y++)
    for (x = 0; x < cx; x++)
        D[y][x] = 0xFF;
    break;
}
```

Of course, if it really were 1985 and you were writing Windows, you wouldn't even be doing it in C. Early Windows *applications* were mostly written in C, but Windows itself was written in 8086 assembly language.

For something as important to Windows as BitBlt, an even more radical solution was required—something even faster than assembly language, as incredible as that may seem. The Microsoft programmers who implemented BitBlt were quite proud of what they had done, and those of us learning Windows programming in the mid-1980s were equally impressed when they bragged of their achievement.

The BitBlt function actually contained a mini compiler of sorts. Based on the raster operation (as well as the graphics format, the number of bits per pixel, and the size of the area), the BitBlt function assembled 8086 machine code instructions on the stack in the form of a subroutine and then executed it. This makeshift machine code routine looped through all the pixels and performed the requested raster operation.

It was the perfect solution to implementing BitBlt and its 256 raster operations. Although this mini compiler required a bit of overhead to put the machine code together on the stack, the per-pixel processing was as fast as possible, and that's what is most important when working with bitmaps. Moreover, the BitBlt code in Windows was probably much shorter than it would have been had it contained explicit code for all 256 raster operations.

It was even possible to get a little glimpse into the workings of this BitBlt mini compiler by examining the documentation of the ternary raster operations. For example, the raster operation identified by the number 0x60 implements a Boolean operation of PDSxa. When calling BitBlt, you actually supply a 32-bit raster operation code, which is documented as 0x00600365 for this operation. Notice the 0x60 byte embedded in that number, but also take note that the bottom two bytes form the number 0x0365.

The raster operation with the result of 11110110 or 0xF6 has the Boolean operation PDSxo, which is very similar to PDSxa except that it performs an OR operation rather than AND. The complete 32-bit raster operation code passed to the BitBlt function is 0x00F70265. The bottom two bytes form the number 0x0265, which is very close to the 0x0365 of PDSxa. If you examine more of these 32-bit raster operation codes, it becomes very obvious that the raster operation code itself serves as a template of sorts for the BitBlt mini compiler to assemble the proper machine code. That technique saves BitBlt both the memory and time required to use a lookup table.

Of course, Windows 1.0 was created over 20 years ago. We have all moved on, and so has Windows itself. These days my preferred programming language is neither assembly language nor C, but C#. I usually write what's called *managed code* that runs under the Microsoft .NET Framework. The C# compiler turns my source code into processor-independent *Intermediate Language* (often referred to as Microsoft Intermediate Language, or MSIL). Only later, when the program is run, does the .NET Common Language Runtime use a just-in-time compiler to convert that Intermediate Language into machine code appropriate for the runtime processor.

And yet digital image processing of all sorts still cries out for unusual approaches to coding. When working with millions of pixels, the per-pixel processing has to be fast, fast, fast. For commercial products, you will probably want to hire an assembly language programmer or someone who knows how to target the Graphics Processing Unit (GPU) found on video boards. Even for casual or noncommercial software, you will probably want something faster than the normal high-level language loop.

I was recently reminded of the on-the-fly code generation of the original Windows BitBlt function while experimenting with some C# code to implement digital image filters, also called *image filters* or *digital filters*. Raster operations such as those implemented in the Windows BitBlt and StretchBlt functions apply only to corresponding pixels of a source, destination, and pattern. Digital filters take *surrounding* pixels into account. You apply a particular digital filter to a bitmap to change it in some way, perhaps to sharpen the edges or even blur the overall image. A blur filter, for example, averages a group of surrounding pixels to calculate a destination pixel.

Simple digital image filters are often implemented as small arrays of numbers. These arrays are usually square and have an odd number of rows and columns. Figure 8-1 shows a simple example.

FIGURE 8-1. Simple digital image filter

Figure 8-1 is a 3×3 filter, and you can think of it as transforming a source bitmap into a destination bitmap. For each pixel of the source bitmap, align this filter so its center is over the desired pixel and the other eight cells are aligned with the surrounding pixels. Multiply the nine values in the filter by the nine source pixels, and add up the results. That's the corresponding pixel for the destination bitmap. If the pixels encode color or transparency, you'll want to apply the filter to each color channel separately. Some filters have different arrays for the different color channels or are implemented with algorithms, but we'll stick to the really simple ones for this exercise.

A filter with the value 1/9 in all its cells is a blur filter. Each pixel in the destination bitmap is an average of nine adjacent pixels in the source bitmap. It's convenient that the numbers add up to 1 so the image doesn't get any brighter or darker, but this filter could easily contain all 1s or any other number. All that would be necessary to compensate would be to divide the sum of the products by the sum of the filter cells (as will become apparent, I actually prefer that method).

Figure 8-2 shows a sharpness filter. This filter tends to highlight areas of high contrast.

FIGURE 8-2. Sharpness filter

Let's suppose we're dealing with gray-shaded bitmaps with one byte per pixel. The pixels of the source bitmap are stored in a two-dimensional array named S. Our job is to calculate the pixels of the destination array named D. The horizontal and vertical sizes of both arrays are stored in the variables cxBitmap and cyBitmap. The Filter is a two-dimensional array named F with dimensions cxFilter and cyFilter. Example 8-1 shows some simple C code for applying the filter.

EXAMPLE 8-1. Naïve C code to apply a digital filter

```c
for (yDestination = 0; yDestination < cyBitmap; yDestination++)
for (xDestination = 0; xDestination < cxBitmap; xDestination++)
{
    double pixelsAccum = 0;
    double filterAccum = 0;

    for (yFilter = 0; yFilter < cyFilter; yFilter++)
    for (xFilter = 0; xFilter < cxFilter; xFilter++)
    {
        int ySource = yDestination + yFilter - cyFilter / 2;
        int xSource = xDestination + xFilter - cxFilter / 2;

        (if ySource >= 0 && ySource < cyBitmap &&
            xSource >= 0 && xSource < cxBitmap)
        {
            pixelsAccum += F[y][x] * S[y][x];
            filterAccum += F[y][x];
        }
    }
    if (filterAccum != 0)
        pixelsAccum /= filterAccum;

    if (pixelsAccum < 0)
        D[y][x] = 0;

    else if (pixelsAccum > 255)
        D[y][x] = 255;

    else
        D[y][x] = (unsigned char) pixelsAccum;
}
```

Notice that looping through the filter cells results in accumulating two totals. The pixelsAccum variable is a sum of the products of the source bitmap values and the filter cells, while filterAccum is a sum of the filter cells only. For destination pixels around the edges of the bitmap, some cells of the filter correspond to pixels outside the extent of the source bitmap. I prefer to ignore those cells by adding nothing to pixelsAccum and filterAccum, but to later divide pixelsAccum by filterAccum so that the destination pixel is approximately correct. That's why filterAccum isn't calculated outside the loop and why the filter cells don't have to be normalized to add up to one. Also notice toward the end of this code that the ratio of pixelsAccum to filterAccum has to be clamped between 0 and 255 so no strange effects result.

For every pixel of the destination bitmap, both the source bitmap and the filter must be accessed nine times. Moreover, as the resolution of bitmaps gets higher, filters must often get larger as well to have a noticeable effect on the image.

It's a lot of processing for a high-level language, but I was curious to discover how C# and .NET would fare in handling the pressure. For my experimentation with C# image processing, I began with some Windows Forms code from my book *Programming Windows with*

C# (Microsoft Press). The `ImageClip` progam in Chapter 24 of that book incorporates code that will load, view, print, and save bitmaps of various popular formats, including JPEG, GIF, and PNG. That code, along with the code I wrote for this exercise, is available for downloading and contributes to a program named `ImageFilterTest`. The project file requires Visual Studio 2005 for compilation; the executable should run under the .NET Framework 2.0 and later. Perform the following steps to use the program:

1. In the File menu, select Open and load in a full-color bitmap. The filter-related code in the program only works with 24-bit-per-pixel or 32-bit-per-pixel bitmaps; it doesn't work with bitmaps that use color palette tables, including those where the palette table contains gray shades.

2. Select one of the filters in the Filter menu. The filter will be applied to the bitmap and the elapsed time will be reported. The first item in the Filter menu ("Use method that generates Intermediate Language") lets you select the method used to apply the filter. By default, the program uses a method called `FilterMethodCS` (short for "Filter Method using C#"). If you enable this menu item, the program uses `FilterMethodIL` ("Filter Method with Intermediate Language"). Both of these methods will be described later in this chapter.

Whenever you attempt to write C# code for best performance, one of the more interesting exercises is to examine the compiled file using a little utility included with the .NET Software Development Kit called *IL Disassembler*. The IL Disassembler shows you the Intermediate Language generated by the C# compiler. Although the program doesn't show you the final step—the conversion of the Intermediate Language into machine code by the just-in-time compiler—you can usually use it to locate some problem areas.

Very early on, I gave up on the idea of storing bitmap pixels in two-dimensional arrays. C# supports multidimensional arrays, but on the Intermediate Language level, getting elements in and out of multidimensional arrays requires method calls. Intermediate Language instructions do, however, support access to one-dimensional arrays. Furthermore, the standard (and fast) code for transferring pixels from a Bitmap object into an array and back into a Bitmap object involves a one-dimensional array. The code I wrote to transfer everything into a two-dimensional array involved a considerable amount of time just by itself.

To encapsulate image filters and the methods that apply these filters to bitmaps, I created a class named `ImageFilter` that contains three private fields and a constructor that sets the fields. The private field `filter` is a one-dimensional array that contains a two-dimensional filter, so the `cxFilter` and `cyFilter` fields are necessary to indicate the implicit number of columns and rows:

```
class ImageFilter
{
    double[] filter;
    int cxFilter;
    int cyFilter;
```

```
    public ImageFilter(int cxFilter, double[] filter)
    {
        this.filter = filter;
        this.cxFilter = cxFilter;
        this.cyFilter = filter.Length / cxFilter;
    }
    ...
}
```

If only square filters were allowed, the cxFilter parameter to the constructor wouldn't be necessary, and the number of rows and columns could simply be calculated as the square root of the size of the filter array, which is available as filter.Length. The cxFilter parameter allows for rectangular filter arrays rather than just square ones. If cxFilter indicates the number of columns in the filter, the number of rows is filter.Length/cxFilter, which my code implicitly assumes is an integer.

The Filter class includes a method named ApplyFilter, which has a parameter of type Bitmap. I won't show you the ApplyFilter method here because it simply contains standard code to first access the pixels of the Bitmap object (using a method named LockBits), and then to transfer the pixels into a one-dimensional array. A second parameter of ApplyFilter is a Boolean named willGenerateCode. If *false*, the ApplyFilter method calls FilterMethodCS.

FilterMethodCS, shown in Example 8-2, is a fairly straightforward implementation of the filtering algorithm from Example 8-1, but it has been translated to C# and uses one-dimensional arrays.

EXAMPLE 8-2. A digital filter algorithm in C#

```
 1  void FilterMethodCS(byte[] src, byte[] dst, int stride, int bytesPerPixel)
 2  {
 3      int cBytes = src.Length;
 4      int cFilter = filter.Length;
 5
 6      for (int iDst = 0; iDst < cBytes; iDst++)
 7      {
 8          double pixelsAccum = 0;
 9          double filterAccum = 0;
10
11          for (int iFilter = 0; iFilter < cFilter; iFilter++)
12          {
13              int yFilter = iFilter / cyFilter;
14              int xFilter = iFilter % cxFilter;
15
16              int iSrc = iDst + stride * (yFilter - cyFilter / 2) +
17                                bytesPerPixel * (xFilter - cxFilter / 2);
18
19              if (iSrc >= 0 && iSrc < cBytes)
20              {
21                  pixelsAccum += filter[iFilter] * src[iSrc];
22                  filterAccum += filter[iFilter];
23              }
24          }
```

EXAMPLE 8-2. A digital filter algorithm in C# (continued)

```
25          if (filterAccum != 0)
26              pixelsAccum /= filterAccum;
27
28          dst[iDst] = pixelsAccum < 0 ? (byte)0 : (pixelsAccum > 255 ?
29                                  (byte)255 : (byte)pixelsAccum);
30      }
31 }
```

The first two parameters are the source and destination arrays src and dst. The third
parameter is stride, which is the number of bytes in each row of the source and destination bitmaps. This stride value is generally equal to the pixel width of the bitmap times
the number of bytes per pixel, but for performance reasons it might be rounded up to a
four-byte boundary. (Because the program only works with full-color bitmaps, the number of bytes per pixel will always be three or four.) It's not necessary to calculate the stride
value because it's provided with the information returned by the LockBits method when
you get access to the bitmap bits. The method begins by saving the number of bytes in
both the src and filter arrays to avoid frequent accesses of the Length property. The variables that begin with the letter *i* are indexes to the three arrays used in the method.

If the goal here is to write a *fast* digital filter algorithm, then FilterMethodCS is a failure.
With a 24-bit-per-pixel 300,000-pixel bitmap and a 5×5 filter, this method requires about
two seconds on my 1.5 GHz Pentium 4. Two seconds might not seem too bad, but a 5×5
filter applied to a 32-bit-per-pixel 4.3 megapixel bitmap requires about half a minute, and
that is *very* long. Yet I can't see any way to improve the C# code to make it more efficient.

Traditionally, if a function isn't working fast enough and you don't feel you can optimize
it any further, you start considering assembly language. In this era of platform independence and managed code, you might instead consider the vaguely equivalent approach of
writing the routine directly in .NET Intermediate Language. This is certainly an entirely
plausible solution, and might even be considered fun (to the right type of mentality).
However, even coding in Intermediate Language might not be sufficient. Use the IL
Disassembler to look at the Intermediate Language generated by the C# compiler for
FilterMethodCS. Do you really think you can improve greatly on that?

The real problem with FilterMethodCS is that it's generalized for bitmaps of any dimension
and for filters of any dimension. Much of the code in FilterMethodCS is just "busy work"
involved with looping and indexing. This method could be improved dramatically if it didn't
have to be so generalized. Suppose you were always dealing with 32-bit-per-pixel bitmaps
of the same size, which I'll symbolize as *CX* and *CY* (think of these uppercase letters as
#defines in C or C++, or const values in C#). And suppose you always used the same filter—
a 3×3 filter with fixed elements whose fields are symbolized like the ones in Figure 8-3.

F11	F12	F13
F21	F22	F23
F31	F32	F33

FIGURE 8-3. Array layout of a 3x3 filter

How would you write the filter method then? You might decide to dispense with the iFilter loop and just hardcode the logic for the nine filter elements:

```
// Filter cell F11
int iSrc = iDst - 4 * CX - 4;

if (iSrc >= 0 && iSrc < 4 * CX * CY)
{
    pixelsAccum += src[iSrc] * F11;
    filterAccum += F11;
}

// Filter cell F12
iSrc = iDst - 4 * CX;

if (iSrc >= 0 && iSrc < 4 * CX * CY)
{
    pixelsAccum += src[iSrc] * F12;
    filterAccum += F12;
}

// Filter cells F13 through F32
...

// Filter cell F33
iSrc = iDst + 4 * CX + 4;

if (iSrc >= 0 && iSrc < 4 * CX * CY)
{
    pixelsAccum += src[iSrc] * F33;
    filterAccum += F33;
}
```

This approach gets rid of the looping logic, simplifies the calculation of iSrc, and eliminates the access of the filter array. Although the code is definitely bulkier, it is guaranteed to be faster. In fact, because you know the values of all the filter elements, you can reduce the code somewhat by eliminating those cases where the filter element is 0, and simplifying those cases where the filter element is 1 or –1.

Of course, hardcoding this logic isn't practical because you really want the ability to deal with many differently sized bitmaps and many types of filters. These properties are not known until it's time to actually apply the filter.

Rather than hardcoding the filter logic, a much better approach would be to generate custom code on the fly based on the size and pixel depth of the bitmap, and the size and elements of the filter. In olden days, you might do as the Windows developers did with BitBlt, which was to generate machine code in memory, and then execute it. Translated to modern times, with our concern for portability, the solution might be to generate .NET Intermediate Language using C#, and then execute it.

This is actually a workable solution. In a C# program you can create a static method in memory that consists of instructions in Intermediate Language, and then execute that method, at which point the .NET just-in-time compiler enters the picture to convert your Intermediate Language to machine code. At no time during this entire process do you stop writing managed code.

The facility to dynamically generate Intermediate Language was introduced in .NET 2.0 and involves classes in the System.Reflection.Emit namespace. You can generate whole classes and even entire assemblies, but for smaller applications (such as the one we're developing), you can simply generate a static method and then call it. This is what I've done in FilterMethodIL in the ImageFilter class.

I'm going to show you all of FilterMethodIL here (but eliminating many of the comments you'll find in the *ImageFilter.cs* source code file) because it involves some interesting interplay between the C# code and the generated Intermediate Language. Keep in mind throughout this exercise that FilterMethodIL generates this Intermediate Language whenever a specific filter is applied to a specific bitmap, so all aspects of the filter can be hardcoded into the Intermediate Language, as well as the size and pixel depth of the bitmap. Obviously, some overhead is required to generate this code, but that cost is dwarfed by the number of operations required by large bitmaps, which might easily have over a million pixels.

All the code in FilterMethodIL is shown below in sequence, with explanations throughout to describe what's going on and introduce new concepts. FilterMethodIL has the same parameters as FilterMethodCS and begins by obtaining the total byte size of the bitmap:

```
void FilterMethodIL(byte[] src, byte[] dst, int stride, int bytesPerPixel)
{
    int cBytes = src.Length;
```

To create a static method in code, you create a new object of type DynamicMethod. The second argument to the constructor indicates the method's return type, and the third argument is an array of the method's parameter types. The fourth argument is the class that's creating this method, and is available from the GetType method:

```
DynamicMethod dynameth = new DynamicMethod("Go", typeof(void),
    new Type[] { typeof(byte[]), typeof(byte[]) }, GetType( ));
```

As you can see by the third argument to the constructor, the two parameters in this dynamic method are both byte arrays, and these will be the src and dst arrays from Example 8-2. Throughout the Intermediate Language, these two arguments are referred to with indexes 0 and 1.

To generate the Intermediate Language that comprises the body of this method, you obtain an object of type ILGenerator:

```
ILGenerator generator = dynameth.GetILGenerator( );
```

Most of what follows will use this generator object. You can begin by defining local variables of the method. I determined that it would be convenient to have three local variables corresponding to three of the local variables in the FilterMethodCS:

```
generator.DeclareLocal(typeof(int));      // Index 0 = iDst
generator.DeclareLocal(typeof(double));   // Index 1 = pixelsAccum
generator.DeclareLocal(typeof(double));   // Index 2 = filterAccum
```

As the comments indicate, these local variables will be referred to by indexes. We are now ready to begin defining a loop based around iDst that will access all the pixels of the destination array. These three statements correspond to the declarations of these variables in lines 3, 4, and 6 of Example 8-2.

Much of the remainder of this exercise requires generating Intermediate Language operation codes, which are similar to machine language op codes. Intermediate Language consists of one-byte op codes, sometimes with arguments. However, you don't need to get your hands dirty with the actual bits and bytes. To generate these op codes, call one of the overloads of the Emit method defined by the IlGenerator class. The first argument to Emit is always an object of type OpCode, and all the available op codes are predefined as static readonly fields of the OpCodes class (notice the plural). As of this writing, the OpCodes class is documented online at *http://msdn2.microsoft.com/library/system.reflection.emit.opcodes.aspx*.

Most of the assignment and operational logic in Intermediate Language is based on a virtual *evaluation stack*. (I say it's virtual because the actual code that will eventually be executed by your computer processor is machine code generated by the just-in-time compiler, and this code might or might not mimic the evaluation stack of the Intermediate Language.) A load instruction pushes a value onto the stack. This can be either a specific number or a value from a local variable, or something else. A store instruction retrieves the value from the stack and stores it in a local variable or someplace else. Arithmetic and logical operations are also performed on the stack. Add, for example, pops two values from the stack, adds them, and pushes the result onto the stack.

Setting the local iDst variable to 0 in Intermediate Language requires a load instruction and a store instruction. The Ldc_I4_0 instruction places a four-byte integer value of 0 on the stack, and the Stloc_0 instruction stores that value in the local variable with index 0, which is the local variable corresponding to iDst:

```
generator.Emit(OpCodes.Ldc_I4_0);
generator.Emit(OpCodes.Stloc_0);
```

Although many high-level programming languages include a goto (or equivalent) instruction, modern programmers are discouraged from using it. However, in assembly language and Intermediate Language, the goto—generally known as a *jump* or *branch* instruction—is the only form of flow control available. All for and if statements must be mimicked with branching.

The .NET Intermediate Language supports an unconditional branch statement and several conditional branch statements. These conditional branches depend on the results of a specified prior comparison. For example a *branch if less than* instruction performs a branch if, in a previous comparison, one value was less than another. Mimicking an if and else construction in Intermediate Language requires two labels, one corresponding to the beginning of the else block, and the other pointing after the else block. If the if condition is not true, a conditional branch goes to the first label; otherwise, the if block is executed. At the end of the if block, an unconditional branch goes to the label following the else block. The two possibilities are illustrated by Figure 8-4.

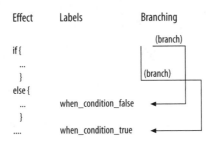

FIGURE 8-4. *Intermediate Language branches to implement if/else*

The actual branch instruction code in Intermediate Language contains a numeric value indicating the address of the destination instruction as an offset to the address of the current instruction. Figuring out these offsets would be too painful for programmers, so a labeling system is provided to make things easier. All that is required is that you define where labels should be inserted in the instruction stream, so that when you indicate a branch to that label, the code generator can calculate the proper numeric offset.

Two method calls are required for using a label. The DefineLabel call defines a label that you can then refer to in branching instructions. The MarkLabel call actually inserts the label into the Intermediate Language instruction stream. This two-step process allows you to define a label and then emit an op code that branches to that label, even though the label won't actually appear until later in the instruction stream. The following lines call both DefineLabel and MarkLabel to put a Label object named labelTop at the top of the *iDst* loop:

```
Label labelTop = generator.DefineLabel();
generator.MarkLabel(labelTop);
```

This label is equivalent to the location of the for statement in line 6 of the C# code listing in Example 8-2. A label is required here because code at the end of the loop has to branch to the top of the loop.

We're now generating code within the iDst loop. This is the per-pixel processing. The first step is to initialize pixelsAccum and filterAccum to 0. The first Emit call shown in the following code snippet has an op code of Ldc_R8, which will load an 8-bit real (that is, a floating-point number) on the stack. The second argument of Emit is the actual number. The type of this number must match the type implied by the op code. If you just use a 0 with no decimal point, the C# compiler will interpret it as an integer, and you won't know you blundered until a runtime exception indicates an invalid program:

```
generator.Emit(OpCodes.Ldc_R8, 0.0);
generator.Emit(OpCodes.Dup);
generator.Emit(OpCodes.Stloc_1);
generator.Emit(OpCodes.Stloc_2);
```

The Dup instruction duplicates the 0 value on the stack, and the Stloc_1 and Stloc_2 op codes store the value in the local variables representing pixelsAccum and filterAccum. Again, you must make sure that all the types agree here; otherwise, a runtime exception will be raised indicating that the just-in-time compiler detected an invalid program.

At this point, we're ready to generate code for each of the elements in the filter array. However, we don't want the Intermediate Language to loop through the filter array and access each element. Instead, we want all the filter elements to be hardcoded in Intermediate Language. If the filter has nine elements, we want nine similar sections of Intermediate Language. For that reason, we use a C# for statement to loop through the filter elements:

```
for (int iFilter = 0; iFilter < filter.Length; iFilter++)
{
```

If a particular element of the filter is 0, that element can be entirely ignored—no Intermediate Language code has to be generated, so we can just skip to the next element of the filter array:

```
if (filter[iFilter] == 0)
    continue;
```

For each filter element, the index of the src array will be a particular offset from the iDst index. The following C# code calculates that offset. The offset value can be calculated in C# code because it only has to be represented as a constant in Intermediate Language:

```
int xFilter = iFilter % cxFilter;
int yFilter = iFilter / cxFilter;
int offset = stride * (yFilter - cyFilter / 2) +
             bytesPerPixel * (xFilter - cxFilter / 2);
```

Accessing or setting an element of an array is a three-step process. First, you need to put a reference to the array on the stack. Then you need to put an index of the array on the stack. Finally, if you're accessing that element, you need a load instruction, and if you're setting the array element, you need a store instruction. The src array must be accessed for each nonzero element of the filter array, so now is a convenient time to put a reference to that array on the evaluation stack:

```
generator.Emit(OpCodes.Ldarg_0);
```

The Ldarg instruction refers to the arguments to the generated method, and the src array will be the first argument associated with an index of 0.

Next, we will specify several labels. Notice that these three labels are defined so that Intermediate Language instructions can refer to them, but they're not marked yet because they will be inserted at a later point in the Intermediate Language instruction stream:

```
Label labelLessThanZero = generator.DefineLabel();
Label labelGreaterThan = generator.DefineLabel();
Label labelLoopBottom = generator.DefineLabel();
```

For each element of the filter, the src array must be accessed with the iDst index plus an offset value that has already been calculated by C# code. The following code puts iDst on the stack, followed by the actual offset value, adds the two together (which effectively pops the two operands from the stack and pushes the sum on the stack), and makes two duplicates of the sum:

```
generator.Emit(OpCodes.Ldloc_0);         // dst index on stack
generator.Emit(OpCodes.Ldc_I4, offset);  // offset on stack
generator.Emit(OpCodes.Add);             // Add the two
generator.Emit(OpCodes.Dup);             // Duplicate twice
generator.Emit(OpCodes.Dup);
```

The resultant index (which was called iSrc in FilterMethodCS) might be outside the bounds of the array. The following code loads an integer 0 on the stack and branches if iSrc is less than 0, effectively popping both operands from the stack. This is a partial equivalent of the if statement conditional in line 19 of Example 8-2:

```
generator.Emit(OpCodes.Ldc_I4_0);
generator.Emit(OpCodes.Blt_S, labelLessThanZero);
```

Blt stands for *branch if less than* and S indicates a *short* branch (one in which the target is fewer than 256 op code bytes away).

A second check determines whether iSrc is greater than the byte size of the bitmap. Notice that the literal cBytes value is pushed on the stack for this comparison. This is the remainder of the if conditional in line 19 of Example 8-2:

```
generator.Emit(OpCodes.Ldc_I4, cBytes);
generator.Emit(OpCodes.Bge_S, labelGreaterThan);
```

If iSrc is good, the source array can be accessed. The Ldelem op code assumes that the array itself and an index to the array are already on the stack. Those two values are effectively popped and replaced with the array element at that index. The U1 part of this op code specifies that the array element is an unsigned one-byte value:

```
generator.Emit(OpCodes.Ldelem_U1);
generator.Emit(OpCodes.Conv_R8);
```

The Conv_R8 op code converts the value on the stack to an eight-byte floating-point value and replaces it on the stack.

At this point, the byte at iSrc is on the stack and has been converted to a floating point. It is ready to be multiplied by a filter element. Because the value of the filter element is known at the time the method is being generated, C# code skips the multiplication if the filter element is 1 (no multiplication is required if the filter element is 1):

```
if (filter[iFilter] == 1)
{
    // src element is on stack, so do nothing
}
```

If the filter element is –1, the source byte can simply be negated, perhaps saving a little processing time over the multiplication:

```
else if (filter[iFilter] == -1)
{
    generator.Emit(OpCodes.Neg);
}
```

Otherwise, the byte is multiplied by the filter element:

```
else
{
    generator.Emit(OpCodes.Ldc_R8, filter[iFilter]);
    generator.Emit(OpCodes.Mul);
}
```

You might recall that pixelsAccum was defined as a local variable with an index of 1. The following code puts pixelsAccum on the stack, adds to it the source byte value multiplied by the filter element, and stores the result back in pixelsAccum:

```
generator.Emit(OpCodes.Ldloc_1);
generator.Emit(OpCodes.Add);
generator.Emit(OpCodes.Stloc_1);
```

Similarly, filterAccum (which has a local variable index of 2) must accumulate the values of the filter elements:

```
generator.Emit(OpCodes.Ldc_R8, filter[iFilter]);
generator.Emit(OpCodes.Ldloc_2);
generator.Emit(OpCodes.Add);
generator.Emit(OpCodes.Stloc_2);
generator.Emit(OpCodes.Br, labelLoopBottom);
```

At this point, we're at the bottom of the inner for loop, equivalent to line 24 of Example 8-2. We are essentially finished with the processing for each filter element, except that the stack has to be cleaned up for cases where the calculated iSrc index is outside the bounds of the bitmap. This section of the generated code (at the bottom of the C# for loop for iFilter) marks the three labels and performs cleanup by popping unused items from the stack:

```
generator.MarkLabel(labelLessThanZero);
generator.Emit(OpCodes.Pop);
generator.MarkLabel(labelGreaterThan);
generator.Emit(OpCodes.Pop);
generator.Emit(OpCodes.Pop);
generator.MarkLabel(labelLoopBottom);
}
```

So far, all the code has been generated to calculate `pixelsAccum` and `filterAccum` for a particular destination pixel. The result is almost ready to be transferred into the `dst` array. The array reference (which has a method argument index of 1) and the `iDst` index (which has a local variable index of 0) are both loaded on the stack:

```
generator.Emit(OpCodes.Ldarg_1);        // dst array
generator.Emit(OpCodes.Ldloc_0);        // iDst index
```

There will be some branching involved, so the following labels are defined:

```
Label labelSkipDivide = generator.DefineLabel( );
Label labelCopyQuotient = generator.DefineLabel( );
Label labelBlack = generator.DefineLabel( );
Label labelWhite = generator.DefineLabel( );
Label labelDone = generator.DefineLabel( );
```

The following code loads both the `pixelsAccum` and `filterAccum` local variables on the stack in preparation for division. The first task is to check for a potential zero-divide by comparing `filterAccum` with 0. This code is equivalent to line 25 in Example 8-2:

```
generator.Emit(OpCodes.Ldloc_1);        // pixelsAccum
generator.Emit(OpCodes.Ldloc_2);        // filterAccum
generator.Emit(OpCodes.Dup);            // Make a copy
generator.Emit(OpCodes.Ldc_R8, 0.0);    // Put 0 on stack
generator.Emit(OpCodes.Beq_S, labelSkipDivide);
```

If the denominator is not 0, the division is executed and the quotient remains on the stack:

```
generator.Emit(OpCodes.Div);
generator.Emit(OpCodes.Br_S, labelCopyQuotient);
```

If `filterAccum` is 0, the following code is executed and the original instance of `filterAccum` is popped from the stack:

```
generator.MarkLabel(labelSkipDivide);
generator.Emit(OpCodes.Pop);            // Pop filterAccum
```

In either case, what remains on the stack is `pixelsAccum`, either divided by `filterAccum` or not. Two copies of that quotient are made:

```
generator.MarkLabel(labelCopyQuotient);
generator.Emit(OpCodes.Dup);            // Make a copy of quotient
generator.Emit(OpCodes.Dup);            // And another
```

Most of what follows is the Intermediate Language equivalent of the statement in lines 28 and 29 of Example 8-2. If the quotient is less than zero, the code branches to a label where the destination pixel will be set to 0:

```
generator.Emit(OpCodes.Ldc_R8, 0.0);
generator.Emit(OpCodes.Blt_S, labelBlack);
```

If the quotient is greater than 255, the following code branches to a label where the destination pixel will be set to 255:

```
generator.Emit(OpCodes.Ldc_R8, 255.0);
generator.Emit(OpCodes.Bgt_S, labelWhite);
```

Otherwise, the value on the stack is converted to an unsigned one-byte value:

```
generator.Emit(OpCodes.Conv_U1);
generator.Emit(OpCodes.Br_S, labelDone);
```

The following code is for the case where a zero byte must be stored in the destination array. The Ldc_I4_S instruction puts a one-byte value on the stack, but it goes onto the stack as a four-byte integer because the slot widths on the stack are in increments of four bytes:

```
generator.MarkLabel(labelBlack);
generator.Emit(OpCodes.Pop);
generator.Emit(OpCodes.Pop);
generator.Emit(OpCodes.Ldc_I4_S, 0);
generator.Emit(OpCodes.Br_S, labelDone);
```

This part of the code is similar to the part in which 255 must be stored in the destination array:

```
generator.MarkLabel(labelWhite);
generator.Emit(OpCodes.Pop);
generator.Emit(OpCodes.Ldc_I4_S, 255);
```

And now we're finally ready to store the byte in the destination array. The dst array is already on the stack, the iDst index is already on the stack, and the value to be stored in the array is on the stack. The Stelem_I1 instruction stores a one-byte value into the array:

```
generator.MarkLabel(labelDone);
generator.Emit(OpCodes.Stelem_I1);
```

We're now at the bottom of the iDst loop, equivalent to line 30 of Example 8-2. The iDst local variable must now be incremented and compared to the number of bytes in the array. If it's less, the code branches to the top of the loop:

```
generator.Emit(OpCodes.Ldloc_0);       // Put iDst on stack
generator.Emit(OpCodes.Ldc_I4_1);      // Put 1 on stack
generator.Emit(OpCodes.Add);           // Add 1 to iDst
generator.Emit(OpCodes.Dup);           // Duplicate
generator.Emit(OpCodes.Stloc_0);       // Store result in iDst
generator.Emit(OpCodes.Ldc_I4, cBytes); // Put cBytes value on stack
generator.Emit(OpCodes.Blt, labelTop);   // Go to top if iDst < cBytes
```

After the loop is finished, the generated method concludes with a return instruction:

```
generator.Emit(OpCodes.Ret);
```

All the Intermediate Language code has now been generated. The DynamicMethod instance created at the beginning of FilterMethodIL is complete and ready to be executed, or *invoked*, as the following method name implies. The second argument to Invoke specifies the two arguments to the generated method as the src and dst arrays:

```
        dynameth.Invoke(this, new object[] { src, dst });
    }
```

And that concludes `FilterMethodIL`. The `DynamicMethod` object and the `ILGenerator` object are now out of scope, and the memory they occupied can be reclaimed by the .NET garbage collector.

Algorithms written in low-level languages are usually faster than those written in high-level languages, and custom algorithms are almost always faster than generalized algorithms. By customizing an algorithm in Intermediate Language on the fly right before it's used, we seem to have the best of both worlds. The algorithm is generalized until it has to be customized, and then it's customized with efficient code.

The downside is that you need to become a compiler writer of sorts, and breach that barrier between code and data, thus entering a strange netherworld where code and data become mirror images of each other.

`FilterMethodIL` was surely a lot of work, but how well does it perform? Generally, `FilterMethodIL`, which generates Intermediate Language instructions on the fly, runs in about one-quarter of the time hogged by the straight C# version, `FilterMethodCS`, and sometimes better.

Now, you might regard `FilterMethodIL` as ugly, and I'd be willing to concede that it sure isn't the prettiest code I've ever seen. But when an algorithm clocks in at a quarter of the execution time of some earlier code, then the only word that I find appropriate is *beautiful*.

## CHAPTER NINE

Top Down Operator Precedence

Douglas Crockford

IN 1973, VAUGHAN PRATT PRESENTED "TOP DOWN OPERATOR PRECEDENCE"[*] at the first annual Principles of Programming Languages Symposium in Boston. In the paper, Pratt described a parsing technique that combines the best properties of Recursive Descent and the Operator Precedence syntax technique of Robert W Floyd.[†] He claimed that the technique is simple to understand, trivial to implement, easy to use, extremely efficient, and very flexible. I will add that it is also beautiful.

It might seem odd that such an obviously utopian approach to compiler construction is completely neglected today. Why is this the case? Pratt suggested in the paper that preoccupation with BNF grammars and their various offspring, along with their related automata and theorems, have precluded development in directions that are not visibly in the domain of automata theory.

---

[*] Pratt's paper is available at *http://portal.acm.org/citation.cfm?id=512931*; more information about Pratt himself can be found at *http://boole.stanford.edu/pratt.html*.

[†] For a description of Floyd, see "Robert W Floyd, In Memoriam," Donald E. Knuth, *http://sigact.acm. org/floyd*.

Another explanation is that his technique is most effective when used in a dynamic, functional programming language. Its use in a static, procedural language would be considerably more difficult. In his paper, Pratt used LISP and almost effortlessly built parse trees from streams of tokens.

But parsing techniques are not greatly valued in the LISP community, which celebrates the Spartan denial of syntax. There have been many attempts since LISP's creation to give the language a rich, ALGOL-like syntax, including:

Pratt's CGOL

http://zane.brouhaha.com/~healyzh/doc/cgol.doc.txt

LISP 2

*http://community.computerhistory.org/scc/projects/LISP/index.html#LISP_2_*

MLISP

ftp://reports.stanford.edu/pub/cstr/reports/cs/tr/68/92/CS-TR-68-92.pdf

Dylan

http://www.opendylan.org

Interlisp's Clisp

http://community.computerhistory.org/scc/projects/LISP/interlisp/Teitelman-3IJCAI.pdf

McCarthy's original M-expressions

http://www-formal.stanford.edu/jmc/history/lisp/lisp.html

All failed to find acceptance. The functional programming community found the correspondence between programs and data to be much more valuable than expressive syntax. But the mainstream programming community likes its syntax, so LISP has never been accepted by the mainstream. Pratt's technique befits a dynamic language, but dynamic language communities historically have had no use for the syntax that Pratt's technique realizes.

JavaScript

The situation changed with the advent of JavaScript. JavaScript is a dynamic, functional language, but in a syntactic sense, it is obviously a member of the C family. JavaScript is a dynamic language with a community that likes syntax. In addition, JavaScript is object oriented. Pratt's 1973 paper anticipated object orientation but lacked an expressive notation for it. JavaScript has an expressive object notation. Thus, JavaScript is an ideal language for exploiting Pratt's technique. I will show that we can quickly and inexpensively produce parsers in JavaScript.

We don't have time in this short chapter to deal with the whole JavaScript language, and perhaps we wouldn't want to because the language is a mess. But it has some brilliant stuff in it, which is worthy of your consideration. We will build a parser that can process Simplified JavaScript, and we will write that parser in Simplified JavaScript. Simplified JavaScript is just the good stuff, including:

Functions as first-class objects

Functions are lambdas with lexical scoping.

Dynamic objects with prototypal inheritance

Objects are class-free. We can add a new member to any object by ordinary assignment. An object can inherit members from another object.

Object literals and array literals.

This is a very convenient notation for creating new objects and arrays. JavaScript literals were the inspiration for the JSON data interchange (*http://www.JSON.org*) format.

We will take advantage of JavaScript's prototypal nature to make token objects that inherit from symbols, and symbols that inherit from an original symbol. We will depend on the `object` function, which makes a new object that inherits members from an existing object. Our implementation will also depend on a tokenizer that produces an array of simple token objects from a string. We will advance through the array of tokens as we weave our parse tree.

Symbol Table

We will use a symbol table to drive our parser:

```
var symbol_table = {};
```

The `original_symbol` object will be the prototype for all other symbols. It contains methods that report errors. These will usually be overridden with more useful methods:

```
var original_symbol = {
    nud: function () {
        this.error("Undefined.");
    },
    led: function (left) {
        this.error("Missing operator.");
    }
};
```

Let's define a function that defines symbols. It takes a symbol `id` and an optional binding power that defaults to zero. It returns a symbol object for that `id`. If the symbol already exists in the `symbol_table`, it returns that symbol object. Otherwise, it makes a new symbol object that inherits from `original_symbol`, stores it in the symbol table, and returns it. A symbol object initially contains an `id`, a value, a left binding power, and the stuff it inherits from the `original_symbol`:

```
var symbol = function (id, bp) {
    var s = symbol_table[id];
    bp = bp || 0;
    if (s) {
        if (bp >= s.lbp) {
            s.lbp = bp;
        }
```

```
        } else {
            s = object(original_symbol);
            s.id = s.value = id;
            s.lbp = bp;
            symbol_table[id] = s;
        }
        return z;
    };
```

The following symbols are popular separators and closers:

```
    symbol(":");
    symbol(";");
    symbol(",");
    symbol(")");
    symbol("]");
    symbol("}");
    symbol("else");
```

The (end) symbol indicates that there are no more tokens. The (name) symbol is the prototype for new names, such as variable names. They are spelled strangely to avoid collisions:

```
    symbol("(end)");
    symbol("(name)");
```

The (literal) symbol is the prototype for all string and number literals:

```
    var itself = function () {
        return this;
    };
    symbol("(literal)").nud = itself;
```

The this symbol is a special variable. In a method invocation, it is the reference to the object:

```
    symbol("this").nud = function () {
        scope.reserve(this);
        this.arity = "this";
        return this;
    };
```

Tokens

We assume that the source text has been transformed into an array of simple token objects (tokens), each containing a type member that is a string ("name", "string", "number", "operator") and a value member that is a string or number.

The token variable always contains the current token:

```
    var token;
```

The advance function makes a new token object and assigns it to the token variable. It takes an optional id parameter, which it can check against the id of the previous token. The new token object's prototype will be a name token in the current scope or a symbol from the symbol table. The new token's arity will be "name", "literal", or "operator". Its arity may be changed later to "binary", "unary", or "statement" when we know more about the token's role in the program:

```
var advance = function (id) {
    var a, o, t, v;
    if (id && token.id !== id) {
        token.error("Expected '" + id + "'.");
    }
    if (token_nr >= tokens.length) {
        token = symbol_table["(end)"];
        return;
    }
    t = tokens[token_nr];
    token_nr += 1;
    v = t.value;
    a = t.type;
    if (a === "name") {
        o = scope.find(v);
    } else if (a === "operator") {
        o = symbol_table[v];
        if (!o) {
            t.error("Unknown operator.");
        }
    } else if (a === "string" || a ===  number") {
        a = "literal";
        o = symbol_table["(literal)"];
    } else {
        t.error("Unexpected token.");
    }
    token = object(o);
    token.value = v;
    token.arity = a;
    return token;
};
```

Precedence

Tokens are objects that bear methods that allow them to make precedence decisions, match other tokens, and build trees (and in a more ambitious project also check types, optimize, and generate code). The basic precedence problem is this: given an operand between two operators, is the operand bound to the left operator or the right? Thus, if *A* and *B* are operators in:

d *A* e *B* f

does operand e bind to *A* or to *B*? In other words, are we talking about:

(d *A* e) *B* f

or:

d *A* (e *B* f)

Ultimately, the complexity in the process of parsing comes down to the resolution of this ambiguity. The technique we will develop here uses token objects whose members include binding powers (or precedence levels), and simple methods called nud (null denotation) and led (left denotation). A nud does not care about the tokens to the left. A led does. A nud method is used by values (such as variables and literals) and by prefix operators. A led method is used by infix operators and suffix operators. A token may have both a nud and a led. For example, - might be both a prefix operator (negation) and an infix operator (subtraction), so it would have both nud and led methods.

Expressions

The heart of Pratt's technique is the expression function. It takes a right binding power that controls the aggressiveness of its consumption of tokens that it sees to the right. It returns the result of calling methods on the tokens it acts upon:

```
var expression = function (rbp) {
    var left;
    var t = token;
    advance();
    left = t.nud();
    while (rbp < token.lbp) {
        t = token;
        advance();
        left = t.led(left);
    }
    return left;
}
```

expression calls the nud method of the token. The nud is used to process literals, variables, and prefix operators. After that, as long as the right binding power is less than the left binding power of the next token, the led methods are invoked. The led is used to process infix and suffix operators. This process can be recursive because the nud and led methods can call expression.

Infix Operators

The + operator is an infix operator, so it will have a led method that makes the token object into a tree, where the two branches are the operand to the left of the + and the operand to the right. The left operand is passed into the led, and the right is obtained by calling the expression method.

The number 60 is the binding power of +. Operators that bind tighter or have higher precedence have greater binding powers. In the course of mutating the stream of tokens into a parse tree, we will use the operator tokens as containers of operand nodes:

```
symbol("+", 60).led = function (left) {
    this.first = left;
    this.second = expression(60);
    this.arity = "binary";
    return this;
};
```

When we define the symbol for *, we see that only the id and binding powers are different. It has a higher binding power because it binds more tightly:

```
symbol("*", 70).led = function (left) {
    this.first = left;
    this.second = expression(70);
    this.arity = "binary";
    return this;
};
```

Not all infix operators will be this similar, but many will, so we can make our work easier by defining an infix function that will help us specify infix operators. The infix function will take an id and a binding power, and optionally a led function. If a led function is not provided, it will supply a default led that is useful in most cases:

```
var infix = function (id, bp, led) {
    var s = symbol(id, bp);
    s.led = led || function (left) {
        this.first = left;
        this.second = expression(bp);
        this.arity = "binary";
        return this;
    };
    return s;
}
```

This allows a more declarative style for specifying operators:

```
infix("+", 60);
infix("-", 60);
infix("*", 70);
infix("/", 70);
```

The string === is JavaScript's exact-equality comparison operator:

```
infix("===", 50);
infix("!==", 50);
infix("<", 50);
infix("<=", 50);
infix(">", 50);
infix(">=", 50);
```

The ternary operator takes three expressions, separated by ? and :. It is not an ordinary infix operator, so we need to supply its led function:

```
infix("?", 20, function (left) {
    this.first = left;
    this.second = expression(0);
    advance(":");
    this.third = expression(0);
    this.arity = "ternary";
    return this;
});
```

The . operator is used to select a member of an object. The token on the right must be a name, but it will be used as a literal:

```
infix(".", 90, function (left) {
    this.first = left;
    if (token.arity !== "name") {
        token.error("Expected a property name.");
    }
    token.arity = "literal";
    this.second = token;
    this.arity = "binary";
    advance();
    return this;
});
```

The [operator is used to dynamically select a member from an object or array. The expression on the right must be followed by a closing]:

```
infix("[", 90, function (left) {
    this.first = left;
    this.second = expression(0);
    this.arity = "binary";
    advance("]");
    return this;
});
```

Those infix operators are left associative. We can also make right associative operators, such as short-circuiting logical operators, by reducing the right binding power:

```
var infixr = function (id, bp, led) {
    var s = symbol(id, bp);
    s.led = led || function (left) {
        this.first = left;
        this.second = expression(bp - 1);
        this.arity = "binary";
        return this;
    };
    return s;
}
```

The && operator returns the first operand if the first operand is falsy. Otherwise, it returns the second operand. The || operator returns the first operand if the first operand is truthy; otherwise, it returns the second operand:

```
infixr("&&", 40);
infixr("||", 40);
```

Prefix Operators

We can do a similar thing for prefix operators. Prefix operators are right associative. A prefix does not have a left binding power because it does not bind to the left. Prefix operators can sometimes be reserved words (reserved words are discussed in the section "Scope," later in this chapter):

```
var prefix = function (id, nud) {
    var s = symbol(id);
    s.nud = nud || function () {
        scope.reserve(this);
        this.first = expression(80);
        this.arity = "unary";
        return this;
    };
    return s;
}
prefix("-");
prefix("!");
prefix("typeof");
```

The nud of (will call advance(")") to match a balancing) token. The (token does not become part of the parse tree because the nud returns the expression:

```
prefix("(", function () {
    var e = expression(0);
    advance(")");
    return e;
});
```

Assignment Operators

We could use infixr to define our assignment operators, but we want to do two extra bits of business, so we will make a specialized assignment function. It will examine the left operand to make sure that it is a proper lvalue. We will also set an assignment flag so that we can later quickly identify assignment statements:

```
var assignment = function (id) {
    return infixr(id, 10, function (left) {
        if (left.id !== "." && left.id !== "[" &&
                left.arity !== "name") {
            left.error("Bad lvalue.");
        }
        this.first = left;
        this.second = expression(9);
        this.assignment = true;
        this.arity = "binary";
        return this;
    });
};
assignment("=");
assignment("+=");
assignment("-=");
```

Notice that we have a sort of inheritance pattern, where assignment returns the result of calling infixr, and infixr returns the result of calling symbol.

Constants

The constant function builds constants into the language. The nud mutates a name token into a literal token:

```
var constant = function (s, v) {
    var x = symbol(s);
    x.nud = function () {
        scope.reserve(this);
        this.value = symbol_table[this.id].value;
        this.arity = "literal";
        return this;
    };
    x.value = v;
    return x;
};
constant("true", true);
constant("false", false);
constant("null", null);
constant("pi", 3.141592653589793);
```

Scope

We use functions such as infix and prefix to define the symbols used in the language. Most languages have some notation for defining new symbols, such as variable names. In a very simple language, when we encounter a new word, we might give it a definition and put it in the symbol table. In a more sophisticated language, we would want a notion of scope, giving the programmer convenient control over the lifespan and visibility of a variable.

A *scope* is a region of a program in which a variable is defined and accessible. Scopes can be nested inside of other scopes. Variables defined in a scope are not visible outside of the scope.

We will keep the current scope object in the scope variable:

```
var scope;
```

original_scope is the prototype for all scope objects. It contains a define method that is used to define new variables in the scope. The define method transforms a name token into a variable token. It produces an error if the variable has already been defined in the scope or if the name has already been used as a reserved word:

```
var original_scope = {
    define: function (n) {
        var t = this.def[n.value];
        if (typeof t === "object") {
            n.error(t.reserved ?
                "Already reserved." :
                "Already defined.");
        }
```

```
            this.def[n.value] = n;
            n.reserved = false;
            n.nud      = itself;
            n.led      = null;
            n.std      = null;
            n.lbp      = 0;
            n.scope    = scope;
            return n;
    },
```

The find method is used to find the definition of a name. It starts with the current scope and will go, if necessary, back through the chain of parent scopes and ultimately to the symbol table. It returns symbol_table["(name")] if it cannot find a definition:

```
    find: function (n) {
        var e = this;
        while (true) {
            var o = e.def[n];
            if (o) {
                return o;
            }
            e = e.parent;
            if (!e) {
                return symbol_table[
                    symbol_table.hasOwnProperty(n) ?
                    n : "(name)"];
            }
        }
    },
```

The pop method closes a scope:

```
    pop: function () {
        scope = this.parent;
    },
```

The reserve method is used to indicate that a name has been used as a reserved word in the current scope:

```
    reserve: function (n) {
        if (n.arity !== "name" || n.reserved) {
            return;
        }
        var t = this.def[n.value];
        if (t) {
            if (t.reserved) {
                return;
            }
            if (t.arity === "name") {
                n.error("Already defined.");
            }
        }
        this.def[n.value] = n;
        n.reserved = true;
    }
};
```

We need a policy for reserved words. In some languages, words that are used structurally (such as if) are reserved and cannot be used as variable names. The flexibility of our parser allows us to have a more useful policy. For example, we can say that in any function, any name may be used as a structure word or as a variable, but not as both. Also, we will reserve words locally only after they are used as reserved words. This makes things better for the language designer because adding new structure words to the language will not break existing programs, and it makes things better for programmers because they are not hampered by irrelevant restrictions on the use of names.

Whenever we want to establish a new scope for a function or a block, we call the new_scope function, which makes a new instance of the original scope prototype:

```
var new_scope = function () {
    var s = scope;
    scope = object(original_scope);
    scope.def = {};
    scope.parent = s;
    return scope;
};
```

Statements

Pratt's original formulation worked with functional languages in which everything is an expression. Most mainstream languages have statements. We can easily handle statements by adding another method to tokens, std (statement denotation). An std is like a nud except that it is only used at the beginning of a statement.

The statement function parses one statement. If the current token has an std method, the token is reserved and the std is invoked. Otherwise, we assume an expression statement terminated with a ;. For reliability, we reject an expression statement that is not an assignment or invocation:

```
var statement = function () {
    var n = token, v;
    if (n.std) {
        advance();
        scope.reserve(n);
        return n.std();
    }
    v = expression(0);
    if (!v.assignment && v.id !== "(") {
        v.error("Bad expression statement.");
    }
    advance(";");
    return v;
};
```

The statements function parses statements until it sees (end) or } signaling the end of a block. It returns a statement, an array of statements, or (if there were no statements present) simply null:

```
var statements = function () {
    var a = [], s;
    while (true) {
        if (token.id === "}" || token.id === "(end)") {
            break;
        }
        s = statement();
        if (s) {
            a.push(s);
        }
    }
    return a.length === 0 ? null : a.length === 1 ? a[0] : a;
};
```

The stmt function is used to add statements to the symbol table. It takes a statement id and an std function:

```
var stmt = function (s, f) {
    var x = symbol(s);
    x.std = f;
    return x;
};
```

The block statement wraps a pair of curly braces around a list of statements, giving them a new scope:

```
stmt("{", function () {
    new_scope();
    var a = statements();
    advance("}");
    scope.pop();
    return a;
});
```

The block function parses a block:

```
var block = function () {
    var t = token;
    advance("{");
    return t.std();
};
```

The var statement defines one or more variables in the current block. Each name can optionally be followed by = and an expression:

```
stmt("var", function () {
    var a = [], n, t;
    while (true) {
        n = token;
        if (n.arity !== "name") {
            n.error("Expected a new variable name.");
        }
        scope.define(n);
        advance();
        if (token.id === "=") {
```

```
            t = token;
            advance("=");
            t.first = n;
            t.second = expression(0);
            t.arity = "binary";
            a.push(t);
        }
        if (token.id !== ",") {
            break;
        }
        advance(",");
    }
    advance(";");
    return a.length === 0 ? null : a.length === 1 ? a[0] : a;
});
```

The while statement defines a loop. It contains an expression in parentheses and a block:

```
stmt("while", function () {
    advance("(");
    this.first = expression(0);
    advance(")");
    this.second = block();
    this.arity = "statement";
    return this;
});
```

The if statement allows for conditional execution. If we see the else symbol after the block, we parse the next block or if statement:

```
stmt("if", function () {
    advance("(");
    this.first = expression(0);
    advance(")");
    this.second = block();
    if (token.id === "else") {
        scope.reserve(token);
        advance("else");
        this.third = token.id === "if" ? statement() : block();
    }
    this.arity = "statement";
    return this;
});
```

The break statement is used to break out of loops. We make sure that the next symbol is }:

```
stmt("break", function () {
    advance(";");
    if (token.id !== "}") {
        token.error("Unreachable statement.");
    }
    this.arity = "statement";
    return this;
});
```

The return statement is used to return from functions. It can return an optional expression:

```
stmt("return", function () {
    if (token.id !== ";") {
        this.first = expression(0);
    }
    advance(";");
    if (token.id !== "}") {
        token.error("Unreachable statement.");
    }
    this.arity = "statement";
    return this;
});
```

Functions

Functions are executable object values. A function has an optional name (so that it can call itself recursively), a list of parameter names wrapped in parentheses, and a body that is a list of statements wrapped in curly braces. A function has its own scope:

```
prefix("function", function () {
    var a = [];
    scope = new_scope();
    if (token.arity === "name") {
        scope.define(token);
        this.name = token.value;
        advance();
    }
    advance("(");
    if (token.id !== ")") {
        while (true) {
            if (token.arity !== "name") {
                token.error("Expected a parameter name.");
            }
            scope.define(token);
            a.push(token);
            advance();
            if (token.id !== ",") {
                break;
            }
            advance(",");
        }
    }
    this.first = a;
    advance(")");
    advance("{");
    this.second = statements();
    advance("}");
    this.arity = "function";
    scope.pop();
    return this;
});
```

Functions are invoked with the (operator. It can take zero or more comma-separated arguments. We look at the left operand to detect expressions that cannot possibly be function values:

```
infix("(", 90, function (left) {
    var a = [];
    this.first = left;
    this.second = a;
    this.arity = "binary";
    if ((left.arity !== "unary" ||
            left.id !== "function") &&
        left.arity !== "name" &&
        (left.arity !== "binary" ||
            (left.id !== "." &&
            left.id !== "(" &&
            left.id !== "["))) {
        left.error("Expected a variable name.");
    }
    if (token.id !== ")") {
        while (true)  {
            a.push(expression(0));
            if (token.id !== ",") {
                break;
            }
            advance(",");
        }
    }
    advance(")");
    return this;
});
```

Array and Object Literals

An array literal is a set of square brackets around zero or more comma-separated expressions. Each of the expressions is evaluated, and the results are collected into a new array:

```
prefix("[", function () {
    var a = [];
    if (token.id !== "]") {
        while (true) {
            a.push(expression(0));
            if (token.id !== ",") {
                break;
            }
            advance(",");
        }
    }
    advance("]");
    this.first = a;
    this.arity = "unary";
    return this;
});
```

An object literal is a set of curly braces around zero or more comma-separated pairs. A *pair* is a key/expression pair separated by a :. The key is a literal or a name treated as a literal:

```
prefix("{", function () {
    var a = [];
    if (token.id !== "}") {
        while (true) {
            var n = token;
            if (n.arity !== "name" && n.arity !== "literal") {
                token.error("Bad key.");
            }
            advance();
            advance(":");
            var v = expression(0);
            v.key = n.value;
            a.push(v);
            if (token.id !== ",") {
                break;
            }
            advance(",");
        }
    }
    advance("}");
    this.first = a;
    this.arity = "unary";
    return this;
});
```

Things to Do and Think About

The simple parser shown in this chapter is easily extensible. The tree could be passed to a code generator, or it could be passed to an interpreter. Very little computation is required to produce the tree. And as we saw, very little effort was required to write the programming that built the tree.

We could make the infix function take an opcode that would aid in code generation. We could also have it take additional methods that would be used to do constant folding and code generation.

We could add additional statements, such as for, switch, and try. We could add statement labels. We could add more error checking and error recovery. We could add lots more operators. We could add type specification and inference.

We could make our language extensible. With the same ease that we can define new variables, we can let the programmer add new operators and new statements.

You can try the demonstration of the parser that was described in this chapter at *http://javascript.crockford.com/tdop/index.html*.

Another example of this parsing technique can be found in JSLint at *http://JSLint.com*.

## CHAPTER TEN

The Quest for an Accelerated Population Count

Henry S. Warren, Jr.

A FUNDAMENTAL COMPUTER ALGORITHM, AND A DECEPTIVELY SIMPLE ONE, is the *population count* or *sideways sum*, which calculates the number of bits in a computer word that are 1. The population count function has applications that range from the very simple to the quite sublime. For example, if sets are represented by bit strings, population count gives the size of the set. It can also be used to generate binomially distributed random integers. These and other applications are discussed at the end of this chapter.

Although uses of this operation are not terribly common, many computers—often the supercomputers of their day—had an instruction for it. These included the Ferranti Mark I (1951), the IBM Stretch computer (1960), the CDC 6600 (1964), the Russian-built BESM-6 (1967), the Cray 1 (1976), the Sun SPARCv9 (1994), and the IBM Power 5 (2004).

This chapter discusses how to compute the population count function on a machine that does not have that instruction, but which has the fundamental instructions generally found on a RISC or CISC computer: *shift, add, and, load, conditional branch*, and so forth. For illustration, we assume the computer has a 32-bit word size, but most of the techniques discussed here can be easily adapted to other word sizes.

Two problems in population counting are addressed: counting the 1-bits in a single computer word, and counting the 1-bits in a large number of words, perhaps arranged in an array. In each case, we show that the obvious solution, even if carefully honed, can be beaten substantially by very different algorithms that take some imagination to find. The first is an application of the divide-and-conquer strategy, and the second is an application of a certain logic circuit that is familiar to computer logic designers but not so familiar to programmers.

Basic Methods

As a first cut, a programmer might count the 1-bits in a word x, as illustrated in the following C-language solution. Here x is an unsigned integer, so the right shift is with 0-fill:

```
pop = 0;
for (i = 0; i < 32; i++){
    if (x & 1) pop = pop + 1;
    x = x >> 1;
}
```

On a typical RISC computer, the loop might compile into about seven instructions, two of which are conditional branches. (One of the conditional branches is for loop control.) These seven instructions are executed 32 times, but one of them is bypassed about half the time (we might presume), so that it executes about $32 \times 6.5 = 208$ instructions.

It would probably not take the programmer long to realize that this code can be easily improved. For one thing, on many computers, counting down from 31 to 0 is more efficient than counting up, because it saves a *compare* instruction. Better yet, why count at all? Just let the loop go until x is 0. This eliminates some iterations if x has high-order 0-bits. Another optimization is to replace the `if` test with code that simply adds the rightmost bit of x to the count. This leads to the code:

```
pop = 0;
while (x) {
    pop = pop + (x & 1);
    x = x >> 1;
}
```

This has only four or five RISC instructions in the loop, depending upon whether or not a *compare* of x to 0 is required, and only one branch. (We assume the compiler rearranges the loop so that the conditional branch is at the bottom.) Thus, it takes a maximum of 128 to 160 instructions. The maximum occurs if x begins with a 1-bit, but it will take far fewer instructions if x has many leading 0s.

Some readers may recall that the simple expression x & $(x-1)$ is x with its least significant 1-bit turned off, or is 0 if $x = 0$. Thus, to count the 1-bits in x, one can turn them off one at a time until the result is 0, keeping count of how many were turned off. This leads to the code:

```
pop = 0;
while (x) {
    pop = pop + 1;
    x = x & (x - 1);
}
```

Like the preceding code, this takes four or five instructions in the loop, but the loop runs only the same number of times as the number of 1s in x. This is surely an improvement.

A complementary approach, applicable if the number of 1-bits is expected to be large, is to keep turning on the rightmost 0-bit with $x = x \mid (x+1)$ until the result is all 1s (-1). Count the number of iterations executed in a variable n, and return $32 - n$. (Alternatively, the original number x can be complemented, or n can be initialized to 32 and counted down.)

The first program in this series is rather dull, but the others might be considered to have some beauty to an eye that values efficiency, conciseness, and useful cleverness. The first program can be made to run substantially faster by unrolling the loop, but the other two programs would be improved very little, if at all, by this change.

One can also employ table lookup, translating perhaps a byte of x at a time to the number of 1-bits in that byte. The code is quite short and will be very fast on many machines (approximately 17 instructions on a basic RISC that doesn't have indexed loads). In the following code, table[i] is the number of 1-bits in i, for i ranging from 0 to 255:

```
static char table[256] = {0, 1, 1, 2, 1, 2, 2, 3, ..., 8};
pop = table[x & 0xFF] + table[(x >> 8) & 0xFF] +
        table[(x >> 16) & 0xFF] + table[x >> 24];
```

Divide and Conquer

Another interesting and useful way to compute the population count of a word is based on the "divide and conquer" paradigm. This algorithm might be devised by reasoning, "Suppose I had a way to compute the population count of a 16-bit quantity. Then I could run that on the left and right halves of the 32-bit word, and add the results, to obtain the population count of the 32-bit word." This strategy won't pay off if the basic algorithm must be run sequentially on the two halves and it takes time proportional to the number of bits being analyzed, because it would then take $16k + 16k = 32k$ units of time, where k is the constant of proportionality, plus another instruction for the addition. But if we can somehow do the operation on the two halfwords in parallel, there will be an improvement from, essentially, $32k$ to $16k + 1$.

To efficiently compute the population count of two 16-bit quantities, we need a way to do it for 8-bit quantities, and to do 4 of them in parallel. Continuing this reasoning, we need a way to compute the population count of 2-bit quantities, and to do 16 of them in parallel.

The algorithm to be described in no way depends on running operations on separate processors, or on unusual instructions such as the SIMD* instructions found on some computers. It uses only the facilities usually found on a conventional uniprocessor RISC or CISC.

The plan is illustrated in Figure 10-1.

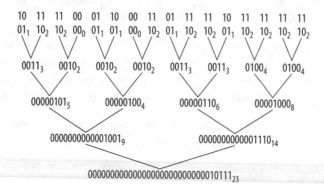

FIGURE 10-1. Counting 1-bits, "divide and conquer" strategy

The first line in Figure 10-1 is the word x for which we wish to count the number of 1-bits. Each 2-bit field of the second line contains the count of the number of 1-bits in the 2-bit field immediately above. The subscripts are the decimal values of these 2-bit fields. Each 4-bit field in the third line contains the sum of the numbers in two adjacent 2-bit fields of the second line, with the subscripts showing the decimal values, and so forth. The last line contains the number of 1-bits in x. The algorithm is executed in $\log_2(32) = 5$ steps, where each step contains some shifting and masking instructions to do the addition of adjacent fields.

The method illustrated in Figure 10-1 may be committed to C code as follows:

```
x = (x & 0x55555555) + ((x >> 1) & 0x55555555);
x = (x & 0x33333333) + ((x >> 2) & 0x33333333);
x = (x & 0x0F0F0F0F) + ((x >> 4) & 0x0F0F0F0F);
x = (x & 0x00FF00FF) + ((x >> 8) & 0x00FF00FF);
x = (x & 0x0000FFFF) + ((x >>16) & 0x0000FFFF);
```

(Constants beginning with 0x in C are hexadecimal.) The first line uses (x >> 1) & 0x55555555 rather than the perhaps more natural (x & 0xAAAAAAAA) >> 1 because the code shown avoids generating two large constants in a register. This would cost an instruction if the machine lacks the *and not* instruction. A similar remark applies to the other lines.

Clearly the last *and* is unnecessary because x >> 16 must begin with 16 0-bits, so the *and* does not alter the value of x >> 16. Other *and*s may be omitted when there is no danger that a field's sum will carry over into the adjacent field. And there is a way to code the first line that uses one less instruction. This leads to the simplification shown in Example 10-1, which executes in 21 instructions and is free of branches and memory references.

* Single-instruction, multiple-data instructions are instructions that operate on multiple fields (such as bytes or halfwords) of a computer word in parallel. For example, an 8-bit SIMD *add* might add the corresponding bytes of two words without propagating the carry from one byte to the next.

EXAMPLE 10-1. Counting 1-bits in a word

```
int pop(unsigned x) {
   x = x - ((x >> 1) & 0x55555555);
   x = (x & 0x33333333) + ((x >> 2) & 0x33333333);
   x = (x + (x >> 4)) & 0x0F0F0F0F;
   x = x + (x >> 8);
   x = x + (x >> 16);
   return x & 0x0000003F;
}
```

The first assignment to x is based on the first two terms of the formula:

$$\text{pop}(x) = x - \left\lfloor \frac{x}{2} \right\rfloor - \left\lfloor \frac{x}{4} \right\rfloor - \left\lfloor \frac{x}{8} \right\rfloor - \ldots - \left\lfloor \frac{x}{2^{31}} \right\rfloor$$

Here we must have $x \geq 0$. By treating x as an unsigned integer, this equation can be implemented with a sequence of 31 *shift right immediate*s of 1, and 31 *subtract*s. The procedure of Example 10-1 uses the first two terms of this on each 2-bit field, in parallel. I leave the proof of this equation to the reader.

Unfortunately, the code of Example 10-1 has lost most of the regularity and elegance of the code from which it was derived. A consequence of this is that it is no longer immediately clear how to extend the code to a 64-bit machine. But it's hard to pass up all those opportunities to save instructions!

Divide and conquer is an important technique that should be near the top of every programmer's bag of tricks. And that goes for computer logic designers, too. Other applications of divide and conquer are the well-known technique of binary search, a sorting method known as Quicksort, and a method for reversing the bits of a word.

Other Methods

Item 169 in the HAKMEM memo* is an algorithm that counts the number of 1-bits in a word x by using the first three terms of the formula shown in the previous section on each 3-bit field of x separately, to produce a word of 3-bit fields, each of which contains the number of 1-bits that were in it. It then adds adjacent 3-bit fields to form 6-bit field sums, and then adds the 6-bit fields by computing the value of the word modulo 63. Although originally developed for a machine with a 36-bit word, the algorithm is easily adapted to a 32-bit word. This is shown below in C (the long constants are in octal):

```
int pop(unsigned x) {
   unsigned n;

   n = (x >> 1) & 033333333333;    // Count bits in
   x = x - n;                      // each three-bit
   n = (n >> 1) & 033333333333;    // field.
```

---

* Michael Beeler, R. William Gosper, and Richard Schroeppel, "HAKMEM," *MIT Artificial Intelligence Laboratory AIM* 239, February 1972. This is now available on the Web at *http://www.inwap.com/ pdp10/hbaker/hakmem/hakmem.html*, thanks to Henry Baker.

```
    x = x - n;
    x = (x + (x >> 3)) & 030707070707; // Six-bit sums.
    return x%63;                       // Add six-bit sums.
}
```

The last line uses the unsigned modulus function. (It could be either signed or unsigned if the word length were a multiple of 3.) It's clear that the modulus function sums the 6-bit fields when you regard the word x as an integer written in base 64. Upon dividing a base b integer by $b - 1$, the remainder is, for $b \geq 3$, congruent to the sum of the digits and, of course, is less than $b - 1$. Because the sum of the digits in this case must be less than or equal to 32, mod(x, 63) must be equal to the sum of the digits of x, which is to say equal to the number of 1-bits in the original x.

This algorithm requires only 10 instructions on the DEC PDP-10, as that machine has an instruction for computing the remainder with its second operand directly referencing a fullword in memory. On a basic RISC, it requires about 15 instructions, assuming the machine offers *unsigned modulus* as one instruction (but not directly referencing a fullword immediate or memory operand). But it is probably not very fast, because division is almost always a slow operation. Also, it doesn't apply to 64-bit word lengths by simply extending the constants, although it does work for word lengths up to 62.

A rather amazing algorithm is to rotate x left one position, 31 times, adding the 32 terms.[*] The sum is the negative of pop(x)! That is:

$$\mathrm{pop}(x) = -\sum_{i=0}^{31} (x \overset{rot}{\ll} i)$$

where the additions are done modulo the word size, and the final sum is interpreted as a two's-complement integer. This is just a novelty; it would not be useful on most machines because the loop is executed 31 times and thus requires 63 instructions plus the loop-control overhead. I leave it to the reader to figure out why this works.

Sum and Difference of Population Counts of Two Words

To compute pop(x) + pop(y) (if your computer does not have the population count instruction), some time can be saved by using the first two executable lines of Example 10-1 on x and y separately, and then adding x and y and executing the last three stages of the algorithm on the sum. After the first two lines of Example 10-1 are executed, x and y consist of eight 4-bit fields, each containing a maximum value of 4. Thus x and y may safely be added, because the maximum value in any 4-bit field of the sum would be 8, so no overflow occurs. (In fact, three words may be combined in this way.)

This idea also applies to subtraction. To compute pop(x) − pop(y), use:[†]

---

[*] Mike Morton, "Quibbles & Bits," *Computer Language*, Vol. 7, No.12, December 1990, pp. 45–55.

[†] $\bar{y}$ denotes the one's-complement of y, which in C is written ~y.

$$pop(x) - pop(y) = pop(x) - (32 - pop(\bar{y}))$$
$$= pop(x) + pop(\bar{y}) - 32$$

Then, use the technique just described to compute $pop(x) + pop(y)$. The code is shown in Example 10-2. It uses 32 instructions, versus 43 for two applications of the code of Example 10-1 followed by a subtraction.

EXAMPLE 10-2. Computing pop(x) – pop(y)

```
int popDiff(unsigned x, unsigned y) {
   x = x - ((x >> 1) & 0x55555555);
   x = (x & 0x33333333) + ((x >> 2) & 0x33333333);
   y = ~y;
   y = y - ((y >> 1) & 0x55555555);
   y = (y & 0x33333333) + ((y >> 2) & 0x33333333);
   x = x + y;
   x = (x & 0x0F0F0F0F) + ((x >> 4) & 0x0F0F0F0F);
   x = x + (x >> 8);
   x = x + (x >> 16);
   return (x & 0x0000007F) - 32;
}
```

Comparing the Population Counts of Two Words

Sometimes one wants to know which of two words has the larger population count, without regard to the actual counts. Can this be determined without doing a population count of the two words? Computing the difference of two population counts, as in Example 10-2, and comparing the result to 0, is one way, but there is another way that is preferable if either the population counts are expected to be low, or if there is a strong correlation between the particular bits that are set in the two words.

The idea is to clear a single bit in each word until one of the words is all zero; the other word then has the larger population count. The process runs faster in its worst and average cases if the bits that are 1 at the same positions in each word are first cleared. The code is shown in Example 10-3. The procedure returns a negative number if $pop(x) < pop(y)$, 0 if $pop(x) = pop(y)$, and a positive number (1) if $pop(x) > pop(y)$.

EXAMPLE 10-3. Comparing pop(x) with pop(y)

```
int popCmpr(unsigned xp, unsigned yp) {
   unsigned x, y;
   x = xp & ~yp;          // Clear bits where
   y = yp & ~xp;          // both are 1.
   while (1) {
      if (x == 0) return y | -y;
      if (y == 0) return 1;
      x = x & (x - 1);    // Clear one bit
      y = y & (y - 1);    // from each.
   }
}
```

After clearing the common 1-bits in each 32-bit word, the maximum possible number of 1-bits in both words together is 32. Therefore the word with the smaller number of 1-bits can have at most 16, and the loop in Example 10-3 is executed a maximum of 16 times, which gives a worst case of 119 instructions executed on a basic RISC ($16 \times 7 + 7$). A simulation using uniformly distributed random 32-bit numbers showed that the average population count of the word with the smaller population count is approximately 6.186, after clearing the common 1-bits. This gives an average execution time of about 50 instructions when executed on random 32-bit inputs, not as good as using Example 10-2. For this procedure to beat that of Example 10-2, the number of 1-bits in either x or y, after clearing the common 1-bits, would have to be three or less.

Counting the 1-Bits in an Array

The simplest way to count the number of 1-bits in an array (vector) of fullwords, in the absence of the *population count* instruction, is to use a procedure such as that of Example 10-1 on each word of the array, and simply add the results. We call this the naïve method. Ignoring loop control, the generation of constants, and loads from the array, it takes 16 instructions per word: 15 for the code of Example 10-1, plus 1 for the addition. We assume the procedure is expanded inline, the masks are loaded outside of the loop, and the machine has a sufficient number of registers to hold all the quantities used in the calculation.

Another way is to use the first two executable lines of Example 10-1 on groups of three words in the array, adding the three partial results. Because each partial result has a maximum value of 4 in each 4-bit field, the sum of the three has a maximum value of 12 in each 4-bit field, so no overflow occurs. This idea can be applied to the 8- and 16-bit fields. Coding and compiling this method indicates that it gives about a 20 percent reduction over the naïve method in total number of instructions executed on a basic RISC. Much of the savings is canceled by the additional housekeeping instructions required. We will not dwell on this method because there is a much better way to do it.

The better way seems to have been invented by Robert Harley and David Seal in about 1996.[*] It is based on a circuit called a *carry-save adder* (CSA) or 3:2 compressor. A CSA is simply a sequence of independent full adders[†] and is often used in binary multiplier circuits.

---

[*] David Seal, Newsgroup *comp.arch.arithmetic*, May 13, 1997. Robert Harley was the first person known to this writer to apply the CSA to this problem, and David Seal showed a particularly good way to use it for counting the bits in a large array (as illustrated in Figure 10-2 and Example 10-5), and also for an array of size 7 (similar to the plan in Figure 10-3).

[†] A full adder is a circuit with three 1-bit inputs (the bits to be added) and two 1-bit outputs (the sum and carry). See John L. Hennessy and David A. Patterson, *Computer Architecture: A Quantitative Approach*. Morgan Kaufmann, 1990.

In Boolean algebra notation (juxtaposition denotes *and*, + denotes *or*, and ⊕ denotes exclusive or), the logic for each full adder is:

```
h ← ab + ac + bc = ab + (a + b)c = ab + (a ⊕ b)c
l ← (a ⊕ b) ⊕ c
```

where a, b, and c are the 1-bit inputs, l is the low-bit output (sum), and h is the high-bit output (carry). Changing $a + b$ on the first line to $a \oplus b$ is justified because when a and b are both 1, the term ab makes the value of the whole expression 1. By first assigning $a \oplus b$ to a temporary, the full adder logic can be evaluated in five logical instructions, each operating on 32 bits in parallel (on a 32-bit machine). We will refer to these five instructions as CSA(h, l, a, b, c). This is a "macro," with h and l being outputs.

One way to use the CSA operation is to process elements of the array A in groups of three, reducing each group of three words to two and applying the population count operation to these two words. In the loop, these two population counts are summed. After executing the loop, the total population count of the array is twice the accumulated population count of the CSA's high-bit outputs plus the accumulated population count of the low-bit outputs.

The following sequence illustrates the process for a 16-bit word:

```
a = 0110 1001 1110 0101   9
b = 1000 1000 0100 0111   6
c = 1100 1010 0011 0101   8
--------------------------
l = 0010 1011 1001 0111   9
h = 1100 1000 0110 0101   7*2 = 14
```

Observe that in each column, the (h, l) pair, written in that order, is a two-bit binary number whose value is the number of 1-bits in a, b, and c, in the column. Thus each 1-bit in h represents two 1-bits in a, b, and c, and each 1-bit in l represents one 1-bit in a, b, and c. Therefore the total population (shown at the right) is twice the number of 1-bits in h plus the number of 1-bits in l, which totals to 23 in the illustration.

Let n_c be the number of instructions required for the CSA steps, and n_p be the number of instructions required to do the population count of one word. On a typical RISC machine, $n_c = 5$ and $n_p = 15$. Ignoring loads from the array and loop control (the code for which may vary quite a bit from one machine to another), the loop discussed previously takes $(n_c + 2n_p + 2) / 3 \approx 12.33$ instructions per word of the array (the "+ 2" is for the two additions in the loop). This contrasts with the 16 instructions per word required by the naïve method.

There is another way to use the CSA operation that results in a more efficient and slightly more compact program. This is shown in Example 10-4. It takes $(n_c + n_p + 1) / 2 = 10.5$ instructions per word (ignoring loop control and loads).

```
#define CSA(h,l, a,b,c) \
   {unsigned u = a ^ b; unsigned v = c; \
      h = (a & b) | (u & v); l = u ^ v;}
int popArray(unsigned A[], int n) {
   int tot, i;
   unsigned ones, twos;
   tot = 0;                    // Initialize.
   ones = 0;
   for (i = 0; i <= n - 2; i = i + 2) {
      CSA(twos, ones, ones, A[i], A[i+1])
      tot = tot + pop(twos);
   }
   tot = 2*tot + pop(ones);
   if (n & 1)                  // If there's a last one,
      tot = tot + pop(A[i]);   // add it in.
   return tot;
}
```

When Example 10-4 is compiled, the CSA operation expands into:

```
u = ones ^ A[i];
v = A[i+1];
twos = (ones & A[i]) | (u & v);
ones = u ^ v;
```

The code relies on the compiler to omit subsequent loads of a quantity that has already been loaded (a process known as *commoning*).

There are ways to use the CSA operation to further reduce the number of instructions required to compute the population count of an array. They are most easily understood by means of a circuit diagram. For example, Figure 10-2 illustrates a way to code a loop that takes array elements eight at a time and compresses them into four quantities, labeled *eights, fours, twos,* and *ones.* The *fours, twos,* and *ones* are fed back into the CSAs on the next loop iteration, the 1-bits in *eights* are counted by an execution of the word-level population count function, and this count is accumulated. When the entire array has been processed, the total population count is:

$$8 \times \text{pop}(\textit{eights}) + 4 \times \text{pop}(\textit{fours}) + 2 \times \text{pop}(\textit{twos}) + \text{pop}(\textit{ones})$$

The code is shown in Example 10-5, which uses the CSA macro defined in Example 10-4. The numbering of the CSA blocks in Figure 10-2 corresponds to the order of the CSA macro calls in Example 10-5. The execution time of the loop, exclusive of array loads and loop control, is $(7n_c + n_p + 1) / 8 = 6.375$ instructions per word of the array.

```
int popArray(unsigned A[], int n) {
   int tot, i;
   unsigned ones, twos, twosA, twosB,
      fours, foursA, foursB, eights;
   tot = 0;                    // Initialize.
   fours = twos = ones = 0;
```

```
for (i = 0; i <= n - 8; i = i + 8) {
    CSA(twosA, ones, ones, A[i], A[i+1])
    CSA(twosB, ones, ones, A[i+2], A[i+3])
    CSA(foursA, twos, twos, twosA, twosB)
    CSA(twosA, ones, ones, A[i+4], A[i+5])
    CSA(twosB, ones, ones, A[i+6], A[i+7])
    CSA(foursB, twos, twos, twosA, twosB)
    CSA(eights, fours, fours, foursA, foursB)
    tot = tot + pop(eights);
}
tot = 8*tot + 4*pop(fours) + 2*pop(twos) + pop(ones);
for (i = i; i < n; i++)      // Simply add in the last
    tot = tot + pop(A[i]);   // 0 to 7 elements.
return tot;
}
```

The CSAs may be connected in many arrangements other than that shown in Figure 10-2. For example, increased instruction-level parallelism might result from feeding the first three array elements into one CSA, and the next three into a second CSA, which allows the instructions of these two CSAs to execute in parallel. One might also be able to permute the three input operands of the CSA macros for increased parallelism. With the plan shown in Figure 10-2, one can easily see how to use only the first three CSAs to construct a program that processes array elements in groups of four, and also how to expand it to construct programs that process array elements in groups of 16 or more. The plan shown also spreads out the loads somewhat, which is advantageous for a machine that has a relatively low limit on the number of loads that can be outstanding at any one time.

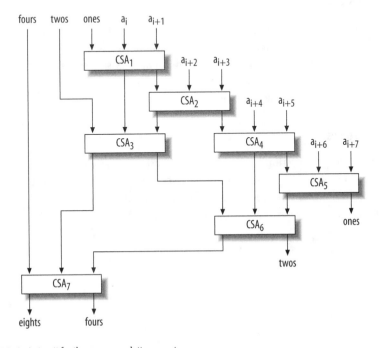

FIGURE 10-2. A circuit for the array population count

Table 10-1 summarizes the number of instructions executed by generalizations of the plan of Figure 10-2 for various group sizes. The values in the middle two columns ignore loads and loop control. The third column gives the total loop instruction execution count per word of the input array, produced by a compiler for a basic RISC machine that does not have indexed loads.

TABLE 10-1. *Instructions per word for the array population count*

Program	Instructions exclusive of loads and loop control		All instructions in loop (compiler output)
	Formula	For $n_c = 5, n_p = 15$	
Naive method	$np + 1$	16	21
Groups of 2	$(n_c + n_p + 1)/2$	10.5	14
Groups of 4	$(3n_c + n_p + 1)/4$	7.75	10
Groups of 8	$(7n_c + n_p + 1)/8$	6.38	8
Groups of 16	$(15n_c + n_p + 1)/16$	5.69	7
Groups of 32	$(31n_c + n_p + 1)/32$	5.34	6.5
Groups of 2^n	$n_c + \dfrac{n_p - n_c + 1}{2^n}$	$5 + \dfrac{11}{2^n}$	

It is a pleasant surprise that in the limit, the number of computational instructions required to compute the population count of n words is reduced from the naïve method's $16n$ to the CSA method's $5n$, where the 5 is the number of instructions required to implement one CSA circuit.

For small arrays, there are better plans than that of Figure 10-2. For example, for an array of seven words, the plan of Figure 10-3 is quite efficient.* It executes in $4n_c + 3n_p + 4 = 69$ instructions, or 9.86 instructions per word. Similar plans exist that apply to arrays of size $2^k - 1$ words, for any positive integer k. The plan for 15 words executes in $11n_c + 4n_p + 6 = 121$ instructions, or 8.07 instructions per word.

Applications

The *population count* instruction has a miscellany of uses. As mentioned at the beginning of this chapter, one use is to compute the size of a set when sets are represented by bit strings. In this representation, there is a "universe" set whose members are numbered sequentially. A set is represented by a bit string in which bit i is 1 if and only if member i is in the set.

---

* Seal, *op. cit.*

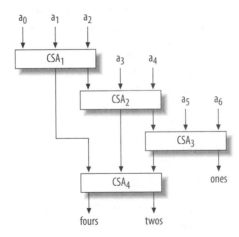

FIGURE 10-3. A circuit for the total population count of seven words

Another simple application is to compute the Hamming distance between two bit vectors, a concept from the theory of error-correcting codes. The *Hamming distance* is simply the number of places where the vectors differ, that is:[*]

    dist(x, y) = pop(x ⊕ y)

The *population count* instruction may be used to compute the number of trailing 0s in a word, using relations such as:

    ntz(x) = pop(¬x & (x - 1)) = 32 - pop(x | -x)

(The reader who is not familiar with these mixtures of arithmetic and logical operations might pause for a few moments to discover why they work.) The function $ntz(x)$ also has a miscellany of uses. For example, some early computers, upon interrupt, would store a "reason for interrupt" bit in a special register. The bits were placed in a position that identified which type of interrupt occurred. The positions were chosen in priority order, usually with the higher-priority interrupts in the less significant positions. Two or more bits could be set at the same time. To determine which interrupt to process, the supervisor program would execute the ntz function on the quantity in the special register.

Another application of *population count* is to allow reasonably fast direct indexed access to a moderately sparse array A that is represented in a certain compact way. In the compact representation, only the defined, or nonzero, elements of the array are stored. There is an auxiliary bit string *bits* that has a 1-bit for each bit position i for which $A[i]$ is defined. Since *bits* is generally quite long, it is broken up into 32-bit words, with the first bit of the long string being at bit 0 (the least significant bit) of the first word of *bits*.

---

* See, for example, the chapter on error-correcting codes in A. K. Dewdney, *The Turing Omnibus.* Computer Science Press, 1989.

As a speedup device, there is also an array of words *bitsum* such that *bitsum[j]* is the total number of 1-bits in all the words of *bits* that precede entry *j*. This is illustrated in the following table for an array in which elements 0, 2, 32, 47, 48, and 95 are defined:

bits	bitsum	data
0x00000005	0	A[0]
0x00018001	2	A[2]
0x80000000	5	A[32]
		A[47]
		A[48]
		A[95]

Here's the key task: given a "logical" index *i* into the full array, translate it into the "physical" index *sparse_i* where the array element is stored, if that element exists, or give some indication if it does not exist. For the array in the previous table, we wish to translate 47 to 3, 48 to 4, and 49 to "does not exist." Given a logical index *i*, the corresponding index *sparse_i* into the *data* array is given by the number of 1-bits in array *bits* that precede the bit corresponding to *i*. This may be calculated as follows:

```
j = i >> 5;                 // j = i/32.
k = i & 31;                 // k = rem(i, 32);
mask = 1 << k;              // A "1" at position k.
if ((bits[j] & mask) == 0) goto no_such_element;
mask = mask - 1;            // 1's to right of k.
sparse_i = bitsum[j] + pop(bits[j] & mask);
```

The space cost of this representation is two bits per position in the full array.

The population count function can be used to generate binomially distributed random integers. To generate an integer drawn from a population given by *Binomial(t, p)* where *t* is the number of trials and $p = 1/2$, generate *t* random bits and count the number of 1s in the *t* bits. This can be generalized to probabilities *p* other than $1/2$.*

According to computer folklore, *population count* is important to the National Security Agency. No one (outside of NSA) seems to know just what they use it for, but it may be in cryptography work or in searching huge amounts of material.

---

* See section 3.4.1, problem 27 in Donald E. Knuth, *The Art of Computer Programming: Seminumerical Algorithms* (Vol. 2, 3rd. ed.). Addison-Wesley, 1998.

## CHAPTER ELEVEN

Secure Communication:
The Technology Of Freedom

Ashish Gulhati

> I speak of none other than the computer that is to come after me. A
> computer whose merest operational parameters I am not worthy to calcu-
> late—and yet I will design it for you. A computer which can calculate the
> Question to the Ultimate Answer, a computer of such infinite and subtle
> complexity that organic life itself shall form part of its operational matrix.

> *Deep Thought*, The Hitchhiker's Guide to the Galaxy

I N MID-1999 I FLEW TO COSTA RICA TO WORK WITH LAISSEZ FAIRE CITY, a group that was working to create software systems to help usher in a new era of individual sovereignty.*

The group at LFC was working primarily to develop a suite of software designed to protect
and enhance individual rights in the digital age, including easy-to-use secure email, online
dispute mediation services, an online stock exchange, and a private asset trading and
banking system. My interest in many of the same technologies had been piqued long ago
by the cypherpunks list and Bruce Schneier's *Applied Cryptography* (Wiley), and I'd already
been working on prototype implementations of some of these systems.

The most fundamental of these were systems to deliver strong and *usable* communications
privacy to just about everybody.

When I stepped into LFC's sprawling "interim consulate" outside San José, Costa Rica,
they had a working prototype of a secure webmail system they called MailVault. It ran on
Mac OS 9, used FileMaker as its database, and was written in Frontier. Not at all the mix

---

* See *The Sovereign Individual: Mastering the Transition to the Information Age*, James Dale Davidson and
  Sir William Rees Mogg, Free Press, 1999.

of technologies you'd want to run a mission-critical communications service on, but that's what the programmers had produced.

It was no surprise the system crashed early and often, and was extremely fragile. It could hardly support two concurrent users. LFC was facing a credibility crisis with its investors, as their software releases had been delayed many times, and their first beta of MailVault, the flagship product, was no gem. So in the free time left over from my contract network and system administration work at LFC, I started writing a new secure mail system from scratch.

This system is now named Cryptonite and has been in constant off-and-on development and testing since then, in between other projects.

The first functioning prototype of Cryptonite was licensed to LFC as MailVault beta 2, and was open for testing in September 1999. It was the first OpenPGP-compatible webmail system available for public use and was almost immediately put to the test by LFC's investors and beta testers. Since that time, Cryptonite has evolved in many ways through interaction with users, the open source community, and the market. While not an open source product itself, it has led to the development of numerous components I decided to release as open source along the way.

The Heart of the Start

Developing Cryptonite and marketing and supporting associated services single-handedly for many years (with unwavering support and many invaluable ideas from my wife, Barkha) has been an incredibly interesting and rewarding journey, not only from a development perspective but also from an entrepreneurial one.

Before jumping into the nitty-gritty of the system, I thought I'd touch upon some points that have impressed themselves strongly in my consciousness over the course of this project:

- My friend Rishab Ghosh once quipped that there's a lot of hype about how the Internet can enable wired hackers to work from anywhere, but most of the people who create this hype live within a small area in California. The great thing about an independent startup project is that it really can be done anywhere, and dropped and picked up again when convenient. I've hacked on Cryptonite over many years on four continents, and it may well be the first high-quality software application developed in large part in the Himalayan mountains. (I used the word "wired" before loosely. In reality, five wireless technologies facilitated our connectivity in the Himalayas: a VSAT satellite Internet link, Wi-Fi, Bluetooth, GPRS, and CDMA.)

- When working on a project as a single developer in your spare time, remember the old hacker wisdom that "six months in the lab can save you ten minutes in the library." It's critical to maximize your reuse of existing code libraries. For this reason, I elected to develop the system in Perl, a popular and flexible high-level language with a rich library of mature, free software modules, and the Perl hacker's first virtue of laziness informed every design decision.

- Especially for end-user application software, ease of use is a critical issue. It is essential to the function of such code to present a simple, accessible interface to the user. The usability considerations of developing an end-user security application are even more significant, and were in fact a key factor in making the Cryptonite system worth developing.

- To get off to a running start, it's a good idea to implement a working prototype first, and use a prototype-to-production path to move to production deployment after the essential functionality is implemented. This can be a huge help in getting the basic design and structure right before you unleash the code on hundreds or (hopefully!) millions of users.

- Keeping your system as simple as possible is always a great idea. Resist the urge to get suckered into using the latest complex buzzword technology, unless the application really demands it.

- Processors are pretty fast now, and programmer time is generally more valuable than processor time, but speed is still critical for application software. Users expect their applications to be snappy. For web applications, which many users will use concurrently, investing some time in optimizing for speed is a Very Good Thing.

- A software application is a living entity, in constant need of attention, updating, enhancement, testing, fixing, tweaking, marketing, and support. Its success and beauty in an economic sense depends directly on the code being flexible enough to evolve over time and meet the requirements of its users, and to do it again and again and again over the course of many years.

- It really does help if the problem you're trying to solve is something that personally interests you. This not only makes it possible to flip between user and developer roles easily, but ensures you'll still be interested in the project five years later—because building and marketing a software application is generally quite a long-term proposition.

The development of Cryptonite has been powered in large measure by my desire to create tools to help individuals all over the world achieve practical liberty. And while developing the system single-handedly has been difficult at times, I find that being a single-developer project has also given the code a certain stylistic and structural unity that's rare in code developed by multiple programmers.

Untangling the Complexity of Secure Messaging

While bringing secure communications capabilities to the world is a whoppingly great idea for the protection of individual human rights (more on this later), getting it right is a trickier task than it may seem. Public-key cryptosystems can, in principle, facilitate ad hoc secure communications, but practical implementations are very often needlessly complex and disconnected from on-the-ground realities concerning who will use such systems, and how.

The fundamental problem to be solved in practical implementations based on public-key cryptography is key authentication. To send an encrypted message to someone, you need her public key. If you can be tricked into using the wrong public key, your privacy vanishes.

There are two very different approaches to the key authentication problem.

The conventional Public Key Infrastructure (PKI) approach, typically based on ISO standard X.509, depends on a system of trusted third-party Certification Authorities (CAs), and is in many ways fundamentally unsuited to meet the real needs of users in ad hoc networks.* PKI implementations have achieved significant success in more structured domains, such as corporate VPNs and the authentication of secure web sites, but have made little headway in the real-world heterogeneous email environment.

The other approach is exemplified by the most popular public-key-based messaging security solution in use today: Phil Zimmermann's PGP and its descendants, now formalized as the IETF OpenPGP protocol. OpenPGP preserves the flexibility and fundamentally decentralized nature of public-key cryptography by facilitating distributed key authentication through "webs of trust" rather than depending on a centralized, hierarchical system of CAs, as PKI approaches do (including OpenPGP's primary competitor, S/MIME). Not surprisingly, S/MIME, which is almost ubiquitously available in popular email clients, enjoys a vastly smaller user base than OpenPGP, despite email clients' general lack of comprehensive support for OpenPGP.

But the web-of-trust approach, which relies on users to build their own chains of trust for certifying and authenticating public keys, has its own issues. Prime among these are the interrelated challenges of ensuring that users understand how to use the web of trust to authenticate keys, and the need to achieve a critical mass of users in order to ensure that any two users can easily find a trust path between each other.

As Figure 11-1 shows, in a web of trust implementation, no third parties are arbitrarily designated as "trusted." Each individual user is her own most trusted certifying authority, and may assign varying levels of trust to others for the purpose of validating keys. You consider a key valid if it is certified directly by you, by another person who is fully trusted by you to certify keys, or by a user-definable number of people, each of whom is partially trusted by you to certify keys.

Because the web-of-trust approach doesn't attempt to outsource key authentication the way PKI approaches do, users must play a central role in building their webs of trust and ascertaining the authenticity of public keys. This puts usability considerations front and center in the design of OpenPGP-based secure messaging systems.

---

* The drawbacks of conventional PKI have been concisely summarized by Roger Clarke at *http:// www.anu.edu.au/people/Roger.Clarke/II/PKIMisFit.html.*

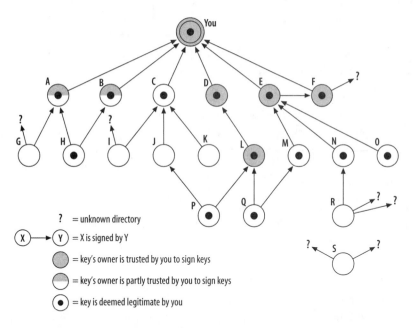

? = unknown directory

(X) ⟶ (Y) = X is signed by Y

⬤ = key's owner is trusted by you to sign keys

◒ = key's owner is partly trusted by you to sign keys

(•) = key is deemed legitimate by you

FIGURE 11-1. How keys are validated through the web of trust

Usability Is the Key

Email privacy software often requires users to jump through too many hoops, so very few bother to use it. Usability is critical to the success of any security solution, because if the system isn't usable, it will end up being bypassed or used in an insecure manner, in either case defeating its whole purpose.

A case study of the usability of PGP conducted at Carnegie Mellon University in 1998 pointed out the specialized challenges of creating an effective and usable interface for email encryption and found that of 12 study participants, all of whom were experienced at using email, "only one-third of them were able to use PGP to correctly sign and encrypt an email message when given 90 minutes in which to do so."*

I saw Cryptonite as an interesting project in terms of designing a secure, reliable, and efficient email system while achieving a very high level of usability. I set out to create a webmail system that would embed OpenPGP security into the very structure of the email experience, and help even casual users to effectively utilize OpenPGP to achieve communications privacy. The webmail format was chosen specifically because it could bring powerful communications privacy technology to anyone with access to an Internet café, or a cellphone with a web browser, not just to the few able to run desktop email encryption software on powerful computers.

---

* "Usability of Security: A Case Study." Alma Whitten and J. D. Tygar, Carnegie Mellon University. *http://reports-archive.adm.cs.cmu.edu/anon/1998/CMU-CS-98-155.pdf.*

Cryptonite was designed to make encryption a normal part of everyday email, not by masking the complexities of the public-key cryptosystems that it relies on, but rather by making the elements of these systems clearer and more accessible to the user. Usability considerations were thus central to Cryptonite's design and development, as was manifested in a number of ways:

Development of UI functionality from user feedback and usability studies

The CMU user study provided many good ideas for the initial design, and many features evolved out of usability testing with Cryptonite itself by casual email users. The interface was kept clean, minimalist, and consistent, with all important actions being at most one or two clicks away at all times.

Significant insights gleaned from usability testing included the need to integrate key management into the email client, the need to offer persistence for decrypted messages, and the desirability of exposing message structure information in the message list view.

The final three-pane layout, similar to that found on desktop email programs, was decided on after testing a simple single-pane HTML interface as well as an AJAX interface. The three-pane interface optimized the user's experience by not forcing a page reload every time one returned to the message list, as a single-pane design does, and a simple three-pane HTML interface was both more portable and cleaner to implement than an AJAX one, while not being much more bandwidth-intensive.

Rich and meaningful exposure of OpenPGP objects to the user in an intuitive way

All key operations are available to the user, including generating, importing and exporting keys; checking key signatures and fingerprints; certifying keys and revoking key certifications; and publishing keys to and retrieving them from a key server. This puts the user in full control of her own web of trust. The validity and trust levels of keys are visible explicitly in text, as well as by color-coding in the key list. Key trust values are always kept updated with the latest state of the key ring and trust database.

The UI's Key Ring view, illustrated in Figure 11-2, shows the validity of all user identities for each key, both in text and by color-coding. It also shows the key type, using icons, and owner trust values for each key (both in text and by color-coding). Full details for any key are available through the "edit" link for the key.

Warnings and feedback about security implications of user actions

Giving users the power to manage keys brings the risk that they will use their abilities in ways that weaken the security of the system. So, it is also the application's job to educate the user about security implications of actions such as certifying a key, altering a key's trust level, or signing a message.

All screens in Cryptonite that allow for actions with security implications contain short, highlighted warnings about these implications. And they're right on the same screen, not in irritating pop-up boxes.

My Key Ring

	Type	Identities	Owner Trust	Edit
☐	⌐	Ashish Gulhati <ashish@neomailbox.net> (Ultimately Valid)	-	edit
☐	⌐	Barkha Gulhati <barkha@neomailbox.com> (Ultimately Valid)	Ultimately trusted certifier	edit
☐	⌐	Ashish Gulhati <ashish@neomailbox.com> (Ultimately Valid) Ashish Gulhati <hash@netropolis.org> (Ultimately Valid) Ashish Gulhati <agul@cpan.org> (Ultimately Valid)	Ultimately trusted certifier	edit
☐	⌐	Vipul Ved Prakash. <mail@vipul.net> (Fully Valid)	Fully trusted certifier	edit
☐	⌐	Adam Back <adam@cypherspace.org> (Fully Valid)	Fully trusted certifier	edit
☐	⌐	Gordon Worley (Mac GPG) <macgpg@rbisland.cx> (Expired) Gordon Worley (Mac GPG) <redbird@rbisland.cx> (Expired)	Marginally trusted certifier	edit
☐	⌐	Ashish Gulhati <ashish@neomailbox.net> (Ultimately Valid)	Ultimately trusted certifier	edit
☐	⌐	Philip R. Zimmermann <prz@pgp.com> (Fully Valid)	Fully trusted certifier	edit
☐	⌐	Rishab Aiyer Ghosh <rishab@dxm.org> (Fully Valid)	Fully trusted certifier	edit
☐	⌐	John Gilmore <gnu@cygnus.com> (Fully Valid) John Gilmore <gnu@toad.com> (Fully Valid) John Gilmore <gnu@freeswan.org> (Fully Valid)	Fully trusted certifier	edit

FIGURE 11-2. The Key Ring view exposes information on keys and trust

Built-in associations

Cryptonite's concept of a user's identity is strongly tied to the private keys in the user's key ring. When sending mail, users can use any "From" address that corresponds to a private key in their key ring. This helps the user grasp in an intuitive and inescapable way the idea of a private key. Public keys can be tied to contacts in the user's address book, so they can be picked up for automatic encryption whenever available.

Full-featured email client

Cryptonite is primarily an email client that just happens to have complete support for OpenPGP-based security and key management built in. An important usability goal was to provide the user with a full-featured email client without letting the security functionality get in the way of its usability for email. This required not only providing the full range of features a user would expect to find in an email client but, most significantly, enabling users to search through their mail folders, including text within encrypted messages, without much more complexity than a regular email client where all messages are stored unencrypted.

The Foundation

Application software today, of course, is many levels removed from the bare hardware and builds on top of many layers of existing code. So when starting a new project, getting the foundation right has to be the crucial starting point.

For a number of reasons, I chose to write Cryptonite in Perl. The rich pool of open source reusable modules on CPAN (*http://www.cpan.org*) helped minimize the need to write new code where existing solutions could be leveraged, and also allowed a great deal of flexibility in interfaces and options. This was borne out well by prior experience with the language as well as by later experiences with the Cryptonite project.

The ability to interface to C and other libraries through Perl's XS API allowed access to even more libraries. Perl's excellent portability and robust support for object-oriented programming were other important advantages. Cryptonite was intended to be easily modifiable by licensees, which would also be facilitated by writing it in Perl.

So, the Cryptonite system is implemented entirely in object-oriented Perl. The project has led to the creation of numerous open source Perl modules, which I have made available on CPAN.

GNU/Linux jumped out as the obvious development platform, because code developed on a Unix-like environment would be easiest to port to whatever deployment platform it would be used on, which could only be another Unix-like platform. No Windows or Mac system at the time (OS X was in pre-beta) had what it took to run mission-critical software to be used concurrently by thousands of users. Linux was my preferred desktop environment anyway, so it was also the default choice.

In 2001, development and deployment moved to OpenBSD, and since 2003, development has proceeded on OS X and OpenBSD (as well as Linux). OS X was chosen for its out-of-box usability as a portable primary desktop, combined with its Unix-like underpinnings and ability to run a wide variety of open source software. OpenBSD was chosen as a deployment platform for its reliability, superlative security record, and focus on code quality and code auditing.

The IDE used for development was Emacs, selected for its power, extensibility, and excellent portability, including portability to handheld and wearable devices that I often used for development on the move. I also appreciated the availability of Emacs's *cperl* mode, which manages to offer pretty good auto-formatting for Perl code, even though "only *perl* can parse Perl."

Design Goals and Decisions

Cryptonite was envisioned as an OpenPGP-compatible webmail system designed to be secure, scalable, reliable, and easy to use. Portability and extensibility were other important goals of the project.

A key decision made early on was to develop a fully independent core engine to facilitate interface diversity and cross-platform access. It was important for interface specialists to be able to build interfaces without needing to modify the core. Clean separation of the core from the interface would allow experimentation with a variety of interface styles, which could then be subjected to usability testing to help evolve the optimal interface. This separation is also the essential design feature that will enable a diversity of interfaces to be built in the future, including interfaces designed for small devices such as cellphones and PDAs.

This design called for a client-server system, with a well-defined internal API and a clear separation of functionality and privilege between the Cryptonite engine and the user interface. Interfaces to the core could then be implemented in any language with any UI framework. A reference interface would be developed to enable live usability testing.

Another consideration was to enable flexibility in deployment, by providing the option to perform cryptographic operations either on the server or on the user's own machine. Both approaches have their advantages and drawbacks.

While in principle it is desirable to restrict cryptographic operations to the user's machine, these machines in practice are very often physically insecure and riddled with spyware. The server, on the other hand, can benefit from both high physical security and dedicated software maintenance by experts, making server-side cryptography (especially in conjunction with hardware token authentication) a more secure option for many users. This was another reason behind the choice of Perl as the implementation language: its high portability would make it possible to run the application (or components of it) on both server and user machines, as needed.

An object-oriented implementation would help keep the code easy to comprehend, extend, maintain, and modify over many years. As the code would be available in source form to licensees and end users, readability and accessibility of the code were themselves important objectives.

Basic System Design

The initial design of Cryptonite is shown in Figure 11-3.

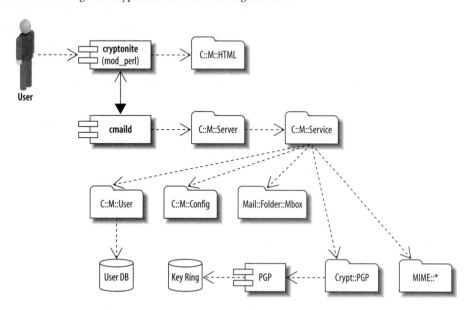

FIGURE 11-3. The initial design of Cryptonite (C::M is shorthand for Cryptonite::Mail)

Most of the work is done by the Cryptonite::Mail::Service class, which defines a high-level service object that implements all the core functionality of the Cryptonite system. The methods of this class simply perform operations based on their arguments and return a status code and the results of the operation, if any. All the methods are noninteractive, and there is no user interface code in this class:

```
package Cryptonite::Mail::Service;

sub new {        #       Object constructor
  ...
}

sub newuser {    #       Create new user account.
  ...
}

sub newkey {     #       Generate a new key for a user.
  ...
}
...
```

Cryptonite::Mail::Service encapsulates all the core functionality of the system, including user creation and management; creating, opening and closing folders; sending, deleting and copying mail; encryption, decryption and signature verification; and parsing multipart MIME messages.

The Service class is used by Cryptonite::Mail::Server to implement a server that receives serialized Cryptonite API calls and dispatches them to a Service object.

Serialization was initially achieved via SOAP calls, but the SOAP object parsing and handling added too much needless complexity and overhead. So, a simple home-brewed serialization scheme was implemented instead. (Seven years in, this looks like a really good move, judging from *http://wanderingbarque.com/nonintersecting/2006/11/15/the-s-stands-for-simple* and its comments.) This is the command dispatcher in Cryptonite::Mail::Server:

```
package Cryptonite::Mail::Server;

use Net::Daemon;

use vars qw(@ISA);
use Cryptonite::Mail::Service;

@ISA = qw(Net::Daemon);

my $debug = 1;
my $cmail = new Cryptonite::Mail::Service;

sub process_request {
  my $self = shift; my ($retcode, $input);

  # Wrap in eval to catch timeout exception.
```

```perl
eval {
  local $SIG{ALRM} = sub { die "Timed Out!\n" };

  # Timeout after 2 minutes of no input.
  my $timeout = 120;

  my $previous_alarm = alarm($timeout);
  while( <STDIN> ){
    s/\r?\n$//;

    # Get caller, command and cmd args.
    my ($caller, $command, @args) = split /(?<!\\):/;
    $debug ? $debug == 2 ? warn "$$: $_\n" :
      warn "$$: $caller:$command:$args[0]\n" : '';

    # Unescape arg separators in the stream.
    for (@args) { s/(?<!;);(?!;)/:/sg; s/;;/;/sg }
    return if $command =~ /^\s*quit\s*$/i;

    # Validate command.
    my $valid = $cmail->valid_cmd;
    if ($command=~/$valid/x) {
      # Call service method.
      $ret = join ("\n", ($cmail->$command (@args), ''));
      print STDOUT $ret;
    }
    else {
      # Invalid command.
      print STDOUT ($cmail->cluebat (ECOMMAND, $command) . "\n");
    }
    alarm($timeout);
  }
  alarm($previous_alarm);
};

if( $@=~/timed out/i ){
  print STDOUT "Timed Out.\r\n";
  return;
}
}
```

The Cryptonite Mail Daemon (*cmaild*) receives serialized method calls via Unix or TCP sockets, calls the method on the service object, and returns a result code (+OK or -ERR) along with a human-readable status message (e.g., "Everything is under control!") and optional return values (such as a list of messages in a folder, or the text of a message part). If multiple lines of return values are being returned, the status message indicates how many lines the client should expect to read.

The server forks a new process every time a new client connects, so Perl's built-in *alarm* function is used to send each new server process a SIGALRM *$timeout* seconds after the last message received from the client, which causes the server to time out and disconnect the client.

The Test Suite

Because automated testing is a crucial component of long-term development, I developed a test suite simultaneously with the project code.

The clean separation of the core from the interface makes it easy to test both components separately, as well as to quickly diagnose bugs and pinpoint where they are in the code. Writing tests for *cmaild* is just a matter of calling its methods with valid (or invalid) inputs and making sure that the return codes and values are as expected.

The test suite for *cmaild* uses the client API calls cmdopen (to open a connection to the Cryptonite Mail Daemon), cmdsend (to send an API call to the daemon), and cmdayt (to send an "Are you there?" ping to the server):

```perl
use strict;
use Test;

BEGIN { plan tests => 392, todo => [] }

use Cryptonite::Mail::HTML qw (&cmdopen &cmdsend &cmdayt);

$Test::Harness::Verbose = 1;

my ($cmailclient, $select, $sessionkey);
my ($USER, $CMAILID, $PASSWORD) = 'test';
my $a = $Cryptonite::Mail::Config::CONFIG{ADMINPW};

ok(sub {                # 1: cmdopen
    my $status;
    ($status, $cmailclient, $select) = cmdopen;
    return $status unless $cmailclient;
    1;
  }, 1);

ok(sub {                # 2: newuser
    my $status = cmdsend('test.pl', $a, $cmailclient, $select,
                         'newuser', $USER);
    return $status unless $status =~ /^\+OK.*with password (.*)$/;
    $PASSWORD = $1;
    1;
  }, 1);

...
```

The Functioning Prototype

For the first prototype, I used a simple object persistence module, Persistence::Object::Simple (which my friend Vipul had written for a project we'd worked on earlier) to whip up a basic user database. Using persistent objects helped keep the code clean and intuitive, and also provided a straightforward upgrade path to production database engines (simply create or derive a compatible Persistence::Object::* class for the database engine).

In late 2002, Matt Sergeant created another simple prototype-to-production path for Perl hackers, DBD::SQLite module, a "self-contained RDBMS in a DBI driver," which can be used for rapid prototyping of database code without the need for a full database engine during development. Personally, though, I prefer the elegance and simplicity of persistent objects to having my code littered with SQL queries and DBI calls.

Mail received into the Cryptonite system was saved to regular *mbox* files, which worked fine for the prototype. Of course, a production implementation would have to use a more sophisticated mail store. I decided to use PGP itself as the encryption backend, to avoid rewriting (and maintaining) all the encryption functionality already contained in PGP.

GnuPG was coming along, and I kept in mind that I might want to use it for cryptography support in the future. So, I wrote Crypt::PGP5 to encapsulate the PGP5 functionality in a Perl module. This module is available from CPAN (though I haven't updated it in ages).

For the cryptographic core of Crypt::PGP5, I could have used the proprietary PGPSDK library, but I would have had to create a Perl interface to it, which would likely have been more work than just using the PGP binary. So, with a healthy dose of Perlish laziness and keeping in mind that TMTOWTDI,* I decided to use the Expect module to automate inter-actions with the PGP binary, using the same interface that's available to human users of the program. This worked well enough for the first prototype.

A basic web interface was developed, using the Text::Template module, to populate HTML templates. The Cryptonite::Mail::HTML module contained all web-interface-related code, including session handling.

The prototype system was ready after just three months of part-time coding. It implemented a full web interface, basic MIME support, OpenPGP encryption, decryption, signing and signature verification, online new user registration, and a new and interesting alternative to login passwords for authentication: PassFaces from ID Arts.

Clean Up, Plug In, Rock On...

After developing the initial prototype of Cryptonite in Costa Rica, I continued working on it independently. After a much needed cleanup of the code (prototype development had been hectic and had left not much time to refactor or test the code), I worked on a number of Perl modules and components that would be needed next, to make the jump from a simple prototype to a scalable product. These included Crypt::GPG (with an interface almost identical to that of Crypt::PGP5, so that switching to GnuPG for the crypto opera-tions in Cryptonite involved little more than a single-line change to the code), and Persis-tence::Database::SQL and Persistence::Object::Postgres (which provide object persistence in a Postgres database, with a similar interface to Persistence::Object::Simple, making the backend database switch quite seamless as well).

* "There's More Than One Way To Do It," a central tenet of the Perl way of life.

Persistence::Object::Postgres, like Persistence::Object::Simple, uses a blessed reference* to a hash container to store key-value pairs, which can be committed to the database with a commit method call. It also uses Perl's Tie mechanism to tie Postgres' large objects (BLOBs) to filehandles, enabling natural filehandle-based access to large binary objects in the database. One of the major benefits of Persistence::Database::SQL over Persistence::Object:: Simple, of course, is that it enables proper queries into a real database. For example, with Persistence::Object::Simple, there's no clean way to quickly search for a particular user's record, whereas with Persistence::Database::SQL, getting a specific user record from the database is straightforward:

```perl
sub _getuser {  # Get a user object from the database.
  my $self = shift; my $username = shift;
  $self->db->table('users'); $self->db->template($usertmpl);
  my ($user) = $self->db->select("WHERE USERNAME = '$username'");
  return $user;
}
```

With Persistence::Object::Simple one would have to either iterate over all the persistent objects in the data directory or resort to a hack such as directly grepping the plaintext persistence files in the data directory.

In most respects, the interface of Persistence::Object::Postgres is very similar to that of Persistence::Object::Simple. To modify an object with either module, the code is identical:

```perl
my $user  = $self->_getuser($username);
return $self->cluebat (EBADLOGIN) unless $user and $user->timestamp;
$user->set_level($level);
$user->commit;
```

The switch from a plaintext database to a real DBMS was made after most of the prototype code was basically working well, and marked the second stage of Cryptonite development: getting the system ready for real-world deployment. For prototype development, Persistence::Object::Simple was great, as it didn't require a database server to be available for development, and objects were stored in plaintext files so they could be easily examined for debugging.

The use of homomorphic interfaces for Crypt::GPG and Persistence::Object::Postgres allowed these major changes (of the encryption and the database backends) to be made with very minor edits to the code in Cryptonite::Mail::Service.

Revamping the Mail Store

Storing user mail in plain *mbox* files worked for the first prototype, but a production system needed to be able to access and update individual messages more efficiently than a single flat file mailbox allowed. I also wanted to move toward the very important objective of providing mail store replication for fault-tolerance.

---

* In Perl, a reference becomes an object when associated to a class by bless, so "blessed reference" is just a Perlish term for an object.

A usability consideration also imposed some requirements on the mail store. In Cryptonite, unlike most email clients, information about MIME structures of messages would be made visible to users in the message list. This would make it possible for a user to visually identify which messages were encrypted and/or signed, directly in the message list. Availability of information about message parts in the message list would also enable the user to open a message subpart directly. The message parts are visible as icons in the rightmost column of the message list view, as shown in Figure 11-4.

	Date	From	Subject	Size	Parts
	6:43 AM	Ashish Gulhati	Photos...	87K	
	6:38 AM	Ashish Gulhati	No subject	2K	
	6:15 AM	feedback	[The Sovereign Cyborg]...	1.5K	
	9:27 AM	Angelina Rowe	Best prices for u	11.6K	
	12:46 AM	"Lora Sheldon"	Cursos completos de Tango	5.5K	
	12:07 AM	"john williams"	Do you know why Katherine the...	1.9K	

FIGURE 11-4. Message list with parts

To enable such visual feedback, the mail store would need to efficiently provide accurate information about the MIME structure of a list of messages. A further complication was the fact that the OpenPGP/MIME spec allows for MIME parts to be nested within signed and/or encrypted parts, so only an OpenPGP/MIME-aware mail store could return accurate information about MIME structures of encrypted or signed messages.

So I decided to implement, based on the Mail::Folder module, an SQL-based mail storage backend with most of the abilities of an IMAP4rev1 server. The core of this system is the Mail::Folder::SQL class, based on Mail::Folder and using Persistence::Object::Postgres. This was back when IMAP had not yet gained much traction. I opted not to use an existing IMAP server as a mail store because I anticipated needing some features that most IMAP servers didn't support well, such as mail store replication and the ability to retrieve detailed information about the structure of a MIME message without having to retrieve and parse the entire message.

Even though some IMAP servers might have suited my needs, I also didn't want Cryptonite to be dependent on and tied down to the capabilities of any specific IMAP server implementation. All in all, this turned out to be a good decision, even though it did lead to a lot of effort being expended on code that was later demoted to a less central role in the system.

Mail store replication was hacked up using two Perl modules I wrote: Replication::Recall and DBD::Recall, which used Eric Newton's Recall replication framework (*http://www.fault-tolerant.org/recall*) to replicate databases across multiple servers. The idea was to use this as a prototype and to custom-build a new database replication system in the future.

With the encryption, database, and mail store backends revamped, and with a new, cleaner theme, the first internal beta of Cryptonite went online in October 2001. It was tested by many users of varying skill levels, some of whom even used it as their primary mail client. Usability testing during the internal beta indicated that novice users were able to successfully generate and import keys, and to send and read encrypted and signed messages without much trouble.

Persistence of Decryption

An essential feature for an encrypted mail client is the ability to keep decrypted messages available in decrypted form for the duration of the user's session. A secure mail client that lacks this facility can get very irritating and inefficient to use, as it would require typing in long passphrases and waiting for decryption every time you want to read an encrypted message or search within encrypted messages.

Persistence for previously decrypted messages in Cryptonite was accomplished by creating a new Mail::Folder class, based on Mail::Folder::SQL. Mail::Folder::Shadow would delegate mailbox accesses to a *shadow folder* if the message had a counterpart in the shadow folder; otherwise, it would access the underlying (or *shadowed*) folder.

By this means, decrypted messages could be kept in the shadow folder while a session was alive, and little modification of the code was necessary to add persistent decrypts, other than to plug in the Mail::Folder::Shadow module everywhere Mail::Folder::SQL was used. Mail::Folder::Shadow implements its magic with a simple, tweakable delegation table:

```
my %method =
qw (get_message 1 get_mime_message 1 get_message_file 1 get_header 1
    get_mime_message 1 mime_type 1 get_mime_header 1 get_fields 1
    get_header_fields 1 refile 1 add_label 2 delete_label 2
    label_exists 2 list_labels 2 message_exists 1 delete_message 5
    sync 2 delete 2 open 2 set_header_fields 2 close 2 DESTROY 2
    get_mime_skeleton 1 get_body_part 1);
```

Mail::Folder::Shadow delegates method calls as appropriate to the shadow folder, the original shadowed folder, or to both. Perl's powerful AUTOLOAD feature, which provides a mechanism to handle methods that are not explicitly defined in a class, is a simple way to accomplish this delegation, while also providing a simple mechanism to tweak at runtime how different methods are handled.

Methods that have to check the shadow store, such as get_message and get_header, are delegated to the shadow if the message concerned exists in the shadow folder; otherwise, they are delegated to the original shadowed folder. Other methods, such as add_label and delete (which deletes a folder), need to be dispatched to both the shadow and the shadowed folder, as these messages must change the state of the original folder, as well as that of the shadow folder.

Yet other methods, such as delete_message, can accept a message list through an array reference. Some of the messages in the message list may be shadowed, and others may not. Mail::Folder::Shadow's AUTOLOAD handles such methods by building two lists from the message list passed to it, one of shadowed messages and one of nonshadowed messages. It then calls the method on both the shadowed and shadow folder for messages that are shadowed, and only on the shadowed folder for messages that aren't.

The practical upshot of all of this is that *cmaild* can continue to use folders just as it did before, and stash decrypted messages in the shadow folder for the duration of a session. There are a few extra methods in Mail::Folder::Shadow to enable this, including `update_shadow`, which is used to save the decrypted message in the shadow folder; `delete_shadow`, used to delete individual shadowed messages at user request; and `unshadow`, used to delete all messages in shadow folders before session termination.

Mail::Folder::Shadow makes it possible to offer persistence of decrypted messages for a session and to implement search within encrypted messages—both essential features from a user's perspective, but rarely implemented in current-generation OpenPGP-compliant email systems.

Hacking in the Himalayas

Through 2000 and 2001 I was able to work on Cryptonite only intermittently, both because of other commitments and because the project needed peace and quiet, which was in limited supply when I was traveling around and living in chaotic, cacophonous, polluted Indian cities.

In the summer of 2002, my wife and I took a vacation in the Himalayas, where I finally managed to get the time to finish writing major chunks of the code, including adding important key management abilities to Crypt::GPG, and creating an integrated interface for key management, which is a critical part of the whole web-of-trust mechanism. The core of this management interface, the Edit Key dialog, is shown in Figure 11-5. It enables fingerprint verification, the viewing and creation of user identity certifications, and the assigning of trust values to keys.

I also ported the system over to OpenBSD, which would be the ultimate deployment platform.

We already had all the other major components for a secure email service in place, and as it would still take some time to get Cryptonite ready for public use, we decided to go ahead and launch a commercial secure email service right away. This would enable me to spend more time on Cryptonite development, and to begin building a community of testers immediately.

So in mid-2003, we launched the Neomailbox secure IMAP, POP3, and SMTP email service. In the following years, this proved to be an excellent move that would help fund development, freeing me from the need to take on other contract work and simultaneously keeping me in close touch with the market for secure, private messaging.

In the fall of 2003, we set up a semi-permanent development base in a small Himalayan hamlet, about 2000 meters above sea level, and this is primarily where development has progressed since then. This kept our cash burn low, which is critical for a bootstrapping startup, and gave me lots of time and peace to work on Neomailbox and Cryptonite.

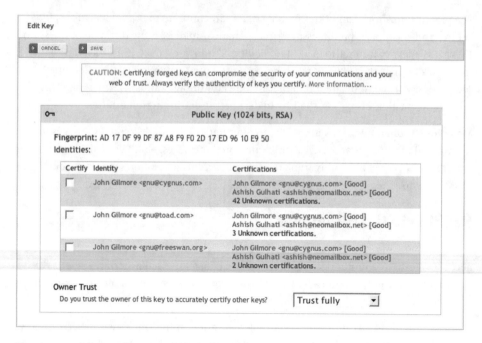

Edit Key

CANCEL   SAVE

CAUTION: Certifying forged keys can compromise the security of your communications and your web of trust. Always verify the authenticity of keys you certify. More information...

Public Key (1024 bits, RSA)

Fingerprint: AD 17 DF 99 DF 87 A8 F9 F0 2D 17 ED 96 10 E9 50
Identities:

Certify	Identity	Certifications
☐	John Gilmore <gnu@cygnus.com>	John Gilmore <gnu@cygnus.com> [Good] Ashish Gulhati <ashish@neomailbox.net> [Good] 42 Unknown certifications.
☐	John Gilmore <gnu@toad.com>	John Gilmore <gnu@cygnus.com> [Good] Ashish Gulhati <ashish@neomailbox.net> [Good] 3 Unknown certifications.
☐	John Gilmore <gnu@freeswan.org>	John Gilmore <gnu@cygnus.com> [Good] Ashish Gulhati <ashish@neomailbox.net> [Good] 2 Unknown certifications.

Owner Trust

Do you trust the owner of this key to accurately certify other keys?   Trust fully ▾

FIGURE 11-5. The Edit Key dialog

Even though we had our share of trials working on mission-critical high-tech systems from a remote Himalayan village that was, for the most part, still stuck in the 19th century, the words of Nikolai Roerich, the prolific Russian artist, writer, and philosopher who lived in the same part of the Himalayas for many years, did to a large extent hold true for us, too: "In truth, only here, only in the Himalayas, exist the unique, unprecedented, calm conditions for achieving results."

Securing the Code

Originally the code was designed as a prototype, and I didn't worry about securing it too much. But as time to make the system available as a public beta came around, it was time to lock down the code with, at least:

- Complete privilege separation

- Paranoid input validation

- Security audit of Crypt::GPG

- Documentation of any potential security issues

Privilege separation was already built in from the ground up, by running *cmaild* as a privileged user and interacting with it via its API. This allowed *cmaild* to perform privileged operations such as modifying system configuration files and performing cryptographic operations in a controlled manner, without giving the web server process access to sensitive resources. Only a few areas required cleanup of the separation between the core and the interface.

One of these was the composition of MIME messages with binary attachments. When the code was built using Persistence::Object::Simple, the *cmaild* protocol had been circumvented for binary MIME message composition. Attachments uploaded by the user were saved in a temporary directory, which both *cmaild* and the web server process had access to. Thus, it was necessary to run *cmaild* and the Cryptonite web interface on the same server.

With the move to Persistence::Object::Postgres, it became possible to easily pass binary objects between the frontend and the backend via the database, without relying on direct filesystem operations. This was important because the interface, the database, and the Cryptonite engine were all intended to run on their own independent servers or in load-balancing clusters.

Input validation (to check the validity of user-supplied inputs, such as folder and message identifiers) was straightforward to add. The Params::Validate module, very slightly modified, was used to add input validation to every method of Cryptonite::Mail::Service. The mvmsgs method, for example, validates its inputs with:

```
sub mvmsgs {      #      Move a list of messages to some other mailbox.
  my ($self, $username, $key, $dest, $copy, @msgnums) =
    (shift, lc shift, shift);
  my ($user, $session, $err) = $self->validateuser($username, $key);
  return $err if $err;
  return $self->cluebat(@{$@}) unless eval {
    ($dest, $copy, @msgnums) = validate_with ( params => \@_,
      extra => [$self], spec = [
        { type => SCALAR, callbacks =>
          { 'Legal Folder Name'   => $self->legal_foldername } },
        { type => SCALAR, callbacks =>
          { 'Boolean Flag' => $self->opt_boolean }, optional => 1 },
        ({ type => SCALAR, callbacks =>
          { 'Legal Message Number'  => $self->legal_msgnum } })
            x (@_ - 2) ]
  )
};
```

The acceptability of user-supplied input for each type of input field is specified via callback subroutine references stored in a hash in the Cryptonite::Mail::Config module:

```
LGL_FOLDERNAME => sub { $_[0] =~ /$_[1]->{"VFOLDER"}/i
                        or die (['EBADFOLDER', $_[0]]) },
OPT_BOOLEAN    => sub { $_[0] eq '' or $_[0] eq 0 or $_[0] eq 1
                        or die (['EBADBOOL', $_[0]]) },
LGL_MSGNUM     => sub { $_[0] =~ /$_[1]->{"VMSGNUM"}/
                        or die (['EBADMSGNUM', $_[0]]) },
```

Similar subroutines are invoked whenever an input parameter is validated. The regular expressions for validity are stored separately in Cryptonite::Mail::Config.

Even though most of the validation subroutines are essentially the same, they are all distinct, to enable each one to be tweaked as necessary without affecting the others or sacrificing clarity in this part of the code. The validation regular expressions and error strings are stored in a table as well, to enable localization in the future.

Persistence::Object::Postgres also performs its own input sanity checks, to protect against SQL injection attacks.

Auditing Crypt::GPG

Crypt::GPG had been written to be a working prototype and needed complete auditing to eliminate any potential security issues before public testing of the system.

Crypt::GPG had been freely available on CPAN since 2001, and I'd received much valuable feedback from its users. While many users said that they really liked the module's clean and simple interface, some had trouble getting it to run on certain platforms, where the Expect module it used to interact with GnuPG didn't work right. (Expect uses Unix pseudoterminals [ptys] as its IPC mechanism, and that doesn't work on Windows, for example.)

The Expect module's interface and syntax were also somewhat convoluted, which made the code a little difficult to read, as can be seen from this section of the sign method:

```
my $expect = Expect->spawn ($self->gpgbin, @opts, '-o-', '--sign',
                            @extras, @secretkey, $tmpnam);
$expect->log_stdout($self->debug);

$expect->expect (undef, '-re',
                 '-----BEGIN', 'passphrase:', 'signing failed');

if ($expect->exp_match_number == 2) {
  $self->doze; print $expect ($self->passphrase . "\r");
  $expect->expect (undef, '-re', '-----BEGIN', 'passphrase:');

  if ($expect->exp_match_number == 2) {    # Passphrase incorrect
    $self->doze;
    print $expect ($self->passphrase . "\r");
    $expect->expect (undef, 'passphrase:'); $self->doze;
    print $expect ($self->passphrase . "\r");
    $expect->expect (undef);
    unlink $tmpnam;
    return;
  }
}

elsif ($expect->exp_match_number == 3) {
  unlink $tmpnam; $expect->close;
  return;
}

$expect->expect (undef);
my $info = $expect->exp_match . $expect->exp_before;
```

Using the Expect-based module also caused *Heisenbugs*—failures that weren't easily reproducible, and that I discovered were the result of sending input to *gpg* too fast. The calls to doze in the previous code are a workaround for this: they introduce a few milliseconds of delay before sending the next bit of input to *gpg*. This generally worked, but failures would still occur on heavily loaded systems.

All these issues pointed to moving away from Expect and using another mechanism to interact with the GnuPG binary. I considered the idea of writing a pure Perl implementation of OpenPGP, but decided against it for basically the same reasons that I had decided to use GnuPG in the first place: Cryptonite is primarily an email client, with integrated Open-PGP support. A full OpenPGP implementation would at least double the complexity of the code I would have to maintain.*

After a little experimenting, it looked like IPC::Run by Barrie Slaymaker might do the trick for communication with GnuPG. With IPC::Run, the previous code became:

```
my ($in, $out, $err, $in_q, $out_q, $err_q);
my $h = start ([$self->gpgbin, @opts, @secretkey, '-o-',
               '--sign', @extras, $tmpnam],
              \$in, \$out, \$err, timeout( 30 ));

my $i = 0;

while (1) {
  pump $h until ($out =~ /NEED_PASSPHRASE (.{16}) (.{16}).*\n/g or
                 $out =~ /GOOD_PASSPHRASE/g);
  if ($2) {
    $in .= $self->passphrase . "\n";
    pump $h until $out =~ /(GOOD|BAD)_PASSPHRASE/g;
    last if $1 eq 'GOOD' or $i++ == 2;
  }
}
finish $h;
my $d = $detach ? 'SIGNATURE' : 'MESSAGE';
$out =~ /(-----BEGIN PGP $d-----.*-----END PGP $d-----)/s;
my $info = $1;
```

IPC::Run works reliably without the mini-delays needed with Expect, is much clearer to read, and works perfectly on most platforms.

Some operations with *gpg* didn't require any interaction, and earlier versions of the module had used Perl's backtick operator for such cases. Because the backtick operator invokes a shell, it's a security risk. With IPC::Run, it was easy to replace the use of the backtick operator with a tiny secure backtick function, thereby bypassing the shell. This made it possible to eliminate all shell invocations in Crypt::GPG.

```
sub backtick {
  my ($in, $out, $err, $in_q, $out_q, $err_q);
  my $h = start ([@_], \$in, \$out, \$err, timeout( 10 ));
  local $SIG{CHLD} = 'IGNORE';
  local $SIG{PIPE} = 'IGNORE';
  finish $h;
  return ($out, $err);
}
```

---

* A pure-Perl OpenPGP implementation, Crypt::OpenPGP, was written by Ben Trott in 2001–2002, and is available from CPAN. I'm looking forward to using it in future versions of Cryptonite that will support multiple cryptographic backends.

Some users had also pointed out that using temporary files to store plaintext could be insecure. This problem could be easily overcome without touching the code, simply by using temporary files on a RAM disk with encrypted swap (such as OpenBSD provides) or an encrypted RAM disk, so plaintext would never be written to disk unencrypted.

Of course, it would be nice to modify the code to avoid writing plaintext to temporary files at all, but as there already existed a practical workaround, eliminating temporary files went on the to-do list rather than being implemented immediately.

The new IPC::Run-based Crypt::GPG was uploaded to CPAN at the end of 2005. It now worked on a larger range of operating systems, and was more reliable and secure than its Expect-based predecessor.

The Invisible Hand Moves

By mid-2004, Neomailbox was a year old and had attracted quite a few paying customers. Cryptonite development was put on hold for a bit while I worked on developing various aspects of the Neomailbox service as well as on a few other projects I just couldn't wait to get started on.

But being out in the market was great, as it brought market forces, from competition to user feedback, to bear on the development process, and helped sharpen and clarify priorities. Customer requests and queries helped keep me intimately connected to what the users and the market wanted. Meeting the market's demands is how application code becomes beautiful in a commercial sense, after all, so interaction with the market became an integral and critical component of the development process.

Cryptonite was designed to be easy to maintain and modify, precisely because I knew that at some point it would have to start to evolve in new ways, both in response to and in anticipation of what the customer wanted. Being in the market enabled me to see that emerging demand: it was clear that IMAP was the future of remote mailbox access.

IMAP has a lot of attractive features that make it a very powerful and practical mail access protocol. One of the most important of these is the ability to access the same mailbox using multiple clients, which becomes increasingly important with the proliferation of computing devices. The typical user now has a desktop, a laptop, a PDA, and a cellphone, all capable of accessing her mailbox.

This posed a slight problem, as I'd already implemented a full mail store for Cryptonite, and it was not IMAP-based. There were two ways forward: either implement a full IMAP server based on the Cryptonite mail store (a big job), or modify Cryptonite to enable it to use an IMAP mail store as a backend. In fact, the second would have to be done either way.

Again, opting to reduce complexity of the system, and focusing on its primary purpose, I decided not to develop the Cryptonite mail store into a full-blown IMAP server. Instead, I modified it into a caching mechanism, which caches MIME skeletons (just the structure information, without the content) of multipart MIME messages listed by the user, and also entire messages read by the user, so that the next time a user opens a message she's read before, Cryptonite doesn't need to go back to the IMAP server to fetch it again.

This gave me the best of both worlds. Cryptonite could reflect the contents of an IMAP mailbox, while simultaneously posessing full information of each message's exact MIME structure, as well as being able to keep decrypted messages available in the shadow folders the Cryptonite mail store supported.

The modifications to the code were straightforward. Whenever the user clicks to read a message that isn't in the cache, Cryptonite caches it in the corresponding Mail::Folder:: Shadow folder:

```
my $folder = $session->folder;                # The folder name
my $mbox = _opencache($username, $folder);  # The M::F::Shadow cache

unless ($msgnum and grep { $_ == $msgnum } $mbox->message_list) {

  # Message is not in cache. Fetch from IMAP server and cache it.

  my $imap = $self->_open_imapconn($username, $user->password)
    or sleep(int(rand(3))+2), return $self->cluebat (EBADLOGIN);

  $imap->select($folder) or return $self->cluebat (ENOFOLDER, $folder);

  $imap->Uid(1);

  my ($tmpfh, $tmpnam) =
    tempfile( $self->tmpfiles, DIR => "$HOME/tmp",
              SUFFIX => $self->tmpsuffix, UNLINK => 1);
  $imap->message_to_file($tmpfh, $msgnum);

  $imap->logout;

  my $parser = new MIME::Parser; $parser->output_dir("$HOME/tmp/");

  $parser->filer->ignore_filename(1);  # Do NOT use suggested filename

  seek ($tmpfh,0,0);
  my $mail = $parser->parse($tmpfh);

  return $self->cluebat (ENOSUCHMSG, 0 + $msgnum) unless $mail;
  $mbox->update_message($msgnum,$mail);
}
```

In a similar manner, MIME skeletons are cached for all messages listed by the user through the message list view. The rest of the code continues to work as before, by operating on the cache for all read operations. Now we have IMAP compatibility, without compromising the features afforded by my mail store or modifying the main code much.

Mail store replication would need to be worked in again because the switch from Mail:: Folder::SQL to an IMAP server for the mail store meant Replication::Recall couldn't be used for replication. But in any case, Replication::Recall wasn't the most elegant or easy to implement replication system, and the Recall library had been rewritten in Python, making my Perl interface to the earlier C++ implementation obsolete anyway.

In hindsight, I spent a lot of time on the replication functionality, which had to be scrapped, and I probably would have been better off not bothering with replication at that stage. On the other hand, it did teach me a lot that will come in handy when I get down to implementing replication again.

Market forces and changing standards mean that application software is always evolving, and much of the beauty of such code from the programmer's point of view is certainly in how easy it is to adapt the code to ever-changing requirements. Cryptonite's object-oriented architecture makes it possible to implement major revisions with ease.

Speed Does Matter

With the Cryptonite mail store, performance had been quite snappy, and most mail store operations had been independent of mailbox size. But with the switch to IMAP, I noticed some major slowdowns with large mailboxes. A little profiling revealed that the performace bottleneck was the pure-Perl Mail::IMAPClient module, which I'd used to implement the IMAP capability.

A quick benchmark script (written using the Benchmark module) helped me check whether another CPAN module, Mail::Cclient, which interfaces to the UW C-Client library, was more efficient than Mail::IMAPClient. The results showed clearly that I'd have to redo the IMAP code using Mail::Cclient:

```
                   Rate IMAPClientSearch   CclientSearch
IMAPClientSearch 39.8/s              --            -73%
CclientSearch    145/s             264%              --


                   Rate IMAPClientSort   CclientSort
IMAPClientSort   21.3/s            --          -99%
CclientSort      2000/s          9280%            --
```

I probably should have thought of benchmarking the different modules before writing the code with Mail::IMAPClient. I'd originally avoided the C-Client library because I wanted to keep the build process as simple as possible, and Mail::IMAPClient's build process is definitely simpler than that of Mail::Cclient.

Fortunately, the switch from the former to the latter was generally quite straightforward. For some operations, I noticed that IMAPClient could do the job better than C-Client without much of a performance penalty, so Cryptonite::Mail::Service now uses both modules, each to do whatever it's better at.

A program like Cryptonite is never "finished," of course, but the code is now mature, robust, full of features, and efficient enough to serve its purpose: to provide thousands of concurrent users a secure, intuitive, and responsive email experience while helping them effectively protect the privacy of their communications.

Communications Privacy for Individual Rights

I mentioned at the beginning of this chapter that making secure communications technology widely available is a very effective means of protecting individual rights. As this recognition is the basic motivation behind the Cryptonite project, I'd like to end with a few observations on this point.

Cryptographic technology can, among other things:*

- Provide strong life-saving protection for activists, NGOs, and reporters working in repressive countries.†

- Preserve the communicability of censored news and controversial ideas.

- Protect the anonymity of whistle-blowers, witnesses, and victims of domestic abuse.

- For dessert, catalyze the geodesic society by enabling the free and unfettered exchange of ideas, goods, and services globally.

The motley crew of hackers known as the Cypherpunks has been developing privacy-enhancing software for years, with the intent of enhancing personal freedom and individual sovereignty in the digital age. Some cryptographic software is already a cornerstone of how the world works today. This includes the Secure SHell (SSH) remote terminal software, which is essential to securing the Internet's infrastructure, and the Secure Sockets Layer (SSL) encryption suite, which secures online commerce.

But these systems target very specific needs: secure server access and secure online credit card transactions, respectively. Both are concerned with securing human-machine interactions. Much more cryptographic technology specifically targeted at human-to-human interactions needs to be deployed in the coming years to combat the advancing menace of ubiquitous surveillance (which "leads to a quick end to civilization"‡).

An easy-to-use, secure webmail system is an enabling technology—it makes possible, for the first time in history, secure and private long-distance communications between individuals all over the globe, who never need meet in person.

Hacking the Civilization

This computer of such infinite and subtle complexity that it includes organic life itself in its operational matrix—the Earth, and the civilizations it hosts—can be reprogrammed in powerful ways by simple pieces of code that hack human culture right back, and rewire the operating system of society itself.

---

* See *http://www.idiom.com/~arkuat/consent/Anarchy.html* and *http://www.chaum.com/articles/Security_Wthout_Identification.htm*.

† See *http://philzimmermann.com/EN/letters/index.html*.

‡ Vernor Vinge, *A Deepness in the Sky*. Tor Books, 1999.

Code has changed the world many times. Consider the medical advances made possible by genetic sequencing software, the impact of business software on large enterprises and small businesses alike, the revolutions enabled by industrial automation software and computer modeling, or the multiple revolutions of the Internet: email, the Web, blogs, social networking services, VoIP.... Clearly, much of the history of our times is the story of software innovation.

Of course, code, like any technology, can cut both ways, either increasing or decreasing the "returns to violence"* in society, increasing the efficacy of privacy-violating technology and giving tyrants more effective tools of censorship, on the one hand, or enhancing and promoting individual rights on the other. Code of either sort hacks the very core of human society itself, by altering fundamental social realities such as the tenability of free speech.

Interestingly, even with a specific technology such as public key cryptography, the implementation chosen can significantly alter cultural realities. For example, a PKI-based implementation reimposes authoritarian properties such as centralized hierarchies and identification requirements on a technology whose entire value arguably lies in its lack of those properties. Despite this, PKI approaches deliver weaker key authentication than does a web-of-trust implementation (which also doesn't dilute other important features of public-key cryptography, such as distributed deployment).

I think that as the weavers of code, it is to a large extent the ethical responsibility of programmers to seek not only that our code be beautiful in its design and implementation, but also that it be beautiful in its results, in a larger social context. This is why I find freedom code so beautiful. It puts computing technology to the most sublime use: protecting human rights and human life.

Laws and international human rights treaties can go only so far in protecting individual rights. History has shown that these are far too easy to bypass or ignore. On the other hand, the mathematics of cryptosystems can, when implemented carefully, provide practically impenetrable shields for individual rights and open expression, and can finally set people across the world free to communicate and trade in privacy and liberty.

Actualizing this global, mathematically protected open society is largely up to us, the gods of the machine.

---

* By "returns to violence," I refer to the social and economic incentives for violating individual rights. As the authors of *The Sovereign Individual* point out, "The key to understanding how societies evolve is to understand factors that determine the costs and rewards of employing violence."

## CHAPTER TWELVE

Growing Beautiful Code in BioPerl

Lincoln Stein

IN THE PAST DECADE, BIOLOGY HAS BLOSSOMED INTO AN INFORMATION SCIENCE. New technologies provide biologists with unprecedented windows into the intricate processes going on inside the cells of animals and plants. DNA sequencing machines allow the rapid readout of complete genome sequences; microarray technologies give snapshots of the complex patterns of gene expression in developing organisms; confocal microscopes produce 3-D movies to track changes in cell architecture as precancerous tissues turn malignant.

These new technologies routinely generate terabytes of data, all of which must be filtered, stored, manipulated and data-mined. The application of computer science and software engineering to the problems of biological data management is called *bioinformatics*.

Bioinformatics is similar in many ways to software engineering on Wall Street. Like software engineers in the financial sector, bioinformaticians need to be fleet of foot: they have to get applications up and running quickly with little time for requirement analysis and design. Data sets are large and mutable, with shelf lives measured in months, not years. For this reason, most bioinformatics developers favor agile development techniques, such as eXtreme Programming, and toolkits that allow for rapid prototyping and deployment. As in the financial sector, there is also a strong emphasis on data visualization and pattern recognition.

BioPerl and the Bio::Graphics Module

One of the rapid development toolkits developed by and for bioinformaticians is BioPerl, an extensive open source library of reusable code for the Perl programming language. BioPerl provides modules to handle most common bioinformatics problems involving DNA and protein analysis, the construction and analysis of evolutionary trees, the interpretation of genetic data, and, of course, genome sequence analysis.

BioPerl allows a software engineer to rapidly create complex pipelines to process, filter, analyze, integrate, and visualize large biological datasets. Because of its extensive testing by the open source community, applications built on top of BioPerl are more likely to work right the first time, and because Perl interpreters are available for all major platforms, applications written with BioPerl will run on Microsoft Windows, Mac OS X, Linux, and Unix machines.

This chapter discusses Bio::Graphics, BioPerl's genome map rendering module. The problem it addresses is how to visualize a genome and its annotations. A genome consists of a set of DNA sequences, each a string of the letters [A,G,C,T], which are nucleotides, also known as base pairs, or *bp*. Some of the DNA sequence strings can be quite long: for example, the human genome consists of 24 DNA sequence strings, one each for chromosomes 1 through 22, plus the X and Y chromosomes. The longest of these, chromosome 1, is roughly 150,000,000 bp long (150 megabases).

Hidden inside these DNA sequences are multiple regions that play roles in cell metabolism, reproduction, defense, and signaling. For example, some sections of the chromosome 1 DNA sequence are protein-coding genes. These genes are "transcribed" by the cell into shorter RNA sequences that are transported from the cell nucleus into the cytoplasm; these RNA sequences are then translated into proteins responsible for generating energy, moving nutrients into and out of the cell, making the cell membrane, and so on. Other regions of the DNA sequence are regulatory in nature: when a regulatory protein binds to a specific regulatory site, a nearby protein-coding gene is "turned on" and starts to be transcribed. Some regions correspond to parasitic DNA: short regions of sequence that can replicate themselves semiautonomously and hitchhike around on the genome. Still other regions are of unknown significance; we can tell that they're important because they have been conserved among humans and other organisms across long evolutionary intervals, but we don't yet understand what they do.

Finding and interpreting functionally significant regions of the genome is called *annotation* and is now the major focus of the genome project. The annotation of a genome typically generates far more data than the raw DNA sequence itself. The whole human genome sequence occupies just three gigabytes uncompressed, but its current annotation uses many terabytes (also see Chapter 13).

Example of Bio::Graphics Output

To home in on "interesting" regions of the genome, biologists need to visualize how multiple annotations relate to each other. For example, a putative regulatory region is more likely to be functionally significant if it is spatially close to a protein-coding gene and overlaps with a region that is conserved between evolutionarily distant species.

Bio::Graphics allows bioinformatics software developers to rapidly visualize a genome and all its annotations. It can be used in a standalone fashion to generate a static image of a region in a variety of graphics formats (including PNG, JPEG, and SVG), or incorporated into a web or desktop application to provide interactive scrolling, zooming, and data exploration.

Figure 12-1 gives an example of an image generated by Bio::Graphics. This image shows a region of the genome of *C. elegans* (a small soil-dwelling worm) that illustrates several aspects of a typical image generated by Bio::Graphics. The image is divided vertically into a series of horizontal tracks. The top track consists of a scale that runs horizontally from left to right. The units are in kilobases ("k"), indicating thousands of DNA bases. The region shown begins at just before position 160,000 of the *C. elegans* chromosome I, and extends to just after position 179,000, covering 20,000 base pairs in toto. There are four annotation tracks, each of which illustrates increasingly complex visualizations.

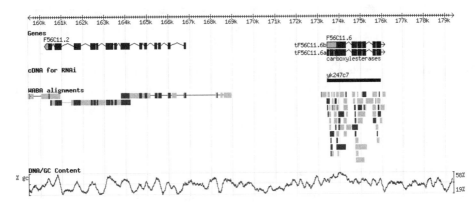

FIGURE 12-1. A sample image generated by Bio::Graphics

The original image is brightly colored, but has been reduced to grayscale here for printing. The simplest track is "cDNA for RNAi," which shows the positions of a type of experimental reagent that the research community has created for studying the regulation of *C. elegans* genes. The image contains a single annotation on the right named *yk247c7*. It consists of a black rectangle that begins at roughly position 173,500 and extends to roughly 176,000. It corresponds to a physical piece of DNA covering this region, which a researcher can order from a biotech supply company and use experimentally to change the activity of the gene that overlaps it—in this case, F56C11.6.

The "WABA alignments" track shows slightly more complex information. It visualizes quantitative data arising from comparing this part of the *C. elegans* genome to similar regions in a different worm. Regions that are highly similar are dark gray. Regions that are weakly similar are light gray. Regions of intermediate similarity are medium gray.

The "DNA/GC Content" track shows continuously variable quantitative information. This records the ratio of G and C nucleotides to A and T nucleotides across a sliding window of the nucleotide sequence. This ratio correlates roughly with the chances that the corresponding region of the genome contains a protein-coding gene.

The "Genes" track contains the most complex data: the positions of two protein-coding genes. Each gene has an internal structure that indicates which parts encode protein (dark gray, but blue in the original) and which have other functions (lighter gray). Notice how the coding of the leftmost gene (F56C11.2) corresponds pretty well to the dark-gray, highly similar regions in the WABA alignment track; this is because the protein-coding regions of genes tend to be very strongly conserved across species.

The gene named F56C11.6 is annotated with a function ("carboxylesterases"), indicating that it is related to a family of proteins responsible for a core part of carbon metabolism. In addition, it is shown with two alternative forms, indicating that it can encode more than one distinct protein. The two alternative forms are grouped together and given a distinct label. Notice that there are numerous alignments beneath this gene; this is a reflection that the gene belongs to a large family of related genes, and each related gene contributes to a different alignment.

The actual DNA nucleotide sequence is not shown in this representation because it isn't physically possible to squeeze a line of 20,000 base pairs into 800 pixels. However, when viewing smaller segments of a genome, Bio::Graphics can draw in the actual letters and ornament them (e.g., change their color or highlighting) to show the start and stop positions of interesting features.

Bio::Graphics Requirements

The job of Bio::Graphics is to take a series of genome annotations (called *features* in BioPerl parlance) and output a graphics file formatted according to the programmer's specifications. Each feature has a start position, an end position, and a direction (pointing left, pointing right, or not pointing in either direction). Features may be associated with other attributes such as a name, a description, and a numeric value. Features may also have an internal structure and contain subfeatures and sub-subfeatures.

When designing this library, I had to address the following issues:

Open-ended nature of the problem
   There are already a large number of genome annotation types, and the number is growing daily. While many annotations can be drawn with simple rectangles of different colors, many of them—particularly the quantitative ones—can be quite complex to represent. Furthermore, different bioinformaticians may want to represent the same

annotation type differently; for example, there are many different ways of representing genes, each best suited for different circumstances.

In order to accommodate the open-ended nature of this problem, I wanted to make it easy to add new visual representations to Bio::Graphics and to extend existing ones. Each representation should be highly configurable; for example, the programmer should be able to exercise exquisite control over the height, weight, boundary color, and fill color of even the simple rectangle. Furthermore, the programmer should be able to alter how each feature is rendered on a case-by-case basis.

Feature density

Some genomic features are very dense, whereas others are more sparse (compare the "Genes" and "WABA alignments" tracks in Figure 12-1). Features can also overlap spatially. Sometimes you want overlapping features to partially obscure each other, and sometimes you'd like to practice collision control, shifting the overlapping features up or down vertically to make them distinct. To add to the problem, features can contain subfeatures that themselves overlap, so collision control and spatial layout need to work in a recursive fashion.

I thought it would be good if collision control could be activated and deactivated in a context-dependent manner. For example, if there are thousands of overlapping features in the region being displayed, collision control might cause a track to become unmanageably busy and should be turned off. The programmer should be able to control at what point this context-sensitive collision control kicks in, or override it entirely.

Handling scale

I wanted Bio::Graphics to be able to draw pictures of a highly detailed 500 bp region of the genome, as well as a whole-genome view spanning 150 million nucleotides. To do this, the visual representation of features needs to change intelligently according to the current scale. At a scale of 500 bp, you can show the internal structure of a gene. At a scale of 1,000,000 bp, you can show only the start and end positions of the gene. At a scale of 100,000,000 bp, genes merge into a single black bar, and you should shift to a representation that shows the gene density as an intensity grayscale.

Useful for interactive web applications

I wanted Bio::Graphics to be suitable for the backend of an interactive web-based genome browser. In particular, I wanted end users to be able to click on the graphical renditions of features in order to bring up pull-down menus, link to other web pages, view tool tips, and so on. To accomplish this, Bio::Graphics had to be relatively fast so as to generate images in real time. It also had to keep track of the positions of each of its rendered features (and, if necessary, their subfeatures) in order to create an image map that could be passed back to the programmer.

Independence from graphic formats

I wanted Bio::Graphics to be useful for generating screen-quality, low-resolution images suitable for embedding in a web page, as well as for generating high-resolution, publication-quality images. To do this, the part of Bio::Graphics that handled the logic of the layout had to be separate from the part that generated graphics. Ideally, it should be able to output both pixmap and vector graphics formats.

Independence from database schemes

The bioinformatics community has designed many dozens of database formats for managing genome annotation data, ranging from simple flat files to sophisticated relational databases. For maximum utility, I wanted to avoid tying Bio::Graphics to any specific database scheme. It should be just as easy to invoke Bio::Graphics to render a genome region described by a flat file as to have it render a segment of a genome described in an Oracle database.

The Bio::Graphics Design Process

I'm not enamored of formal design engineering; instead, I typically write out little snippets of pseudocode that describe how I want something to work (a "code story"), play a bit with input and output formats, do a bit of coding, and—if I'm not satisfied with how the system is fitting together—go back and rework the code story. For anything larger than a toy application, I implement little bits of the system and test them out in standalone programs before deciding whether to move forward with that part of the design. I keep my notes in a "stream of consciousness" text file, and commit code to my CVS repository often. I try to make all the code visually appealing and elegant. If it isn't elegant, something's wrong with the design, and I go back to the drawing board.

Designing How the Developer Interacts with the Module

My first design task was to figure out the flow of a typical Bio::Graphics application. I started with the code story shown in Example 12-1.

EXAMPLE 12-1. Basic story for BioPerl::Graphics use (pseudocode)

```
1 use Bio::Graphics::Panel;

2 @first_set_of_features  = get_features_somehow( );
3 @second_set_of_features = get_more_features_somehow( );

4 $panel_object = Bio::Graphics::Panel->new(panel_options...)
5 $panel_object->add_track(\@first_set_of_features,
                           track_options...);
6 $panel_object->add_track(\@second_set_of_features,
                           track_options...);

7 print $panel_object->png;
```

The code story starts out by bringing in the main Bio::Graphics object class, Bio::Graphics:: Panel (line 1). This object, I reasoned, would hold configuration options for the image as a whole, such as the dimensions of the resulting diagram and its scale (base pairs per pixel), and would be the main object that users interact with.

The code story continues with two calls to fetch arrays of sequence features (lines 2–3). In order to maintain independence from feature databases, I decided that Bio::Graphics would operate on lists of features that had already been retrieved from a database. Fortunately, BioPerl already supported a variety of annotation databases via a nicely generic interface. A sequence feature is represented by an interface called Bio::SeqFeatureI, which specifies a set of methods that all sequence features should support. The methods are mostly straightforward; for example, *$feature*->start( ) gets the starting position of the feature, *$feature*->end( ) gets its end position, and *$feature*->get_SeqFeatures( ) gets its sub-features. To retrieve features from a database, BioPerl has an interface called Bio::Seq-Feature::CollectionI, which provides a standard API for retrieving features sequentially or randomly via queries.

The code story then calls `Bio::Graphics::Panel->new( )` (line 4), creating a new panel object, and calls `add_track( )` twice (line 5–6). This adds two tracks, one each for the first and second sets of features. Each call to `add_track( )` takes an initial argument consisting of a reference to the array of features to add, followed by additional arguments controlling the appearance of the track.

The last step in the code story is to convert the panel into a PNG file and immediately print the result to standard output.

Initially this looked like a reasonable story, but as I thought about it further, I realized there were some basic deficiencies in the API. The biggest problem was that it forces the programmer to load all features into memory before beginning to construct the image. However, it is often convenient to read sequence features one at a time from a file or database. Several of the implementations of Bio::SeqFeature::CollectionI allow you to do this:

```
$iterator = Bio::SeqFeature::CollectionI->get_seq_stream(@query_parameters);
while ($feature = $iterator->next_seq) {
    # do something with the feature
}
```

Another problem was that once you called $panel->add_track( ), you couldn't change the track's configuration settings. However, I could envision situations in which a developer would want to add a bunch of tracks in advance, and then go back and change an earlier track configuration later.

Finally, it seemed to me that add_track( ) was too inflexible, in that it forced the developer to add the tracks in a fixed order (top to bottom). However, there should be a way to insert tracks at arbitrary positions.

These considerations mandated the creation of a Track object:

```
$track1 = $panel_object->add_track(\@set_of_gene_features,
                                    track_options..);
$track2 = $panel_object->add_track(\@set_of_variation_features,
                                    track_options...);
```

One could then add features to an existing track like this:

```
$track1->add_features(feature1,feature2,feature3....)
```

or change its configuration this way:

```
$track1->configure(new_options)
```

This led to the alternative code story shown in Example 12-2.

EXAMPLE 12-2. Story for BioPerl::Graphics use with tracks (pseudocode)

```
1 use Bio::Graphics::Panel;

2 $panel_object = Bio::Graphics::Panel->new(panel_options...)
3 $track1 = $panel_object->add_track(bump_true,other_track_options...);
4 $track2 = $panel_object->add_track(bump_true,other_track_options...);

5 $collection = Bio::SeqFeature::CollectionI->new(@args);
6 $iterator   = $collection->get_seq_stream(@query_parameters);

7 $genes=0; $variations=0;
8 while ($feature = $iterator->next_seq) {

9      if ($feature->method eq 'gene') {
10          $track1->add_feature($feature);
11          $genes++;

12     } elsif ($feature->method eq 'variation') {
13          $track2->add_feature($feature);
14          $variations++;
15     }
16 }

17 $track1->configure(bump_false) if $genes     > 100;
18 $track2->configure(bump_false) if $variations > 100;

19 print $panel_object->png;
```

In this version of the story, we first create two tracks without providing any features up front (lines 3–4). We do, however, provide add_track( ) with a set of options, including a "bump" option that is initially set to true. When designing this story, I posited that a bump option of true would activate collision control, while a bump option of false would turn collision control off.

We then create a feature collection object using BioPerl; ordinarily this will be connected to a database of some sort and initiate a query (lines 5–6), returning an iterator across the results. We then call $iterator->next_seq repeatedly to return all features that satisify the query (lines 8–16). For each returned feature, we interrogate its type using a method from Bio::SeqFeatureI called method. If the feature is of type gene, we add it to track1 and bump up a counter for genes. If the feature is of type variation, we add it to track2 and bump up a different counter.

After all features are added, we interrogate the number of genes and variations added. If the total number of either feature exceeds 100, we call the corresponding track's configure( ) method in order to set the bump option to false (17–18). What this achieves is to turn on collision control for tracks that contain a manageable number of features, so that overlapping features are moved up and down to avoid covering each other. Tracks with a large number of features, where collision control might create unreasonably tall tracks, have bumping set to false, so that overlapping features can be superimposed.

READING THE CODE IN THIS CHAPTER

Bio::Graphics and BioPerl are written in Perl, a language which is deceptively similar to C or Java, but has many cryptic idiosyncrasies. If you don't know Perl, don't sweat it. Just read through the code examples to get a general sense of the logic of the design. To help you understand what's going on, here's a quick summary of the quirkier parts of Perl syntax:

$*variable_name*
> A variable name that starts with a dollar sign ($) is a scalar variable. It holds a single-valued string or number.

@*variable_name*
> A variable name that starts with an at-sign (@) is an ordered array. It holds multiple strings or numbers, indexed by their numeric position in the array. When addressing a member of the array, one places the index in square brackets:
>
> ```
>     $foo[3] = 'element three';
> ```
>
> There's a $ in front of the variable name because the individual element is scalar.
>
> Within subroutine and method definitions, a special array named @_ holds the list of arguments passed to the subroutine.

%*variable_name*
> A variable name that starts with a percent sign (%) is an unordered hash. It holds multiple strings or numbers (the hash *values*) indexed by strings (the hash *keys*). When assigning a list of key/value pairs to a hash, one uses this notation:
>
> ```
>     %clade = (monkey=>'mammal',
>              frog=>'amphibian',
>              gazelle=>'mammal');
> ```
>
> When addressing a member of the hash, one places the key in curly braces:
>
> ```
>     print "The clade of a monkey is ", $clade{monkey};
> ```

$*object*->method('*arg1*','*arg2*','*arg3*')
> The -> arrow indicates an object-oriented method call. The object is stored in the scalar variable $*object*. The method call takes zero or more arguments.
>
> If there are no arguments, the parentheses can be omitted, which looks weird to C and Java folk:
>
> ```
>     $object->method;
> ```
>
> Within the definition of a method, the object is usually stored in a scalar named $self, although this is a matter of coding style.

Setting Options

Up to this point I hadn't figured out how options would be set. I decided that for consistency with the BioPerl coding style, options should be passed as tag/value pairs in the format *-option_name=>option_value*. For example, the following method call would create a track with feature drawings 10 pixels high, a background color of blue, and collision control (bump) turned on:

```
$track1 = $panel_object->add_track(\@features,
                            -height   => 10,
                            -bgcolor  => 'blue',
                            -bump     => 1);
```

Later on, one would be able to change any of these options by calling configure( ). This example turns off collision control:

```
$track1->configure(-bump => 0);
```

Eventually, I extended the power of track configuration options by making it possible to use code references (a type of callback) as option values, but the first iteration of the module did not have this feature. I'll discuss it later in this chapter.

What configuration options should the track object support? I quickly came up with a small number of standard track options, the most important of which was glyph:

```
-glyph => 'glyph_type'
```

As described earlier, I wanted to be able to support a wide range of visual representations for features. The -glyph option was the end developer's way of accessing this range of representations. For example -glyph=>'box' should render features as simple rectangles, -glyph=>'oval' should render features as appropriately sized ovals, and -glyph=>'arrow' should draw arrows.

In addition to -glyph, other options included in the original design were:

-fgcolor
> Foreground (line) color of features rendered in the track

-bgcolor
> Background (fill) color of features rendered in the track

-bump
> Whether to turn on collision control

-label
> Whether to print each feature's name above it

-description
> Whether to print each feature's description below it

-height
> The height of each feature

`-key`

A label for the track as a whole

`-tkcolor`

Background color for the track

I was aware that fancy glyphs might have special-purpose options that the simple ones wouldn't, so I had to design the code library in such a way that the list of options passed to add_track( ) was extensible.

The Panel also needed to take options for such things as the desired image width and the conversion scale between pixels and base pairs. I made up a small number of panel-specific options that included:

`-width`

Width of the image, in pixels

`-length`

Length of the sequence segment, in base pairs

I could now flesh out the code story to show the specifics of each of the Bio::Graphics calls, as shown in Example 12-3.

EXAMPLE 12-3. Detailed story for BioPerl::Graphics use (pseudocode)

```
1 use Bio::Graphics::Panel;

2 $panel_object = Bio::Graphics::Panel->new(-width  => 800,
                                            -length => 50000);
3 $track1 = $panel_object->add_track(-glyph  => 'box',
                                     -height => 12,
                                     -bump   => 1,
                                     -key    => 'Protein-coding Genes');

4 $track2 = $panel_object->add_track(-glyph  => 'triangle',
                                     -height => 6,
                                     -bump   => 1,
                                     -key    => 'Sequence Variants');

5 $collection = Bio::SeqFeature::CollectionI->new(@args);
6 $iterator   = $collection->get_seq_stream(@query_parameters);

7 $genes=0; $variations=0;
8 while ($feature = $iterator->next_seq) {

9      if ($feature->method eq 'gene') {
10         $track1->add_feature($feature);
11         $genes++;

12     } elsif ($feature->method eq 'variation') {
13         $track2->add_feature($feature);
14         $variations++;
15     }
16 }
```

```
17 $track1->configure(-bump => 0) if $genes      > 100;
18 $track2->configure(-bump => 0) if $variations > 100;

19 print $panel_object->png;
```

Choosing Object Classes

The last major design task was selecting the main object classes that the developer would interact with. From the code story, it first seemed that there were two main classes:

Bio::Graphics::Panel
> Objects of this class would represent the entire diagram and would typically be divided into a series of horizontal tracks. Bio::Graphics::Panel would be responsible for positioning each track in its drawing area and for converting feature coordinates (expressed in base pairs) into glyph coordinates (expressed in pixels).

Bio::Graphics::Track
> Objects of this class would represent the tracks that make up the panel. Tracks would primarily be responsible for positioning and drawing glyphs.

What about glyphs? It seemed natural to me that glyphs should be objects and should contain the internal logic for drawing themselves. All glyphs should inherit from a generic Bio::Graphics::Glyph object that knew how to do basic drawing. As one called the Track object's add_feature( ) method, it would create new glyphs by calling the Glyph constructor like this:

```
$glyph = Bio::Graphics::Glyph->new(-feature=>$feature);
```

Then, when the Track needed to draw itself, it would have a draw( ) method similar to this:

```
sub draw {
  @glyphs  = $self->get_list_of_glyphs();

  for $glyph (@glyphs) {
      $glyph->draw;
  }

  # draw other stuff in the track, for example, its label
}
```

This subroutine starts by fetching a list of the Glyph objects that we created during add_feature( ). It then invokes each glyph's draw( ) method to have it draw itself. Finally, it draws stuff specific to the track, such as the track label.

As I thought more about Bio::Graphics::Glyph, I realized that they had to embody a bit of cleverness. Recall that a sequence feature can have an internal structure with subfeatures, sub-subfeatures, and so forth, and that each of the components of the internal structure needs to be laid out using collision control, and then drawn according to user preferences. This layout and draw behavior is very glyph-like, and so it seemed to make sense to let glyphs contain subglyphs in parallel to the feature/subfeature structure. The Glyph new( ) routine would look something like this:

```
sub new {
  $self    = shift;  # get self
  $feature = shift;  # get feature
  for $subfeature ($feature->get_SeqFeatures) {
      $subglyph = Bio::Graphics::Glyph->new(-feature=>$subfeature);
      $self->add_subpart($subglyph);
  }
}
```

For each of the feature's subfeatures we create a new subglyph, and add the subglyph to
an internal list. Because we call new( ) recursively, if a subfeature has subfeatures itself, it
creates another level of nested glyphs.

To draw itself and all its subglyphs, a top-level glyph's drawing routine would look something like this:

```
sub draw {
  @subglyphs   = $self->get_subparts( )

  for $subglyph (@subglyphs) {
     $subglyph->draw;
  }

  # draw ourself somehow
}
```

This bit of pseudocode calls get_subparts( ) to get all the subglyphs created by our constructor. It loops through each subglyph and calls its draw( ) methods. The code then does
its own drawing.

At this point, I was struck by the fact that the Glyph draw( ) pseudocode routine was essentially identical to the Track draw( ) method shown earlier. I realized that I could unify the
two classes by simply arranging for add_track( ) to create and manage a single internal feature object associated with the track. Subsequent calls to add_feature( ) would in fact add
subfeatures to the feature.

I fooled around with some test code and found out that this worked quite well. In addition
to the benefits of removing redundant drawing code, I was able to consolidate all the code
dealing with passing and configuring track and glyph options. So, tracks became a subclass
of Bio::Graphics::Glyph named Bio::Graphics::Glyph::track, and the Panel's add_track( )
method ended up looking like this (simplified somewhat):

```
sub add_track {
  my $self     = shift;
  my $features = shift;
  my @options  = @_;
  my $top_level_feature = Bio::Graphics::Feature->new(-type=>'track');
  my $track_glyph =
      Bio::Graphics::Glyph::track->new(\@options);

  if ($features) {
      $track_glyph->add_feature($_) foreach @$features;
  }
```

```
    $self->do_add_track($track_glyph);
    return $track_glyph;
}
```

To accommodate the very first code story, in which the caller passes a list of features to add_track( ), I allow the first argument to be a list of features. In the actual code, I do run-time type checking on the first argument to distinguish a list of features from the first option. This allows the caller to call add_track( ) either using the style from the first code story:

```
$panel->add_track(\@list_of_features,@options)
```

or using the style from the second code story:

```
$panel->add_track(@options)
```

add_track( ) then creates a new feature of type track using a lightweight feature class that I wrote for Bio::Graphics (this was necessary for performance reasons; the standard BioPerl feature objects are memory- and performance-intensive). This class is passed to the constructor for Bio::Graphics::Glyph::track.

If the list of features was provided, the method loops through the list and calls the track glyph's add_feature( ) method.

Lastly, the add_track( ) method adds the track to an internal list of tracks that have been added to the panel and returns the track glyph to the caller.

The track's add_feature( ) method is used to create subglyphs contained within the track. It is called either by the glyph constructor or later on by the developer when he calls $track->add_feature( ). Conceptually, the code looks like this:

```
sub add_feature {
  my $self = shift;
  my $feature = shift;
  my $subglyph = Bio::Graphics::Glyph->new(-feature=>$feature);
  $self->add_subpart($subglyph);
}
```

I show the constructor for Bio::Graphics::Glyph being called in a hardcoded manner, but in practice there will be many different types of glyphs, so the choice of what subclass of Bio::Graphics::Glyph to create must be done at runtime based on options provided by the user. I discuss how I decided to do this in the next section.

Option Processing

The next step in the design process was to figure out how glyphs would be created dynamically. This was part and parcel of the general problem of handling user-configurable options. Recall from the code stories that I wanted options to be specified at track creation like this:

```
$panel->add_track(-glyph   => 'arrow',
                  -fgcolor => 'blue',
                  -height  => 22)
```

This example asks the panel to create a track containing `arrow` glyphs whose foreground color is blue and whose height is 22 pixels. As decided in the previous section, `add_track()` will create a hardcoded track glyph of type `Bio::Graphics::Glyph::track` and pass these options to its `new()` constructor. Later, when the track glyph's `add_feature()` method is called, it will create a new subglyph for each feature to display.

However, this leaves three unresolved questions:

1. How does the track glyph's `add_feature()` method figure out what type of subglyph to create?

   We want to create different glyphs to display different types of features based on user preferences. Thus, in the previous example, the user wants to populate the track with a series of `arrow` glyphs, based on the value of the `-glyph` option. The pseudocode for `$track->add_feature()` in the previous section hardcoded a call to `Bio::Graphics::Glyph->new()`, but in the production code, we would want to dynamically select the appropriate glyph subclass—for example, `Bio::Graphics::Glyph::arrow`.

2. How do these subglyphs know what type of sub-subglyphs to create?

   Recall that features can contain subfeatures, and that each subfeature is represented by a subglyph that is part of the main glyph. In the previous example, the track glyph first created a series of arrow glyphs based on the value of the `-glyph` option. The arrow glyph was then responsible for creating any subglyphs that it needed; these subglyphs were responsible for creating sub-subglyphs, and so forth. How does the arrow glyph decide what type of subglyph to create?

3. How are the other options passed to the newly created glyph?

   For instance, what object keeps track of the values for the `-fgcolor` and `-height` options in the example?

Because choosing the glyph type is a special case of processing configuration options, I decided to attack this problem first. My first thought was that each glyph should have the responsibility of managing its options, but I quickly lost enthusiasm for this idea. Since a track may contain thousands of glyphs, it would be quite inefficient for each one to keep a complete copy of its configuration. I also thought of storing options in the `Panel` object, but this didn't feel right, since the panel has its own options that are distinct from track-specific options.

The solution that I came up with was to create a series of glyph "factories," of type `Bio::Graphics::Glyph::Factory`. Each time a track is created, the `Panel` creates a corresponding factory initialized with the caller's desired options. Each glyph and subglyph in the track contains a reference to the factory, and makes calls to the factory to get its options. Hence, if the panel has four tracks, there are four `Bio::Graphics::Glyph::Factory` objects.

Once I came up with the idea of a factory, the problems of how to create the appropriate glyph and subglyph types became easy. The factory stores the user's choice of glyph (e.g., arrow) along with all the other options. The factory has a method named `make_glyph()` that creates glyphs and subglyphs as needed, using the stored option to decide what glyph sub-class to use.

This choice implies that all glyphs contained inside the track share the same class. In other words, if a particular feature contains three nested levels of subfeatures, and the user has selected the arrow glyph to use for the features in the track, then each arrow glyph contains arrow subglyphs, and these contain arrow sub-subglyphs. This sounds like a serious limitation, but it actually makes some sense. Typically, a glyph and its subparts act together, and making them all of the subclass allows one to keep all the relevant code in one place. Furthermore, glyphs can escape this restriction by overriding their new( ) constructors in order to create subglyphs of whatever type they choose.

The final Bio::Graphics::Glyph::Factory class has just a few methods:

The constructor

The constructor creates a new factory:

```
$factory = Bio::Graphics::Glyph::Factory->new(-options=> \%options, -panel => $panel);
```

During construction, it takes a list of options passed to it by the panel's add_track( ) method and stores them internally. The factory can also hold a copy of the panel. I added this so that the factory could provide information about the panel, such as the panel's scale.

The options are actually passed as a reference to a hash (a Perl dictionary of name/value pairs). The Panel's add_track( ) method has the minor duty of turning the list of *-option=>$value* pairs passed to it into a hash to pass to the factory's new( ) method.

The option( ) *method*

Given an option name, the factory looks up its value and returns it:

```
$option_value = $factory->option('option_name')
```

If no option by this name is set, option( ) looks to see whether there is a default value and returns that.

The make_glyph( ) *method*

Given a list of features, the factory creates a list of glyphs of the appropriate class:

```
@glyphs = $factory->make_glyph($feature1,$feature2,$feature3...)
```

Now we'll look at a simplified version of the Bio::Graphics::Glyph::Factory code:

```
1  package Bio::Graphics::Glyph::Factory;

2  use strict;

3  my %GENERIC_OPTIONS = (
4                      bgcolor   => 'turquoise',
5                      fgcolor   => 'black',
6                      fontcolor => 'black',
7                      font2color => 'turquoise',
8                      height    => 8,
9                      font      => 'gdSmallFont',
10                     glyph     => 'generic',
11                     );
```

```
12  sub new {
13    my $class = shift;
14    my %args  = @_;
15    my $options    = $args{-options};      # the options, as a hash reference
16    my $panel      = $args{-panel};
17    return bless {
18                  options   => $options,
19                  panel     => $panel,
20                  },$class;
21  }

22  sub option {
23    my $self = shift;
24    my $option_name = shift;
25    $option_name    = lc $option_name; # all options are lower case
26    if (exists $self->{options}{$option_name}) {
27      return $self->{options}{$option_name};
28    } else {
29      return $GENERIC_OPTIONS{$option_name};
30    }
31  }

32  sub make_glyph {
33    my $self  = shift;
34    my @result;

35    my $glyph_type  = $self->option('glyph');
36    my $glyph_class = 'Bio::Graphics::Glyph::' . $glyph_type;
37    eval("require $glyph_class") unless $glyph_class->can('new');

38    for my $feature (@_) {
39      my $glyph = $glyph_class->new(-feature  => $f,
40                                    -factory  => $self);

41      push @result,$glyph;

42    }
43    return @result;
44  }

45  1;
```

I start by declaring the package name and turning on strict type checking (lines 1 and 2).

I then define a package-specific hash containing some generic glyph options to use as fallback defaults. Among the options are a default background color, a default height, and a default font (lines 3–11).

The new( ) constructor reads its arguments from @_ (the Perl subroutine argument list) into a hash named %args. It then looks for two named arguments, -options and -panel. It saves these options into an internal anonymous hash under the keys options and panel, creates the object using the Perl bless function, and returns it (lines 12–21).

The definition of the option( ) method occupies lines 22–31. I read the factory object and the requested option name from the subroutine argument list. I then call the built-in lc( )

function to put the option name into lowercase, in order to shield the method's behavior from developers who forget whether an option is named -height or -Height. I look for the existence of a like-named key in the options hash that I created in new( ), and if it is present, I return the corresponding value. Otherwise, I use the option name to index into %GENERIC_OPTIONS and return that value. If there is no corresponding key in either the options hash or %GENERIC_OPTIONS, I end up returning an undefined value.

The make_glyph( ) method (lines 32–44) demonstrates how Perl can dynamically load a module at runtime. I first look up the desired glyph type by using option( ) to look up the value of the glyph option. Note that the key/value pair glyph=>'generic' is defined in %GENERIC_OPTIONS; this means that if the programmer neglected to ask for a specific glyph type, option( ) returns generic.

I now load the requested glyph class if needed. By convention, all subclasses of Bio:: Graphics::Glyph are named Bio::Graphics::Glyph::*subclass_name*. The generic glyph has a Perl class of Bio::Graphics::Glyph::generic, the arrow glyph lives in Bio::Graphics::Glyph:: arrow, and so forth. I use a string concatention operation (.) to create the fully qualified class name. I then compile and load this class into memory using require $glyph_class. The call to require is wrapped inside a string and passed to the Perl compiler using eval( ). This is done to prevent Perl from trying to invoke require( ) at the time the Factory definition is compiled. To avoid unnecessary recompilation, I load the class only if I detect that its new( ) constructor does not already exist, indicating that the class is not yet loaded.

I loop through each feature passed in the @_ subroutine argument array, invoking the selected glyph class's new( ) constructor. Each newly created glyph is placed on an array, which I then return to the caller.

The last line of the module is 1, which ends all Perl modules for mostly historical reasons.

Notice that the design of the glyph constructor has now been extended so that each glyph is constructed using two named arguments: the feature and the factory object. By passing a copy of the factory, each glyph can get at its relevant options. Here are excerpts of two relevant methods from Bio::Graphics::Glyph:

factory( )
    This returns the factory object that was passed to the glyph when it was constructed:

```
sub factory {
  my $self = shift;
  return $self->{factory};
}
```

option( )
    This is a pass-through method to get the value of a named option:

```
sub option {
  my $self = shift;
  my ($option_name) = @_;
  return $self->factory->option($option_name);
}
```

The glyph calls factory( ) to get its factory and immediately calls the factory's option( ) method to get the value of the option specified on the subroutine argument list.

Code Example

To put it all together, Example 12-4 is a simple illustration of Bio::Graphics in action. Its output is shown in Figure 12-2.

EXAMPLE 12-4. A script that uses Bio::Graphics

```
1   #!/usr/bin/perl

2   use strict;

3   use Bio::Graphics;
4   use Bio::SeqFeature::Generic;
5   my $bsg = 'Bio::SeqFeature::Generic';

6   my $span        = $bsg->new(-start=>1,-end=>1000);

7   my $test1_feat  = $bsg->new(-start=>300,-end=>700,
8                               -display_name=>'Test Feature',
9                               -source_tag=>'This is only a test');

10  my $test2_feat = $bsg->new(-start=>650,-end=>800,
11                              -display_name=>'Test Feature 2');

12  my $panel       = Bio::Graphics::Panel->new(-width=>600,-length=>$span->length,
13                                              -pad_left=>12,-pad_right=>12);

14  $panel->add_track($span,-glyph=>'arrow',-double=>1,-tick=>2);

15  $panel->add_track([$test1_feat,$test2_feat],
16                    -glyph     => 'box',
17                    -bgcolor   => 'orange',
18                    -font2color => 'red',
19                    -height    => 20,
20                    -label     => 1,
21                    -description => 1,
22      );

23  print $panel->png;
```

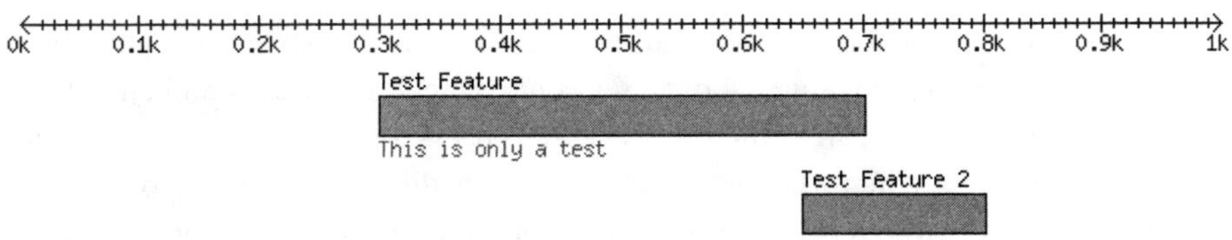

FIGURE 12-2. The output from Example 12-4

We load the Bio::Graphics library and one of BioPerl's standard Bio::SeqFeatureI classes, Bio::SeqFeature::Generic (lines 3–4). In order to avoid repeatedly typing out the full name of the feature class, we store it in a variable (line 5).

We then create three Bio::SeqFeature::Generic objects. One feature starts at position 1 and ends at position 1000, and will be used to draw a track containing the scale for the image (line 6). Two others will be features in a second track (lines 7–11).

We create the panel, passing it options that specify its width in pixels, its length in base pairs, and additional whitespace to pad the image with on the left and right (lines 12–13).

Next, we create a track for the image scale (line 14). It consists of a single feature, contained in the variable $span, and options that select the arrow glyph, make the arrow double-headed (-double=>1), and print both major and minor tick marks on the arrow (-tick=>2).

Now it's time to create a track for the two features, $test1_feat and $test2_feat. We add a second track, this time specifying options to use the box glyph with a background color of orange, a description font color of red, and a height of 20 pixels. We also selectively turn on the printing of the feature name and description (lines 15–22).

The last step is to call the panel object's png( ) method to convert it into a PNG graphic, and to print the graphic to standard output where it can be saved to a file or piped to a graphics display program (line 23).

Dynamic Options

The original Bio::Graphics::Glyph::Factory design was based around the idea of simple static option values. However, as I started working with the first version of Bio::Graphics, I realized that it would be handy to give the developer the ability to compute some options dynamically.

For example, scattered along the genome are sites on the DNA where regulatory proteins attach. When a regulatory protein attaches to a specific site of the DNA (a process called "binding"), a nearby gene is typically turned on or off. Some binding sites are strong, while others are weak, and the strength of the DNA/protein binding interaction is often of great importance to understanding how the regulatory interaction works.

To create a track showing the positions and relative strengths of DNA/protein binding site features, a developer might want to show a series of rectangles. The start and end of each rectangle would show the span of the feature, and its background (interior) color would show the strength of binding: white for weak, pink for medium, and red for strong. Under the original design the developer could specify the background color for all features in the track like this:

```
@features = get_features_somehow( );
$panel->add_track(\@features,
                 -glyph  => 'generic',
                 -bgcolor => 'pink');
```

However, this offered no way to set the color on a feature-by-feature basis.

When I realized this limitation, I went back and extended the API to allow the values of options to be CODE references. These are anonymous subroutines that Perl programmers can define in a variety of ways and are used in much the same way that function pointers are used in C. Here is a revised add_track( ) call that takes advantage of this facility:

```
$panel->add_track(\@features,
                 -glyph  => 'box',
                 -bgcolor => sub {
                       my $feature = shift;
                       my $score   = $feature->score;
                       return 'white' if $score < 0.25;
                       return 'pink'  if $score < 0.75;
                       return 'red';
                 }
      );
```

This works as follows: the value of -bgcolor is an anonymous CODE reference created using the sub keyword without a subroutine name. The code is invoked at runtime each time the glyph wants to access the value of its bgcolor option. The subroutine receives the corresponding feature on its argument array and calls its score( ) method to get the binding-site strength. Assuming that the binding-site strength is represented as a floating-point number between 0 and 1.0, I return an option value of white if the score is less than 0.25, a value of pink if the score is greater than 0.25 but less than 0.75, and red if it is greater than 0.75. Figure 12-3 shows how this might look.

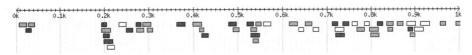

FIGURE 12-3. Colorizing the background according to dynamically changing values

In the end, I made it possible to use code callbacks for every option passed to add_track( ), including the -glyph option itself. This gives the end user an amazing amount of flexibility for customizing and extending the library. For example, it greatly simplifies "semantic zooming," or changing the appearance of tracks depending on the size of the region to display. The following callback turns off collision control when the region gets larger than 50,000 bp:

```
-bump => sub {
    my ($feature,$option_name,$glyph) = @_; # get all args
    return $glyph->panel->length < 50_000;
}
```

Let's now have a look at a simplified version of the revised option-processing code. First, I modified Bio::Graphics::Glyph::Factory to look like this:

```
# In Bio::Graphics::Glyph::Factory
sub option {
  my $self = shift;
  my ($glyph,$option_name) = @_;
```

```
$option_name    = lc $option_name; # all options are lowercase
my $value;
if (exists $self->{options}{$option_name}) {
   $value = $self->{options}{$option_name};
} else {
   $value = $GENERIC_OPTIONS{$option_name};
}

return $value unless ref $value eq 'CODE';

my $feature = $glyph->feature;
my $eval    = eval {$value->($feature,$option_name,$glyph)};
warn "Error while evaluating "$option_name' option for glyph $glyph, feature
$feature: ",$@,"\n"
      if $@;

return defined $eval && $eval eq '*default*' ?
$GENERIC_OPTIONS{$option_name}
                                        : $eval;
}
```

The method now takes two arguments rather than one. The first argument is the current glyph, while the second one is the option name as before. Once again, the factory looks first in its hash of track-specific options and then in the defaults hash (%GENERIC_OPTIONS) if the option wasn't named in the track configuration.

However, additional logic now comes after retrieving the option value. I call Perl's ref( ) function to look up the data type of the contents of $value. If it is a code reference, ref( ) returns the string CODE. If I don't get CODE, I just return the value as before. Otherwise, I get the corresponding feature by calling the glyph's feature( ) method, and then invoke the code reference by using Perl's anonymous code reference invocation syntax:

  $value->($feature,$option_name,$glyph)

The first argument passed to the callback is the feature, the second is the option name, and the third is the glyph itself.

Because the callback might cause a runtime error, I defend against this possibility by wrapping the entire call in an eval {} block. In case of a fatal error in the callback, this will return an undefined value and place Perl error diagnostics into the special scalar $@. After invoking the callback, I check whether $@ is nonempty and, if so, print a nonfatal warning.

The last step is to return the value derived from the callback. I thought it would be useful for the callback to be able to indicate that it wanted to use the default value for the named option. The last line of code simply checks whether the callback returned the string *default* and, if so, returns the value from the defaults hash.

To accommodate this change in the factory's option( ) method, I had to make a corresponding change to Bio::Graphics::Glyph->option( ):

```
# In Bio::Graphics::Glyph
sub option {
```

```
    my $self = shift;
    my ($option_name) = @_;
    return $self->factory->option($self,$option_name);
}
```

As I worked with callbacks, I found them to be an increasingly useful concept. For example, I realized that callbacks handle semantic zooming very nicely. The gene glyph draws a detailed representation of a protein-coding gene's internal structure, which is fine at high magnifications, but doesn't work when viewing very large regions, where the details become so small that they are indistinguishable. However, one can apply a callback to the -glyph option in order to dynamically select the simple rectangular box glyph rather than the gene glyph whenever the gene is smaller than five percent of the displayed region:

```
$panel->add_track(
    -glyph => sub {
        my ($feature,$panel) = @_;
        return 'box'  if $feature->length/$panel->length < 0.05;
        return 'gene';
           },
    -height => 12,
    -font2color => 'red',
    -label_transcripts => 1,
    -label => 1,
    -description => 1,
    );
```

Note that the callback arguments for the -glyph option are different from other options because this value is needed before the glyph is created. Instead of passing the feature, option name, and glyph, the callback passes the feature and the panel object.

As it happens, the callback feature became one of the most popular features of Bio::Graphics. As time went on, I added callbacks liberally to other parts of the API, including when processing options passed to the Panel constructor, and in the code that decides in what order to sort features from top to bottom.

On various occasions, users found uses for callbacks that I hadn't anticipated. To give one nice example, I provided a way for users to specify a callback to do some direct drawing on the Panel after it drew its gridlines but before it drew the glyphs. Years later, an enterprising genome biologist figured out how to use this feature to create diagrams that compare the genomes of species whose chromosomes have undergone structural changes relative to one other. The gridline callback draws colored polygons that connect features of one chromosome to the corresponding features in the other (Figure 12-4).

There is also a dark side to the Bio::Graphics::Factory story. In my initial burst of enthusiasm, I added a slew of other features to the option-getting and -setting methods that I omitted from the code examples shown here. One feature was the ability to initialize a factory using a web-style cascading stylesheet. Another feature provided detailed information to each callback concerning the current glyph's relationship to other glyphs in its track or to the top-level glyph. In practice, these features have never been used and are now hanging around as dead code.

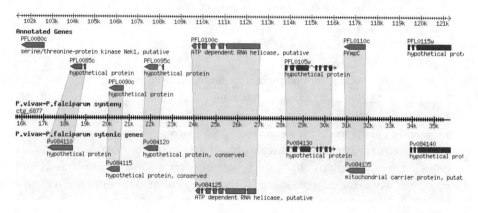

FIGURE 12-4. Clever use of Bio::Graphics callbacks allows related features on two chromosomes to be compared

Extending Bio::Graphics

We'll now look at some of the Bio::Graphics extensions that were added after the initial release. This illustrates how code evolves in response to user input.

Supporting Web Developers

One of the objectives of Bio::Graphics was to support interactive browsable views of the genome using web-based applications. My basic idea for this was that a CGI script would process a fill-out form indicating the genome to browse and a region to display. The script would make the database connection, process the user's request, find the region or regions of interest, pull out the features in the corresponding region, and pass them to Bio::Graphics. Bio::Graphics would render the image, and the CGI script would incorporate this data into an <IMG> tag for display.

The one thing missing from this picture was the ability to generate an image map for the generated image. An image map is necessary to support the user's ability to click on a glyph and get more information about it. Image maps also make it possible to make tool tips appear when the user mouses over the glyph and to perform such dynamic HTML tasks as populating a pull-down menu when the user right-clicks on the glyph.

To support image map generation, the original version of Bio::Graphics had a single method called boxes( ). This returned an array containing the glyph bounding rectangles, the features associated with each glyph, and the glyph objects themselves. To generate an image map, developers had to step through this array and generate the image map HTML manually.

Unfortunately, this was not as easy to do as I hoped it would be, judging from the number of user-support requests I received. So, after some experience writing my own Bio:: Graphics-based genome browser, I added an image_and_map( ) method to Bio::Graphics:: Panel. Here is a code fragment that illustrates how to use this method:

```
$panel = Bio::Graphics::Panel->new(@args);
$panel->add_track(@args);
$panel->add_track(@args);
...

($url,$map,$mapname) = $panel->image_and_map(
                           -root => '/var/www/html',
                           -url  => '/images',
                           -link => sub {
                                 my $feature = shift;
                                 my $name    = $feature->display_name;
                                 return "http://www.google.com/search?q=$name";
                           }
print "<H2>My Genome</H2>";
print "<IMG SRC='$url' USEMAP='#$mapname' BORDER='0' />";
print $map;
```

We set up a Panel and add tracks to it as before. We then call image_and_map() with three argument/value pairs. The -root argument gives the physical location of the web server's document root—the place where the tree of HTML files starts. -url indicates where, relative to the document root, Bio::Graphics-generated images should be stored. The -link argument is a callback that Bio::Graphics invokes to attach a clickable link to a glyph. In this case, we recover the feature object from the callback's argument list, get the feature's human-readable name by calling display_name( ), and generate a Google search link. Several other image_and_map( ) options can be used to customize and extend the resulting image map.

The method generates the image and stores it into the filesystem at the location indicated by -root and -url—in this case, */var/www/html/images*. It then returns a three-member result list consisting of a URL for the generated image, the HTML for the image map, and the name of the image map for use in the <IMG> tag. We then simply print the appropriate fragments of HTML to use the image and its map.

To date there are two web-based genome browsers based on Bio::Graphics. The one that I wrote, called GBrowse (*http://www.gmod.org/gbrowse*), is now widely used to display a large number of genomes ranging from bacteria to man. However, it was written in 2002 before Ajax-based asynchronous page refreshes were invented; one moves along the genome by clicking arrow buttons and waiting for the screen to reload. A new browser that is currently in prototype stage, the Ajax Generic Genome Browser (*http://genome.biowiki.org/gbrowse*), provides Google Maps-style functionality for the genome. To navigate, one simply grabs the view and slides it.

Supporting Publication-Quality Images

Another original requirement was support for multiple graphics formats. To satisfy this, I designed Bio::Graphics to use the Perl GD library for its low-level graphics calls. This library, which is based on Tom Boutell's *libgd* (*http://www.libgd.org*), generates pixmap-based images in a variety of formats, including PNG, JPEG, and GIF.

The Panel object creates and maintains a GD graphics object internally and passes this object to each of its tracks' draw( ) routines. The tracks, in turn, pass the GD object to their glyphs, and the glyphs to their subglyphs.

The Bio::Graphics::Panel->png( ) method is simply a pass-through to GD's png( ) method:

```
# in Bio::Graphics::Panel
sub png {
    my $self = shift;
    my $gd   = $self->gd;
    return $gd->png;
}
```

The jpeg( ) and gif( ) methods are similar. The developer also has the option of recovering the raw GD object and calling its png( ) method:

```
$gd = $panel->gd;
print $gd->png;
```

The advantage of making the internal GD object available to the public interface is that the developer can do additional things with the GD object, such as embedding it in a larger picture or manipulating its colors.

One consequence of my choice to use GD was that Bio::Graphics was originally limited to the generation of pixmap images. This problem was solved by Todd Harris when he wrote the Perl GD:::SVG module (*http://toddot.net/projects/GD-SVG*). GD::SVG has the same API as GD, but generates Scalable Vector Graphics (SVG) images, which can be printed at high resolution without loss of detail, and manipulated in various image-drawing applications such as Adobe Illustrator.

After I added support for GD::SVG in Bio::Graphics, it became possible to produce SVGs simply by passing an -image_class argument to the Panel constructor:

```
$panel = Bio::Graphics::Panel->new(-length=>1000,
                                   -width=>600,
                                   -image_class => 'GD::SVG'
                                  );
$panel->add_track.... etc...
print $panel->gd->svg;
```

Internally, the only change I had to make to Bio::Graphics was to process the -image_class option and to load the indicated image library. This allows for forward compatibility with new GD-compatible libraries. For example, if someone writes a GD::PDF that generates PDF-format graphic files, Bio::Graphics will be able to accommodate it.

Adding New Glyphs

At the time it was first published, Bio::Graphics supported about a dozen simple glyphs, including rectangles, ovals, arrows, the gene glyph, and a glyph that draws protein and DNA sequences. Each of these glyphs had multiple configuration options, leading to a very large number of possible displays. However, this number was still finite, whereas the number of feature types on the genome is potentially infinite. Fortunately, it is relatively easy to add new glyphs, and over time, I and other BioPerl developers have added many new glyphs to Bio::Graphics. Currently there are nearly 70 glyph types, ranging from whimsical (a Star of David) to sophisticated (a ternary plot for comparing frequencies of sequence variants in multiple populations).

The ability to easily extend existing glyphs to create new ones is a valuable feature. I will illustrate this in Example 12-5 by showing you how to create a new Glyph called hourglass.

EXAMPLE 12-5. The hourglass glyph

```
1   package Bio::Graphics::Glyph::hourglass;

2   use strict;
3   use base 'Bio::Graphics::Glyph::box';

4   sub draw_component {
5       my $self = shift;
6       my ($gd,$dx,$dy) = @_;
7       my ($left,$top,$right,$bottom) = $self->bounds($dx,$dy);

8       # draw the hourglass as a polygon
9       my $poly = GD::Polygon->new;
10      $poly->addPt($left,$top);
11      $poly->addPt($right,$bottom);
12      $poly->addPt($right,$top);
13      $poly->addPt($left,$bottom);
14      $poly->addPt($left,$top);
15      $gd->filledPolygon($poly,$self->bgcolor);
16      $gd->polygon($poly,$self->fgcolor);
17  }

18  1;
```

This glyph generates an hourglass (Figure 12-5). The glyph starts by defining its package name, which by convention must begin with Bio::Graphics::Glyph:: (line 1). It then declares that it is inheriting from Bio::Graphics::Glyph::box, which is a simple glyph that draws a rectangle (line 3).

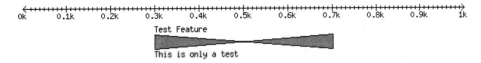

FIGURE 12-5. The hourglass glyph, a twisted version of the standard box glyph

The glyph then overrides the inherited draw_component( ) method (lines 4–17). The draw_component( ) method is called by a draw( ) method of Bio::Graphics::Glyph after setting up the drawing environment. The method receives the GD object along with horizontal and vertical coordinates indicating the position of the glyph relative to its enclosing glyph. We pass the relative coordinates to the inherited bounds( ) method to convert them into the absolute coordinates of the rectangle enclosing the glyph (line 7).

Now we actually draw the glyph. We create a polygon using GD's polygon library and add vertices corresponding to the top-left, bottom-right, top-right, and bottom-left corners of the hourglass (lines 9–14). We then pass the polygon object first to the GD object's `filledPolygon( )` method to draw the solid contents of the polygon (line 15), and then to the GD object's `polygon( )` method to draw the outline of the hourglass (line 16). Notice our use of the inherited `bgcolor( )` and `fgcolor( )` methods to get the appropriate colors to use for the fill and the outline.

This demonstrates the simplicity of adding new glyphs to Bio::Graphics. In many cases, one can create a new glyph by inheriting from an existing glyph that does almost what one wants, and then modifying one or two methods to customize it.

Conclusions and Lessons Learned

Designing software to be used by other developers is a challenge. It has to be easy and straightforward to use because developers are just as impatient as everyone else, but it can't be so dumbed-down that it loses functionality. Ideally, a code library must be immediately usable by naïve developers, easily customized by more sophisticated developers, and readily extensible by experts.

I think Bio::Graphics hits this sweet spot. Developers new to BioPerl can get started right away by writing simple scripts that use familiar BioPerl objects such as Bio::SeqFeature::Generic. Intermediate developers can customize the library's output by writing callbacks, while the most sophisticated developers can extend the library with custom glyphs.

Bio::Graphics also illustrates the power of standard interfaces. Because it was designed to render any object that follows BioPerl's Bio::SeqFeatureI interface, it will work hand-in-hand with any of BioPerl's sequence data access modules. Bio::Graphics can generate diagrams of handcoded sequence features as easily as it can display features read from a flat file, retrieved from a database query, or generated by a web service and transmitted across the network.

The module also has a few warts, and if I had to reimplement it now, I would have done several things differently. A major issue is the way that subglyphs are generated. In the current implementation, if you assign a glyph to a feature and the feature has subfeatures, the subglyphs will all be of the same type as the top-level glyph.

This has two drawbacks. First, one must use subclassing to create composite glyphs in which the subglyphs reuse code from a previously defined class and the parent glyph is something new. Second, glyph methods always have to be aware of which level of features they are currently rendering. For example, to create a glyph in which the top level is represented as a dotted octagon and the subfeatures are represented as rectangles, the `draw_component( )` routine must be sure to call the glyph's `level( )` method to find out the current nesting level and then draw the appropriate shape. If I were to do it again, I would provide an API to select the right glyph to use at each level of nesting.

Another annoyance is the box model. Glyphs are allowed to allocate additional space around themselves in order to draw decorations such as arrows, highlights, or labels. They do this by overriding methods called `pad_left( )`, `pad_right( )`, and so on.

This works fine until you define a new glyph class that inherits from the old one, and you need to adjust the padding for additional decoration. The derived class must be careful to find out how much padding its parent requests (by calling the inherited pad method) and then add its own padding needs to this value. This can get tricky. If I were to do it over, I would simply keep track of where the glyph draws in its `draw_component( )` routine, and increase its bounding rectangle as needed.

Unfortunately, implementing either of these fixes will change the glyph API in pretty fundamental ways and would require someone, most likely myself, to rewrite all 60+ existing glyph classes in order not to break them. So for the time being, I will accept that the module will always be Pretty Good but will never achieve Perfection. And this is the last, and maybe the best, lesson learned.

## CHAPTER THIRTEEN

The Design of the Gene Sorter

Jim Kent

THIS CHAPTER IS ABOUT A MODERATE-SIZED PROGRAM I WROTE CALLED THE **GENE SORTER.** The size of the Gene Sorter code is larger than the projects described in most of the other chapters, about 20,000 lines in all. Though there are some smaller pieces of the Gene Sorter that are quite nice, for me the real beauty is how easy it is to read, understand, and extend the program as a whole. In this chapter, I'll present an overview of what the Gene Sorter does, highlight some of the more important parts of the code, and then discuss the issues involved in making programs longer than a thousand lines enjoyable and even beautiful to work with.

The Gene Sorter helps scientists rapidly sift through the roughly 25,000 genes in the human genome to find those most relevant to their research. The program is part of the *http://genome.ucsc.edu* web site, which also contains many other tools for working with data generated by the Human Genome Project. The Gene Sorter design is simple and flexible. It incorporates many lessons we learned in two previous generations of programs that serve biomedical data over the Web. The program uses CGI to gather input from the user, makes queries into a MySQL database, and presents the results in HTML. About half of the program code resides in libraries shared with other *genome.ucsc.edu* tools.

The human genome is a digital code that somehow contains all of the information needed to build a human body, including that most remarkable of organs, the human brain. The information is stored in three billion bases of DNA. Each base can be an A, C, G, or T. Thus, there are two bits of information per base, or 750 megabytes of information in the genome.

It is remarkable that the information to build a human being could fit easily into a memory stick in your pocket. Even more remarkably, we know from an evolutionary analysis of many genomes that only about 10 percent of that information is actually needed. The other 90 percent of the genome consists primarily of relics from evolutionary experiments that turned into dead ends, and in the clutter left by virus-like elements known as *transposons*.

Most of the currently functional parts of the genome are found in genes. Genes consist of regulatory elements that determine how much of the gene product will be made, and the code for the gene product itself. The regulation of genes is often quite complex. Different types of cells use different genes. The same cell type uses different genes in different situations.

The gene products are diverse, too. A large and important class of genes produce *messenger RNA* (mRNA), which is then translated into proteins. These proteins include the receptors molecules that let the cell sense the environment and interact with other cells, the enzymes that help convert food to more usable forms of energy, and the transcription factors that control the activity of other genes. Though it has not been an easy job, science has identified about 90 percent of the genes in the genome, over 20,000 genes in all.

Most scientific research projects are interested in just a few dozen of these genes. People researching a rare genetic disease examine the patterns of inheritance of the disease to link the disease to perhaps a 10,000,000-base region of a single chromosome. In recent years scientists have tried to associate 100,000-base regions with more common diseases such as diabetes that are partly but not entirely genetic in nature.

The User Interface of the Gene Sorter

The Gene Sorter can collect all the known genes in disease-related regions of DNA into a list of candidate genes. This list is displayed in a table, illustrated in Figure 13-1, that includes summary information on each gene and hyperlinks to additional information. The candidate list can be filtered to eliminate genes that are obviously not relevant, such as genes expressed only in the kidneys when the viewer is researching a genetic disease of the lungs. The Gene Sorter is also useful in other contexts where one wants to look at more than one gene at once, such as when one is studying genes that are expressed in similar ways or genes that have similar known functions. The Gene Sorter is available currently for the human, mouse, rat, fruit fly, and *C. elegans* genomes.

The controls on the top of the screen specify which version of which genome to use. The table underneath contains one row per gene.

#	Name	VisiGene	fetal brain	whole brain	amygdala	thymus	bone marrow	PB-CD4+ Tcells	skin	adipocyte	pancreatic islets	heart	lung	kidney	liver	ovary	testis	Genome Position	Description
1	SYP	181524																chrX 48,937,407	synaptophysin
2	LMO6	221																chrX 48,924,285	LIM domain only 6
3	PLP2	181508																chrX 48,916,798	proteolipid protein 2 (colonic
4	CACNA1F	174590																chrX 48,962,622	calcium channel, voltage-dependent, alpha 1F
5	FLJ21687	179636																chrX 48,909,468	PDZ domain containing, X chromosome
6	CCDC22	185850																chrX 48,986,613	coiled-coil domain containing 22
7	FOXP3	1768																chrX 49,001,293	forkhead box P3
8	GPKOW	n/a																chrX 48,862,156	G patch domain and KOW motifs
9	PPP1R3F	179945	n/a					n/a			n/a							chrX 49,022,141	protein phosphatase 1, regulatory (inhibitor)
10	WDR45	35149																chrX 48,832,019	WD repeat domain 45 isoform 1
11	PRAF2	175866																chrX 48,817,185	JM4 protein
12	JM11	185851																chrX 48,808,956	hypothetical protein LOC90060
13	TFE3	986																chrX 48,779,619	Hypothetical protein DKFZp761J1810.
14	GRIPAP1	30802																chrX 48,729,348	GRIP1 associated protein 1 isoform 1
15	KCND1	178025																chrX 48,708,389	potassium voltage-gated channel, Shal-related
16	OTUD5	62197																chrX 48,682,134	hypothetical protein LOC55593

FIGURE 13-1. Main page of the Gene Sorter

A separate configuration page controls which columns are displayed in the table and how they are displayed. A filter page can be used to filter out genes based on any combination of column values.

The table can be sorted a number of ways. In this case, it is sorted by proximity to the selected gene, SYP. SYP is a gene involved with the release of neurotransmitters.

Maintaining a Dialog with the User over the Web

The Gene Sorter is a CGI script. When the user points her web browser to the Gene Sorter's URL (*http://genome.ucsc.edu/cgi-bin/hgNear*), the web server runs the script and sends the output over the network. The script's output is an HTML form. When the user hits a button on the form, the web browser sends a URL to the web server that includes the values in the drop-down menus and other controls encoded as a series of *variable=value* pairs. The web server runs the script once more, passing the *variable=value* pairs as input. The script then generates a new HTML form in response.

CGI scripts can be written in any language. The Gene Sorter script is actually a moderately large program written in C.

A CGI script has both advantages and disadvantages compared to other programs that interact with users on the desktop. CGI scripts are quite portable and do not need different versions to support users on Windows, Macintosh, and Linux desktops. On the other hand, their interactivity is only modest. Unless one resorts to JavaScript (which introduces serious portability issues of its own), the display will be updated only when the user presses a button and waits a second or two for a new web page. However, for most genomic purposes, CGI provides an acceptably interactive and very standard user interface.

The lifetime of a CGI script is very limited. It starts in response to the user clicking on something and finishes when it generates a web page. As a consequence, the script can't keep long-term information in program variables. For very simple CGI scripts, all of the necessary information is stored in the *variable=value* pairs (also known as *CGI variables*).

However, for more complex scripts such as the Gene Sorter, this is not sufficient because the script might need to remember the result of a control that the user set several screens back, but the web server sends only the CGI variables corresponding to the controls in the most recently submitted page. Our CGI scripts therefore need a way to store data for the long term.

There are two mechanisms CGI provides for storing data not visible in a form's controls: hidden CGI variables and cookies. In a hidden CGI variable, the data is stored in the HTML in the form of <INPUT> tags of type hidden. With cookies, the data is stored by the web browser and sent in the HTTP header.

Cookies were somewhat controversial when they were first released, and some users would disable them. However, cookies can persist for years, while hidden variables disappear as soon as a web page is closed. Neither cookies nor hidden variable can store truly large amounts of data. The exact amount varies between web browsers, but generally it's not safe to try to save more than 4 KB of data via these mechanisms.

To exploit both cookies and hidden variables, the Gene Sorter team developed a "cart" object that integrates the cookie and hidden variable mechanisms with an SQL database. The cart maintains two tables, one associated with a user and one associated with a web session. The tables are of the same format, consisting of a key column, a blob field containing all of the *variable=value* pairs in the same format they are passed in the URL, and fields that track the usage times and access counts.

A key into the user table is kept in a persistent cookie, and a key into the session table is kept in a hidden CGI variable. On startup, the script looks for the user key in a cookie. If it finds it, it loads the associated *variable=value* pairs into a hash table. If it doesn't find the cookie, it generates a new user key, and the hash table remains empty.

Next, the script looks for the session key and loads the variables from it, replacing any variables that are already in the hash. Finally, any new CGI variables are loaded on top of whatever is in hash.

A series of library routines allows the script to read and write variables in the cart's hash. As the script exits, it updates the database tables with the current contents of the cart. If the user does not have cookies enabled, he will still be able to interact with Gene Sorter during a single session because the session key is not kept in cookies. Separating the session from the user keys also lets the user have the Gene Sorter going in two separate windows, without the two windows interfering with each other. The user level of the cart allows the Gene Sorter to start up in the same place it was last used, even after the user has moved onto another site in the meantime.

In the *genome.ucsc.edu* implementation of the Gene Sorter, all of the CGI scripts on the site share the same cart. Thus, the cart contains variables that are even more global than normal program variables. This is often useful. If the user is focusing on the mouse genome rather than the human genome in one of our programs, she probably wants to be using the mouse on other programs as well.

However, as our programs have grown, to avoid inadvertent name conflicts between cart variables, we have adopted the convention that cart variables (unless they truly are meant to be global) start with the name of the CGI script that uses them. Thus, most of the Gene Sorter's cart variables start with hgNear_. (We use the underline character rather than a period as a separator because the period would interfere with JavaScript.)

All in all, the cart makes it relatively straightforward for the Gene Sorter to maintain the illusion of continuity to users, even though a separate instance of the program runs on each user click.

The short lifetime of a CGI script does have some advantages. In particular, a CGI script does not need to worry much about memory leaks and closing files because these are all cleaned up by the operating system on program exit. This is particularly nice in the C language, which does not have automatic resource management.

A Little Polymorphism Can Go a Long Way

Inside most programs of any flexibility, there is likely to be a polymorphic object of some sort. The table that takes up most of the main page of the Gene Sorter is composed of a series of polymorphic column objects.

Making polymorphic objects in C is not as easy as it is in more modern object-oriented languages, but it can be done in a relatively straightforward manner using a struct in place of an object, and function pointers in place of polymorphic methods. Example 13-1 shows a somewhat abbreviated version of the C code for the column object.

EXAMPLE 13-1. The column structure, a polymorphic object in C

```
struct column
/* A column in the big table. The central data structure for
 * hgNear. */
    {
    /* Data set guaranteed to be in each column.  */
    struct column *next;   /* Next column in list. */
    char *name;            /* Column name, not seen by user. */
    char *shortLabel;      /* Column label. */
    char *longLabel;       /* Column description. */

    /* -- Methods -- */
    void (*cellPrint)(struct column *col, struct genePos *gp,
        struct sqlConnection *conn);
    /* Print one cell of this column in HTML. */

    void (*labelPrint)(struct column *col);
    /* Print the label in the label row. */
```

EXAMPLE 13-1. The column structure, a polymorphic object in C (continued)

```
void (*filterControls)(struct column *col,
    struct sqlConnection *conn);
/* Print out controls for advanced filter. */

struct genePos *(*advFilter)(struct column *col,
    struct sqlConnection *conn,
/* Return list of positions for advanced filter. */

/* Lookup tables use the next few fields. */
char *table;              /* Name of associated table. */
char *keyField;           /* GeneId field in associated table. */
char *valField;           /* Value field in associated table. */

/* Association tables use these as well as the lookup fields. */
char *queryFull;    /* Query that returns 2 columns key/value. */
char *queryOne;     /* Query that returns value, given key. */
char *invQueryOne;  /* Query that returns key, given value. */
};
```

The structure starts with data shared by all types of columns. Next come the polymorphic methods. Finally, there's a section containing type-specific data.

Each column object contains space for the data of all types of columns. It would be possible, using a union or some related mechanism, to avoid this waste of space. However, this would complicate the use of the type-specific fields, and because there are fewer than 100 columns, the total space saved would be no more than a few kilobytes.

Most of the functionality of the program resides in the column methods. A column knows how to retrieve data for a particular gene either as a string or as HTML. A column can search for genes where the column data fits a simple search string. The columns also implement the interactive controls to filter data, and the routine to do the filtering itself.

The columns are created by a factory routine based on information in the *columnDb.ra* files. An excerpt of one of these files is shown in Example 13-2. All columnDb records contain fields describing the column name, user-visible short and long labels, the default location of the column in the table (priority), whether the column is visible by default, and a type field. The type field controls what methods the column has. There may be additional fields, some of which are type-specific. In many cases, the SQL used to query the tables in the database associated with a column is included in the columnDb record, as well as a URL to hyperlink to each item in the column.

EXAMPLE 13-2. A section of a columnDb.ra file containing metadata on the columns

```
name proteinName
shortLabel UniProt
longLabel UniProt (SwissProt/TrEMBL) Protein Display ID
priority 2.1
visibility off
type association kgXref
queryFull select kgID,spDisplayID from kgXref
queryOne select spDisplayId,spID from kgXref where kgID = '%s'
```

```
invQueryOne select kgID from kgXref where spDisplayId = '%s'
search fuzzy
itemUrl http://us.expasy.org/cgi-bin/niceprot.pl?%s

name proteinAcc
shortLabel UniProt Acc
longLabel UniProt (SwissProt/TrEMBL) Protein Accession
priority 2.15
visibility off
type lookup kgXref kgID spID
search exact
itemUrl http://us.expasy.org/cgi-bin/niceprot.pl?%s

name refSeq
shortLabel RefSeq
longLabel NCBI RefSeq Gene Accession
priority 2.2
visibility off
type lookup knownToRefSeq name value
search exact
itemUrl http://www.ncbi.nlm.nih.gov/entrez/query.
fcgi?cmd=Search&db=Nucleotide&term=%s&doptcmdl=GenBank&tool=genome.ucsc.edu
```

The format of a *columnDb.ra* file is simple: one field per line, and records separated by blank lines. Each line begins with the field name, and the remainder of the line is the field value.

This simple, line-oriented format is used for a lot of the metadata at *genome.ucsc.edu*. At one point, we considered using indexed versions of these files as an alternative to a relational database (*.ra* stands for relational alternative). But there are a tremendous number of good tools associated with relational databases, so we decided keep the bulk of our data relational. The *.ra* files are very easy to read, edit, and parse, though, so they see continued use in applications such as these.

The *columnDb.ra* files are arranged in a three-level directory hierarchy. At the root lies information about columns that appear for all organisms. The mid-level contains information that is organism-specific. As our understanding of a particular organism's genome progresses, we'll have different assemblies of its DNA sequence. The lowest level contains information that is assembly-specific.

The code that reads a columnDb constructs a hash of hashes, where the outer hash is keyed by the column name and the inner hashes are keyed by the field name. Information at the lower levels can contain entirely new records, or add or override particular fields of records first defined at a higher level.

Some types of columns correspond very directly to columns in the relational database. The lookup type columns refer to a table that contains an indexed gene ID field with no more than one row per gene ID. The type line contains the table, the gene ID field, and the field displayed by the column. The proteinAcc and refSeq columns in Example 13-2 are examples of type lookup.

If the relational table can contain more than one row per gene, its type becomes association. Associations with multiple values for a single gene are displayed as a comma-separated list in the Gene Sorter. Associations include the SQL code to fetch the data either one gene at a time (queryOne), for all genes (queryFull), or for the genes associated with a particular value (invQueryOne). The queryOne SQL actually returns two values, one to display in the Gene Sorter and another to use in the hyperlink, although these can be the same.

Most of the columns in the Gene Sorter are of type lookup or association, and given any relational table that is keyed by gene ID, it is a simple matter to make it into Gene Sorter columns.

Other columns, such as the gene expression columns, are relatively complex. Figure 13-1 shows a gene expression column as colored boxes underneath the names of various organs such as brain, liver, kidney, etc. The colors indicate how much of the mRNA for the gene is found in these specific organs in comparison to the level of mRNA in the body as a whole. Red indicates a higher-than-average expression, green a lower-than-average expression, and black an average expression level.

The entire set of gene expression information from fetal brain to testis in Figure 13-1 is considered a single Gene Sorter column. It's broken into three columns from the HTML table point of view, to provide the gray lines between groups of five organs for better readability.

Filtering Down to Just the Relevant Genes

Filters are one of the most powerful features of the gene sorter. Filters can be applied to each of the columns in order to view just the genes relevant to a particular purpose. For instance, a filter on the gene expression column can be used to find genes that are expressed in the brain but not in other tissues. A filter on the genome position can find genes on the X chromosome. A combination of these filters could find brain-specific genes found on the X chromosome. These genes would be particularly interesting to researchers on autism, since that condition appears to be to a fairly strong degree sex-linked.

Each column has two filter methods: filterControls to write the HTML for the filter user interface and advFilter to actually run the filter. These two methods communicate with each other through cart variables that use a naming convention that includes the program name, the letters as, and the column name as prefixes to the specific variable name. In this way, different columns of the same type have different cart variables, and filter variables can be distinguished from other variables. A helpful routine named cartFindPrefix, which returns a list of all variables with a given prefix, is heavily used by the filter system.

The filters are arranged as a chain. Initially, the program constructs a list of all genes. Next it checks the cart to see whether any filters are set. If so, it calls the filters for each column. The first filter gets the entire gene list as input. Subsequent filters start with the output of the previous filter. The order in which the filters are applied doesn't matter.

The filters are the most speed-critical code in the Gene Sorter. Most of the code is executed on just 50 or 100 genes, but the filters work on tens of thousands. To keep good interactive response time, the filter should spend less than 0.0001 of a second per gene. A modern CPU operates so fast that generally 0.0001s is not much of a limitation. However, a disk seek still takes about 0.005s, so the filter must avoid causing seeks.

Most filters start by checking the cart to see whether any of their variables are set, and if not, just quickly return the input list unchanged. Next, the filters read the tables associated with a column. Reading the entire table avoids potentially causing a disk seek for each item, and while it is slower if just processing a few genes, it is much faster when processing a large set of genes.

Genes that pass the filter are put into a hash, keyed by gene ID. Finally, the filter calls a routine named weedUnlessInHash that loops through each gene in the input to see whether it is in the hash and, if so, copies the gene to the output. The net result is a fast and flexible system in a relatively small amount of code.

Theory of Beautiful Code in the Large

The Gene Sorter is one of the more beautiful programs at the design and code level that I've worked on. Most of the major parts of the system, including the cart, the directory of *.ra* riles, and the interface to the genomics database, are on their second or third iterations and incorporate lessons we learned from previous programs. The structure of the program's objects nicely parallels the major components of the user interface and the relational databases. The algorithms used are simple but effective, and make good trade-offs between speed, memory usage, and code complexity. The program has had very few bugs compared to most programs its size. Other people are able to come up to speed on the code base and contribute to it relatively quickly.

Programming is a human activity, and perhaps the resource that limits us most when programming is our human memory. We can typically keep a half-dozen things in our short-term memory. Any more than that requires us to involve our long-term memory as well. Our long-term memory system actually has an amazingly large capacity, but we enter things into it relatively slowly, and we can't retrieve things from it randomly, only by association.

While the structure of a program of no more than a few hundred lines can be dictated by algorithmic and machine considerations, the structure of larger programs must be dictated by human considerations, at least if we expect humans to work productively to maintain and extend them in the long term.

Ideally, everything that you need to understand a piece of code should fit on a single screen. If not, the reader of the code will be forced at best to hop around from screen to screen in hopes of understanding the code. If the code is complex, the reader is likely to have forgotten what is defined on each screen by the time he gets back to the initial screen, and will actually have to *memorize* large amounts of the code before he can understand any part of it. Needless to say, this will slow down programmers, and many of them will find it frustrating as well.

Well-chosen names are very important to making code locally understandable. It's OK to have a few local variables (no more than can fit in short-term memory) with one- and two-letter names. All other names should be words, short phrases, or commonly used (and short) abbreviations. In most cases, the reader should be able to tell the purpose of a variable or function just from its name.

These days, with our fancy integrated development environments, the reader can, at the click of a mouse, go from where a symbol is used to where it is defined. However, we want to write our code so that the user needs to go to the symbol definition only when she is curious about the details. We shouldn't force her to follow a couple of hyperlinks to understand each line.

Names can be too long as well as too short, though most programmers, influenced by the mathematical descriptions of algorithms and such evils as Hungarian notation, err on the short side. It may take some time to come up with a good name, but it is time well spent.

For a local variable, a well-chosen name may be sufficient documentation. Thus, Example 13-3 shows a reasonably nicely done function from the Gene Sorter. It filters associations according to criteria that can contain wildcards. (There is also a simpler, faster method that handles only exact matches.) The code fits on one screen, which is always a virtue in a function, though not always possible.

EXAMPLE 13-3. The filter method for association type columns that handle wildcards

```
static struct genePos *wildAssociationFilter(
        struct slName *wildList, boolean orLogic. struct column *col,
        struct sqlConnection *conn, struct genePos *list)
/* Filter associations that match any of a list of wildcards. */
{
/* Group associations by gene ID. */
struct assocGroup *ag = assocGroupNew(16);
struct sqlResult *sr = sqlGetResult(conn, col->queryFull);
char **row;
while ((row = sqlNextRow(sr)) != NULL)
    assocGroupAdd(ag, row[0], row[1]);
sqlFreeResult(&sr);

/* Look for matching associations and put them on passHash. */
struct hash *passHash = newHash(16); /* Hash of items passing filter */
struct genePos *gp;
for (gp = list; gp != NULL; gp = gp->next)
    {
    char *key = (col->protKey ? gp->protein : gp->name);
    struct assocList *al = hashFindVal(ag->listHash, key);
    if (al != NULL)
        {
        if (wildMatchRefs(wildList, al->list, orLogic))
            hashAdd(passHash, gp->name, gp);
        }
    }
```

```
/* Build up filtered list, clean up, and go home. */
list = weedUnlessInHash(list, passHash);
hashFree(&passHash);
assocGroupFree(&ag);
return list;
}
```

The function prototype is followed by a one-sentence comment that summarizes what the function does. The code within the function is broken into "paragraphs," each starting with a comment summarizing what the block does in English.

Programmers can read this function at several different levels of details. For some, the name itself tells them all they need. Others will want to read the opening comment as well. Still others will read all the comments, ignoring the code. Those interested in the full details will read every line.

Because human memory is so strongly associative, once a reader has read the function at one level of detail, reading it at a higher level will generally be enough to recall the more detailed levels. This happens in part because the higher levels form a framework for organizing your memory of the function even as you are reading the lower levels.

In general, the larger the programming entity, the more documentation it deserves. A variable needs at least a word, a function at least a sentence, and larger entities such as modules or objects perhaps a paragraph. It's very helpful if a program as a whole can have a few pages of documentation providing an overview.

It's possible to have too much documentation as well as too little. Documentation is of no use if people don't read it, and people tend to avoid reading long text, especially if it is repetitious.

Humans tend to remember the important things best, though a few people are blessed (or cursed) with a good memory for trivia. The words used in a programming name are important, but whether the style is *varName, VarName, varname, var_name, VARNAME, vrblnam,* or *Variable_Name* is not so important. What is important is that a single convention be adopted and followed consistently, so that the programmer need not waste time and memory remembering which style is used in any particular case.

Other keys to keeping code understandable are:

- Use a scope as local as possible. Never use a global variable when an object variable will do, and never use an object variable when a local variable will do.

- Minimize side effects. In particular, avoid *altering* any variables except the return value in a function. A function that obeys this rule is called "reentrant," and is a thing of beauty. Not only is it easy to understand, it is automatically thread-safe and capable of being used recursively. Beyond readability, code with few side effects is easier to reuse in different contexts.

These days, many programmers are well aware of the negative impact of global variables on code reuse. Another thing that can discourage code reuse is dependence on data structures. The object-oriented programming style sometimes can end up backfiring in this regard. If useful code is embedded in an object method, one must construct an object to use the code. For some objects, this task can be pretty complex.

A function that is not embedded in an object, and which takes as parameters standard data types, is a lot more likely to be used in many different contexts than a method deeply embedded in a complex object hierarchy. For instance, the previously mentioned weedUnlessInHash function, although written for use by the column object in the Gene Sorter, was designed not to depend on being in a column. So, this useful little function may see application in other contexts now as well.

Conclusion

This chapter has been about one of the prettier pieces of code I've written. The program serves a useful purpose for biomedical researchers. The cart system makes it relatively easy to construct an interactive program over the Web, even though it uses a CGI interface. Both the user's model and the programmer's model of the program revolve around the idea of a big table with one row per gene and a variable number of columns that can represent many different types of data.

Although the Gene Sorter is written in C, the column code is done in a straightforward, polymorphic, object-oriented design. Additional columns can be added by editing simple text files with no additional programming required, and these same files help make it easy for a single version of the program to work on different genomic databases associated with a variety of organisms.

The design minimizes disk seeks, which continue to be a bottleneck, lagging CPU and memory speeds by a large margin. The code is written to be readable and reusable. I hope you will find some of the principles it is built on useful in your own programs.

## CHAPTER FOURTEEN

How Elegant Code Evolves with Hardware: The Case of Gaussian Elimination

Jack Dongarra and Piotr Luszczek

THE INCREASING AVAILABILITY OF ADVANCED-ARCHITECTURE COMPUTERS, at affordable costs, has had a significant effect on all spheres of scientific computation. In this chapter, we'll show the need for designers of computing algorithms to make expeditious and substantial adaptations to algorithms, in reaction to architecture changes, by closely examining one simple but important algorithm in mathematical software: Gaussian elimination for the solution of linear systems of equations.

At the application level, science has to be captured in mathematical models, which in turn are expressed algorithmically and ultimately encoded as software. At the software level, there is a continuous tension between performance and portability on the one hand, and understandability of the underlying code. We'll examine these issues and look at trade-offs that have been made over time. Linear algebra—in particular, the solution of linear systems of equations—lies at the heart of most calculations in scientific computing. This chapter focuses on some of the recent developments in linear algebra software designed to exploit advanced-architecture computers over the decades.

There are two broad classes of algorithms: those for dense matrices and those for sparse matrices. A matrix is called *sparse* if it contains a substantial number of zero elements. For sparse matrices, radical savings in space and execution time can be achieved through specialized storage and algorithms. To narrow our discussion and keep it simple, we will look only at the *dense matrix problem* (a dense matrix is defined as one with few zero elements).

Much of the work in developing linear algebra software for advanced-architecture computers is motivated by the need to solve large problems on the fastest computers available. In this chapter, we'll discuss the development of standards for linear algebra software, the building blocks for software libraries, and aspects of algorithm design as influenced by the opportunities for parallel implementation. We'll explain motivations for this work, and say a bit about future directions.

As representative examples of dense matrix routines, we will consider Gaussian elimination, or LU factorization. This examination, spanning hardware and software advances over the past 30 years, will highlight the most important factors that must be considered in designing linear algebra software for advanced-architecture computers. We use these factorization routines for illustrative purposes not only because they are relatively simple, but also because of their importance in several scientific and engineering applications that make use of boundary element methods. These applications include electromagnetic scattering and computational fluid dynamics problems.

The past 30 years have seen a great deal of activity in the area of algorithms and software for solving linear algebra problems. The goal of achieving high performance in code that is portable across platforms has largely been realized by the identification of linear algebra kernels, the Basic Linear Algebra Subprograms (BLAS). We will discuss the LINPACK, LAPACK, and ScaLAPACK libraries, which are expressed in successive levels of the BLAS. See the section "Further Reading" at the end of this chapter for discussions of these libraries.

The Effects of Computer Architectures on Matrix Algorithms

The key motivation in the design of efficient linear algebra algorithms for advanced-architecture computers involves the storage and retrieval of data. Designers wish to minimize the frequency with which data moves between different levels of the memory hierarchy. Once data is in registers or the fastest cache, all processing required for this data should be performed before it gets evicted back to the main memory. Thus, the main algorithmic approach for exploiting both vectorization and parallelism in our implementations uses *block-partitioned* algorithms, particularly in conjunction with highly tuned kernels for performing matrix-vector and matrix-matrix operations (the Level-2 and Level-3 BLAS). Block partitioning means that the data is divided into blocks, each of which should fit within a cache memory or a vector register file.

The computer architectures considered in this chapter are:

- Vector machines
- RISC computers with cache hierarchies

- Parallel systems with distributed memory

- Multi-core computers

Vector machines were introduced in the late 1970s and early 1980s. They were able in one step to perform a single operation on a relatively large number of operands stored in vector registers. Expressing matrix algorithms as vector-vector operations was a natural fit for this type of machine. However, some of the vector designs had a limited ability to load and store the vector registers in main memory. A technique called *chaining* allowed this limitation to be circumvented by moving data between the registers before accessing main memory. Chaining required recasting linear algebra in terms of matrix-vector operations.

RISC computers were introduced in the late 1980s and early 1990s. While their clock rates might have been comparable to those of the vector machines, the computing speed lagged behind due to their lack of vector registers. Another deficiency was their creation of a deep memory hierarchy with multiple levels of cache memory to alleviate the scarcity of bandwidth that was, in turn, caused mostly by a limited number of memory banks. The eventual success of this architecture is commonly attributed to the right price point and astonishing improvements in performance over time as predicted by Moore's Law. With RISC computers, the linear algebra algorithms had to be redone yet again. This time, the formulations had to expose as many matrix-matrix operations as possible, which guaranteed good cache reuse.

A natural way of achieving even greater performance levels with both vector and RISC processors is by connecting them together with a network and letting them cooperate to solve a problem bigger than would be feasible on just one processor. Many hardware configurations followed this path, so the matrix algorithms had to follow yet again as well. It was quickly discovered that good local performance has to be combined with good global partitioning of the matrices and vectors.

Any trivial divisions of matrix data quickly uncovered scalability problems dictated by so-called Amdahl's Law: the observation that the time taken by the sequential portion of a computation provides the minimum bound for the entire execution time, and therefore limits the gains achievable from parallel processing. In other words, unless most computations can be done independently, the point of diminishing returns is reached, and adding more processors to the hardware mix will not result in faster processing.

For the sake of simplicity, the class of multi-core architectures includes both symmetric multiprocessing (SMP) and single-chip multi-core machines. This is probably an unfair simplification, as the SMP machines usually have better memory systems. But when applied to matrix algorithms, both yield good performance results with very similar algorithmic approaches: these combine local cache reuse and independent computation with explicit control of data dependences.

A Decompositional Approach

At the basis of solutions to dense linear systems lies a decompositional approach. The general idea is the following: given a problem involving a matrix A, one factors or decomposes A into a product of simpler matrices from which the problem can easily be solved. This divides the computational problem into two parts: first determine an appropriate decomposition, and then use it in solving the problem at hand.

Consider the problem of solving the linear system:

$Ax = b$

where A is a nonsingular matrix of order n. The decompositional approach begins with the observation that it is possible to factor A in the form:

$A = LU$

where L is a lower triangular matrix (a matrix that has only zeros above the diagonal) with ones on the diagonal, and U is upper triangular (with only zeros below the diagonal). During the decomposition process, diagonal elements of A (called pivots) are used to divide the elements below the diagonal. If matrix A has a zero pivot, the process will break with division-by-zero error. Also, small values of the pivots excessively amplify the numerical errors of the process. So for numerical stability, the method needs to interchange rows of the matrix or make sure pivots are as large (in absolute value) as possible. This observation leads to a row permutation matrix P and modifies the factored form to:

$P^T A = LU$

The solution can then be written in the form:

$x = A^{-1} Pb$

which then suggests the following algorithm for solving the system of equations:

1. Factor A

2. Solve the system $Ly = Pb$

3. Solve the system $Ux = y$

This approach to matrix computations through decomposition has proven very useful for several reasons. First, the approach separates the computation into two stages: the computation of a decomposition, followed by the use of the decomposition to solve the problem at hand. This can be important, for example, if different right hand sides are present and need to be solved at different points in the process. The matrix needs to be factored only once and reused for the different righthand sides. This is particularly important because the factorization of A, step 1, requires $O(n^3)$ operations, whereas the solutions, steps 2 and 3, require only $O(n^2)$ operations. Another aspect of the algorithm's strength is in storage: the L and U factors do not require extra storage, but can take over the space occupied initially by A.

For the discussion of coding this algorithm, we present only the computationally intensive part of the process, which is step 1, the factorization of the matrix.

A Simple Version

For the first version, we present a straightforward implementation of LU factorization. It consists of $n–1$ steps, where each step introduces more zeros below the diagonal, as shown in Figure 14-1.

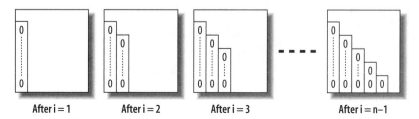

FIGURE 14-1. LU factorization

A tool often used to teach Gaussian elimination is MATLAB. It features a scripting language (also called MATLAB) that makes developing matrix algorithms very simple. The language might seem very unusual to people familiar with other scripting languages because it is oriented to process multidimensional arrays. The unique features of the language that we use in the example code are:

- Transposition operator for vectors and matrices: ' (single quote)
- Matrix indexing specified as:
  - Simple integer values: A(m, k)
  - Ranges: A(k:n, k)
  - Other matrices: A([k m], :)
- Built-in matrix functions such as size (returns matrix dimensions), tril (returns the lower triangular portion of the matrix), triu (returns the upper triangular portion of the matrix), and eye (returns an identity matrix, which contains only zero entries, except for the diagonal, which is all ones)

Example 14-1 shows the simple implementation.

EXAMPLE 14-1. Simple variant (MATLAB coding)

```
function [L,U,p] = lutx(A)
%LUTX   Triangular factorization, textbook version
%   [L,U,p] = lutx(A) produces a unit lower triangular matrix L,
%   an upper triangular matrix U, and a permutation vector p,
%   so that L*U = A(p,:)

[n,n] = size(A);
p = (1:n)';
```

EXAMPLE 14-1. Simple variant (MATLAB coding) (continued)

```matlab
for k = 1:n-1

    % Find index 'm' of largest element 'r' below diagonal in k-th column
    [r,m] = max(abs(A(k:n,k)));
    m = m+k-1; % adjust 'm' so it becomes a global index

    % Skip elimination if column is zero
    if (A(m,k) ~= 0)

        % Swap pivot row
        if (m ~= k)
            A([k m],:) = A([m k],:); % swap rows 'k' and 'm' of 'A'
            p([k m]) = p([m k]);     % swap entrix 'k' and 'm' of 'p'
        end

        % Compute multipliers
        i = k+1:n;
        A(i,k) = A(i,k)/A(k,k);

        % Update the remainder of the matrix
        j = k+1:n;
        A(i,j) = A(i,j) - A(i,k)*A(k,j);
    end
end

% Separate result
L = tril(A,-1) + eye(n,n);
U = triu(A);
```

The algorithm presented in Example 14-1 is row-oriented, in the sense that we are taking a scalar multiple of the "pivot" row and adding it to the rows below to introduce zeros below the diagonal. The beauty of the algorithm lies in its similarity to the mathematical notation. Hence, this is the preferred way of teaching the algorithm for the first time so that students can quickly turn formulas into running code.

This beauty, however, has its price. In the 1970s, Fortran was the language for scientific computations. Fortran stores two-dimensional arrays by column. Accessing the array in a row-wise fashion within the matrix could involve successive memory reference to locations separated from each other by a large increment, depending on the size of the declared array. The situation was further complicated by the operating system's use of memory pages to effectively control memory usage. With a large matrix and a row-oriented algorithm in a Fortran environment, an excessive number of page swaps might be generated in the process of running the software. Cleve Moler pointed this out in the 1970s (see "Further Reading" at the end of this chapter).

To avoid this situation, one needed simply to interchange the order of the innermost nested loops on *i* and *j*. This simple change resulted in more than 30 percent savings in wall-clock time to solve problems of size 200 on an IBM 360/67. Beauty was thus traded for efficiency by using a less obvious ordering of loops and a much more obscure (by today's standard) language.

LINPACK's DGEFA Subroutine

The performance issues with the MATLAB version of the code continued as, in the mid-1970s, vector architectures became available for scientific computations. Vector architectures exploit pipeline processing by running mathematical operations on arrays of data in a simultaneous or pipelined fashion. Most algorithms in linear algebra can be easily vectorized. Therefore, in the late 1970s there was an effort to standardize vector operations for use in scientific computations. The idea was to define some simple, frequently used operations and implement them on various systems to achieve portability and efficiency. This package came to be known as the Level-1 Basic Linear Algebra Subprograms (BLAS) or Level-1 BLAS.

The term *Level-1* denotes vector-vector operations. As we will see, Level-2 (matrix-vector operations), and Level-3 (matrix-matrix operations) play important roles as well.

In the 1970s, the algorithms of dense linear algebra were implemented in a systematic way by the LINPACK project. LINPACK is a collection of Fortran subroutines that analyze and solve linear equations and linear least-squares problems. The package solves linear systems whose matrices are general, banded, symmetric indefinite, symmetric positive definite, triangular, and tridiagonal square. In addition, the package computes the QR and singular value decompositions of rectangular matrices and applies them to least-squares problems.

LINPACK uses column-oriented algorithms, which increase efficiency by preserving locality of reference. By column orientation, we mean that the LINPACK code always references arrays down columns, not across rows. This is important since Fortran stores arrays in column-major order. This means that as one proceeds down a column of an array, the memory references proceed sequentially through memory. Thus, if a program references an item in a particular block, the next reference is likely to be in the same block.

The software in LINPACK was kept machine-independent partly through the introduction of the Level-1 BLAS routines. Almost all of the computation was done by calling Level-1 BLAS. For each machine, the set of Level-1 BLAS would be implemented in a machine-specific manner to obtain high performance.

Example 14-2 shows the LINPACK implementation of factorization.

EXAMPLE 14-2. LINPACK variant (Fortran 66 coding)

```
      subroutine dgefa(a,lda,n,ipvt,info)
      integer lda,n,ipvt(1),info
      double precision a(lda,1)
      double precision t
      integer idamax,j,k,kp1,l,nm1
c
c
c     gaussian elimination with partial pivoting
c
```

EXAMPLE 14-2. LINPACK variant (Fortran 66 coding) (continued)

```
      info = 0
      nm1 = n - 1
      if (nm1 .lt. 1) go to 70
      do 60 k = 1, nm1
         kp1 = k + 1
c
c        find l = pivot index
c
         l = idamax(n-k+1,a(k,k),1) + k - 1
         ipvt(k) = l
c
c        zero pivot implies this column already triangularized
c
         if (a(l,k) .eq. 0.0d0) go to 40
c
c           interchange if necessary
c
            if (l .eq. k) go to 10
               t = a(l,k)
               a(l,k) = a(k,k)
               a(k,k) = t
   10       continue
c
c           compute multipliers
c
            t = -1.0d0/a(k,k)
            call dscal(n-k,t,a(k+1,k),1)
c
c           row elimination with column indexing
c
            do 30 j = kp1, n
               t = a(l,j)
               if (l .eq. k) go to 20
                  a(l,j) = a(k,j)
                  a(k,j) = t
   20          continue
               call daxpy(n-k,t,a(k+1,k),1,a(k+1,j),1)
   30       continue
         go to 50
   40    continue
            info = k
   50    continue
   60 continue
   70 continue
      ipvt(n) = n
      if (a(n,n) .eq. 0.0d0) info = n
      return
      end
```

The Level-1 BLAS subroutines DAXPY, DSCAL, and IDAMAX are used in the routine DGEFA. The main difference between Examples 14-1 and 14-2 (other than the programming language and the interchange of loop indexes) is the use of routine DAXPY to encode the inner loop of the method.

It was presumed that the BLAS operations would be implemented in an efficient, machine-specific way suitable for the computer on which the subroutines were executed. On a vector computer, this could translate into a simple, single vector operation. This would avoid leaving the optimization up to the compiler and explicitly exposing a performance-critical operation.

In a sense, then, the beauty of the original code was regained with the use of a new vocabulary to describe the algorithms: the BLAS. Over time, the BLAS became a widely adopted standard and were most likely the first to enforce two key aspects of software: modularity and portability. Again, these are taken for granted today, but at the time they were not. One could have the cake of compact algorithm representation and eat it, too, because the resulting Fortran code was portable.

Most algorithms in linear algebra can be easily vectorized. However, to gain the most out of such architectures, simple vectorization is usually not enough. Some vector computers are limited by having only one path between memory and the vector registers. This creates a bottleneck if a program loads a vector from memory, performs some arithmetic operations, and then stores the results. In order to achieve top performance, the scope of the vectorization must be expanded to facilitate chaining operations together and to minimize data movement, in addition to using vector operations. Recasting the algorithms in terms of matrix-vector operations makes it easy for a vectorizing compiler to achieve these goals.

Thus, as computer architectures became more complex in the design of their memory hierarchies, it became necessary to increase the scope of the BLAS routines from Level-1 to Level-2 and Level-3.

LAPACK DGETRF

As mentioned before, the introduction in the late 1970s and early 1980s of vector machines brought about the development of another variant of algorithms for dense linear algebra. This variant was centered on the multiplication of a matrix by a vector. These subroutines were meant to give improved performance over the dense linear algebra subroutines in LINPACK, which were based on Level-1 BLAS. Later on, in the late 1980s and early 1990s, with the introduction of RISC-type microprocessors (the "killer micros") and other machines with cache-type memories, we saw the development of LAPACK Level-3 algorithms for dense linear algebra. A Level-3 code is typified by the main Level-3 BLAS, which, in this case, is matrix multiplication.

The original goal of the LAPACK project was to make the widely used LINPACK library run efficiently on vector and shared-memory parallel processors. On these machines, LINPACK is inefficient because its memory access patterns disregard the multilayered memory hierarchies of the machines, thereby spending too much time moving data instead of doing useful floating-point operations. LAPACK addresses this problem by reorganizing the algorithms to use block matrix operations, such as matrix multiplication, in the innermost loops (see the paper by E. Anderson and J. Dongarra listed under "Further Reading"). These block operations can be optimized for each architecture to account for its memory hierarchy, and so provide a transportable way to achieve high efficiency on diverse modern machines.

Here, we use the term "transportable" instead of "portable" because, for fastest possible performance, LAPACK requires that highly optimized block matrix operations be implemented already on each machine. In other words, the correctness of the code is portable, but high performance is not—if we limit ourselves to a single Fortran source code.

LAPACK can be regarded as a successor to LINPACK in terms of functionality, although it doesn't always use the same function-calling sequences. As such a successor, LAPACK was a win for the scientific community because it could keep LINPACK's functionality while getting improved use out of new hardware.

Example 14-3 shows the LAPACK solution to LU factorization.

EXAMPLE 14-3. LAPACK solution factorization

```
SUBROUTINE DGETRF( M, N, A, LDA, IPIV, INFO )
      INTEGER           INFO, LDA, M, N
      INTEGER           IPIV( * )
      DOUBLE PRECISION  A( LDA, * )
      DOUBLE PRECISION  ONE
      PARAMETER         ( ONE = 1.0D+0 )
      INTEGER           I, IINFO, J, JB, NB
      EXTERNAL          DGEMM, DGETF2, DLASWP, DTRSM, XERBLA
      INTEGER           ILAENV
      EXTERNAL          ILAENV
      INTRINSIC         MAX, MIN
      INFO = 0
      IF( M.LT.0 ) THEN
         INFO = -1
      ELSE IF( N.LT.0 ) THEN
         INFO = -2
      ELSE IF( LDA.LT.MAX( 1, M ) ) THEN
         INFO = -4
      END IF
      IF( INFO.NE.0 ) THEN
         CALL XERBLA( 'DGETRF', -INFO )
         RETURN
      END IF
      IF( M.EQ.0 .OR. N.EQ.0 ) RETURN
      NB = ILAENV( 1, 'DGETRF', ' ', M, N, -1, -1 )
      IF( NB.LE.1 .OR. NB.GE.MIN( M, N ) ) THEN
         CALL DGETF2( M, N, A, LDA, IPIV, INFO )
      ELSE
         DO 20 J = 1, MIN( M, N ), NB
            JB = MIN( MIN( M, N )-J+1, NB )
*           Factor diagonal and subdiagonal blocks and test for exact
*           singularity.
            CALL DGETF2( M-J+1, JB, A( J, J ), LDA, IPIV( J ), IINFO )
*           Adjust INFO and the pivot indices.
```

EXAMPLE 14-3. LAPACK solution factorization (continued)

```
              IF( INFO.EQ.0 .AND. IINFO.GT.0 ) INFO = IINFO + J - 1
              DO 10 I = J, MIN( M, J+JB-1 )
                 IPIV( I ) = J - 1 + IPIV( I )
   10         CONTINUE
*             Apply interchanges to columns 1:J-1.
              CALL DLASWP( J-1, A, LDA, J, J+JB-1, IPIV, 1 )
*
              IF( J+JB.LE.N ) THEN
*                Apply interchanges to columns J+JB:N.
                 CALL DLASWP( N-J-JB+1, A( 1, J+JB ), LDA, J, J+JB-1, IPIV, 1 )
*                Compute block row of U.
                 CALL DTRSM( 'Left', 'Lower', 'No transpose', 'Unit', JB,
     $                       N-J-JB+1, ONE, A( J, J ), LDA, A( J, J+JB ), LDA )
                 IF( J+JB.LE.M ) THEN
*                   Update trailing submatrix.
                    CALL DGEMM( 'No transpose', 'No transpose', M-J-JB+1,
     $                          N-J-JB+1, JB, -ONE, A( J+JB, J ), LDA,
     $                          A( J, J+JB ), LDA, ONE, A( J+JB, J+JB ), LDA )
                 END IF
              END IF
   20      CONTINUE
        END IF
        RETURN
        end
```

Most of the computational work in the algorithm from Example 14-3 is contained in three routines:

DGEMM

Matrix-matrix multiplication

DTRSM

Triangular solve with multiple righthand sides

DGETF2

Unblocked LU factorization for operations within a block column

One of the key parameters in the algorithm is the block size, called NB here. If NB is too small or too large, poor performance can result—hence the importance of the ILAENV function, whose standard implementation was meant to be replaced by a vendor implementation encapsulating machine-specific parameters upon installation of the LAPACK library. At any given point of the algorithm, NB columns or rows are exposed to a well-optimized Level-3 BLAS. If NB is 1, the algorithm is equivalent in performance and memory access patterns to the LINPACK's version.

Matrix-matrix operations offer the proper level of modularity for performance and transportability across a wide range of computer architectures, including parallel systems with memory hierarchy. This enhanced performance is primarily due to a greater opportunity for reusing data. There are numerous ways to accomplish this reuse of data to reduce memory traffic and to increase the ratio of floating-point operations to data movement through the memory hierarchy. This improvement can bring a three- to ten-fold improvement in performance on modern computer architectures.

The jury is still out concerning the productivity of writing and reading the LAPACK code: how hard is it to generate the code from its mathematical description? The use of vector notation in LINPACK is arguably more natural than LAPACK's matrix formulation. The mathematical formulas that describe algorithms are usually more complex if only matrices are used, as opposed to mixed vector-matrix notation.

Recursive LU

Setting the block size parameter for the LAPACK's LU might seem like a trivial matter at first. But in practice, it requires a lot of tuning for various precisions and matrix sizes. Many users end up leaving the setting unchanged, even if the tuning has to be done only once at installation. This problem is exacerbated by the fact that not just one but many LAPACK routines use a blocking parameter.

Another issue with LAPACK's formulation of LU is the factorization of tall and narrow panels of columns performed by the DGETF2 routine. It uses Level-1 BLAS and was found to become a bottleneck as the processors became faster throughout the 1990s without corresponding increases in memory bandwidth.

A solution came from a rather unlikely direction: divide-and-conquer recursion. In place of LAPACK's looping constructs, the newer recursive LU algorithm splits the work in half, factorizes the left part of the matrix, updates the rest of the matrix, and factorizes the right part. The use of Level-1 BLAS is reduced to an acceptable minimum, and most of the calls to Level-3 BLAS operate on larger portions of the matrix than LAPACK's algorithm. And, of course, the block size does not have to be tuned anymore.

Recursive LU required the use of Fortran 90, which was the first Fortran standard to allow recursive subroutines. A side effect of using Fortran 90 was the increased importance of the LDA parameter, the leading dimension of A. It allows more flexible use of the subroutine, as well as performance tuning for cases when matrix dimension m would cause memory bank conflicts that could significantly reduce available memory bandwidth.

The Fortran 90 compilers use the LDA parameter to avoid copying the data into a contiguous buffer when calling external routines, such as one of the BLAS. Without LDA, the compiler has to assume the worst-case scenario when input matrix a is not contiguous and needs to be copied to a temporary contiguous buffer so the call to BLAS does not end up with an out-of-bands memory access. With LDA, the compiler passes array pointers to BLAS without any copies.

Example 14-4 shows recursive LU factorization.

EXAMPLE 14-4. Recursive variant (Fortran 90 coding)

```
recursive subroutine rdgetrf(m, n, a, lda, ipiv, info)
implicit none

integer, intent(in) :: m, n, lda
double precision, intent(inout) :: a(lda,*)
```

EXAMPLE 14-4. *Recursive variant (Fortran 90 coding) (continued)*

```
      integer, intent(out) :: ipiv(*)
      integer, intent(out) :: info

      integer :: mn, nleft, nright, i
      double precision :: tmp

      double precision :: pone, negone, zero
      parameter (pone=1.0d0)
      parameter (negone=-1.0d0)
      parameter (zero=0.0d0)

      intrinsic min

      integer idamax
      external dgemm, dtrsm, dlaswp, idamax, dscal

      mn = min(m, n)

      if (mn .gt. 1) then
         nleft = mn / 2
         nright = n - nleft

         call rdgetrf(m, nleft, a, lda, ipiv, info)

         if (info .ne. 0) return
         call dlaswp(nright, a(1, nleft+1), lda, 1, nleft, ipiv, 1)

         call dtrsm('L', 'L', 'N', 'U', nleft, nright, pone, a, lda,
     $       a(1, nleft+1), lda)

         call dgemm('N', 'N', m-nleft, nright, nleft, negone,
     $       a(nleft+1,1) , lda, a(1, nleft+1), lda, pone,
     $       a(nleft+1, nleft+1), lda)

         call rdgetrf(m - nleft, nright, a(nleft+1, nleft+1), lda,
     $       ipiv(nleft+1), info)
         if (info .ne. 0) then
           info = info + nleft
           return
         end if

         do i = nleft+1, m
           ipiv(i) = ipiv(i) + nleft
         end do

         call dlaswp(nleft, a, lda, nleft+1, mn, ipiv, 1)

      else if (mn .eq. 1) then
         i = idamax(m, a, 1)
         ipiv(1) = i
         tmp = a(i, 1)

         if (tmp .ne. zero .and. tmp .ne. -zero) then
            call dscal(m, pone/tmp, a, 1)
```

EXAMPLE 14-4. *Recursive variant (Fortran 90 coding) (continued)*

```
        a(i,1) = a(1,1)
        a(1,1) = tmp
    else
        info = 1
    end if

end if

return
end
```

There is a certain degree of elegance in the recursive variant. No loops are exposed in the routine. Instead, the algorithm is driven by the recursive nature of the method (see the paper by F. G. Gustavson listed under "Further Reading").

The Recursive LU Algorithm consists of four basic steps, illustrated in Figure 14-2:

1. Split the matrix into two rectangles ($m * n/2$); if the left part ends up being only a single column, scale it by the reciprocal of the pivot and return.

2. Apply the *LU* algorithm to the left part.

3. Apply transformations to the right part (perform the triangular solve $A_{12} = L^{-1}A_{12}$ and matrix multiplication $A_{22}=A_{22} - A_{21}*A_{12}$).

4. Apply the LU algorithm to the right part.

FIGURE 14-2. *Recursive LU factorization*

Most of the work is performed in the matrix multiplications, which operate on successive matrices of size $n/2$, $n/4$, $n/8$, etc. The implementation in Example 14-4 can show about a 10 percent improvement in performance over the LAPACK implementation given in Example 14-3.

In a sense, any of the previous renditions of the LU algorithm could be considered a step backward in terms of code elegance. But divide-and-conquer recursion was a tremendous leap forward (even dismissing the modest performance gains). The recursive algorithm for matrix factorization can now be taught to students alongside other recursive algorithms, such as various kinds of sorting methods.

By changing just the size of matrix parts, it is possible to achieve the same memory access pattern as in LINPACK or LAPACK. Setting nleft to 1 makes the code operate on vectors, just as in LINPACK, whereas setting nleft to NB>1 makes it behave like LAPACK's blocked code. In both cases, the original recursion deteriorates from divide-and-conquer to the tail kind. The behavior of such variations of the recursive algorithm can be studied alongside a Quicksort algorithm with various partitioning schemes of the sorted array.

Finally, we leave as an exercise to the reader to try to mimic the recursive code without using recursion and without explicitly handling the recursive call stack—an important problem to solve if the Fortran compiler cannot handle recursive functions or subroutines.

ScaLAPACK PDGETRF

LAPACK is designed to be highly efficient on vector processors, high-performance "super-scalar" workstations, and shared-memory multiprocessors. LAPACK can also be used satisfactorily on all types of scalar machines (PCs, workstations, and mainframes). However, LAPACK in its present form is less likely to give good performance on other types of parallel architectures—for example, massively parallel Single Instruction Multiple Data (SIMD) machines, or Multiple Instruction Multiple Data (MIMD) distributed-memory machines. The ScaLAPACK effort was intended to adapt LAPACK to these new architectures.

By creating the ScaLAPACK software library, we extended the LAPACK library to scalable MIMD, distributed-memory, concurrent computers. For such machines, the memory hierarchy includes the off-processor memory of other processors, in addition to the hierarchy of registers, cache, and local memory on each processor.

Like LAPACK, the ScaLAPACK routines are based on block-partitioned algorithms in order to minimize the frequency of data movement between different levels of the memory hierarchy. The fundamental building blocks of the ScaLAPACK library are distributed-memory versions of the Level-2 and Level-3 BLAS, and a set of Basic Linear Algebra Communication Subprograms (BLACS) for communication tasks that arise frequently in parallel linear algebra computations. In the ScaLAPACK routines, all interprocessor communication occurs within the distributed BLAS and the BLACS, so the source code of the top software layer of ScaLAPACK looks very similar to that of LAPACK.

The ScaLAPACK solution to LU factorization is shown in Example 14-5.

EXAMPLE 14-5. ScaLAPACK variant (Fortran 90 coding)

```
      SUBROUTINE PDGETRF( M, N, A, IA, JA, DESCA, IPIV, INFO )
       INTEGER          BLOCK_CYCLIC_2D, CSRC_, CTXT_, DLEN_, DTYPE_,
      $                 LLD_, MB_, M_, NB_, N_, RSRC_
       PARAMETER        ( BLOCK_CYCLIC_2D = 1, DLEN_ = 9, DTYPE_ = 1,
      $                    CTXT_ = 2, M_ = 3, N_ = 4, MB_ = 5, NB_ = 6,
      $                    RSRC_ = 7, CSRC_ = 8, LLD_ = 9 )
       DOUBLE PRECISION ONE
       PARAMETER        ( ONE = 1.0D+0 )
       CHARACTER        COLBTOP, COLCTOP, ROWBTOP
       INTEGER          I, ICOFF, ICTXT, IINFO, IN, IROFF, J, JB, JN,
      $                 MN, MYCOL, MYROW, NPCOL, NPROW
       INTEGER          IDUM1( 1 ), IDUM2( 1 )
       EXTERNAL         BLACS_GRIDINFO, CHK1MAT, IGAMN2D, PCHK1MAT, PB_TOPGET,
      $                 PB_TOPSET, PDGEMM, PDGETF2, PDLASWP, PDTRSM, PXERBLA
       INTEGER          ICEIL
       EXTERNAL         ICEIL
       INTRINSIC        MIN, MOD
```

EXAMPLE 14-5. ScaLAPACK variant (Fortran 90 coding) (continued)

```
*     Get grid parameters
      ICTXT = DESCA( CTXT_ )
      CALL BLACS_GRIDINFO( ICTXT, NPROW, NPCOL, MYROW, MYCOL )
*     Test the input parameters
      INFO = 0
      IF( NPROW.EQ.-1 ) THEN
         INFO = -(600+CTXT_)
      ELSE
         CALL CHK1MAT( M, 1, N, 2, IA, JA, DESCA, 6, INFO )
         IF( INFO.EQ.0 ) THEN
            IROFF = MOD( IA-1, DESCA( MB_ ) )
            ICOFF = MOD( JA-1, DESCA( NB_ ) )
            IF( IROFF.NE.0 ) THEN
               INFO = -4
            ELSE IF( ICOFF.NE.0 ) THEN
               INFO = -5
            ELSE IF( DESCA( MB_ ).NE.DESCA( NB_ ) ) THEN
               INFO = -(600+NB_)
            END IF
         END IF
         CALL PCHK1MAT( M, 1, N, 2, IA, JA, DESCA, 6, 0, IDUM1, IDUM2, INFO )
      END IF
      IF( INFO.NE.0 ) THEN
         CALL PXERBLA( ICTXT, 'PDGETRF', -INFO )
         RETURN
      END IF
      IF( DESCA( M_ ).EQ.1 ) THEN
         IPIV( 1 ) = 1
         RETURN
      ELSE IF( M.EQ.0 .OR. N.EQ.0 ) THEN
         RETURN
      END IF
*     Split-ring topology for the communication along process rows
      CALL PB_TOPGET( ICTXT, 'Broadcast', 'Rowwise', ROWBTOP )
      CALL PB_TOPGET( ICTXT, 'Broadcast', 'Columnwise', COLBTOP )
      CALL PB_TOPGET( ICTXT, 'Combine', 'Columnwise', COLCTOP )
      CALL PB_TOPSET( ICTXT, 'Broadcast', 'Rowwise', 'S-ring' )
      CALL PB_TOPSET( ICTXT, 'Broadcast', 'Columnwise', ' ' )
      CALL PB_TOPSET( ICTXT, 'Combine', 'Columnwise', ' ' )
*     Handle the first block of columns separately
      MN = MIN( M, N )
      IN = MIN( ICEIL( IA, DESCA( MB_ ) )*DESCA( MB_ ), IA+M-1 )
      JN = MIN( ICEIL( JA, DESCA( NB_ ) )*DESCA( NB_ ), JA+MN-1 )
      JB = JN - JA + 1
*     Factor diagonal and subdiagonal blocks and test for exact
*     singularity.
      CALL PDGETF2( M, JB, A, IA, JA, DESCA, IPIV, INFO )
      IF( JB+1.LE.N ) THEN
*        Apply interchanges to columns JN+1:JA+N-1.
         CALL PDLASWP('Forward', 'Rows', N-JB, A, IA, JN+1, DESCA, IA, IN, IPIV )
*        Compute block row of U.
         CALL PDTRSM( 'Left', 'Lower', 'No transpose', 'Unit', JB,
     $                N-JB, ONE, A, IA, JA, DESCA, A, IA, JN+1, DESCA )
```

EXAMPLE 14-5. ScaLAPACK variant (Fortran 90 coding) (continued)

```
*
          IF( JB+1.LE.M ) THEN
*             Update trailing submatrix.
              CALL PDGEMM( 'No transpose', 'No transpose', M-JB, N-JB, JB,
     $                     -ONE, A, IN+1, JA, DESCA, A, IA, JN+1, DESCA,
     $                     ONE, A, IN+1, JN+1, DESCA )
          END IF
      END IF
*     Loop over the remaining blocks of columns.
      DO 10 J = JN+1, JA+MN-1, DESCA( NB_ )
         JB = MIN( MN-J+JA, DESCA( NB_ ) )
         I = IA + J - JA
*
*        Factor diagonal and subdiagonal blocks and test for exact
*        singularity.
*
         CALL PDGETF2( M-J+JA, JB, A, I, J, DESCA, IPIV, IINFO )
*
         IF( INFO.EQ.0 .AND. IINFO.GT.0 ) INFO = IINFO + J - JA
*
*        Apply interchanges to columns JA:J-JA.
*
         CALL PDLASWP('Forward', 'Rowwise', J-JA, A, IA, JA, DESCA, I,I+JB-1, IPIV)
         IF( J-JA+JB+1.LE.N ) THEN
*            Apply interchanges to columns J+JB:JA+N-1.
             CALL PDLASWP( 'Forward', 'Rowwise', N-J-JB+JA, A, IA, J+JB,
     $                     DESCA, I, I+JB-1, IPIV )
*            Compute block row of U.
             CALL PDTRSM( 'Left', 'Lower', 'No transpose', 'Unit', JB,
     $                    N-J-JB+JA, ONE, A, I, J, DESCA, A, I, J+JB,
     $                    DESCA )
             IF( J-JA+JB+1.LE.M ) THEN
*                Update trailing submatrix.
                 CALL PDGEMM( 'No transpose', 'No transpose', M-J-JB+JA,
     $                        N-J-JB+JA, JB, -ONE, A, I+JB, J, DESCA, A,
     $                        I, J+JB, DESCA, ONE, A, I+JB, J+JB, DESCA )
             END IF
         END IF
  10  CONTINUE
      IF( INFO.EQ.0 ) INFO = MN + 1
      CALL IGAMN2D(ICTXT, 'Rowwise', ' ', 1, 1, INFO, 1, IDUM1,IDUM2, -1,-1, MYCOL)
      IF( INFO.EQ.MN+1 ) INFO = 0
      CALL PB_TOPSET( ICTXT, 'Broadcast', 'Rowwise', ROWBTOP )
      CALL PB_TOPSET( ICTXT, 'Broadcast', 'Columnwise', COLBTOP )
      CALL PB_TOPSET( ICTXT, 'Combine', 'Columnwise', COLCTOP )
      RETURN
      END
```

In order to simplify the design of ScaLAPACK, and because the BLAS have proven to be very useful tools outside LAPACK, we chose to build a Parallel BLAS, or PBLAS (described in the paper by Choi et al. listed under "Further Reading"), whose interface is as similar to the BLAS as possible. This decision has permitted the ScaLAPACK code to be quite similar, and sometimes nearly identical, to the analogous LAPACK code.

It was our aim that the PBLAS would provide a distributed memory standard, just as the BLAS provided a shared memory standard. This would simplify and encourage the development of high-performance and portable parallel numerical software, as well as providing manufacturers with just a small set of routines to be optimized. The acceptance of the PBLAS requires reasonable compromises between competing goals of functionality and simplicity.

The PBLAS operate on matrices distributed in a two-dimensional block cyclic layout. Because such a data layout requires many parameters to fully describe the distributed matrix, we have chosen a more object-oriented approach and encapsulated these parameters in an integer array called an *array descriptor*. An array descriptor includes:

- The descriptor type
- The BLACS context (a virtual space for messages that is created to avoid collisions between logically distinct messages)
- The number of rows in the distributed matrix
- The number of columns in the distributed matrix
- The row block size
- The column block size
- The process row over which the first row of the matrix is distributed
- The process column over which the first column of the matrix is distributed
- The leading dimension of the local array storing the local blocks

By using this descriptor, a call to a PBLAS routine is very similar to a call to the corresponding BLAS routine:

```
CALL DGEMM ( TRANSA, TRANSB, M, N, K, ALPHA,
             A( IA, JA ), LDA,
             B( IB, JB ), LDB, BETA,
             C( IC, JC ), LDC )

CALL PDGEMM( TRANSA, TRANSB, M, N, K, ALPHA,
             A, IA, JA, DESC_A,
             B, JB, DESC_B, BETA,
             C, IC, JC, DESC_C )
```

DGEMM computes $C = BETA * C + ALPHA * op(A) * op(B)$, where $op(A)$ is either A or its transpose depending on *TRANSA, op(B)* is similar, *op(A) is M-by-K*, and *op(B)* is *K-by-N*. *PDGEMM* is the same, with the exception of the way submatrices are specified. To pass the submatrix starting at *A(IA,JA)* to *DGEMM*, for example, the actual argument corresponding to the formal argument *A* is simply *A(IA,JA)*. *PDGEMM*, on the other hand, needs to understand the global storage scheme of *A* to extract the correct submatrix, so *IA* and *JA* must be passed in separately.

DESC_A is the array descriptor for *A*. The parameters describing the matrix operands *B* and *C* are analogous to those describing *A*. In a truly object-oriented environment, matrices and *DESC_A* would be synonymous. However, this would require language support and detract from portability.

Using message passing and scalable algorithms from the ScaLAPACK library makes it possible to factor matrices of arbitrarily increasing size, given machines with more processors. By design, the library computes more than it communicates, so for the most part, data stays locally for processing and travels only occasionally across the interconnect network.

But the number and types of messages exchanged between processors can sometimes be hard to manage. The context associated with every distributed matrix lets implementations use separate "universes" for message passing. The use of separate communication contexts by distinct libraries (or distinct library invocations) such as the PBLAS insulates communication internal to the library from external communication. When more than one descriptor array is present in the argument list of a routine in the PBLAS, the individual BLACS context entries must be equal. In other words, the PBLAS do not perform "inter-context" operations.

In the performance sense, ScaLAPACK did to LAPACK what LAPACK did to LINPACK: it broadened the range of hardware where LU factorization (and other codes) could run efficiently. In terms of code elegance, the ScaLAPACK's changes were much more drastic: the same mathematical operation now required large amounts of tedious work. Both the users and the library writers were now forced into explicitly controlling data storage intricacies, because data locality became paramount for performance. The victim was the readability of the code, despite efforts to modularize the code according to the best software engineering practices of the day.

Multithreading for Multi-Core Systems

The advent of multi-core chips brought about a fundamental shift in the way software is produced. Dense linear algebra is no exception. The good news is that LAPACK's LU factorization runs on a multi-core system and can even deliver a modest increase of performance if multithreaded BLAS are used. In technical terms, this is the fork-join model of computation: each call to BLAS (from a single main thread) forks a suitable number of threads, which perform the work on each core and then join the main thread of computation. The fork-join model implies a synchronization point at each join operation.

The bad news is that the LAPACK's fork-join algorithm gravely impairs scalability even on small multi-core computers that do not have the memory systems available in SMP systems. The inherent scalability flaw is the heavy synchronization in the fork-join model (only a single thread is allowed to perform the significant computation that occupies the critical section of the code, leaving other threads idle) that results in lock-step execution and prevents hiding of inherently sequential portions of the code behind parallel ones. In other words, the threads are forced to perform the same operation on different data. If there is not enough data for some threads, they will have to stay idle and wait for the rest of the threads that perform useful work on their data. Clearly, another version of the LU algorithm is needed such that would allow threads to stay busy all the time by possibly making them perform different operations during some portion of the execution.

The multithreaded version of the algorithm recognizes the existence of a so-called *critical path* in the algorithm: a portion of the code whose execution depends on previous calculations and can block the progress of the algorithm. The LAPACK's LU does not treat this critical portion of the code in any special way: the DGETF2 subroutine is called by a single thread and doesn't allow much parallelization even at the BLAS level. While one thread calls this routine, the other ones wait idly. And since the performance of DGETF2 is bound by memory bandwidth (rather than processor speed), this bottleneck will exacerbate scalability problems as systems with more cores are introduced.

The multithreaded version of the algorithm attacks this problem head-on by introducing the notion of look-ahead: calculating things ahead of time to avoid potential stagnation in the progress of the computations. This of course requires additional synchronization and bookkeeping not present in the previous versions—a trade-off between code complexity and performance. Another aspect of the multithreaded code is the use of recursion in the panel factorization. It turns out that the use of recursion can give even greater performance benefits for tall panel matrices than it does for the square ones.

Example 14-6 shows a factorization suitable for multithreaded execution.

EXAMPLE 14-6. Factorization for multithreaded execution (C code)

```
void SMP_dgetrf(int n, double *a, int lda, int *ipiv, int pw,
                            int tid, int tsize, int *pready,ptm *mtx, ptc *cnd) {
  int pcnt, pfctr, ufrom, uto, ifrom, p;
  double *pa = a, *pl, *pf, *lp;

  pcnt = n / pw; /* number of panels */

  pfctr = tid + (tid ? 0 : tsize); /* first panel that should be factored by this
                      thread after the very first panel (number 0) gets factored */

  /* this is a pointer to the last panel */
  lp = a + (size_t)(n - pw) * (size_t)lda;

  /* for each panel (that is used as source of updates) */
  for (ufrom = 0; ufrom < pcnt; ufrom++, pa += (size_t)pw * (size_t)(lda + 1)){
    p = ufrom * pw; /* column number */

    /* if the panel to be used for updates has not been factored yet; 'ipiv'
       does not be consulted, but it is to possibly avoid accesses to 'pready'*/
    if (! ipiv[p + pw - 1] || ! pready[ufrom]) {

      if (ufrom % tsize == tid) { /* if this is this thread's panel */
        pfactor( n - p, pw, pa, lda, ipiv + p, pready, ufrom, mtx, cnd );
      } else if (ufrom < pcnt - 1) { /* if this is not the last panel */
```

```
            LOCK( mtx );
            while (! pready[ufrom]) { WAIT( cnd, mtx ); }
            UNLOCK( mtx );
        }
    }
    /* for each panel to be updated */
    for (uto = first_panel_to_update( ufrom, tid, tsize ); uto < pcnt;
            uto += tsize) {
        /* if there are still panels to factor by this thread and preceding panel
           has been factored; test to 'ipiv' could be skipped but is in there to
           decrease number of accesses to 'pready' */
        if (pfctr < pcnt && ipiv[pfctr * pw - 1] && pready[pfctr - 1]) {
            /* for each panel that has to (still) update panel 'pfctr' */
            for (ifrom = ufrom + (uto > pfctr ? 1 : 0); ifrom < pfctr; ifrom++) {
                p = ifrom * pw;
                pl = a + (size_t)p * (size_t)(lda + 1);
                pf = pl + (size_t)(pfctr - ifrom) * (size_t)pw * (size_t)lda;
                pupdate( n - p, pw, pl, pf, lda, p, ipiv, lp );
            }
            p = pfctr * pw;
            pl = a + (size_t)p * (size_t)(lda + 1);
            pfactor( n - p, pw, pl, lda, ipiv + p, pready, pfctr, mtx, cnd );
            pfctr += tsize; /* move to this thread's next panel */
        }

        /* if panel 'uto' hasn't been factored (if it was, it certainly has been
           updated, so no update is necessary) */
        if (uto > pfctr || ! ipiv[uto * pw]) {
            p = ufrom * pw;
            pf = pa + (size_t)(uto - ufrom) * (size_t)pw * (size_t)lda;
            pupdate( n - p, pw, pa, pf, lda, p, ipiv, lp );
        }
    }
}
```

The algorithm is the same for each thread (the SIMD paradigm), and the matrix data is partitioned among threads in a cyclic manner using panels with pw columns in each panel (except maybe the last). The pw parameter corresponds to the blocking parameter NB of LAPACK. The difference is the logical assignment of panels (blocks of columns) to threads. (Physically, all panels are equally accessible because the code operates in a shared memory regimen.) The benefits of blocking in a thread are the same as they were in LAPACK: better cache reuse and less stress on the memory bus. Assigning a portion of the matrix to a thread seems an artificial requirement at first, but it simplifies the code and the bookkeeping data structures; most importantly, it provides better memory affinity. It turns out that multi-core chips are not symmetric in terms of memory access bandwidth, so minimizing the number of reassignments of memory pages to cores directly benefits performance.

The standard components of LU factorization are represented by the pfactor( ) and pupdate( ) functions. As one might expect, the former factors a panel, whereas the latter updates a panel using one of the previously factored panels.

The main loop makes each thread iterate over each panel in turn. If necessary, the panel is factored by the owner thread while other threads wait (if they happen to need this panel for their updates).

The look-ahead logic is inside the nested loop (prefaced by the comment for each panel to be updated) that replaces DGEMM or PDGEMM from previous algorithms. Before each thread updates one of its panels, it checks whether it's already feasible to factor its first unfactored panel. This minimizes the number of times the threads have to wait because each thread constantly attempts to eliminate the potential bottleneck.

As was the case for ScaLAPACK, the multithreaded version detracts from the inherent elegance of the LAPACK's version. Also in the same spirit, performance is the main culprit: LAPACK's code will not run efficiently on machines with ever-increasing numbers of cores. Explicit control of execution threads at the LAPACK level rather than the BLAS level is critical: parallelism cannot be encapsulated in a library call. The only good news is that the code is not as complicated as ScaLAPACK's, and efficient BLAS can still be put to a good use.

A Word About the Error Analysis and Operation Count

The key aspect of all of the implementations presented in this chapter is their numerical properties.

It is acceptable to forgo elegance in order to gain performance. But numerical stability is of vital importance and cannot be sacrificed because it is an inherent part of the algorithm's correctness. While these are serious considerations, there is some consolation to follow. It may be surprising to some readers that all of the algorithms presented are the same, even though it's virtually impossible to make each excerpt of code produce exactly the same output for exactly the same inputs.

When it comes to repeatability of results, the vagaries of floating-point representation may be captured in a rigorous way by *error bounds*. One way of expressing the numerical robustness of the previous algorithms is with the following formula:

$$\|r\|/\|A\| \leq \|e\| \leq \|A^{-1}\| \, \|r\|$$

where error $e = x - y$ is the difference between the computed solution y and the correct solution x, and $r = Ay - b$ is a so-called "residual." The previous formula basically says that the size of the error (the parallel bars surrounding a value indicate a norm—a measure of absolute size) is as small as warranted by the quality of the matrix A. Therefore, if the matrix is close to being singular in numerical sense (some entries are so small that they might as well be considered to be zero), the algorithms will not give an accurate answer. But, otherwise, a relatively good quality of result can be expected.

Another feature that is common to all the versions presented is the operation count: they all perform $2/3n^3$ floating-point multiplications and/or additions. The order of these operations is what differentiates them. There are algorithms that increase the amount of floating-point work to save on memory traffic or network transfers (especially for distribute-memory parallel algorithms). But because the algorithms shown in this chapter have the same operation count, it is valid to compare them for performance. The computational rate (number of floating-point operations per second) may be used instead of the time taken to solve the problem, provided that the matrix size is the same. But comparing computational rates is sometimes better because it allows a comparison of algorithms when the matrix sizes differ. For example, a sequential algorithm on a single processor can be directly compared with a parallel one working on a large cluster on a much bigger matrix.

Future Directions for Research

In this chapter, we have looked at the evolution of the design of a simple but important algorithm in computational science. The changes over the past 30 years have been necessary to follow the lead of the advances in computer architectures. In some cases, these changes have been simple, such as interchanging loops. In other cases, they have been as complex as the introduction of recursion and look-ahead computations. In each case, however, the code's ability to efficiently utilize the memory hierarchy is the key to high performance on a single processor as well as on shared and distributed memory systems.

The essence of the problem is the dramatic increase in complexity that software developers have had to confront, and still do. Dual-core machines are already common, and the number of cores is expected to roughly double with each processor generation. But contrary to the assumptions of the old model, programmers will not be able to consider these cores independently (i.e., multi-core is *not* "the new SMP") because they share on-chip resources in ways that separate processors do not. This situation is made even more complicated by the other nonstandard components that future architectures are expected to deploy, including the mixing of different types of cores, hardware accelerators, and memory systems.

Finally, the proliferation of widely divergent design ideas shows that the question of how to best combine all these new resources and components is largely unsettled. When combined, these changes produce a picture of a future in which programmers will have to overcome software design problems vastly more complex and challenging than those in the past in order to take advantage of the much higher degrees of concurrency and greater computing power that new architectures will offer.

So, the bad news is that none of the presented code will work efficiently someday. The good news is that we have learned various ways to mold the original simple rendition of the algorithm to meet the ever-increasing challenges of hardware designs.

Further Reading

- *LINPACK User's Guide*, J. J. Dongarra, J. R. Bunch, C. B. Moler, and G. W. Stewart, SIAM: Philadelphia, 1979, ISBN 0-89871-172-X.

- *LAPACK Users' Guide*, Third Edition, E. Anderson, Z. Bai, C. Bischof, S. Blackford, J. Demmel, J. Dongarra, J. Du Croz, A. Greenbaum, S. Hammaring, A. McKenney, and D. Sorensen, SIAM: Philadelphia, 1999, ISBN 0-89871-447-8.

- *ScaLAPACK Users' Guide*, L. S. Blackford, J. Choi, A. Cleary, E. D'Azevedo, J. Demmel, I. Dhillon, J. Dongarra, S. Hammarling, G. Henry, A. Petitet, K. Stanley, D. Walker, and R. C. Whaley, SIAM Publications, Philadelphia, 1997, ISBN 0-89871-397-8.

- "Basic Linear Algebra Subprograms for FORTRAN usage," C. L. Lawson, R. J. Hanson, D. Kincaid, and F. T. Krogh, *ACM Trans. Math. Soft., Vol. 5*, pp. 308–323, 1979.

- "An extended set of FORTRAN Basic Linear Algebra Subprograms," J. J. Dongarra, J. Du Croz, S. Hammarling, and R. J. Hanson, *ACM Trans. Math. Soft., Vol. 14*, pp. 1–17, 1988.

- "A set of Level 3 Basic Linear Algebra Subprograms," J. J. Dongarra, J. Du Croz, I. S. Duff, and S. Hammarling, *ACM Trans. Math. Soft., Vol. 16*, pp. 1–17, 1990.

- *Implementation Guide for LAPACK*, E. Anderson and J. Dongarra, UT-CS-90-101, April 1990.

- *A Proposal for a Set of Parallel Basic Linear Algebra Subprograms*, J. Choi, J. Dongarra, S. Ostrouchov, A. Petitet, D. Walker, and R. C. Whaley, UT-CS-95-292, May 1995.

- *LAPACK Working Note 37: Two Dimensional Basic Linear Algebra Communication Subprograms*, J. Dongarra and R. A. van de Geijn, University of Tennessee Computer Science Technical Report, UT-CS-91-138, October 1991.

- "Matrix computations with Fortran and paging," Cleve B. Moler, *Communications of the ACM*, 15(4), pp. 268–270, 1972.

- *LAPACK Working Note 19: Evaluating Block Algorithm Variants in LAPACK*, E. Anderson and J. Dongarra, University of Tennessee Computer Science Technical Report, UT-CS-90-103, April 1990.

- "Recursion leads to automatic variable blocking for dense linear-algebra algorithms," Gustavson, F. G. *IBM J. Res. Dev.* Vol. 41, No. 6 (Nov. 1997), pp. 737–756.

## CHAPTER FIFTEEN

The Long-Term Benefits
of Beautiful Design

Adam Kolawa

SOME ALGORITHMS FOR SEEMINGLY STRAIGHTFORWARD AND SIMPLE mathematical equations are actually extremely difficult to implement. For instance, rounding problems can compromise accuracy, some mathematical equations can cause values to exceed the range of a floating-point value on the system, and some algorithms (notably the classic Fourier Transform) take much too long if done in a brute-force fashion. Furthermore, different sets of data work better with different algorithms. Consequently, beautiful code and beautiful mathematics are not necessarily one and the same.

The programmers who wrote the code for the CERN mathematical library recognized the difference between mathematical equations and computed solutions: the difference between theory and practice. In this chapter, I will explore the beauty in a few of the programming strategies that they used to bridge that gap.

My Idea of Beautiful Code

My idea of beautiful code stems from my belief that the ultimate purpose of code is to work. In other words, code should accurately and efficiently perform the task that it was designed to complete, in such a way that there are no ambiguities as to how it will behave.

I find beauty in code that I can trust—code that I am confident will produce results that are correct and applicable to my problem. What I am defining here as my first criterion of beautiful code is code that I can use and reuse without any shred of doubt in the code's ability to deliver results. In other words, my primary concern is not what the code looks like, but what I can do with it.

It's not that I don't appreciate the beauty in code's implementation details; I do indeed, and I will discuss criteria and examples of code's inner beauty later in this chapter. My point here is that when code satisfies my somewhat nontraditional notion of beauty in utility, it's rarely necessary to look at its implementation details. Such code promotes what I believe to be one of the most important missions in the industry: the ability to share code with others, without requiring them to analyze the code and figure out exactly how it works. Beautiful code is like a beautiful car. You rarely need to open it up to look at its mechanics. Rather, you enjoy it from the outside and trust that it will drive you where you want to go.

For code to be enjoyed in this way, it must be designed so that it's clear how it should be used, easy to understand how you can apply it to solve your own problems, and easy to verify if you are using it correctly.

Introducing the CERN Library

I believe that the mathematical library developed by CERN (European Organization for Nuclear Research) is a prime example of beautiful code. The code in this library performs algebraic operations, integrates functions, solves differential equations, and solves a lot of physics problems. It was written over 30 years ago and has been widely used over the years. The linear algebra part of the CERN Library evolved into the LAPACK library, which is the code that I will discuss here. The LAPACK library is currently developed by multiple universities and organizations.

I have used this code since I was young, and I am still fascinated by it. The beauty of this code is that it contains many complicated mathematical algorithms that are very well tested and difficult to reproduce. You can reuse it and rely on it without having to worry about whether it works.

The library's high accuracy and reliability are why—even after all these years—it remains the mathematical library of choice for anyone who needs to accurately and reliably solve equations. There are other mathematical libraries available, but they can't compete with the CERN library's proven reliability and accuracy.

The first part of this chapter discusses this code's outer beauty: the things that make it so accurate and reliable that developers want to reuse it and the elements that make this reuse as simple as possible. The second part explores the inner beauty of its implementation details.

Outer Beauty

If you've ever tried to solve a system of linear equations or perform an equally complicated mathematical operation, you know that many times the code you write to achieve this does not deliver the correct results. One of the greatest problems with mathematical libraries is that rounding errors and floating-point operations lead to solution instabilities and incorrect results.

If you design a mathematical library, you need to carefully define the range in which each algorithm will work. You need to write each algorithm in such a way that it will adhere to these conditions, and you also need to write it in such a way that the rounding errors will cancel out. This can be very complicated.

In the CERN library, the algorithms are specified in a very precise way. Basically, if you look at any routine, you will notice that it has a description of what it is going to do. It really doesn't matter in which language the routine is written. In fact, these routines were written in Fortran but have interfaces that allow them to be called from almost any other place. That's also a beautiful thing. In some sense, the routine is a black box: you don't care what goes on inside, only that it delivers the appropriate results for your inputs. It carefully defines what every routine is doing, under which conditions it is working, what input data it accepts, and what constraints must be put on the input data in order to get the correct answer.

For example, let's look at the LAPACK library's SGBSV routine, which solves a system of linear equations for a banded matrix. If you try to solve a system of linear equations numerically, you use different algorithms. Different algorithms operate better in different domains, and you need to know the structure of the matrix to choose the best one. For instance, you would want to use one algorithm to solve the problem if you had a banded matrix (a matrix where most of the elements are around the diagonal), and a different one if you had a sparse matrix (a matrix that has a lot of zeros and few numbers).

Because different routines are optimized for different situations, the best routine to use really depends on the matrix structure that you have. However, in order to understand the range of this, you need to understand how to input data to these routines. Sometimes you input data in the form of a matrix. Sometimes—for instance, with a banded matrix—you send it like a very narrow array. Each of these routines and their requirements are described very clearly in the library:

```
      SUBROUTINE SGBSV( N, KL, KU, NRHS, AB, LDAB, IPIV, B, LDB, INFO )
*
*  -- LAPACK driver routine (version 2.0) --
*     Univ. of Tennessee, Univ. of California Berkeley, NAG Ltd.,
*     Courant Institute, Argonne National Lab, and Rice University
*     March 31, 1993
*
*     .. Scalar Arguments ..
      INTEGER            INFO, KL, KU, LDAB, LDB, N, NRHS
*     ..
```

```
*         .. Array Arguments ..
          INTEGER            IPIV( * )
          REAL               AB( LDAB, * ), B( LDB, * )
*         ..
*
*  Purpose
*  =======
*
*  SGBSV computes the solution to a real system of linear equations
*  A * X = B, where A is a band matrix of order N with KL subdiagonals
*  and KU superdiagonals, and X and B are N-by-NRHS matrices.
*
*  The LU decomposition with partial pivoting and row interchanges is
*  used to factor A as A = L * U, where L is a product of permutation
*  and unit lower triangular matrices with KL subdiagonals, and U is
*  upper triangular with KL+KU superdiagonals.  The factored form of A
*  is then used to solve the system of equations A * X = B.
*
*  Arguments
*  =========
*
*  N       (input) INTEGER
*          The number of linear equations, i.e., the order of the
*          matrix A.  N >= 0.
*
*  KL      (input) INTEGER
*          The number of subdiagonals within the band of A.  KL >= 0.
*
*  KU      (input) INTEGER
*          The number of superdiagonals within the band of A.  KU >= 0.
*
*  NRHS    (input) INTEGER
*          The number of right hand sides, i.e., the number of columns
*          of the matrix B.  NRHS >= 0.
*
*  AB      (input/output) REAL array, dimension (LDAB,N)
*          On entry, the matrix A in band storage, in rows KL+1 to
*          2*KL+KU+1; rows 1 to KL of the array need not be set.
*          The j-th column of A is stored in the j-th column of the
*          array AB as follows:
*          AB(KL+KU+1+i-j,j) = A(i,j) for max(1,j-KU)<=i<=min(N,j+KL)
*          On exit, details of the factorization: U is stored as an
*          upper triangular band matrix with KL+KU superdiagonals in
*          rows 1 to KL+KU+1, and the multipliers used during the
*          factorization are stored in rows KL+KU+2 to 2*KL+KU+1.
*          See below for further details.
*
*  LDAB    (input) INTEGER
*          The leading dimension of the array AB.  LDAB >= 2*KL+KU+1.
*
*  IPIV    (output) INTEGER array, dimension (N)
*          The pivot indices that define the permutation matrix P;
*          row i of the matrix was interchanged with row IPIV(i).
*
*  B       (input/output) REAL array, dimension (LDB,NRHS)
*          On entry, the N-by-NRHS right hand side matrix B.
*          On exit, if INFO = 0, the N-by-NRHS solution matrix X.
*
```

```
*  LDB     (input) INTEGER
*          The leading dimension of the array B.  LDB >= max(1,N).
*
*  INFO    (output) INTEGER
*          = 0:  successful exit
*          < 0:  if INFO = -i, the i-th argument had an illegal value
*          > 0:  if INFO = i, U(i,i) is exactly zero.  The factorization
*                has been completed, but the factor U is exactly
*                singular, and the solution has not been computed.
*
*  Further Details
*  ===============
*
*  The band storage scheme is illustrated by the following example, when
*  M = N = 6, KL = 2, KU = 1:
*
*  On entry:                       On exit:
*
*      *    *    *    +    +    +       *    *    *   u14  u25  u36
*      *    *    +    +    +    +       *    *   u13  u24  u35  u46
*      *   a12  a23  a34  a45  a56      *   u12  u23  u34  u45  u56
*     a11  a22  a33  a44  a55  a66     u11  u22  u33  u44  u55  u66
*     a21  a32  a43  a54  a65   *      m21  m32  m43  m54  m65   *
*     a31  a42  a53  a64   *    *      m31  m42  m53  m64   *    *
*
*  Array elements marked * are not used by the routine; elements marked
*  + need not be set on entry, but are required by the routine to store
*  elements of U because of fill-in resulting from the row interchanges.
*
*  ======================================================================
*
*     .. External Subroutines ..
      EXTERNAL           SGBTRF, SGBTRS, XERBLA
*     ..
*     .. Intrinsic Functions ..
      INTRINSIC          MAX
*     ..
*     .. Executable Statements ..
*
*     Test the input parameters.
*
      INFO = 0
      IF( N.LT.0 ) THEN
         INFO = -1
      ELSE IF( KL.LT.0 ) THEN
         INFO = -2
      ELSE IF( KU.LT.0 ) THEN
         INFO = -3
      ELSE IF( NRHS.LT.0 ) THEN
         INFO = -4
      ELSE IF( LDAB.LT.2*KL+KU+1 ) THEN
         INFO = -6
      ELSE IF( LDB.LT.MAX( N, 1 ) ) THEN
         INFO = -9
      END IF
```

```
          IF( INFO.NE.O ) THEN
             CALL XERBLA( 'SGBSV ', -INFO )
             RETURN
          END IF
*
*        Compute the LU factorization of the band matrix A.
*
          CALL SGBTRF ( N, N, KL, KU, AB, LDAB, IPIV, INFO )
          IF( INFO.EQ.O ) THEN
*
*           Solve the system A*X = B, overwriting B with X.
*
             CALL SGBTRS( 'No transpose', N, KL, KU, NRHS, AB, LDAB, IPIV,
     $                    B, LDB, INFO )
          END IF
          RETURN
*
*        End of SGBSV
*
          END
```

One of the first things to notice in the code for the SGBSV routine is that it starts with a long comment that describes the routine's purpose and use. In fact, the comment is exactly the same as the manual page for that routine. Having the full documentation of the routine's usage in the code is important because it connects the routine's internal structure with its usage. In many other cases, I have found that the manual description and code documentation have nothing in common. I think this practice of marrying the two is one thing that makes code beautiful.

Following the initial comments, the algorithm that the routine uses is detailed in the routine's description. This helps anyone using the code to understand what the code will do and how it should react. Next comes a detailed description of the arguments, with their ranges explicitly specified.

The AB argument is an interesting one to consider. This argument contains the elements of the matrix A. Because the matrix is banded, it contains a lot of zero values, which are not clustered close to the diagonal. In principle, the input to the routine could be presented as a two-dimensional array of the dimensions of the matrix. However, this would be a waste of memory space. Instead, the AB argument contains only nonzero elements of the matrix next to its diagonal.

The format of the AB argument not only conserves memory space, but also has another purpose. In this routine, the algorithm is using the properties of the system of equations to solve the problem in a more efficient way. This means that the algorithm relies on the user to provide the correct matrix type as an input. If the AB argument contains all the elements of the matrix, one or more of the elements outside the band could accidentally be set to nonzero. This could lead to errors in the solution. The format chosen for AB makes it impossible to make this mistake. This was done on purpose, and it contributes to the code's beauty.

The AB argument also plays another role: it serves as an output argument as well as an input argument. In this context, the design solves a different problem. By having the routine reuse the space that the original program allocated, the developers of this code ensured that the routine would work as long as the original program had sufficient memory. If it had been written so that the routine needed additional memory allocation, then it might not run if the system was unable to allocate more memory. This can be especially problematic when there is a really large system of equations, and the routine needs a significant amount of memory space in which it can operate. The sample code is immune to such problems because it was written so that the routine can return the solution as long as the original program has sufficient memory space to store the problem. This is very beautiful.

Before I move on to the other arguments, I want to discuss this issue further. I have seen a lot of code written in my lifetime. Very often, developers write code and unconsciously place intrinsic restrictions on it. Most commonly, they restrict the size of the problem that can be solved. This occurs as a result of the following thought process:

1. I have something to write.

2. I'll write it fast so I can see if it works.

3. Once it works, I will generalize it for the real problem.

This process prompts developers to build restrictions into code, which very often leads to difficult-to-find errors that may take years to clean. During this process, developers commonly place explicit or implicit restrictions on the size of the problem they may solve. For example, an explicit restriction may be the definition of a large data space, which should be large enough for all the problems. This is bad and relatively easy to spot. An implicit restriction may be improper usage of dynamic memory—for instance, writing code so that once the problem is presented to the code, the program dynamically allocates the space and solves the problem. For large problems, this can create out-of-memory errors and significantly impact performance. The performance penalty stems from the program's reliance on the operating system's paging utility. If the algorithm is computationally intensive and needs data from many different chunks of memory, the program will fall into constant paging and execute very slowly.

Another example of this type of problem manifests itself in programs that use database systems. If such a program is written in the manner I just described, it could start constantly accessing the database when it is operating on the data. The programmer might think that the program's operations are trivial and fast, but they are actually very inefficient because they contain calls to the database.

So what is the lesson here? When writing beautiful code, one needs to think about its scalability. Contrary to popular belief, scalability does not come from code optimization; rather, it comes from using the right algorithm. Code profiling can provide hints about symptoms of poor performance, but the root cause of performance issues can generally be traced back to design issues. The SGBSV routine is designed so that it does not have this performance problem, and that is another thing that makes it beautiful.

Looking now at the other input arguments, it becomes clear that the same principle that applied to the AB array also applies to the others.

The final argument, INFO, is the error communication mechanism. It is interesting to see how the diagnostics are presented to the user. It is possible that the system of equations does not have a solution, and this case is also reported here. Notice that the INFO argument reports failure as well as success, and that it provides diagnostics to help you identify the problem.

This is something often lacking in code written today. Nowadays, code is commonly written to handle positive use cases: it is written to perform the actions detailed in the specification. With the sample code, this means that the code will work fine if the solution for the system of equations exists. However, reality is messy. In real life, code can break, and code dumps core or throw exceptions when it is presented with a system of equations that lacks a solution. This is a common case of failure to specify requirements about unexpected usages.

Many systems today are programmed to do as little as possible; then—once they are in use—they are "fixed" to do the things nobody initially anticipated they would need to do. A similar problem is the failure to specify requirements about how to gracefully handle errors and other unexpected situations. Such a response to exceptional circumstances is critical to application reliability and should be treated as a fundamental functionality requirement.

When writing code to a specification, developers need to recognize that specifications are usually incomplete. The developer must have a deep understanding of the problem at hand so that she can extend the specification with the additional use cases and unexpected usages that need to be implemented in order for the code to perform in an intelligent way. Our sample routine is one example of what happens when such careful consideration is applied. This routine will either do the job, or it will tell you that it cannot do it—it won't crash on you. This is beautiful.

Next, let's look at the routine's Further Details section. This section describes how the memory is used and makes it obvious that the space is used as the scratch space during internal operations. This is a good example of beautifully implemented code, so I'll be discussing this in the next section, "Inner Beauty."

Another example of the code's outer beauty is that many routines in the CERN library provide simple test and example programs. This is very important for beautiful code. You should be able to tell whether the code is doing what it's supposed to be doing in your application. The developers of this library have written test programs that show you how the library is being called for specific data. You can use these test programs to verify whether you are going to get the correct results for your data, thus building your confidence in the library.

The beautiful design here is that the tests not only tell you under which conditions you can use the routines, but also give you a validation example that allows you to build confidence and know what's going on—without really looking into the code.

Inner Beauty

Now, let's start looking at the code's implementation details.

Beauty in Brevity and Simplicity

I believe that beautiful code is short code, and I find that lengthy, complicated code is generally quite ugly. The SGBSV routine is a prime example of the beauty of short code. It begins with a quick verification of the consistency of the input arguments, then continues with two calls that logically follow the mathematical algorithm.

From the first glance, it is obvious what this code is doing: it begins by performing LU factorization with the SGBTRF routine, then solves the system with the SGBTRS routine. This code is very easy to read. There's no need to pore over hundreds of lines of code to understand what the code does. The main task is split into two subtasks, and the subtasks are pushed into a subsystem.

Note that the subsystem adheres to the same design assumptions regarding memory usage as the main system. This is a very important and beautiful aspect of the design.

The routines from the subsystem are reused in different "driver" routines (the SGBSV routine is called a driver routine). This creates a hierarchical system that encourages code reuse. This is beautiful, too. Code reuse significantly reduces the effort required for code development, testing, and maintenance. In fact, it is one of the best ways to increase developers' productivity and reduce their stress. The problem is that reuse is typically difficult. Very often, code is so complicated and difficult to read that developers find it easier to rewrite code from scratch than to reuse somebody else's code. Good design and clear, concise code are vital to promoting code reuse.

Unfortunately, much of the code written today falls short in this respect. Nowadays, most of the code written has an inheritance structure, which is encouraged in the hope that it will bring clarity to the code. However, I must admit that I've spent hours on end staring at a few lines of such code...and still could not decipher what it was supposed to do. This is not beautiful code; it is bad code with a convoluted design. If you cannot tell what the code does by glancing at the naming conventions and several code lines, then the code is too complicated.

Beautiful code should be easy to understand. I hate reading code that was written to show off the developer's knowledge of the language, and I shouldn't need to go through 25 files before I can really understand what a piece of it is really doing. The code does not necessarily need to be commented, but its purpose should be explicit, and there should be no ambiguity in each operation. The problem with the new code being written today—especially in the C++ language—is that developers use so much inheritance and overloading that it's almost impossible to tell what the code is really doing, why it's doing it, and whether it's correct. To figure this out, you need to understand all of the hierarchy of inheritance and overloading. If the operation is some kind of complicated overloaded operation, this code is not beautiful to me.

Beauty in Frugality

My next criterion for beautiful code is that you can tell that a lot of thought went into how the code will be running on the computer. What I'm trying to say is that beautiful code never forgets that it will be running on a computer, and that a computer has limitations. As I said earlier in this chapter, computers have limited speed, sometimes operate better on floating-point numbers or integer numbers, and have finite amounts of memory. Beautiful code must consider these limitations of reality. Quite often, people writing code assume that memory is infinite, computer speed is infinite, and so on. This is not beautiful code; it's arrogant code. Beautiful code is frugal about things like memory use and reuses memory whenever possible.

For example, let's look at the LU decomposition subroutine SGBTRF, which is in the second level of subroutines. To save space, I removed the initial comments in the header and other excepts that I do not directly discuss (you can view the complete subroutine at *http://www.netlib.org/lapack/explore-html/sgbtrf.f.html*):

```
      SUBROUTINE SGBTRF( M, N, KL, KU, AB, LDAB, IPIV, INFO )
*
*  -- LAPACK routine (version 2.0) --
*     Univ. of Tennessee, Univ. of California Berkeley, NAG Ltd.,
*     Courant Institute, Argonne National Lab, and Rice University
*     February 29, 1992
.
.
.

Initial comments, description of parameters
.
,
,

*     Test the input parameters.
*
      INFO = 0
      IF( M.LT.0 ) THEN
.
.


.
Checking parameters
.
.
.

         CALL XERBLA( 'SGBTRF', -INFO )
        RETURN
      END IF
*
*     Quick return if possible
*
      IF( M.EQ.0 .OR. N.EQ.0 )
     $   RETURN
*
```

```
*     Determine the block size for this environment
*
      NB = ILAENV( 1, 'SGBTRF', ' ', M, N, KL, KU )
*
*     The block size must not exceed the limit set by the size of the
*     local arrays WORK13 and WORK31.
*
      NB = MIN( NB, NBMAX )
*
      IF( NB.LE.1 .OR. NB.GT.KL ) THEN
*
*        Use unblocked code
*
         CALL SGBTF2( M, N, KL, KU, AB, LDAB, IPIV, INFO )
      ELSE
*
*        Use blocked code
*
*        Zero the superdiagonal elements of the work array WORK13
*
         DO 20 J = 1, NB
            DO 10 I = 1, J - 1
               WORK13( I, J ) = ZERO
   10       CONTINUE
   20    CONTINUE
*
*        Zero the subdiagonal elements of the work array WORK31
*
         DO 40 J = 1, NB
            DO 30 I = J + 1, NB
               WORK31( I, J ) = ZERO
   30       CONTINUE
   40    CONTINUE
*
*        Gaussian elimination with partial pivoting
*
*        Set fill-in elements in columns KU+2 to KV to zero
*
         DO 60 J = KU + 2, MIN( KV, N )
            DO 50 I = KV - J + 2, KL
               AB( I, J ) = ZERO
   50       CONTINUE
   60    CONTINUE
*
*        JU is the index of the last column affected by the current
*        stage of the factorization
*
         JU = 1
*
         DO 180 J = 1, MIN( M, N ), NB
            JB = MIN( NB, MIN( M, N )-J+1 )
*
*           The active part of the matrix is partitioned
*
```

```
*              A11    A12    A13
*              A21    A22    A23
*              A31    A32    A33
*
*         Here A11, A21 and A31 denote the current block of JB columns
*         which is about to be factorized. The number of rows in the
*         partitioning are JB, I2, I3 respectively, and the numbers
*         of columns are JB, J2, J3. The superdiagonal elements of A13
*         and the subdiagonal elements of A31 lie outside the band.

          I2 = MIN( KL-JB, M-J-JB+1 )
          I3 = MIN( JB, M-J-KL+1 )
*
*         J2 and J3 are computed after JU has been updated.
*
*         Factorize the current block of JB columns
*
          DO 80 JJ = J, J + JB - 1
*
*            Set fill-in elements in column JJ+KV to zero
*
             IF( JJ+KV.LE.N ) THEN
                DO 70 I = 1, KL
                   AB( I, JJ+KV ) = ZERO
   70           CONTINUE
             END IF
*
*            Find pivot and test for singularity. KM is the number of
*            subdiagonal elements in the current column.
*
             KM = MIN( KL, M-JJ )
             JP = ISAMAX( KM+1, AB( KV+1, JJ ), 1 )
             IPIV( JJ ) = JP + JJ - J
             IF( AB( KV+JP, JJ ).NE.ZERO ) THEN
                JU = MAX( JU, MIN( JJ+KU+JP-1, N ) )
                IF( JP.NE.1 ) THEN
*
*                  Apply interchange to columns J to J+JB-1
*
                   IF( JP+JJ-1.LT.J+KL ) THEN
*
                      CALL SSWAP( JB, AB( KV+1+JJ-J, J ), LDAB-1,
     $                            AB( KV+JP+JJ-J, J ), LDAB-1 )
                   ELSE
*
*                     The interchange affects columns J to JJ-1 of A31
*                     which are stored in the work array WORK31
*
                      CALL SSWAP( JJ-J, AB( KV+1+JJ-J, J ), LDAB-1,
     $                            WORK31( JP+JJ-J-KL, 1 ), LDWORK )
                      CALL SSWAP( J+JB-JJ, AB( KV+1, JJ ), LDAB-1,
     $                            AB( KV+JP, JJ ), LDAB-1 )
                   END IF
                END IF
*
*               Compute multipliers
*
```

```
                  CALL SSCAL( KM, ONE / AB( KV+1, JJ ), AB( KV+2, JJ ),
     $                        1 )
*
   .
   .
   .
Continue direct solution
   .
   .
   .

  170      CONTINUE
  180      CONTINUE
        END IF
*
        RETURN
*
*       End of SGBTRF
*
        END
```

Again, the subroutine starts with argument verification and then proceeds to the problem solution. This is followed by an optimization check, which looks at the problem size to determine whether it can be solved in the "cache" arrays WORK13 and WORK31, or whether it needs to be sent to a lower level for more complicated operations. This is an excellent example of code that is built realistically, for a computer with inherent limitations. The work array can be adjusted for the standard memory of the computer that is solving the problem; in problems with a small enough size, this can prevent performance penalties from possible paging. Problems above that size are so large that that the performance penalty cannot be avoided.

Beauty in Flow

The previous problem solution provides a step-by-step representation of the algorithm. Reading this code is almost like reading a book, since it is so easy to follow. The parts of the problem that are common to other algorithms are reused, and the parts that would complicate the code are passed to subroutines. The result is a very clear, understandable flow.

Each step in the flow corresponds to the mathematical expression. At each step, the code describes what a lower system is expected to do and calls that lower system. The main routine, which is a driver routine, branches into lower routines, each of which branches into more lower routines, and so on. This flow is represented in Figure 15-1.

This is an excellent example of how to apply the "divide and conquer" principle to code design. Every time you move to a lower step, there is a smaller problem to conquer, and you can focus on well-defined circumstances that make the code smaller and better focused. If the problem fits in the computer's memory, the algorithm will solve it directly, as I discussed previously. If not, it goes to the next level of subroutines, and so on.

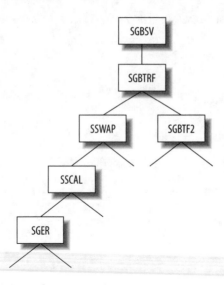

FIGURE 15-1. Logical subdivision of tasks into subroutines

As a result, very computation-intensive routines can be written in assembly language and then optimized for the architecture. Another benefit of this design is that many people can work on the code simultaneously because each subroutine is independent and so well defined.

Conclusion

In sum, I believe that beautiful code must be short, explicit, frugal, and written with consideration for reality. However, I think that the true test of beauty—for code as well as art—is whether the work stands the test of time. Lots of code has been written over the years, but little of it was still in use even several years after it was written. That the CERN library code is still in use more than 30 years after it was written confirms that it is truly beautiful.

## CHAPTER SIXTEEN

The Linux Kernel Driver Model: The Benefits of Working Together

Greg Kroah-Hartman

THE **LINUX KERNEL DRIVER MODEL ATTEMPTS TO CREATE A SYSTEM-WIDE TREE** of all different types of devices managed by the operating system. The core data structures and code used to do this have changed over the years from a very simplistic system meant for handling a few devices to a highly scalable system that can control every different type of device that the real world needs to interact with.

As the Linux kernel has evolved over the years, handling more and more different types of devices,* the core of the kernel has had to change and evolve in order to come up with easier and more manageable ways to handle the range of device types.

Almost all devices consist of two different portions: the physical portion that defines how the operating system talks to the device (be it through the PCI bus, SCSI bus, ISA bus, USB bus, etc.) and the virtual portion that defines how the operating system presents the device to the user so that it can be operated properly (keyboard, mouse, video, sound, etc.). Through the 2.4 kernel releases, each physical portion of devices was controlled by a bus-specific portion of code. This bus code was responsible for a wide range of different tasks, and each individual bus code had no interaction with any other bus code.

---

* Linux now supports more different types of devices and processors than any other operating system ever has in the history of computing.

In 2001, Pat Mochel was working on solving the issue of power management in the Linux kernel. He came to realize that in order to shut down or power up individual devices properly, the kernel had to know the linkages between the different devices. For example, a USB disk drive should be shut down before the PCI controller card for the USB controller is shut down, in order to properly save the data on the device. To solve this issue, the kernel needed to know the tree of all devices in the system, showing what device controlled what other device, and the order in which everything was connected.

Around the same time, I was running into another device-related problem: Linux did not properly handle devices in a persistent manner. I wanted my two USB printers to always have the same name, no matter which one was turned on first, or the order in which they were discovered by the Linux kernel.

Some other operating systems have solved this issue by placing a small database in the kernel to handle device naming, or have attempted to export all possible unique characteristics of a device through a *devfs* type of filesystem* that can be used to directly access the device. For Linux, placing a database inside the kernel was not going to be an acceptable solution. Also, the Linux's *devfs* filesystem implementation contained a number of well-known and incurable race conditions, preventing almost all Linux distributions from relying on it. The *devfs* solution also forced a specific naming policy on the user. Although some people considered this an advantage, it went against the published Linux device-naming standard, and did not allow anyone to use a different naming policy if they so desired.

Pat and I realized that both of our problems could be solved by a unified driver and device model within the Linux kernel. Such a unified model was not a new idea by any means, as other operating systems had embodied such unified models in the past. Now it was time for Linux to do the same. Such a model would allow for the creation of a tree of all devices and also allow a userspace program outside the kernel to handle persistent device naming of any device, in any way that the user desired.

This chapter will describe the evolution of the data structures and supporting functions inside the Linux kernel to do this work, and how this evolution caused changes that could have never been anticipated by anyone at the beginning of the development process.

Humble Beginnings

To start with, a simple structure, struct device, was created as the "base" class for all devices in the kernel. This structure started out looking like the following:

```
struct device {
        struct list_head node;            /* node in sibling list */
        struct list_head children;
        struct device *parent;
```

---

* *devfs* is one way for an operating system to show users all the different devices that are available to be used. It does this by showing all of the different device names, and sometimes a limited relationship between those devices.

```
    char    name[DEVICE_NAME_SIZE]; /* descriptive ascii string */
    char    bus_id[BUS_ID_SIZE];    /* position on parent bus */

    spinlock_t      lock;           /* lock for the device to ensure two
                                       different layers don't access it at
                                       the same time. */
    atomic_t        refcount;       /* refcount to make sure the device
                                     * persists for the right amount of time */

    struct driver_dir_entry * dir;

    struct device_driver *driver;   /* which driver has allocated this
                                       device */
    void            *driver_data;   /* data private to the driver */
    void            *platform_data; /* Platform-specific data (e.g. ACPI,
                                       BIOS data relevant to device */

    u32             current_state;  /* Current operating state. In
                                       ACPI-speak, this is D0-D3, D0
                                       being fully functional, and D3
                                       being off. */

    unsigned char *saved_state;     /* saved device state */
};
```

Every time this structure was created and registered with the kernel driver core, a new entry in a virtual filesystem was created that showed the device and any different attributes it contained. This allowed all devices in the system to be shown to userspace, in the order in which they were connected. This virtual filesystem is now called *sysfs* and can be seen on a Linux machine in the */sys/devices* directory. An example of this structure showing a few PCI and USB devices follows:

```
$ tree -d /sys/devices/
/sys/devices/pci0000:00/
|-- 0000:00:00.0
|-- 0000:00:02.0
|-- 0000:00:07.0
|-- 0000:00:1b.0
|   |-- card0
|   |   |-- adsp
|   |   |-- audio
|   |   |-- controlC0
|   |   |-- dsp
|   |   |-- mixer
|   |   |-- pcmC0D0c
|   |   |-- pcmC0D0p
|   |   |-- pcmC0D1p
|   |   `-- subsystem -> ../../../../class/sound
|   `-- driver -> ../../../bus/pci/drivers/HDA Intel
|-- 0000:00:1c.0
|   |-- 0000:00:1c.0:pcie00
|   |-- 0000:00:1c.0:pcie02
|   |-- 0000:00:1c.0:pcie03
|   |-- 0000:01:00.0
|   |   `-- driver -> ../../../../bus/pci/drivers/sky2
|   `-- driver -> ../../../../bus/pci/drivers/pcieport-driver
```

```
|-- 0000:00:1d.0
|   |-- driver -> ../../../bus/pci/drivers/uhci_hcd
|   `-- usb2
|       |-- 2-0:1.0
|       |   |-- driver -> ../../../../../bus/usb/drivers/hub
|       |   |-- subsystem -> ../../../../../bus/usb
|       |   `-- usbdev2.1_ep81
|       |-- driver -> ../../../../bus/usb/drivers/usb
|       `-- usbdev2.1_ep00
|-- 0000:00:1d.2
|   |-- driver -> ../../../bus/pci/drivers/uhci_hcd
|   `-- usb4
|       |-- 4-0:1.0
|       |   |-- driver -> ../../../../../bus/usb/drivers/hub
|       |   `-- usbdev4.1_ep81
|       |-- 4-1
|       |   |-- 4-1:1.0
|       |   |   |-- driver -> ../../../../../../bus/usb/drivers/usbhid
|       |   |   `-- usbdev4.2_ep81
|       |   |-- driver -> ../../../../../bus/usb/drivers/usb
|       |   |-- power
|       |   `-- usbdev4.2_ep00
|       |-- 4-2
|       |   |-- 4-2.1
|       |   |   |-- 4-2.1:1.0
|       |   |   |   |-- driver -> ../../../../../../../bus/usb/drivers/usbhid
|       |   |   |   `-- usbdev4.4_ep81
|       |   |   |-- 4-2.1:1.1
|       |   |   |   |-- driver -> ../../../../../../../bus/usb/drivers/usbhid
|       |   |   |   `-- usbdev4.4_ep82
|       |   |   |-- driver -> ../../../../../../bus/usb/drivers/usb
|       |   |   `-- usbdev4.4_ep00
|       |   |-- 4-2.2
|       |   |   |-- 4-2.2:1.0
|       |   |   |   |-- driver -> ../../../../../../../bus/usb/drivers/usblp
|       |   |   |   |-- usbdev4.5_ep01
|       |   |   |   `-- usbdev4.5_ep81
|       |   |   |-- driver -> ../../../../../../bus/usb/drivers/usb
|       |   |   `-- usbdev4.5_ep00
|       |   |-- 4-2:1.0
|       |   |   |-- driver -> ../../../../../../bus/usb/drivers/hub
|       |   |   `-- usbdev4.3_ep81
|       |   |-- driver -> ../../../../../bus/usb/drivers/usb
|       |   `-- usbdev4.3_ep00
|       |-- driver -> ../../../../bus/usb/drivers/usb
|       `-- usbdev4.1_ep00
...
```

To use this structure, it is required that you embed it within another structure, causing the new structure to "inherit," in a sense, from the base structure:

```
struct usb_interface {
        struct usb_interface_descriptor *altsetting;

        int act_altsetting;            /* active alternate setting */
        int num_altsetting;            /* number of alternate settings */
        int max_altsetting;            /* total memory allocated */
```

```
        struct usb_driver *driver;        /* driver */
        struct device dev;                /* interface specific device info */
};
```

The driver core operates by passing around pointers to a struct device, operating on the basic fields that are in that structure and thus are common to all types of devices. When the pointer is handed off to the bus-specific code for various functions, it needs to be converted to the real type of structure that contains it. To handle this conversion, the bus-specific code casts the pointer back to the original structure, based on where it is in memory. This is accomplished by the following fun macro:

```
#define container_of(ptr, type, member) ({                        \
        const typeof( ((type *)0)->member ) *__mptr = (ptr);      \
        (type *)( (char *)__mptr - offsetof(type,member) );})
```

This macro deserves some explanation, for those not up on their pointer arithmetic in the C language. To take an example, the previous struct usb_interface could convert a pointer to the struct device member of the structure back to the original pointer through:

```
int probe(struct device *d) {
        struct usb_interface *intf;

        intf = container_of(d, struct usb_interface, dev);

        ...
}
```

where d is a pointer to a struct device.

Expanding the container_of macro just shown creates the following code:

```
intf = ({
    const typeof( ((struct usb_interface *)0)->dev) *__mptr = d;
    (struct usb_interface *)( (char *)__mptr - offsetof(struct usb_interface, dev));
});
```

To understand this, remember that dev is a member of the struct usb_interface structure. The first line of the macro sets up a pointer that points to the struct device passed to the code. The second line of the macro finds the real location in memory of the struct usb_interface that we want to access.

So, with the type of the dev structure known, the macro can be reduced to:

```
intf = ({
    const struct device *__mptr = d;
    (struct usb_interface *)( (char *)__mptr - offsetof(struct usb_interface, dev));
});
```

Based on the definition of the struct usb_interface recently shown, the dev variable is probably placed 16 bytes into the structure on a 32-bit processor. This is automatically calculated by the compiler with the offsetof macro. Replacing this information in the macro now yields:

```
intf = ({
    const struct device *__mptr = d;
    (struct usb_interface *)( (char *)__mptr - 16));
});
```

The container_of macro has now been reduced to simple pointer arithmetic, subtracting 16 from the original pointer to get to the desired struct usb_interface pointer. The compiler does this quickly at runtime.

With this very simple method, the Linux kernel allows normal C structures to be inherited and manipulated in very powerful ways. Well, very powerful as long as you know exactly what you are doing.

If you notice, there is no runtime type checking to ensure that the pointer that was originally passed as a struct device really was of the struct usb_interface type. Traditionally, most systems that do this kind of pointer manipulation also have a field in the base structure that defines the type of the pointer being manipulated, to catch sloppy programming errors. It also allows for code to be written to dynamically determine the type of the pointer and do different things with it based on the type.

The Linux kernel developers made the decision to do none of this checking or type definition. These types of checks can catch basic programming errors at the initial time of development, but allow programmers to create hacks that can have much more subtle problems later on that can't be easily caught.

The lack of runtime checking forces the developers who are manipulating these pointers to be absolutely sure they know exactly what type of pointer they are manipulating and passing around the system. Sure, at moments, a developer really wishes that there would be some way to determine what type of struct device he is staring at, but the feeling eventually passes when the problem is properly debugged.

Is this lack of type checking good enough to be called "beautiful code"? After working with it for over five years, yes, I think it is. It keeps easy hacks from springing up within the kernel and forces everyone to be very exact in their logic, never falling back on any checks for types that might prevent bugs from happening later.

I should note here that only a relatively small number of developers—those who code up subsystems for common buses—work on these parts of the kernel, and that they are expected to develop considerable expertise; that is why no hand-holding in the form of type-checking is done here.

With this method of inheriting the basic struct device structure, all the different driver subsystems were unified during the 2.5 kernel development process. They now shared the common core code, which allowed the kernel to show users how all devices were interconnected. This enabled the creation of tools such as udev, which does persistent device naming in a small userspace program, and power management tools, which can walk the tree of devices and shut devices down in the proper order.

Reduced to Even Smaller Bits

As the initial driver core rework was happening, another kernel developer, Al Viro, was working on fixing a number of issues regarding object reference counting in the virtual filesystem layer.

The main problem with structures in multithreaded programs written in the C language is that it's very hard to determine when it is safe to free up any memory used by a structure. The Linux kernel is a massively multithreaded program that must properly handle hostile users as well as large numbers of processors all running at the same time. Because of this, reference counting on any structure that can be found by more than one thread is a necessity.

The `struct device` structure was one such reference-counted structure. It had a single field that was used to determine when it was safe to free the structure:

```
atomic_t        refcount;
```

When the structure was initialized, this field was set to 1. Whenever any code wished to use the structure, it had to first increment the reference count by calling the function get_ device, which checked that the reference count was valid and incremented the reference count of the structure:

```
static inline void get_device(struct device * dev)
{
        BUG_ON(!atomic_read(&dev->refcount));
        atomic_inc(&dev->refcount);
}
```

Similarly, when a thread was finished with the structure, it decremented the reference count by calling put_device, which was a bit more complex:

```
void put_device(struct device * dev)
{
        if (!atomic_dec_and_lock(&dev->refcount,&device_lock))
                return;

    ...

        /* Tell the driver to clean up after itself.
         * Note that we likely didn't allocate the device,
         * so this is the driver's chance to free that up...
         */
        if (dev->driver && dev->driver->remove)
                dev->driver->remove(dev,REMOVE_FREE_RESOURCES);
}
```

This function decremented the reference count and then, if it was the last user of the object, would tell the object to clean itself up and call a function that was previously set up to free it from the system.

Al Viro liked the unification of the struct device structure, the virtual filesystem that showed all of the different devices and how they were linked together, and the automatic reference counting. The only problem was that his virtual filesystem core did not work on "devices," nor did it have "drivers" that would attach to these objects. So, he decided to refactor things a bit and make the code simpler.

Al convinced Pat to create something called struct kobject. This structure had the basic properties of the struct device structure, but was smaller and did not have the "driver" and "device" relationship. It contained the following fields:

```
struct kobject {
        char                    name[KOBJ_NAME_LEN];
        atomic_t                refcount;
        struct list_head        entry;
        struct kobject          *parent;
        struct subsystem        *subsys;
        struct dentry           *dentry;
};
```

This structure is a type of empty object. It has only the very basic ability to be reference-counted and to be inserted into a hierarchy of objects. The struct device structure could now include this smaller struct kobject "base" structure to inherit all of its functionality:

```
struct device {
        struct list_head g_list;        /* node in depth-first order list */
        struct list_head node;          /* node in sibling list */
        struct list_head bus_list;      /* node in bus's list */
        struct list_head driver_list;
        struct list_head children;
        struct list_head intf_list;
        struct device   *parent;

        struct kobject kobj;
        char    bus_id[BUS_ID_SIZE];  /* position on parent bus */

    ...
}
```

The container_of macro is used to cast back from the core kobject, to the main struct device:

```
#define to_dev(obj) container_of(obj, struct device, kobj)
```

During this development process, many other people were increasing the robustness of the Linux kernel by allowing it to scale up to larger and larger numbers of processors all running in the same system image.* Because of this, many other developers were adding reference counts to their structures to properly handle their memory usage. Each developer had to duplicate the ability to initialize, increment, decrement, and clean up the

---

* The current record for the number of processors with Linux running in a single system image is 4096 processors, so the scalability work has succeeded.

structure. So it was decided that this simple functionality could be taken from the struct kobject and made into its own structure. Thus was the struct kref structure born:

```
struct kref {
        atomic_t refcount;
};
```

struct kref has only three simple functions: kref_init to initialize the reference count, kref_get to increment the reference count, and kref_put to decrement the reference count. The first two functions are very simple; it is the last one that's a bit interesting:

```
int kref_put(struct kref *kref, void (*release)(struct kref *kref))
{
        WARN_ON(release == NULL);
        WARN_ON(release == (void (*)(struct kref *))kfree);

        if (atomic_dec_and_test(&kref->refcount)) {
                release(kref);
                return 1;
        }
        return 0;
}
```

The kref_put function has two parameters: a pointer to the struct kref whose reference count you wish to decrement, and a pointer to the function that you wish to have called if this was the last reference held on the object.

The first two lines of the function were added a while after the struct kref was added to the kernel, as a number of programmers were trying to get around the reference counting by passing in either no pointer to a release function or, when they realized that the kernel would complain about that, a pointer to the basic kfree function. (Sad to say, but even these two checks are not enough these days. Some programmers have taken to just creating empty release functions that do not do anything, as they are trying to ignore the reference count altogether. Unfortunately, C doesn't have a simple way to determine whether a pointer to a function really does anything within that function; otherwise, that check would be added to kref_put, too.)

After these two checks are made, the reference count is atomically decremented, and if this is the last reference, the release function is called and 1 is returned. If this is not the last reference on the object, 0 is returned. This return value is used just to determine whether the caller was the last holder of the object, not whether the object is still in memory (it can't guarantee that the object still exists because someone else might come in and release it after the call returns).

With the creation of struct kref, the struct kobject structure was changed to use it:

```
struct kobject {
        char                    name[KOBJ_NAME_LEN];
        struct kref             kref;
    ...
};
```

With all of these different structures embedded within other structures, the result is that the original struct usb_interface described earlier now contains a struct device, which contains a struct kobject, which contains a struct kref. And who said it was hard to do object-oriented programming in the C language....

Scaling Up to Thousands of Devices

As Linux runs on everything from cellphones, radio-controlled helicopters, desktops, and servers to 73 percent of the world's largest supercomputers, scaling the driver model was very important and always in the backs of our minds. As development progressed, it was nice to see that the basic structures used to hold devices, struct kobject and struct devices, were relatively small. The number of devices connected to most systems is directly proportional to the size of the system. So small, embedded systems had only a few—one to ten— different devices connected and in their device tree. Larger "enterprise" systems had many more devices connected, but these systems also had a lot of memory to spare, so the increased number of devices was still only a very small proportion of the kernel's overall memory usage.

This comfortable scaling model, unfortunately, was found to be completely false when it came to one class of "enterprise" system, the s390 mainframe computer. This computer could run Linux in a virtual partition (up to 1,024 instances at the same time on a single machine) and had a huge number of different storage devices connected to it. Overall, the system had a lot of memory, but each virtual partition would have only a small slice of that memory. Each virtual partition wanted to see all different storage devices (20,000 could be typical), while only being allocated a few hundred megabytes of RAM.

On these systems, the device tree was quickly found to suck up a huge percentage of memory that was never released back to the user processes. It was time to put the driver model on a diet, and some very smart IBM kernel developers went to work on the problem.

What the developers found was initially surprising. It turned out that the main struct device structure was only around 160 bytes (for a 32-bit processor). With 20,000 devices in the system, that amounted to only 3 to 4 MB of RAM being used, a very manageable usage of memory. The big memory hog was the RAM-based filesystem mentioned earlier, *sysfs*, which showed all of these devices to userspace. For every device, *sysfs* created both a struct inode and a struct dentry. These are both fairly heavy structures, with the struct inode weighing in around 256 bytes and struct dentry about 140 bytes.*

For every struct device, at least one struct dentry and one struct inode were being created. Generally, many different copies of these filesystem structures were created, one for every virtual file per device in the system. As an example, a single block device would create about 10 different virtual files, so that meant that a single structure of 160 bytes would

---

* Both of these structures have since been shrunk, and therefore are smaller in current kernel versions.

end up using 4 KB. In a system of 20,000 devices, about 80 MB were wasted on the virtual filesystem. This memory was consumed by the kernel, unable to be used by any user programs, even if they never wanted to look at the information stored in *sysfs*.

The solution for this was to rewrite the *sysfs* code to put these `struct inode` and `struct dentry` structures in the kernel's caches, creating them on the fly when the filesystem was accessed. The solution was just a matter of dynamically creating the directories and files on the fly as a user walked through the tree, instead of preallocating everything when the device was originally created. Because these structures are in the main caches of the kernel, if memory pressure is placed on the system by userspace programs, or other parts of the kernel, the caches are freed and the memory is returned to those who need it at the time. This was all done by touching the backend *sysfs* code, and not the main `struct device` structures.

Small Objects Loosely Joined

The Linux driver model shows how the C language can be used to create a heavily object-oriented model of code by creating numerous small objects, all doing one thing well. These objects can be embedded in other objects, all without any runtime type identification, creating a very powerful and flexible object tree. And based on the real-world usage of these objects, their memory footprint is minimal, allowing the Linux kernel to be flexible enough to work from the same code base for tiny embedded systems up to the largest supercomputers in the world.

The development of this model also shows two very interesting and powerful aspects of the way Linux kernel development works.

First, the process is very iterative. As the requirements of the kernel change, and the systems on which it runs also change, the developers have found ways to abstract different parts of the model to make it more efficient where it is needed. This is responding to a basic evolutionary need of the system to survive in these environments.

Second, the history of device handling shows that the process is extremely collaborative. Different developers come up independently with ideas for improving and extending different aspects of the kernel. Through the source code, others can then see the goals of the developers exactly as they describe them, and then help change the code in ways the original developers never considered. The end result is something that meets the goals of many different developers by finding a common solution that would not have been seen by any one individual.

These two characteristics of development have helped Linux evolve into the most flexible and powerful operating system ever created. And they ensure that as long as this type of development continues, Linux will remain this way.

CHAPTER SEVENTEEN

Another Level of Indirection

Diomidis Spinellis

ALL PROBLEMS IN COMPUTER SCIENCE CAN BE SOLVED BY ANOTHER LEVEL OF INDIRECTION," is a
famous quote attributed to Butler Lampson, the scientist who in 1972 envisioned the
modern personal computer. The quote rings in my head on various occasions: when I am
forced to talk to a secretary instead of the person I wish to communicate with, when I first
travel east to Frankfurt in order to finally fly west to Shanghai or Bangalore, and—yes—
when I examine a complex system's source code.

Let's start this particular journey by considering the problem of a typical operating system
that supports disparate filesystem formats. An operating system may use data residing on
its native filesystem, a CD-ROM, or a USB stick. These storage devices may, in turn,
employ different filesystem organizations: NTFS or ext3fs for a Windows or Linux native
filesystem, ISO-9660 for the CD-ROM, and, often, the legacy FAT-32 filesystem for the
USB stick. Each filesystem uses different data structures for managing free space, for storing file metadata, and for organizing files into directories. Therefore, each filesystem
requires different code for each operation on a file (open, read, write, seek, close, delete,
and so on).

From Code to Pointers

I grew up in an era where different computers more often than not had incompatible file-systems, forcing me to transfer data from one machine to another over serial links. Therefore, the ability to read on my PC a flash card written on my camera never ceases to amaze me. Let's consider how the operating system would structure the code for accessing the different filesystems. One approach would be to employ a switch statement for each operation. Consider as an example a hypothetical implementation of the read system call under the FreeBSD operating system. Its kernel-side interface would look as follows:

```
int VOP_READ(
        struct vnode *vp,        /* File to read from */
        struct uio *uio,         /* Buffer specification */
        int ioflag,              /* I/O-specific flags */
        struct ucred *cred)      /* User's credentials */
{
    /* Hypothetical implementation */
        switch (vp->filesystem) {
        case FS_NTFS:                    /* NTFS-specific code */
        case FS_ISO9660:                 /* ISO-9660-specific code */
        case FS_FAT32:                   /* FAT-32-specific code */
        /* [...] */
        }
}
```

This approach would bundle together code for the various filesystems, limiting modularity. Worse, adding support for a new filesystem type would require modifying the code of each system call implementation and recompiling the kernel. Moreover, adding a processing step to all the operations of a filesystem (for example, the mapping of remote user credentials) would also require the error-prone modification of each operation with the same boilerplate code.

As you might have guessed, our task at hand calls for some additional levels of indirection. Consider how the FreeBSD operating system—a code base I admire for the maturity of its engineering—solves these problems. Each filesystem defines the operations that it supports as functions and then initializes a vop_vector structure with pointers to them. Here are some fields of the vop_vector structure:

```
struct vop_vector {
        struct vop_vector *vop_default;
        int (*vop_open)(struct vop_open_args *);
        int (*vop_access)(struct vop_access_args *);
```

and here is how the ISO-9660 filesystem initializes the structure:

```
struct vop_vector cd9660_vnodeops = {
        .vop_default =          &default_vnodeops,
        .vop_open =             cd9660_open,
        .vop_access =           cd9660_access,
        .vop_bmap =             cd9660_bmap,
        .vop_cachedlookup =     cd9660_lookup,
        .vop_getattr =          cd9660_getattr,
        .vop_inactive =         cd9660_inactive,
```

```
    .vop_ioctl =            cd9660_ioctl,
    .vop_lookup =           vfs_cache_lookup,
    .vop_pathconf =         cd9660_pathconf,
    .vop_read =             cd9660_read,
    .vop_readdir =          cd9660_readdir,
    .vop_readlink =         cd9660_readlink,
    .vop_reclaim =          cd9660_reclaim,
    .vop_setattr =          cd9660_setattr,
    .vop_strategy =         cd9660_strategy,
};
```

(The .field = value syntax is a nifty C99 feature that allows fields of a structure to be initialized in an arbitrary order and in a readable way.) Note that although the complete vop_vector structure contains 52 fields, only 16 are defined in the preceding code. As an example, the vop_write field is left undefined (getting a value of NULL) because writing to files is not supported on ISO-9660 CD-ROMs. Having initialized one such structure for every filesystem type (see the bottom of Figure 17-1), it is then easy to tie this structure to the administrative data associated with each file handle. Then, in the FreeBSD kernel, the filesystem-independent part of the read system call implementation appears simply as (see Figure 17-1):

```
    struct vop_vector *vop;

    rc = vop->vop_read(a);
```

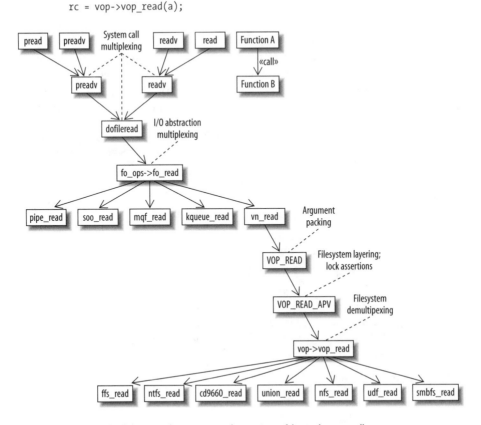

FIGURE 17-1. Layers of indirection in the FreeBSD implementation of the read system call

So, when reading from a CD containing an ISO-9660 filesystem, the previous call through a pointer would actually result in a call to the function cd9660_read; in effect:

```
rc = cd9660_read(a);
```

From Function Arguments to Argument Pointers

Most Unix-related operating systems, such as FreeBSD, Linux, and Solaris, use function pointers to isolate the implementation of a filesystem from the code that accesses its contents. Interestingly, FreeBSD also employs indirection to abstract the read function's arguments.

When I first encountered the call vop->vop_read(a), shown in the previous section, I asked myself what that a argument was and what happened to the original four arguments of the hypothetical implementation of the VOP_READ function we saw earlier. After some digging, I found that the kernel uses another level of indirection to layer filesystems on top of each other to an arbitrary depth. This layering allows a filesystem to offer some services (such as translucent views, compression, and encryption) based on the services of another underlying filesystem. Two mechanisms work cleverly together to support this feature: one allows a single bypass function to modify the arguments of any vop_vector function, while another allows all undefined vop_vector functions to be redirected to the underlying filesystem layer.

You can see both mechanisms in action in Figure 17-2. The figure illustrates three filesystems layered on top of one another. On top lies the *umapfs* filesystem, which the system administrator mounted in order to map user credentials. This is valuable if the system where this particular disk was created used different user IDs. For instance, the administrator might want user ID 1013 on the underlying filesystem to appear as user ID 5325.

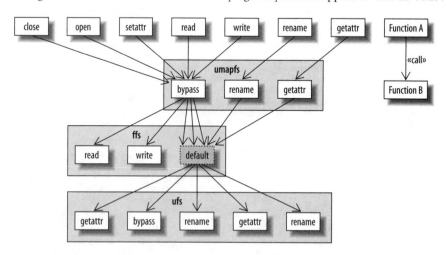

FIGURE 17-2. Example of filesystem layering

Beneath the top filesystem lies the Berkeley Fast Filesystem (*ffs*), the time- and space-efficient filesystem used by default in typical FreeBSD installations. The *ffs* in turn, for most of its operations, relies on the code of the original 4.2 BSD filesystem implementation *ufs*.

In the example shown in the figure, most system calls pass through a common bypass function in *umapfs* that maps the user credentials. Only a few system calls, such as rename and getattr, have their own implementations in *umapfs*. The *ffs* layer provides optimized implementations of read and write; both rely on a filesystem layout that is more efficient than the one employed by *ufs*. Most other operations, such as open, close, getattr, setatr, and rename, are handled in the traditional way. Thus, a vop_default entry in the *ffs* vop_vector structure directs all those functions to call the underlying *ufs* implementations. For example, a read system call will pass through umapfs_bypass and ffs_read, whereas a rename call will pass through umapfs_rename and ufs_rename.

Both mechanisms, the bypass and the default, pack the four arguments into a single structure to provide commonality between the different filesystem functions, and also support the groundwork for the bypass function. This is a beautiful design pattern that is easily overlooked within the intricacies of the C code required to implement it.

The four arguments are packed into a single structure, which as its first field (a_gen.a_desc) contains a description of the structure's contents (vop_read_desc, in the following code). As you can see in Figure 17-1, a read system call on a file in the FreeBSD kernel will trigger a call to vn_read, which will set up the appropriate low-level arguments and call VOP_READ. This will pack the arguments and call VOP_READ_APV, which finally calls vop->vop_read and thereby the actual filesystem read function:

```
struct vop_read_args {
        struct vop_generic_args a_gen;
        struct vnode *a_vp;
        struct uio *a_uio;
        int a_ioflag;
        struct ucred *a_cred;
};

static __inline int VOP_READ(
        struct vnode *vp,
        struct uio *uio,
        int ioflag,
        struct ucred *cred)
{
        struct vop_read_args a;

        a.a_gen.a_desc = &vop_read_desc;
        a.a_vp = vp;
        a.a_uio = uio;
        a.a_ioflag = ioflag;
        a.a_cred = cred;
        return (VOP_READ_APV(vp->v_op, &a));
}
```

This same elaborate dance is performed for calling all other vop_vector functions (stat, write, open, close, and so on). The vop_vector structure also contains a pointer to a bypass function. This function gets the packed arguments and, after possibly performing some modifications on them (such as, perhaps, mapping user credentials from one administrative domain to another) passes control to the appropriate underlying function for the specific call through the a_desc field.

Here is an excerpt of how the *nullfs* filesystem implements the bypass function. The *nullfs* filesystem just duplicates a part of an existing filesystem into another location of the global filesystem namespace. Therefore, for most of its operations, it can simply have its bypass function call the corresponding function of the underlying filesystem:

```
#define VCALL(c) ((c)->a_desc->vdesc_call(c))
int
null_bypass(struct vop_generic_args *ap)
{
    /* ... */
        error = VCALL(ap);
```

In the preceding code, the macro VCALL(ap) will bump the *vnode* operation that called null_bypass (for instance VOP_READ_APV) one filesystem level down. You can see this trick in action in Figure 17-3.

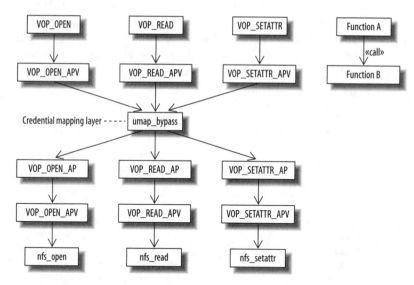

FIGURE 17-3. *Routing system calls through a bypass function*

In addition, the vop_vector contains a field named default that is a pointer to the vop_vector structure of the underlying filesystem layer. Through that field, if a filesystem doesn't implement some functionality, the request is passed on to a lower level. By populating the bypass and the default fields of its vop_vector structure, a filesystem can choose among:

- Handling an incoming request on its own

- Bypassing the request to a lower-level filesystem after modifying some arguments

- Directly calling the lower-level filesystem

In my mind, I visualize this as bits sliding down the ramps, kickers, and spinners of an elaborate pinball machine. The following example from the read system call implementation shows how the system locates the function to call:

```
int
VOP_READ_APV(struct vop_vector *vop, struct vop_read_args *a)
{
    [...]
      /*
 * Drill down the filesystem layers to find one
 * that implements the function or a bypass
 */
while (vop != NULL &&
          vop->vop_read == NULL && vop->vop_bypass == NULL)
              vop = vop->vop_default;
      /* Call the function or the bypass */
        if (vop->vop_read != NULL)
              rc = vop->vop_read(a);
        else
              rc = vop->vop_bypass(&a->a_gen);
```

Elegantly, at the bottom of all filesystem layers lies a filesystem that returns the Unix "operation not supported" error (EOPNOTSUPP) for any function that wasn't implemented by the filesystems layered on top of it. This is our pinball's drain:

```
#define VOP_EOPNOTSUPP  ((void*)(uintptr_t)vop_eopnotsupp)

struct vop_vector default_vnodeops = {
        .vop_default =          NULL,
        .vop_bypass =           VOP_EOPNOTSUPP,
}

int
vop_eopnotsupp(struct vop_generic_args *ap)
{
        return (EOPNOTSUPP);
}
```

From Filesystems to Filesystem Layers

For a concrete example of filesystem layering, consider the case where you mount on your computer a remote filesystem using the NFS (Network File System) protocol. Unfortunately, in your case, the user and group identifiers on the remote system don't match those used on your computer. However, by interposing a *umapfs* filesystem over the actual NFS implementation, we can specify through external files the correct user and group mappings. Figure 17-3 illustrates how some operating system kernel function calls first get routed through the bypass function of *umapfs*—umap_bypass—before continuing their journey to the corresponding NFS client functions.

In contrast to the null_bypass function, the implementation of umap_bypass actually does some work before making a call to the underlying layer. The vop_generic_args structure passed as its argument contains a description of the actual arguments for each *vnode* operation:

```
/*
 * A generic structure.
 * This can be used by bypass routines to identify generic arguments.
 */
struct vop_generic_args {
        struct vnodeop_desc *a_desc;
        /* other random data follows, presumably */
};

/*
 * This structure describes the vnode operation taking place.
 */
struct vnodeop_desc {
        char    *vdesc_name;          /* a readable name for debugging */
        int     vdesc_flags;          /* VDESC_* flags */
        vop_bypass_t   *vdesc_call;   /* Function to call */

        /*
         * These ops are used by bypass routines to map and locate arguments.
         * Creds and procs are not needed in bypass routines, but sometimes
         * they are useful to (for example) transport layers.
         * Nameidata is useful because it has a cred in it.
         */
        int     *vdesc_vp_offsets;    /* list ended by VDESC_NO_OFFSET */
        int     vdesc_vpp_offset;     /* return vpp location */
        int     vdesc_cred_offset;    /* cred location, if any */
        int     vdesc_thread_offset;  /* thread location, if any */
        int     vdesc_componentname_offset; /* if any */
};
```

For instance, the vnodeop_desc structure for the arguments passed to the vop_read operation is the following:

```
struct vnodeop_desc vop_read_desc = {
        "vop_read",
        0,
        (vop_bypass_t *)VOP_READ_AP,
        vop_read_vp_offsets,
        VDESC_NO_OFFSET,
        VOPARG_OFFSETOF(struct vop_read_args,a_cred),
        VDESC_NO_OFFSET,
        VDESC_NO_OFFSET,
};
```

Importantly, apart from the name of the function (used for debugging purposes) and the underlying function to call (VOP_READ_AP), the structure contains in its vdesc_cred_offset field the location of the user credential data field (a_cred) within the read call's arguments. By using this field, umap_bypass can map the credentials of *any* vnode operation with the following code:

```
if (descp->vdesc_cred_offset != VDESC_NO_OFFSET) {
        credpp = VOPARG_OFFSETTO(struct ucred**,
            descp->vdesc_cred_offset, ap);
        /* Save old values */
        savecredp = (*credpp);
        if (savecredp != NOCRED)
                (*credpp) = crdup(savecredp);
        credp = *credpp;
        /* Map all ids in the credential structure. */
        umap_mapids(vp1->v_mount, credp);
}
```

What we have here is a case of data describing the format of other data: a redirection in terms of data abstraction. This *metadata* allows the credential mapping code to manipulate the arguments of arbitrary system calls.

From Code to a Domain-Specific Language

You may have noticed that some of the code associated with the implementation of the read system call, such as the packing of its arguments into a structure or the logic for calling the appropriate function, is highly stylized and is probably repeated in similar forms for all 52 other interfaces. Another implementation detail, which we have not so far discussed and which can keep me awake at nights, concerns locking.

Operating systems must ensure that various processes running concurrently don't step on each other's toes when they modify data without coordination between them. On modern multithreaded, multi-core processors, ensuring data consistency by maintaining one mutual exclusion lock for all critical operating system structures (as was the case in older operating system implementations) would result in an intolerable drain on performance. Therefore, locks are nowadays held over fine-grained objects, such as a user's credentials or a single buffer. Furthermore, because obtaining and releasing locks can be expensive operations, ideally once a lock is held it should not be released if it will be needed again in short order. These locking specifications can best be described through preconditions (what the state of a lock must be before entering a function) and postconditions (the state of the lock at a function's exit).

As you can imagine, programming under those constraints and verifying the code's correctness can be hellishly complicated. Fortunately for me, another level of indirection can be used to bring some sanity into the picture. This indirection handles both the redundancy of packing code and the fragile locking requirements.

In the FreeBSD kernel, the interface functions and data structures we've examined, such as VOP_READ_AP, VOP_READ_APV, and vop_read_desc, aren't directly written in C. Instead, a domain-specific language is used to specify the types of each call's arguments and their locking pre- and postconditions. Such an implementation style always raises my pulse, because the productivity boost it gives can be enormous. Here is an excerpt from the read system call specification:

```
#
#% read           vp      L L L
#
vop_read {
        IN struct vnode *vp;
        INOUT struct uio *uio;
        IN int ioflag;
        IN struct ucred *cred;
};
```

From specifications such as the above, an *awk* script creates:

- C code for packing the arguments of the functions into a single structure

- Declarations for the structures holding the packed arguments and the functions doing the work

- Initialized data specifying the contents of the packed argument structures

- The boilerplate C code we saw used for implementing filesystem layers

- Assertions for verifying the state of the locks when the function enters and exits

In the FreeBSD version 6.1 implementation of the *vnode* call interface, all in all, 588 lines of domain-specific code expand into 4,339 lines of C code and declarations.

Such compilation from a specialized high-level domain-specific language into C is quite common in the computing field. For example, the input to the lexical analyzer generator *lex* is a file that maps regular expressions into actions; the input to the parser generator *yacc* is a language's grammar and corresponding production rules. Both systems (and their descendants *flex* and *bison*) generate C code implementing the high-level specifications. A more extreme case involves the early implementations of the C++ programming language. These consisted of a preprocessor, *cfront*, that would compile C++ code into C.

In all these cases, C is used as a portable assembly language. When used appropriately, domain-specific languages increase the code's expressiveness and thereby programmer productivity. On the other hand, a gratuitously used obscure domain-specific language can make a system more difficult to comprehend, debug, and maintain.

The handling of locking assertions deserves more explanation. For each argument, the code lists the state of its lock for three instances: when the function is entered, when the function exits successfully, and when the function exits with an error—an elegantly clear separation of concerns. For example, the preceding specification of the read call indicated that the vp argument should be locked in all three cases. More complex scenarios are also possible. The following code excerpt indicates that the rename call arguments fdvp and fvp are always unlocked, but the argument tdvp has a process-exclusive lock when the routine is called. All arguments should be unlocked when the function terminates:

```
#
#% rename        fdvp    U U U
#% rename        fvp     U U U
#% rename        tdvp    E U U
#
```

The locking specification is used to instrument the C code with assertions at the function's entry, the function's normal exit, and the function's error exit. For example, the code at the entry point of the rename function contains the following assertions:

```
ASSERT_VOP_UNLOCKED(a->a_fdvp, "VOP_RENAME");
ASSERT_VOP_UNLOCKED(a->a_fvp, "VOP_RENAME");
ASSERT_VOP_ELOCKED(a->a_tdvp, "VOP_RENAME");
```

Although assertions, such as the preceding one, don't guarantee that the code will be bug-free, they do at least provide an early-fail indication that will diagnose errors during system testing, before they destabilize the system in a way that hinders debugging. When I read complex code that lacks assertions, it's like watching acrobats performing without a net: an impressive act where a small mistake can result in considerable grief.

Multiplexing and Demultiplexing

As you can see back in Figure 17-1, the processing of the read system call doesn't start from VOP_READ. VOP_READ is actually called from vn_read, which itself is called through a function pointer.

This level of indirection is used for another purpose. The Unix operating system and its derivatives treat all input and output sources uniformly. Thus, instead of having separate system calls for reading from, say, a file, a socket, or a pipe, the read system call can read from any of those I/O abstractions. I find this design both elegant and useful; I've often relied on it, using tools in ways their makers couldn't have anticipated. (This statement says more about the age of the tools I use than my creativity.)

The indirection appearing in the middle of Figure 17-1 is the mechanism FreeBSD uses for providing this high-level I/O abstraction independence. Associated with each file descriptor is a function pointer leading to the code that will service the particular request: pipe_read for pipes, soo_read for sockets, mqf_read for POSIX message queues, kqueue_read for kernel event queues, and, finally, vn_read for actual files.

So far, in our example, we have encountered two instances where function pointers are used to dispatch a request to different functions. Typically, in such cases, a function pointer is used to demultiplex a single request to multiple potential providers. This use of indirection is so common that it forms an important element of object-oriented languages, in the form of dynamic dispatch to various subclass methods. To me, the manual implementation of dynamic dispatch in a procedural language like C is a distinguishing mark of an expert programmer. (Another is the ability to write a structured program in assembly language or Fortran.)

Indirection is also often introduced as a way to factor common functionality. Have a look at the top of Figure 17-1. Modern Unix systems have four variants of the vanilla read system call. The system call variants starting with p (pread, preadv) allow the specification of a file position together with the call. The variants ending with a v (readv, preadv) allow the specification of a vector of I/O requests instead of a single one. Although I consider this proliferation of system calls inelegant and against the spirit of Unix, applications programmers seem to depend on them for squeezing every bit of performance out of the Web or database servers they implement.

All these calls share some common code. The FreeBSD implementation introduces indirection through additional functions in order to avoid code duplication. The function kern_preadv handles the common parts of the positional system call variants, while kern_readv handles the remaining two system calls. The functionality common in all four is handled by another function, dofileread. In my mind, I can picture the joy developers got from factoring out the code common to those functions by introducing more levels of indirection. I always feel elated if, after committing a refactoring change, the lines I add are less than the lines I remove.

The journey from our call to a read function in our user-level program to the movement of a disk head to fetch our data from a platter is a long and tortuous one. In our description, we haven't considered what happens above the kernel layer (virtual machines, buffering, data representation), or what happens when a filesystem handles a request (buffering again, device drivers, data representation). Interestingly, there's a pleasant symmetry between the two ends we haven't covered: both involve hardware interfaces (virtual machines, such as the JVM at the top, and real interfaces at the bottom), buffering (to minimize system calls at the top, and to optimize the hardware's performance at the bottom), and data representation (to interact with the user's locale at the top, and to match the physical layer's requirements at the bottom). It seems that indirection is everywhere we care to cast our eyes. In the representative chunk we've looked at, nine levels of function calls, two indirections through function pointers, and a domain-specific language provided us with a representative view of its power.

Layers Forever?

We could continue looking at more code examples forever, so it is worth bringing our discussion to an end by noting that Lampson attributes the aphorism that started our exploration (all problems in computer science can be solved by another level of indirection) to David Wheeler, the inventor of the subroutine. Significantly, Wheeler completed his quote with another phrase: "But that usually will create another problem." Indeed, indirection and layering add space and time overhead, and can obstruct the code's comprehensibility.

The time and space overhead is often unimportant, and should rarely concern us. In most cases, the delays introduced by an extra pointer lookup or subroutine call are insignificant in the greater scheme of things. In fact, nowadays the tendency in modern programming languages is for some operations to always happen through a level of indirection in order to provide an additional measure of flexibility. Thus, for example, in Java and C#, almost all accesses to objects go through one pointer indirection, to allow for automatic garbage collection. Also, in Java, almost all calls to instance methods are dispatched through a lookup table, in order to allow inheriting classes to override a method at runtime.

Despite these overheads that burden all object accesses and method calls, both platforms are doing fine in the marketplace, thank you very much. In other cases, compilers optimize away the indirection we developers put in our code. Thus, most compilers detect cases where calling a function is more expensive than substituting its code inline, and automatically perform this inlining.

Then again, when we're operating at the edge of performance, indirection can be a burden. One trick that developers trying to feed gigabit network interfaces use to speed up their code is to combine functionality of different levels of the network stack, collapsing some layers of abstraction. But these are extreme cases.

On the other hand, the effect that indirection has on the comprehensibility of our code is a very important concern, because over the last 50 years, in contrast to the dizzying increases in CPU speeds, the ability of humans to understand code hasn't improved much. Therefore, the proponents of agile processes advise us to be especially wary when introducing layering to handle some vague, unspecified requirements we imagine might crop up in the future rather than today's concrete needs. As Bart Smaalders quipped when discussing performance anti-patterns: "Layers are for cakes, not for software."

## CHAPTER EIGHTEEN

Python's Dictionary Implementation: Being All Things to All People

Andrew Kuchling

DICTIONARIES ARE A FUNDAMENTAL DATA TYPE IN THE PYTHON PROGRAMMING LANGUAGE. Like *awk's* associative arrays and Perl's hashes, dictionaries store a mapping of unique keys to values. Basic operations on a dictionary include:

- Adding a new key/value pair

- Retrieving the value corresponding to a particular key

- Removing existing pairs

- Looping over the keys, values, or key/value pairs

Here's a brief example of using a dictionary at the Python interpreter prompt. (To try out this example, you can just run the *python* command on Mac OS and most Linux distributions. If Python isn't already installed, you can download it from *http://www.python.org*.)

In the following interactive session, the >>> signs represent the Python interpreter's prompts, and d is the name of the dictionary I'm playing with:

```
>>> d = {1: 'January', 2: 'February',
...    'jan': 1, 'feb': 2, 'mar': 3}
```

```
{'jan': 1, 1: 'January', 2: 'February', 'mar': 3, 'feb': 2}
>>> d['jan'], d[1]
(1, 'January')
>>> d[12]
Traceback (most recent call last):
  File "<stdin>", line 1, in <module>
KeyError: 12
>>> del d[2]
>>> for k, v in d.items(): print k,v      # Looping over all pairs.
jan 1
1 January
mar 3
feb 2
...
```

Two things to note about Python's dictionary type are:

- A single dictionary can contain keys and values of several different data types. It's legal to store the keys 1, 3+4j (a complex number), and "abc" (a string) in the same dictionary. Values retain their type; they aren't all converted to strings.

- Keys are not ordered. Methods such as .values( ) that return the entire contents of a dictionary will return the data in some arbitrary arrangement, not ordered by value or by insertion time.

It's important that retrieval of keys be a very fast operation, so dictionary-like types are usually implemented as hash tables. For the C implementation of Python (henceforth referred to as CPython), dictionaries are even more pivotal because they underpin several other language features. For example, classes and class instances use a dictionary to store their attributes:

```
>>> obj = MyClass()           # Create a class instance
>>> obj.name = 'object'       # Add a .name attribute
>>> obj.id = 14               # Add a .id attribute
>>> obj.__dict__              # Retrieve the underlying dictionary
{'name': 'object', 'id': 14}
>>> obj.__dict__['id'] = 12   # Store a new value in the dictionary
>>> obj.id                    # Attribute is changed accordingly
12
```

Module contents are also represented as a dictionary, most notably the __builtin__ module that contains built-in identifiers such as int and open. Any expression that uses such built-ins will therefore result in a few dictionary lookups. Another use of dictionaries is to pass keyword arguments to a function, so a dictionary could potentially be created and destroyed on every function call. This internal use of the dictionary type means that any running Python program has many dictionaries active at the same time, even if the user's program code doesn't explicitly use a dictionary. It's therefore important that dictionaries can be created and destroyed quickly and not use an overly large amount of memory.

The implementation of dictionaries in Python teaches several lessons about performance-critical code. First, one has to trade off the advantages of an optimization against the overhead it adds in space or calculation time. There were places where the Python developers found that a relatively naïve implementation was better in the long run than an extra optimization that seemed more appealing at first. In short, it often pays to keep things simple.

Second, real-life benchmarking is critical; only that way can you discover what's really worth doing.

Inside the Dictionary

Dictionaries are represented by a C structure, PyDictObject, defined in *Include/dictobject.h*. Here's a schematic of the structure representing a small dictionary mapping "aa", "bb", "cc", ..., "mm" to the integers 1 to 13:

```
int ma_fill        13
int ma_used        13
int ma_mask        31

PyDictEntry ma_table[]:
[0]: aa, 1          hash(aa) == -1549758592, -1549758592 & 31 = 0
[1]: ii, 9          hash(ii) == -1500461680, -1500461680 & 31 = 16
[2]: null, null
[3]: null, null
[4]: null, null
[5]: jj, 10         hash(jj) == 653184214, 653184214 & 31 = 22
[6]: bb, 2          hash(bb) == 603887302, 603887302 & 31 = 6
[7]: null, null
[8]: cc, 3          hash(cc) == -1537434360, -1537434360 & 31 = 8
[9]: null, null
[10]: dd, 4         hash(dd) == 616211530, 616211530 & 31 = 10
[11]: null, null
[12]: null, null
[13]: null, null
[14]: null, null
[15]: null, null
[16]: gg, 7         hash(gg) == -1512785904, -1512785904 & 31 = 16
[17]: ee, 5         hash(ee) == -1525110136, -1525110136 & 31 = 8
[18]: hh, 8         hash(hh) == 640859986, 640859986 & 31 = 18
[19]: null, null
[20]: null, null
[21]: kk, 11        hash(kk) == -1488137240, -1488137240 & 31 = 8
[22]: ff, 6         hash(ff) == 628535766, 628535766 & 31 = 22
[23]: null, null
[24]: null, null
[25]: null, null
[26]: null, null
[27]: null, null
[28]: null, null
[29]: ll, 12        hash(ll) == 665508394, 665508394 & 31 = 10
[30]: mm, 13        hash(mm) == -1475813016, -1475813016 & 31 = 8
[31]: null, null
```

The `ma_` prefix in the field names comes from the word *mapping*, Python's term for data types that provide key/value lookups. The fields in the structure are:

`ma_used`

Number of slots occupied by keys (in this case, 13).

`ma_fill`

Number of slots occupied by keys or by dummy entries (also 13).

`ma_mask`

Bitmask representing the size of the hash table. The hash table contains `ma_mask+1` slots—in this case, 32. The number of slots in the table is always a power of 2, so this value is always of the form 2^n-1 for some *n*, and therefore consists of *n* set bits.

`ma_table`

Pointer to an array of `PyDictEntry` structures. `PyDictEntry` contains pointers to:

- The key object
- The value object
- A cached copy of the key's hash code

The hash value is cached for the sake of speed. When searching for a key, the exact hash values can be quickly compared before performing a slower, full equality comparison of the keys. Resizing a dictionary also requires the hash value for each key, so caching the value saves having to rehash all the keys when resizing.

We don't keep track directly of the number of slots in the table, but derive it instead as needed from `ma_mask`. When looking up the entry for a key, `slot = hash & mask` is used to figure out the initial slot for a particular hash value. For instance, the hash function for the first entry generated a hash of –1549758592, and –1549758592 mod 31 is 0, so the entry is stored in slot 0.

Because the mask is needed so often, we store it instead of the number of slots. It's easy to calculate the number of slots by adding 1, and we never need to do so in the most speed-critical sections of code.

`ma_fill` and `ma_used` are updated as objects are added and deleted. `ma_used` is the number of keys present in the dictionary; adding a new key increases it by 1, and deleting a key decreases it by 1. To delete a key, we make the appropriate slot point to a dummy key; `ma_fill` therefore remains the same when a key is deleted, but may increase by 1 when a new key is added. (`ma_fill` is never decremented, but will be given a new value when a dictionary is resized.)

Special Accommodations

When trying to be all things to all people—a time- and memory-efficient data type for Python users, an internal data structure used as part of the interpreter's implementation, and a readable and maintainable code base for Python's developers—it's necessary to complicate a pure, theoretically elegant implementation with special-case code for particular cases…but not too much.

A Special-Case Optimization for Small Hashes

The PyDictObject also contains space for an eight-slot hash table. Small dictionaries with five elements or fewer can be stored in this table, saving the time cost of an extra malloc( ) call. This also improves cache locality; for example, PyDictObject structures occupy 124 bytes of space when using x86 GCC and therefore can fit into two 64-byte cache lines. The dictionaries used for keyword arguments most commonly have one to three keys, so this optimization helps improve function-call performance.

When Special-Casing Is Worth the Overhead

As previously explained, a single dictionary can contain keys of several different data types. In most Python programs, the dictionaries underlying class instances and modules have only strings as keys. It's natural to wonder whether a specialized dictionary object that only accepted strings as keys might provide benefits. Perhaps a special-case data type would be useful and make the interpreter run faster?

The Java implementation: another special-case optimization

In fact, there *is* a string-specialized dictionary type in Jython (*http://www.jython.org*), an implementation of Python in Java. Jython has an org.python.org.PyStringMap class used only for dictionaries in which all keys are strings; it is used for the __dict__ dictionary underpinning class instances and modules. Jython code that creates a dictionary for user code employs a different class, org.python.core.PyDictionary, a heavyweight object that uses a java.util.Hashtable to store its contents and does extra indirection to allow PyDictionary to be subclassed.

Python's language definition doesn't allow users to replace the internal __dict__ dictionaries by a different data type, making the overhead of supporting subclassing unnecessary. For Jython, having a specialized string-only dictionary type makes sense.

The C implementation: selecting the storage function dynamically

CPython does *not* have a specialized dictionary type, as Jython does. Instead, it employs a different trick: an individual dictionary uses a string-only function until a search for non-string data is requested, and then a more general function is used. The implementation is simple. PyDictObject contains one field, ma_lookup, that's a pointer to the function used to look up keys:

```
struct PyDictObject {
    ...
    PyDictEntry *(*ma_lookup)(PyDictObject *mp, PyObject *key, long hash);
};
```

PyObject is the C structure that represents any Python data object, containing basic fields such as a reference count and a pointer to a type object. Specific types such as PyIntObject and PyStringObject extend the structure with additional fields as necessary. The dictionary implementation calls (dict->ma_lookup)(dict, key, hash) to find a key; key is a pointer to the PyObject representing the key, and hash is the hash value derived for the key.

ma_lookup is initially set to lookdict_string, a function that assumes that both the keys in the dictionary and the key being searched for are strings represented as Python's standard PyStringObject type. lookdict_string can therefore take a few shortcuts. One shortcut is that string-to-string comparisons never raise exceptions, so some unnecessary error checking can be skipped. Another is that there's no need to check for rich comparisons on the object; arbitrary Python data types can provide their own separate versions of <, >, <=, >=, ==, and !=, but the standard string type has no such special cases.

If a nonstring key is encountered, either because it's used as a dictionary key or the program makes an attempt to search for it, the ma_lookup field is changed to point to the more general lookdict function. lookdict_string checks the type of its input and changes ma_lookup if necessary, then calls the chosen function to obtain a correct answer. (CPython trivia: this means that a dictionary with only string keys will become slightly slower if you issue d.get(1), even though the search can't possibly succeed. All subsequent code in the program that refers to the dictionary will also go through the more general function and incur a slight slowdown.) Subclasses of PyStringObject have to be treated as nonstrings because the subclass might define a new equality test.

Collisions

For any hash table implementation, an important decision is what to do when two keys hash to the same slot. One approach is *chaining* (see *http://en.wikipedia.org/wiki/Hash_table#Chaining*): each slot is the head of a linked list containing all the items that hash to that slot. Python doesn't take this approach because creating linked lists would require allocating memory for each list item, and memory allocations are relatively slow operations. Following all the linked-list pointers would also probably reduce cache locality.

The alternative approach is *open addressing* (see *http://en.wikipedia.org/wiki/Hash_table#Open_addressing*): if the first slot i that is tried doesn't contain the key, other slots are tried in a fixed pattern. The simplest pattern is called *linear probing*: if slot i is full, try i+1, i+2, i+3, and so on, wrapping around to slot 0 when the end of the table is reached. Linear probing would be wasteful in Python because many programs use consecutive integers as keys, resulting in blocks of filled slots. Linear probing would frequently scan these blocks, resulting in poor performance. Instead, Python uses a more complicated pattern:

```
/* Starting slot */
slot = hash;

/* Initial perturbation value */
perturb = hash;
```

```
while (<slot is full> && <item in slot doesn't equal the key>) {
    slot = (5*slot) + 1 + perturb;
    perturb >>= 5;
}
```

In the C code, 5*slot is written using bit shifts and addition as (slot << 2) + slot. The perturbation factor perturb starts out as the full hash code; its bits are then progressively shifted downward 5 bits at a time. This shift ensures that every bit in the hash code will affect the probed slot index fairly quickly. Eventually the perturbation factor becomes zero, and the pattern becomes simply slot = (5*slot) + 1. This eventually generates every integer between 0 and ma_mask, so the search is guaranteed to eventually find either the key (on a search operation) or an empty slot (on an insert operation).

The shift value of 5 bits was chosen by experiment; 5 bits minimized collisions slightly better than 4 or 6 bits, though the difference wasn't significant. Earlier versions of this code used more complicated operations such as multiplication or division, but though these versions had excellent collision statistics, the calculation ran slightly more slowly. (The extensive comments in *Objects/dictobject.c* discuss the history of this optimization in more detail.)

Resizing

The size of a dictionary's hash table needs to be adjusted as keys are added. The code aims to keep the table two-thirds full; if a dictionary is holding *n* keys, the table must have at least $n/(2/3)$ slots. This ratio is a trade-off: filling the table more densely results in more collisions when searching for a key, but uses less memory and therefore fits into cache better. Experiments have been tried where the 2/3 ratio is adjusted depending on the size of the dictionary, but they've shown poor results; every insert operation has to check whether the dictionary needed to be resized, and the complexity that the check adds to the insert operation slows things down.

Determining the New Table Size

When a dictionary needs to be resized, how should the new size be determined? For small- or medium-size dictionaries with 50,000 keys or fewer, the new size is ma_used * 4. Most Python programs that work with large dictionaries build up the dictionary in an initial phase of processing, and then look up individual keys or loop over the entire contents. Quadrupling the dictionary size like this keeps the dictionary sparse (the fill ratio starts out at 1/4) and reduces the number of resize operations performed during the build phase. Large dictionaries with more than 50,000 keys use ma_used * 2 to avoid consuming too much memory for empty slots.

On deleting a key from a dictionary, the slot occupied by the key is changed to point to a dummy key, and the ma_used count is updated, but the number of full slots in the table isn't checked. This means dictionaries are never resized on deletion. If you build a large dictionary and then delete many keys from it, the dictionary's hash table may be larger than if you'd constructed the smaller dictionary directly. This usage pattern is quite infrequent, though. Keys are almost never deleted from the many small dictionaries used for objects and for passing function arguments. Many Python programs will build a dictionary, work with it for a while, and then discard the whole dictionary. Therefore, very few Python programs will encounter high memory usage because of the no-resize-on-deletion policy.

A Memory Trade-Off That's Worth It: The Free List

Many dictionary instances are used by Python itself to hold the keyword arguments in function calls. These are therefore created very frequently and have a very short lifetime, being destroyed when the function returns. An effective optimization when facing a high creation rate and short lifetime is to recycle unused data structures, reducing the number of malloc( ) and free( ) calls.

Python therefore maintains a free_dicts array of dictionary structures no longer in use. In Python 2.5, this array is 80 elements long. When a new PyDictObject is required, a pointer is taken from free_dicts and the structure is reused. Dictionaries are added to the array when deletion is requested; if free_dicts is full, the structure is simply freed.

Iterations and Dynamic Changes

A common use case is looping through the contents of a dictionary. The keys( ), values( ), and items( ) methods return lists containing all of the keys, values, or key/value pairs in the dictionary. To conserve memory, the user can call the iterkeys( ), itervalues( ), and iteritems( ) methods instead; they return an iterator object that returns elements one by one. But when these iterators are used, Python has to forbid any statement that adds or deletes an entry in the dictionary during the loop.

This restriction turns out to be fairly easy to enforce. The iterator records the number of items in the dictionary when an iter*( ) method is first called. If the size changes, the iterator raises a RuntimeError exception with the message dictionary changed size during iteration.

One special case that modifies a dictionary while looping over it is code that assigns a new value for the same key:

```
for k, v in d.iteritems( ):
    d[k] = d[k] + 1
```

It's convenient to avoid raising a RuntimeError exception during such operations. Therefore, the C function that handles dictionary insertion, PyDict_SetItem( ), guarantees not to resize the dictionary if it inserts a key that's already present. The lookdict( ) and lookdict_string search functions support this feature by the way they report failure (not finding the searched-for key): on failure, they return a pointer to the empty slot where the searched-for key would have been stored. This makes it easy for PyDict_SetItem to store the new value in the returned slot, which is either an empty slot or a slot known to be occupied by the same key. When the new value is recorded in a slot already occupied by the same key, as in d[k] = d[k] + 1, the dictionary's size isn't checked for a possible resize operation, and the RuntimeError is avoided. Code such as the previous example therefore runs without an exception.

Conclusion

Despite the many features and options presented by Python dictionaries, and their widespread use internally, the CPython implementation is still mostly straightforward. The optimizations that have been done are largely algorithmic, and their effects on collision rates and on benchmarks have been tested experimentally where possible. To learn more about the dictionary implementation, the source code is your best guide. First, read the *Objects/dictnotes.txt* file at *http://svn.python.org/view/python/trunk/Objects/dictnotes.txt?view= markup* for a discussion of the common use cases for dictionaries and of various possible optimizations. (Not all the approaches described in the file are used in the current code.) Next, read the *Objects/dictobject.c* source file at *http://svn.python.org/view/python/trunk/Objects/ dictobject.c?view=markup*.

You can get a good understanding of the issues by reading the comments and taking an occasional clarifying glance at the code.

Acknowledgments

Thanks to Raymond Hettinger for his comments on this chapter. Any errors are my own.

## CHAPTER NINETEEN

Multidimensional Iterators in NumPy

Travis E. Oliphant

NUMPY IS AN OPTIONAL PACKAGE FOR THE PYTHON LANGUAGE that provides a powerful N-dimensional array object. An *N*-dimensional array is a data structure that uses *N* integers, or indices, to access individual elements. It is a useful model for a wide variety of data processed by a computer.

For example, a one-dimensional array can store the samples of a sound wave, a two-dimensional array can store a grayscale image, a three-dimensional array can store a color image (with one of the dimensions having a length of 3 or 4), and a four-dimensional array can store the value of pressure in a room during a concert. Even higher-dimensional arrays are often useful.

NumPy provides an environment for the mathematical and structural manipulation of arrays of arbitrary dimensions. These manipulations are at the heart of much scientific, engineering, and multimedia code that routinely deals with large amounts of data. Being able to perform these mathematical and structural manipulations in a high-level language can considerably simplify the development and later reuse of these algorithms.

NumPy provides an assortment of mathematical calculations that can be done on arrays, as well as providing very simple syntax for structural operations. As a result, Python (with NumPy) can be successfully used for the development of significant and fast-performing engineering and scientific code.

One feature that allows fast structural manipulation is that any subregion of a NumPy array can be selected using the concept of *slicing*. In Python, a slice is defined by a starting index, a stopping index, and a stride, using the notation start:stop:stride (inside square brackets).

For example, suppose we want to crop and shrink a 656×498 image to a 160×120 image by selecting a region in the middle of the image. If the image is held in the NumPy array, im, this operation can be performed using:

```
im2=im[8:-8:4, 9:-9:4]
```

An important feature of NumPy, however, is that the new image selected in this way actually shares data with the underlying image. A copy is not performed. This can be an important optimization when calculating with large data sets where indiscriminate copying can overwhelm the computing resources.

Key Challenges in N-Dimensional Array Operations

In order to provide fast implementations of all mathematical operations, NumPy implements loops (in C) that work quickly over an array or several arrays of any number of dimensions. Writing such generic code that works quickly on arrays of arbitrary dimension can be a mind-stretching task. It may be easy to write a for loop to process all the elements of a one-dimensional array, or two nested for loops to process all the elements of a two-dimensional array. Indeed, if you know ahead of time how many dimensions the array consists of, you can use the right number of for loops to directly loop over all of the elements of the array. But how do you write a general for loop that will process all of the elements of an *N*-dimensional array when *N* can be an arbitrary integer?

There are two basic solutions to this problem. One solution is to use recursion by thinking about the problem in terms of a recursive case and a base case. Thus, if copy_ND(a, b, N) is a function that copies an *N*-dimensional array pointed to by b to another *N*-dimensional array pointed to by a, a simple recursive implementation might look like:

```
if (N==0)
    copy memory from b to a
    return
set up ptr_to_a and ptr_to_b
for n=0 to size of first dimension of a and b
    copy_ND(ptr_to_a, ptr_to_b, N-1)
    add stride_a[0] to ptr_to_a and stride_b[0] to ptr_b
```

Notice the use of the single for loop and the check for the base case that stops the recursion when *N* reaches 0.

It is not always easy to think about how to write every algorithm as a recursive algorithm, even though the code just shown can often be used as a starting model. Recursion also requires the use of a function call at each iteration of the loop. So it can be all too easy for recursion to create slow code, unless some base-case optimization is performed (such as stopping when N==1 and doing the memory copy in a for loop locally).

Most languages will not do that kind of optimization automatically, so an elegant-looking recursive solution might end up looking much more contrived by the time optimizations are added.

In addition, many algorithms require the storage of intermediate information that will be used during later recursions. For example, what if the maximum or minimum value in the array must be tracked? Typically, such values become part of the recursive call structure and are passed along as arguments in the recursive call. In the end, each algorithm that uses recursion must be written in a slightly different way. Thus, it is hard to provide the programmer with additional simplifying tools for recursive solutions.

Instead of using recursion, NumPy uses iteration to accomplish most of its N-dimensional algorithms. Every recursive solution can be written using an iterative solution. Iterators are an abstraction that simplifies thinking about these algorithms. Therefore, using iterators, N-dimensional routines can be developed that run quickly, while the code can still be read and understood using a single looping structure.

An iterator is an abstract concept that encapsulates the idea of walking through all of the elements of an array with just one loop. In Python itself, iterators are objects that can be used as the predicate of any for loop. For example:

```
for x in iterobj:
    process(x)
```

will run the function process on all of the elements of iterobj. The most important requirement of iterobj is that it has some way to get its "next" element. Thus, the concept of an iterator refocuses the problem of looping over all the elements of a data structure to one of finding the next element.

In order to understand how iterators are implemented and used in NumPy, it is crucial to have at least some conception of how NumPy views the memory in an N-dimensional array. The next section should clarify this point.

Memory Models for an N-Dimensional Array

The simplest model for an N-dimensional array in computer memory can be used whenever all of the elements of the array are sitting next to each other in a contiguous segment. Under such circumstances, getting to the next element of the array is as simple as adding a fixed constant to a pointer to the memory location of the current data pointer. As a result, an iterator for contiguous memory arrays requires just adding a fixed constant to the current data pointer. Therefore, if every N-dimensional array in NumPy were contiguous, discussing iterators would be rather uninteresting.

The beauty of the iterator abstraction is that it allows us to think about processing and manipulating noncontiguous arrays with the same ease as contiguous arrays. Noncontiguous arrays arise in NumPy because an array can be created that is a "view" of some other contiguous memory area. This new array may not itself be contiguous.

For example, consider a three-dimensional array, a, that is contiguous in memory. With NumPy, you can create another array consisting of a subset of this larger array using Python's slicing notation. Thus, the statement b=a[::2,3:,1::3] returns another NumPy array consisting of every other element in the first dimension, all elements starting at the fourth element (with zero-based indexing) in the second dimension, and every third element starting at the second element in the third dimension. This new array is not a copy of the memory at those locations; it is a view of the original array and shares memory with it. But this new array cannot be represented as a contiguous chunk of memory.

A two-dimensional illustration should further drive home the point. Figure 19-1 shows a contiguous, two-dimensional, 4×5 array with memory locations labeled from 1 through 20. Above the representation of the 4×5 array is a linear representation of the memory for the array as the computer might see it. If a represents the full memory block, b=a[1:3,1:4] represents the shaded region (memory locations 7, 8, 9, 12, 13, and 14). As emphasized in the linear representation, these memory locations are not contiguous.

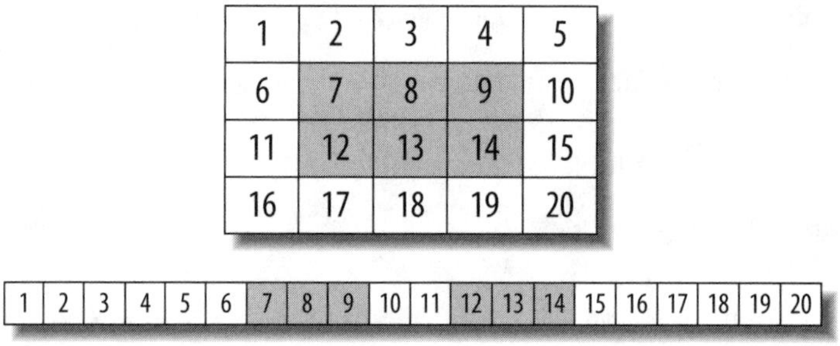

FIGURE 19-1. A two-dimensional array slice and its linear representation in memory

NumPy's general memory model for an N-dimensional array supports the creation of these kinds of noncontiguous views of arrays. It is made possible by attaching to the array a sequence of integers that represent the values for the "striding" through each dimension.

The stride value for a particular dimension specifies how many bytes must be skipped to get from one element of the array to another along the associated dimension, or axis. This stride value can even be negative, indicating that the next element in the array is obtained by moving backward in memory. The extra complication of the (potentially) arbitrary striding means that constructing an iterator to handle the generic case is more difficult.

NumPy Iterator Origins

Loops that traverse all the elements of an array in compiled code are an essential feature that NumPy offers the Python programmer. The use of an iterator makes it relatively easy to write these loops in a straightforward and readable way that works for the most general (arbitrarily strided) arrays supported by NumPy. The iterator abstraction is an example in my mind of beautiful code because it allows simple expression of a simple idea, even though the underlying implementation details might actually be complicated. This kind of beautiful code does not just drop into existence, but it is often the result of repeated attempts to solve a set of similar problems until a general solution crystallizes.

My first attempt at writing a general-purpose, *N*-dimensional looping construct occurred around 1997 when I was trying to write code for both an *N*-dimensional convolution and a general-purpose arraymap that would perform a Python function on every element of an *N*-dimensional array.

The solution I arrived at then (though not formalized as an iterator) was to keep track of a C array of integers as indices for the *N*-dimensional array. Iteration meant incrementing this *N*-index counter with special code to wrap the counter back to zero and increment the next counter by 1 when the index reached the size of the array in a particular dimension.

While writing NumPy eight years later, I became more aware of the concept of, and use of, iterator objects in Python. I thus considered adapting the arraymap code as a formal iterator. In the process, I studied how Peter Vevreer (author of SciPy's *ndimage* package) accomplished *N*-dimensional looping and discovered an iterator very similar to what I had already been using. With this boost in confidence, I formalized the iterator, applying ideas from *ndimage* to the basic structural elements contained in the arraymap and *N*-dimensional convolution code.

Iterator Design

As described previously, an iterator is an abstract concept that encapsulates the idea of walking through each element of an array. The basic pseudocode for an iterator-based loop used in NumPy is:

```
set up iterator
  (including pointing the current value to the first value in the array)
while iterator not done:
    process the current value
    point the current value to the next value
```

Everything but *process the current value* must be handled by the iterator and deserves discussion. As a result, there are basically three parts to the iterator design:

1. Moving to the next value

2. Termination

3. Setup

These will each be discussed separately. The design considerations that went into NumPy's iterators included making the overhead for using them inside of a loop as small as possible and making them as fast as possible.

Iterator Progression

The first decision is the order in which the elements will be taken. Although one could conceive of an iterator with no guarantee of the order in which the elements are taken, it is useful most of the time for the programmer to know the order. As a result, iterators in NumPy follow a specific order. The order is obtained using a relatively simple approach patterned after simple counting (with wrap-around) using a tuple of digits. Let a tuple of N integers represent the current position in the array, with $(0,...,0)$ representing the first element of the $n_1 \times n_2 \times ... \times n_N$ array, and $(n_1-1, n_2-1,..., n_N-1)$ representing the last element.

This tuple of integers represents an N-digit counter. The next position is found by incrementing the last digit by one. If, during this process, the ith digit reaches n_i, it is set to 0, and the $(i-1)^{th}$ digit is incremented by 1.

For example, the counting for a $3 \times 2 \times 4$ array would proceed as follows:

(0,0,0) (0,0,1) (0,0,2) (0,0,3) (0,1,0) (0,1,1) (0,1,2) (0,1,3) (1,0,0) ... (2,1,2) (2,1,3)

The next increment would produce (0,0,0), and the iterator would be set up to start all over again.

This counter is the essence of the NumPy iterator. The way it is incremented plays an important part in the iterator implementation. As a result, the implementation of the counter will be discussed in a subsequent section. Assuming that this counter that specifies the current position in the array is available, a pointer to the current value in the array can always be obtained by multiplying the integers of the counter by the stride values defined with the array, yielding the number of bytes to add to the memory address of the first element of the array.

For example, if data is a pointer to the start of the array, counter is the counter (or coordinate) array, and strides is an array of stride values, the following operations:

```
currptr = (char *)data;
for (i=0; i<N; i++) currptr += counter[i]*strides[i];
```

set currptr to the (first byte of the) current value of the array.

In fact, rather than compute this multiplication every time a pointer to the current value is needed, the implementation can keep track of the pointer at the same time that it keeps track of the counter, making adjustments every time the counter is altered. For example, when the ith index of the counter is incremented by 1, currptr is incremented by strides[i]. When the ith index is reset to 0, this is the same as subtracting n_i-1 from the current index, and therefore the memory address of the current value of the array should be decremented by $(n_i-1) \times$ strides[i].

For the general case, the iterator maintains the counter specifying the position in the array along with a pointer to the current value. In the case of an array whose elements are all next to each other in memory, keeping track of this counter is unnecessary extra work because the memory address of the current value of the array can be maintained just by incrementing its value by the size of each element in the array when the next value is desired.

Iterator Termination

Another important aspect of the iterator (especially when it is used in a loop) is figuring out when the iterator is finished and how to signal that information. The most general approach to signaling is to attach a flag variable to the iterator that is checked each time around the loop, and set when there are no more elements to iterate through.

One possible way to set this flag would be to look for the transition in the first-dimension counter from n_1-1 to 0. The problem with this approach is that it requires a temporary variable to store the last counter value, so it doesn't work for contiguous arrays, which do not keep track of the counter.

The easiest thing to do, however, is just remember that a particular number ($n_1 \times ... \times n_N$) of iterations will take place given the size of the array. This number can be stored in the iterator structure. Then, during each iterator stage, this number can be decremented. When it reaches 0, the iterator should terminate.

NumPy uses a slight modification of this countdown. In order to preserve the total number of iterations as another piece of information, as well as to keep a running counter of the total number of iterations so far, NumPy uses an integer counter that counts *up* from zero. The iteration terminates when this number reaches the total number of elements.

Iterator Setup

When the iterator is created, the size of the underlying array must be computed and stored. In addition, the integer counter must be set to 0, and the coordinate counter must be initialized to $(0,0,...,0)$. Finally, NumPy determines whether the iterator can be based on simple contiguous memory and sets a flag to remember the answer.

In order to speed up the "back-tracking step" that occurs whenever an index in the counter moves from n_i-1 to 0, the product of $(n_i-1) \times \texttt{strides[i]}$ is precalculated and stored for each index. In addition to avoid repeatedly computing n_i-1, this is also precomputed and stored in the structure.

While it is doubtful that there is any speed increase in storing this easily computed quantity, it is still very useful to have the dimensions of the array stored in the iterator structure. In the same manner, it is useful to have information about strides stored directly in the iterator, along with a variable tracking how many dimensions the underlying array has. With the dimensions and strides of the array stored in the iterator, modifications to how the array is interpreted later can be easily accomplished by modifying these values in the iterator and not in the underlying array itself. This is especially useful in implementing *broadcasting*, which makes arrays that are not shaped the same appear as if they were shaped the same (as will be explained later).

Finally, an array of precomputed factors is stored to simplify the calculations involved in the one-to-one mapping between the single integer counter into the array and its N-index counterpart. For example, every item in the array can be referenced by a single integer k between 0 and $n_1 \times \ldots \times n_{N-1} - 1$ or by a tuple of integers: $(k_1, \ldots, k_N)$. The relationship can be defined by $l_1 = k$ and:

$$
k_i = \left\lfloor \frac{l_i}{\displaystyle\prod_{j=i+1}^{N} n_j} \right\rfloor
$$

$$
l_i = l_{i-1} \bmod \left(\prod_{j=i}^{N} n_j \right)
$$

Going back the other way, the relationship is:

$$
k = \sum_{i=1}^{N} k_i \left(\prod_{j=i+1}^{N} n_j \right)
$$

The terms within the parentheses of the previous equation are precomputed and stored in the iterator as an array of factors, to facilitate mapping back and forth between the two ways of thinking about the N-dimensional index.

Iterator Counter Tracking

Code for keeping track of the N-dimensional index counter is fairly straightforward. A distinction must be made between the case when the iterator will simply add 1 to the last index and when wrapping might occur. Whenever wrapping occurs, it has the potential to cause other indices to wrap as well. Therefore, there must be some kind of for loop to handle all the altered indices.

A straightforward approach is to start at the end of the counter, or coordinate, array and work backward. At each index position, the code checks to see whether the coordinate is currently smaller than $n_i - 1$. If it is, it just adds 1 to that coordinate position and adds strides[i] to the memory address of the current value pointer. Whenever this happens, the for loop can break early, and the counter increment is done.

If the ith coordinate is greater than or equal to $n_i - 1$, it needs to be reset to 0 and $(n_i - 1) \times$ strides[i] must be subtracted from the memory address of the current value pointer (to move back to the beginning of that dimension). In this case, the previous index position is checked.

All the necessary information can be represented in a structure we'll call it. The contents are:

coords

    The coordinate index, N

dims_m1

    The index of the highest element n_i-1 for each dimension

strides

    The stride in each dimension

backstrides

    The amount to move back in order to return from the end of each dimension to the beginning: $(n_i-1) \times$ strides[i]

nd_m1

    The number of dimensions

currptr

    A pointer to memory for the current position in the array

The code for the counter-tracking can then be written in C as follows:

```
for (i=it->nd_m1; i>=0; i--) {
    if (it->coords[i] < it->dims_m1[i]) {
        it->coords[i]++;
        it->dataptr += it->strides[i];
        break;
    }
    else {
        it->coords[i] = 0;
        it->dataptr -= it->backstrides[i];
    }
}
```

This implementation uses the break statement and a for loop. We could instead have used a while statement and a flag indicating whether to continue looping:

```
done = 0;
i = it->nd_m1;
while (!done || i>=0) {
    if (it->coords[i] < it->dims_m1[i]) {
        it->coords[i]++;
        it->dataptr += it->strides[i];
        done = 1;
    }
    else {
        it->coords[i] = 0;
        it->dataptr -= it->backstrides[i];
    }
    i--;
}
```

Part of the reason I chose the for loop implementation is that the while loop looks a lot like the for loop (initialize counter, check against a value, decrement the counter), anyway. I typically reserve while loops for situations where the iteration requires more than a single iteration index. A bigger reason for choosing the for loop version, however, is that this code snippet implementing the counter increment will be used as a macro inside of every iterator loop. I wanted to avoid defining the extra variable done.

Iterator Structure

We are now in a position to understand the entire structure of the NumPy iterator. It's represented as the following struct in C:

```
typedef struct {
    PyObject_HEAD
    int nd_m1;
    npy_intp index, size;
    npy_intp coords[NPY_MAXDIMS];
    npy_intp dims_m1[NPY_MAXDIMS];
    npy_intp strides[NPY_MAXDIMS];
    npy_intp backstrides[NPY_MAXDIMS];
    npy_intp factors[NPY_MAXDIMS];
    PyArrayObject *ao;
    char *dataptr;
    npy_bool contiguous;
} PyArrayIterObject;
```

The arrays in this structure (coords, dims_m1, strides, backstrides, and factors) are fixed-size arrays with dimensions controlled by the NPY_MAXDIMS constant. This choice was made to simplify memory management. However, it does limit the number of dimensions that can be used. It could easily be handled differently by dynamically allocating the needed memory when the iterator is created; such a change would not alter the fundamental behavior.

The npy_intp variables are integers just large enough to hold a pointer for the platform. npy_bool is a flag that should be either TRUE or FALSE. The PyObject_HEAD part of the structure contains the required portion that all Python objects must contain.

All of the variables have been explained before, but for clarity they are:

nd_m1
   One less than the number of dimensions of the array: $N-1$.

index
   A running counter indicating which element the iterator is currently at in the array. This counter runs from 0 to size-1.

size
   The total number of elements in the array: $n_1 \times n_2 \times \ldots \times n_N$.

coords
   An array of N integers providing the counter, or the N-dimensional location of the current element.

dims_m1

An array of N integers providing one less than the number of elements along each dimension: n_1-1, n_2-1,..., n_N-1.

strides

An array of N integers providing the number of bytes to skip when advancing to the next element in a particular dimension.

backstrides

An array of N integers providing the number of bytes to subtract when the internal index counter rolls from n_i-1 to 0 in a particular dimension.

factors

An array of factors useful in rapidly calculating the mapping between the one-dimensional index and the N-dimensional coords array. This array is needed only if PyArray_ITER_GOTO1D is called.

ao

A pointer to the underlying array this iterator is built from.

datapr

A pointer to the (first byte of) the current value of the array.

contiguous

TRUE (1) if this iterator is for a contiguous array and FALSE (0) if otherwise. This is the same as (ao->flags & NPY_C_CONTIGUOUS). It's much simpler to find the next element in the array each time when the array is contiguous, so it is worth checking for.

Iterator Interface

The iterator is implemented in NumPy using a combination of macros and function calls. An iterator is created using the C-API function call it = PyArray_IterNew(ao). The check for iterator termination can be accomplished using the macro PyArray_ITER_NOTDONE(it). Finally, the next position in the iterator is accomplished using PyArray_ITER_NEXT(it), which is a macro to ensure that it occurs inline (avoiding the function call). Ideally, this macro would be an inline function because it is sufficiently complicated. However, because NumPy is written to ANSI C, which does not define inline functions, a macro is used. Finally, the pointer to the first byte of the current value can be obtained using PyArray_ITER_DATA(it), which avoids referencing the structure member dataptr directly (allowing for future name changes to the structure members).

An example of the iterator interface is the following code snippet, which computes the largest value in an N-dimensional array. We assume that the array is named ao, has elements of type double, and is correctly aligned:

```
#include <float.h>
double *currval, maxval=-DBL_MAX;
PyObject *it;
it = PyArray_IterNew(ao);
while (PyArray_ITER_NOTDONE(it)) {
```

```
      currval = (double *)PyArray_ITER_DATA(it);
      if (*currval > maxval) maxval = *currval;
      PyArray_ITER_NEXT(it);
   }
```

This code shows how relatively easy it is to construct a loop for a noncontiguous, *N*-dimensional array using the iterator structure. The simplicity of this code also illustrates the elegance of iterator abstraction. Notice how similar the code is to the simple iterator pseudocode shown at the beginning of the earlier section "Iterator Design." Consider also that this code works for arrays of arbitrary dimensions and arbitrary strides in each dimension, and you begin to appreciate the beauty of the multidimensional iterator.

The iterator-based code is fast for both contiguous and noncontiguous arrays. However, the fastest contiguous-array loop is still something like:

```
   double *currval, maxval=-MAX_DOUBLE;
   int size;
   currval = (double *)PyArray_DATA(ao);
   size = PyArray_SIZE(ao);
   while (size--) {
       if (*currval > maxval) maxval = *currval;
       currval += 1;
   }
```

The real benefit of the NumPy iterator is that it allows programmers to write contiguous-like code that is still fairly fast without worrying about whether their arrays are contiguous. It should be remembered that forcing a contiguous algorithm has performance costs as well because noncontiguous data must be copied to another array for processing.

The speed difference between the NumPy iterator solution and the fastest contiguous-case solution could be largely eliminated if a remaining problem with the current NumPy iterator interface could be fixed. The problem is that the PyArray_ITER_NEXT macro checks each time through the loop whether the iterator can use the simplified contiguous approach. Ideally, this check should be made only once outside of the loop, and then a single approach to finding the next value should be used inside the loop. However, this kind of interface is a bit messy to implement in C. It would require two different macros similar to ITER_NEXT and two different while loops. As a result, nothing to this effect was implemented in NumPy at the time of the writing of this chapter. People wishing to get the small speed gain available for contiguous cases are assumed to be knowledgeable enough to write the simple loop themselves (bypassing the iterator entirely).

Iterator Use

A good abstraction proves its worth when it makes coding simpler under diverse conditions, or when it ends up being useful in ways that were originally unintended. Both of these affirmations of value are definitely true of the NumPy iterator object. With only slight modifications, the original simple NumPy iterator has become a workhorse for implementing other NumPy features, such as iteration over all but one dimension and iteration over multiple arrays at the same time. In addition, when we had to quickly add some enhancements to the code for generating random numbers and for broadcast-based copying, the existence of the iterator and its extensions made implementation much easier.

Iteration Over All But One Dimension

A common motif in NumPy is to gain speed by concentrating optimizations on the loop over a single dimension where simple striding can be assumed. Then an iteration strategy that iterates over all but the last dimension is used. This was the approach introduced by NumPy's predecessor, Numeric, to implement the math functionality.

In NumPy, a slight modification to the NumPy iterator makes it possible to use this basic strategy in any code. The modified iterator is returned from the constructor as follows:

    it = PyArray_IterAllButAxis(array, &dim).

The `PyArray_IterAllButAxis` function takes a NumPy array and the address of an integer representing the dimension to remove from the iteration. The integer is passed by reference (the & operator) because if the dimension is specified as –1, the function determines which dimension to remove from iteration and places the number of that dimension in the argument. When the input dimension is –1, the routine chooses the dimension with the smallest nonzero stride.

Another choice for the dimension to remove might have been the dimension with the largest number of elements. That choice would minimize the number of outer loop iterations and reserve the most elements for the presumably fast inner loop. The problem with that choice is that getting information in and out of memory is often the slowest part of an algorithm on general-purpose processors.

As a result, the choice made by NumPy is to make sure that the inner loop is proceeding with data that is as close together as possible. Such data is more likely to be accessed more quickly during the speed-critical inner loop.

The iterator is modified by:

1. Dividing the iteration size by the length of the dimension being removed.

2. Setting the number of elements in the selected dimension to 1 (so the array storing one less than the total number is set to 0): `dims_m1[i] = 0`.

3. Setting the backstrides entry for that dimension to 0 so that the continual re-wrapping of the counter in the given dimension back to 0 will never alter the data pointer.

4. Resetting the contiguous flag to 0 because processing will not be contiguous in memory (each iteration has to skip an entire dimension of the array).

The altered iterator is returned by the function. It can now be used everywhere an iterator was previously used. Each time through the loop, the iterator will point to the first element of the selected dimension of the array.

Multiple Iterations

Another common task in NumPy is to iterate over several arrays in concert. For example, the implementation of array addition requires iterating over both arrays using a connected iterator so that the output array is the sum of each element of the first array multiplied by each element of the second array. This can be accomplished using a different iterator for each of the input elements and an iterator for the output array in the normal fashion.

Alternatively, NumPy provides a multi-iterator object that can simplify dealing with several iterators at once. This multi-iterator object also handles the broadcasting functionality of NumPy automatically. *Broadcasting* is the name given to the feature in NumPy that allows arrays with different shapes to be used together in operations that are supposed to work element-by-element. For example, broadcasting allows a (4,1)-shaped array to be added to a (3)-shaped array resulting in a (4,3)-shaped array. Broadcasting also allows simultaneous iteration over a (4,1)-shaped array, a (3)-shaped array, and a (5,1,1)-shaped array to produce a broadcasted iteration covering the elements of a (5,4,3)-shaped array.

The rules of broadcasting are:

- Arrays with fewer dimensions are treated as occupying the last dimensions of an array that has the full number of dimensions, so that all arrays have the same number of dimensions. The new, initial dimensions are filled in with 1s.

- The length of each dimension in the final broadcast shape is the greatest length of that dimension in any of the arrays.

- For each dimension, all inputs must either have the same number of elements as the broadcast result or a 1 as the number of elements.

- Arrays with a single element in a particular dimension act as if that element were virtually copied to all positions during the iteration. In effect, the element is "broadcast" to the additional positions.

The key to the implementation of broadcasting consists of surprisingly simple modifications to the array iterators. With these alterations, standard iterator loops can be used to implement the resulting calculations in a straightforward way. The modifications needed are changes to the shape of the iterators (not the underlying array) and changes to the strides and backstrides. The shape stored in the iterator is changed to match the broadcast shape. The strides and backstrides for broadcast dimensions are changed to 0. With a stride of 0, the standard iterator does not actually move the data pointer to the element in memory as the index in that dimension proceeds. This creates the desired effect of broadcasting without actually copying the memory.

The following code illustrates usage of the multi-iterator object:

```
PyObject *multi;
PyObject *in1, *in2;
double *i1p, *i2p, *op;
/* get in1 and in2 (assumed to be arrays of NPY_DOUBLE) */
/* first argument is the number of input arrays; the
```

```
        next (variable number of) arguments are the
        array objects */
multi = PyArray_MultiNew(2, in1, in2);
/* construct output array */
out = PyArray_SimpleNew(PyArray_MultiIter_NDIM(multi),
                        PyArray_MultiIter_DIMS(multi),
                        NPY_DOUBLE);
op = PyArray_DATA(out);
while(PyArray_MultiIter_NOTDONE(multi)) {
    /* get (pointers to) the current value in each array */
    i1p = PyArray_MultiIter_DATA(multi, 0);
    i2p = PyArray_MultiIter_DATA(multi, 1);
    /* perform the operation for this element */
    *op = *ip1 + *ip2
    op += 1;  /* Advance output array pointer */
    /* Advance all the input iterators */
    PyArray_MultiIter_NEXT(multi);
}
```

The code is very similar to a standard iterator loop, except the multi-iterator handles adjustments of the input iterators to accomplish broadcasting, as well as incrementing all the other input iterators. This code handles the broadcasting automatically as part of the iterator processing, so that the addition of a (3,1)-shaped array to a (4)-shaped one will produce a (3,4)-shaped output array.

Anecdotes

The NumPy iterator is used throughout the NumPy code base to simplify the construction of *N*-dimensional loops. Having the iterator available allowed me to code algorithms for more general (noncontiguous) arrays. Normally, the difficulty of thinking about how to handle the noncontiguous arrays would have convinced me to just force an array to be contiguous (by making a new copy if necessary) and then use an easy looping algorithm. The existence of the NumPy iterator allowed me to write much more general code that is still as readable, with a very minor cost in speed for arrays that are actually contiguous. This slight disadvantage is offset by the very great decrease in memory requirements for arrays that are noncontiguous. The improved productivity in writing such loops is sufficient to justify the existence of the NumPy iterator.

However, it is NumPy's encapsulation for broadcasting where the utility of the abstraction really shines. It shone particularly bright when the multi-iterator allowed me to enhance the random-number generators of NumPy to deal with arrays of parameters pertaining to the random number generators. The change took about two hours with only a few lines of code.

The random-number generator facility of NumPy was written by Robert Kern. He was not familiar with the C broadcasting API that had only been recently added. As a result, the original implementation required all parameters used to specify the random numbers to be scalar values (i.e., the value of λ for an exponential distribution).

This was an unfortunate restriction. It is quite common to need an array of random numbers drawn from a particular distribution where different parts of the array should have different parameters. For instance, a programmer might need a matrix of random numbers drawn from the exponential distribution where each row of numbers should be sampled using a different value of λ. To allow arrays of parameters, the bulk of the change was to use the multi-iterator loop (with its built-in broadcasting facility) and fill in the output array with the random samples.

Another opportunity to use the iterator surfaced when the code that copied data from one array to another needed to be altered to copy in a manner consistent with NumPy's definition of broadcasting. Previously, an array was copied over to another using the standard iterator. The only shape checking done was to ensure that the destination array got filled only once. If the destination ran out of elements, its iterator started over again. Eventually, it became clear that this was not the desired copying behavior because it basically implemented a different kind of "broadcasting" (as long as the total number of elements of one array was a multiple of another, any array could be copied into any other array regardless of shape). The kind of data replication that resulted from this copy command was inconsistent with the definition of broadcasting used in other places in NumPy. It became clear that it needed to be changed. Again, the multi-iterators and its built-in concept of iterator broadcasting was a useful abstraction because it allowed me to write the code to accomplish the copy (including size checking) very quickly with only very few lines of actual new code.

Conclusion

The iterator object in NumPy is an example of a coding abstraction that simplifies programming. Since its construction in 2005, it has been extremely useful in writing N-dimensional algorithms that work on general NumPy arrays regardless of whether or not they are contiguous in memory or actually represent noncontiguous N-dimensional slices of some other contiguous chunk of memory. In addition, simple modifications to the iterator have made it much simpler to implement some of the more difficult ideas of NumPy, such as optimizing loops (looping over all but the least-striding dimension) and broadcasting.

Iterators are a beautiful abstraction because they save valuable programmer attention in the implementation of a complicated algorithm. This has been true in NumPy as well. The NumPy implementation of a standard array iterator has made general-purpose code much more pleasant to write and debug, and it has allowed the encapsulation and exposure of some of the important (but hard-to-write) internal features of NumPy, such as broadcasting.

## CHAPTER TWENTY

A Highly Reliable Enterprise System for NASA's Mars Rover Mission

Ronald Mak

HOW OFTEN DO YOU HEAR THAT BEAUTY IS IN THE EYE OF THE BEHOLDER? In our case, the beholder was NASA's Mars Exploration Rover mission, and it had very strict requirements that the mission's software systems be functional, reliable, and robust. Oh, and the software also had to be completed on schedule—Mars would not accept any excuses for schedule slips. When NASA talks about meeting "launch windows," it means it in more ways than one!

This chapter describes the design and development of Collaborative Information Portal, or CIP, which is a large enterprise information system developed at NASA and used by mission managers, engineers, and scientists worldwide.

Martians have zero tolerance for ugly software. For CIP, the notion of beauty is not so much about elegant algorithms or programs that you can stand back and admire. Rather, beauty is embodied in a complex software structure built by master builders who knew just where to pound in the nails. Large applications can be beautiful in ways that small programs often are not. This is due both to increased necessity and to greater opportunity— large applications often have to do things that small programs don't need to. We'll take a look at CIP's overall Java-based service-oriented architecture, and then, by focusing on one of its services as a case study, examine some code snippets and study some of the nails that enable the system to meet the functionality, reliability, and robustness requirements.

As you can imagine, software used on NASA space missions must be highly reliable. Missions are expensive, and years of planning and many millions of dollars cannot be jeopardized by faulty programs. The most difficult part of the software work, of course, is to debug and patch software used onboard a spacecraft that is millions of miles from Earth. But even ground-based systems must be reliable; nobody wants a software bug to interrupt mission operations or cause the loss of valuable data.

There is a bit of irony in writing about beauty for this type of software. In a multitiered service-oriented architecture, the services are implemented in a middleware tier that resides on a server. (We developed shared reusable components in the middleware, which greatly reduced development time.) The middleware decouples the client applications from the backend data sources; in other words, an application doesn't have to know where and how the data it needs is stored. Client applications make remote service requests to the middleware and then receive responses that contain the requested data. When all the middleware services are doing their jobs well, the end users of the enterprise system should not even know that their client applications are making remote service requests. When the middleware is operating smoothly, users should believe that they are directly accessing the data sources and that all the data processing is happening locally on their workstations or laptops. Therefore, the more successful the middleware is, the less visible it becomes. Beautiful middleware should be invisible!

The Mission and the Collaborative Information Portal

The primary goal of the Mars Exploration Rover, or MER, mission is to discover whether liquid water once flowed on the Martian surface. In June and July 2003, NASA launched two identical rovers to Mars to operate as robotic geologists. In January 2004, after separate seven-month journeys, they landed on opposite sides of the planet.

Each rover is solar-powered and can drive itself over the surface. Each one has scientific instruments such as spectrometers mounted at the end of an articulated arm. The arm has a drill and a microscopic imager to examine what's beneath the surface of rocks. Each rover has several cameras and antennas to send data and images back to earth (see Figure 20-1).

Unmanned NASA missions are a combination of hardware and software. Different software packages onboard each Mars rover control its operation autonomously and in response to remote commands issued from mission control at NASA's Jet Propulsion Laboratory (JPL) near Pasadena, California. Earth-based software packages at mission control enable the mission managers, engineers, and scientists to download and analyze the information sent by the rovers, to plan and develop new command sequences to send to the rovers, and to collaborate with each other.

At the NASA Ames Research Center near Mountain View, California, we designed and developed the Collaborative Information Portal (CIP) for the MER mission. The project team consisted of 10 software engineers and computer scientists. Another nine team members included project managers and the support engineers who took care of QA, software system build, hardware configuration, and bug-tracking tasks.

FIGURE 20-1. A Mars rover (image courtesy of JPL)

Mission Needs

We designed CIP to meet three primary needs of the MER mission. By satisfying these needs, CIP provides vital "situational awareness" among mission personnel:

Time management

Keeping everybody synchronized during any large complex mission is critical for success, and MER presented some special time management challenges. Because mission personnel work at locations around the world, CIP displays time in various terrestrial time zones. Because the rovers landed on opposite sides of Mars, there are also two Martian time zones.

Initially, the mission ran on Mars time, which meant that all scheduled meetings and events (such as data downloads from Mars) were given in the time of one Mars time zone or the other, depending on to which rover the meeting or event pertained. A Martian day is nearly 40 minutes longer than an Earth day, and so relative to Earth time, mission personnel shifted later by that amount of time each day as seen by their families and colleagues who remained on Earth time. This made CIP's time management functions even more important.

Personnel management

With two rover teams (one per rover) and some people moving between the teams, keeping track of everybody is another critical function. CIP manages a personnel roster and displays schedules (as Gantt charts) that show who is working where, when, and in what role.

CIP also enables some collaboration among mission personnel. They can send out broadcast messages, share analyses of data and image, upload reports, and annotate each other's reports.

Data management

Getting data and images from the far reaches of the universe is the key to every NASA planetary and deep space mission, and here, too, CIP plays a major role. An array of terrestrial antennas receive the data and images sent by the Mars rovers, and once on Earth, they are transmitted to JPL to be processed and stored in the mission file servers.

Once the mission managers release the processed data and image files, CIP generates metadata that categorizes the files by various criteria, such as which rover instrument generated the data, which camera took the image, at which setting, using what configuration, when and where, etc. CIP users can then search for the data and images by these criteria and download them from the mission file servers over the Internet onto their personal laptops and workstations.

CIP also implements data security. For example, depending on a user's role (and whether she is a U.S. citizen), certain data and images can be off-limits.

System Architecture

Code beauty for an enterprise system is derived partly from architecture, the way the code is put together. Architecture is more than aesthetics. In a large application, architecture determines how the software components interoperate and contributes to overall system reliability.

We implemented CIP using a three-tiered service-oriented architecture (SOA). We adhered to industry standards and best practices, and where practicable, we used commercial off-the-shelf (COTS) software. We programmed mostly in Java and used the Java 2 Enterprise Edition (J2EE) standards (see Figure 20-2).

The client tier consists mostly of standalone GUI-based Java applications implemented with Swing components and a few web-based applications. A J2EE-compliant application server runs in the middleware and hosts all the services that respond to requests from the client applications. We implemented the services using Enterprise JavaBeans (EJBs). The data tier consists of the data sources and data utility programs. Also written in Java, these utilities monitor the file server for the processed data and image files. The utilities generate metadata for the files as soon as they're released by the mission managers.

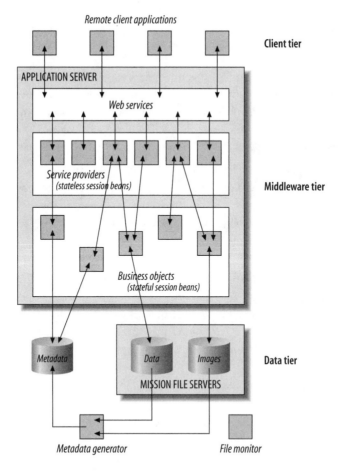

Remote client applications

Client tier

APPLICATION SERVER

Web services

Service providers
(stateless session beans)

Middleware tier

Business objects
(stateful session beans)

Metadata

Data   Images

Data tier

MISSION FILE SERVERS

Metadata generator   File monitor

FIGURE 20-2. CIP's three-tiered service-oriented architecture

Using an SOA based on J2EE gave us the option to use these well-defined beans (and others) wherever appropriate in the design of a large enterprise application. Stateless session beans handle service requests without remembering any state from one request to the next. On the other hand, stateful session beans maintain state information for clients and typically manage persisted information that the beans read from and write to a data store. Having multiple options in any design situation is important when developing large complex applications.

In the middleware, we implemented a stateless session bean as a service provider for each service. This was the facade from which we generated a web service that the client applications use to make service requests and get back responses. Each service may also access one or more stateful session beans that are business objects supplying any necessary logic that must maintain state between service requests, such as where to read the next block of information from a database in response to a data request. In effect, the stateless beans are often the service dispatchers for the stateful beans that do the actual work.

There is much beauty in this type of architecture! The architecture embodies some key design principles:

Standards-based

> Especially at a research institution (like the NASA Ames Research Center, where we designed and developed CIP), there is always a strong temptation to invent something new, even if the result is reinventing the wheel. The MER mission afforded the CIP development team neither the time nor the resources, and our goal was to develop production-quality code for the mission, not necessarily to do research.

> *In any large application, the key to success is integration, not coding.* The beauty behind adhering to industry standards and best practices is that we did less coding by using COTS components, and because of common interfaces, these components were able to work well with each other. This enabled us to make guarantees to the mission managers that we would deliver functional and reliable code on time.

Loose coupling

> We loosely coupled the client applications and the middleware services. This meant that once the application programmer and the service programmer agreed on an interface between the two, they could develop their respective code in parallel. Any changes on one side didn't affect the other as long as the interface remained stable. Loose coupling was another major factor that allowed us to complete a large multitiered SOA application on time.

Language independence

> The client applications and the middleware services used web services to communicate with each other. The web services protocol is an industry standard that is language-independent. Most of the CIP client applications were written in Java, but the middleware also served some C++ and C# applications. Once we got a service to work with a Java client, it was relatively simple to get it to work with another client written in any language that supported web services. This greatly expanded the usefulness and usability of CIP with little extra cost in time or resources.

Modularity

> The importance of modularity increases exponentially with the size of the application. In CIP, each service is a self-contained middleware component that is independent of the other services. If one service needs to work with another service, it makes a service request of the other service just as if it were a client application. This allowed us to create the services separately and added another dimension of parallelism in our development. Modular services are beautiful artifacts that are often found in large, successful SOA applications.

> In the client tier, the application programs often compounded the services, either combining the results of multiple services or using the results of one service to pass in a request to another service.

CIP usage levels spike whenever mission control releases processed data and image files, especially after an interesting discovery by one of the rovers. We had to ensure that the CIP middleware can handle such spikes, particularly when the users are anxious to download and view the latest files. A slowdown or, worse, a crash, at such times would be highly intolerable and highly visible.

One of the beauties of the J2EE infrastructure is how it handles scalability. The application server maintains bean pools, and based on demand, it can automatically create more instances of our stateless session bean service providers. This is a significant "free" J2EE feature that the middleware service developers were happy to accept.

Reliability

As a standard that had undergone much vetting by industry, the J2EE infrastructure proved to be extremely reliable. We avoided pushing the envelope of what it was designed to do. So after two years of operation, CIP achieved an uptime record of over 99.9 percent.

We went beyond what J2EE intrinsically provided for reliability. As you'll see in the following case study, we pounded a few extra nails into our services to further increase their reliability.

Case Study: The Streamer Service

You've seen some of the beauty of CIP at the architectural level. It's time to focus on one of its middleware services—the streamer service—as a case study, and examine some of the nails that allowed us to meet the mission's strict functional, reliability, and robustness requirements. You'll see that the nails were not particularly fancy; the beauty was in knowing just where to pound them in.

Functionality

One of the MER mission's data management needs is to allow users to download data and image files from the mission file servers located at JPL to their personal workstations and laptops. As described earlier, CIP data-tier utilities generate metadata that allow users to find the files they want based on various search criteria. Users also need to upload files that contain their analysis reports to the servers.

CIP's streamer service performs file downloading and uploading. We gave the service that name because it streams the file data securely across the Internet between the mission file servers at JPL and users' local computers. It uses the web services protocol, so client applications can be written in any language that supports the protocol, and these applications are free to devise whatever GUI they deem suitable.

Service Architecture

Like each of the other middleware services, the streamer service uses web services to receive client requests and to return responses. Each request is first fielded by the streamer service provider, which is implemented by a stateless session bean. The service provider creates a file reader, implemented by a stateful session bean, to do the actual work of downloading the requested file contents to the client. Conversely, the service provider creates a file writer, also implemented by a stateful session bean, to upload file contents (see Figure 20-3).

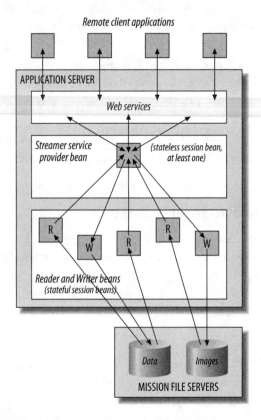

FIGURE 20-3. The streamer service architecture

At any given moment, multiple users can be downloading or uploading files, and any single user can also have several download or upload operations going at once. So, there can be numerous file reader and file writer beans active in the middleware. A single stateless Streamer Service Provider bean handles all the requests, unless the load becomes heavy, at which time the application server can create more provider beans.

Why does each file reader and file writer have to be a *stateful* session bean? Unless the file is small, the streamer service transfers the file contents one block at a time in response to "Read Data Block" or "Write Data Block" requests from the client. (The download block size is configurable on the middleware server. The client application chooses the upload block size.) From one request to the next, the stateful bean keeps track of the open source or destination file on the mission file servers and the position within the file of the next block to be read or written.

This is a very simple architecture, but it very effectively handles multiple downloads simultaneously from multiple users. Figure 20-4 shows the sequence of events for downloading a file from the mission file servers to a user's local machine.

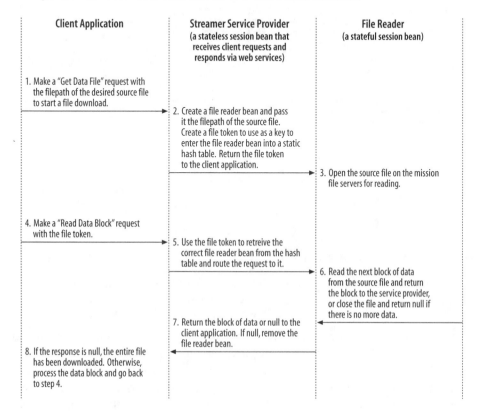

FIGURE 20-4. How the two-layer service handles a file read

Note that the Streamer Service Provider bean does not maintain any state between service requests. It functions as a rapid service dispatcher that parcels work out to the stateful File Reader beans. Because it doesn't need to track requests or maintain state, it can handle requests intermingled from several client applications. Each File Reader bean maintains state information (where to get the next block of data) for a single client application as the application makes multiple "Read Data Block" requests to download a complete file. This architecture enables the streamer service to download multiple files to multiple clients simultaneously while providing acceptable throughput for all.

The sequence of events for a file upload from a user's local machine to the mission file servers is just as straightforward. It's shown in Figure 20-5.

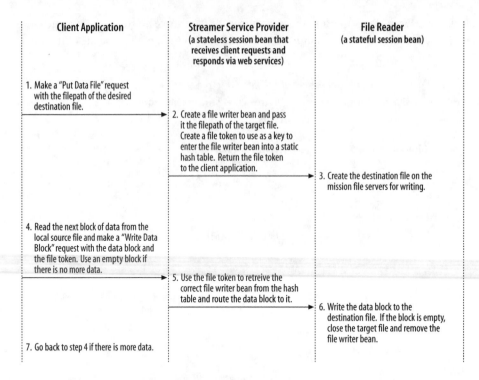

Client Application	Streamer Service Provider (a stateless session bean that receives client requests and responds via web services)	File Reader (a stateful session bean)
1. Make a "Put Data File" request with the filepath of the desired destination file.		
	2. Create a file writer bean and pass it the filepath of the target file. Create a file token to use as a key to enter the file writer bean into a static hash table. Return the file token to the client application.	
		3. Create the destination file on the mission file servers for writing.
4. Read the next block of data from the local source file and make a "Write Data Block" request with the data block and the file token. Use an empty block if there is no more data.		
	5. Use the file token to retreive the correct file writer bean from the hash table and route the data block to it.	
		6. Write the data block to the destination file. If the block is empty, close the target file and remove the file writer bean.
7. Go back to step 4 if there is more data.		

FIGURE 20-5. How the two-layer service handles a file write

These tables don't show it, but besides a file token, each client request also includes a user token. A client application first obtains a user token when it makes a successful login request (with a user name and password) to the middleware's user management service, thus authenticating the user. A user token contains information that identifies a particular user session, including the user's role. It enables the streamer service to verify that a request is coming from a legitimate user. It checks the user's role to ensure that she has the right to download a particular file. For example, the MER mission disallowed users from foreign (non-U.S.) countries from accessing certain files, and CIP respected all such security restrictions.

Reliability

Reliable code continues to perform well without problems. It rarely crashes, if ever. As you can imagine, code that is on board the Mars rovers must be extremely reliable because making on-site maintenance calls is somewhat difficult. But the MER mission wanted earthbound software used by mission control to be reliable, too. Once the mission was underway, no one wanted software problems to disrupt operations.

As noted earlier, the CIP project took several measures to ensure the intrinsic reliability of the system:

- Adhering to industry standards and best practices, including J2EE

- Using proven COTS software wherever practicable, including a commercial application server from an established middleware vendor

- Using a service-oriented architecture with modular services

- Implementing simple, straightforward middleware services

We further enhanced reliability with extra nails: service logging and monitoring. While these features can be useful for debugging even small programs, they become essential for keeping track of the runtime behavior of large applications.

Logging

During development, we used the open source Apache Log4J Java package to log nearly everything that occurred in the middleware services. It was certainly useful for debugging during development. Logging enabled us to write code that was more reliable. Whenever there was a bug, the logs told us what was going on just prior to the problem, and so we were better able to fix the bug.

We originally intended to reduce the logging only to serious messages before CIP went into operation. But we ended up leaving most of the logging on since it had a negligible impact on overall performance. Then we discovered that the logs gave us much useful information not only about what was going on with each service, but also *how* client applications were using the services. By analyzing the logs (which we called "log mining"), we were able to tune the services for better performance based on empirical data (see "Dynamic Reconfiguration," later in this chapter).

Here are some code snippets from the streamer service provider bean that show how we did logging for file downloading. The getDataFile( ) method processes each "Get Data File" request (via web services) from the client applications. The method immediately logs the request (lines 15–17), including the user ID of the requester and the filepath of the desired source file:

```
1   public class StreamerServiceBean implements SessionBean
2   {
3       static {
4           Globals.loadResources("Streamer");
5       };
6
7       private static Hashtable readerTable = new Hashtable( );
8       private static Hashtable writerTable = new Hashtable( );
9
10      private static BeanCacheStats cacheStats = Globals.queryStats;
11
12      public FileToken getDataFile(AccessToken accessToken, String filePath)
13          throws MiddlewareException
14      {
15          Globals.streamerLogger.info(accessToken.userId( ) +
16                                  ": Streamer.getDataFile("
17                                  + filePath + ")");
18          long startTime = System.currentTimeMillis( );
19
```

```
20          UserSessionObject.validateToken(accessToken);
21          FileToken fileToken = doFileDownload(accessToken, filePath);
22          cacheStats.incrementTotalServerResponseTime(startTime);
23          return fileToken;
24      }
25
```

The doFileDownload( ) method creates a new file token (line 30) and file reader bean (line 41), and then calls the reader bean's getDataFile( ) method (line 42). The cacheStats field deals with runtime monitoring, which is described later:

```
26      private static FileToken doFileDownload(AccessToken accessToken,
27                                              String filePath)
28          throws MiddlewareException
29      {
30          FileToken fileToken = new FileToken(accessToken, filePath);
31          String    key      = fileToken.getKey();
32
33          FileReaderLocal reader = null;
34          synchronized (readerTable) {
35              reader = (FileReaderLocal) readerTable.get(key);
36          }
37
38          // Create a file reader bean to start the download.
39          if (reader == null) {
40              try {
41                  reader = registerNewReader(key);
42                  reader.getDataFile(filePath);
43
44                  return fileToken;
45              }
46              catch(Exception ex) {
47                  Globals.streamerLogger.warn("Streamer.doFileDownload("
48                                              + filePath + "): " +
49                                              ex.getMessage());
50                  cacheStats.incrementFileErrorCount();
51                  removeReader(key, reader);
52                  throw new MiddlewareException(ex);
53              }
54          }
55          else {
56              throw new MiddlewareException("File already being downloaded: " +
57                                            filePath);
58          }
59      }
60
```

The readDataBlock( ) method processes each "Read Data Block" request from the client applications. It looks up the correct file reader bean (line 71) and calls the reader bean's readDataBlock( ) method (line 79). At the end of the source file, it removes the file reader bean (line 91):

```
61      public DataBlock readDataBlock(AccessToken accessToken, FileToken fileToken)
62          throws MiddlewareException
63      {
```

```
64          long startTime = System.currentTimeMillis( );
65          UserSessionObject.validateToken(accessToken);
66
67          String key = fileToken.getKey( );
68
69          FileReaderLocal reader = null;
70          synchronized (readerTable) {
71              reader = (FileReaderLocal) readerTable.get(key);
72          }
73
74          // Use the reader bean to download the next data block.
75          if (reader != null) {
76              DataBlock block = null;
77
78              try {
79                  block = reader.readDataBlock( );
80              }
81              catch(MiddlewareException ex) {
82                  Globals.streamerLogger.error("Streamer.readDataBlock("
83                                              + key + ")", ex);
84                  cacheStats.incrementFileErrorCount( );
85                  removeReader(key, reader);
86                  throw ex;
87              }
88
89              // End of file?
90              if (block == null) {
91                  removeReader(key, reader);
92              }
93
94              cacheStats.incrementTotalServerResponseTime(startTime);
95              return block;
96          }
97          else {
98              throw new MiddlewareException(
99                  "Download source file not opened: " +
100                 fileToken.getFilePath( ));
101         }
102     }
103
```

The registerNewReader( ) and removeReader( ) methods create and destroy the stateful file reader beans, respectively:

```
104     private static FileReaderLocal registerNewReader(String key)
105         throws Exception
106     {
107         Context context = MiddlewareUtility.getInitialContext( );
108         Object queryRef = context.lookup("FileReaderLocal");
109
110         // Create the reader service bean and register it.
111         FileReaderLocalHome home = (FileReaderLocalHome)
112             PortableRemoteObject.narrow(queryRef, FileReaderLocalHome.class);
113         FileReaderLocal reader = home.create( );
114
```

```
115        synchronized (readerTable) {
116            readerTable.put(key, reader);
117        }
118
119        return reader;
120    }
121
122    private static void removeReader(String key, FileReaderLocal reader)
123    {
124        synchronized (readerTable) {
125            readerTable.remove(key);
126        }
127
128        if (reader != null) {
129            try {
130                reader.remove();
131            }
132            catch(javax.ejb.NoSuchObjectLocalException ex) {
133                // ignore
134            }
135            catch(Exception ex) {
136                Globals.streamerLogger.error("Streamer.removeReader("
137                                        + key + ")", ex);
138                cacheStats.incrementFileErrorCount();
139            }
140        }
141    }
142 }
```

Now, here are code snippets from the file reader bean. The cacheStats and fileStats fields are for runtime monitoring, as described later. The getDataFile( ) method logs the start of the file download (lines 160–161):

```
143 public class FileReaderBean implements SessionBean
144 {
145    private static final String FILE = "file";
146
147    private transient static BeanCacheStats cacheStats = Globals.queryStats;
148    private transient static FileStats      fileStats  = Globals.fileStats;
149
150    private transient int              totalSize;
151    private transient String           type;
152    private transient String           name;
153    private transient FileInputStream     fileInputStream;
154    private transient BufferedInputStream inputStream;
155    private transient boolean          sawEnd;
156
157    public void getDataFile(String filePath)
158        throws MiddlewareException
159    {
160        Globals.streamerLogger.debug("Begin download of file '"
161                                + filePath + "'");
162        this.type  = FILE;
163        this.name  = filePath;
164        this.sawEnd = false;
165
```

```
166         try {
167
168             // Create an input stream from the data file.
169             fileInputStream = new FileInputStream(new File(filePath));
170             inputStream     = new BufferedInputStream(fileInputStream);
171
172             fileStats.startDownload(this, FILE, name);
173         }
174         catch(Exception ex) {
175             close();
176             throw new MiddlewareException(ex);
177         }
178     }
179
```

The readDataBlock( ) method reads each data block from the source file. When it has read the entire source file, it logs the completion (lines 191–193):

```
180     public DataBlock readDataBlock( )
181         throws MiddlewareException
182     {
183         byte buffer[] = new byte[Globals.streamerBlockSize];
184
185         try {
186             int size = inputStream.read(buffer);
187
188             if (size == -1) {
189                 close();
190
191                 Globals.streamerLogger.debug("Completed download of " +
192                                             type + " '" + name + "': " +
193                                             totalSize + " bytes");
194
195                 cacheStats.incrementFileDownloadedCount( );
196                 cacheStats.incrementFileByteCount(totalSize);
197                 fileStats.endDownload(this, totalSize);
198
199                 sawEnd = true;
200                 return null;
201             }
202             else {
203                 DataBlock block = new DataBlock(size, buffer);
204                 totalSize += size;
205                 return block;
206             }
207         }
208         catch(Exception ex) {
209             close();
210             throw new MiddlewareException(ex);
211         }
212     }
213 }
```

Here are some sample streamer service log entries:

```
2004-12-21 19:17:43,320 INFO : jqpublic:
Streamer.getDataFile(/surface/tactical/sol/120/jpeg/1P138831013ETH2809P2845L2M1.JPG)
2004-12-21 19:17:43,324 DEBUG: Begin download of file '/surface/tactical/sol/120/
    jpeg/1P138831013ETH2809P2845L2M1JPG'
2004-12-21 19:17:44,584 DEBUG: Completed download of file '/surface/tactical/sol/120/
    jpeg/1P138831013ETH2809P2845L2M1.JPG': 1876 bytes
```

Figure 20-6 shows a useful graph of information we can glean from log mining. The graph shows the trend in the amount of downloading (the number of files and the number of bytes downloaded) over a period of several months during the mission. Over shorter periods of time, the graph can show spikes whenever one of the rovers makes an interesting discovery.

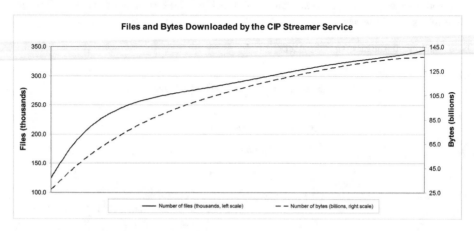

FIGURE 20-6. A graph generated from "mining" the CIP streamer service logs

Monitoring

Logging enables us to analyze the performance of the services by examining what they have been doing over a period of time. Unlike log entries, which are most helpful in pinpointing problems and their causes, runtime monitoring helps us see how well the services are currently performing. It gives us a chance to make dynamic adjustments to improve performance or to head off any potential problems. As mentioned earlier, the ability to monitor operational behavior is often critical to the success of any large application.

The code listings previously shown included statements that update the performance data kept by global static objects referenced by the fields cacheStats and fileStats. A middleware monitoring service probes this performance data upon request. The global objects to which these fields refer aren't shown, but you should be able to imagine what they contain. The key point is that it's not complicated to gather useful runtime performance data.

We wrote the CIP Middleware Monitor Utility as a client application that periodically sends requests to the middleware monitoring service to obtain the current performance data. Figure 20-7 shows a screenshot of the utility's Statistics tab that displays, among other runtime statistics, the number of files and bytes that have been downloaded and uploaded by the streamer service, and the number of file errors (such as an invalid filename specified by a client application) that have occurred.

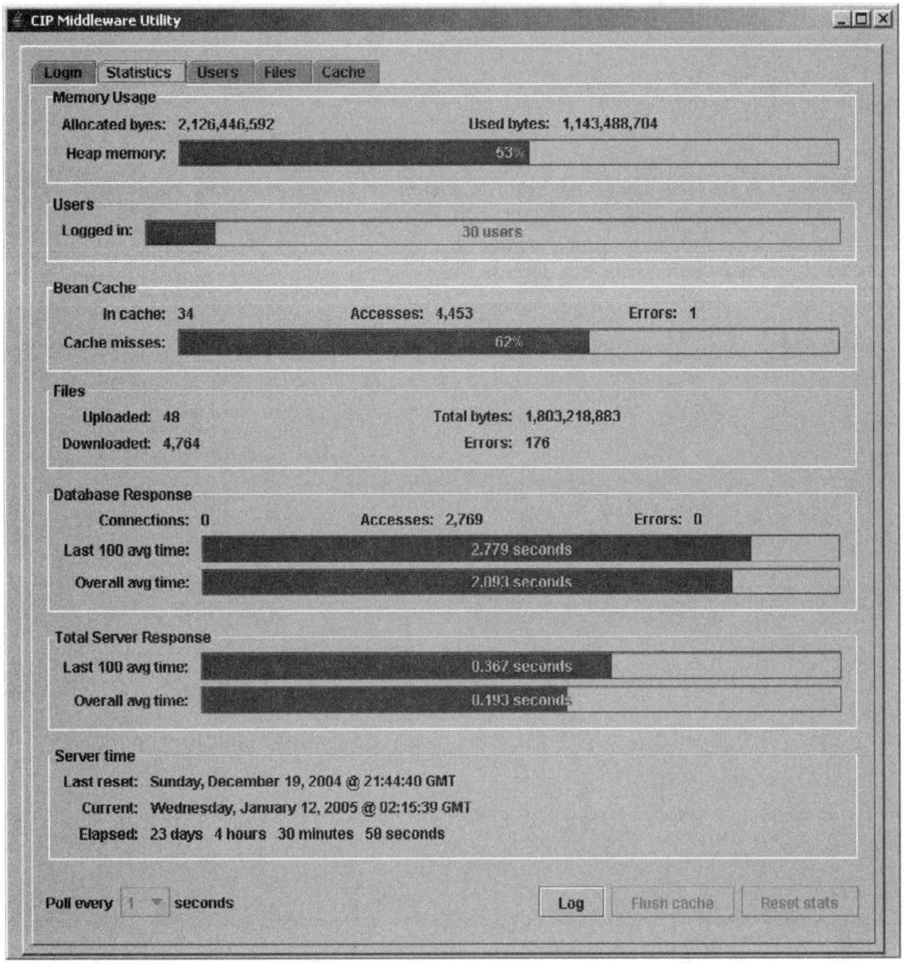

FIGURE 20-7. Screenshot of the Statistics tab of the Middleware Monitor Utility

The streamer service provider bean's doFileDownload( ) and readDataBlock( ) methods both update the global file error count (lines 50 and 84 in the code shown earlier in the section "Logging"). The getDataFile( ) and readDataBlock( ) methods increment the global total service response time (lines 22 and 94). As seen in Figure 20-7, the middleware monitor utility displays average response times under the "Total Server Response" label.

The file reader bean's getDataFile( ) method records the start of each file download (line 172). The readDataBlock( ) method increments the global total file and byte counts (lines 195 and 196) and records the completion of a download (line 197). Figure 20-8 shows a screenshot of the Files tab of the monitor utility, which displays current and recent file downloading and uploading activity.

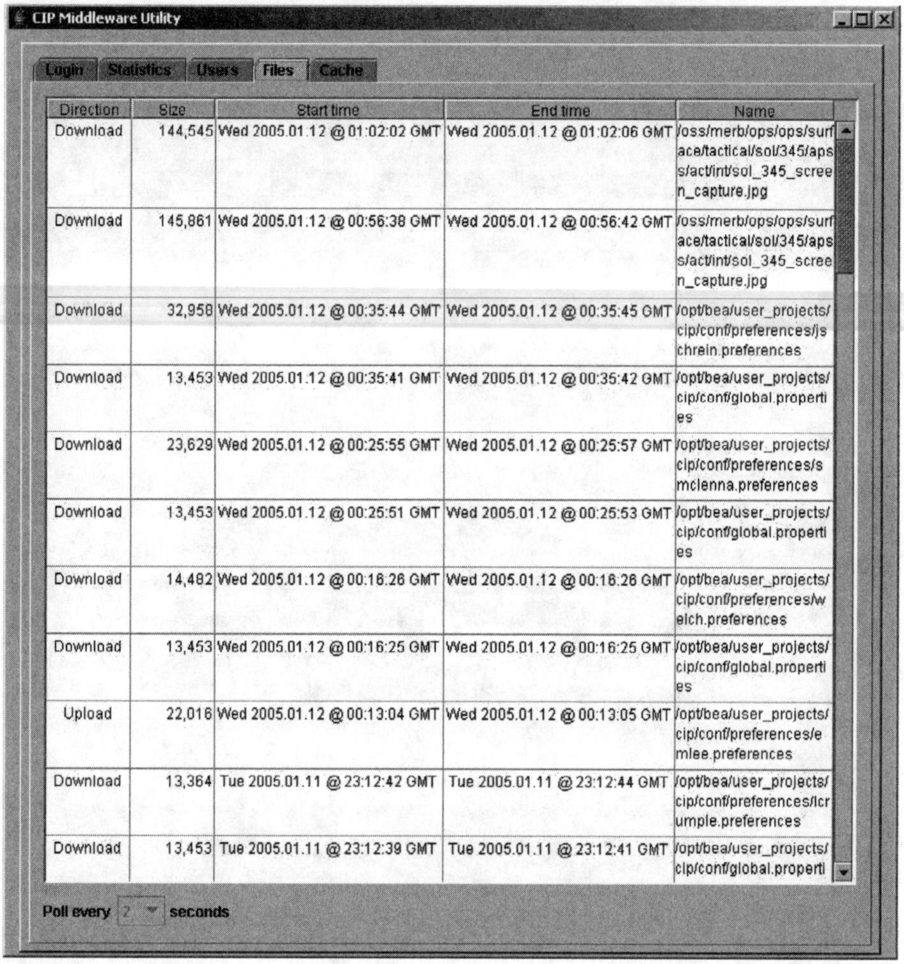

FIGURE 20-8. Screenshot of the Files tab of the Middleware Monitor Utility

Robustness

Change is inevitable, and beautiful code can handle change gracefully even after going into operation. We took a couple of measures to ensure that CIP is robust and can deal with changes in operational parameters:

- We avoided hardcoding parameters in the middleware services.

- We made it possible to make changes to the middleware services that are already in operation with minimal interruption to the client applications.

Dynamic Reconfiguration

Most of the middleware services have certain key operational parameters. For example, as seen above, the streamer service downloads file contents in blocks, and so it has a block size. Instead of hardcoding the block size, we put the value in a parameter file that the service reads each time it first starts up. This happens whenever the streamer service provider bean is loaded (lines 3–5 in the code under the section "Logging").

A *middleware.properties* file, which all the middleware services share and load, contains the line:

```
middleware.streamer.blocksize = 65536
```

The file reader bean's readDataBlock( ) method can then refer to the value (line 183).

Each middleware service can load several parameter values at startup. One of the skills of a master software builder is knowing which key values of a service to expose as loadable parameters. They are certainly helpful during development; for instance, we were able to try different block sizes during development without having to recompile the streamer service each time.

But loadable parameters are even more critical for putting code into operation. In most production environments, it is difficult and expensive to make changes to software that is already in operation. This was certainly true for the MER mission, which had a formal Change Control Board that scrutinized the justifications for making code changes once the mission was under way.

Avoiding hardcoded parameter values is, of course, a basic Programming 101 dictum that applies to small and large applications alike. But it is especially important with large applications, which may have many more parameter values that are scattered throughout large bodies of code.

Hot Swapping

Hot swapping is an important feature of the commercial application server that we employed in the CIP middleware. It is possible to deploy a middleware service that replaces one that is already running without first bringing down the middleware (and CIP altogether).

We use hot swapping whenever we need to force a service to reload its parameter values after a change, which we accomplish simply by reloading a service on top of itself. Of course, a service such as the streamer service that uses stateful session beans (the file reader and writer beans) would lose all state information. So, we can hot swap such a service only during "quiet" periods when we know the service is not currently being used. For the streamer service, we can use the Middleware Monitor Utility's Files tab (see Figure 20-8) to let us know when that's the case.

Hot swapping makes most sense in the context of a large enterprise application, where it's important to keep the rest of the application running while you are replacing part of it. With a small program, you'd probably just rerun the program to make a change.

Conclusion

The Collaborative Information Portal proves that it is possible—yes, even at a huge government agency like NASA—to develop a large complex enterprise software system on time that successfully meets strict requirements for functionality, reliability, and robustness. The Mars rovers have far exceeded expectations, a testament of how well the hardware and the software, both on Mars and on Earth, were designed and built, and of the skills of the builders.

Unlike smaller programs, beauty for a large application is not necessarily found only in elegant algorithms. For CIP, beauty is in its implementation of a service-oriented architecture and in the numerous simple but well-chosen components—the nails that master software builders know just where to pound in.

## CHAPTER TWENTY-ONE

ERP5: Designing for Maximum Adaptability

Rogerio Atem de Carvalho and Rafael Monnerat

ENTERPRISE **R**ESOURCE **P**LANNING SYSTEMS ARE GENERALLY KNOWN as large, proprietary, and highly expensive products. In 2001, work on an open source ERP system known as ERP5 (*http://www.erp5.com*) began in two French companies, Nexedi (its main developer) and Coramy (its first user). ERP5 is named after the five main concepts that compose its core. It is based on the Zope project and the Python scripting language, both of which are also open source.

We have found that ERP5 is exceptionally easy to enhance, and easy for both developers and users to build on. One reason is that we adopted an innovative document-centric approach, instead of a process- or data-centric paradigm. The core idea of a document-centric paradigm is that every business process relies on a series of documents to make it happen. The document's fields correspond to the structure of the process—that is, the fields reflect the data and the relationships among this data. Thus, if you watch how the business experts who use the ERP5 system navigate through the documents, you will discover the process workflow.

Zope's Content Management Framework (CMF) tools and concepts supply the technology behind this approach. Each instance of the CMF, called a *portal*, contains objects to which it offers services such as viewing, printing, workflow, and storage. A document structure is implemented as a Python portal class, and its behavior is implemented as a portal workflow. Therefore, users interact with web documents that are in fact views of system objects controlled by proper workflows.

This chapter will show how this document-centric paradigm and a unified set of core concepts make ERP5 a highly flexible ERP. We will illustrate these ideas by explaining how we used rapid development techniques to create ERP5's project management module, Project.

General Goals of ERP

ERP is software that aims to integrate all the data and processes of an organization into a unique system. Since this is a real challenge, the ERP industry offers different versions of the same ERP software for different economic segments, such as oil and gas, mechanical, pharmaceutical, automobile, and government.

ERP software generally consists of a series of modules that automate the operations of the organization. The most common modules include finance, inventory control, payroll, production planning and control, sales, and accounting. Those modules are designed for customization and adaptation at the user's site, because even though the organizations of a given economic segment share certain common practices, every organization wants to adapt the ERP system to its specific needs. ERP software also evolves quickly to accompany the evolution of the businesses it serves, and more and more modules are added to it over time.

ERP5

ERP5 is developed and used by a growing business and academic community in France, Brazil, Germany, Luxembourg, Poland, Senegal, and India, among other countries. It offers an integrated business management solution based on the open source Zope platform (*http://www.zope.org*), written in the Python language (*http://www.python.org*). Among the key components of Zope used by ERP5 are:

ZODB
  An object database

DCWorkflow
  A workflow engine

Content Management Framework (CMF)
  An infrastructure for adding and moving content

Zope Page Templates (ZPT)
  Rapid GUI scripting based on XML

In addition, ERP5 heavily relies on XML technologies. Every object can be exported and imported in XML format, and two or more ERP5 sites can share synchronized objects through the SyncML protocol. ERP5 also implements an object-to-relational mapping scheme that stores the indexing attributes of each object in a relational database and allows much faster object search and retrieval than ZODB. In that way, objects are kept in ZODB, but searches are made using SQL, which is a standard query language.

ERP5 was conceived to be a very flexible framework for developing enterprise applications. Being flexible means being adaptable to various business models without incurring high costs for changes and maintenance. To accomplish this, it is necessary to define a core object-oriented model from which new components can be easily derived for specific purposes. This model must be abstract enough to embrace all basic business concepts.

As the name indicates, ERP5 therefore defines five abstract concepts that lay the basis for representing business processes:

Resource

Describes a resource necessary to realize a business process, such as individual skills, products, machines, and so on.

Node

A business entity that receives and sends resources. It can be related to a physical entity (such as industrial facilities) or an abstract one (such as a bank account). Metanodes are nodes containing other nodes, such as companies.

Path

Describes how a node accesses resources it needs from another node. For instance, a path may be a trade procedure that defines how a client obtains a product from a supplier.

Movement

Describes a movement of resources among nodes at a given moment and for a given period of time. For example, one such movement can be the shipping of raw material from the warehouse to the factory. Movements are realizations of Paths.

Item

A unique instance of a resource. For instance, a CD driver is a resource for assembling a computer, while the CD driver Part Number 23E982 is an item.

These, along with some other supporting concepts like Order and Delivery, form the ERP5 Unified Business Model (UBM). It is possible to implement a new business process by combining and extending the five concepts, as we will see in this chapter. The relationships among the five core concepts are shown in Figure 21-1. A Path is related to a source node that sends a Resource to a destination node. A Movement is similar, representing a movement of an item that is described by a Resource from a source node to a destination node.

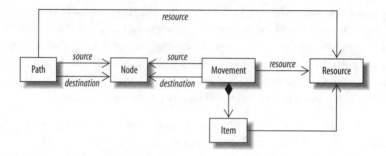

FIGURE 21-1. ERP5 core classes

The Underlying Zope Platform

To understand why ERP5 is said to be document-driven, it is necessary first to understand how Zope and its Content Management Framework (CMF) work. Zope was originally developed as a web content management environment that provides a series of services to manage the life cycle of web documents. With time, people started to note that it can be also used to implement any kind of web-based application.

In keeping with Zope's web content focus, its CMF is a framework that aims to speed the development of applications based on content types. It provides a series of services associated to these types, such as workflow, searching, security, design, and testing. From Zope, CMF inherits access to the ZODB (Zope Object Database), which provides transactions and undo functionality.

CMF implements the structural part of applications through CMF Types, maintained by the portal_types service, which is in turn a kind of registry tool for the recognized types of a given portal. The visible part of a portal type is a document that represents it. To implement behavior, portal types have actions associated with them, composing a workflow, which in turn is the implementation of a business process. An action on a document changes its state and is implemented by a Python script that realizes some business logic; for instance, calculating the total cost of an order. Given this framework, when developing an application in ERP5, we have to think in terms of documents that hold business process data and whose life cycles are kept by workflows, which implement the business process behavior.

To take advantage of the CMF structure, ERP5 code is divided into a four-level architecture that implements a chain of concept transformations, with configuration tasks at the highest level.

The first level comprises the five conceptual core classes. They have no code, only a skeleton, for the sake of simple documentation:

```
class Movement:
    """
    Movement of a quantity of a resource in a given variation
    from a source to a destination.
    """
```

At the second level is the real core classes' implementation in Python. But here, they are still abstract classes. Still, there is already some Zope stuff in the classes, and they inherit from XMLObject, which means that every object can be serialized into XML for synchronization or exporting.

Class attributes are organized into *property sheets*. Property sheets are configurable sets of attributes that facilitate the creation of different object *views*, potentially manipulated by different sets of class methods. Moreover, these views allow system administrators to set up security in a very flexible and sophisticated way.

For instance, the SimpleItem sheet bears title, short_title, and description attributes. The system administrator can set a security scheme where some users can only view these attributes, while others can write to them:

```
class Movement(XMLObject):
    """
    Movement of a quantity of a resource in a given variation
    from a source to a destination.
    """
    # defines the name of the type
    meta_type = 'ERP5 Movement'
    # defines the CMF type name
    portal_type = 'Movement'
    # adds basic Zope security configuration
    add_permission = Permissions.AddPortalContent
    # the type is listed as a valid content type
    isPortalContent = 1
    # this type is enabled for ERP5 Rapid Application Development facilities
    isRADContent = 1
    # used for trade and inventory operations
    isMovement = 1

    # Declarative security
          # stores basic class's security information
    security = ClassSecurityInfo()
          # as default, allows authenticated users to view the object
    security.declareObjectProtected(Permissions.AccessContentsInformation)

    # Declarative properties
      property_sheets = ( PropertySheet.Base
                        , PropertySheet.SimpleItem
                        , PropertySheet.Amount
                        , PropertySheet.Task
                        , PropertySheet.Arrow
                        , PropertySheet.Movement
                        , PropertySheet.Price
                        )
```

The third level holds the Meta classes, which are instantiable classes. At this tier, classes already represent specific business entities:

```
class DeliveryLine(Movement):
    """
    A DeliveryLine object allows lines to be implemented in
    Deliveries (packing list, order, invoice etc).
```

```
    It may include a price (for insurance, for customs, for invoices,
    for orders etc).
    """

    meta_type = 'ERP5 Delivery Line'
    portal_type = 'Delivery Line'

    # Declarative properties
        # it is necessary the overload the property_sheets property
        # inherited from Movement
    property_sheets = ( PropertySheet.Base
                      , PropertySheet.XMLObject
                      , PropertySheet.CategoryCore
                      , PropertySheet.Amount
                      , PropertySheet.Task
                      , PropertySheet.Arrow
                      , PropertySheet.Movement
                      , PropertySheet.Price
                      , PropertySheet.VariationRange
                      , PropertySheet.ItemAggregation
                      , PropertySheet.SortIndex
                      )
```

Finally, at the fourth level are the Portal classes, which are CMF-based. This is the level at which configuration takes place. For instance, Figure 21-2 shows the main part of the Properties tab. This screenshot shows, in particular, the properties of Task Report Line. This type is an implementation of the Delivery Line Meta type. It is interesting to note that new property sheets can be added at this tab, but they are not needed for our project tool.

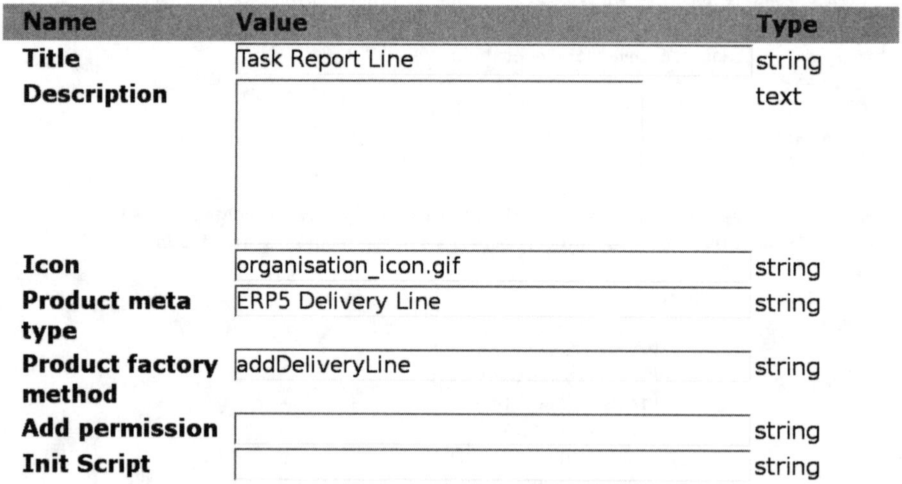

Name	Value	Type
Title	Task Report Line	string
Description		text
Icon	organisation_icon.gif	string
Product meta type	ERP5 Delivery Line	string
Product factory method	addDeliveryLine	string
Add permission		string
Init Script		string

FIGURE 21-2. Properties tab

Figure 21-3 shows the Actions tab, listing actions associated with the Task Report Line type. Actions implement specific services for this type. In the figure, you can see the View and Print services.

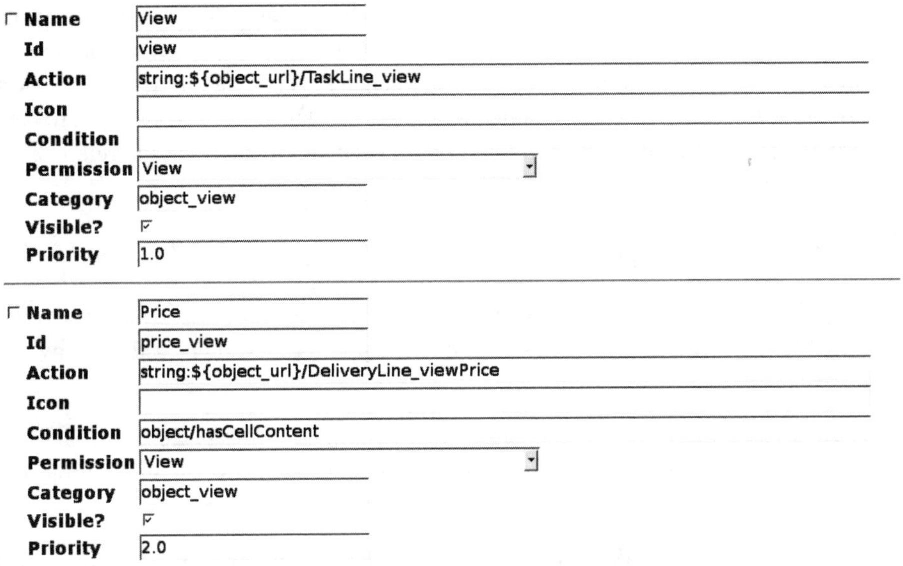

Name	View
Id	view
Action	string:${object_url}/TaskLine_view
Icon	
Condition	
Permission	View
Category	object_view
Visible?	☑
Priority	1.0

Name	Price
Id	price_view
Action	string:${object_url}/DeliveryLine_viewPrice
Icon	
Condition	object/hasCellContent
Permission	View
Category	object_view
Visible?	☑
Priority	2.0

FIGURE 21-3. Actions tab

The four-level structure representing system classes makes it easy to add functionality and platform features incrementally. It also allows a practice that is very common in ERP5: implementing new portal types without creating new classes in the system. All the programmer has to do is change the appearance of one, because ERP5's core concepts can represent entities of specific business domains.

For instance, a Movement can be used to represent both a cash withdrawal in the finances module and a transference of material from the warehouse to the factory in the inventory module. To do so, we create one portal type to represent a cash withdrawal and another to represent a material transfer, each using the appropriate business terms that appear in the GUI.

Besides using basic CMF features, ERP5 also implements some extra features to enhance programming productivity. Perhaps the most interesting is the concept of relationship managers, which are objects responsible for keeping the relationships between pairs of objects. Coding relationship logic into each business class is often tedious and error-prone. Also, traditional relationship code spreads the implementation (back-pointers, deletion notifications, and so on) among many business classes, which is more difficult to track, maintain, and keep in sync than mediated approaches.

In ERP5, a portal service called Portal Categories records all the one-to-one, one-to-many, and many-to-many relationships between groups of related objects. Query methods, getters and setters, and relationship code are automatically generated.

This service holds *base category* objects, which connect classes that collaborate to carry out a given business process. For every base category, ERP5 automatically generates all necessary getters and setters. As an example, the base category source is a reference for objects of the Node type. If, in a given ERP5 implementation, the class Order is configured to have this base category, the system will automatically include all the methods and references necessary to navigate from orders to nodes, and vice versa if desired.

ERP5 Project Concepts

To exemplify how ERP5 modules are coded, we'll spend most of the rest of this chapter exploring ERP5 Project, a flexible project management tool that can be used in many ways.

Due to the fast and competitive global business environment, projects are the usual form through which businesses develop innovative products and services. Therefore, project management is gaining interest in every industry segment.

But what is a project? According to Wikipedia, a project is "a temporary endeavor undertaken to create a unique product or service" (*http://en.wikipedia.org/wiki/Project*, last visited April 13, 2007).

The uniqueness of projects makes their management difficult, even for a small project sometimes. Hence the need for project management, which is "the discipline of organizing and managing resources in such a way that these resources deliver all the work required to complete a project within defined scope, quality, time, and cost constraints" (*http://en. wikipedia.org/wiki/Project_management*, last visited April 13, 2007).

Project management therefore must control a series of data related to resources such as money, time, and people to keep everything going as planned. Because of this, information tools are needed to ease the analysis of large amounts of data.

The first use for ERP5 Project was as an "internal" project management tool to support ERP5 instance creation projects. Afterwards, it was redesigned to support other types of projects in general. Even more broadly, this tool can manage order planning and execution wherever a project viewpoint can aid production planning and control. In other words, ERP5 Project should be adaptable to every situation where it is interesting to think in terms of a project composed of a series of tasks and limited by a series of constraints.

ERP5 allows the developer to reuse the current packages in delivering other packages as completely new modules. Following this concept, a new business template (BT) is created by basing it on an existing one.

By the time ERP5 Project started to be implemented, ERP5 already contained the Trade BT. The development team thus decided to base Project on Trade, representing the planning part of a project by reusing the logic developed for trading operations. After finishing the first Project version, they could improve the Project BT and then use the improvements to refactor Trade BT, making it yet more flexible.

In building Project, the interesting parts of Trade are the Order and Delivery classes. These classes, also part of the UBM, are containers for Order Line and Delivery Line objects, which in turn are Movements that contain ordered and delivered items, as shown in Figure 21-4. In that figure, the subclasses at the lowest level are all portal types. Therefore, they have basically the same structure as their superclasses, but each portal type has a different GUI and modifications in its workflow to act according to project management logic.

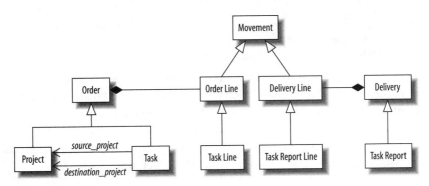

FIGURE 21-4. Relations between Trade and Project

The relation between Order and Delivery is maintained by *causalities*, which basically determine that for every confirmed order there will be a mirroring delivery sometime in the future. Tasks and task reports inherit the same behavior. Accordingly, order lines represent planned movements of resources between two nodes, which, after being confirmed, will be executed and generate delivery lines. Therefore, from a project management point of view, tasks implement project planning, and task reports implement project control.

Coding the ERP5 Project

The first thing we thought about in creating the Project BT was the main project class. Initially, instead of creating a new class, we decided to simply use Order itself, without change. But after some time, we realized that the business definitions for an order and a project are so different that we should simply create Project as a subclass of Order, without any new code in it, just for the sake of separating concerns. In this design, a project is an object that is described by a series of goals or milestones with one or more tasks associated with each of them.

Then, we had to decide how to implement task management since there are differences between a project and a trade operation. The first thing to consider is that tasks can occur outside projects—for instance, in production planning. Therefore, we consider a task as a composition of task lines, or smaller activities inside a task. In that way, we decouple tasks from projects, allowing them to be used in other situations, while keeping the relation with Project through source_project and destination_project base categories.

Tasks are implemented through configuration, as we did for Task Report Line in Figure 21-2, with the difference of using Order as a metaclass. The creation of a task associated with a project is shown here:

```
# Add a task in task_module. Context represents the current project object.
context_obj = context.getObject()
# newContent is an ERP5 API method that creates a new content.
task = context.task_module.newContent(portal_type = 'Task')
# Set the source_project reference to the task.
task.setSourceProjectValue(context_obj)
# Redirect the user to Task GUI, so that the user can edit its properties.
return context.REQUEST.RESPONSE.redirect(task.absolute_url() + '?portal_status_
message=Created+Task.')
```

Remember that for retrieving the tasks of a certain project, the programmer needs to use only the base category source_project. With this category, ERP5 RAD automatically generates signatures and algorithms of accessors. It is interesting to note that the same accessors will be created for both Task and Project. The programmer decides which ones to use through configuration, using the Actions tab shown in Figure 21-3. In that tab, the programmer can define a new GUI for using the following methods:

```
### These accessors are used to navigate from task to project

# This method returns the related Project reference
getSourceProject()

# This method sets the related Project reference
setSourceProject()

# This method returns the related Project object
getSourceProjectValue()

# This method sets the related Project object
setSourceProjectValue()

### These accessors are used to navigate from project to task

# This method returns references to related tasks
getSourceProjectRelated()

# This method is not generated in order to avoid an encapsulation break
# setSourceProjectRelated()

# This method returns the related tasks objects
getSourceProjectRelatedValue()

# This method is not generated in order to avoid an encapsulation break
# setSourceProjectRelatedValue()
```

You must be asking where the typical project domain attributes and behavior are. The answer for the attributes, in most cases, is that they are attributes of Movement and some other UBM classes, masked in the GUI with other names. In other cases, the attribute is implemented through a base category, with all the accessors automatically generated as expected.

One example of this is the task predecessors, a list of tasks that need to be executed before a given task—a very basic project management concept, not found on trade operations. This list is also implemented by a base category named predecessor, which links a task to its predecessor in a configurable way because the category takes care of all the code needed.

Workflows implement task behavior. Again, basic Movement and more specialized Order behavior is reused. These workflows manipulate the objects in a way that makes sense for project management, and include some scripts for doing so. Workflows make development easier because they are configurable, and the programmer needs to write scripts only for specific object manipulation.

Figure 21-5 shows the Task workflow. In each box, words in parentheses represent the state ID. Transitions with the _action suffix are trigged by GUI events; the others are internally trigged by workflow events. For each transition, it is possible to define pre- and post-scripts. These scripts are the ones that will manipulate the objects according to the business logic—in this case, the task execution logic. Task represents the planning view of the process, which essentially goes through planned, ordered, and confirmed states.

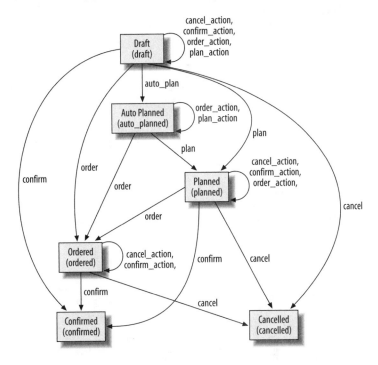

FIGURE 21-5. Task workflow

This workflow is the same as Order, but some scripts were changed according to project domain logic. As an example, here is the script order_validateData, which is called before every _action as follows:

```
### This script check that necessary data exists on Task
# gets the task object in use
task = state_change.object
error_message = ''
message_list = []
# checks if the task is attached to some project or not
if task.getSource() is None:
  message_list.append('No Source')
# if the initial date is null, but there is a final date, makes
# initialDate = finalDate
if task.getStartDate() is None and task.getStopDate() is not None:
  task.setStartDate(task.getStopDate())
if task.getStartDate () is None:
  message_list.append("No Date")
if task.getDestination() is None:
  message_list.append('No Destination')
# for each contained object, filters the one that are movements.
# A typical return would be something like
#('Task Line', 'Sale Order Line', 'Purchase Order Line')
for line in task.objectValues(portal_type=task.getPortalOrderMovementTypeList ()):
  # checks if all movements have a associated resource
  if line.getResourceValue() is None:
    message_list.append("No Resource for line with id: %s" % line.getId())
# if any error happened, raises a warning
if len(message_list) > 0:
  raise ValidationFailed, "Warning: " + " --- ".join(message_list)
```

Figure 21-6 shows the Task Report workflow. It follows the same logic as the Delivery workflow, with some added scripts, such as taskReport_notifyAssignee, shown here.

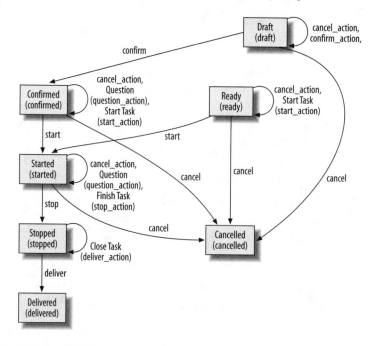

FIGURE 21-6. Task Report workflow

```
task_report = state_change.object
# searches for the assigner for the task
source_person = task_report.getSourceValue(portal_type="Person")
# searches for the assignee
destination_person = task_report.getDestinationValue(portal_type="Person")
# get the assigner email
if source_person is not None:
  from_email = destination_person.getDefaultEmailText()
  email = source_person.getDefaultEmailValue()
  if email is not None:
    msg = """
# preformmated string with message plus task data goes here
"""
    email.activate().send(from_url = from_email,
                          subject="New Task Assigned to You",
                          msg = msg)
```

Conclusion

The ERP5 team was able to implement a highly flexible tool, used for both "traditional" project management and for order planning and execution control, by making substantial reuse of already existing core concepts and code. Actually, reuse is a daily operation in ERP5 development, to the point where entire new modules are created just by changing GUI elements and adjusting workflows.

Because of this emphasis on reuse, queries on the object database can be done at the abstraction levels of portal types or meta classes. In the first case, the specific business domain concept is retrieved, such as a project task. In the second case, all objects related to the UBM generic concepts are retrieved, which is quite interesting for such requirements as statistics gathering.

In this chapter, we have edited some code snippets to make them more readable. All ERP5 code in its raw state is available at *http://svn.erp5.org/erp5/trunk*.

Acknowledgments

We would like to thank Jean-Paul Smets-Solanes, ERP5 creator and chief architect, and all the guys on the team, especially Romain Courteaud and Thierry Faucher. When the authors say *we* during the discussion of ERP5 design and implementation, they are referring to all those nice folks at Nexedi.

## CHAPTER TWENTY-TWO

A Spoonful of Sewage

Bryan Cantrill

If you put a spoonful of sewage in a barrel full of wine, you get sewage.

Schopenhauer's Law of Entropy

UNLIKE MOST THINGS THAT WE ENGINEER, SOFTWARE HAS A BINARY NOTION OF CORRECTNESS: either it is correct, or it is flawed. That is, unlike a bridge or an airplane or a microprocessor, software doesn't have physical parameters that limit the scope of its correctness; software doesn't have a rated load or a maximum speed or an environmental envelope. In this regard, software is much more like mathematical proof than physical machine: a proof's elegance or inelegance is subjective, but its correctness is not.

And indeed, this lends a purity to software that has traditionally only been enjoyed by mathematics: software, like mathematics, can be correct in an absolute and timeless sense. But if this purity of software is its Dr. Jekyll, software has a brittleness that is its Mr. Hyde: given that software can only be correct or flawed, a single flaw can become the difference between unqualified success and abject failure.

Of course, this is not to say that every bug is necessarily fatal—just that the possibility always exists that a single bug will reveal something much larger than its manifestations: a design flaw that calls into question the fundamental assumptions upon which the software was built. Such a flaw can shake software to its core and, in the worst case, invalidate it completely. That is, a single software bug can be the proverbial spoonful of sewage in the barrel of wine, turning what would otherwise be an enjoyable pleasure into a toxic stew.

For me personally, this fine line between wine and sewage was never so stark as in one incident in the development of a critical subsystem of the Solaris kernel in 1999. This problem—and its solution—are worth discussing at some length, for they reveal how profound design defects can manifest themselves as bugs, and how devilish the details can become when getting a complicated and important body of software to function perfectly.

A word of caution before we begin: this journey will take us deep into the core of the Solaris kernel, into some of the most fundamental and subtlest mechanism of the operating system. As such, the detail may seem crushing; like adventurous spelunkers, we will at times be wading through dark, cold water or squeezing through suffocatingly tight passages—but for those that make the trip, a hidden and beautiful underground cavern awaits. So if you're ready, don your headlamp, grab a water bottle, and let's descend into the Solaris kernel....

The subsystem that is the center of our story is the turnstile subsystem. A *turnstile* is the mechanism used to block and wake up threads in Solaris—it is the underpinning of synchronization primitives such as mutexes and reader/writer locks. Or, to let the code speak for itself:*

```
/*
 * Turnstiles provide blocking and wakeup support, including priority
 * inheritance, for synchronization primitives (e.g. mutexes and rwlocks).
 * Typical usage is as follows:
 *
 * To block on lock 'lp' for read access in foo_enter():
 *
 *      ts = turnstile_lookup(lp);
 *      [ If the lock is still held, set the waiters bit
 *      turnstile_block(ts, TS_READER_Q, lp, &foo_sobj_ops);
 *
 * To wake threads waiting for write access to lock 'lp' in foo_exit():
 *
 *      ts = turnstile_lookup(lp);
 *      [ Either drop the lock (change owner to NULL) or perform a direct
 *      [ handoff (change owner to one of the threads we're about to wake).
 *      [ If we're going to wake the last waiter, clear the waiters bit.
 *      turnstile_wakeup(ts, TS_WRITER_Q, nwaiters, new_owner or NULL);
 *
 * turnstile_lookup() returns holding the turnstile hash chain lock for lp.
 * Both turnstile_block() and turnstile_wakeup() drop the turnstile lock.
 * To abort a turnstile operation, the client must call turnstile_exit().
 *
 ...
```

The turnstile abstraction thus allows synchronization primitives to focus on their own particular policy without worrying about the delicate mechanics of blocking and awakening. As the block comment mentions, turnstile_block( ) is the function called to actually block the current thread on a synchronization primitive, and it is in this function that our subterranean journey begins in earnest with this cryptic comment of mine:

---

* This code is open source and is available at *http://src.opensolaris.org/source/xref/onnv/onnv-gate/usr/src/uts/common/os/turnstile.c.*

```
/*
 * Follow the blocking chain to its end, willing our priority to
 * everyone who's in our way.
 */
while (t->t_sobj_ops != NULL &&
    (owner = SOBJ_OWNER(t->t_sobj_ops, t->t_wchan)) != NULL) {
        if (owner == curthread) {
                if (SOBJ_TYPE(sobj_ops) != SOBJ_USER_PI) {
                        panic("Deadlock: cycle in blocking chain");
                }
                /*
                 * If the cycle we've encountered ends in mp,
                 * then we know it isn't a 'real' cycle because
                 * we're going to drop mp before we go to sleep.
                 * Moreover, since we've come full circle we know
                 * that we must have willed priority to everyone
                 * in our way.  Therefore, we can break out now.
                 */
                if (t->t_wchan == (void *)mp)
                        break;
```

For me, this comment (and the two lines of code to which it refers, all highlighted in bold) will always be the canonical difference between sewage and wine: they were added in the final, frenzied moments of Solaris 8, in one of the more intense experiences of my engineering career—a week-long collaboration with fellow Sun engineer Jeff Bonwick that required so much shared mental state that he and I both came to call it "the mind-meld."

We will come back to this code and the mind-meld behind it, but to get there, we first need to journey much deeper into the inner workings of turnstiles, exploring in particular how turnstiles address the classic problem of *priority inversion*.

If you are unfamiliar with the problem of priority inversion, it can be described as follows: given three threads at three different priorities, if the highest priority thread blocks on a synchronization object held by the lowest priority thread, the middling priority thread could (in a pure priority preemptive system running on a uniprocessor) run in perpetuity, starving the highest priority thread. The result is illustrated in Figure 22-1.

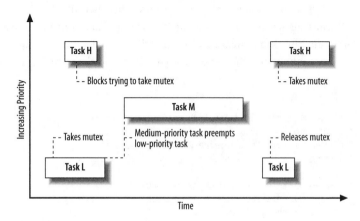

FIGURE 22-1. Priority inversion

One mechanism to solve priority inversion is a technique called *priority inheritance*. Under priority inheritance, when one thread is going to block on a resource held by a lower priority thread, the higher priority thread *wills* its priority to the lower priority thread for the duration of the critical section. That is, the priority of the lower priority thread is *boosted* to that of the higher priority thread as long as the lower priority thread owns a resource that the higher priority thread needs. When the lower priority thread (running with a boosted priority) exits the critical section—when it releases the synchronization primitive upon which the higher priority thread is blocked—it awakens the blocked higher priority thread and returns itself to the lower priority. In this way, no middling priority thread ever has the opportunity to run—the inversion is averted.

Now, in Solaris we have long had priority inheritance for kernel synchronization primitives; indeed, this is one of the architectural differences between SunOS 4.x and Solaris 2.x, and it is one of the core services of the turnstile subsystem. And just getting priority inheritance right for kernel synchronization primitives is nasty: one must know who owns a lock, and one must know which lock the owner is blocked on (if any). That is, if a thread is blocking on a lock that is owned by a thread that is *itself* blocked, we need to be able to determine what lock the owning thread is blocked on, and which thread owns *that* lock. We call this chain of blocked threads the *blocking chain*, and because its nuances are central to the implementation of priority inheritance, it's worth fleshing out a plausible and concrete example of how one might develop.

For an example of a blocking chain, we can look to the interaction between two well-known Solaris subsystems: the kernel memory allocator and the Zettabyte Filesystem (ZFS). For purposes of our example, we don't need to understand these grand subsystems in any detail; we're just shining a flashlight into them, not exploring their many nooks and crannies. The salient bits about the kernel memory allocator are that it is an *object-caching* allocator—all allocations are served from caches that manage objects of a fixed size—and that it caches allocated buffers in per-CPU structures called *magazines*. When a magazine is exhausted, allocations are satisfied out of a structure called a *depot*. This tiered structure is highly scalable with respect to CPUs: by satisfying most allocations out of the per-CPU magazine structure (upon which contention is highly unlikely), the allocator exhibits near-linear CPU scalability. And while it is orthogonal to our purpose at the moment, I can't help but illuminate an elegant detail in the code that executes when a per-CPU magazine is empty and the depot lock (which is global per-cache) must be acquired:

```
/*
 * If we can't get the depot lock without contention,
 * update our contention count.  We use the depot
 * contention rate to determine whether we need to
 * increase the magazine size for better scalability.
 */
if (!mutex_tryenter(&cp->cache_depot_lock)) {
        mutex_enter(&cp->cache_depot_lock);
        cp->cache_depot_contention++;
}
```

This code doesn't simply acquire the lock, it *attempts* to acquire the lock, keeping track of the number of times that this attempt fails because the lock was held. The resulting count is a rough indicator of contention at the global layer, and if the count becomes too high in a given interval of time, the system increases the number of buffers stored at the per-CPU layer, reducing the contention at the global layer. This simple mechanism thus allows the subsystem to dynamically adjust its structures to reduce its own contention! Beautiful code, for certain.

Let's return to the construction of our example, and now to ZFS, where all we need to know is that files and directories have an in-memory structure called a znode.

Given this background about the kernel memory allocator and ZFS, we can envision the following sequence of events:

1. A thread T1, attempts an allocation from the kmem_alloc_32 cache on CPU 2, which requires taking the lock for CPU 2's kmem_alloc_32 magazine. Discovering that the magazines for CPU 2 are all empty, T1 acquires the depot lock for the kmem_alloc_32 cache, and it is then preempted, with both the CPU 2 magazine lock and the depot lock held.

2. A second thread T2, running on CPU 3, attempts an unrelated allocation from the kmem_alloc_32 cache. As bad luck would have it, its magazines are also empty. T2 attempts to acquire the depot lock for the kmem_alloc_32 cache—but it sees that the lock is held by T1, and it blocks.

3. A third thread T3, runs on CPU 3 after T2 has blocked. This thread is attempting to create the ZFS file */foo/bar/mumble*. As part of this operation, it must create a ZFS directory entry lock for the entry *mumble* in the directory */foo/bar*. It acquires the lock on the znode that corresponds to */foo/bar* and then attempts to allocate a zfs_dirlock_t. Because a zfs_dirlock_t is 32 bytes in size, this allocation is to be satisfied from the kmem_alloc_32 cache, and T3 therefore attempts to acquire the magazine lock for the kmem_alloc_32 cache on CPU 3—but it sees that the lock is held by T2, and it blocks.

4. A fourth thread, T4, attempts to examine the contents of the directory */foo/bar*. As a part of this operation, it attempts to acquire the lock on the znode that corresponds to */foo/bar*—but it sees that the lock is held by T3, and it blocks.

When T4 blocks, it is blocking on T3, which is in turn blocked on T2, which is in turn blocked on T1—and it is this chain of threads that constitutes the blocking chain. Having seen what a blocking chain might actually look like in the wild, it might be easier to appreciate the essential subtlety of getting priority inheritance correct: when a blocking thread wills its priority to its blocking chain, we must iterate over the entire blocking chain *coherently*. That is, when we iterate over the blocking chain, we must see a consistent snapshot of all of the threads that were on the blocking chain at that instant—no more and no less. In the context of this example, we wouldn't want to will our priority to T1 *after* it released the lock blocking T2 (and thus, transitively, T4)—this would potentially leave T1 at an artificially high priority.

So, how can we iterate over the blocking chain coherently? In Solaris, a thread's dispatcher state (e.g., whether it's running, enqueued to run, or sleeping) is protected by acquiring a special spin lock known as its *thread lock*; it might be tempting to believe that in order to process the blocking chain coherently, we should simply acquire all of the thread locks at once. This won't work, however, in part because of the way that thread locks are implemented.

A thread lock is a very special lock because it is not a spin lock in any traditional sense, but rather a *pointer* to a spin lock, with the lock that it points to being the lock that protects the structure currently managing the thread; as the management of a thread is changed from one structure to another, its thread lock is changed to point to the correct lock.

For example, if a thread is enqueued to run on a CPU, its thread lock points to a lock for the dispatch queue on that CPU for the thread's priority level, but when the thread is running on a CPU, the thread lock is changed to point to a lock within the CPU's cpu_t structure. And if the thread should block on a synchronization primitive, its thread lock is changed to point to a lock in the (cue ominous, foreshadowing music) turnstile table.

This last structure will become much more important as we descend deeper, but for now, the critical point is this: we cannot simply acquire every thread lock because multiple threads can point to the *same* underlying dispatcher lock; if we simply tried to acquire them all, we might deadlock on ourselves as we spin, attempting to acquire a lock that we ourselves have already acquired!*

Fortunately, we don't actually have to hold every thread lock to assure a consistent snapshot of the blocking chain, thanks to an important (if self-evident) property of blocking chains: they can only become unwound from their *unblocked* ends. That is, the only way for a thread blocked on a synchronization primitive to become unblocked is to be explicitly awoken by the thread owning the synchronization primitive.

So in our example, the only way for (say) T3 to become runnable is to be awoken by T2. So if we proceed atomically from T3 to T2, and then atomically from T2 to T1, we're guaranteed that there is no window by which T3 can be awoken—even if we have dropped the thread lock for T3.

This means that we need not lock the *entire* chain—we need only lock *two consecutive elements* at a time: when T4 is to block, we can grab the lock for T3, then grab the lock for T2, then drop the lock for T3 and acquire the lock for T1, then drop the lock for T2, and so on. Because we're only looking to hold two thread locks at a time, it's easy to deal with the case where they point to the same underlying lock: if they point to the same underlying lock, we just retain that lock as we iterate over that element in the blocking chain.

This has *almost* resolved the issue of iterating over blocking chains, but a substantial hurdle remains—one that is the ramification of a different design decision. Recall that we

---

* There is a subtler problem here, too, of lock ordering; suffice it to say that acquiring all thread locks in a blocking chain is a nonstarter, for myriad reasons.

mentioned that thread locks can point to dispatcher locks in the turnstile table. We now need to explain the turnstile table, as we will be encountering it several more times in our journey.

The turnstile table is a hash table keyed by the virtual address of the synchronization primitive; it is the table of queues upon which blocked threads are queued. Each queue is locked at its head, by a *turnstile lock*—and it is one of these locks that a thread's thread lock will point to if the thread is blocked on a synchronization primitive.

This is a critical, if subtle, design decision: when a thread is blocked on a synchronization primitive, it is *not* enqueued on a queue that is unique to the synchronization primitive, but rather one that may be shared by several synchronization primitives that happen to map to the same turnstile table entry.

Why was it done this way? As a highly parallel operating system, Solaris has fine-grained synchronization, meaning that there are many (many!) instances of synchronization primitives, and that they are manipulated very frequently—nearly always with zero contention. Thus, the structures that represent kernel synchronization primitives—kmutex_t and krwlock_t—must be as small as possible, and their manipulation must optimize for the common, uncontended case. Embedding the queue for the blocking chain in the synchronization primitive itself would lead to an unacceptable impact, either on space (by bloating the size of the primitive with a queue pointer and dispatcher lock) or on time (by slowing down the uncontended case to maintain a more complicated structure). Either way, it is unacceptable to situate the data structure for a blocking chain with the synchronization primitive itself—a turnstile table (or something like it) is required.

To restate the ramifications of the turnstile table: threads blocked on *different* synchronization primitives can have their thread locks point to the *same* turnstile lock. Given that we must hold two locks at a time while traversing the blocking chain, this creates a nasty lock ordering problem. When Jeff encountered this problem in his original implementation, he solved it in an elegant way; his comment in turnstile_interlock() explains the problem and his solution:

```
/*
 * When we apply priority inheritance, we must grab the owner's thread lock
 * while already holding the waiter's thread lock.  If both thread locks are
 * turnstile locks, this can lead to deadlock: while we hold L1 and try to
 * grab L2, some unrelated thread may be applying priority inheritance to
 * some other blocking chain, holding L2 and trying to grab L1.  The most
 * obvious solution -- do a lock_try() for the owner lock -- isn't quite
 * sufficient because it can cause livelock: each thread may hold one lock,
 * try to grab the other, fail, bail out, and try again, looping forever.
 * To prevent livelock we must define a winner, i.e. define an arbitrary
 * lock ordering on the turnstile locks.  For simplicity we declare that
 * virtual address order defines lock order, i.e. if L1 < L2, then the
 * correct lock ordering is L1, L2.  Thus the thread that holds L1 and
 * wants L2 should spin until L2 is available, but the thread that holds
 * L2 and can't get L1 on the first try must drop L2 and return failure.
```

```
 * Moreover, the losing thread must not reacquire L2 until the winning
 * thread has had a chance to grab it; to ensure this, the losing thread
 * must grab L1 after dropping L2, thus spinning until the winner is done.
 * Complicating matters further, note that the owner's thread lock pointer
 * can change (i.e. be pointed at a different lock) while we're trying to
 * grab it.  If that happens, we must unwind our state and try again.
 */
```

This lock ordering issue is part of what made it difficult to implement priority inheritance for kernel synchronization objects—and unfortunately, kernel-level priority inheritance solves only part of the priority inversion problem.

Providing priority inheritance exclusively for kernel synchronization objects has an obvious shortcoming: to build a multithreaded real-time system, one needs priority inheritance not just for kernel-level synchronization primitives, but also for *user-level* synchronization primitives. And it was this problem—user-level priority inheritance—that we decided to address in Solaris 8. We assigned an engineer to solve it, and (with extensive guidance from those of us who best understand the guts of scheduling and synchronization), the new facility was integrated in October 1999.

A few months later—in December of 1999—I was looking at an operating system failure that a colleague had encountered. It was immediately clear that this was some sort of defect in our implementation of user-level priority inheritance, but as I understood the bug, I came to realize that this was no surface problem: this was a design defect—and I could practically smell our wine turning to sewage.

Before explaining this bug—and the design defect that it revealed—it's worth discussing the methodology used to debug it. An important skill for any software engineer is the ability to analyze the failure of a complicated software system, and to present that analysis rigorously. And in any sufficiently complicated system, failure analysis will often be forensic: it will be based on a snapshot of system state at the time of failure. Indeed, such a snapshot of state is so fundamental to debugging that it carries with it a moniker from the dawn of computing: it is a "core dump."

This variant of debugging—*postmortem debugging*—can be contrasted to the more traditional *in situ* debugging by which one is debugging a live and running (albeit stopped) system. Whereas with *in situ* debugging one can use breakpoints to iteratively test hypotheses about the system, with postmortem debugging one can use only the state of the system at the time of failure to test hypotheses. While this means that postmortem debugging is necessarily a less complete methodology than *in situ* debugging (as there are bugs for which there simply does not exist enough state at the time of failure to eliminate a significant number of hypotheses), there are many bugs that are not sufficiently reproducible to apply *in situ* debugging—there is no other way to debug them *but* postmortem.

Moreover, because the more limited options afforded by postmortem debugging require more rigorous thinking around both hypothesis generation and validation, developing one's ability to debug postmortem makes one much more efficient at *in situ* debugging.

Finally, because the state of the system is static, one can present specific, rigorous analysis to peers, who can then perform their own analysis—in parallel—and draw their own conclusions. And even if not actively validated by others, this analysis is valuable, for drafting it forces one to address the holes in one's own logic. In short, postmortem debugging is an essential part of our craft—a skill that every serious software engineer should develop.

Given that background on (and plug for) postmortem debugging, and with the caveat that this analysis will not yet be completely (or perhaps not at all) comprehensible, here is my analysis of the bug at hand, as it appeared verbatim in my initial bug report:*

```
[ bmc, 12/13/99 ]

The following sequence of events can explain the state in the dump (the arrow
denotes an ordering):

            Thread A (300039c8580)                  Thread B (30003c492a0)
            (executing on CPU 10)                   (executing on CPU 4)
+----------------------------------+ +------------------------------------+
|                                  | |                                    |
|  Calls lwp_upimutex_lock() on    | |                                    |
|  lock 0xff350000                 | |                                    |
|                                  | |                                    |
|  lwp_upimutex_lock() acquires    | |                                    |
|  upibp->upib_lock                | |                                    |
|                                  | |                                    |
|  lwp_upimutex_lock(), seeing the | |                                    |
|  lock held, calls turnstile_block()| |                                  |
|                                  | |                                    |
|  turnstile_block():              | |                                    |
|  - Acquires A's thread lock      | |                                    |
|  - Transitions A into TS_SLEEP   | |                                    |
|  - Drops A's thread lock         | |                                    |
|  - Drops upibp->upib_lock        | |                                    |
|  - Calls swtch()                 | |                                    |
|                                  | |                                    |
|                                  | |                                    |
:                                  : :                                    :


    +---------------------------------------------------------------+
    | Holder of 0xff350000 releases the lock, explicitly handing it off to |
    | thread A (and thus setting upi_owner to 300039c8580)          |
    +---------------------------------------------------------------+


:                                  : :                                    :
|                                  | |                                    |
|  Returns from turnstile_block()  | |                                    |
|                                  | |  Calls lwp_upimutex_lock() on      |
|                                  | |  lock 0xff350000                   |
|                                  | |                                    |
|                                  | |  lwp_upimutex_lock() acquires      |
|                                  | |  upibp->upib_lock                  |
|                                  | |                                    |
```

* "Beautiful Bug Reports," anyone?

```
|                                  | | Seeing the lock held (by A), calls |
|                                  | | turnstile_block()                  |
| Calls lwp_upimutex_owned() to    | |                                    |
| check for lock hand-off          | | turnstile_block():                 |
|                                  | | - Acquires B's thread lock         |
| lwp_upimutex_owned() attempts    | | - Transitions B into TS_SLEEP,     |
| to acquire upibp->upib_lock      | |   setting B's wchan to upimutex    |
|                                  | |   corresponding to 0xff350000      |
| upibp->upib_lock is held by B;   | | - Attempts to promote holder of    |
| calls into turnstile_block()     | |   0xff350000 (Thread A)            |
| through mutex_vector_enter()     | | - Acquires A's thread lock         |
|                                  | | - Adjusts A's priority             |
| turnstile_block():               | | - Drops A's thread lock            |
|                     <------------+                                      |
| - Acquires A's thread lock       | | - Drops B's thread lock            |
| - Attempts to promote holder of  | |                                    |
|   upibp->upib_lock (Thread B)    | |                                    |
| - Acquires B's thread lock       | | - Drops upibp->upib_lock           |
| - Adjusts B's priority           | |                                    |
| - Drops B's thread lock          | |                                    |
| - Seeing that B's wchan is not   | |                                    |
|   NULL, attempts to continue     | |                                    |
|   priority inheritance           | |                                    |
| - Calls SOBJ_OWNER() on B's wchan| |                                    |
| - Seeing that owner of B's wchan | |                                    |
|   is A, panics with "Deadlock:   | |                                    |
|   cycle in blocking chain"       | |                                    |
|                                  | |                                    |
+----------------------------------+ +------------------------------------+
```

As the above sequence implies, the problem is in turnstile_block():

```
        THREAD_SLEEP(t, &tc->tc_lock);
        t->t_wchan = sobj;
        t->t_sobj_ops = sobj_ops;
        ...
        /*
         * Follow the blocking chain to its end, or until we run out of
         * inversions, willing our priority to everyone who's in our way.
         */
        while (inverted && t->t_sobj_ops != NULL &&
            (owner = SOBJ_OWNER(t->t_sobj_ops, t->t_wchan)) != NULL) {
                ...
        }
(1) --> thread_unlock_nopreempt(t);
        /*
         * At this point, "t" may not be curthread. So, use "curthread", from
         * now on, instead of "t".
         */
        if (SOBJ_TYPE(sobj_ops) == SOBJ_USER_PI) {
(2) -->         mutex_exit(mp);
                ...
```

We're dropping the thread lock of the blocking thread (at (1)) before we drop
the upibp->upib_lock at (2). From (1) until (2) we are violating one of
the invariants of SOBJ_USER_PI locks: when sleeping on a SOBJ_USER_PI lock,
_no_ kernel locks may be held; any held kernel locks can yield a deadlock
panic.

Understanding the analysis requires some knowledge of implementation nomenclature:

upibp

A pointer to the in-kernel state associated with a held user-level priority inheriting lock; the upib_lock is the lock that protects this state.

t_wchan

The member of the thread structure that contains the pointer to the synchronization primitive upon which the thread (if any) is blocked.*

SOBJ_TYPE

A macro that takes the ops vector for a synchronization primitive and returns a constant denoting the type; SOBJ_USER_PI is the constant that denotes a user-level, priority-inheriting lock.

The essence of the problem is this: for user-level locks, we normally keep track of the state associated with the lock (e.g., whether or not there's a waiter) at user-level—that information is considered purely advisory by the kernel. (There are several situations in which the waiters bit can't be trusted, and the kernel knows not to trust it in these situations.)

To implement priority inheritance for user-level locks, however, one must become much more precise about ownership; the ownership must be tracked the same way we track ownership for kernel-level synchronization primitives. That is, when we're doing the complicated thread lock dance in turnstile_interlock( ), we can't be doing loads from user-level memory to determine ownership. The nasty implication of this is that the kernel-level state tracking the ownership of the user-level lock must itself be protected by a lock, and that (in-kernel) lock must itself implement priority inheritance to avoid a potential inversion.

This leads us to a deadlock that we did not predict: the in-kernel lock must be acquired and dropped both to acquire the user-level lock *and* to drop it. That is, there are conditions in which a thread owns the in-kernel lock and wants the user-level lock, and there are conditions in which a thread owns the user-level lock and wants the in-kernel lock. As a result, there can exist blocking chains that appear circular—which will cause the kernel to induce an explicit panic. And indeed, that's exactly what happened in the failure analyzed above: thread A owned the user-level lock and wanted the in-kernel lock (upib_lock), and thread B owned the in-kernel lock and wanted the user-level lock—deadlock!

Once I understood the problem, it was disconcertingly easy to reproduce: in a few minutes I was able to pound out a test case that panicked the system in the same manner as seen in the dump. (As an aside, this is one of the most gratifying feelings in software engineering: analyzing a failure postmortem, discovering that the bug should be easily reproduced, writing a test case testing the hypothesis, and then watching the system blow up just as you predicted. Nothing quite compares to this feeling; it's the software equivalent of the walk-off home run.)

---

* wchan stands for *wait channel*, a term that dates back to the earliest days of UNIX at Bell Labs, and is itself almost certainly a bastardization of *event channels* from Multics.

While I had some ideas on how to fix this, the late date in the release and the seriousness of the problem prompted me to call Jeff at home to discuss. As Jeff and I discussed the problem, we couldn't seem to come up with a potential solution that didn't introduce a new problem. Indeed, the more we talked about the problem, the harder it seemed—and we realized that we had erred originally, both by underestimating the problem and by delegating its solution.

Worse, Jeff and I began to realize that there must be another manifestation lurking. We knew that if one were blocking on the in-kernel lock when the false deadlock was discovered, the kernel would explicitly panic. But what if one were blocking on the user-level lock when the false deadlock was discovered? We quickly determined (and a test case confirmed) that in this case, the attempt to acquire the user-level lock would (erroneously) return EDEADLK. That is, the kernel would see that the "deadlock" was induced by a user-level synchronization primitive, and therefore assume that it was an application-induced deadlock—a bug in the application.

So in this failure mode, a correct program would have one of its calls to pthread_mutex_lock erroneously fail—a failure mode even more serious than a panic, because any application that didn't check the return value of pthread_mutex_lock (as one well might not) could easily corrupt its own data by assuming that it owned a lock that, in fact, it had failed to acquire.

This problem, if encountered in the wild, would be virtually undebuggable—it absolutely had to be fixed.

So, how to solve these problems? We found this to be a hard problem because we kept trying to find a way to avoid that in-kernel lock. I have presented the in-kernel lock as a natural constraint on the problem, but that was a conclusion that we came to only with tremendous reluctance. Whenever one of us came up with some scheme to avoid the lock, the other would find some window invalidating the scheme.

After exhausting ourselves on the alternatives, we were forced to the conclusion that an in-kernel lock was a constraint on the user-level priority inheritance problem—and our focus switched from avoiding the situation to detecting it.

There are two cases to detect: the panic case and the false deadlock case. The false deadlock case is actually pretty easy to detect and handle, because we always find ourselves at the end of the blocking chain—and we always find that the lock that we own that induced the deadlock is the in-kernel lock passed as a parameter to turnstile_block. Because we know that we have willed our priority to the entire blocking chain, we can just detect this and break out—and that is exactly what that cryptic comment that I added to turnstile_block described, and what those two lines effected (the in-kernel lock that is passed to turnstile_block is stored in the local variable mp).

The panic case is nastier to deal with. As a reminder, in this case the thread owns the user-level synchronization object and is blocking trying to acquire the in-kernel lock. We might wish to handle this case in a similar way, by reasoning as follows: if the deadlock ends in the current thread, and the last thread in the blocking chain is blocked on a user-level synchronization object, the deadlock is false. (That is, we might wish to handle this case by a more general handling of the above case.) This is simple, but it's also wrong: it ignores the possibility of an *actual* application-level deadlock (i.e., an application bug), in which EDEADLK *must* be returned; a more precise approach is required.

To deal with this case, we observe that if a blocking chain runs from threads blocked on in-kernel synchronization objects to threads blocked on user-level synchronization objects, we know that we're in this case and *only* this case.* Because we know that we've caught another thread in code in which it can't be preempted (because we know that the other thread must be in the midst of turnstile_block, which explicitly disables preemption), we can fix this by busy-waiting until the lock changes, and then restarting the priority inheritance dance.

Here's the code to handle this case:†

```
/*
 * We now have the owner's thread lock.  If we are traversing
 * from non-SOBJ_USER_PI ops to SOBJ_USER_PI ops, then we know
 * that we have caught the thread while in the TS_SLEEP state,
 * but holding mp.  We know that this situation is transient
 * (mp will be dropped before the holder actually sleeps on
 * the SOBJ_USER_PI sobj), so we will spin waiting for mp to
 * be dropped.  Then, as in the turnstile_interlock() failure
 * case, we will restart the priority inheritance dance.
 */
if (SOBJ_TYPE(t->t_sobj_ops) != SOBJ_USER_PI &&
    owner->t_sobj_ops != NULL &&
    SOBJ_TYPE(owner->t_sobj_ops) == SOBJ_USER_PI) {
        kmutex_t *upi_lock = (kmutex_t *)t->t_wchan;

        ASSERT(IS_UPI(upi_lock));
        ASSERT(SOBJ_TYPE(t->t_sobj_ops) == SOBJ_MUTEX);

        if (t->t_lockp != owner->t_lockp)
                thread_unlock_high(owner);
        thread_unlock_high(t);
        if (loser)
                lock_clear(&turnstile_loser_lock);

        while (mutex_owner(upi_lock) == owner) {
                SMT_PAUSE();
                continue;
        }
}
```

* Presumably like most other operating systems, Solaris never executes user-level code with kernel-level locks held—and never acquires user-level locks from in-kernel subsystems. This case is thus the only one in which we acquire a user-level lock with a kernel-level lock held.

† The code dealing with turnstile_loser_lock didn't actually exist when we wrote this case; that was added to deal with (yet) another problem we discovered as a result of our four-day mind-meld. This problem deserves its own chapter, if only for the great name that Jeff gave it: "dueling losers." Shortly after Jeff postulated its existence, I actually saw a variant of this in the wild—a variant that I dubbed "cascading losers." But the losers—both dueling and cascading—will have to wait for another day.

```
        if (loser)
                lock_set(&turnstile_loser_lock);
        t = curthread;
        thread_lock_high(t);
        continue;
    }
```

Once these problems were fixed, we thought we were done. But further stress testing revealed that an even darker problem lurked—one that I honestly wasn't sure that we would be able to solve.

This time, the symptoms were different: instead of an explicit panic or an incorrect error value, the operating system simply hung—hard. Taking (and examining) a dump of the system revealed that a thread had deadlocked attempting to acquire a thread lock from turnstile_block( ), which had been called recursively from turnstile_block( ) via mutex_vector_exit( ), the function that releases a mutex if it is found to have waiters. Given just this state, the problem was clear—and it felt like a punch in the gut.

Recall that the diabolical (but regrettably required) in-kernel lock needs to be acquired and dropped to either acquire or drop a user-level priority-inheriting lock. When blocking on the user-level lock, the kernel-level lock must be dropped after the thread has willed its priority, as essentially the last thing it does before it actually gives up the CPU via swtch( ). (This was the code quoted in part in my original analysis; the code marked (2) in that analysis is the dropping of the kernel-level lock.)

But if another thread blocks on the kernel-level lock while we are dealing with the mechanics of blocking on the user-level lock, we will need to wake that waiter as part of dropping the kernel-level lock. Waking the waiter requires taking the thread lock in the turnstile table associated with the synchronization primitive, and then—in order to *waive* any inherited priority—acquiring the thread lock of the former holder of the lock (which is to say, the current thread).

Here's the problem: we are entering the function that waives inherited priority (the turnstile_pi_waive( ) function) *from* turnstile_block( ), *after* we already appear to be blocked. In particular, the current thread's thread lock has already been changed to point not to the current CPU's lock, but to the lock for the entry *in the turnstile table* that corresponds to the user-level lock on which we are actually blocking. So, if the kernel-level lock and the user-level lock happen to hash to the same entry in the turnstile table (as they did in the failure in which we first saw this), the turnstile lock acquired in turnstile_lookup( ) and the thread lock acquired in turnstile_pi_waive( ) will be the *same lock*—and we will have single-thread deadlock. Even if these locks happen not to hash to the same entry in the turnstile table, but happen not to be in the lock ordering dictated by turnstile_interlock( ), we have the potential for a classic AB/BA deadlock. Sewage, either way.

When we understood the problem, it seemed intractable. Given that the fundamental problem was that we were dropping the in-kernel lock after we appeared to be blocked, the tempting course would have been to find a way to eliminate the kernel-level lock. But we knew from our work on the earlier bugs that this line of thought was a dead end; we understood that the in-kernel lock was required, and we knew that it couldn't be dropped until priority had been willed down the entire blocking chain.

This left us challenging more fundamental assumptions: could we somehow flip the order in turnstile_block( ) such that we willed priority *before* modifying the current thread's data structures to indicate that it's asleep? (No, it would introduce a window for priority inversion.) Could we somehow indicate that we are in this state such that the call to turnstile_pi_waive( ) from turnstile_block( ) via mutex_vector_enter( ) didn't induce the deadlock? (No, as this didn't address the multithreaded deadlock scenario.)

Whenever we came up with a hypothetical solution, we were quick to see its fatal flaws—and the more we thought about the problem, the more we saw flaws instead of solutions.

Hopelessness was beginning to set in; it was very frustrating that merely adding the new dimension of user-level priority inheritance could invalidate what had seemed to be a perfect mechanism. The spoon had become the barrel, and we felt adrift in sewage.

As we got up to seek solace in a nearby coffee shop, an idea occurred to us: if user-level priority inheritance was the problem, perhaps we were being overly general in our thinking. Instead of solving this problem at its most abstract, why not deal specifically with *this* problem by, say, partitioning the turnstile table? We could hash the in-kernel locks protecting the user-level priority inheritance state to one half of the table, and hash every other lock to the other half.

This would guarantee us that the lock that we would be dropping immediately before calling swtch( ) in turnstile_block( ) would *necessarily* hash to a different entry in the turnstile table than the lock upon which we were blocking. Moreover, by *guaranteeing* that any kernel-level lock protecting the state of a user-level priority-inheriting lock hashed to a turnstile table entry with a lower virtual address than any turnstile table entry for any other kind of lock, we would also be guaranteeing that the locking order dictated by turnstile_interlock( ) would always be observed; we would be solving both the single-threaded and multithreaded cases.

On the one hand, this solution seemed like some pretty gross special-casing; it would mean putting knowledge of one specific kind of lock (the lock protecting in-kernel, user-level priority inheritance state) into the generic turnstile system. On the other hand, we were certain that it would work, and it would be a reasonably straightforward and low-risk change—which was very important considering that we were in the final days of a two-year release cycle. It was also clarifying that we didn't have any other ideas; if and until we came up with something more elegant, this was going to have to be it.

So, Jeff and I discussed the details of our solution over coffee, and he returned to write the block comment explaining our deceptively simple code change. Frankly, given the arguable inelegance of our solution, I was expecting the comment to be something of a confessional, adorned with the usual adjectives used in such comments, like "gross," "disgusting," or "vile."* But Jeff surprised me with what I believe is the best comment in all of Solaris—if not all of software:

```
/*
 * The turnstile hash table is partitioned into two halves: the lower half
 * is used for upimutextab[] locks, the upper half for everything else.
 * The reason for the distinction is that SOBJ_USER_PI locks present a
 * unique problem: the upimutextab[] lock passed to turnstile_block()
 * cannot be dropped until the calling thread has blocked on its
 * SOBJ_USER_PI lock and willed its priority down the blocking chain.
 * At that point, the caller's t_lockp will be one of the turnstile locks.
 * If mutex_exit() discovers that the upimutextab[] lock has waiters, it
 * must wake them, which forces a lock ordering on us: the turnstile lock
 * for the upimutextab[] lock will be acquired in mutex_vector_exit(),
 * which will eventually call into turnstile_pi_waive(), which will then
 * acquire the caller's thread lock, which in this case is the turnstile
 * lock for the SOBJ_USER_PI lock.  In general, when two turnstile locks
 * must be held at the same time, the lock order must be the address order.
 * Therefore, to prevent deadlock in turnstile_pi_waive(), we must ensure
 * that upimutextab[] locks *always* hash to lower addresses than any
 * other locks.  You think this is cheesy?  Let's see you do better.
 */
#define TURNSTILE_HASH_SIZE    128            /* must be power of 2 */
#define TURNSTILE_HASH_MASK    (TURNSTILE_HASH_SIZE - 1)
#define TURNSTILE_SOBJ_HASH(sobj)    \
        ((((ulong_t)sobj >> 2) + ((ulong_t)sobj >> 9)) & TURNSTILE_HASH_MASK)
#define TURNSTILE_SOBJ_BUCKET(sobj)          \
        ((IS_UPI(sobj) ? 0 : TURNSTILE_HASH_SIZE) + TURNSTILE_SOBJ_HASH(sobj))
#define TURNSTILE_CHAIN(sobj)    turnstile_table[TURNSTILE_SOBJ_BUCKET(sobj)]

typedef struct turnstile_chain {
        turnstile_t    *tc_first;    /* first turnstile on hash chain */
        disp_lock_t    tc_lock;      /* lock for this hash chain */
} turnstile_chain_t;

turnstile_chain_t      turnstile_table[2 * TURNSTILE_HASH_SIZE];
```

The tone of Jeff's comment much more accurately conveyed our sentiment than the confessional that I was envisioning: we implemented this solution not because we were defeated, but because it was the only way to conquer one of the most challenging problems that either of us had ever faced. And some may think it cheesy, but in the seven years since this code has integrated, no one has done better—and as of this writing, it seems unlikely that anyone ever will. To me at least, that's about as beautiful as code can get—cheesy or not.

So, the story had a happy ending: we integrated the fixes, and shipped the product on time. But the experience served to remind us of several principles of good software engineering:

---

* Which brings up a good tip: search for these words—along with classic standbys such as "XXX" and "FIXME"—in any source base for which you're curious where the bodies are buried.

Implement early

None of the problems that we faced was foreseen by Jeff or me, despite the fact that we had both spent time thinking about the problem during its design and implementation. Indeed, even after we encountered the initial bugs and were thus revisiting the problem very closely, the deeper problem still didn't occur to us; we had to encounter it to understand it.

Pound on it

We would have encountered these issues much, much earlier if the original engineer had implemented stress tests instead of relying exclusively on functional tests. As software engineers, *we are responsible for our own stress tests*. Those that don't believe this—those have some patrician notion that writing such tests is too coarse for the delicate hands of a Gentleman Engineer—will deliver chronically broken software. This is not to say that one shouldn't have test engineers or organizations—just that the tests generated by those engineers and organizations should be thought of as supplementing the tests written by the original implementers, not replacing them.

Focus on the edge conditions

Part of the reason that young software engineers should cut their teeth debugging complicated systems is that it inculcates a lifelong skill: the ability to analyze a solution to a problem in terms of the ways that it *won't* work instead of the ways that it might—the ability to focus on the edge conditions. When conceiving of new software, we software engineers should not try to convince ourselves why our design will work; we should invalidate the reasons why it will not. This is not to advocate overanalysis in lieu of writing code, but rather to suggest that the first code written on any project should be the code in which bugs may invalidate larger design ideas.

If these principles are applied, one will naturally gravitate to implementing the hardest problems at the earliest phase in any given project, and to putting in place the infrastructure to validate that that infrastructure works (and remains working). This won't eliminate the sewage, but it will assure that the most fetid spoonfuls are caught as early as possible, when design changes are still possible—and when the wine can still be saved.

## CHAPTER TWENTY-THREE

Distributed Programming with MapReduce

Jeffrey Dean and Sanjay Ghemawat

THIS CHAPTER DESCRIBES THE DESIGN AND IMPLEMENTATION OF **MAPREDUCE,** a programming system for large-scale data processing problems. MapReduce was developed as a way of simplifying the development of large-scale computations at Google. MapReduce programs are automatically parallelized and executed on a large cluster of commodity machines. The runtime system takes care of the details of partitioning the input data, scheduling the program's execution across a set of machines, handling machine failures, and managing the required intermachine communication. This allows programmers without any experience with parallel and distributed systems to easily utilize the resources of a large distributed system.

A Motivating Example

Suppose that you have 20 billion documents, and you want to generate a count of how often each unique word occurs in the documents. With an average document size of 20 KB, just reading through the 400 terabytes of data on one machine will take roughly four months. Assuming we were willing to wait that long and that we had a machine with sufficient memory, the code would be relatively simple. Example 23-1 (all the examples in this chapter are pseudocode) shows a possible algorithm.

EXAMPLE 23-1. Naïve, nonparallel word count program

```
map<string, int> word_count;
for each document d {
  for each word w in d {
    word_count[w]++;
  }
}
... save word_count to persistent storage ...
```

One way of speeding up this computation is to perform the same computation in parallel across each individual document, as shown in Example 23-2.

EXAMPLE 23-2. Parallelized word count program

```
Mutex lock;    // Protects word_count
map<string, int> word_count;
for each document d in parallel {
  for each word w in d {
    lock.Lock();
    word_count[w]++;
    lock.Unlock();
  }
}
... save word_count to persistent storage ...
```

The preceding code nicely parallelizes the input side of the problem. In reality, the code to start up threads would be a bit more complex, since we've hidden a bunch of details by using pseudocode. One problem with Example 23-2 is that it uses a single global data structure for keeping track of the generated counts. As a result, there is likely to be significant lock contention with the word_count data structure as the bottleneck. This problem can be fixed by partitioning the word_count data structure into a number of buckets with a separate lock per bucket, as shown in Example 23-3.

EXAMPLE 23-3. Parallelized word count program with partitioned storage

```
struct CountTable {
  Mutex lock;
  map<string, int> word_count;
};
const int kNumBuckets = 256;
CountTable tables[kNumBuckets];
for each document d in parallel {
  for each word w in d {
    int bucket = hash(w) % kNumBuckets;
    tables[bucket].lock.Lock();
    tables[bucket].word_count[w]++;
    tables[bucket].lock.Unlock();
  }
}
for (int b = 0; b < kNumBuckets; b++) {
  ... save tables[b].word_count to persistent storage ...
}
```

The program is still quite simple. However, it cannot scale beyond the number of processors in a single machine. Most affordable machines have eight or fewer processors, so even with perfect scaling, this approach will still require multiple weeks of processing to complete. Furthermore, we have been glossing over the problem of where the input data is stored and how fast it can be read by one machine.

Further scaling requires that we distribute the data and the computation across multiple machines. For the moment, let's assume that the machines do not fail. One way to increase scaling is to start many processes on a cluster of networked machines. We will have many input processes, each one responsible for reading and processing a subset of the documents. We will also have many output processes, each responsible for managing one of the word_count buckets. Example 23-4 shows the algorithm.

EXAMPLE 23-4. Parallelized word count program with partitioned processors

```
const int M = 1000;    // Number of input processes
const int R = 256;     // Number of output processes
main( ) {
  // Compute the number of documents to assign to each process
  const int D = number of documents / M;
  for (int i = 0; i < M; i++) {
    fork InputProcess(i * D, (i + 1) * D);
  }
  for (int i = 0; i < R; i++) {
    fork OutputProcess(i);
  }
  ... wait for all processes to finish ...
}

void InputProcess(int start_doc, int end_doc) {
  map<string, int> word_count[R];     // Separate table per output process
  for each doc d in range [start_doc .. end_doc-1] do {
    for each word w in d {
      int b = hash(w) % R;
      word_count[b][w]++;
    }
  }

  for (int b = 0; b < R; b++) {
    string s = EncodeTable(word_count[b]);
    ... send s to output process b ...
  }
}

void OutputProcess(int bucket) {
  map<string, int> word_count;
  for each input process p {
    string s = ... read message from p ...
    map<string, int> partial = DecodeTable(s);
    for each <word, count> in partial do {
      word_count[word] += count;
    }
  }
  ... save word_count to persistent storage ...
}
```

This approach scales nicely on a network of workstations, but is significantly more complicated and hard to understand (even though we've hidden the details of marshaling and unmarshaling, as well as starting and synchronizing different processes). It also does not deal gracefully with machine failures. To deal with failures, we would extend Example 23-4 to re-execute processes that failed before completion. To avoid double-counting data when we re-execute an input process, we would mark each piece of intermediate data with a generation number of the input process and modify the output processing so that it uses these generation numbers to discard duplicates. As you can imagine, adding this failure-handling support would further complicate things.

The MapReduce Programming Model

If you compare Example 23-1 with Example 23-4, you'll find that the simple task of counting words has been buried under lots of details about managing parallelism. If we can somehow separate the details of the original problem from the details of parallelization, we may be able to produce a general parallelization library or system that can be applied not just to this word-counting problem, but other large-scale processing problems. The parallelization pattern that we are using is:

- For each input record, extract a set of key/value pairs that we care about from each record.

- For each extracted key/value pair, combine it with other values that share the same key (perhaps filtering, aggregating, or transforming values in the process).

Let's rewrite our program to implement the application-specific logic of counting word frequencies for each document and summing these counts across documents in two functions that we'll call Map and Reduce. The result is Example 23-5.

EXAMPLE 23-5. Division of word counting problem into Map and Reduce

```
void Map(string document) {
  for each word w in document {
    EmitIntermediate(w, "1");
  }
}

void Reduce(string word, list<string> values) {
  int count = 0;
  for each v in values {
    count += StringToInt(v);
  }
  Emit(word, IntToString(count));
}
```

A simple driver program that uses these routines to accomplish the desired task on a single machine would look like Example 23-6.

EXAMPLE 23-6. Driver for Map and Reduce

```
map<string, list<string> > intermediate_data;

void EmitIntermediate(string key, string value) {
  intermediate_data[key].append(value);
}

void Emit(string key, string value) {
  ... write key/value to final data file ...
}

void Driver(MapFunction mapper, ReduceFunction reducer) {
  for each input item do {
    mapper(item)
  }
  for each key k in intermediate_data {
    reducer(k, intermediate_data[k]);
  }
}

main( ) {
  Driver(Map, Reduce);
}
```

The Map function is called once for each input record. Any intermediate key/value pairs emitted by the Map function are collected together by the driver code. Then, the Reduce function is called for each unique intermediate key, together with a list of intermediate values associated with that key.

We're now back to an implementation that runs on a single machine. However, with things separated in this manner, we can now change the implementation of the driver program to make it deal with distribution, automatic parallelization, and fault tolerance without affecting the application-specific logic in the Map and Reduce functions. Furthermore, the driver is independent of the particular application logic implemented by the Map and Reduce functions, and therefore the same driver program can be reused with other Map and Reduce functions to solve different problems. Finally, notice that the Map and Reduce functions that implement the application-specific logic are nearly as understandable as the simple sequential code shown in Example 23-1.

Other MapReduce Examples

We'll examine the implementation of a much more sophisticated driver program that automatically runs MapReduce programs on large-scale clusters of machines in a moment, but first, let's consider a few other problems and how they can be solved using Map-Reduce:

Distributed grep
   The Map function emits a line if it matches a supplied regular expression pattern. The Reduce function is an identity function that just copies the supplied intermediate data to the output.

Reverse web-link graph

A forward web-link graph is a graph that has an edge from node URL1 to node URL2 if the web page found at URL1 has a hyperlink to URL2. A reverse web-link graph is the same graph with the edges reversed. MapReduce can easily be used to construct a reverse web-link graph. The Map function outputs *<target, source>* pairs for each link to a target URL found in a document named *source*. The Reduce function concatenates the list of all source URLs associated with a given target URL and emits the pair *<target, list of source URLs>*.

Term vector per host

A term vector summarizes the most important words that occur in a document or a set of documents as a list of *<word, frequency>* pairs. The Map function emits a *<hostname, term vector>* pair for each input document (where the hostname is extracted from the URL of the document). The Reduce function is passed all per-document term vectors for a given host. It adds these term vectors, throwing away infrequent terms, and then emits a final *<hostname, term vector>* pair.

Inverted index

An inverted index is a data structure that maps from each unique word to a list of documents that contain the word (where the documents are typically identified with a numeric identifier to keep the inverted index data relatively compact). The Map function parses each document and emits a sequence of *<word, docid>* pairs. The Reduce function accepts all docids for a given word, sorts the corresponding document IDs, and emits a *<word, list of docids>* pair. The set of all output pairs forms a simple inverted index. It is easy to augment this computation to keep track of word positions within each document.

Distributed sort

MapReduce can also be used to sort data by a particular key. The Map function extracts the key from each record, and emits a *<key, record>* pair. The Reduce function emits all pairs unchanged (i.e., the identity Reduce function). This computation depends on the partitioning facilities and ordering properties described later in this chapter.

There are many more examples of computations that can easily be expressed as a MapReduce computation. For more complex computations, it is often easy to express them as a sequence of MapReduce steps or as an iterative application of a MapReduce computation, where the output of one MapReduce step is the input to the next MapReduce step.

One you start thinking of data processing problems in terms of MapReduce, they are often relatively easy to express. As some testament to this, over the last four years, the number of MapReduce programs at Google has gone from a small handful of candidate problems in March 2003 (when we started to design MapReduce) to more than 6,000 distinct MapReduce programs in December 2006. These programs were written by more than a thousand different software developers, many of whom had never written a parallel or distributed program before using MapReduce.

A Distributed MapReduce Implementation

Much of the benefit of the MapReduce programming model is that it nicely separates the expression of the desired computation from the underlying details of parallelization, failure handling, etc. Indeed, different implementations of the MapReduce programming model are possible for different kinds of computing platforms. The right choice depends on the environment. For example, one implementation may be suitable for a small shared-memory machine, another for a large NUMA multiprocessor, and yet another for an even larger collection of networked machines.

A very simple single-machine implementation that supports the programming model was shown in the code fragment in Example 23-6. This section describes a more complex implementation that is targeted to running large-scale MapReduce jobs on the computing environment in wide use at Google: large clusters of commodity PCs connected together with switched Ethernet (see "Further Reading," at the end of this chapter). In this environment:

- Machines are typically dual-processor x86 processors running Linux, with 2–4 GB of memory per machine.

- Machines are connected using commodity-networking hardware (typically 1 gigabit/ second switched Ethernet). Machines are organized into racks of 40 or 80 machines. These racks are connected to a central switch for the whole cluster. The bandwidth available when talking to other machines in the same rack is 1 gigabit/second per machine, while the per-machine bandwidth available at the central switch is much smaller (usually 50 to 100 megabits/second per machine).

- Storage is provided by inexpensive IDE disks attached directly to individual machines. A distributed filesystem called GFS (see the reference to "The Google File System" under "Further Reading," at the end of this chapter) is used to manage the data stored on these disks. GFS uses replication to provide availability and reliability on top of unreliable hardware by breaking files into chunks of 64 megabytes and storing (typically) 3 copies of each chunk on different machines.

- Users submit jobs to a scheduling system. Each job consists of a set of tasks and is mapped by the scheduler to a set of available machines within a cluster.

Execution Overview

The Map function invocations are distributed across multiple machines by automatically partitioning the input data into a set of M splits. The input splits can be processed in parallel by different machines. Reduce invocations are distributed by partitioning the intermediate key space into R pieces using a partitioning function (e.g., hash(key) % R).

Figure 23-1 shows the actions that occur when the user program calls the MapReduce function (the numbered labels in Figure 23-1 correspond to the numbers in the following list).

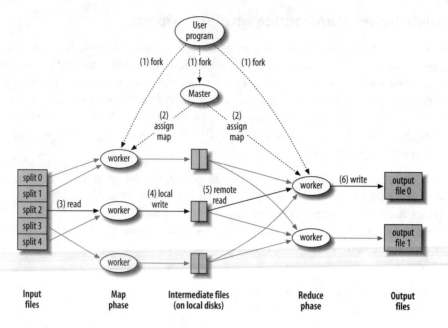

FIGURE 23-1. Relationships between processes in MapReduce

1. The MapReduce library first splits the input files into *M* pieces (typically 16 megabytes to 64 megabytes per piece). It then starts up many copies of the program on a cluster of machines, by making a request to the cluster scheduling system.

2. One of the copies is special and is called the MapReduce *master*. The remaining tasks are assigned chunks of Map and Reduce work by the master. There are *M* map tasks and *R* reduce tasks. The master picks idle workers and assigns a map and/or a reduce task to each.

3. A worker that is assigned a map task reads the contents of the corresponding input split. It passes each input record to the user-defined Map function. The intermediate key/value pairs produced by the Map function are buffered in memory.

4. Periodically, the buffered pairs are written to local disk, partitioned into *R* separate buckets by the partitioning function. When the map task is completed, the worker notifies the master. The master forwards information about the location of the intermediate data generated by this map task to any workers that have been assigned reduce tasks. If there are remaining map tasks, the master assigns one of the remaining tasks to the newly idle worker.

5. When a reduce worker is told the locations of intermediate data for its reduce task, it issues remote procedure calls to read the buffered intermediate data from the local disk of the map workers. When a reduce worker has finished reading all intermediate data for its reduce task, it sorts it by the intermediate keys so that all occurrences of the same intermediate key are grouped together. If the intermediate data is too large to fit in memory on the reduce worker, an external sort is used.

6. The reduce worker iterates over the sorted intermediate key/value pairs. For each unique intermediate key encountered, it passes the key and the corresponding list of intermediate values to the user's Reduce function. Any key/value pairs generated by the user's Reduce function are appended to a final output file for this reduce partition. When the reduce task is done, the worker notifies the master. If there are remaining reduce tasks, the master assigns one of the remaining reduce tasks to the newly idle worker.

When all map tasks and reduce tasks have been completed, the MapReduce function call in the user program returns, giving control back to the user code. At this point, the output of the MapReduce job is available in the R output files (one file per reduce task).

Several details of the implementation allow it to perform well in our environment.

Load balancing

A MapReduce job typically has many more tasks than machines, which means that each worker will be assigned many different tasks by the master. The master assigns a new task to a machine when it finishes its previous task. This means that a faster machine will be assigned more tasks than a slower machine. Therefore, the assignment of tasks to machine is properly balanced even in a heterogeneous environment, and workers tend to be kept busy with useful work throughout the computation.

Fault tolerance

Because this implementation of MapReduce is designed to run jobs distributed across hundreds or thousands of machines, the library must transparently handle machine failures.

The master keeps state about which map and reduce tasks have been done by which workers. The master periodically sends a ping remote procedure call to each worker. If a worker does not respond to several consecutive pings, the master declares that worker as dead and assigns any work that was done by that worker to other machines for re-execution. Since a typical MapReduce execution might have 50 times as many map tasks as worker machines, recovery is very fast, because 50 separate machines can each pick up one map task for re-execution when a machine fails.

The master logs all updates of its scheduling state to a persistent logfile. If the master dies (a rare occurrence, since there is only one master), it is restarted by the cluster scheduling system. The new master instance reads the logfile to reconstruct its internal state.

Locality

Our MapReduce implementation conserves network bandwidth by taking advantage of the fact that the input data (managed by GFS) is stored on the same machines or racks on which the map computation is executed. For any given Map task, the MapReduce master finds the locations of the input data (there are typically multiple locations due to GFS's replication). The master then tries to schedule the map task on a machine that is close to one of the replicas of the tasks's input data. For large MapReduce jobs that use thousands of workers, most input data is read directly from local disk.

Backup tasks

The running time of MapReduce is often dominated by a few stragglers. (A straggler is any machine that takes a long time to execute one of the last few map or reduce tasks.) A task may take a long time to execute either because it is intrinsically expensive, or because it is running on a slow machine.

A machine might be slow for a wide variety of reasons. For example, the machine might be busy with other unrelated CPU-intensive processes, or the machine might have a faulty hard drive that causes frequent retries of read operations that slow disk reads by factors of 10 or 100.

We use backup tasks to solve the problem of stragglers. When there are only a few map tasks left, the master schedules (on idle workers) one backup execution for each of the remaining in-progress map tasks. Each remaining map task is marked as completed whenever one of the instances of the task finishes (the primary or the backup). A similar strategy is used for reduce tasks. We typically use just 1–2 percent additional computational resources for backup tasks, but have found that they significantly shorten the typical completion time of large MapReduce operations.

Extensions to the Model

Although most uses of MapReduce require just writing Map and Reduce functions, we have extended the basic model with a few features that we have found useful in practice.

Partitioning function

MapReduce users specify the number of reduce tasks/output files that they desire (*R*). Intermediate data gets partitioned across these tasks using a partitioning function on the intermediate key. A default partitioning function is provided that uses hashing (hash(key) % R) to evenly balance the data across the *R* partitions.

In some cases, however, it is useful to partition data by some other function of the key. For example, sometimes the output keys are URLs, and we want all entries for a single host to end up in the same output file. To support situations like this, the users of the MapReduce library can provide their own custom partitioning function. For example, using hash(Hostname(urlkey)) % R as the partitioning function causes all URLs from the same host to end up in the same output file.

Ordering guarantees

Our MapReduce implementation sorts the intermediate data to group together all intermediate values that share the same intermediate key. Since many users find it convenient to have their Reduce function called on keys in sorted order, and we have already done all of the necessary work, we expose this to users by guaranteeing this ordering property in the interface to the MapReduce library.

Skipping bad records

Sometimes there are bugs in user code that cause the Map or Reduce functions to crash deterministically on certain records. Such bugs may cause a large MapReduce execution to fail after doing large amounts of computation. The preferred course of action is to fix the bug, but sometimes this is not feasible; for instance, the bug may be in a third-party library for which source code is not available. Also, it is sometimes acceptable to ignore a few records, such as when doing statistical analysis on a large data set. Thus, we provide an optional mode of execution where the MapReduce library detects records that cause deterministic crashes and skips these records in subsequent re-executions, in order to make forward progress.

Each worker process installs a signal handler that catches segmentation violations and bus errors. Before invoking a user Map or Reduce operation, the MapReduce library stores the sequence number of the record in a global variable. If the user code generates a signal, the signal handler sends a "last gasp" UDP packet that contains the sequence number to the MapReduce master. When the master has seen more than one failure on a particular record, it indicates that the record should be skipped when it issues the next re-execution of the corresponding Map or Reduce task.

A number of other extensions are discussed in a lengthier paper about MapReduce (see "Further Reading," below).

Conclusion

MapReduce has proven to be a valuable tool at Google. As of early 2007, we have more than 6,000 distinct programs written using the MapReduce programming model, and run more than 35,000 MapReduce jobs per day, processing about 8 petabytes of input data per day (a sustained rate of about 100 gigabytes per second). Although we originally developed the MapReduce programming model as part of our efforts to rewrite the indexing system for our web search product, it has shown itself to be useful across a very broad range of problems, including machine learning, statistical machine translation, log analysis, information retrieval experimentation, and general large-scale data processing and computation tasks.

Further Reading

A more detailed description of MapReduce appeared in the OSDI '04 conference:

> "MapReduce: Simplified Data Processing on Large Clusters." Jeffrey Dean and Sanjay Ghemawat. Appeared in *OSDI '04: Sixth Symposium on Operating System Design and Implementation*, San Francisco, CA, December, 2004. Available from *http://labs.google.com/papers/mapreduce.html*.

A paper about the design and implementation of the Google File System appeared in the SOSP '03 conference:

> "The Google File System." Sanjay Ghemawat, Howard Gobioff, and Shun-Tak Leung. *19th ACM Symposium on Operating Systems Principles*, Lake George, NY, October, 2003. Available from *http://labs.google.com/papers/gfs.html*.

A paper describing the general hardware infrastructure at Google appeared in IEEE Micro:

"Web Search for a Planet: The Google Cluster Architecture." Luiz Barroso, Jeffrey Dean, and Urs Hoelzle. *IEEE Micro*, Volume 23, Issue 2 (March 2003), pp. 22–28. Available from *http://labs.google.com/papers/googlecluster.html*.

A language called Sawzall developed at Google for logs analysis runs on top of Map-Reduce:

"Interpreting the Data: Parallel Analysis with Sawzall." Rob Pike, Sean Dorward, Robert Griesemer, Sean Quinlan. *Scientific Programming Journal* Special Issue on Grids and Worldwide Computing Programming Models and Infrastructure 13:4, pp. 227–298. Available from *http://labs.google.com/papers/sawzall.html*.

Acknowledgments

A number of people have made substantial contributions to the continued development and improvement of MapReduce, including Tom Annau, Matt Austern, Chris Colohan, Frank Dabek, Walt Drummond, Xianping Ge, Victoria Gilbert, Shan Lei, Josh Levenberg, Nahush Mahajan, Greg Malewicz, Russell Power, Will Robinson, Ioannis Tsoukalidis, and Jerry Zhao. MapReduce builds on a number of pieces of infrastructure developed at Google, including the Google File System and our cluster scheduling system. We would like to especially thank the developers of those systems. Finally, we thank all the users of MapReduce within Google's engineering organization for providing helpful feedback, suggestions, and bug reports.

Appendix: Word Count Solution

This section contains the full C++ implementation of the word frequency counting example that was used in the early part of this chapter. The code can also be found on the O'Reilly web site for this book (*http://www.oreilly.com/catalog/9780596510046*):

```
#include "mapreduce/mapreduce.h"

// User's map function
class WordCounter : public Mapper {
 public:
  virtual void Map(const MapInput& input) {
    const string& text = input.value();
    const int n = text.size();
    for (int i = 0; i < n; ) {
      // Skip past leading whitespace
      while ((i < n) && isspace(text[i]))
        i++;

      // Find word end
      int start = i;
      while ((i < n) && !isspace(text[i]))
        i++;
```

```
      if (start < i)
        EmitIntermediate(text.substr(start,i-start),"1");
    }
  }
};
REGISTER_MAPPER(WordCounter);

// User's reduce function
class Adder : public Reducer {
  virtual void Reduce(ReduceInput* input) {
    // Iterate over all entries with the
    // same key and add the values
    int64 value = 0;
    while (!input->done()) {
      value += StringToInt(input->value());
      input->NextValue();
    }

    // Emit sum for input->key()
    Emit(IntToString(value));
  }
};
REGISTER_REDUCER(Adder);

int main(int argc, char** argv) {
  ParseCommandLineFlags(argc, argv);

  MapReduceSpecification spec;

  // Store list of input files into "spec"
  for (int i = 1; i < argc; i++) {
    MapReduceInput* input = spec.add_input();
    input->set_format("text");
    input->set_filepattern(argv[i]);
    input->set_mapper_class("WordCounter");
  }

  // Specify the output files:
  //     /gfs/test/freq-00000-of-00100
  //     /gfs/test/freq-00001-of-00100
  //     ...
  MapReduceOutput* out = spec.output();
  out->set_filebase("/gfs/test/freq");
  out->set_num_tasks(100);
  out->set_format("text");
  out->set_reducer_class("Adder");

  // Optional: do partial sums within map
  // tasks to save network bandwidth
  out->set_combiner_class("Adder");

  // Tuning parameters: use at most 2,000
  // machines and 100 MB of memory per task
  spec.set_machines(2000);
  spec.set_map_megabytes(100);
  spec.set_reduce_megabytes(100);
```

```
    // Now run it
    MapReduceResult result;
    if (!MapReduce(spec, &result)) abort();

    // Done: 'result' structure contains info
    // about counters, time taken, number of
    // machines used, etc.

    return 0;
}
```

## CHAPTER TWENTY-FOUR

Beautiful Concurrency

Simon Peyton Jones

THE FREE LUNCH IS OVER.[*] **W**E HAVE GROWN USED TO THE IDEA that our programs will go faster when we buy a next-generation processor, but that time has passed. While that next-generation chip will have more CPUs, each individual CPU will be no faster than the previous year's model. If we want our programs to run faster, we must learn to write parallel programs.[†]

Parallel programs execute in a nondeterministic way, so they are hard to test, and bugs can be almost impossible to reproduce. For me, a beautiful program is one that is so simple and elegant that it obviously has no mistakes, rather than merely having no obvious mistakes.[‡] If we want to write parallel programs that work reliably, we must pay particular attention to beauty. Sadly, parallel programs are often *less* beautiful than their sequential cousins; in particular they are, as we shall see, less *modular*.

---

[*] Herb Sutter, "The free lunch is over: a fundamental turn toward concurrency in software," *Dr. Dobb's Journal*, March 2005.

[†] Herb Sutter and James Larus, "Software and the concurrency revolution," *ACM Queue*, Vol. 3, No. 7, September 2005.

[‡] This turn of phrase is due to Tony Hoare.

In this chapter, I'll describe *Software Transactional Memory* (STM), a promising new approach to programming shared-memory parallel processors that seems to support modular programs in a way that current technology does not. By the time we are done, I hope you will be as enthusiastic as I am about STM. It is not a solution to every problem, but it is a beautiful and inspiring attack on the daunting ramparts of concurrency.

A Simple Example: Bank Accounts

Here is a simple programming task.

> Write a procedure to transfer money from one bank account to another. To keep things simple, both accounts are held in memory: no interaction with databases is required. The procedure must operate correctly in a concurrent program, in which many threads may call transfer simultaneously. No thread should be able to observe a state in which the money has left one account, but not arrived in the other (or vice versa).

This example is somewhat unrealistic, but its simplicity allows us to focus in this chapter on what is new about the solution: the language Haskell and transactional memory. But first let us briefly look at the conventional approach.

Bank Accounts Using Locks

The dominant technologies used for coordinating concurrent programs today are *locks* and *condition variables*. In an object-oriented language, every object has an implicit lock, and the locking is done by *synchronized methods*, but the idea is the same. So, one might define a class for bank accounts something like this:

```
class Account {
  Int balance;
  synchronized void withdraw( Int n ) {
    balance = balance - n; }
  void deposit( Int n ) {
    withdraw( -n ); }
}
```

We must be careful to use a synchronized method for withdraw, so that we do not get any missed decrements if two threads call withdraw at the same time. The effect of synchronized is to take a lock on the account, run withdraw, and then release the lock.

Now, here is how we might write the code for transfer:

```
void transfer( Account from, Account to, Int amount ) {
  from.withdraw( amount );
  to.deposit( amount ); }
```

This code is fine for a sequential program, but in a concurrent program, another thread could observe an intermediate state in which the money has left account from but has not arrived in to. The fact that both methods are synchronized does not help us at all. Account from is first locked and then unlocked by the call to method withdraw, and then to is locked and unlocked by deposit. In between the two calls, the money is (visibly) absent from both accounts.

In a finance program, that might be unacceptable. How do we fix it? The usual solution would be to add explicit locking code like so:

```
void transfer( Account from, Account to, Int amount ) {
  from.lock(); to.lock();
    from.withdraw( amount );
    to.deposit( amount );
  from.unlock(); to.unlock() }
```

But this program is fatally prone to deadlock. In particular, consider the (unlikely) situation in which another thread is transferring money in the opposite direction between the same two accounts. Then each thread might get one lock and then block indefinitely waiting for the other.

Once recognized—and the problem is not always so obvious—the standard fix is to put an arbitrary global order on the locks, and to acquire them in increasing order. The locking code would then become:

```
if from < to
  then { from.lock(); to.lock(); }
  else { to.lock(); from.lock(); }
```

That works fine when the full set of required locks can be predicted in advance, but that is not always the case. For example, suppose from.withdraw is implemented by transferring money out of the from2 account if from does not have enough funds. We don't know whether to acquire from2's lock until we have read from, and by then it is too late to acquire the locks in the "right" order. Furthermore, the very existence of from2 may be a private matter that should be known by from, but not by transfer. And even if transfer did know about from2, the locking code must now take three locks, presumably by sorting them into the right order.

Matters become even more complicated when we want to *block*. For example, suppose that transfer should block if from has insufficient funds. This is usually done by waiting on a *condition variable*, while simultaneously releasing from's lock. It gets much trickier if we want to block until there are sufficient funds in from and from2 considered together.

Locks Are Bad

To make a long story short, today's dominant technology for concurrent programming—locks and condition variables—is fundamentally flawed. Here are some standard difficulties, some of which we have just seen:

Taking too few locks

It is easy to forget to take a lock and thereby end up with two threads that modify the same variable simultaneously.

Taking too many locks

It is easy to take too many locks and thereby inhibit concurrency (at best) or cause deadlock (at worst).

Taking the wrong locks

In lock-based programming, the connection between a lock and the data it protects often exists only in the mind of the programmer and is not explicit in the program. As a result, it is all too easy to take or hold the wrong locks.

Taking locks in the wrong order

In lock-based programming, one must be careful to take locks in the "right" order. Avoiding the deadlock that can otherwise occur is always tiresome and error-prone, and sometimes extremely difficult.

Error recovery

Error recovery can be very hard because the programmer must guarantee that no error can leave the system in a state that is inconsistent, or in which locks are held indefinitely.

Lost wakeups and erroneous retries

It is easy to forget to signal a condition variable on which a thread is waiting, or to retest a condition after a wakeup.

But the fundamental shortcoming of lock-based programming is that *locks and condition variables do not support modular programming*. By "modular programming," I mean the process of building large programs by gluing together smaller programs. Locks make this impossible. For example, we could not use our (correct) implementations of `withdraw` and `deposit` unchanged to implement `transfer`; instead, we had to expose the locking protocol. Blocking and choice are even less modular. For example, suppose we had a version of `withdraw` that blocked if the source account had insufficient funds. Then we would not be able to use `withdraw` directly to withdraw money from A or B (depending on which had sufficient funds), without exposing the blocking condition—and even then it wouldn't be easy. This critique is elaborated elsewhere.*

Software Transactional Memory

Software Transactional Memory is a promising new approach to the challenge of concurrency, as I will explain in this section. I shall explain STM using Haskell, the most beautiful programming language I know, because STM fits into Haskell particularly elegantly. If you don't know any Haskell, don't worry; we'll learn it as we go.

Side Effects and Input/Output in Haskell

Here is the beginning of the code for `transfer` in Haskell:

```
transfer :: Account -> Account -> Int -> IO ()
-- Transfer 'amount' from account 'from' to account 'to'
transfer from to amount = ...
```

---

* Edward A. Lee, "The problem with threads,"*IEEE Computer*, Vol. 39, No. 5, pp. 33–42, May 2006; J. K. Ousterhout, "Why threads are a bad idea (for most purposes)," Invited Talk, *USENIX Technical Conference*, January 1996; Tim Harris, Simon Marlow, Simon Peyton Jones, and Maurice Herlihy, "Composable memory transactions," *ACM Symposium on Principles and Practice of Parallel Programming (PPoPP '05)*, June 2005.

The second line of this definition, starting with --, is a comment. The first line gives the *type signature* for transfer.* This signature says that transfer takes as its arguments two values of type Account (the source and destination accounts) and an Int (the amount to transfer), and returns a value of type IO ( ). This result type says, "transfer returns an action that, when performed, may have some side effects, and then returns a value of type ( )." The type ( ), pronounced "unit," has just one value, which is also written ( ); it is akin to void in C. So, transfer's result type IO ( ) announces that its side effects constitute the only reason for calling it. Before we go further, we must explain how side effects are handled in Haskell.

A *side effect* is anything that reads or writes mutable state. Input/output is a prominent example of a side effect. For example, here are the signatures of two Haskell functions with input/output effects:

```
hPutStr  :: Handle -> String -> IO ()
hGetLine :: Handle -> IO String
```

We call any value of type IO t an *action*. So, (hPutStr h "hello") is an action† that, when performed, will print hello on handle‡ h and return the unit value. Similarly, (hGetLine h) is an action that, when performed, will read a line of input from handle h and return it as a String. We can glue together little side-effecting programs to make bigger side-effecting programs using Haskell's do notation. For example, hEchoLine reads a string from the input and prints it:

```
hEchoLine :: Handle -> IO String
hEchoLine h = do { s <- hGetLine h
                 ; hPutStr h ("I just read: " ++ s ++ "\n")
                 ; return s }
```

The notation do $\{a_1; ...; a_n\}$ constructs an action by gluing together the smaller actions $a_1...a_n$ in sequence. So hEchoLine h is an action that, when performed, will first perform hGetLine h to read a line from h, naming the result s. Then it will perform hPutStr to print s, preceded§ by "I just read: ". Finally, it will return the string s. This last line is interesting because return is not a built-in language construct: rather, it is a perfectly ordinary function with type:

```
return :: a -> IO a
```

---

* You may think it odd that there are three function arrows in this type signature, rather than one. That's because Haskell supports *currying*, which you can find described in any book about Haskell (*Haskell: The Craft of Functional Programming*, by S.J. Thompson [Addison-Wesley]), or on Wikipedia. For the purposes of this chapter, simply treat all the types except the final one as arguments.

† In Haskell, we write function application using simple juxtaposition. In most languages you would write hPutStr(h,"hello"), but in Haskell you write simply (hPutStr h "hello").

‡ A Handle in Haskell plays the role of a file descriptor in C: it says which file or pipe to read or write. As in Unix, there are three predefined handles: stdin, stdout, and stderr.

§ The ++ operator concatenates two strings.

The action return v, when performed, returns v without having caused any side effects.*
This function works on values of any type, and we indicate this by using a type variable a
in its type.

Input/output is one important sort of side effect. Another is the act of reading or writing a
mutable variable. For example, here is a function that increments the value of a mutable
variable:

```
incRef :: IORef Int -> IO ()
incRef var = do { val <- readIORef var
               ; writeIORef var (val+1) }
```

Here, incRef var is an action that first performs readIORef var to read the value of the variable, naming its value val, and then performs writeIORef to write the value (val+1) into the
variable. The types of readIORef and writeIORef are as follows:

```
readIORef  :: IORef a -> IO a
writeIORef :: IORef a -> a -> IO ()
```

A value of type IORef t should be thought of as a pointer, or reference, to a mutable location containing a value of type t, a bit like the type (t *) in C. In the case of incRef, the
argument has type IORef Int because incRef applies only to locations that contain an Int.

So far, I have explained how to build big actions by combining smaller ones together—but
how does an action ever actually get performed? In Haskell, the whole program defines a
single IO action, called main. To run the program is to perform the action main. For example,
here is a complete program:

```
main :: IO ()
main = do { hPutStr stdout "Hello"
          ; hPutStr stdout " world\n" }
```

This program is a sequential program because the do notation combines IO actions in
sequence. To construct a concurrent program we need one more primitive, forkIO:

```
forkIO :: IO a -> IO ThreadId
```

The function forkIO, which is built into Haskell, takes an IO action as its argument, and
spawns it as a concurrent Haskell thread. Once created, it is run concurrently with all the
other Haskell threads by the Haskell runtime system. For example, suppose we modified
our main program thus:†

```
main :: IO ()
main = do { forkIO (hPutStr stdout "Hello")
          ; hPutStr stdout " world\n" }
```

* The IO type indicates the *possibility* of side effects, not the *certainty*.

† In the first line of main, we could instead have written tid <- forkIO (hPutStr ...), to bind the
ThreadId returned by forkIO to tid. However, because we do not use the returned ThreadId, we are
free to discard it by omitting the tid <- part.

Now, the two hPutStr actions would run concurrently. Which of them would "win" (by printing its string first) is unspecified. Haskell threads spawned by forkIO are extremely lightweight: they occupy a few hundred bytes of memory, and it is perfectly reasonable for a single program to spawn thousands of them.

Gentle reader, you may by now be feeling that Haskell is a very clumsy and verbose language. After all, our three-line definition of incRef accomplishes no more than x++ does in C! Indeed, in Haskell side effects are extremely explicit and somewhat verbose. However, remember first that Haskell is primarily a *functional* language. Most programs are written in the functional core of Haskell, which is rich, expressive, and concise. Haskell thereby gently encourages you to write programs that make sparing use of side effects.

Second, notice that being explicit about side effects reveals a good deal of useful information. Consider two functions:

```
f :: Int -> Int
g :: Int -> IO Int
```

From looking only at their types, we can see that f is a pure function: it has no side effects. Given a particular Int, say 42, the call (f 42) will return the same value every time it is called. In contrast, g has side effects, and this is apparent in its type. Each time g is performed, it may give a different result—for example, it may read from stdin or modify a mutable variable—even if its argument is the same every time. This ability to make side effects explicit will prove very useful in what follows.

Lastly, actions are first-class values: they may be passed as arguments, as well as returned as results. For example, here is the definition of a (simplified) for loop function, written entirely in Haskell rather than being built-in:

```
nTimes :: Int -> IO () -> IO ()
nTimes 0 do_this = return ()
nTimes n do_this = do { do_this; nTimes (n-1) do_this }
```

This recursive function takes an Int saying how many times to loop, and an action do_this; it returns an action that, when performed, performs the do_this action n times. Here is an example that uses nTimes to print Hello 10 times:

```
main = nTimes 10 (hPutStr stdout "Hello\n")
```

In effect, by treating actions as first-class values, Haskell supports *user-defined control structures*.

This chapter is not the place for a full introduction to Haskell, or even to side effects in Haskell. A good starting point for further reading is my tutorial "Tackling the awkward squad."[*]

---

[*] Simon Peyton Jones, "Tackling the awkward squad: monadic input/output, concurrency, exceptions, and foreign-language calls in Haskell," C. A. R. Hoare, M. Broy, and R. Steinbrueggen, editors, *Engineering theories of software construction*, Marktoberdorf Summer School 2000, NATO ASI Series, pp. 47–96, IOS Press, 2001.

Transactions in Haskell

Now, we can return to our transfer function. Here is its code:

```
transfer :: Account -> Account -> Int -> IO ()
-- Transfer 'amount' from account 'from' to account 'to'
transfer from to amount
  = atomically (do { deposit    to    amount
                   ; withdraw from amount })
```

The inner do block should by now be fairly self-explanatory: we call deposit to deposit amount in to, and withdraw to withdraw amount from account from. We will write these auxiliary functions in a moment, but first let's look at the call to atomically. It takes an action as its argument and performs it atomically. More precisely, it makes two guarantees:

Atomicity

The effects of atomically act become visible to another thread all at once. This ensures that no other thread can see a state in which money has been deposited in to but not yet withdrawn from from.

Isolation

During a call atomically act, the action act is completely unaffected by other threads. It is as if act takes a snapshot of the state of the world when it begins running, and then executes against that snapshot.

Here is a simple execution model for atomically. Suppose there is a single, global lock. Then atomically act grabs the lock, performs the action act, and releases the lock. This implementation brutally ensures that no two atomic blocks can be executed simultaneously, and thereby ensures atomicity.

There are two problems with this model. First, it does not ensure isolation at all: while one thread is accessing an IORef inside an atomic block (holding the Global Lock), there is nothing to stop *another* thread from writing the same IORef directly (i.e., outside atomically, without holding the Global Lock), thereby destroying the isolation guarantee. Second, performance is dreadful because every atomic block is serialized even if no actual interference is possible.

I will discuss the second problem shortly, in the section "Implementing Transactional Memory." Meanwhile, the first objection is easily addressed with the type system. We give atomically the following type:

```
atomically :: STM a -> IO a
```

The argument of atomically is an action of type STM a. An STM action is like an IO action, in that it can have side effects, but the range of side effects for STM actions is much smaller. The main thing you can do in an STM action is to read or write a transactional variable, of type (TVar a), much as we could read or write IORefs in an IO action:*

---

* The nomenclature is inconsistent here: it would be more consistent to use either TVar and IOVar, or TRef and IORef. But it would be disruptive to change at this stage; for better or worse, we have TVar and IORef.

```
readTVar  :: TVar a -> STM a
writeTVar :: TVar a -> a -> STM ()
```

STM actions can be composed together with the same do notation as IO actions—the do notation is overloaded to work on both types, as is return.* Here, for example, is the code for withdraw:

```
type Account = TVar Int

withdraw :: Account -> Int -> STM ()
withdraw acc amount
  = do { bal <- readTVar acc
       ; writeTVar acc (bal - amount) }
```

We represent an Account by a transactional variable containing an Int for the account balance. Then withdraw is an STM action that decrements the balance in the account by amount.

To complete the definition of transfer, we can define deposit in terms of withdraw:

```
deposit :: Account -> Int -> STM ()
deposit acc amount = withdraw acc (- amount)
```

Notice that transfer ultimately performs four primitive read/write actions: a read and then write on account to, followed by a read and then write on account from. These four actions execute atomically, and that meets the specification given at the start of the section "A Simple Example: Bank Accounts."

The type system neatly prevents us from reading or writing a TVar outside of a transaction. For example, suppose we tried this:

```
bad :: Account -> IO ()
bad acc = do { hPutStr stdout "Withdrawing..."
             ; withdraw acc 10 }
```

This program is rejected because the hPutStr is an IO action, while the withdraw is an STM action, and the two cannot be combined in a single do block. If we wrap a call to atomically around the withdraw, all is well:

```
good :: Account -> IO ()
good acc = do { hPutStr stdout "Withdrawing..."
              ; atomically (withdraw acc 10) }
```

---

* This overloading of do notation and return is not an ad hoc trick to support IO and STM. Rather, IO and STM are both examples of a common pattern, called a *monad* (described in P. L. Wadler, "The essence of functional programming," *20th ACM Symposium on Principles of Programming Languages [POPL '92]*, Albuquerque, pp. 1–14, ACM, January 1992), and the overloading is achieved by expressing that common pattern using Haskell's very general *type-class* mechanism (described in P. L. Wadler and S. Blott, "How to make ad-hoc polymorphism less ad hoc," *Proc 16th ACM Symposium on Principles of Programming Languages*, Austin, Texas, ACM, January 1989; and Simon Peyton Jones, Mark Jones, and Erik Meijer, "Type classes: an exploration of the design space," J. Launchbury, editor, *Haskell workshop*, Amsterdam, 1997).

Implementing Transactional Memory

The guarantees of atomicity and isolation that I described earlier should be all that a programmer needs in order to use STM. Even so, I often find it helpful to have a reasonable implementation model to guide my intuitions, and I will sketch one such implementation in this section. But remember that this is just *one* possible implementation. One of the beauties of the STM abstraction is that it presents a small, clean interface that can be implemented in a variety of ways, some simple and some sophisticated.

One particularly attractive implementation is well established in the database world, namely *optimistic execution*. When atomically act is performed, a thread-local *transaction log* is allocated, initially empty. Then the action act is performed, without taking any locks at all. While performing act, each call to writeTVar writes the address of the TVar and its new value into the log; it does not write to the TVar itself. Each call to readTVar first searches the log (in case the TVar was written by an earlier call to writeTVar); if no such record is found, the value is read from the TVar itself, and the TVar and value read are recorded in the log. In the meantime, other threads might be running their own atomic blocks, reading and writing TVars like crazy.

When the action act is finished, the implementation first *validates* the log and, if validation is successful, *commits* the log. The validation step examines each readTVar recorded in the log and checks that the value in the log matches the value currently in the real TVar. If so, validation succeeds, and the commit step takes all the writes recorded in the log and writes them into the real TVars.

These steps are performed truly indivisibly: the implementation disables interrupts, or uses locks or compare-and-swap instructions—whatever is necessary to ensure that validation and commit are perceived by other threads as completely indivisible. All of this is handled by the implementation, however, and the programmer does not need to know or care how it is done.

What if validation fails? Then the transaction has had an inconsistent view of memory. So, we abort the transaction, reinitialize the log, and run act all over again. This process is called *re-execution*. Because none of act's writes have been committed to memory, it is perfectly safe to run it again. However, notice that it is crucial that act contains no effects *other than* reads and writes on TVars. For example, consider:

```
atomically (do { x <- readTVar xv
               ; y <- readTVar yv
               ; if x>y then launchMissiles
                        else return () })
```

where launchMissiles :: IO ( ) causes serious international side effects. Because the atomic block is executed without taking locks, it might have an inconsistent view of memory if other threads are concurrently modifying xv and yv. If that happens, it would be a mistake to launch the missiles, and only *then* discover that validation fails so the transaction should be rerun. Fortunately, the type system prevents us from running IO actions inside STM actions, so the above fragment would be rejected by the type checker. This is another big advantage of distinguishing the types of IO and STM actions.

Blocking and Choice

Atomic blocks as we have introduced them so far are utterly inadequate to coordinate concurrent programs. They lack two key facilities: *blocking* and *choice*. In this section, I'll describe how the basic STM interface is elaborated to include them in a fully modular way.

Suppose that a thread should *block* if it attempts to overdraw an account (i.e., withdraw more than the current balance). Situations like this are common in concurrent programs: for example, a thread should block if it reads from an empty buffer, or when it waits for an event. We achieve this in STM by adding the single function retry, whose type is:

```
retry :: STM a
```

Here is a modified version of withdraw that blocks if the balance would go negative:

```
limitedWithdraw :: Account -> Int -> STM ()
limitedWithdraw acc amount
  = do { bal <- readTVar acc
       ; if amount > 0 && amount > bal
         then retry
         else writeTVar acc (bal - amount) }
```

The semantics of retry are simple: if a retry action is performed, the current transaction is abandoned and retried at some later time. It would be correct to retry the transaction immediately, but it would also be inefficient: the state of the account will probably be unchanged, so the transaction will again hit the retry. An efficient implementation would instead block the thread until some other thread writes to acc. How does the implementation know to wait on acc? Because the transaction reads acc on the way to the retry, and that fact is conveniently recorded in the transaction log.

The conditional in limitedWithdraw has a very common pattern: check that a Boolean condition is satisfied and, if not, retry. This pattern is easy to abstract as a function, check:

```
check :: Bool -> STM ()
check True  = return ()
check False = retry
```

Now, we can use check to re-express limitedWithdraw a little more neatly:

```
limitedWithdraw :: Account -> Int -> STM ()
limitedWithdraw acc amount
  = do { bal <- readTVar acc
       ; check (amount <= 0 || amount <= bal)
       ; writeTVar acc (bal - amount) }
```

We now turn our attention to *choice*. Suppose you want to withdraw money from account A if it has enough money, but if not then withdraw it from account B? For that, we need the ability to choose an alternative action if the first one retries. To support choice, STM Haskell has one further primitive action, called orElse, whose type is:

```
orElse :: STM a -> STM a -> STM a
```

Like atomically, orElse takes actions as its arguments, and glues them together to make a bigger action. Its semantics are as follows. The action (orElse a1 a2) first performs a1. If a1 retries (i.e., calls retry), it tries a2 instead. If a2 also retries, the whole action retries. It may be easier to see how orElse is used:

```
limitedWithdraw2 :: Account -> Account -> Int -> STM ()
-- (limitedWithdraw2 acc1 acc2 amt) withdraws amt from acc1,
-- if acc1 has enough money, otherwise from acc2.
-- If neither has enough, it retries.
limitedWithdraw2 acc1 acc2 amt
  = orElse (limitedWithdraw acc1 amt) (limitedWithdraw acc2 amt)
```

Because the result of orElse is itself an STM action, you can feed it to another call to orElse and so choose among an arbitrary number of alternatives.

Summary of Basic STM Operations

In this section, I have introduced all the key transactional memory operations supported by STM Haskell. They are summarized in Table 24-1. This table includes one operation that has not so far arisen: newTVar is the way in which you can create new TVar cells, and we will use it in the following section.

TABLE 24-1. The key operations of STM Haskell

Operation	Type signature
atomically	STM a -> IO a
retry	STM a
orElse	STM a -> STM a -> STM a
newTVar	a -> STM (TVar a)
readTVar	TVar a -> STM a
writeTVar	TVar a -> a -> STM ()

The Santa Claus Problem

I want to show you a complete, runnable concurrent program using STM. A well-known example is the so-called Santa Claus problem,* originally attributed to Trono:†

> Santa repeatedly sleeps until wakened by either all of his nine reindeer, back from their holidays, or by a group of three of his ten elves. If awakened by the reindeer, he harnesses each of them to his sleigh, delivers toys with them and finally unharnesses them (allowing them to go off on holiday). If awakened by a group of elves, he shows each of the group into his study, consults with them on toy R&D and finally shows them each out (allowing them to go back to work). Santa should give priority to the reindeer in the case that there is both a group of elves and a group of reindeer waiting.

---

* My choice was influenced by the fact that I am writing these words on December 22.

† J. A. Trono, "A new exercise in concurrency," *SIGCSE Bulletin*, Vol. 26, pp. 8–10, 1994.

Using a well-known example allows you to directly compare my solution with well-described solutions in other languages. In particular, Trono's paper gives a semaphore-based solution that is partially correct. Ben-Ari gives a solution in Ada95 and in Ada.[*] Benton gives a solution in Polyphonic C#.[†]

Reindeer and Elves

The basic idea of the STM Haskell implementation is this. Santa makes one "Group" for the elves and one for the reindeer. Each elf (or reindeer) tries to join its Group. If it succeeds, it gets two "Gates" in return. The first Gate allows Santa to control when the elf can enter the study and also lets Santa know when they are all inside. Similarly, the second Gate controls the elves leaving the study. Santa, for his part, waits for either of his two Groups to be ready, and then uses that Group's Gates to marshal his helpers (elves or reindeer) through their task. Thus the helpers spend their lives in an infinite loop: try to join a group, move through the gates under Santa's control, and then delay for a random interval before trying to join a group again.

Rendering this informal description in Haskell gives the following code for an elf:[‡]

```
elf1 :: Group -> Int -> IO ()
elf1 group elf_id = do { (in_gate, out_gate) <- joinGroup group
                       ; passGate in_gate
                       ; meetInStudy elf_id
                       ; passGate out_gate }
```

The elf is passed its Group and an Int that specifies its elfin identity. This identity is used only in the call to meetInStudy, which simply prints out a message to say what is happening:[§]

```
meetInStudy :: Int -> IO ()
meetInStudy id = putStr ("Elf " ++ show id ++ " meeting in the study\n")
```

The elf calls joinGroup to join its group and passGate to pass through each of the gates:

```
joinGroup :: Group -> IO (Gate, Gate)
passGate  :: Gate  -> IO ()
```

The code for reindeer is identical, except that reindeer deliver toys rather than meet in the study:

```
deliverToys :: Int -> IO ()
deliverToys id = putStr ("Reindeer " ++ show id ++ " delivering toys\n")
```

---

[*] Mordechai Ben-Ari, "How to solve the Santa Claus problem," *Concurrency: Practice and Experience*, Vol. 10, No. 6, pp. 485–496, 1998.

[†] Nick Benton, "Jingle bells: Solving the Santa Claus problem in Polyphonic C#," Technical report, Microsoft Research, 2003.

[‡] I have given this function a suffix 1 because it deals with only one iteration of the elf, whereas in reality the elves rejoin the fun when they are done with their task. We will define elf in the section "The Main Program."

[§] The function putStr is a library function that calls hPutStr stdout.

Because IO actions are first-class, we can abstract over the common pattern, like this:

```
helper1 :: Group -> IO () -> IO ()
helper1 group do_task = do { (in_gate, out_gate) <- joinGroup group
                           ; passGate in_gate
                           ; do_task
                           ; passGate out_gate }
```

The second argument of helper1 is an IO action that is the helper's task, which the helper performs between the two passGate calls. Now we can specialize helper1 to be either an elf or a reindeer:

```
elf1, reindeer1 :: Group -> Int -> IO ()
elf1      gp id = helper1 gp (meetInStudy id)
reindeer1 gp id = helper1 gp (deliverToys id)
```

Gates and Groups

The first abstraction is a Gate, which supports the following interface:

```
newGate     :: Int -> STM Gate
passGate    :: Gate -> IO ()
operateGate :: Gate -> IO ()
```

A Gate has a fixed *capacity*, n, which we specify when we make a new Gate, and a mutable *remaining capacity*. This remaining capacity is decremented whenever a helper calls passGate to go through the gate; if the remaining capacity is zero, passGate blocks. A Gate is created with zero remaining capacity, so that no helpers can pass through it. Santa opens the gate with operateGate, which sets its remaining capacity back to n.

Here, then, is a possible implementation of a Gate:

```
data Gate  = MkGate Int (TVar Int)

newGate :: Int -> STM Gate
newGate n = do { tv <- newTVar 0; return (MkGate n tv) }

passGate :: Gate -> IO ()
passGate (MkGate n tv)
  = atomically (do { n_left <- readTVar tv
                   ; check (n_left > 0)
                   ; writeTVar tv (n_left-1) })

operateGate :: Gate -> IO ()
operateGate (MkGate n tv)
  = do { atomically (writeTVar tv n)
       ; atomically (do { n_left <- readTVar tv
                        ; check (n_left == 0) }) }
```

The first line declares Gate to be a new *data type*, with a single *data constructor* MkGate.* The constructor has two *fields*: an Int giving the gate capacity, and a TVar whose contents says how many helpers can go through the gate before it closes. If the TVar contains zero, the gate is closed.

---

* A data type declaration is not unlike a C struct declaration, with MkGate being the structure tag.

The function newGate makes a new Gate by allocating a TVar and building a Gate value by calling the MkGate constructor. Dually, passGate uses pattern-matching to take apart the MkGate constructor; then, it decrements the contents of the TVar, using check to ensure there is still capacity in the gate, as we did with withdraw in the section "Blocking and Choice." Finally, operateGate first opens the Gate by writing its full capacity into the TVar, and then waits for the TVar to be decremented to zero.

A Group has the following interface:

```
newGroup   :: Int -> IO Group
joinGroup  :: Group -> IO (Gate,Gate)
awaitGroup :: Group -> STM (Gate,Gate)
```

Again, a Group is created empty, with a specified capacity. An elf may join a group by calling joinGroup, a call that blocks if the group is full. Santa calls awaitGroup to wait for the group to be full; when it is full, he gets the Group's gates, *and* the Group is immediately reinitialized with fresh Gates, so that another group of eager elves can start assembling.

Here is a possible implementation:

```
data Group = MkGroup Int (TVar (Int, Gate, Gate))

newGroup n = atomically (do { g1 <- newGate n; g2 <- newGate n
                            ; tv <- newTVar (n, g1, g2)
                            ; return (MkGroup n tv) })
```

Again, Group is declared as a fresh data type, with constructor MkGroup and two fields: the Group's full capacity, and a TVar containing its number of empty slots and its two Gates. Creating a new Group is a matter of creating new Gates, initializing a new TVar, and returning a structure built with MkGroup.

The implementations of joinGroup and awaitGroup are now more or less determined by these data structures:

```
joinGroup (MkGroup n tv)
  = atomically (do { (n_left, g1, g2) <- readTVar tv
                   ; check (n_left > 0)
                   ; writeTVar tv (n_left-1, g1, g2)
                   ; return (g1,g2) })

awaitGroup (MkGroup n tv)
  = do { (n_left, g1, g2) <- readTVar tv
       ; check (n_left == 0)
       ; new_g1 <- newGate n; new_g2 <- newGate n
       ; writeTVar tv (n,new_g1,new_g2)
       ; return (g1,g2) }
```

Notice that awaitGroup makes new gates when it reinitializes the Group. This ensures that a new group can assemble while the old one is still talking to Santa in the study, with no danger of an elf from the new group overtaking a sleepy elf from the old one.

Reviewing this section, you may notice that I have given some of the Group and Gate operations IO types (e.g., newGroup, joinGroup), and some STM types (e.g., newGate, awaitGroup). How did I make these choices? For example, newGroup has an IO type, which means that I can never call it from within an STM action. But this is merely a matter of convenience: I could instead have given newGroup an STM type, by omitting the atomically in its definition. In exchange, I would have had to write atomically (newGroup n) at each call site, rather than merely newGroup n. The merit of giving newGate an STM type is that it is more composable, a generality that newGroup did not need in this program. In contrast, I wanted to call newGate inside newGroup, and so I gave newGate an STM type.

In general, when designing a library, you should give the functions STM types wherever possible. You can think of STM actions as Lego bricks that can be glued together—using do {...}, retry, and orElse—to make bigger STM actions. However, as soon as you wrap a block in atomically, making it an IO type, it can no longer be combined atomically with other actions. There is a good reason for that: a value of IO type can perform arbitrary, irrevocable input/output (such as launchMissiles).

It is therefore good library design to export STM actions (rather than IO actions) whenever possible, because they are composable; their type advertises that they have no irrevocable effects. The library client can readily get from STM to IO (using atomically), but not vice versa.

Sometimes, however, it is *essential* to use an IO action. Look at operateGate. The two calls to atomically cannot be combined into one, because the first has an externally visible side effect (opening the gate), while the second blocks until all the elves have woken up and gone through it. So, operateGate *must* have an IO type.

The Main Program

We will first implement the outer structure of the program, although we have not yet implemented Santa himself. Here it is:

```
main = do { elf_group <- newGroup 3
          ; sequence_ [ elf elf_group n | n <- [1..10] ]

          ; rein_group <- newGroup 9
          ; sequence_ [ reindeer rein_group n | n <- [1..9] ]

          ; forever (santa elf_group rein_group) }
```

The first line creates a Group for the elves with capacity 3. The second line is more mysterious: it uses a so-called *list comprehension* to create a list of IO actions and calls sequence_ to execute them in sequence. The list comprehension [e|x<-xs] is read, "the list of all e where x is drawn from the list xs." So, the argument to sequence_ is the list:

```
[elf elf_group 1, elf elf_group 2, ..., elf elf_group 10]
```

Each of these calls yields an IO action that spawns an elf thread. The function sequence_ takes a list of IO actions and returns an action that, when performed, runs each of the actions in the list in order:*

```
sequence_ :: [IO a] -> IO ()
```

An elf is built from elf1, but with two differences. First, we want the elf to loop indefinitely, and second, we want it to run in a separate thread:

```
elf :: Group -> Int -> IO ThreadId
elf gp id = forkIO (forever (do { elf1 gp id; randomDelay }))
```

The forkIO part spawns its argument as a separate Haskell thread (see the earlier section "Side Effects and Input/Output in Haskell"). In turn, forkIO's argument is a call to forever, which runs *its* argument repeatedly (compare to the definition of nTimes in "Side Effects and Input/Output in Haskell"):

```
forever :: IO () -> IO ()
-- Repeatedly perform the action
forever act = do { act; forever act }
```

Finally, the expression (elf1 gp id) is an IO action, and we want to repeat that action indefinitely, followed each time by a random delay:

```
randomDelay :: IO ()
-- Delay for a random time between 1 and 1,000,000 microseconds
randomDelay = do { waitTime <- getStdRandom (randomR (1, 1000000))
                 ; threadDelay waitTime }
```

The rest of the main program should be self-explanatory. We make 9 reindeer in the same way that we made 10 elves, except that we call reindeer instead of elf:

```
reindeer :: Group -> Int -> IO ThreadId
reindeer gp id = forkIO (forever (do { reindeer1 gp id; randomDelay }))
```

The code for main finishes by reusing forever to run santa repeatedly. All that remains is to implement Santa himself.

Implementing Santa

Santa is the most interesting participant of this little drama because he makes choices. He must wait until there is *either* a group of reindeer waiting *or* a group of elves. Once he has made his choice of which group to attend to, he must take them through their task. Here is his code:

```
santa :: Group -> Group -> IO ()
santa elf_gp rein_gp
  = do { putStr "----------\n"
```

---

* The type [IO a] means "a list of values of type IO a." You may also wonder about the underscore in the name sequence_: it's because there is a related function sequence, whose type is [IO a] -> IO [a], that gathers the results of the argument actions into a list. Both sequence and sequence_ are defined in the Prelude library, which is imported by default.

```
; (task, (in_gate, out_gate))
        <- atomically (orElse
              (chooseGroup rein_gp "deliver toys")
              (chooseGroup elf_gp  "meet in my study"))

; putStr ("Ho! Ho! Ho! let's " ++ task ++ "\n")
; operateGate in_gate
-- Now the helpers do their task
; operateGate out_gate }
where
  chooseGroup :: Group -> String -> STM (String, (Gate,Gate))
  chooseGroup gp task = do { gates <- awaitGroup gp
                           ; return (task, gates) }
```

The choice is made by the orElse, which first attempts to choose the reindeer (thereby giving them priority), and otherwise chooses the elves. The chooseGroup function does an awaitGroup call on the appropriate group, and returns a pair consisting of a string that indicates the task (delivering toys or meeting in the study) and the two gates that Santa must operate to take the group through the task. Once the choice is made, Santa prints out a message and operates the two gates in sequence.

This implementation works fine, but we will also explore an alternative, more general version, because santa demonstrates a very common programming pattern. The pattern is this: a thread (Santa in this case) makes a choice in one atomic transaction, followed by one or more further consequential transactions. Another typical example might be: take a message from one of several message queues, act on the message, and repeat. In the Santa scenario, the consequential action was very similar for both elves and reindeer—in both cases, Santa had to print a message and operate two gates. But that would not work if Santa had to do very different things for elves and reindeer. One approach would be to return a Boolean indicating which was chosen, and dispatch on that Boolean after the choice, but that becomes inconvenient as more alternatives are added. Here is another approach that works better:

```
santa :: Group -> Group -> IO ()
santa elf_gp rein_gp
  = do { putStr "----------\n"
       ; choose [(awaitGroup rein_gp, run "deliver toys"),
                 (awaitGroup elf_gp,  run "meet in my study")] }
where
  run :: String -> (Gate,Gate) -> IO ()
  run task (in_gate,out_gate)
    = do { putStr ("Ho! Ho! Ho! let's " ++ task ++ "\n")
         ; operateGate in_gate
         ; operateGate out_gate }
```

The function choose is like a guarded command: it takes a list of pairs, waits until the first component of a pair is ready to "fire," and then executes the second component. So choose has this type:*

---

* In Haskell, the type [ty] means a list whose elements have type ty. In this case, choose's argument is a list of pairs, written (ty_1,ty_2); the first component of the pair has type STM a, while the second is a function with type a->IO ().

```
choose :: [(STM a, a -> IO ())] -> IO ()
```

The guard is an STM action delivering a value of type a; when the STM action is ready (that is, does not retry), choose can pass the value to the second component, which must therefore be a function expecting a value of type a. With this in mind, santa should be easy reading. He uses awaitGroup to wait for a ready Group; the choose function gets the pair of Gates returned by awaitGroup and passes it to the run function. The latter operates the two gates in succession—recall that operateGate blocks until all the elves (or reindeer) have gone through the gate.

The code for choose is brief, but a little mind-bending:

```
choose :: [(STM a, a -> IO ())] -> IO ()
choose choices = do { act <- atomically (foldr1 orElse actions)
                    ; act }
  where
    actions :: [STM (IO ())]
    actions = [ do { val <- guard; return (rhs val) }
              | (guard, rhs) <- choices ]
```

First, it forms a list, actions, of STM actions, which it then combines with orElse. (The call foldr1 $\oplus$ $[x_1,\ldots,x_n]$ returns $x_1 \oplus x_2 \oplus \ldots \oplus x_n$.) Each of these STM actions itself returns an IO action, namely *the thing to be done when the choice is made*. That is why each action in the list has the cool type STM (IO ()). The code first makes an atomic choice among the list of alternatives, getting the action act, with type IO () in return—and then performs the action act. The list of choices, actions, is constructed by taking each pair (guard,rhs) from the list of choices, running the guard (an STM action), and returning the IO action gotten by applying the rhs to the guard's return value.

Compiling and Running the Program

I have presented *all* the code for this example. If you simply add the appropriate import statements at the top, listed here, you should be good to go:*

```
module Main where
  import Control.Concurrent.STM
  import Control.Concurrent
  import System.Random
```

To compile the code, use the Glasgow Haskell Compiler, GHC:†

```
$ ghc Santa.hs -package stm -o santa
```

Finally, you can run the program:

```
$ ./santa
----------
Ho! Ho! Ho! let's deliver toys
Reindeer 8 delivering toys
Reindeer 7 delivering toys
```

---

* You can get the code online at *http://research.microsoft.com/~simonpj/papers/stm/Santa.hs.gz*.

† GHC is available for free at *http://haskell.org/ghc*.

```
Reindeer 6 delivering toys
Reindeer 5 delivering toys
Reindeer 4 delivering toys
Reindeer 3 delivering toys
Reindeer 2 delivering toys
Reindeer 1 delivering toys
Reindeer 9 delivering toys
----------
Ho! Ho! Ho! let's meet in my study
Elf 3 meeting in the study
Elf 2 meeting in the study
Elf 1 meeting in the study
...and so on...
```

Reflections on Haskell

Haskell is, first and foremost, a *functional* language. Nevertheless, I think that it is also the world's most beautiful *imperative* language. Considered as an imperative language, Haskell's unusual features are that:

- Actions (which have effects) are rigorously distinguished from pure values by the type system.

- Actions are first-class values. They can be passed to functions, returned as results, formed into lists, and so on, all without causing any side effects.

Using actions as first-class values, the programmer can define *application-specific control structures*, rather than make do with the ones provided by the language designer. For example, nTimes is a simple for loop, and choose implements a sort of guarded command. We also saw other applications of actions as values. In the main program, we used Haskell's rich expression language (in this case, list comprehensions) to generate a list of actions, which we then performed in order, using sequence_. Earlier, when defining helper1, we improved modularity by abstracting out an action from a chunk of code. To illustrate these points, I have perhaps overused Haskell's abstraction power in the Santa code, which is a very small program. For large programs, though, it is hard to overstate the importance of actions as values.

On the other hand, I have underplayed other aspects of Haskell—higher-order functions, lazy evaluation, data types, polymorphism, type classes, and so on—because of the focus on concurrency. Not many Haskell programs are as imperative as this one! You can find a great deal of information about Haskell at *http://haskell.org*, including books, tutorials, Haskell compilers and interpreters, Haskell libraries, mailing lists, and much more besides.

Conclusion

My main goal is to persuade you that you can write programs in a fundamentally more modular way using STM than you can with locks and condition variables. First, though, note that transactional memory allows us to completely avoid many of the standard problems that plague lock-based concurrent programs (as explained earlier in the section

"Locks Are Bad"). *None of these problems arises in STM Haskell.* The type system prevents you from reading or writing a TVar outside an atomic block, and because there *are* no programmer-visible locks, the questions of which locks to take, and in which order, simply do not arise. Other benefits of STM, which I lack the space to describe here, include freedom from lost wakeups and the treatment of exceptions and error recovery.

However, as we also discussed in the section "Locks Are Bad," the worst problem with lock-based programming is that *locks do not compose*. In contrast, any function with an STM type in Haskell can be composed, using sequencing or choice, with any other function with an STM type to make a new function of STM type. Furthermore, the compound function will guarantee all the same atomicity properties that the individual functions did. In particular, blocking (retry) and choice (orElse), which are fundamentally non-modular when expressed using locks, are fully modular in STM. For example, consider this transaction, which uses functions we defined in the section "Blocking and Choice":

```
atomically (do { limitedWithdraw a1 10
               ; limitedWithdraw2 a2 a3 20 })
```

This transaction blocks until a1 contains at least 10 units, and either a2 or a3 has 20 units. However, that complicated blocking condition is not written explicitly by the programmer, and indeed if the limitedWithdraw functions are implemented in a sophisticated library, the programmer might have no idea what their blocking conditions are. STM is modular: small programs can be glued together to make larger programs *without exposing their implementations*.

There are many aspects of transactional memory that I have not covered in this brief overview, including important topics such as nested transactions, exceptions, progress, starvation, and invariants. You can find many of them discussed in papers about STM Haskell.[*]

Transactional memory is a particularly good "fit" for Haskell. In STM, the implementation potentially must track every memory load and store, but a Haskell STM need only track TVar operations, and these form only a tiny fraction of all the memory loads and stores executed by a Haskell program. Furthermore, the treatment of actions as first-class values, and the rich type system, allow us to offer strong static guarantees without extending the language in any way. However, there is nothing to stop the adoption of transactional memory in mainstream imperative languages, although it may be less elegant and require more language support. Indeed doing so is a hot research topic; Larus and Rajwar give a comprehensive summary.[†]

---

[*] Tim Harris, Simon Marlow, Simon Peyton Jones, and Maurice Herlihy, "Composable memory transactions," *ACM Symposium on Principles and Practice of Parallel Programming (PPoPP '05)*, June 2005; Tim Harris and Simon Peyton Jones, "Transactional memory with data invariants," *First ACM SIGPLAN Workshop on Languages, Compilers, and Hardware Support for Transactional Computing (TRANSACT '06)*, Ottawa, June 2006, ACM; Anthony Discolo, Tim Harris, Simon Marlow, Simon Peyton Jones, and Satnam Singh, "Lock-free data structures using STMs in Haskell," *Eighth International Symposium on Functional and Logic Programming (FLOPS '06)*, April 2006.

[†] James Larus and Ravi Rajwar, *Transactional Memory*, Morgan & Claypool, 2006.

Using STM is like using a high-level language instead of assembly code—you can still write buggy programs, but many tricky bugs simply cannot occur, and it is much easier to focus attention on the higher-level aspects of the program. There is, alas, no silver bullet that will make concurrent programs easy to write. But STM looks like a promising step forward, and one that will help you to write beautiful code.

Acknowledgments

I would like to thank those who helped me to improve the chapter with their feedback: Bo Adler, Justin Bailey, Matthew Brecknell, Paul Brown, Conal Elliot, Tony Finch, Kathleen Fisher, Greg Fitzgerald, Benjamin Franksen, Jeremy Gibbons, Tim Harris, Robert Helgesson, Dean Herington, David House, Brian Hulley, Dale Jordan, Marnix Klooster, Chris Kuklewicz, Evan Martin, Greg Meredith, Neil Mitchell, Jun Mukai, Michal Palka, Sebastian Sylvan, Johan Tibell, Aruthur van Leeuwen, Wim Vanderbauwhede, David Wakeling, Dan Wang, Peter Wasilko, Eric Willigers, Gaal Yahas, and Brian Zimmer. My special thanks go to Kirsten Chevalier, Andy Oram, and Greg Wilson for their particularly detailed reviews.

## CHAPTER TWENTY-FIVE

Syntactic Abstraction:
The syntax-case Expander

R. Kent Dybvig

WHEN WRITING COMPUTER PROGRAMS, CERTAIN PATTERNS ARISE OVER AND OVER AGAIN. For example, programs must often loop through the elements of arrays, increment or decrement the values of variables, and perform multiway conditionals based on numeric or character values. Programming language designers typically acknowledge this by including special-purpose syntactic constructs that handle the most common patterns. C, for instance, provides multiple looping constructs, multiple conditional constructs, and multiple constructs for incrementing or otherwise updating the value of a variable.*

Some patterns are less common but may occur frequently in a certain class of programs, or perhaps just within a single program. These patterns may not even be anticipated by a language's designers, who in any case would typically choose not to incorporate syntactic constructs to handle such patterns in the language core.

Yet, recognizing that such patterns do arise and that special-purpose syntactic constructs can make programs both simpler and easier to read, language designers sometimes include

---

* *The C Programming Language*, Second Edition, Brian W. Kernighan and Dennis M. Ritchie, Prentice Hall, 1988.

a mechanism for *syntactic abstraction,* such as C's preprocessor macros or Common Lisp[*] macros. When such facilities are absent or are inadequate for a specific purpose, an external tool, such as the *m4* macro expander,[†] may be brought to bear.

Syntactic abstraction facilities differ in several significant ways. C's preprocessor macros are essentially token-based, allowing the replacement of a macro call with a sequence of tokens; text passed to the macro call is substituted for the macro's formal parameters, if any. Lisp macros are expression-based, allowing the replacement of a single expression with another expression, computed in Lisp itself and based on the subforms of the macro call, if any.

In both cases, identifiers appearing within a macro-call subform are scoped where they appear in the output, rather than where they appear in the input, possibly leading to unintended *capture* of a variable reference by a variable binding.

For example, consider the simple transformation of Scheme's or form[‡] into let and if in the following example:

```
(or e₁ e₂) → (let ([t e₁]) (if t t e₂))
```

> **NOTE**
> Readers unfamiliar with Scheme might want to read the first few chapters of *The Scheme Programming Language,* Third Edition (R. Kent Dybvig, MIT Press), which is available online at *http://www.scheme.com/tspl3.*

An or form must return the value of its first subform, if it evaluates to a true (any non-false) value. The let expression is used to name this value so that it is not computed twice.

The previous transformation works fine in most cases, but it breaks down if the identifier t appears free in e_2 (i.e., outside of any binding for t in e_2), as in the following expression:

```
(let ([t #t]) (or #f t))
```

This should evaluate to the true value #t. With the simple transformation of or specified previously, however, the expression expands to:

```
(let ([t #t])
  (let ([t #f])
    (if t t t)))
```

which evaluates to the false value #f.

[*] *Common Lisp: The Language,* Second Edition, Guy L. Steele Jr., Digital Press, 1990.

[†] *The M4 Macro Processor,* Brian W. Kernighan and Dennis M. Ritchie, 1979.

[‡] "Revised report on the algorithmic language Scheme," Richard Kelsey, William Clinger, and Jonathan Rees, editors, *Higher-Order and Symbolic Computation,* Vol. 11, No. 1, pp. 7–105, 1998. Also appeared in *ACM SIGPLAN Notices,* Vol. 33, No. 9, September 1998.

Once seen, this problem is easily addressed by using a generated identifier for the introduced binding:

```
(or e₁ e₂) → (let ([g e₁]) (if g g e₂))
```

where g is a generated (fresh) identifier.

As Kohlbecker, Friedman, Felleisen, and Duba observe in their seminal paper on hygienic macro expansion* variable capture problems like this are insidious, because a transformation may work correctly for a large body of code only to fail sometime later in a way that may be difficult to debug.

While unintended captures caused by introduced identifier *bindings* can always be solved by using generated identifiers, no such simple solution is available for introduced identifier *references*, which may be captured by bindings in the context of the macro call. In the following expression, if is lexically bound in the context of an or expression:

```
(let ([if (lambda (x y z) "oops")]) (or #f #f))
```

With the second transformation for or, this expression expands into:

```
(let ([if (lambda (x y z) "oops")])
  (let ([g #f])
    (if g g #f)))
```

where g is a fresh identifier. The value of the expression should be #f, but will actually be "oops" because the locally bound procedure if is used in place of the original if conditional syntax.

Limiting the language by reserving the names of keywords such as let and if would solve this problem for keywords, but it would not solve the problem generally. For instance, the same situation can arise with the introduced reference to the user-defined variable add1 in the following transformation of increment:

```
(increment x) → (set! x (add1 x))
```

Kohlbecker et al. invented the concept of *hygienic* macro expansion to solve both kinds of capturing problems, borrowing the term "hygiene" from Barendregt.† Barendregt's hygiene condition for the λ-calculus holds that the free variables of one expression substituted into another are assumed not to be captured by bindings in the other, unless such capture is explicitly required. Kohlbecker et al. adapted this into the following *hygiene condition for macro expansion*:

> Generated identifiers that become binding instances in the completely expanded program must only bind variables that are generated at the same transcription step.

---

* "Hygienic macro expansion," Eugene Kohlbecker, Daniel P. Friedman, Matthias Felleisen, and Bruce Duba, *Proceedings of the 1986 ACM Conference on Lisp and Functional Programming*, pp. 151–161, 1986.

† "Introduction to the lambda calculus," H. P. Barendregt, *Nieuw Archief voor Wisenkunde*, Vol. 4, No. 2, pp. 337–372, 1984.

In practice, this requirement forces the expander to rename identifiers as necessary to avoid unintended captures. For example, with the original or transformation:

```
(or e₁ e₂) → (let ([t e₁]) (if t t e₂))
```

the expression:

```
(let ([t #t]) (or #f t))
```

expands into the equivalent of:

```
(let ([t0 #t])
  (let ([t1 #f])
    (if t1 t1 t0)))
```

which properly evaluates to #t. Similarly, the expression:

```
(let ([if (lambda (x y z) "oops")]) (or #f #f))
```

expands into the equivalent of:

```
(let ([if0 (lambda (x y z) "oops")])
  (let ([t #f])
    (if t t #f)))
```

which properly evaluates to #f.

In essence, hygienic macro expansion implements lexical scoping with respect to the source code, whereas unhygienic expansion implements lexical scoping with respect to the code after expansion.

Hygienic expansion can preserve lexical scope only to the extent that the scope is preserved by the transformations it is told to perform. A transformation can still produce code that apparently violates lexical scoping. This can be illustrated with the following (incorrect) transformation of let:

```
(let ((x e)) body) → (letrec ((x e)) body)
```

The expression *e* should appear outside the scope of the binding of the variable *x*, but in the output it appears inside, due to the semantics of letrec.

The hygienic macro expansion algorithm (KFFD) described by Kohlbecker et al. is both clever and elegant. It works by adding a timestamp to each variable introduced by a macro, and then uses the timestamps to distinguish like-named variables as it renames lexically bound variables. KFFD has some shortcomings that prevent its direct use in practice, however. The most serious are a lack of support for local macro bindings and quadratic overhead resulting from the complete rewrite of each expression as timestamping and renaming are performed.

These shortcomings are addressed by the syntax-rules system, developed by Clinger, Dybvig, Hieb, and Rees for the Revised Report on Scheme.* The simple pattern-based

---

* "Revised report on the algorithmic language Scheme," William Clinger and Jonathan Rees, editors, *LISP Pointers*, Vol. 4, No. 3, pp. 1–55, July–September 1991.

nature of the syntax-rules system permits it to be implemented easily and efficiently.[*] Unfortunately, it also limits the utility of the mechanism, so that many useful syntactic abstractions are either difficult or impossible to write.

The syntax-case system[†] was developed to address the shortcomings of the original algorithm without the limitations of syntax-rules. The system supports local macro bindings and operates with constant overhead, yet allows macros to use the full expressive power of the Scheme language. It is upwardly compatible with syntax-rules, which can be expressed as a simple macro in terms of syntax-case, and it permits the same pattern language to be used even for "low-level" macros for which syntax-rules cannot be used. It also provides a mechanism for allowing *intended* captures—i.e., allowing hygiene to be "bent" or "broken" in a selective and straightforward manner. In addition, it handles several practical aspects of expansion that must be addressed in a real implementation, such as internal definitions and tracking of source information through macro expansion.

This all comes at a price in terms of the complexity of the expansion algorithm and the size of the code required to implement it. A study of a complete implementation in all its glory is therefore beyond the scope of this chapter. Instead, we'll investigate a simplified version of the expander that illustrates the underlying algorithm and the most important aspects of its implementation.

Brief Introduction to syntax-case

We'll start with a few brief syntax-case examples, adapted from the *Chez Scheme Version 7 User's Guide* (R. Kent Dybvig, Cadence Research Systems, 2005). Additional examples and a more detailed description of syntax-case are given in that document and in *The Scheme Programming Language*, Third Edition.

The following definition of or illustrates the form of a syntax-case macro definition:

```
(define-syntax or
  (lambda (x)
    (syntax-case x ()
      [(_ e1 e2)
       (syntax (let ([t e1]) (if t t e2)))])))
```

The define-syntax form creates a keyword binding, associating the keyword or in this case with a transformation procedure, or *transformer*. The transformer is obtained by evaluating, at expansion time, the lambda expression on the righthand side of the define-syntax form. The syntax-case form is used to parse the input, and the syntax form is used to construct the output, via straightforward pattern matching. The *pattern* (_ e1 e2) specifies the shape of the input, with the underscore (_) marking where the keyword or appears,

* "Macros that work," William Clinger and Jonathan Rees, *Conference Record of the Eighteenth Annual ACM Symposium on Principles of Programming Languages*, pp. 155–162, January 1991.

† "Syntactic abstraction in Scheme," R. Kent Dybvig, Robert Hieb, and Carl Bruggeman, *Lisp and Symbolic Computation*, Vol. 5, No. 4, pp. 295–326, 1993.

and the pattern variables e1 and e2 bound to the first and second subforms. The *template* (let ([t e1]) (if t t e2)) specifies the output, with e1 and e2 inserted from the input.

The form (syntax *template*) may be abbreviated to #'*template*, so the previous definition may be rewritten as follows:

```
(define-syntax or
  (lambda (x)
    (syntax-case x ()
      [(_ e1 e2)
       (syntax (let ([t e1]) (if t t e2)))])))
```

Macros may also be bound within a single expression via letrec-syntax.

```
(letrec-syntax ([or (lambda (x)
                      (syntax-case x ()
                        [(_ e1 e2)
                         #'(let ([t e1]) (if t t e2))]))])
  (or a b))
```

Macros can be recursive (i.e., expand into occurrences of themselves), as illustrated by the following version of or that handles an arbitrary number of subforms. Multiple syntax-case clauses are required to handle the two base cases and the recursion case:

```
(define-syntax or
  (lambda (x)
    (syntax-case x ()
      [(_) #'#f]
      [(_ e) #'e]
      [(_ e1 e2 e3 ...)
       #'(let ([t e1]) (if t t (or e2 e3 ...)))])))
```

An input or output form followed by an ellipsis in the syntax-case pattern language matches or produces zero or more forms.

Hygiene is ensured for the definitions of or in this example, so that the introduced binding for t and the introduced references to let, if, and even or are scoped properly. If we want to bend or break hygiene, we do so with the procedure datum->syntax, which produces a syntax object from an arbitrary s-expression. The identifiers within the s-expression are treated as if they appeared in the original source where the first argument, the *template identifier*, appeared.

We can use this fact to create a simple method syntax that implicitly binds the name this to the first (object) argument:

```
(define-syntax method
  (lambda (x)
    (syntax-case x ()
      [(k (x ...) e1 e2 ...)
       (with-syntax ([this (datum->syntax #'k 'this)])
         #'(lambda (this x ...) e1 e2 ...))])))
```

By using the keyword k, extracted from the input, as the template variable, the variable this is treated as if it were present in the method form, so that:

```
(method (a) (f this a))
```

is treated as the equivalent of:

```
(lambda (this a) (f this a))
```

with no renaming to prevent the introduced binding from capturing the source-code reference.

The with-syntax form used in the definition of method creates local pattern-variable bindings. It is a simple macro written in terms of syntax-case:

```
(define-syntax with-syntax
  (lambda (x)
    (syntax-case x ()
      [(_ ((p e0) ...) e1 e2 ...)
       #'(syntax-case (list e0 ...) ()
           [(p ...) (begin e1 e2 ...)])])))
```

The datum->syntax procedure can be used for arbitrary expressions, as illustrated by the following definition of include:

```
(define-syntax include
  (lambda (x)
    (define read-file
      (lambda (fn k)
        (let ([p (open-input-file fn)])
          (let f ([x (read p)])
            (if (eof-object? x)
                (begin (close-input-port p) '())
                (cons (datum->syntax k x) (f (read p))))))))
    (syntax-case x ()
      [(k filename)
       (let ([fn (syntax->datum #'filename)])
         (with-syntax ([(e ...) (read-file fn #'k)])
           #'(begin e ...)))])))
```

The form (include "filename") has the effect of treating the forms within the named file as if they were present in the source code in place of the include form. In addition to using datum->syntax, include also uses its inverse operator, syntax->datum, to convert the filename subform into a string it can pass to open-input-file.

Expansion Algorithm

The syntax-case expansion algorithm is essentially a lazy variant of the KFFD algorithm that operates on an abstract representation of the input expression rather than on the traditional s-expression representation. The abstract representation encapsulates both a representation of an input form and a *wrap* that enables the algorithm to determine the scope of all identifiers within the form. The wrap consists of *marks* and *substitutions*.

Marks are like KFFD timestamps and are added to the portions of a macro's output that are introduced by the macro.

Substitutions map identifiers to bindings with the help of a compile-time environment. Substitutions are created whenever a binding form, such as `lambda`, is encountered, and they are added to the wraps of the syntax objects representing the forms within the scope of the binding form's bindings. A substitution applies to an identifier only if the identifier has the same name and marks as the substituted identifier.

Expansion operates in a recursive, top-down fashion. As the expander encounters a macro call, it invokes the associated transformer on the form, marking it first with a fresh mark and then marking it again with the same mark. Like marks cancel, so only the introduced portions of the macro's output—i.e., those portions not simply copied from the input to the output—remain marked.

When a core form is encountered, a core form in the output language of the expander (in our case, the traditional s-expression representation) is produced, with any subforms recursively expanded as necessary. Variable references are replaced by generated names via the substitution mechanism.

Representations

The most important aspect of the `syntax-case` mechanism is its abstract representation of program source code as *syntax objects*. As described above, a syntax object encapsulates not only a representation of the program source code but also a wrap that provides sufficient information about the identifiers contained within the code to implement hygiene:

```
(define-record syntax-object (expr wrap))
```

The `define-record` form creates a new type of value with the specified name (in this case, `syntax-object`) and fields (in this case, `expr` and `wrap`), along with a set of procedures to manipulate it. The procedures in this case are:

`make-syntax-object`
  Returns a new syntax object with the `expr` and `wrap` fields initialized to the values of its arguments

`syntax-object?`
  Returns true if and only if its argument is a syntax object

`syntax-object-expr`
  Returns the value of the `expr` field of a `syntax-object`

`syntax-object-wrap`
  Returns the value of the `wrap` field of a syntax object

A complete implementation of `syntax-case` might also include, within each syntax object, source information to be tracked through the expansion process.

Each wrap, as explained previously, consists of a list of marks and substitutions. Marks are distinguished by their object identity and do not require any fields:

```
(define-record mark ())
```

A substitution maps a symbolic name and list of marks to a label:

```
(define-record subst (sym mark* label))
```

Labels, like marks, are distinguished by their identity and require no fields:

```
(define-record label ())
```

The expand-time environment maintained by the expander maps labels to *bindings*. The environment is structured as a traditional *association list*—i.e., a list of pairs, each car of which contains a label and each cdr of which contains a binding. Bindings consist of a type (represented as a symbol) and a value:

```
(define-record binding (type value))
```

The type identifies the nature of the binding: macro for keyword bindings and lexical for lexical variable bindings. The value is any additional information required to specify the binding, such as the transformation procedure when the binding is a keyword binding.

Producing Expander Output

The expander's output is a simple s-expression in the core language and is thus constructed for the most part using Scheme's quasiquote syntax for creating list structure. For example, a lambda expression may be created with formal parameter *var* and body *body* as follows:

```
`(lambda (,var) ,body)
```

The expander does need to create fresh names, however, and does so via the gen-var helper, which makes use of the Scheme primitives for converting strings to symbols and vice versa, along with a local sequence counter:

```
(define gen-var
  (let ([n 0])
    (lambda (id)
      (set! n (+ n 1))
      (let ([name (syntax-object-expr id)])
        (string->symbol (format "~s.~s" name n)))))))
```

Stripping Syntax Objects

Whenever a quote form is encountered in the input, the expander must return a representation of the constant contents appearing within the quote form. To do this, it must strip off any embedded syntax objects and wraps using the strip procedure, which traverses the syntax object and list structure of its input and recreates an s-expression representation of its input:

```
(define strip
  (lambda (x)
    (cond
      [(syntax-object? x)
       (if (top-marked? (syntax-object-wrap x))
           (syntax-object-expr x)
           (strip (syntax-object-expr x)))]
      [(pair? x)
       (let ([a (strip (car x))] [d (strip (cdr x))])
         (if (and (eq? a (car x)) (eq? d (cdr x)))
             x
             (cons a d)))]
      [else x])))
```

Traversal terminates along any branch of the input expression when something other than a syntax object or pair is found—i.e., when a symbol or immediate value is found. It also terminates when a syntax object is found to be "top marked"—i.e., when its wrap contains a unique *top mark*:

```
(define top-mark (make-mark))

(define top-marked?
  (lambda (wrap)
    (and (not (null? wrap))
         (or (eq? (car wrap) top-mark)
             (top-marked? (cdr wrap))))))
```

When the expander creates a syntax object representing the original input, it uses a wrap that contains the top mark at its base, specifically to allow the stripping code detect when it has reached the syntax-object base and need not traverse the object further. This feature prevents the expander from traversing constants unnecessarily so that it can easily preserve shared and cyclic structure, and not be confused by the presence of quoted syntax objects in the input.

Syntax Errors

The expander reports syntax errors via syntax-error, which is defined as follows:

```
(define syntax-error
  (lambda (object message)
    (error #f "~a ~s" message (strip object))))
```

If the implementation attaches source information to syntax objects, this source information can be used to construct an error message that incorporates the source line and character position.

Structural Predicates

The nonatomic structure of a syntax object is always determined with the patterns of a syntax-case form. The identifier? predicate determines whether a syntax object represents an identifier:

```
(define identifier?
  (lambda (x)
    (and (syntax-object? x)
         (symbol? (syntax-object-expr x)))))
```

Similarly, the self-evaluating? predicate is used, after stripping a syntax object, to determine whether it represents a constant:

```
(define self-evaluating?
  (lambda (x)
    (or (boolean? x) (number? x) (string? x) (char? x))))
```

Creating Wraps

A mark or substitution is added to a syntax object by extending the wrap:

```
(define add-mark
  (lambda (mark x)
    (extend-wrap (list mark) x)))

(define add-subst
  (lambda (id label x)
    (extend-wrap
      (list (make-subst
              (syntax-object-expr id)
              (wrap-marks (syntax-object-wrap id))
              label))
      x)))
```

If the syntax object is only partially wrapped, the wrap is extended simply by creating a syntax object encapsulating the partially wrapped structure. Otherwise, the syntax object is rebuilt with the new wrap joined to the old wrap:

```
(define extend-wrap
  (lambda (wrap x)
    (if (syntax-object? x)
        (make-syntax-object
          (syntax-object-expr x)
          (join-wraps wrap (syntax-object-wrap x)))
        (make-syntax-object x wrap))))
```

Joining two wraps is almost as simple as appending the lists of marks. The only complication is that the expansion algorithm requires that two like marks cancel when they meet.

```
(define join-wraps
  (lambda (wrap1 wrap2)
    (cond
      [(null? wrap1) wrap2]
      [(null? wrap2) wrap1]
      [else
       (let f ([w (car wrap1)] [w* (cdr wrap1)])
         (if (null? w*)
             (if (and (mark? w) (eq? (car wrap2) w))
                 (cdr wrap2)
                 (cons w wrap2))
             (cons w (f (car w*) (cdr w*)))))])))
```

Manipulating Environments

Environments map labels to bindings and are represented as association lists. Extending an environment therefore involves adding a single pair mapping a label to a binding:

```
(define extend-env
  (lambda (label binding env)
    (cons (cons label binding) env)))
```

Identifier Resolution

Determining the binding associated with an identifier is a two-step process. The first step is to determine the label associated with the identifier in the identifier's wrap, and the second is to look the label up in the current environment:

```
(define id-binding
  (lambda (id r)
    (label-binding id (id-label id) r)))
```

The marks and substitutions that appear in an identifier's wrap determine the associated label, if any. Substitutions map names and lists of marks to labels. Any substitution whose name is not the name of the identifier is ignored, as is any whose marks do not match. The names are symbols and are thus compared using the pointer equivalence operator, eq?.

The set of marks considered relevant are those that were layered onto the wrap before the substitution. Thus, the set of marks to which a substitution's marks are compared changes as the search through the wrap proceeds. The starting set of marks is the entire set that appears in the wrap. Each time a mark is encountered during the search for a matching substitution in the wrap, the first mark in the list is removed:

```
(define id-label
  (lambda (id)
    (let ([sym (syntax-object-expr id)]
          [wrap (syntax-object-wrap id)])
      (let search ([wrap wrap] [mark* (wrap-marks wrap)])
        (if (null? wrap)
            (syntax-error id "undefined identifier")
            (let ([w0 (car wrap)])
              (if (mark? w0)
                  (search (cdr wrap) (cdr mark*))
                  (if (and (eq? (subst-sym w0) sym)
                           (same-marks? (subst-mark* w0) mark*))
                      (subst-label w0)
                      (search (cdr wrap) mark*)))))))))
```

If no matching substitution exists in the wrap, the identifier is undefined, and a syntax error is signaled. It would be possible instead to treat all such identifier references as global variable references.

The id-label procedure obtains the starting list of marks via wrap-marks and uses the same-marks? predicate to compare lists of marks:

```
(define wrap-marks
  (lambda (wrap)
    (if (null? wrap)
        '()
        (let ([w0 (car wrap)])
          (if (mark? w0)
              (cons w0 (wrap-marks (cdr wrap)))
              (wrap-marks (cdr wrap)))))))

(define same-marks?
  (lambda (m1* m2*)
    (if (null? m1*)
        (null? m2*)
        (and (not (null? m2*))
             (eq? (car m1*) (car m2*))
             (same-marks? (cdr m1*) (cdr m2*))))))
```

Once a label has been found, `id-binding` is used to find the associated binding, if any, using the assq procedure for performing association-list lookups. If an association is found, the binding in the cdr of the association is returned:

```
(define label-binding
  (lambda (id label r)
    (let ([a (assq label r)])
      (if a
          (cdr a)
          (syntax-error id "displaced lexical")))))
```

If no binding is found, the identifier is a "displaced lexical." This occurs when a macro improperly inserts into its output a reference to an identifier that is not visible in the context of the macro output.

The Expander

With the mechanisms for handling wraps and environments in place, the expander is straightforward. The expression expander, exp, handles macro calls, lexical variable references, applications, core forms, and constants. Macro calls come in two forms: singleton macro-keyword references and structured forms with a macro keyword in the first position.

The exp procedure takes three arguments: a syntax object *x*, a runtime environment *r*, and a meta environment *mr*. The runtime environment is used to process ordinary expressions whose code will appear in the expander's output, while the meta environment is used to process transformer expressions (e.g., on the righthand sides of `letrec-syntax` bindings), which are evaluated and used at expansion time. The difference between the runtime and meta environments is that the meta environment does not contain lexical variable bindings, because these bindings are not available when the transformer is evaluated and used:

```
(define exp
  (lambda (x r mr)
    (syntax-case x ()
```

```
[id
 (identifier? #'id)
 (let ([b (id-binding #'id r)])
   (case (binding-type b)
     [(macro) (exp (exp-macro (binding-value b) x) r mr)]
     [(lexical) (binding-value b)]
     [else (syntax-error x "invalid syntax")]))]
[(e0 e1 ...)
 (identifier? #'e0)
 (let ([b (id-binding #'e0 r)])
   (case (binding-type b)
     [(macro) (exp (exp-macro (binding-value b) x) r mr)]
     [(lexical)
      `(,(binding-value b) ,@(exp-exprs #'(e1 ...) r mr))]
     [(core) (exp-core (binding-value b) x r mr)]
     [else (syntax-error x "invalid syntax")]))]
[(e0 e1 ...)
 `(,(exp #'e0 r mr) ,@(exp-exprs #'(e1 ...) r mr))]
[_
 (let ([d (strip x)])
   (if (self-evaluating? d)
       d
       (syntax-error x "invalid syntax")))])])))
```

Macro calls are handled by exp-macro (described shortly) and then re-expanded. Lexical variables are rewritten into the binding value, which is always a generated variable name. Applications are rewritten into lists as in the traditional s-expression syntax for Lisp and Scheme, with the subforms expanded recursively. Core forms are handled by exp-core (described shortly); any recursion back to the expression expander is performed explicitly by the core transformer. A constant is rewritten into the constant value, stripped of its syntax wrapper.

The expander uses syntax-case and syntax (in its abbreviated form—i.e., #'*template*) to parse and refer to the input or portions thereof. Because the expander is also charged with implementing syntax-case, this may seem like a paradox. In actuality, it is handled by bootstrapping one version of the expander using a previous version. The expander would be much more tedious to write if syntax-case and syntax were not used.

The exp-macro procedure applies the transformation procedure (the value part of the macro binding) to the entire macro form, which may either be a single macro keyword or a structured expression with the macro keyword at its head. The exp-macro procedure first adds a fresh mark to the wrap of the input form, then applies the same mark to the wrap of the output form. The first mark serves as an "anti-mark" that cancels out the second mark, so the net effect is that the mark adheres only to the portions of the output that were introduced by the transformer, thus uniquely identifying the portions of the code introduced at this transcription step:

```
(define exp-macro
  (lambda (p x)
    (let ([m (make-mark)])
      (add-mark m (p (add-mark m x))))))
```

The exp-core procedure simply applies the given core transformer (the value part of the core binding) to the input form:

```
(define exp-core
  (lambda (p x r mr)
    (p x r mr)))
```

The exp-exprs procedure used to process application subforms simply maps the expander over the forms:

```
(define exp-exprs
  (lambda (x* r mr)
    (map (lambda (x) (exp x r mr)) x*)))
```

Core Transformers

Transformers for several representative core forms (quote, if, lambda, let, and letrec-syntax) are described here. Adding transformers for other core forms, such as letrec or let-syntax, is straightforward.

The exp-quote procedure produces an s-expression representing a quote form, with the data value stripped of its syntax wrap:

```
(define exp-quote
  (lambda (x r mr)
    (syntax-case x ()
      [(_ d) `(quote ,(strip #'d))])))
```

The exp-if procedure produces an s-expression representation of an if form, with the subforms recursively expanded:

```
(define exp-if
  (lambda (x r mr)
    (syntax-case x ()
      [(_ e1 e2 e3)
       `(if ,(exp #'e1 r mr)
            ,(exp #'e2 r mr)
            ,(exp #'e3 r mr))])))
```

The exp-lambda procedure handles lambda expressions that have only a single formal parameter and only a single body expression. Extending it to handle multiple parameters is straightforward. It is less straightforward to handle arbitrary lambda bodies, including internal definitions, but support for internal definitions is beyond the scope of this chapter.

When the s-expression representation of a lambda expression is produced, a generated variable name is created for the formal parameter. A substitution mapping the identifier to a fresh label is added to the wrap on the body, and the environment is extended with an association from the label to a lexical binding whose value is the generated variable, during the recursive processing of the body:

```
(define exp-lambda
  (lambda (x r mr)
    (syntax-case x ()
```

```
[(_ (var) body)
 (let ([label (make-label)] [new-var (gen-var #'var)])
   `(lambda (,new-var)
      ,(exp (add-subst #'var label #'body)
            (extend-env label
              (make-binding 'lexical new-var)
              r)
            mr)))])))
```

The meta environment is not extended because the meta environment should not include lexical variable bindings.

The exp-let procedure that transforms single-binding let forms is similar to the transformer for lambda, but a bit more involved:

```
(define exp-let
  (lambda (x r mr)
    (syntax-case x ()
      [(_ ([var expr]) body)
       (let ([label (make-label)] [new-var (gen-var #'var)])
         `(let ([,new-var ,(exp #'expr r mr)])
            ,(exp (add-subst #'var label #'body)
                  (extend-env label
                    (make-binding 'lexical new-var)
                    r)
                  mr)))])))
```

The body is in the scope of the binding created by let, so it is expanded with the extended wrap and environment. The righthand-side expression, expr, is not within the scope, so it is expanded with the original wrap and environment.

The exp-letrec-syntax procedure handles single-binding letrec-syntax forms. As with lambda and let, a substitution mapping the bound identifier—in this case, a keyword rather than a variable—to a fresh label is added to the wrap on the body, and an association from the label to a binding is added to the environment while the body is recursively processed. The binding is a macro binding rather than a lexical binding, and the binding value is the result of recursively expanding and evaluating the righthand-side expression of the letrec-syntax form.

In contrast with let, the righthand-side expression is also wrapped with a substitution from the keyword to the label and expanded with the extended environment; this allows the macro to be recursive. This would not be done if the form were a let-syntax form instead of a letrec-syntax form. The output produced by expanding a letrec-syntax form consists only of the output of the recursive call to the expander on the body of the form:

```
(define exp-letrec-syntax
  (lambda (x r mr)
    (syntax-case x ()
      [(_ ((kwd expr)) body)
       (let ([label (make-label)])
         (let ([b (make-binding 'macro
                    (eval (exp (add-subst #'kwd label #'expr)
                               mr mr)))])
```

```
(exp (add-subst #'kwd label #'body)
     (extend-env label b r)
     (extend-env label b mr)))))])))
```

Both the runtime and meta environments are extended in this case, since transformers are available both in runtime and transformer code.

Parsing and Constructing Syntax Objects

Macros are written in a pattern-matching style using syntax-case to match and take apart the input, and syntax to reconstruct the output. The implementation of the pattern matching and reconstruction is outside the scope of this chapter, but the following low-level operators can be used as the basis for the implementation. The syntax-case form can be built from the following set of three operators that treat syntax objects as abstract s-expressions:

```
(define syntax-pair?
  (lambda (x)
    (pair? (syntax-object-expr x))))

(define syntax-car
  (lambda (x)
    (extend-wrap
      (syntax-object-wrap x)
      (car (syntax-object-expr x)))))

(define syntax-cdr
  (lambda (x)
    (extend-wrap
      (syntax-object-wrap x)
      (cdr (syntax-object-expr x)))))
```

The definitions of syntax-car and syntax-cdr employ the extend-wrap helper defined in the earlier section "Creating Wraps" to push the wrap on the pair onto the car and cdr.

Similarly, syntax can be built from the following more basic version of syntax that handles constant input, but not pattern variables and ellipses:

```
(define exp-syntax
  (lambda (x r mr)
    (syntax-case x ()
      [(_ t) `(quote ,#'t)])))
```

In essence, the simplified version of syntax is just like quote except that syntax does not strip the encapsulated value but rather leaves the syntax wrappers intact.

Comparing Identifiers

Identifiers are compared based on their intended use. They may be compared as symbols by using the pointer equivalence operator eq? on the symbolic names of the identifiers. They may also be compared according to their intended use as free or bound identifiers in the output of a macro.

Two identifiers are considered equivalent by `free-identifier=?` if they would resolve to the same binding if introduced into the output of a macro outside of any binding introduced by the macro. Equivalency is tested by comparing the labels to which the identifiers resolve, as described previously in the section "Identifier Resolution":

```
(define free-identifier=?
  (lambda (x y)
    (eq? (id-label x) (id-label y))))
```

The `free-identifier=?` predicate is often used to check for auxiliary keywords, such as `else` in `cond` or `case`.

Two identifiers are considered equivalent by `bound-identifier=?` if a reference to one would be captured by an enclosing binding for another. This is accomplished by comparing the names and marks of the two identifiers:

```
(define bound-identifier=?
  (lambda (x y)
    (and (eq? (syntax-object-expr x) (syntax-object-expr y))
         (same-marks?
           (wrap-marks (syntax-object-wrap x))
           (wrap-marks (syntax-object-wrap y))))))
```

The `bound-identifier=?` predicate is often used to check for duplicate identifier errors in a binding form, such as `lambda` or `let`.

Conversions

The conversion from s-expression to syntax object performed by `datum->syntax` requires only that the wrap be transferred from the template identifier to the s-expression:

```
(define datum->syntax
  (lambda (template-id x)
    (make-syntax-object x (syntax-object-wrap template-id))))
```

The opposite conversion involves stripping the wrap away from a syntax object, so `syntax->datum` is just `strip`:

```
(define syntax->datum strip)
```

Starting Expansion

All of the pieces are now in place to expand Scheme expressions containing macros into expressions in the core language. The main expander merely supplies an initial wrap and environment that include names and bindings for the core forms and primitives:

```
(define expand
  (lambda (x)
    (let-values ([(wrap env) (initial-wrap-and-env)])
      (exp (make-syntax-object x wrap) env env))))
```

The initial wrap consists of a set of substitutions mapping each predefined identifier to a fresh label, and the initial environment associates each of these labels with the corresponding binding:

```
(define initial-wrap-and-env
  (lambda ()
    (define id-binding*
      `((quote . ,(make-binding 'core exp-quote))
        (if . ,(make-binding 'core exp-if))
        (lambda . ,(make-binding 'core exp-lambda))
        (let . ,(make-binding 'core exp-let))
        (letrec-syntax . ,(make-binding 'core exp-letrec-syntax))
        (identifier? . ,(make-binding 'lexical 'identifier?))
        (free-identifier=? . ,(make-binding 'lexical 'free-identifier=?))
        (bound-identifier=? . ,(make-binding 'lexical 'bound-identifier=?))
        (datum->syntax . ,(make-binding 'lexical 'datum->syntax))
        (syntax->datum . ,(make-binding 'lexical 'syntax->datum))
        (syntax-error . ,(make-binding 'lexical 'syntax-error))
        (syntax-pair? . ,(make-binding 'lexical 'syntax-pair?))
        (syntax-car . ,(make-binding 'lexical 'syntax-car))
        (syntax-cdr . ,(make-binding 'lexical 'syntax-cdr))
        (syntax . ,(make-binding 'core exp-syntax))
        (list . ,(make-binding 'core 'list))))
    (let ([label* (map (lambda (x) (make-label)) id-binding*)])
      (values
        `(,@(map (lambda (sym label)
                   (make-subst sym (list top-mark) label))
                 (map car id-binding*)
                 label*)
          ,top-mark)
        (map cons label* (map cdr id-binding*))))))
```

In addition to the entries listed, the initial environment should also include bindings for the built-in syntactic forms we have not implemented (e.g., letrec and let-syntax), as well as for all built-in Scheme procedures. It should also include a full version of syntax and, in place of syntax-pair?, syntax-car, and syntax-cdr, it should include syntax-case.

Example

We now trace through the following example from the beginning of this chapter:

```
(let ([t #t]) (or #f t))
```

We assume that or has been defined to do the transformation given at the beginning of the chapter, using the equivalent of the following definition of or from the section "Brief Introduction to syntax-case":

```
(define-syntax or
  (lambda (x)
    (syntax-case x ()
      [(_ e1 e2) #'(let ([t e1]) (if t t e2))])))
```

At the outset, the expander is presented with a syntax object whose expression is (let ([t #t]) (or #f t)), and the wrap is empty, except for the contents of the initial wrap, which we suppress for brevity. (We identify syntax objects by enclosing the expression and wrap entries, if any, in angle brackets.)

    <(let ((t #t)) (or #f t))>

The expander is also presented with the initial environment, which we assume contains a binding for the macro or as well as for the core forms and built-in procedures. Again, these environment entries are omitted for brevity, along with the meta environment, which plays no role here since we are not expanding any transformer expressions.

The let expression is recognized as a core form because let is present in the initial wrap and environment. The transformer for let recursively expands the righthand-side expression #t in the input environment, yielding #t. It also recursively expands the body with an extended wrap that maps x to a fresh label l1:

    <(or #f t) [t × () → l1]>

Substitutions are shown with enclosing brackets, the name and list of marks separated by the symbol ×, and the label following a right arrow.

The environment is also extended to map the label to a binding of type lexical with the fresh name t.1:

    l1 → lexical(t.1)

The or form is recognized as a macro call, so the transformer for or is invoked, producing a new expression to be evaluated in the same environment. The input of the or transformer is marked with a fresh mark m2, and the same mark is added to the output, yielding:

    <(<let> ((<t> #f))
       (<if> <t> <t> <t m2 [t × () → l1]>))
     m2>

The differences between the syntax objects representing the introduced identifier t and the identifier t extracted from the input are crucial in determining how each is renamed when the expander reaches it, which will be described shortly.

The #f appearing on the righthand side of the let is technically a syntax object with the same wraps as the occurrence of t extracted from the input, but the wrap is unimportant for constants, so we treat it, for the sake of simplicity, as if it were not wrapped.

We have another core let expression. In the process of recognizing and parsing the let expression, the mark m2 is pushed onto the subforms:

    (<let m2> ((<t m2> #f))
       <(<if> <t> <t> <t m2 [t × () → l1]>)
        m2>)

The transformer for let recursively expands the righthand-side expression #f, yielding #f, then recursively expands the body with an extended wrap mapping the introduced t with mark m2 to a fresh label l2:

```
<(<if> <t> <t> <t m2 [t × () → l1]>)
 [t × (m2)  →  l2]
 m2>
```

The environment is also extended to map the label to a binding of type lexical with the fresh name t.2:

```
l2 → lexical(t.2), l1 → lexical(t.1)
```

The resulting expression is recognized as an if core form. In the process of recognizing and parsing it, the expander pushes the outer substitution and marks onto the component parts. The mark m2 that already appears in the wrap for the last occurrence of t cancels the mark m2 on the outer wrap, leaving that occurrence of t unmarked:

```
(<if [t × (m2) → l2] m2>
   <t [t × (m2) → l2] m2>
   <t [t × (m2) → l2] m2>
   <t [t × (m2) → l2] [t × () → l1]>)
```

The transformer for if recursively processes its subforms in the input environment. The first:

```
<t [t × (m2) → l2] m2>
```

is recognized as an identifier reference because the expression is a symbol (t). The substitution appearing in the wrap applies in this case, since the name (t) and marks (m2) are the same. So the expander looks for l2 in the environment and finds that it maps to the lexical variable t.2. The second subform is the same and so also maps to t.2. The third, however, is different:

```
<t [t × (m2) → l2] [t × () → l1]>
```

This identifier lacks the m2 mark, so the first substitution does not apply, even though the name is the same. The second does apply because it has the same name and the same set of marks (none beyond the top mark from the suppressed initial wrap). The expander thus looks for l1 in the environment and finds that it maps to t.1.

On the way out, the if expression is reconstructed as:

```
(if t.2 t.2 t.1)
```

The inner let expression is reconstructed as:

```
(let ([t.2 #f]) (if t.2 t.2 t.1))
```

And the outer let expression is reconstructed as:

```
(let ([t.1 #t]) (let ([t.2 #f]) (if t.2 t.2 t.1)))
```

which is exactly what we want, although the particular choice of fresh names is not important as long as they are distinct.

Conclusion

The simplified expander described here illustrates the basic algorithm that underlies a complete implementation of syntax-case, without the complexities of the pattern-matching mechanism, handling of internal definitions, and additional core forms that are usually handled by an expander. The representation of environments is tailored to the single-binding lambda, let, and letrec-syntax forms implemented by the expander; a more efficient representation that handles groups of bindings would typically be used in practice. While these additional features are not trivial to add, they are conceptually independent of the expansion algorithm.

The syntax-case expander extends the KFFD hygienic macro-expansion algorithm with support for local syntax bindings and controlled capture, among other things, and also eliminates the quadratic expansion overhead of the KFFD algorithm.

The KFFD algorithm is simple and elegant, and an expander based on it could certainly be a beautiful piece of code. The syntax-case expander, on the other hand, is of necessity considerably more complex. It is not, however, any less beautiful, for there can still be beauty in complex software as long as it is well structured and does what it is designed to do.

## CHAPTER TWENTY-SIX

Labor-Saving Architecture:
An Object-Oriented Framework for
Networked Software

William R. Otte and Douglas C. Schmidt

DEVELOPING SOFTWARE FOR NETWORKED APPLICATIONS IS HARD, and developing reusable software for networked applications is even harder. First, there are the complexities inherent to distributed systems, such as optimally mapping application services onto hardware nodes, synchronizing service initialization, and ensuring availability while masking partial failures. These complexities can stymie even experienced software developers because they arise from fundamental challenges in the domain of network programming.

Unfortunately, developers must also master *accidental complexities*, such as low-level and nonportable programming interfaces and the use of function-oriented design techniques that require tedious and error-prone revisions as requirements and/or platforms evolve. These complexities arise largely from limitations with the software tools and techniques applied historically by developers of networked software.

Despite the use of object-oriented technologies in many domains, such as graphical user interfaces and productivity tools, much networked software still uses C-level operating system (OS) application programmatic interfaces (APIs), such as the Unix socket API or the Windows threading API. Many accidental complexities of networked programming stem from the use of these C-level OS APIs, which are not type-safe, often not reentrant, and not portable across OS platforms. The C APIs were also designed before the widespread adoption of modern design methods and technologies, so they encourage developers to decompose their problems functionally in terms of processing steps in a top-down design, instead of using OO design and programming techniques. Experience over the past several decades has shown that functional decomposition of nontrivial software complicates maintenance and evolution because functional requirements are rarely stable design centers.*

Fortunately, two decades of advances in design/implementation techniques and programming languages have made it much easier to write and reuse networked software. In particular, object-oriented (OO) programming languages (such as C++, Java, and C#) combined with *patterns* (such as Wrapper Facades,† Adapters, and the Template Method‡), and frameworks (such as host infrastructure middleware like ACE§ and the Java class libraries for network programming,** and similar host infrastructure middleware) help to encapsulate low-level functional OS APIs and mask syntactic and semantic differences between platforms. As a result, developers can focus on application-specific behavior and properties in their software, rather than repeatedly wrestling with the accidental complexities of programming the low-level networking and OS infrastructure.

A key benefit of applying patterns and frameworks to networked software is that they can help developers craft reusable architectures that (1) capture the common structure and behavior in a particular domain, and (2) make it easy to change or replace various algorithms, policies, and mechanisms selectively without affecting other existing parts of the architecture. While most developers of networked software can apply well-designed OO frameworks to their applications, the knowledge of how to create such a framework remains a black art that has historically been learned only by extensive (and expensive) trial and error.

In addition to the conventional challenges of devising a flexible OO design that can expand and contract to meet new requirements, networked software must often run efficiently and scalably in a range of operating environments. The goal of this chapter is to help demystify the black art of OO frameworks for networked software by using a case study to systematically dissect the design and implementation of a representative networked software application.

---

* *Object-Oriented Software Construction,* Second Edition, Bertrand Meyer, Prentice Hall, 1997.

† *Pattern-Oriented Software Architecture, Vol. 2: Patterns for Concurrent and Networked Objects,* Douglas Schmidt, Michael Stal, Hans Rohnert, and Frank Buschmann, John Wiley and Sons, 2000.

‡ *Design Patterns: Elements of Reusable Object-Oriented Software,* Erich Gamma, Richard Helm, Ralph Johnson, and John Vlissides, Addison-Wesley, 1995.

§ *C++ Network Programming, Vol. 2: Systematic Reuse with ACE and Frameworks,* Douglas C. Schmidt and Stephen D. Huston, Addison-Wesley Longman, 2003.

** *Java Network Programming,* Third Edition, Elliotte Rusty Harold, O'Reilly, 2004.

In general, the beauty of our solution stems from its use of patterns and OO techniques to balance key domain forces, such as reusability, extensibility, and performance. In particular, our approach enables developers to identify common design/programming artifacts, thereby enhancing reuse. It also provide a means to encapsulate variabilities in a common and parameterizable way, thereby enhancing extensibility and portability.

Sample Application: Logging Service

The OO software that we use as the basis of our case study is a networked logging service. As shown in Figure 26-1, this service consists of client applications that generate log records and send them to a central logging server that receives and stores the log records for later inspection and processing.

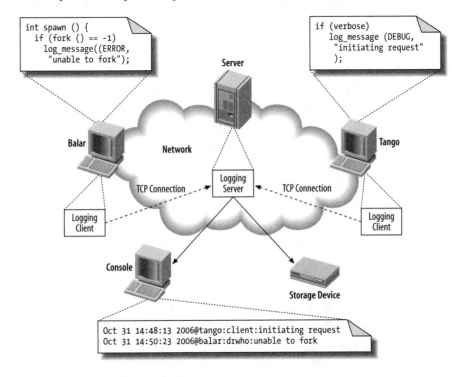

FIGURE 26-1. Architecture of a networked logging service

The logging server portion (at the center of Figure 26-1) of our networked logging service provides an ideal context for demonstrating the beauty of OO networked software because it exhibits the following dimensions of design-time variability that developers can choose from when implementing such a server:

- Different interprocess communication (IPC) mechanisms (such as sockets, SSL, shared memory, TLI, named pipes, etc.) that developers can use to send and receive log records.

- Different concurrency models (such as iterative, reactive, thread-per-connection, process-per-connection, various types of thread pools, etc.) that developers can use to process log records.

- Different locking strategies (such as thread-level or process-level recursive mutex, nonrecursive mutex, readers/writer lock, null mutex, etc.) that developers can use to serialize access to resources, such as a count of the number of requests, shared by multiple threads.

- Different log record formats that can be transmitted from client to server. Once received by the server, the log records can be handled in different ways—e.g., printed to console, stored to a single file, or even one file per client to maximize parallel writes to disk.

It is relatively straightforward to implement any one of these combinations, such as running one thread per connection-logging server using socket-based IPC and a thread-level nonrecursive mutex. A one-size-fits-all solution, however, is inadequate to meet the needs of all logging services because different customer requirements and different operating environments can have significantly different impacts on time/space trade-offs, cost, and schedule. A key challenge is therefore to design a configurable logging server that is *easily extensible* to meet new needs with a *minimum of effort*.

At the heart of the solution to this challenge is a thorough understanding of the patterns and associated design techniques needed to develop OO frameworks that efficiently:

- Capture common structure and behavior in base classes and generic classes

- Enable selective customization of behavior via subclasses and by providing concrete parameters to generic classes

Figure 26-2 illustrates the design of an OO logging server framework that realizes these goals. The core of this design is the Logging_Server class, which defines the common structure and functionality for the logging server via the use of:

- C++ parameterized types, which allow developers to defer the selection of data types used in generic classes or functions until their point of instantiation

- The Template Method pattern, which defines the skeleton of an algorithm, delegating individual steps to methods that may be overridden by subclasses

- The Wrapper Facade pattern, which encapsulates non-object-oriented APIs and data within type-safe object-oriented classes

Subclasses and concrete instantiations of Logging_Server refine this common reusable architecture to customize variable steps in the logging server behavior by selecting desired IPC mechanisms, concurrency models, and locking strategies. The Logging_Server is thus a *product-line architecture** that defines an integrated set of classes that collaborate to define a reusable design for a family of related logging servers.

---

* *Software Product Lines: Practices and Patterns*, Paul Clements and Linda Northrop, Addison-Wesley, 2001.

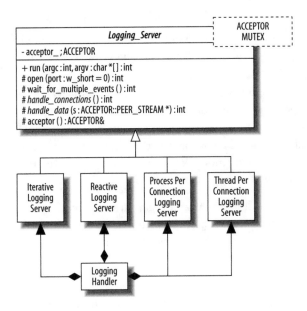

FIGURE 26-2. Object-oriented design for the logging server framework

The remainder of this chapter is organized as follows. The next section describes the OO design of the logging server framework, exploring its architecture and the forces that influence the design of the OO framework to illustrate why we selected certain patterns and language features, as well as summarizing alternative approaches that we rejected for various reasons. Two further sections present several C++ sequential programming instantiations of the logging server framework and of concurrent programming instantiations of this framework. We conclude by summarizing the beauty of the OO software concepts and techniques in this chapter.

Object-Oriented Design of the Logging Server Framework

Before we discuss the OO design of our logging server, it is important to understand several key concepts about OO frameworks. Most programmers are familiar with the concept of a class library, which is a set of reusable classes that provides functionality that may be used when developing OO programs. OO frameworks extend the benefits of OO class libraries in the following ways:*

They define "semi-complete" applications that embody domain-specific object structures and functionality

    Classes in a framework work together to provide a generic architectural skeleton for applications in a particular domain, such as graphical user interfaces, avionics mission computing, or networked logging services. Complete applications can be composed by inheriting from and/or instantiating framework components. In contrast, class libraries

---

* "Frameworks = Patterns + Components," Ralph Johnson, *Communications of the ACM*, Vol. 40, No. 10, October 1997.

are less domain-specific and provide a smaller scope of reuse. For instance, class library components such as classes for strings, complex numbers, arrays, and bitsets are relatively low-level and ubiquitous across many application domains.

Frameworks are active and exhibit "inversion of control" at runtime

Class libraries are typically passive—i.e., they perform isolated bits of processing when invoked by threads of control from self-directed application objects. In contrast, frameworks are active—i.e., they direct the flow of control within an application via event-dispatching patterns, such as Reactor* and Observer.† The "inversion of control" in the runtime architecture of a framework is often referred to as "The Hollywood Principle," which states "Don't call us, we'll call you."‡

Frameworks are typically designed by analyzing various potential problems that the framework might address and identifying which parts of each solution are the same and which areas of each solution are unique. This design method is called *commonality/ variability analysis*,§ which covers the following topics:

Scope

Defines the domains (i.e., the problem areas a framework addresses) and the context of the framework.

Commonalities

Describe the attributes that recur across all members of the family of products based on the framework.

Variabilities

Describe the attributes unique to the different members of the family of products.

Understanding the Commonalities

The first step in designing our logging server framework is therefore to understand the parts of the system that should be implemented by the framework (commonalities) and the parts of the system left to be specialized in subclasses or parameters (variabilities). This analysis is straightforward because the steps involved in processing a log record sent over a network can be decomposed into the steps shown in Figure 26-3, which are common to all logging server implementations.

During this stage of the design process, we define each step as abstractly as possible. For example, at this stage we've made minimal assumptions about the type of IPC mechanisms, other than they are connection-oriented to ensure reliable delivery of log records. Likewise, we've avoided specifying the type of concurrency strategy (e.g., whether the

---

* Schmidt et al., *op. cit.*

† Gamma et al., *op. cit.*

‡ "Pattern Hatching - Protection, Part I: The Hollywood Principle," John Vlissides, *C++ Report*, February 1996.

§ "Commonality and Variability in Software Engineering." J. Coplien, D. Hoffman, and D. Weiss, *IEEE Software*, Vol. 15, No. 6, November/December 1998.

server can handle multiple requests, and if so, how they are dispatched) or the synchronization mechanism used by each step. The actual choice of specific behavior for a step is thus deferred to the subsequent concrete implementations that provide a particular variant for each step.

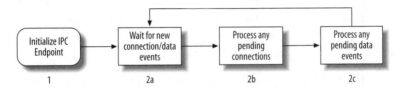

FIGURE 26-3. Logging server main loop

The Template Method pattern is a useful way to define abstract steps and defer implementation of their specific behaviors to later steps in the design process. This pattern defines a base class that implements the common—but abstract—steps in the *template method* in terms of *hook methods* that can be overridden selectively by concrete implementations. Programming language features, such as pure virtual functions in C++ or abstract methods in Java, can be used to ensure that all concrete implementations define the hook methods. Figure 26-4 shows the structure of the Template Method pattern and demonstrates how this pattern is applied to the design of our OO logging server framework.

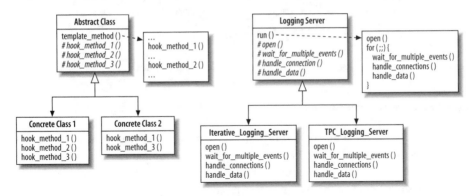

FIGURE 26-4. Template Method pattern and its application to the logging server

Accommodating Variation

Although the Template Method pattern addresses the overall design of the steps in our logging server framework, we're left with the question of how to accommodate all three dimensions of variability defined earlier (IPC, concurrency, and synchronization mechanisms) needed to support our design. One approach would simply use the Template Method pattern and implement one IPC/concurrency/synchronization combination per concrete subclass. Unfortunately, this approach would yield exponential growth in the number of concrete subclasses, as each addition to any dimension could generate another implementation for each possible combination of the other dimensions. A pure Template Method design, therefore, would not be substantially better than handcrafting one-off implementations of a logging server for each variant.

A more effective and scalable design could leverage the fact that our variability dimensions are largely independent. The choice of a different IPC mechanism, for instance, is unlikely to require changes in the concurrency or synchronization mechanisms used. Moreover, there is a high-level commonality in how different types of IPC and synchronization mechanisms function—e.g., IPC mechanisms can initiate/accept connections and send/receive data on connections, whereas synchronization mechanisms have operations to acquire and release locks. The design challenge is to encapsulate the accidental complexities in these APIs so that they can be used interchangeably.

A solution to this challenge is to use the Wrapper Facade pattern, which presents a single unified OO interface for the underlying non-OO IPC and synchronization mechanisms provided by system functions in an OS. Wrapper facades are particularly useful for enhancing portability by hiding accidental complexities between mechanisms, as well as making it less tedious and error-prone to work with these APIs. For instance, a wrapper facade can define a higher-level type system that ensures that only correct operations are called on the underlying non-OO (and less type-safe) OS IPC and synchronization data structures. The role of a wrapper facade is shown in Figure 26-5.

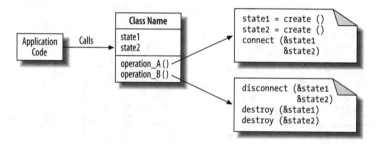

FIGURE 26-5. Wrapper facade design pattern

ACE is a widely used example of host infrastructure middleware that defines unified OO interfaces using wrapper facades for both IPC and synchronization mechanisms. We base the wrapper facades in this chapter on simplified versions of those provided by ACE. Figure 26-6 shows some of the ACE wrapper facades.

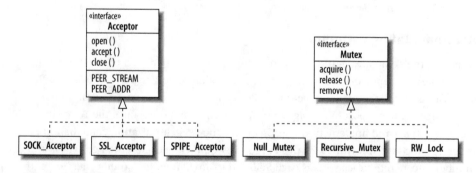

FIGURE 26-6. Some ACE wrapper facades for passive connection establishment and synchronization

The `Acceptor` wrapper facade provides the means to create passive-mode connections and provides "traits" to represent aspects of a mechanism that work essentially the same way across different implementations, just with different APIs. For instance, `PEER_STREAM` and `PEER_ADDR` designate dependent wrapper facades appropriate for sending/receiving data and for addressing by the IPC mechanism, respectively. `SOCK_Acceptor` is a subclass of `Acceptor` used in this chapter to implement a factory for passively establishing connections implemented using the socket API.

The `Mutex` wrapper facade provides an interface whose methods acquire and release locks, including a `Recursive_Mutex` implemented using a mutex that will not deadlock when acquired multiple times by the same thread, a `RW_Lock` that implements readers/writer semantics, and a `Null_Mutex` whose acquire()/release( ) methods are inline no-ops. The last class mentioned is an example of the Null Object pattern* and is useful for eliminating synchronization without changing application code. Figure 26-6 makes it appear as if each family of classes is related by inheritance, but they are actually implemented by classes unrelated by inheritance that have a common interface and can be used as type parameters to C++ templates. We made this design choice to avoid virtual method call overhead.

Tying It All Together

Another design challenge is how to associate a concurrency strategy with an IPC and synchronization mechanism. One approach would be to use the Strategy pattern,† which encapsulates algorithms as objects so they can be swapped at runtime. This approach would provide the `Logging_Server` with a pointer to abstract base classes of `Acceptor` and `Mutex`, and then rely on dynamic binding and polymorphism to dispatch the virtual methods to the appropriate subclass instances.

While a Strategy-based approach is feasible, it is not ideal. Each incoming log record may generate several calls to methods in the `Acceptor` and `Mutex` wrapper facades. Performance could therefore degrade, because virtual methods incur more overhead than nonvirtual method calls. Given that dynamically swapping IPC or synchronization mechanisms are not a requirement for our logging servers, a more efficient solution is to use C++ parameterized types to instantiate our logging server classes with the wrapper facades for IPC and synchronization.

We therefore define the following generic abstract base class called `Logging_Server` from which all logging servers in this chapter will inherit:

```
template <typename ACCEPTOR, typename MUTEX>
class Logging_Server {
 public:
   typedef Log_Handler<typename ACCEPTOR::PEER_STREAM> HANDLER;
```

---

* "The Null Object Pattern," Bobby Woolf, in *Pattern Languages of Program Design, Volume 3*, Robert C. Martin, Dirk Riehle, and Frank Buschmann, Addison-Wesley, 1997.

† Gamma et al., *op. cit.*

```
        Logging_Server (int argc, const char *argv);

        // Template method that runs each step in the main event loop.
        virtual void run (void);

    protected:
        // Hook methods that enable each step to be varied.
        virtual void open (void);
        virtual void wait_for_multiple_events (void) = 0;
        virtual void handle_connections (void) = 0;
        virtual void handle_data
                    (typename ACCEPTOR::PEER_STREAM *stream = 0) = 0;

        // Increment the request count, protected by the mutex.
        virtual void count_request (size_t number = 1);

        // Instance of template parameter that accepts connections.
        ACCEPTOR acceptor_;

        // Keeps a count of the number of log records received.
        size_t request_count_;

        // Instance of template parameter that serializes access to
        // the request_count_.
        MUTEX mutex_;

        // Address that the server will listen on for connections.
        std:string server_address_;
    };
```

Most methods in Logging_Server are pure virtual, which ensures that subclasses implement
them. The open( ) and count_request( ) methods that follow, however, are reused by all
logging servers in this chapter:

```
template <typename ACCEPTOR, typename MUTEX>
Logging_Server<ACCEPTOR, MUTEX>::Logging_Server
(int argc, char *argv[]): request_count_ (0) {
  // Parse the argv arguments and store the server address_...
}

template <typename ACCEPTOR, typename MUTEX> void
Logging_Server<ACCEPTOR, MUTEX>::open (void) {
  return acceptor_.open (server_address_);
}

template <typename ACCEPTOR, typename MUTEX> void
Logging_Server<ACCEPTOR, MUTEX>::count_request (size_t number) {
  mutex_.acquire (); request_count_ += number; mutex_.release ();
}
```

The Log_Handler class is responsible for demarshaling a log record from a connected data
stream whose IPC mechanism is designated by the ACCEPTOR type parameter. The implementation of this class is outside the scope of this chapter, and could itself be another
dimension of variability—that is, logging servers might want to support different log

message formats. If we were to support varying the format of method of storing incoming log messages, this class could be yet another template parameter in our logging framework. For our purposes, it is sufficient to know that it is parameterized by the IPC mechanism and provides two methods: peer( ), which returns a reference to the data stream, and log_record( ), which reads a single log record from the stream.

The primary entry point into Logging_Server is the template method called run( ), which implements the steps outlined in Figure 26-3, delegating the specific steps to the hook methods declared in the protected section of Logging_Server, as shown in the following code fragment:

```
template <typename ACCEPTOR, typename MUTEX> void
Logging_Server<ACCEPTOR, MUTEX>::run (void) {
  try {
    // Step 1: initialize an IPC factory endpoint to listen for
    // new connections on the server address.
    open ();

    // Step 2: Go into an event loop
    for (;;) {
      // Step 2a: wait for new connections or log records
      // to arrive.
wait_for_multiple_events ();

// Step 2b: accept a new connection (if available)
      handle_connections ();

      // Step 2c: process received log record (if available)
      handle_data ();
    }
  } catch (...) { /* ... Handle the exception ... */ }
}
```

The beauty of this code is that:

- Its pattern-based design makes it easy to handle variation in concurrency models, such as by varying the behavior of the run( ) template method by providing specific implementations of the hook methods in the implementation of subclasses.

- Its template-based design makes it easy to handle variation in IPC and synchronization mechanisms, such as by plugging different types into the ACCEPTOR and MUTEX template parameters.

Implementing Sequential Logging Servers

This section demonstrates the implementation of logging servers that feature sequential concurrency models—i.e., all processing is performed in a single thread. We cover both iterative and reactive implementations of sequential logging servers.

An Iterative Logging Server

Iterative servers process all log records from each client before handling any log records from the next client. Since there is no need to spawn or synchronize threads, we use the Null_Mutex facade to parameterize the Iterative_Logging_Server subclass template, as follows:

```
template <typename ACCEPTOR>
   class Iterative_Logging_Server :
   virtual Logging_Server<ACCEPTOR, Null_Mutex> {
public:
   typedef Logging_Server<ACCEPTOR, Null_Mutex>::HANDLER HANDLER;
   Iterative_Logging_Server (int argc, char *argv[]);

protected:
   virtual void open (void);
   virtual void wait_for_multiple_events (void) {};
   virtual void handle_connections (void);
   virtual void handle_data
     (typename ACCEPTOR::PEER_STREAM *stream = 0);
   HANDLER log_handler_;

   // One log file shared by all clients.
   std::ofstream logfile_;
};
```

Implementing this version of our server is straightforward. The open( ) method decorates the behavior of the method from the Logging_Server base class by opening an output file before delegating to the parent's open( ), as follows:

```
template <typename ACCEPTOR> void
Interative_Logging_Server<ACCEPTOR>::open (void) {
  logfile_.open (filename_.c_str ());
  if (!logfile_.good ()) throw std::runtime_error;
  // Delegate to the parent's open() method.
  Logging_Server<ACCEPTOR, Null_Mutex>::open ();
}
```

The wait_for_multiple_events( ) method is a no-op. It is not needed because we just handle a single connection at any one time. The handle_connections( ) method therefore simply blocks until a new connection is established, as follows:

```
template <typename ACCEPTOR> void
Iterative_Logging_Server<ACCEPTOR>::handle_connections (void)
{ acceptor_.accept (log_handler_.peer ()); }
```

Finally, handle_data( ) simply reads log records from the client and writes them to the logfile until the client closes the connection or an error occurs:

```
template <typename ACCEPTOR> void
Iterative_Logging_Server<ACCEPTOR>::handle_data (void) {
    while (log_handler_.log_record (logfile _))
      count_request ();
    }
```

While the iterative server is straightforward to implement, it suffers from the drawback of being able to service only one client at a time. A second client that attempts to connect may time out while waiting for the first to finish its request.

A Reactive Logging Server

The reactive logging server alleviates one of the primary drawbacks with the iterative logging server in the previous section by processing multiple client connections and log record requests via operating system synchronous event demultiplexing APIs provided by the OS, such as select( ) and WaitForMultipleObjects( ). These APIs can monitor multiple clients by waiting in a single thread of control for I/O-related events to occur on a group of I/O handles, and then interleave the processing of log records. Since a reactive logging server is still fundamentally sequential, however, it inherits from the iterative logging server implemented earlier, as shown in Figure 26-7.

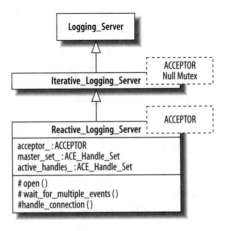

FIGURE 26-7. Reactive logging server interface

The Reactive_Logging_Server class overrides all four hook methods that it inherits from base class Iterative_Logging_Server. Its open( ) hook method decorates the behavior of the base class method to initialize the ACE_Handle_Set member variables, which are part of the wrapper facades that simplify the use of select( ), as shown here:

```
template <typename ACCEPTOR> void
Reactive_Logging_Server<ACCEPTOR>::open () {
  // Delegate to base class.
  Iterative_Logging_Server<ACCEPTOR>::open ();

  // Mark the handle associated with the acceptor as active.
  master_set_.set_bit (acceptor_.get_handle ());

  // Set the acceptor's handle into non-blocking mode.
  acceptor_.enable (NONBLOCK);
}
```

The `wait_for_multiple_events( )` method is needed in this implementation, unlike its counterpart in `Iterative_Server`. As shown in Figure 26-8, this method uses a synchronous event demultiplexer (in this case, the `select( )` call) to detect which I/O handles have connection or data activity pending.

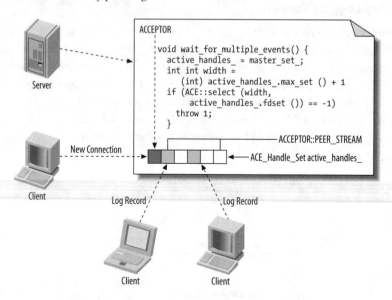

FIGURE 26-8. *Using an asynchronous event demultiplexer in the Reactive_Logging_Server program*

After `wait_for_multiple_events( )` has executed, the `Reactive_Logging_Server` has a cached set of handles with pending activity (i.e., either new connection requests or new incoming data events), which will then be handled by its other two hook methods: `handle_data( )` and `handle_connections( )`. The `handle_connections( )` method checks whether the acceptors handle is active and, if so, accepts as many connections as possible and caches them in the `master_handle_set_`. Similarly, the `handle_data( )` method iterates over the remaining active handles marked by `select( )` earlier. This activity is simplified by the ACE socket wrapper facade that implements an instance of the Iterator pattern* for socket handle sets, as shown in Figure 26-9.

The following code implements a `Reactive_Logging_Server` main program that uses the socket API:

```
int main (int argc, char *argv[]) {
  Reactive_Logging_Server<SOCK_Acceptor> server (argc, argv);
  server.run ();
  return 0;
}
```

---

* Gamma et al., *op. cit.*

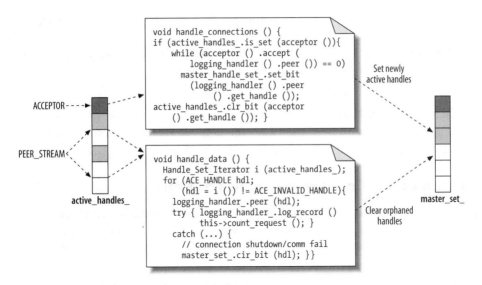

```
void handle_connections () {
    if (active_handles_.is_set (acceptor ()){
        while (acceptor () .accept (
            logging_handler () .peer ()) == 0)
            master_handle_set_.set_bit
                (logging_handler () .peer
                    () .get_handle ());
    active_handles_.clr_bit (acceptor
        () .get_handle ()); }
```

Set newly
active handles

ACCEPTOR

PEER_STREAM

active_handles_

```
void handle_data () {
    Handle_Set_Iterator i (active_handles_);
    for (ACE_HANDLE hdl;
        (hdl = i ()) != ACE_INVALID_HANDLE){
        logging_handler_.peer (hdl);
        try { logging_handler_.log_record ()
            this->count_request (); }
        catch (...) {
            // connection shutdown/comm fail
            master_set_.cir_bit (hdl); }}
```

Clear orphaned
handles

master_set_

FIGURE 26-9. Reactive server connection/data event handling

The first line of our main function parameterizes the Reactive_Logging_Server with the SOCK_Acceptor type, which will cause the C++ compiler to generate code for a reactive logging server that is able to communicate over sockets. This will, in turn, parameterize its Logging_Server base class with both the SOCK_Acceptor and Null_Mutex, by virtue of the hard-coded template argument provided when we inherited from it. The second line calls the run( ) template method, which is delegated to the Logging_Server base class, which itself delegates to the various hook methods we implemented in this class.

Evaluating the Sequential Logging Server Solutions

The Reactive_Logging_Server improves upon the Iterative_Logging_Server by interleaving its servicing of multiple clients, rather than just handling one client in its entirety at a time. It does not take advantage of OS concurrency mechanisms, however, so it cannot leverage multiprocessors effectively. Nor can it overlap computation and communication by processing log records while reading new records. These limitations impede its scalability as the number of clients increases, even if the underlying hardware supports multiple simultaneous threads of execution.

Although Iterative_Logging_Server and Reactive_Logging_Server run only in a single thread of control—and are thus not scalable for most production systems—their simplicity highlights several more beautiful aspects of our OO framework-based design:

- Our use of hook methods in the Logging_Server::run( ) template method shields application developers from low-level details—e.g., how a logging server performs IPC and event demulxiplexing operations—thereby enabling the developers to focus on domain-specific application logic by leveraging the expertise of framework designers.

- Our use of wrapper facades allows us to lock/unlock mutexes, listen on a particular IPC mechanism to accept new connections, and wait for multiple I/O events concisely, efficiently, and portably. Without these useful abstractions, we would have had to write many lines of tedious and error-prone code that would be hard to understand, debug, and evolve.

The benefits from these abstractions become more apparent with more complex concurrent logging servers shown next, as well as with more complex framework use cases, such as graphical user interfaces* or communication middleware.†

Implementing Concurrent Logging Servers

To overcome the scalability limitations of the iterative and reactive servers shown in the previous sections, the logging servers in this section use OS concurrency mechanisms: processes and threads. Using the APIs provided by operating systems to spawn threads or processes, however, can be a daunting task due to accidental complexities in their design. These complexities stem from semantic and syntactic differences that exist not only between different operating systems, but also different versions of the same operating system. Our solution to these complexities is again to apply wrapper facades that provide a consistent interface across platforms and integrate these wrapper facades into our OO Logging_Server framework.

A Thread-per-Connection Logging Server

Our thread-per-connection logging server (TPC_Logging_Server) runs a main thread that waits for and accepts new connections from clients. After accepting a new connection, a new worker thread is spawned to handle incoming log records from that connection. Figure 26-10 shows the steps in this process.

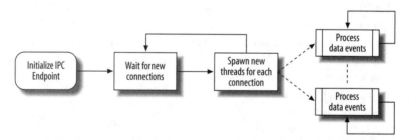

FIGURE 26-10. Steps in the thread-per-connection logging server

The main loop for this particular logging server differs from the steps depicted in Figure 26-3 because the call to handle_data( ) is not necessary, as the worker threads are responsible for that call. There are two ways to handle this situation:

* Gamma et al., *op. cit.*
† Schmidt et al., *op. cit.*

- We could note that the base run( ) method calls handle_data( ) with the default argument of a NULL pointer, and simply have our implementation exit immediately for that input.

- We could simply override the run( ) method with our own implementation that omits this call.

The second solution may at first appear advantageous because it avoids a virtual method call to handle_data( ). The first solution is better in this case, however, because the performance hit of that virtual call is not a limiting factor, and overriding the run( ) template method would prevent this class from benefiting from changes to the base class implementation, potentially causing it to fail in subtle and pernicious ways.

The main challenge here is implementing the concurrency strategy itself. As with the Iterative_Server in the earlier section "An Iterative Logging Server," the wait_for_multiple_events( ) method is superfluous because our main loop simply waits for new connections, so it is sufficient for handle_connections( ) to block on accept( ) and subsequently spawn worker threads to handle connected clients. Our TPC_Logging_Server class must therefore provide a method to serve as an entry point for the thread. In C and C++, a class method may serve as an entry point to a thread only if the class is defined as static, so we define the TPC_Logging_Server::svc( ) static class method.

At this point, we have an important design decision to make: what exactly does the thread entry point do? It is tempting to simply have the svc( ) method itself perform all of the work necessary to receive log records from its associated connection. This design is less than ideal, however, because static methods cannot be virtual, as that would cause problems if we later derive a new logging server from this implementation to change the way it handles data events. Application developers would then be forced to provide an implementation of handle_connections( ) that is textually identical to this class to call the proper static method.

Moreover, to leverage our existing design and code, it is preferable to have the log record processing logic inside the handle_data( ) method and to define a Thread_Args helper object that holds the peer returned from accept( ) and a pointer to the Logging_Server object itself. Our class interface will therefore look like the diagram in Figure 26-11.

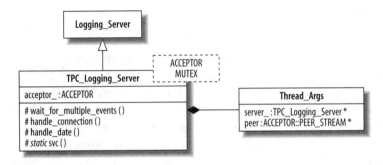

FIGURE 26-11. Thread-per-connection server interface

The remainder of TPC_Logging_Server is straightforward to implement, requiring only that our thread entry point delegate processing to the virtual method handle_data( ) using the server_pointer contained within the Thread_Args helper object passed to the svc( ) method, as shown in Figure 26-12.

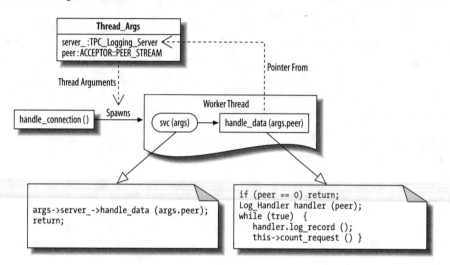

FIGURE 26-12. Thread-per-connection thread behavior

The following code implements a TPC_Logging_Server main program that uses the secure socket API and the readers/writer lock:

```
int main (int argc, char *argv[]) {
  TPC_Logging_Server<SSL_Acceptor, RW_Lock> server (argc, argv);
  server.run ();
  return 0;
}
```

This main( ) function instantiates a TPC_Logging_Server that communicates using SSL connections, and uses an RW_Lock to synchronize the count_connections( ) function in the Logging_Server base class. Except for the name of the class we are instantiating, this main( ) function is identical to the one that was written earlier in this chapter for the Reactive_Logging_Server. This commonality is another beautiful aspect of our design: regardless of the particular combination of concurrency, IPC, and synchronization mechanisms we choose to use, the instantiation and invocation of our server remains the same.

The thread-per-connection logging service addresses the scalability limitations with the sequential implementations described earlier in the section "Evaluating the Sequential Logging Server Solutions." The design of our OO framework makes it straightforward to integrate this concurrency model with minimal changes to the existing code. In particular, TPC_Logging_Server inherits implementations of open( ), count_request( ), and most importantly run( ), allowing this class to leverage bug fixes and improvements to our main event loop transparently. Moreover, adding the necessary synchronization around the request_count_ is simply a matter of parameterizing the TPC_Logging_Server with the RW_LOCK class.

A Process-per-Connection Logging Server

The process-per-connection logging server described next is similar to the thread-per-connection design shown in Figure 26-10, except that instead of spawning a thread, we spawn a new process to handle incoming log records from each client. The choice of processes over threads for concurrency forces us to make design choices to accommodate the variations in process-creation semantics between platforms. There are two key semantic differences between the process APIs on Linux and Windows that our server design must encapsulate:

- In Linux (and other POSIX systems) the primary vehicle for creating new processes is the fork( ) system function, which generates an exact duplicate of the calling program image, including open I/O handles. The processes differ only in their return value from fork( ). At this point, child processes can choose to proceed from that point, or load a different program image using the exec*( ) family of system calls.

- Windows, however, uses the CreateProcess( ) API call, which is functionally equivalent to a POSIX fork( ), followed immediately by a call to one of the exec*( ) system functions. The impact of this difference is that in Windows you have an *entirely new process* that by default *does not* have access to I/O handles open in the parent. To use a connection accepted by the parent process, therefore, the handle must be explicitly duplicated and passed to the child on the command line.

We therefore define a set of wrapper facades that not only hide the syntactic differences between platforms, but also provide a way to hide the semantic differences as well. These wrappers consist of the three cooperating classes shown in Figure 26-13. The Process class represents a single process and is used to create and synchronize processes. The Process_Options class provides a way to set both platform-independent process options (such as command-line options and environment variables) and platform-specific process options (such as avoiding zombie processes). Finally, the Process_Manager class portably manages the life cycle of groups of processes. We won't cover all the uses of these wrapper facades in this chapter, though they are based on the wrapper facades in ACE.* It is sufficient to know that not only can processes be created portably on Linux and Windows, but also that I/O handles can be duplicated and passed portably and automatically to the new process.

The design challenge is therefore to accommodate the fact that processes spawned after new connections are accepted will start at the beginning of our program. We certainly don't want child processes to attempt to open a new acceptor and listen for connections of their own; instead, they should listen for data events only on their assigned handle. A naïve solution to this problem would rely on applications to detect this condition and call a special entry point defined in the interface to our process-based Logging_Server class.

---

* *C++ Network Programming, Vol. 1: Mastering Complexity with ACE and Patterns*, Douglas C. Schmidt and Stephen D. Huston, Addison-Wesley, 2001.

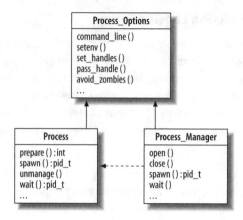

FIGURE 26-13. Portable process wrapper facades

This simple solution, however, is less than ideal. It would require us not only to change the public interface of our process-based Logging_Server, but to expose intimate implementation details to applications, violating encapsulation. A better solution is to override the run() template method inherited from the Logging_Server base class, which is passed a copy of the command-line argument by users, to determine whether it has been passed any I/O handles. If not, the process assumes it is a parent and delegates to the base class run() method. Otherwise, the process assumes it's a child, so it decodes the handle and calls handle_data(), as shown in Figure 26-14.

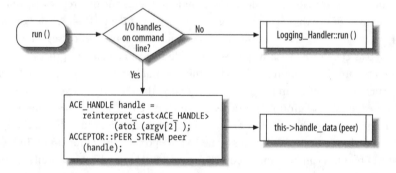

FIGURE 26-14. Process-per-connection run() template method

The remainder of this server implementation is straightforward. As shown in Figure 26-15, the process wrapper facade makes the procedure for spawning our worker processes fairly simple. The implementation for handle_data() should be textually identical to that shown in Figure 26-12.

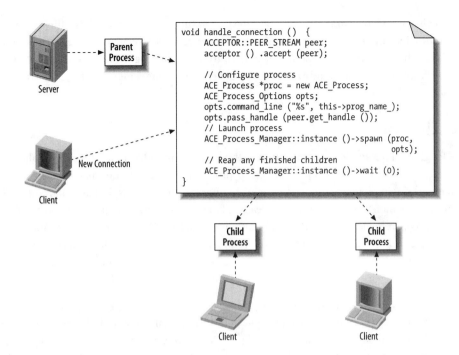

```
void handle_connection () {
    ACCEPTOR::PEER_STREAM peer;
    acceptor () .accept (peer);

    // Configure process
    ACE_Process *proc = new ACE_Process;
    ACE_Process_Options opts;
    opts.command_line ("%s", this->prog_name_);
    opts.pass_handle (peer.get_handle ());
    // Launch process
    ACE_Process_Manager::instance ()->spawn (proc,
                                                opts);

    // Reap any finished children
    ACE_Process_Manager::instance ()->wait (0);
}
```

FIGURE 26-15. Connection handling for the process-per-connection server

Our reimplementation of the run( ) method from the Logging_Server base class allows us to maintain the beautifully simple, straightforward, and uniform invocation used by our other logging servers:

```
int main (int argc, char *argv[]) {
    PPC_Logging_Server<SSL_Acceptor, Null_Mutex> server (argc, argv);
    server.run ();
    return 0;
}
```

This main( ) program differs from the thread-per-connection server only in the name of the class that is instantiated and the choice of a Null_Mutex for synchronization. The dispatch of either a parent or a child process is handled transparently by the run( ) method, driven by the command-line arguments passed to the PPC_Logging_Server constructor.

Evaluating the Concurrent Logging Server Solutions

Both concurrent logging servers described in this section significantly enhance the Reactive_Logging_Server and Iterative_Logging_Server in their ability to scale as the number of clients increases by taking leveraging hardware and OS support for multiple threads of execution. It is hard, however, to develop thread-per-connection and process-per-connection concurrency strategies in a platform-agnostic manner. We accomplished this task by using wrapper facades to hide platform differences. Our framework-based server design also provided a common external interface to the Logging_Server class, shielding the bulk of the logging server from the configured concurrency strategy. Moreover, our design leveraged the run( ) template method inherited from the Logging_Server base class, allowing our implementations to integrate bug fixes or other enhancements to the main server event loop.

Conclusion

The logging server application presented in this chapter provides a digestible but realistic vehicle for showing how to apply OO design/programming techniques, patterns, and frameworks to implementation software for networked applications. In particular, our OO framework demonstrates a number of beautiful design elements, ranging from abstract design to concrete elements in the implementations of the different concurrency models. Our design also uses C++ features, such as templates and virtual functions, in conjunction with design patterns, such as Wrapper Facade and the Template Method, to create a family of logging servers that is portable, reusable, flexible, and extensible.

The Template Method pattern in the Logging_Server base class's run( ) method allowed us to define common steps in a logging server, deferring specialization of individual steps of its operation to hook methods in derived classes. While this pattern helped factor out common steps into the base class, it did not adequately address all our required points of variability, such as synchronization and IPC mechanisms, For these remaining dimensions, therefore, we used the Wrapper Facade pattern to hide semantic and syntactic differences, ultimately making use of these dimensions entirely orthogonal to the implementation of individual concurrency models. This design allowed us to use parameterized classes to address these dimensions of variability, which increased the flexibility of our framework without affecting its performance adversely.

Finally, our individual implementations of concurrency models, such as thread-per-connection and process-per-connection, used wrapper facades to make their implementations more elegant and portable. The end result was a labor-saving software architecture that enabled developers to reuse common design and programming artifacts, as well as provide a means to encapsulate variabilities in a common, parameterizable way.

A concrete implementation of this logging server framework may be found at *http://www.dre.vanderbilt.edu/~schmidt/DOC_ROOT/ACE/examples/Beautiful_Code*, and in the ACE distribution in the file *ACE_wrappers/examples/Beautiful_Code*.

## CHAPTER TWENTY-SEVEN

Integrating Business Partners the RESTful Way

Andrew Patzer

A FEW YEARS BACK, WHEN I WAS A CONSULTANT, I went through a period of a year or two when it seemed that every client I spoke with was absolutely certain he needed a Web Services solution for his business. Of course, not many of my clients actually understood what that meant or the reasons why they might need that kind of architecture, but since they kept hearing about Web Services on the Internet, in magazines, and at trade shows, they figured they'd better get on the bus before it was too late.

Don't get me wrong. I'm not against Web Services. I'm just not a big fan of making technical decisions based solely on whatever happens to be in style at the moment. This chapter will address some of the reasons for using a Web Services architecture, as well as explore some of the options to consider when integrating systems with the outside world.

In this chapter, I'll walk you through a real-life project that involves exposing a set of services to a business partner, and discuss some design choices that were made along the way. Technologies that were used included Java (J2EE), XML, the Rosettanet E-Business protocol, and a function library used to communicate with a program running on an AS/400 system. I will also cover the use of interfaces and the factory design pattern as I show how I made the system extensible for future distributors who may use different protocols and may need to access different services.

Project Background

The project I'll be discussing in this chapter began with a call from one of our clients: "We need a set of Web Services to integrate our systems with one of our distributors." The client was a large manufacturer of electrical components. The system they were referring to was MAPICS, a manufacturing system written in RPG and running on their AS/400 machines. Their main distributor was upgrading its own business systems and needed to modify the way it tied into the order management system to check product availability and order status.

Previously, an operator at the distributor simply connected remotely to the manufacturer's AS/400 system and pressed a "hot key" to access the necessary screens (F13 or F14 as I recall). As you'll see in the code later, the new system I developed for them was named *hotkey*, since that had become part of their common language, much like the way *google* has become a modern-day verb.

Now that the distributor was implementing a new e-business system, it required an automated way to integrate manufacturer data with its own system. Since this was just a single distributor for this client, albeit the largest, the system also needed to allow for the future addition of other distributors and whatever protocols and requirements they might have. Another factor was the relatively low skill level of the staff that would maintain and extend this software. While they were very good in other areas, Java development (as well as any kind of web development) was still very new to them. So, I knew that whatever I built had to be simple and easy to extend.

Exposing Services to External Clients

Prior to this project, I had delivered several technical presentations to user groups and conferences regarding SOAP (Simple Object Access Protocol) and web service architecture. So, when the call came in, it seemed I'd be a natural fit for what the client was looking to accomplish. Once I understood what they really needed, though, I decided that they would be much better off with a set of services exposed through simple GET and POST requests over HTTP, exchanging XML data describing the requests and responses. Although I didn't know it at the time, this architectural style is now commonly referred to as *REST*, or *Representational State Transfer*.

How did I decide to use REST over SOAP? Here are a few of the decision points to consider when choosing a Web Services architecture:

How many different systems will require access to these services, and are all of them known at this time?
>   This manufacturer knew of a single distributor that needed to access its systems, but also acknowledged that others might decide to do the same in the future.

Do you have a tight set of end users that will have advance knowledge of these services, or do these services need to be self-describing for anonymous users to automatically connect to?

Because there has to be a defined relationship between the manufacturer and all its distributors, it is guaranteed that each of the potential users will have advance knowledge of how to access the manufacturer's systems.

What kind of state needs to be maintained throughout a single transaction? Will one request depend on the results of a previous one?

In our case, each transaction will consist of a single request and a corresponding result that doesn't depend on anything else.

Answering the above questions for this project yielded the obvious choice of simply exposing a set of known services over the HTTP protocol and exchanging data using a standard e-business protocol that both systems could understand. If the manufacturer would have liked to allow anonymous users to query product availability, then I might have opted for a full SOAP solution because that would allow systems to discover the services and programmatically interface with them without prior knowledge of the systems.

I currently work in the field of bioinformatics, where there is a definite need for SOAP-style Web Service architectures. We make use of a project called BioMoby (*http://www. biomoby.org*) to define Web Services and publish them to a central repository that allows other groups to literally drag and drop our services into a workflow that builds data pipelines to help biologists integrate diverse sets of data and perform varied analysis on the results. This is a perfect example of why someone would choose SOAP over REST. Anonymous users can access our data and tools without any prior knowledge that they even existed.

Define the Service Interface

The first step, as I decided how to implement this software, was to determine how the users will make requests and receive responses. After speaking with a technical representative from the distributor (the primary user), I learned that its new system can send XML documents via an HTTP POST request and examine the results as an XML document. The XML had to be in a format following the Rosettanet e-business protocol (more on that later), but for now it was enough to know that it can communicate over HTTP by posting XML-formatted requests and responses. Figure 27-1 illustrates the general interaction between each of the systems.

The manufacturer had recently been acquired by a larger corporation that dictated the use of IBM products throughout the organization. Therefore, I already knew what application server and corresponding technology to use. I implemented the service interface as a Java Servlet running on an IBM WebSphere application server. This decision was made easier by my knowledge that the software would need to access functions running on an AS/400 server using a Java-based API.

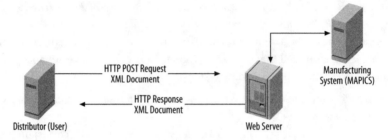

FIGURE 27-1. Service interface to backend systems

The following code is found in the *web.xml* file describing the servlet that will provide the necessary interface to the users:

```
<servlet>
    <servlet-name>HotKeyService</servlet-name>
    <display-name>HotKeyService</display-name>
    <servlet-class>com.xxxxxxxxxxxxx.hotkey.Service</servlet-class>
</servlet>
<servlet-mapping>
    <servlet-name>HotKeyService</servlet-name>
    <url-pattern>/HotKeyService</url-pattern>
</servlet-mapping>
```

The servlet itself handles only POST requests, which it does by overriding the doPost method of the Servlet interface and providing default implementations of the standard life cycle methods. The following code shows the complete implementation of the service, but when I first start breaking down a problem and designing a solution, I typically write a series of comments in the code as placeholders where I'll insert the real code later. I then systematically attack each pseudocode comment until I have a working implementation. This helps keep me focused on how each piece relates to the entire solution:

```
public class Service extends HttpServlet implements Servlet {

    public void doPost(HttpServletRequest req, HttpServletResponse resp)
        throws ServletException, IOException {

        // Read in request data and store in a StringBuffer
        BufferedReader in = req.getReader();
        StringBuffer sb = new StringBuffer();
        String line;
        while ((line = in.readLine())!= null) {
            sb.append(line);
        }

        HotkeyAdaptor hotkey = null;

        if (sb.toString().indexOf("Pip3A2PriceAndAvailabilityRequest") > 0) {
            // Price and Availability Request
            hotkey = HotkeyAdaptorFactory.getAdaptor(
                HotkeyAdaptorFactory.ROSETTANET,
                HotkeyAdaptorFactory.PRODUCTAVAILABILITY);
```

```
        }
        else if (sb.toString( ).indexOf("Pip3A5PurchaseOrderStatusQuery ") > 0) {
            // Order Status
            hotkey = HotkeyAdaptorFactory.getAdaptor(
                HotkeyAdaptorFactory.ROSETTANET,
                HotkeyAdaptorFactory.ORDERSTATUS);
        }

        boolean success = false;

        if (hotkey != null) {
            /* Pass in the XML request data */
            hotkey.setXML(sb.toString( ));
            /* Parse the request data */
            if (hotkey.parseXML( )) {
                /* Execute AS/400 Program */
                if (hotkey.executeQuery( )) {
                    /* Return response XML */
                    resp.setContentType("text/xml");
                    PrintWriter out = resp.getWriter( );
                    out.println(hotkey.getResponseXML( ));
                    out.close( );
                    success = true;
                }
            }
        }

        if (!success) {
            resp.setContentType("text/xml");
            PrintWriter out = resp.getWriter( );
            out.println("Error retrieving product availability.");
            out.close( );
        }

    }

}
```

Looking through this code, you can see that it first reads in the request data and stores it for later use. It then searches this data to determine which type of request this is: pricing and availability, or an order status inquiry. Once it determines the type of request, the appropriate helper object is created. Notice how I used an interface, HotkeyAdaptor, to allow multiple implementations without having to write a bunch of duplicate code for each type of request.

The rest of this method involves parsing the XML request data, executing the appropriate query on the AS/400 system, creating an XML response, and writing it back to the user via HTTP. In the next section, you'll see how I hid the implementation details using interfaces and the very popular factory design pattern.

Routing the Service Using the Factory Pattern

One of the requirements of this system was that it be able to accommodate a wide variety of future requests from several different types of systems with minimal programming effort. I believe I accomplished this by simplifying the implementation down to a single command interface that exposed the basic methods needed to respond to a wide variety of requests:

```
public interface HotkeyAdaptor {

    public void setXML(String _xml);
    public boolean parseXML();
    public boolean executeQuery();
    public String getResponseXML();

}
```

So, how does the servlet decide which concrete implementation of the interface to instantiate? It first looks inside the request data for a specific string to tell it what type of request it is. Then, it uses a static method of a factory object to pick the appropriate implementation.

As far as the servlet knows, whatever implementation we're using will provide appropriate responses to each of these methods. By using an interface in the main servlet, we only have to write the execution code once, without any regard to which type of request it's dealing with or who may have made the request. All of the details are encapsulated in each individual implementation of this interface. Here's that snippet of code again from the servlet:

```
HotkeyAdaptor hotkey = null;

if (sb.toString().indexOf("Pip3A2PriceAndAvailabilityRequest") > 0) {
    // Price and Availability Request
    hotkey = HotkeyAdaptorFactory.getAdaptor(
        HotkeyAdaptorFactory.ROSETTANET,
        HotkeyAdaptorFactory.PRODUCTAVAILABILITY);
}
else if (sb.toString().indexOf("Pip3A5PurchaseOrderStatusQuery ") > 0) {
    // Order Status
    hotkey = HotkeyAdaptorFactory.getAdaptor(
        HotkeyAdaptorFactory.ROSETTANET,
        HotkeyAdaptorFactory.ORDERSTATUS);
}
```

The factory object, HotkeyAdaptorFactory, has a static method that takes two parameters telling it which XML protocol to use and what type of request it is. These are defined as static constants in the factory object itself. As you can see by the following code, the factory object simply uses a switch statement to select the appropriate implementation:

```
public class HotkeyAdaptorFactory {

    public static final int ROSETTANET = 0;
    public static final int BIZTALK = 1;
    public static final int EBXML = 2;

    public static final int PRODUCTAVAILABILITY = 0;
    public static final int ORDERSTATUS = 1;

    public static HotkeyAdaptor getAdaptor(int _vocab, int _target) {

        switch (_vocab) {
            case (ROSETTANET) :
                switch (_target) {
                    case (PRODUCTAVAILABILITY) :
                        return new HotkeyAdaptorRosProdAvailImpl();
                    case (ORDERSTATUS) :
                        return new HotkeyAdaptorRosOrdStatImpl();
                    default :
                        return null;
                }
            case (BIZTALK) :
            case (EBXML) :
            default :
                return null;
        }

    }

}
```

While this may seem to be a rather simple abstraction, it goes a long way in making the code readable and understandable by an inexperienced programming staff. When it comes time to add a new distributor that happens to be using Microsoft's BizTalk product and wants to place orders electronically, the programmer has a simple template for adding this new requirement.

Exchanging Data Using E-Business Protocols

Something that was new to me on this project was the use of standard e-business protocols. When the distributor informed me of the requirement to exchange requests and responses using the Rosettanet standard, I had to do a little research. I started by going to the Rosettanet web site (*http://www.rosettanet.org*) and downloading the specific standards I was interested in. I found a diagram detailing a typical exchange between business partners, along with a specification for the XML request and response.

Since I had a lot of trial-and-error type work to do, the first thing I did was set up a test that I could run myself to simulate an interaction with the distributor without having to coordinate testing with their staff for each iteration of development. I used the Apache Commons HttpClient to manage the HTTP exchanges:

```java
public class TestHotKeyService {

    public static void main (String[] args) throws Exception {

        String strURL = "http://xxxxxxxxxxx/HotKey/HotKeyService";
        String strXMLFilename = "SampleXMLRequest.xml";
        File input = new File(strXMLFilename);

        PostMethod post = new PostMethod(strURL);
        post.setRequestBody(new FileInputStream(input));
        if (input.length() < Integer.MAX_VALUE) {
            post.setRequestContentLength((int)input.length());
        } else {
            post.setRequestContentLength(
                EntityEnclosingMethod.CONTENT_LENGTH_CHUNKED);
        }

        post.setRequestHeader("Content-type", "text/xml; charset=ISO-8859-1");

        HttpClient httpclient = new HttpClient();
        System.out.println("[Response status code]: " +
                httpclient.executeMethod(post));
        System.out.println("\n[Response body]: ");
        System.out.println("\n" + post.getResponseBodyAsString());

        post.releaseConnection();

    }

}
```

This allowed me to accelerate my learning curve as I tried out several different types of requests and examined the results. I'm a firm believer in diving right into coding as soon as possible. You can only learn so much from a book, an article on a web site, or a set of API documents. By getting your hands dirty early on in the process, you'll uncover a lot of things you may not have thought about by simply studying the problem.

The Rosettanet standard, like many others, is very detailed and complete. Chances are, you'll end up needing and using only a small fraction of it to accomplish any given task. For this project, I only needed to set a few standard identification fields, along with a product number and availability date for pricing inquiries, or an order number for order status inquiries.

Parsing the XML Using XPath

The XML request data was far from simple XML. As mentioned earlier, the Rosettanet standard is very detailed and thorough. Parsing such a document could have proved to be quite a nightmare if it were not for XPath. Using XPath mappings, I was able to define the exact path to each node that I was interested in and easily pull out the necessary data. I chose to implement these mappings as a HashMap, which I later iterated over, grabbing the specified nodes and creating a new HashMap with the values. These values were then used later in both the executeQuery and getResponseXML methods that I'll describe next:

```java
public class HotkeyAdaptorRosProdAvailImpl implements HotkeyAdaptor {

    String inputFile;              // request XML
    HashMap requestValues;         // stores parsed XML values from request
    HashMap as400response;         // stores return parameter from RPG call

    /* Declare XPath mappings and populate with a static initialization block */
    public static HashMap xpathmappings = new HashMap();
    static {
        xpathmappings.put("from_ContactName",
"//Pip3A2PriceAndAvailabilityRequest/fromRole/PartnerRoleDescription/
ContactInformation/contactName/FreeFormText");
        xpathmappings.put("from_EmailAddress", "//Pip3A2PriceAndAvailabilityRequest/
fromRole/PartnerRoleDescription/ContactInformation/EmailAddress");
    }
        // Remaining xpath mappings omitted for brevity...

    public HotkeyAdaptorRosProdAvailImpl() {
        this.requestValues = new HashMap();
        this.as400response = new HashMap();
    }

    public void setXML(String _xml) {
        this.inputFile = _xml;
    }

    public boolean parseXML() {

        try {
            Document doc = null;
            DocumentBuilderFactory dbf = DocumentBuilderFactory.newInstance();
            DocumentBuilder db = dbf.newDocumentBuilder();
            StringReader r = new StringReader(this.inputFile);
            org.xml.sax.InputSource is = new org.xml.sax.InputSource(r);
            doc = db.parse(is);

            Element root    = doc.getDocumentElement();

            Node node = null;

            Iterator xpathvals = xpathmappings.values().iterator();
            Iterator xpathvars = xpathmappings.keySet().iterator();
            while (xpathvals.hasNext() && xpathvars.hasNext()) {
                node = XPathAPI.selectSingleNode(root, String)xpathvals.next());
                requestValues.put((String)xpathvars.next(),
                        node.getChildNodes().item(0).getNodeValue());
            }

        }
        catch (Exception e) {
            System.out.println(e.toString());
        }

        return true;
    }
```

```
public boolean executeQuery( ) {
    // Code omitted...
}

public String getResponseXML( ) {
    // Code omitted...
}

}
```

The executeQuery method contains all of the code necessary to access the RPG code running on the AS/400 systems, in order to get the necessary response data we'll use later to
construct the response XML document. Many years ago, I worked on a project that integrated a MAPICS system (RPG on the AS/400) with a new system that I wrote using
Visual Basic. I had written code for both sides of the exchange, in RPG and CL on the
AS/400, and Visual Basic on the PC. This led to several speaking engagements where I
attempted to show legions of RPG programmers how to integrate their legacy systems
with modern client/server software. At the time, it really was a complicated and almost
mystical thing to do.

Since then, IBM has made it very easy and provided us with a library of Java functions
that do all the work for us. (So much for all the consulting gigs and book deals I could
have had with that one!) Here's the code, using the much better Java library from IBM:

```
public boolean executeQuery( ) {

    StringBuffer sb = new StringBuffer( );

    sb.append(requestValues.get("from_ContactName")).append("|");
    sb.append(requestValues.get("from_EmailAddress")).append("|");
    sb.append(requestValues.get("from_TelephoneNumber")).append("|");
    sb.append(requestValues.get("from_BusinessIdentifier")).append("|");
    sb.append(requestValues.get("prod_BeginAvailDate")).append("|");
    sb.append(requestValues.get("prod_EndAvailDate")).append("|");
    sb.append(requestValues.get("prod_Quantity")).append("|");
    sb.append(requestValues.get("prod_ProductIdentifier")).append("|");

    try {
        AS400 sys = new AS400("SS100044", "ACME", "HOUSE123");

        CharConverter ch = new CharConverter( );
        byte[] as = ch.stringToByteArray(sb.toString( ));

        ProgramParameter[] parmList = new ProgramParameter[2];
        parmList[0] = new ProgramParameter(as);
        parmList[1] = new ProgramParameter(255);

        ProgramCall pgm = new ProgramCall(sys,
                "/QSYS.LIB/DEVOBJ.LIB/J551231.PGM", parmList);
        if (pgm.run( ) != true) {
            AS400Message[] msgList = pgm.getMessageList( );
            for (int i=0; i < msgList.length; i++) {
                System.out.println(msgList[i].getID( ) + " : " +
                        msgList[i].getText( ));
```

```
                }
            }
            else {
                CharConverter chconv = new CharConverter();
                String response =
                        chconv.byteArrayToString(parmList[1].getOutputData());

                StringTokenizer st = new StringTokenizer(response, "|");

                String status = (String) st.nextToken().trim();
                as400response.put("Status", status);
                String error = (String) st.nextToken().trim();
                as400response.put("ErrorCode", error);
                String quantity = (String) st.nextToken().trim();
                as400response.put("Quantity",
                        String.valueOf(Integer.parseInt(quantity)));

                if (status.toUpperCase().equals("ER")) {
                    if (error.equals("1")) {
                        as400response.put("ErrorMsg",
                                "Account not authorized for item availability.");
                    }
                    if (error.equals("2")) {
                        as400response.put("ErrorMsg", "Item not found.");
                    }
                    if (error.equals("3")) {
                        as400response.put("ErrorMsg", "Item is obsolete.");
                        as400response.put("Replacement",
                                (String) st.nextToken().trim());
                    }
                    if (error.equals("4")) {
                        as400response.put("ErrorMsg",
                                "Invalid quantity amount.");
                    }
                    if (error.equals("5")) {
                        as400response.put("ErrorMsg",
                                "Preference profile processing error.");
                    }
                    if (error.equals("6")) {
                        as400response.put("ErrorMsg",
                                "ATP processing error.");
                    }
                }

            }
        }
        catch (Exception e) {
            System.out.println(e.toString());
        }

        return true;
    }
```

This method begins by assembling a parameter string (pipe-delimited) that gets passed into the AS/400 program, where it parses the string, retrieves the requested data, and returns a pipe-delimited string with a status and error code as well as the result of the operation.

Assuming there isn't an error, the results of this AS/400 interaction get stored in another HashMap, which we'll use when constructing the XML response document. If there is an error, then that gets written to the response instead.

Assembling the XML Response

I've always enjoyed seeing the many ways people have tried to create XML documents programmatically. What I always tell people is that XML documents are just big text strings. Therefore, it's usually easier to just write one out using a StringBuffer rather than trying to build a DOM (Document Object Model) or using a special XML generator library.

For this project, I simply created a StringBuffer object and appended each individual line of the XML document following the Rosettanet standard. In the following code example, I omitted several lines of code, but this should give you an idea of how the response was constructed:

```
public String getResponseXML() {

        StringBuffer response = new StringBuffer();
        response.append("<Pip3A2PriceAndAvailabilityResponse>").append("\n");
        response.append("    <ProductAvailability>").append("\n");
        response.append("    <ProductQuantity>").append(as400response.get("Quantity")).
append("</ProductQuantity>").append("\n");
        response.append("    </ProductAvailability>").append("\n");
        response.append("    <ProductIdentification>").append("\n");
        response.append("      <PartnerProductIdentification>").append("\n");
        response.append("        <GlobalPartnerClassificationCode>Manufacturer</
GlobalPartnerClassificationCode>").append("\n");
        response.append("        <ProprietaryProductIdentifier>").append(requestValues.
get("prod_ProductIdentifier")).append("</ProprietaryProductIdentifier>").append("\n");
        response.append("      </PartnerProductIdentification>").append("\n");
        response.append("    </ProductIdentification>").append("\n");
        response.append("  </ProductPriceAndAvailabilityLineItem>").append("\n");
        response.append("</Pip3A2PriceAndAvailabilityResponse>").append("\n");

        return response.toString();
    }
```

Conclusion

In looking back on this code I wrote over two years ago, I think it's pretty normal to second-guess myself and think of better ways I could have written it. While I may have written some of the implementation code differently, I think I'd still design the overall solution the same way. This code has stood the test of time, as the client has since added new distributors and new request types all on its own, with minimal help from outside service providers like me.

Currently, as director of a bioinformatics department, I have used this code to demonstrate several things to my staff as I teach them object-oriented design principles and XML parsing techniques. I could have written about code I have developed more recently, but I think this demonstrates several basic principles that are important for any young software developer to understand.

## CHAPTER TWENTY-EIGHT

Beautiful Debugging

Andreas Zeller

MY NAME IS ANDREAS, AND I HAVE BEEN DEBUGGING.** Welcome to Debuggers Anonymous, where you can tell your debugging story and find relief in the stories of others. So you have spent another night away from home? Good thing you've only been in front of the debugger. So you still cannot tell your manager when that showstopper will be fixed? Let's hope for the best! The fellow in the cubicle next to you brags about searching for a bug for 36 consecutive hours? Now that's impressive!

No, there is nothing glamorous about debugging. It is the ugly duckling of our profession, the admission that we are far from perfect, the one activity that is the least predictable or accountable—and a constant impetus to feelings of remorse and guilt: "If only we had done better right from the start, we wouldn't be stuck in this mess." The defect is the crime; debugging is the punishment.

Let us assume, though, that we have done all we can to prevent errors. Yet, from time to time, we will find ourselves in a situation where we need to debug. And as with all other activities, we need to handle debugging in the most professional, maybe even "beautiful" way.

So, can there be any beauty in debugging? I believe there can. In my own life as a programmer, there have been a number of moments when I encountered true beauty in debugging. These moments not only helped me solve a problem at hand, but actually evolved into new approaches to debugging as a whole—approaches that are not only "beautiful" in some way, but actually boost your productivity in debugging. This is because they are *systematic*—they guarantee to guide you toward the problem solution—and partly even *automatic*—they do all the work while you pursue other tasks.

Curious? Read on.

Debugging a Debugger

My first experience of beauty in debugging was granted by one of my students. In her 1994 Master's thesis, Dorothea Lütkehaus built a visual debugger interface that provided a textbook visualization of data structures. Figure 28-1 shows a screenshot of her tool, called the *data display debugger*, or *ddd* for short. As Dorothea demoed her debugger, the audience and myself were amazed: one could grasp complex data within seconds, and explore and manipulate it just by using the mouse.

ddd was a wrapper for the command-line debuggers in use at this time (in particular *gdb*, the GNU debugger), which were very powerful tools but difficult to use. Since graphical user interfaces for programming tools were still scarce, *ddd* was a small revolution. In the following months, Dorothea and I did our best to make *ddd* the most beautiful debugger interface around, and it eventually became part of the GNU ecosystem.

While debugging with *ddd* is usually more fun than using a command-line tool, it does not necessarily make you a more efficient debugger. For this, the debugging *process* is far more important than the tool. Incidentally, I learned this through *ddd* as well. It all started with a *ddd* bug report I received on July 31, 1998, which started my second experience of beauty in debugging. Here is the bug report:

> When using DDD with GDB 4.16, the run command correctly uses any prior command-line arguments, or the value of set args. However, when I switched to GDB 4.17, this no longer worked: If I entered a run command in the console window, the prior command-line options would be lost.

Those *gdb* developers had done it again—releasing a new *gdb* version that behaved slightly differently from the earlier version. Because *ddd* was a frontend, it actually sent commands to *gdb*, just like a human would do, and parsed the *gdb* replies to present its information in the user interface. Something in this process had apparently failed.

All I needed to do was grab and install the new *gdb* version, run *ddd* as its frontend, and see whether I could reproduce the problem. If I could, I would have to launch another debugger instance to walk through the problem. All in all, this was business as usual.

It turned out, though, that at this time, I was pretty fed up with running debuggers, debugging our own debugger, and in particular debugging because of third-party changes.

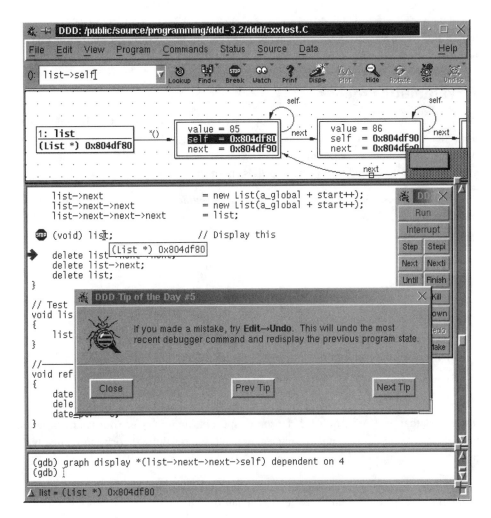

FIGURE 28-1. The ddd debugger in action

So, I sat back and wondered: is there a way to solve this problem without actually launching the debugger? Or: *can I debug something without debugging?*

Since the problem was caused by a change to the *gdb* source code, I could simply look into the *gdb* code—or, more precisely, at the differences between the two releases. The code difference, so I thought, would point me directly to the failure-inducing change. All I needed to do was to run the two code bases through *diff*, a tool for detecting text differences. And this I did.

The *diff* results surprised me. The log had a length of 178,200 lines, which was enormous—especially considering that the total *gdb* source code contained roughly 600,000 lines of code. In no less than 8,721 locations, developers had inserted, deleted, or changed the source code. This was quite a lot for a "minor" release and, of course, far more than I could handle. Even if it took me just 10 seconds to check a single location, I would still spend 24 hours searching for the troublesome change. I sighed, invoked the debugger, and braced myself for yet another boring debugging session. Still, I thought, there must be a better way to do this—a more "beautiful" way.

A Systematic Process

When programmers debug a program, they search for a failure cause, which could lie in the code, the input, or the environment. This cause must be found and eliminated. Once the cause is eliminated, the program works. (Should the program still fail once the cause is eliminated, we may need to revise our beliefs about the cause.)

The general process for finding causes is called the *scientific method*. Applied to program failures, it works as follows:

1. Observe a program failure.

2. Invent a *hypothesis* for the failure cause that is consistent with the observations.

3. Use the hypothesis to make *predictions*.

4. Put your predictions to the test by experiments and further observations:

   a. If experiment and observation satisfy the prediction, refine the hypothesis.

   b. If not, find an alternate hypothesis.

5. Repeat steps 3 and 4 until the hypothesis can no longer be refined.

Eventually, the hypothesis thus becomes a *theory*. This means that you have a conceptual framework that explains (and predicts) some aspect of the universe. Your failing program may be a very small aspect of the universe, but still, the resulting theory should neatly predict where you should fix your program.

To obtain such a theory, programmers apply the scientific method as they walk back through the cause-effect-chain that led to the failure. They:

1. Observe a failure ("The output is wrong").

2. Come up with a hypothesis about the failure cause ("The problem may be that y has a wrong value").

3. Make a prediction ("If y is wrong, its value may come from f( ) in line 632").

4. Put their prediction to the test ("Indeed, y has a wrong value in line 632").

5. Draw appropriate conclusions ("This means that f( ) returns a wrong value. Now where does this come from?").

Among all methods, hints, and tricks, the consistent and disciplined use of the scientific method is the key to becoming a debugging master. This means three things:

Be explicit

   Formulate your hypothesis explicitly. Write it down or explain your problem to other people. Keep a written track of your hypotheses and observations so you can interrupt your work and start the next morning with a fresh mind.

Be systematic

Make sure you know what you're doing. Don't investigate (or change) something at random without having a clear hypothesis and a resulting prediction. Be sure you do not miss possible failure causes.

Look for the most likely causes first

The scientific method guarantees you will find a cause, but it does not tell you when. Identify possible failure causes first, and then focus on those where the product of likelihood and effort is minimal.

Unfortunately, interactive debuggers as they stand do not support the scientific method. To be sure, debuggers are great tools to poke around and investigate code and its results at will. This is a good thing—but only for skilled programmers who know how to use debuggers systematically. I'd rather see programmers trained in systematic debugging methods than in fancy debugging tools. (And I still feel guilty having written a fancy debugging tool myself.)

A Search Problem

Let's come back to our initial problem of debugging the debugger. Even after isolating and fixing the bug, I wondered: is there a way to find the failure-inducing change automatically? What one would need is a test that is automatically invoked each time the programmer changes something. As soon as the test broke, we would know what had changed most recently so we could immediately fix it. (A few years later, David Saff and Michael Ernst implemented this idea under the name *continuous testing*.)

In my situation, I knew the change that had caused the test to fail—it was the change from *gdb* 4.16 to *gdb* 4.17. The problem was that the change was so *huge*, affecting 8,721 locations. There should be a way to break down this change into smaller pieces.

What if I tried to split it into 8,721 smaller changes, each affecting just one location? This way, I could apply and test one change after the other until the test failed—and the last change applied would be the one that broke the test. In other words, I would simulate the 4.17 version's development history. (Actually, it would not be me who would simulate the history; instead, it would be a tool I built. And while I would be sitting sipping my tea, playing a game with my kids, or catching up my email stream, this nifty little tool would search and find the failure-inducing change. Neat.)

There was a catch, though. *I had no clue about the order in which the changes had to be applied.* And this was crucial because the individual changes may depend on each other. For instance, change A may introduce a variable that would be used in new code included in other changes B or C. Whenever B or C are applied, A must be applied, too; otherwise, building *gdb* would fail. Likewise, change X may rename some function definition; other changes (Y, Z) in other locations may reflect this renaming. If X is applied, Y and Z must be applied as well, because again, otherwise, *gdb* would not build.

How does one determine whether one change depends upon another? This problem looked quite hard—and almost intractable without very fancy (and not yet existing) multiversion program analysis.

How about just trying out various orderings of changes? 8,721 individual changes can be ordered in $8,721 \times 8,720 \times 8,719 \times \ldots \times 1 = 8,721!$ different ways. No way anyone could test all of them. Trying out all subsets is somewhat better: 8,721 changes mean $2^{8,721} = 10^{2,625}$ possible subsets, which means a lot fewer tests than 8,721 orderings. I could try to console myself with the thought that by the time these computations had ended on my machine, quantum computing, time travel, and universally correct programs would long have gone mainstream, eliminating the need for such futile attempts.

So, I made another try. How about good old divide and conquer? We could start applying the first half of changes to the *gdb* 4.16 source and test it. If *ddd* failed, we would know that the failure-inducing change was in that first half; if it did not fail, we'd keep on searching in the other half. With each test, we'd reduce the search space by one-half, and thus finally end up in the failure-inducing change. That's it, I thought: an automatic application of the scientific method, systematically creating, testing, and refining hypotheses.

But again—what do we do if applying a set of changes ends in inconsistent code? I had no idea.

Finding the Failure Cause Automatically

It took me three months to come up with a solution—which came to me, incidentally, lying in my bed at six in the morning. The sun was rising, the birds were singing, and I finally had an idea. The reasoning was as follows:

- Applying *half* of the changes has a small chance of getting a consistent build; the risk of skipping a dependent change is simply too high. On the other hand, if we get a consistent build (or a "resolved" outcome), we can very quickly narrow down the set of changes.

- On the other hand, applying *individual* changes has a far greater chance of getting something meaningful—in particular, if the version being changed was already consistent. As an example, think of changing a single function; unless its interface changes, we will most likely get a running program. On the other hand, trying out one change after the other would still take ages.

Therefore, I'd call for a *compromise:* I would start with two halves. If neither half of the changes would result in a testable build, I would split the set of changes into *four* subsets instead, and then apply each subset individually to the *gdb* 4.16 source. In addition, I would also *unapply* the subset from the *gdb* 4.17 source (which would be realized by applying the complement of the subset to the *gdb* 4.16 source).

Splitting in four (rather than two) would mean that *smaller* change sets would be applied, which means that the changed versions would be closer to the (working) original versions—and which would imply higher chances of getting a consistent build.

And if four subsets would not suffice, then I would go for 8, 16, 32, and so on, until, eventually, I would apply each single change individually, one after the other—which should give me the greatest chance of getting a consistent build. As soon as I had a testable build, the algorithm would restart from scratch.

I calculated that in the worst case, the algorithm would still require $8,721^2 = 76,055,841$ tests. This number was still way too high, but much lower than the exponential-approaches thought of earlier. At the other extreme, if all builds succeeded, the algorithm would work as a binary search, and require just $\log_2 8,721 = 14$ tests. Given the odds, was it worth doing?

I implemented a simple Python script with a very crude version of the preceding algorithm. The key part was the testing function. It would take a set of changes, run *patch* to apply the changes to the *gdb* 4.16 source, and then invoke *make* to build the changed *gdb*. Finally, it would run *gdb* and see whether the failure occurred (returning "fail" if it did) or not (returning "pass"). As any of these steps could fail, the testing function could also return "unresolved" as a test result.

As I started the script, it quickly turned out that "unresolved" was still by far the most frequent return value. Actually, for the first 800 tests or so, the testing function returned nothing but "unresolved." The number of change subsets had gone up from two to four to eight…until we had 64 subsets, each containing 136 changes. And these tests took some time. As one *gdb* build took about six minutes, I was already waiting for three days. (Actually, I was not waiting, but writing my Ph.D. thesis. But still….)

I was just examining the log as something unusual happened. A test had just failed! Now, finally, I would see how the algorithm would focus on the smaller set, narrowing the search space. But when I checked the results, it turned out that the test printed the following message on the screen and stopped:

```
NameError: name 'next_c_fial' is not defined
```

After three days of constant calculation, my script had stumbled on a dumb misspelling. I truly wished I had used a language with static checking rather than Python.

I fixed the problem and ran the script again. Now, finally, it would work. After five more days, and roughly 1,200 tests, the script finally isolated the failure-inducing change: the change to *gdb* that had caused *ddd* to fail. It was a one-line change—and it was not even a change to program code, but instead a change to some built-in text:

```
diff -r gdb-4.16/gdb/infcmd.c gdb-4.17/gdb/infcmd.c
1239c1278
< "Set arguments to give program being debugged when it is started.\n\
---
> "Set argument list to give program being debugged when it is started.\n\
```

This change from arguments to argument list was the cause for *gdb* 4.17 no longer working with *ddd*. This text is output by *gdb* when the user requests help for the set args command. However, it is also used in other places. When given the command show args, *gdb* 4.16 replies:

```
Arguments to give program being debugged is "11 14"
```

gdb 4.17, however, replies:

```
Argument list to give program being debugged is "11 14"
```

This new reply was what confused *ddd* because it expected the reply to start with Arguments. Thus, my script had actually determined the failure-inducing change—after five days of work, but yet in a fully automatic version.

Delta Debugging

Over the next several months, I refined and optimized the algorithm as well as the tool, such that eventually it would need just one hour to find the failure-inducing change. I eventually published the algorithm under the name *delta debugging* because it "debugs" programs by isolating a delta, or difference between two versions.

Here I'll show my Python implementation of the delta debugging algorithm. The function dd( ) takes three arguments—two lists of changes as well as a test:

- The list c_pass contains the "working" configuration—in our case, the list of changes that must be applied to make the program work. In our case (which is typical), this is the empty list.

- The list c_fail contains the "failing" configuration—in our case, the list of changes required to make the program fail. In our case, this would be a list of 8,721 changes (which we would encapsulate in, say, Change objects).

- The test function accepts a list of changes, applies them, and runs a test. It returns PASS, FAIL, or UNRESOLVED as the outcome, depending on whether the test was successful, failed, or had an unresolved outcome. In our case, the test function would apply the changes via *patch* and run the test as just described.

- The dd( ) function systematically narrows down the difference between c_pass and c_fail, and eventually returns a triple of values. The first of these values would be the isolated delta—in our case, a single Change object containing the one-line change to the *gdb* source code.

If you plan to implement dd( ) yourself, you can easily use the code shown here (and included on the O'Reilly web site for this book). You also need three supporting functions:

split(*list*, *n*)
    Splits a list into *n* sublists of equal length (except for possibly the last). Thus:

```
split([1, 2, 3, 4, 5], 3)
```

yields:

    [[1, 2], [3, 4], [5]]

`listminus()` and `listunion()`

Return the difference or union of two sets represented as lists, respectively. Thus:

    listminus([1, 2, 3], [1, 2])

yields:

    [3]

whereas:

    listunion([1, 2, 3], [3, 4])

yields:

    [1, 2, 3, 4]

The Python code is shown in Example 28-1.

EXAMPLE 28-1. An implementation of the delta debugging algorithm

```python
def dd(c_pass, c_fail, test):
    """Return a triple (DELTA, C_PASS', C_FAIL') such that
       - C_PASS subseteq C_PASS' subset C_FAIL' subseteq C_FAIL holds
       - DELTA = C_FAIL' - C_PASS' is a minimal difference
         between C_PASS' and C_FAIL' that is relevant with respect
         to TEST."""

    n = 2   # Number of subsets

    while 1:
        assert test(c_pass) == PASS   # Invariant
        assert test(c_fail) == FAIL   # Invariant
        assert n >= 2

        delta = listminus(c_fail, c_pass)

        if n > len(delta):
            # No further minimizing
            return (delta, c_pass, c_fail)

        deltas = split(delta, n)
        assert len(deltas) == n

        offset = 0
        j = 0
        while j < n:
            i = (j + offset) % n
            next_c_pass = listunion(c_pass, deltas[i])
            next_c_fail = listminus(c_fail, deltas[i])

            if test(next_c_fail) == FAIL and n == 2:
                c_fail = next_c_fail
                n = 2; offset = 0; break
            elif test(next_c_fail) == PASS:
                c_pass = next_c_fail
                n = 2; offset = 0; break
```

```
        elif test(next_c_pass) == FAIL:
            c_fail = next_c_pass
            n = 2; offset = 0; break
        elif test(next_c_fail) == FAIL:
            c_fail = next_c_fail
            n = max(n - 1, 2); offset = i; break
        elif test(next_c_pass) == PASS:
            c_pass = next_c_pass
            n = max(n - 1, 2); offset = i; break
        else:
            j = j + 1

    if j >= n:
        if n >= len(delta):
            return (delta, c_pass, c_fail)
        else:
            n = min(len(delta), n * 2)
```

Minimizing Input

The interesting thing about delta debugging (or any other automation of the scientific method) is that it is very general. Rather than search for causes in a set of changes, you can also search for causes in other search spaces. For instance, you can easily apply delta debugging to search for failure causes in program input, which Ralf Hildebrandt and I did in 2002.

When searching for causes in program input, the program code stays the same: no application of changes, no reconstruction, just execution. Instead, it is the input that changes. Think of a program that works on most inputs, but fails on one specific input. One can easily have delta debugging isolate the failure-inducing difference between the two inputs: "The cause of the web browser crashing is the <SELECT> tag in line 40."

One can also modify the algorithm so that it returns a minimized input: "To have the web browser crash, just feed it a web page containing <SELECT>." In minimized input, every single remaining character is relevant for the failure to occur. Minimized inputs can be very valuable for debuggers because they make things simple: they lead to shorter executions and smaller states to be examined. As an important (and perhaps beautiful) side effect, they capture the essence of the failure.

I once met some programmers who were dealing with bugs in a third-party database. They had very complex, machine-generated SQL queries that sometimes would cause the database to fail. The vendor did not categorize these bugs as high priority because "you are our only customer dealing with such complex queries." Then the programmers simplified a one-page SQL query to a single line that still triggered the failure. Faced with this single line, the vendor immediately gave the bug the highest priority and fixed it.

How does one achieve minimization? The easiest way is to feed dd( ) with an empty c_pass, and to have a passing test return "pass" only if the input is empty, and "unresolved" otherwise. c_pass remains unchanged while c_fail becomes smaller and smaller with each failing test.

Again, all that is required to isolate such failure causes is an automated test and a means to split the input into smaller pieces—that is, a splitting function that has some basic knowledge about the syntax of the input.

Hunting the Defect

In principle, delta debugging could also minimize an entire program code so as to keep only what is relevant. Suppose your web browser crashes while printing a HTML page. Applying delta debugging on the program code means that only the bare code required to reproduce the failure would remain. Doesn't this sound neat? Unfortunately, it would hardly work in practice. The reason is that the elements of program code are heavily dependent on each other. Remove one piece, and everything breaks apart. The chances of getting something meaningful by randomly removing parts are very slim. Therefore, delta debugging would almost certainly require a quadratic number of tests. Even for a 1,000-line program, this would already mean a million tests—and years and years of waiting. We never had that much time, so we never implemented that feat.

Nonetheless, we still wanted to hunt down failure causes not only in the input or the set of changes, but in the actual source code—in other words, we wanted to have the statements that caused the program to fail. (And, of course, we wanted to get them automatically.)

Again, this was a task that turned out to be achievable by delta debugging. However, we did not get there directly. We wanted to make a detour via program states—that is, the set of all program variables and their values. In this set, we wanted to determine failure causes automatically, as in "At the call to shell_sort( ), variable size causes the failure." How would that work?

Let us recapitulate what we had done so far. We had done delta debugging on program versions—one that worked and one that failed—and isolated the minimal difference that caused the failure. We had done delta debugging on program inputs—again, one that worked and one that failed—and isolated minimal differences that caused the failure. If we applied delta debugging on program states, we would take one program state from a working run, and one program state from a failing run, and eventually obtain the minimal difference that caused the failure.

Now, there are three problems in here. Problem number one: *How does one obtain a program state?* Eventually, I would instrument the *gdb* debugger to query all named variables first, and then *unfold* all data structures. If I encountered an array or a structure, I would query its elements; if I found a pointer, I would query the variable it pointed to, and so on—until I reached a fix point, or the set of all accessible variables. This program state would be represented as a graph of variables (vertices) and references (edges), as shown in Figure 28-2, abstracting away concrete memory addresses.

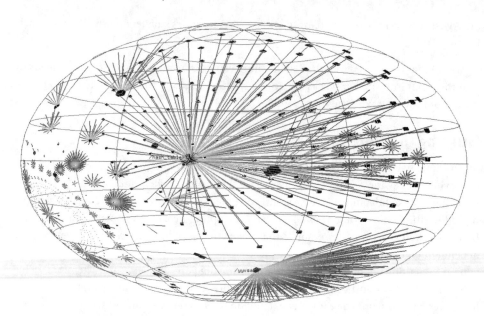

FIGURE 28-2. A program state of the GNU compiler

Next problem: *How does one compare two program states?* This was rather easy: there are known algorithms for computing common subgraphs between two graphs—and anything that would not be part of the subgraph became a difference. With such an algorithm properly implemented, we now could actually extract and determine the difference between two program states.

Third and last problem: *How does one apply differences between states?* This was a real challenge, as it involved not only observing but actually manipulating program states. To apply a difference in program state, we would have to set variables to new values, but also to replicate entire complex data structures, including allocating and deleting elements. Once this was done, we could do something quite fun; we could arbitrarily transfer program states between running processes. And not only entire program states, but also partial program states—ranging from small changes to a single variable to large changes of, say, half of a symbol table.

This idea of transferring program states while the program is executing is something that one needs time getting used to. I remember one of my first presentations at IBM where I explained the algorithm, its application on states, and came to the ultimate example: "We now have 879 differences between these two states. We now let delta debugging narrow down the failure cause. To this end, the algorithm takes half of the differences, that is, 439 state differences, and applies them. This means that in the passing run, 439 variables are now set to the values found in the failing run...."

At this moment, a fellow from the audience stepped up and said: "But doesn't this sound like a very insane thing to do?"

Of course, he was right. Nothing meaningful came out of setting 439 variables to values found in another run; nor did it help setting the other 440 variables. But this is just the situation in which delta debugging comes up with the idea of making smaller changes—that is, it tries 220 variables, 110, and so on. Eventually, it isolates the variable that caused the failure: "The compiler crash was caused by a loop in the abstract syntax tree." And this end, of course, justifies the means—in particular, for the people at IBM, who were all pretty busy developing (and debugging) compilers.

Thus, the demonstration that it worked helped people forget it was a pretty weird approach. Still, my first publication on the topic had a hard time getting accepted. One reviewer frankly admitted he was so appalled by the weird approach, he would not even bother to read on toward the results.

Nonetheless, finding failure causes in program state was only a detour toward the ultimate end. It was Holger Cleve who gave this technique the ultimate touch. Since he knew the failure-causing variables, he would simply trace back their values to the statements that caused them—and presto! We would end up in the statements that caused the failure: "The statement in line 437 caused a loop, which again caused the failure." Now this was true magic—and this paper had no trouble getting published, either.

So, as we had a complete automatic debugging solution on our hands, why do people today still use interactive debuggers? Why didn't we go public and become millionaires with automated debugging?

A Prototype Problem

There is a difference between what you can do in a lab and what you can do in production. The main trouble with our approach was that it was fragile. Very fragile. Extracting accurate program states is a tricky business. Suppose you are working on a C program that just stopped in a debugger. You find a pointer. Does it point to something? If so, what is the C data type of the variable is it pointing to? And how many elements does it point to? In C, all this is left to the discretion of the programmer—and it's awfully hard to guess the memory management used in the program at hand.

Another problem is to determine where the program state ends and the system state begins. Some state is shared between applications, or between applications and the system. Where would we stop extracting and comparing?

For lab experiments, these issues could be addressed and confined, but for a full-fledged, robust industrial approach, we found them insurmountable. And this is why, today, people still have to use interactive debuggers.

The future is not that bleak, though. Command-line tools that implement delta debugging on input are available. The *ddchange* plug-in for Eclipse brings delta debugging on changes to your desktop. Researchers apply delta debugging on method calls, nicely integrating capture/replay with test case minimization. And finally, through all these automated approaches, we have gained a much better understanding of how debugging works and how it can be done in a systematic, sometimes even automatic way—a way that is hopefully most effective, and maybe even "beautiful."

Conclusion

If by any chance, you are forced to debug something, you can strive to make your debugging experience as painless as possible. Being systematic (by following the scientific method) helps a lot. Automating the scientific method helps even more. The best thing you can do, though, is invest effort into your code and your development process. By following the advice in this very book, you will write beautiful code—and, as a side effect, also achieve the most beautiful debugging. And what is the most beautiful debugging? Of course: no debugging at all!

Acknowledgments

I'd like to thank the students with whom I have experienced beauty in debugging tools. Martin Burger took great part in the AskIgor effort and implemented the *ddchange* plug-in for Eclipse. Holger Cleve researched and implemented automated isolation of failure-inducing statements. Ralf Hildebrandt implemented isolation of failure-inducing input. Karsten Lehmann contributed to AskIgor and implemented isolation of failure-inducing program states for Java. Dorothea Lütkehaus wrote the original version of *ddd*. Thomas Zimmermann implemented the graph-comparison algorithms. Christian Lindig and Andrzey Wasylkowski provided helpful comments on earlier revisions of this chapter.

Further Reading

I have compiled my experiences on systematic and automatic debugging in a university course. This is where you can learn more about the scientific method and delta debugging—but also about many more debugging and analysis techniques, such as statistical debugging, automated testing, or static bug detection. All lecture slides and references are available at *http://www.whyprogramsfail.com*.

If you are looking specifically for scientific publications of my group, see the delta debugging home page at *http://www.st.cs.uni-sb.de/dd*.

Finally, a web search on "delta debugging" will point you to a variety of resources, including further publications and implementations.

## CHAPTER TWENTY-NINE

Treating Code As an Essay

Yukihiro Matsumoto

PROGRAMS SHARE SOME ATTRIBUTES WITH ESSAYS. For essays, the most important question readers ask is, "What is it about?" For programs, the main question is, "What does it do?" In fact, the purpose should be sufficiently clear that neither question ever needs to be uttered. Still, for both essays and computer code, it's always important to look at how each one is written. Even if the idea itself is good, it will be difficult to transmit to the desired audience if it is difficult to understand. The style in which they are written is just as important as their purpose. Both essays and lines of code are meant—before all else—to be read and understood by human beings.*

You may ask: "Are human beings actually supposed to be the ones reading computer programs?" The assumption is that people use programs to tell computers what to do, and computers then use compilers or interpreters to compile and understand the code. At the end of the process, the program is translated into machine language that is normally read only by the CPU. That is, of course, the way things work, but this explanation only describes one aspect of computer programs.

---

* This chapter was translated from the Japanese by Nevin Thompson.

Most programs are not write-once. They are reworked and rewritten again and again in their lives. Bugs must be debugged. Changing requirements and the need for increased functionality mean the program itself may be modified on an ongoing basis. During this process, human beings must be able to read and understand the original code; it is therefore more important by far for humans to be able to understand the program than it is for the computer.

Computers can, of course, deal with complexity without complaint, but this is not the case for human beings. Unreadable code will reduce most people's productivity significantly. On the other hand, easily understandable code will increase it. And we see beauty in such code.

What makes a computer program readable? In other words, what is beautiful code? Although different people have different standards about what a beautiful program might be, judging the attributes of computer code is not simply a matter of aesthetics. Instead, computer programs are judged according to how well they execute their intended tasks. In other words, "beautiful code" is not an abstract virtue that exists independent of its programmers' efforts. Rather, beautiful code is really meant to help the programmer be happy and productive. This is the metric I use to evaluate the beauty of a program.

Brevity is one element that helps make code beautiful. As Paul Graham says, "Succinctness is power." In the vocabulary of programming, brevity is a virtue. Because there is a definite cost involved in scanning code with the human eye, programs should ideally contain no unnecessary information.

For example, when type declarations are unnecessary, or when the design does not require class declarations and main routine definitions, brevity mandates that it should be possible to simply avoid them. To illustrate this principle, Example 29-1 shows a Hello World program in Java and Ruby.

EXAMPLE 29-1. "Hello World" in Java versus Ruby

Java	Ruby

```class Sample {}```
 	
 ```public static void main(String[] argv) {```
 ```System.out.println("Hello World");```
 ```}```
	```print "Hello World\n"```

Both programs accomplish exactly the same task—simply displaying the words "Hello World"—but Java and Ruby approach it in radically different ways. In Ruby's version of the program, all that's necessary is to describe the essence of the task. Print "Hello World". No declaration. No data type. In Java, though, it is necessary to include a variety of descriptions that are not immediately related to our intent. Of course, there is merit in including all of the things that Java does. However, because it is impossible to omit anything, brevity is lost. (To digress a little, Ruby's "Hello World" is trilingual: it also works in Perl and Python.)

Brevity can also mean the elimination of redundancy. Redundancy is defined as the duplication of information. When information is duplicated, the cost of maintaining consistency can be quite high. And because a considerable amount of time can be spent maintaining consistency, redundancy will lower programming productivity.

Although it could be argued that redundancy lowers costs when interpreting meaning, the truth is actually the opposite because redundant code contains so much surplus information. One consequence of this extra weight is that the redundant approach relies on the use of supporting tools. Although relying on IDEs to input information has become popular recently, these tools are not intended to help interpret meaning. The real shortcut for developing elegant code is to choose an elegant programming language. Ruby and other lightweight languages like it support this approach.

In order to eliminate redundancy, we follow the DRY principle: Don't Repeat Yourself. If the same code exists in multiple places, whatever you're trying to say becomes obscured.

The concept of DRY is the antithesis of copy-and-paste coding. In the past, some organizations measured productivity by the number of lines of code a programmer produced, so redundancy was actually tacitly encouraged. I've even heard that copying as much code as possible was sometimes considered a virtue. But this is wrong.

The real virtue, I believe, lies in brevity. The recent popularity of Ruby on Rails is driven by its dogged pursuit of brevity and DRY. The Ruby language is serious about "never writing the same thing twice" and "making descriptions concise." Rails inherits this philosophy from the Ruby language.

A more controversial aspect of beautiful code may be its *familiarity*. Human beings are more conservative than you might think; most people find it difficult to embrace new concepts or change their ways of thinking. Instead, many prefer to continue suffering rather than change. Most people are unwilling to replace familiar tools or learn a new language without a good reason. Whenever they can, human beings will compare new processes they are trying to learn with what they have always regarded as common sense, with a resulting negative assessment of the new process that may be undeserved.

The cost of changing one's ways of thinking is far higher than is commonly thought. In order to easily switch between totally different concepts (for example, from procedural programming to logical or functional programming), it is necessary to become acquainted with a wide variety of concepts. Steep learning curves create pain in humans' brains. Therefore, they reduce programmers' productivity.

According to this point of view, because Ruby supports the concept of "beautiful code," it is an extremely conservative programming language. While called a pure object-oriented language, Ruby does not use innovative control structures based on object message passing like Smalltalk. Instead, Ruby sticks to traditional control structures programmers are familiar with, such as if, while, etc. It even inherits the end keyword to terminate code blocks from good old Algol-family languages.

Compared to other contemporary programming languages, Ruby does sometimes look old-fashioned. But it's important to keep in mind that "never be too innovative" is also a key to creating beautiful code.

Simplicity is the next element of beautiful code. We often feel beauty in simple code. If a program is hard to understand, it cannot be considered beautiful. And when programs are obscure rather than comprehensible, the results are bugs, mistakes, and confusion.

Simplicity is one of most misunderstood concepts in programming. People who design languages frequently want to keep those languages simple and clean. While the sentiment is noble, doing this can make programs written in that language more complex. Mike Cowlishaw, who designed the Rexx scripting language at IBM, once pointed out that because language users are more common than language implementers, the needs of the latter must give way to those of the former:

> The general principle is that very few people have to implement interpreters or compilers for a language, whereas millions of people have to use and live with the language. One should therefore optimize for the millions, rather than the few. Compiler writers didn't love me for that, because Rexx got to be a hard language to interpret or compile, but I think it has paid off for people in general, certainly programmers in general.*

I agree from the bottom of my heart. Ruby is meant to be the personification of this ideal, and while it is far from simple, it supports simple solutions for programming. Because Ruby is not simple, the programs that use it can be. This is true of other lightweight languages as well; they are not lightweight in the sense of ease of implementation, but they are called lightweight because of their intention to lighten the workload of the programmer.

To see what this means in practice, consider Rake, a build tool like *make* that is widely used by Ruby programmers. Unlike *Makefile*s, which are written in a single-purpose file format, *Rakefile*s are written in Ruby, as sort of Domain Specific Language (DSL) with full-featured programmability. Example 29-2 shows a *Rakefile* that runs a set of tests.

EXAMPLE 29-2. Sample Rakefile

```
task :default => [:test]
task :test do
  ruby "test/unittest.rb"
end
```

The *Rakefile* takes advantage of the following shortcuts in Ruby syntax:

- Parentheses for method arguments can be eliminated.
- Unbraced hash key/value pairs can appear at the end of methods.
- Code blocks can be attached at the tails of method calls.

---

* *Dr. Dobb's Journal*, March 1996.

You can program in Ruby without these syntax elements, so in theory, they are redundant. They are often criticized for making language more complex. However, Example 29-3 shows how Example 29-2 would be written without using these features.

EXAMPLE 29-3. Rakefile without abbreviated syntax

```
task({:default => [:test]})
task(:test, &lambda( ){
  ruby "test/unittest.rb"
})
```

As you can see, if Ruby's syntax were stripped of redundancies, Ruby the language might become more elegant, but programmers would have to do more work, and their programs would be harder to read. So, when simpler tools are used to solve a complex problem, complexity is merely shifted to the programmer, which is really putting the cart before the horse.

The next important element in the concept of "beautiful code" is flexibility. I define flexibility here as *freedom from enforcement from tools*. When programmers are forced to do something against their intentions, for the tools' sake, the result is stress. This stress negatively affects the programmer. The end result is far from happiness, and far from beauty as well, according to our definitions of beauty in code. Humans are more valuable than any tools or languages. Computers should serve programmers to maximize their productivity and happiness, but in reality, they often increase the burden instead of lightening it.

Balance is the final element of beautiful code. So far I have talked about brevity, conservatism, simplicity, and flexibility. No element by itself will ensure a beautiful program. When balanced together and kept in mind from the very beginning, each element will work harmoniously with the others to create beautiful code. And if you also make sure to have fun writing and reading code, you will experience happiness as a programmer.

Happy Hacking!

## CHAPTER THIRTY

When a Button Is All That Connects You to the World

Arun Mehta

PROFESSOR STEPHEN HAWKING CAN ONLY PRESS ONE BUTTON," was the one-line spec we were given.

Professor Hawking, the eminent theoretical physicist, has ALS. This disease is "marked by gradual degeneration of the nerve cells in the central nervous system that control voluntary muscle movement. The disorder causes muscle weakness and atrophy throughout the body."* He writes and speaks using the software Equalizer, which he operates via a single button. It uses an external box for text-to-speech, which is no longer manufactured. The source code for Equalizer has also been lost.

In order to continue to be able to function should his outdated hardware fail, he approached some software companies, requesting that they write software that might allow persons with extreme motor disabilities to access computers. Radiophony, the company that Vickram Crishna and I started, was happy to take up this challenge. We named the software eLocutor† and decided to make it free and open source, so that the problem with Equalizer should never reoccur.

---

* *http://en.wikipedia.org/wiki/Amyotrophic_lateral_sclerosis.*

† Downloadable from *http://holisticit.com/eLocutor/elocutorv3.htm.*

The importance of such software in the life of a disabled person can hardly be overstated. Indeed, Professor Hawking himself is the best example of this. He has been able to become not only one of our leading scientists, but also an immensely successful author and motivator, only because software allows him to write and to speak. Who knows how much genius we have left undiscovered, simply because a child could not speak or write clearly enough for the teacher to understand.

Professor Hawking still continues to use the software Equalizer, which he has been familiar with for decades. Meanwhile, however, eLocutor is proving to be useful for persons with a variety of disabilities, particularly since it is easily customizable to the changing needs of the individual.

Our first question, and that of every engineer we explained this problem to, was: could we not find a way to increase the number of inputs Professor Hawking could provide? But his assistant was steadfast: Equalizer worked with a single button, and they saw no reason to change. We too saw the wisdom in writing software for the most extreme case of physical disability, for there were many kinds of binary switch that even a severely disabled person could press, operated by a shoulder, eyebrow, or tongue, or even directly by the brain.* Having devised a solution that the largest possible number of people could use, we might then see how to speed up input for those with greater dexterity.

We also saw a niche market for an adaptation of eLocutor for a wider community. Software that could be operated using a single button might come in quite handy for mobile phones, for instance: the hands-free attachment typically has only one button. With appropriate text-to-speech conversion to eliminate dependence on the screen, it could also be operated by the driver of a car. Or, for another scenario, imagine sitting in a meeting with a client, and, without taking your eyes off her, you might be able to Google a name she dropped and have the search result unobtrusively spoken into your ear.

Of course, for a software writer, devising an editor that functioned efficiently using only a single button was quite an interesting technical challenge. First, we had to pick a basic set of functions for eLocutor to perform. We selected file retrieval and storage, typing, deleting, speaking, scrolling, and searching.

Next, we had to find ways to perform all these activities using only a single button. This was the most exciting part, for it is not often that a programmer gets to work at the level of designing basic communication paradigms. This is also the activity that takes up most of this chapter.

Basic Design Model

Needless to say, the software needed to be efficient, so that the user can type quickly without having to click too often. It sometimes takes Professor Hawking minutes to type a single word, so every improvement in editing speed would be useful for a busy man.

---

* See, for instance, *http://www.brainfingers.com/*.

The software certainly needed to be highly customizable. The nature and size of the vocabulary of our users might vary vastly. The software would need to be able to adapt to these. Further, we were keen to ensure that the disabled person could change as many settings and configurations as possible herself, without the intervention of a helper.

Since we had so little by way of job specification to go on, and no experience in writing such software, we expected to make fairly serious changes in the design as our understanding grew. Keeping all these requirements in mind, we decided to write the software in Visual Basic version 6, an excellent rapid prototyping tool with a large variety of readymade controls. VB made it easy to build a graphical user interface and provided convenient access to database features.

Unique to this problem was the unusually high asymmetry in data flow. A user who could see reasonably well would have a large capacity for taking in information. From persons with extreme motor disability, however, very little data flowed in the other direction: just the occasional bit.

The software offers choices one by one to the user, who accepts a choice by clicking when the desired one is presented. The problem is, of course, that there are so many choices at any point. She may wish to type any one of dozens of characters, or save, scroll, find, or delete text. It would take too long if eLocutor were to cycle through all choices, so it organizes them in groups and subgroups, structured as a tree.

To speed up typing, eLocutor looks ahead, offering ways to complete the word being typed, and choices for the next word and the rest of the phrase. The user needs to be kept aware of these guesses, so that he can spot opportunities for a shortcut, should one become available.

We therefore decided to create a visual interface in which the elements are dynamically resized or even hidden, depending on what we thought the user might wish to see, in order to present shortcuts that would help her key in the desired sentence speedily. So, when the user is typing, the eLocutor screen contains a window with suggestions for how she might complete the current word, and another window that helps her select the following word. (Groups of punctuation characters are treated as words, too.) If the start of the sentence she is typing is identical to any sentences in the database, they are displayed, too. Figure 30-1 shows a typical eLocutor display.

Sometimes the choices are far too many to fit into a small window. A scan feature helps the user quickly select among them. This opens up a large window, showing all the choices, with smaller groups out of these successively appearing in a smaller window. A word appearing in the large window informs the user that eLocutor is able to offer him a shortcut to typing that word. He now waits for it to appear in the smaller window, when he clicks. The large window disappears, and the choices from the smaller window, about a dozen, now become available to the user through the tree, as usual.

The middle box, where typing and deleting takes palce

The highlighted tree item, enlarged

Tree

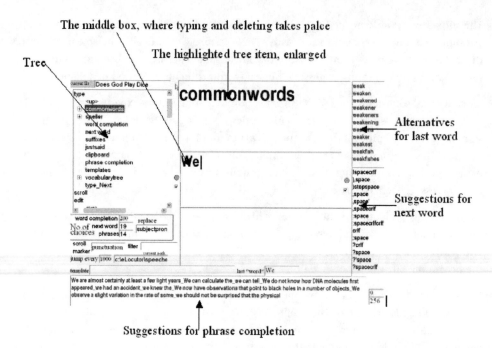

Alternatives for last word

Suggestions for next word

Suggestions for phrase completion

FIGURE 30-1. The eLocutor screen

Screen real estate is again rezoned when the user stops typing and starts to scroll the text, at which time the screen displays as much text as it can before and after the insertion point.

We needed to be as smart in prediction as we could manage, so as to make best possible use of the clicks a disabled user laboriously produces. The intelligence we built in is of three kinds:

A relational database

When the user enters the first few characters of a word, a search in the dictionary table provides suggestions for how to complete it. An analysis of previous text produced by the user also indicates what word the user might select next.

A cache

This takes advantage of patterns in user behavior. We cache not only frequently used words, but also filenames, search terms, spoken text, and paths in decision-making, so that the user can easily reproduce a sequence of steps.

Special groupings

This kind of intelligence takes advantage of natural grouping of words, such as city names, food items, parts of speech, etc. These groupings allow the user to construct new sentences out of old ones, by quickly replacing words in commonly used phrases with others that are similar. For instance, if the sentence "Please bring me some salt" is in the database, a few clicks allow the construction of "Please take her some sugar."

Uniting all the available options is the tree, similar to a menu hierarchy. In the tree, the choices are highlighted one after another, revolving at a fixed rate. The tree structure also extends naturally to subsets of options, such as the special groupings of words just described.

The various elements of the screen in Figure 30-1 need some explanation. The active portion of text that the user wishes to edit is shown in the middle box, while the contents of the boxes above and below it adapt to what the user is doing. To the right, and below, are predictions the software makes about what you might wish to type next.

The text in the upper-righthand corner (shown in red on the user's screen) consists of suggestions for replacing the last word, which are useful if you have typed a few characters of a word and would like eLocutor to guess the rest. Below that, in black, are suggestions for the next word if you have finished typing the last one. Groups of punctuation characters are treated as words, too, and since the last word consists of alphanumeric characters, the next one will be punctuation characters, as shown on the right side of Figure 30-1.

When the user is typing sentences similar to ones already typed, the suggestions at the bottom come in handy. The attention of the user, however, is mostly on the tree to the left, which is the only way she can take advantage of all the information on offer to influence the text in the middle box.

Below the tree, the user can see how many choices of various kinds are available to her, as well as other useful information discussed later.

The interface moves through the tree sequentially. With the one button at her disposal, the user clicks at the right time when the item she wishes to select is highlighted. The different windows in the screen show the user the options available for the next word, word completion, phrase completion, etc. To take advantage of these options, she must navigate until the corresponding choice is offered to her in the menu tree.

Input Interface

As the single binary input, we selected the right mouse button. This allowed a variety of buttons to easily be connected to eLocutor. By opening up the mouse and soldering the desired button in parallel with the right mouse button, any electrician or hobbyist should be able to make the connection.

Figure 30-2 shows how we made a temporary connection for Professor Hawking's special switch: the circuit board at the left bottom is taken from the inside of a mouse, and the points at which the external switch was soldered are the ones where the right mouse button is connected.

FIGURE 30-2. Connecting Professor Hawking's switch in parallel to the right mouse button

The Tree

If you can provide the software only a single binary input, one part of the graphic user interface is obvious: all choices have to be presented turn by turn in the form of a binary tree. At each node, if the user clicks within a fixed time, the interface selects it, which might open up further choices in the form of a subtree. If the user does not click, the software automatically takes him to the next sibling of the node and waits again for a click.

To implement this tree, we used the Visual Basic TreeView control.* This should be looked upon as a tree that grows from left to right. If, at any node, you click within a user-selected time interval—which is set using a Timer control—you expand the node and climb up the tree (i.e., move to the right), or, if it is a leaf node, carry out some action. If you don't click, eLocutor shifts its focus to the next sibling of the node. If the bottom is reached without a click, eLocutor starts again with the node at the top.

We populated the tree such that it provides, at each level in the tree, a node called Up that, if selected, takes the highlight to its parent, one level closer to the root.

The top-level nodes are Type, Scroll, Edit (the primary editing functions), and Commands (miscellaneous). Leaf nodes in the Type subtree enter text into the typing buffer. Those in the Edit subtree delete or copy text from this buffer, while those in the Scroll buffer control the movement of text between buffers.

The intelligence of eLocutor expresses itself by dynamically repopulating the tree, so that you can relatively quickly find the next action you wish to take: it learns in several different ways from your actions, to be better able to predict in the future.

* *http://www.virtualsplat.com/tips/visual-basic-treeview-control.asp.*

The biggest problem with binary input is navigation. If you are in the middle of typing and need to delete something at the start of the sentence, it takes a long time to wait for Up many times to get to the root, then down into Scroll to find the correct position to start deleting, then Up several times again to get to the root, then down into Edit for the deletion, then up and down again to scroll to the end, and again to return to typing. We were very relieved to find an answer to this dilemma.

The Long Click

From observing Professor Hawking use Equalizer, I discovered a new mode of operation: besides simply just clicking the button, he could hold down the button and release it at a strategic moment. The button, in effect, is not merely a binary input device, but actually an analog one, for it can provide a signal of varying duration. We thought long and hard about how best to use this new power we were presented with: we could now get more information out of a click than a simple bit. We could, for instance, allow the user to pick from a list of choices. A short click would now be used for the default action, while a long click opened up many other options.

Clearly, we wanted to use this newfound power for some extra choices for rapid navigation. We also were delighted with the ability to perform different operations on the text highlighted in the tree, such as to type it, copy it into the filter, etc. Without the long-click ability, we were limited to one action per leaf node, whereas now we could offer the user other choices regarding what to do with the highlighted tree node, which need not even be a leaf node.

The list of extra choices could not be too large, for that would require the user to hold down the button for relatively long periods of time. Consequently, we wanted these choices to change depending on where in the tree we were. "Type this" for instance, made no sense when we were in the Scroll subtree but was quite handy in the Speller.

What we came up with was a simple, easy-to-understand mode of operation. Clicking a node performs its default action. But if you keep the button pressed, a separate menu opens up whose options roll by one by one, from which you pick one by releasing the button when the desired choice shows up. We use this a bit like the right-click button under Microsoft Windows, to present the user context-sensitive menu choices. These typically include a jump to the root node of the tree, reverse traversal, etc.

The importance of this extra mode of operation can hardly be overstated: not only did it substantially increase the speed of text entry and correction, it provided tremendous flexibility to the developers.

An elegant solution was needed to make the long-click menu context-sensitive, for it would have been too cumbersome to create a special long-click menu for each node of the binary tree. Like the tree, long-click menus are stored in the form of text files, which are editable in eLocutor. In selecting the appropriate long-click menu, eLocutor looks to see which node is highlighted. If a text file exists with the same name as the node in the long-click directory, it is picked up as the menu. If it doesn't, eLocutor looks for the name of the node one level above in the tree, and so on.

In this way, each subtree can have its own long-click menu, entirely under the control of the user. Another way to present this design is to say that unless a child menu item chooses to override the long-click menu defined for its parent, the child automatically inherits the parent's menu.

Partial code for implementing the long click is shown in Example 30-1. OpenLongClick-File looks for and opens a file with the same name as the parameter passed to it, and if that is not found, recursively looks for one with the name of its parent. Each time the long-click timer times out, a fresh line from this file is displayed in the text box *tblongclick*. When the button is released, the command in *tblongclick* is selected. Depending on how long the button is held pressed, the long-click timer runs out repeatedly. Each time the timer runs out, it causes the code in Example 30-1 to check and set the Boolean variable ThisIsALongClick, and then to execute some code that needs to run only once in each long click in order to select and open the appropriate long-click file for reading.

The portion that repeats upon each expiration of the long-click timer reads a line from the file and displays it in the *tblongclick* text box. When the file reaches the end, it is closed and reopened, and the first line is read in. When the button is released, ThisIsALongClick is reset.

EXAMPLE 30-1. Implementing context-sensitive menu selection for the long click

```
Private Sub longclick_Timer( )
Dim st As String
Dim filenum As Long
    If Not ThisIsALongClick Then
        ThisIsALongClick = True
        If MenuTree.SelectedItem.Text = stStart Then
        'we are at the root already
            OpenLongClickFile MenuTree.SelectedItem
        Else
            OpenLongClickFile MenuTree.SelectedItem.Parent
'find the list of long-click menu choices suited for this context
        End If
    End If
    If EOF(longclickfilenum) Then
'list of choices finished, cycle to the first one by reopening file
        Close #longclickfilenum
        Open stlongclickfilename For Input As #longclickfilenum
    End If
    Line Input #longclickfilenum, st
    tblongclick = st
End Sub
```

Commands made available using the long click include:

>Start

Takes you to the root of the tree (the > indicates a "go to").

Upwards

Moves the cursor backward and upward in the tree until the right mouse button is clicked. Useful when you did not press the button when the desired menu choice was highlighted—i.e., you missed your turn.

Type This

> Types whatever is highlighted in the tree into the middle box. Available only under the Type subtree.

Set Filter

> Copies whatever is highlighted in the tree into the filter; useful for searching text. Also available as a long-click option only when the highlighted item is under the Type subtree.

Words Up, Words Down

> For rapid scrolling during typing, described later.

Pause

> Useful when a command has to be executed repeatedly. When the user holds the button down for a long click, the menu tree freezes, with one of its items highlighted. Selecting the long-click Pause option maintains this state of suspension. Now, each time the user clicks, the command highlighted in the menu tree is executed. To come out of pause, a long click must again be used.

Help

> Opens up and plays a context-sensitive *.avi* video file that explains the choices the tree is offering the user. The Help subdirectory contains a bunch of *.avi* files. It must contain at least one file, which is called *Start.avi*. When the Help long-click item is selected, the appropriate *.avi* file is played, based on where the user currently is in the menu tree.

The correct file to play is found in a fashion similar to the long-click menu. The software first looks for a file with an *.avi* extension in the *helpvideos* subdirectory of *C:\eLocutor*. If such a file is found, it is played; otherwise, eLocutor looks for an *.avi* file with the name of the parent of the highlighted node. If an *.avi* file with this name is not found in the *helpvideos* directory, eLocutor climbs recursively up the menu tree until it finds a node with a corresponding help video. This feature allowed us to ship only overview videos to start with, and gradually add more and more detailed videos, which the user only needed to copy into the *helpvideos* subdirectory for eLocutor to start showing them.

Some help videos are available at *http://www.holisticit.com/eLocutor/helpvideos.zip*. Given the dynamic nature of this software, watching some videos will help the reader understand this chapter faster and more thoroughly.

Dynamic Tree Repopulation

The contents of the tree are stored on disk in the form of text files. The big advantage of this approach is that these files can be edited dynamically both by eLocutor and by the user. In other words, they gave us an easy way to meet one of our design criteria: to allow the user herself to adapt eLocutor to her own needs, by making data structures transparent and easily user-editable.

Because eLocutor tries to predict what you may wish to do next, the binary tree needs to be dynamic; subtrees such as Next Word are frequently repopulated. The name of each file is the same as that of a node (with a *.txt* extension), and contains a list of names of its immediate children. If any of the node names end in *.txt*, they represent the root of a sub-tree, and the names of its children can be found in the corresponding file. For instance, the root file is named *Start.txt* and contains the lines *type.txt*, *edit.txt*, *scroll.txt*, and *commands.txt*, each line corresponding to a set of options displayed to the user for one of the menus described in the earlier section "The Tree."

A node name not ending in *.txt* represents a leaf node. Selecting it results in some action being taken. For instance, if the leaf node is in the Type subtree, its selection results in the corresponding text being typed into the buffer.

To indicate nodes that are dynamically repopulated, the prefix ^ is used. For instance, the following list shows the contents of *type.txt*, which form the child nodes of Type in the tree shown in Figure 30-1:

```
commonwords.txt
speller
^word completion.txt
^next word.txt
suffixes.txt
^justsaid.txt
^clipboard.txt
^phrase completion.txt
^templates.txt
vocabularytree.txt
```

Subtrees whose names are prefixed with ^ are populated only when the user clicks on the corresponding root node.

The Visual Basic TreeView control has an indexing feature to speed up retrieval. This feature made us think of creating nodes in the tree with words as names, grouped together such that siblings in a tree might replace one another in a sentence without making it sound absurd. For instance, a sentence including the word "London" could easily appear in another context with the word "Boston" in its place.

Using the index in this fashion allowed us to implement two critical features of eLocutor, Replace and Template, which are discussed shortly. The downside, though, was that we had to live with the limitations of the indexing feature of the Tree View control, which does not allow duplicate keys. Nothing prevented us from inserting more than one node with the same name into the tree. Only one of those, however, could be indexed.

The subnode vocabulary tree of Type is the root node of a large subtree, which groups words that might meaningfully replace one other in a sentence. For Replace and Template to work, these need to be indexed. However, the same word might show up at other places in the tree, perhaps as a suggestion for word completion or a next word. Those instances cannot be indexed. To keep it simple, we decided not to index the contents of dynamically repopulated subtrees.

Speller is treated as a special case. Its contents are not dynamic. However, the large number of leaf nodes it contains, besides the fact that it contains every word in the vocabulary tree, means it could not be indexed either. It is populated only as needed—i.e., the children of a node in the speller subtree are created only when it is selected.

Simple Typing

The Type subtree contains three nodes that help you do plain typing. Under Speller appear all the letters from a through z, which allow you to pick the first letter of the word you desire. You are then presented similar choices for the next letter, but only if that combination occurs at the start of a word in the dictionary. In this way, you pick letter by letter, until you have the full word. At this point, the node at which you find yourself may or may not be a leaf node. If it is a leaf node, you can type it by simply clicking it. But often it is not.

"Vocabularytree" and "commonwords," described later, are other nodes that make it easy for you to type. However, if the system's prediction feature is working well, which happens if you are trying to make a sentence similar to one in the database, you do not need these facilities often.

Prediction: Word Completion and Next Word

In the predictor database are several tables. One is a simple list of roughly 250,000 words used to populate the Word Completion subtree. A user who has typed one or more starting characters of a word can use this list to type the rest of the word, suggestions for which are shown to the right of the screen, in the above half, as shown in Figure 30-1. This table is available to the user in its entirety via the Speller subtree.

Say you wish to type the word *instant*. This is not a leaf node because words such as *instantaneous* exist that begin with *instant*. Hence, to type *instant*, you select each of the seven characters in turn, and then when *instant* is highlighted, you use a long click to invoke the Type This option.

Another table has the fields *word1*, *word2*, and *frequency*. To populate this table, a long list of sentences are provided to a piece of companion software, *dbmanager*, which tabulates how often each word follows each other word. Once you have typed a word, this table is queried and the Next Word subtree populated, so that it provides the user a list of words that are likely to follow this one.

Each sentence entered by the user through eLocutor is copied into the file *mailtomehtaatvsnldotcom.txt*. The reason for this filename was to gently encourage the user to mail me samples of text he had generated using eLocutor, so that I might get some ideas about how to make it more efficient. Users are advised to edit this file and remove whatever is inappropriate before feeding it to *dbmanager*, so that with time, prediction gets better. In case a software writer wishes to implement a better method of predicting the next word, all she has to do is to alter the query in the Access database; there is no need to delve into the eLocutor code for this.

A separate table lists combinations of punctuation characters occurring in the text supplied to the database, which are treated by eLocutor more or less as words.

It is hard for software to predict what the user might wish to type next, without a knowledge of semantics. We tried talking to linguists to see whether there was a reasonably easy way to make such predictions, but soon gave up. What we did instead was laboriously combine words into semantic groups under the "Vocabulary tree" subtree. For instance, the ancestry of "Boston" in the vocabulary tree is Nouns → Places → Cities. Of course, the user can use this subtree to actually type in words, but that isn't very convenient. The semantic subgroups are better for allowing the user to "fill in the blanks" in the Template and Replace features.

Templates and Replace

The user can select any sentence out of the database as a template to create new ones. This is done by first typing its starting word or words, and then looking under the Template subtree. At the bottom of the screen in Figure 30-1 are suggestions for completing the phrase or sentence. To populate this list, eLocutor looks in its database for sentences beginning with what has already been typed since the last sentence terminator. The same suggestions are also available under the Template subtree, with which the user can create new sentences by simply filling in the blanks in old ones. Should there be too many suggestions, a word or phrase can be put into the filter. Only phrases or sentences containing what is in the filter show up.

eLocutor processes templates by looking at the phrase selected as a template, word by word. Any word in the template not found in the vocabulary tree is directly typed into the buffer. For each word found in the vocabulary tree, using the TreeView indexing feature, eLocutor takes the user to that part of the tree, allowing him to pick it or one of its siblings. So, if the sentence "How are you?" is in the database, the user needs just a few rapid clicks to type, "How is she?" While such "fill in the blanks" is taking place, the portion of the template not yet used is visible in the Template box under the tree.

The Template feature takes advantage of the logical grouping of words under the vocabulary tree to transform the contents of an entire sentence or phrase. The Replace feature allows the user a similar facility on just a single word, the last one found in the middle box. However, not all words are listed under the vocabulary tree. A text box on the screen is therefore needed to tell the user which category, if any, the word in question is found under. On the screen is a box captioned Replace. If the last word in the buffer is found in the vocabulary tree, the name of its parent is written into the Replace text box.

For instance, if the last word in the buffer is Boston, the Replace text box contains the word Cities. This tells the user that the software has recognized the category of the last word. If she then selects the Replace command (under the Word Completion subtree), the last word is deleted from the buffer and the user is taken to the place in the vocabulary tree where it was found, allowing her to easily find another city name to replace it with.

In Figure 30-1, the last word typed is We. The Replace box shows subjectpronoun (which doesn't entirely fit in the space provided). Selecting Replace deletes the We and takes the user to the subjectpronoun subtree, where she could easily select You, for instance.

The Cache Implementation

Caching in eLocutor relies on the subroutine SaveReverse, which takes two parameters: the name of the file in which the text is to be saved, and the text itself. The subroutine replaces the file with a fresh one, in which the text passed to SaveReverse is the first line of the file, followed by the first 19 lines of the original contents that do not match the first line.

This is achieved by first writing the text represented by the variable stringtoadd into the first element of starray, then filling the rest of the array with lines from the file as long as they are not the same as stringtoadd (HistoryLength is a constant of value 20). Finally, the file is opened for writing, which causes its previous contents to be deleted, and the entire contents of starray are copied to the file.

Thus, if a city name already listed in *favouritecities.txt* is used, it simply changes position to become the first name in the file. If a new city name is used, it also becomes the first name, followed by the first 19 lines of the previous contents of the file. In other words, the last line of the file is dropped, and it gets a new first line. As the name of the routine suggests, lines of text are saved in reverse, so the last used word becomes the first.

The code for SaveReverse is shown in Example 30-2.

EXAMPLE 30-2. Adding text to the start of a text file, without duplication

```
Sub SaveReverse(ByVal filest As String, ByVal stringtoadd As String) 'not
'an append, a prepend...
'with elimination of duplicates
    Dim starray(HistoryLength) As String
    Dim i As Long
    Dim arrlength As Long
    Dim st As String
    Dim filenum As Long
    starray(0) = stringtoadd
    filenum = FreeFile
    i = 1
    On Error GoTo err1
    Open filest For Input As #filenum
    While Not EOF(filenum) And (i < HistoryLength)
        Line Input #filenum, st
        If (st <> stringtoadd) Then      'only save non-duplicates
            starray(i) = st
            i = i + 1
        End If
    Wend
    arrlength = i - 1
    Close #filenum
    Open filest For Output As #filenum     'this deletes the existing file contents
    For i = 0 To arrlength
        Print #filenum, starray(i)
    Next
    Close #filenum
    Exit Sub
```

```
err1:
'    MsgBox "error with file " + filest
     Open filest For Output As #filenum
     Close #filenum
     Open filest For Input As #filenum       'this creates an empty file if one does 'not
exist
     Resume Next
End Sub
```

Common Words and Favorites

Frequently used words are collected in the "common words" subtree, which has two components. Part of this subtree is static, consisting of very frequently used words such as *a*, *and*, *but*, etc. The dynamic part contains additional words frequently used by the user, which are found under its "favouritechoices" subtree.

The last 20 words found by the user in Speller can be found under its "favouritespeller" subtree. Likewise, if a node exists in the vocabulary tree called "cities," the user needs only to create a blank file, *favouritecities.txt*. Thereafter, the last 20 selections made by the user of words found under the cities subtree will be available under "favouritecities" in the "favouritechoices" subtree. In this way, the user can decide himself what kind of words, if used frequently, are worth remembering, and how they should be slotted.

Example 30-3 shows the subroutine that creates a new "favourites" and inserts it into the tree. Please note that stfavourite is the constant favorite, and MakeFullFileName returns a proper filename including the path, filename, and *.txt* extension.

EXAMPLE 30-3. How eLocutor files words already typed under "favourites"

```
Public Sub AddToFavourites(parentnode As Node, stAdd As String)
Dim tempfilename As String
     If parentnode.Text = stStart Then
         Exit Sub
     End If
     tempfilename = MakeFullFileName(App.Path, stfavourite + parentnode.Text)
     If FileExists(tempfilename) Then
         SaveReverse tempfilename, stAdd
     Else
         AddToFavourites parentnode.Parent, stAdd
     End If
End Sub
```

Whenever a word is typed, eLocutor looks to see whether it also can be found in the vocabulary tree. Suppose the word Boston has just been typed. In that case, Boston is inserted at the top of the file *favouritecities.txt*, if it exists, using the subroutine SaveReverse. If not, eLocutor looks for *favouriteplaces.txt*, because the parent of Cities is Places. If that file doesn't exist, eLocutor tries a higher ancestor. If *favouriteplaces.txt* does exist, Boston is added to that file using the same subroutine. This provides the user with some control over what the software should consider her "favourites." By creating a file called *favouritecities.txt*, she is telling eLocutor that she uses city names a lot.

Retracing Paths

To aid in rapid navigation in a rather large tree, eLocutor automatically remembers, for each subtree in which the user has made a selection, what the user did the last 20 times after making a selection here. These destinations are presented conveniently to the user. Each parent node *x* has a subtree *x*_Next. After selecting a leaf node, the user should look under the sibling _Next node and select a destination close to where she wants to go next. Effectively, eLocutor detects patterns in operations performed by the user and allows her to repeat them easily. The software also remembers the last 20 files that were opened, the last 20 items of text searched for, and the last 20 statements spoken by the user. All of these were easily implemented using SaveReverse.

The Typing Buffer, Editing, and Scrolling

There were several different ways we could have handled the scrolling of text, and its selection for cutting and pasting. Most editors work with a single window. In the case of a large document, of course, the entire text does not fit in the window displayed, and scrollbars are used to navigate through the text. When text needs to be copied or cut, it has to be first selected. The selected text is highlighted using different foreground and background colors. We had some problems with this standard approach.

We wanted eLocutor to also be usable by persons with cerebral palsy, who often have severe motor disabilities resulting in speech and vision impairment. For them, we needed to show at least part of the text in a very large font. If we were to use this for all text on the screen, we wouldn't have much on the screen at all. We felt it would be awkward to use a substantially larger font for part of the text in a window. Text highlighted for cutting and pasting by changing background color was found by some to be distracting and difficult to read. Our experience in, and fondness of, audio editing led us to select a different paradigm.

In the old days, when audio recording was done using spools of tape, the editor would listen to the tape until he found the start of the portion he wanted to cut, clamp it there, then listen for the end of the portion that was to be deleted, and clamp there again. Now, the portion in between the clamps could easily be cut, or replaced with something else. The tape, therefore, is divided by the two clamps into three sections: that before clamp 1, that after clamp 2, and the portion between clamps.

We adopted the same approach with text, dividing it into three text boxes, with gates between them. Typing is all done at the end of the text in the middle box. This is where the text actually gets inserted and deleted. The Backspace option under Edit deletes text in the middle box from the end. You can decide whether you want to get rid of a character, word, phrase, sentence, paragraph, or the entire middle box.

If you select Cut or Copy under Edit, the entire text in the middle box is copied into the clipboard. Cut, of course, leaves the middle box empty. To compare this with conventional editors, which allow you to set the beginning and the ending of the block of text you wish to cut or copy, imagine that the block begins at the boundary between the upper and the middle box, and ends at the boundary between the middle box and the lower box. Cut or Copy always lifts the entire contents of the middle box.

Having the text in multiple boxes in this way allowed us to make more intensive use of screen real estate. We showed the text in the upper box only during scrolling. At other times, we could use it to show the highlighted tree item in large font, as in Figure 30-1, or the contents of lower levels of the tree to provide the user with a "look ahead." Similarly, we reused the space for the lower box to display the long-click menu at the appropriate time.

There was much trial and error in figuring out what worked best, in use of screen real estate. When individual users make special requests with regard to what they wish to view on the screen, we try to accommodate those in the spaces for the upper and lower boxes.

Analogous to the clamps in audio editing, we have gates. If you wish to cut out a large segment of text, you first scroll until the start of the segment is at the beginning of the middle box. We now close the gate between it at the upper box, so that scrolling does not move text past this boundary: the text is "clamped" at this point. You continue scrolling up or down until the end of the segment you wish to cut is at the end of the middle box. You can now select Cut under Edit.

Menu choices under Scroll allow one or both gates to be opened. Red and green circles show the status of the gates. In Figure 30-1, both gates are open, indicated by green circles to the left and right of the middle box. Two commands, Text Up and Text Down, are available to move text between the boxes. For text to be able to move between the top and the middle box, or between the middle box and the bottom box, the corresponding gate must be open.

The amount of text moved by the text up/down commands depends on the marker selected by the user, which can be character, word, punctuation mark, sentence, or paragraph. The scroll marker currently selected is shown on the screen below the tree. Commands are also available to move the entire contents of the text boxes from one to the other.

In order to be able to scroll a small amount during typing, Words Down and Words Up options are available using the long click. When one of these is selected, words scroll in the selected direction until the right mouse button is clicked again. Note that combinations of punctuation characters are treated as words, too. This allows the user to make quick corrections in the immediate vicinity of the point of insertion or deletion of text, to rapidly scroll a bit while typing.

The Clipboard

When the user selects Cut or Copy in the Edit subtree, SaveReverse is invoked to prepend the contents of the middle box to the file *clipboard.txt*, keeping a total of 20 paragraphs. The advantage of this approach is that it allows paragraphs to be easily rearranged, and older cuts to be pasted again and again. In most text editors, each time Cut or Copy is selected, the previous contents of the clipboard are lost. In eLocutor, older clipboard information hangs around for a while.

Searching

No self-respecting editor can lack a search function, but eLocutor allowed us to look at this basic function afresh. We realized that searching is indeed just a special case of scrolling, so we merely extended our scroll implementation. The user can copy text from the middle box into the filter buffer, or select Set Filter with the desired text highlighted in the tree via a long click. When text is present in the filter, and a scroll command is given, scrolling does not stop until the contents of the filter are also found in the middle box, or the end of text reached.

Macros

An interesting point came up in one of our discussions with Professor Hawking's office. They told me he sometimes had problems with Equalizer when delivering a speech, if the lighting made it hard for him to read the screen. Without being able to read the screen, he found it hard to alternately scroll the text, then issue a speak command.

In eLocutor, it already was possible to put the entire text of the speech in the middle box and issue a command to the software to say it, but that was insufficient. People might clap or laugh in the middle, so he needed to be able to wait for them to subside before continuing to deliver the lecture.

It would not have been hard to build in a function to scroll and speak a sentence each time the user selected a particular menu item, but rather than hardcode this, we thought it would be better to address this problem at a more general level, by providing a macro function that would allow other such combinations to be made in the future.

In the Commands subtree is a node called Macros, under which all files in the subdirectory *C:\eLocutor\macros* are listed. If any of these is selected, the file is opened, and the commands listed in it are executed one by one. No complexities are possible in macro design: no jumps, loops, or branching.

For speech delivery, we created two short macros, preparespeech and scrollspeak. preparespeech opens both gates if they aren't already, and pushes the entire text into the lower box. Having executed this macro, the user then selects Pause via a long click when scrollspeak is highlighted. All this could be done in advance.

Once on stage, the user does not need to look at the screen. Each time he now clicks, he executes scrollclick, so that effectively two commands are executed. First is a Text Up command, which sends as much text as decided by the scroll marker from the lower box into the middle box, and from the middle box to the top box. The second command speaks the contents of the middle box. Typically, for speech delivery, the scroll marker would be set to a sentence, so that the speech is delivered a sentence at a time, but if greater flexibility were desired, it could be set to a paragraph as well.

Efficiency of the User Interface

In order to help in evaluating the efficiency of eLocutor in helping you type, the bottom right of the screen shows two numbers (see Figure 30-2). These indicate the number of clicks and the number of seconds between the last click and the first, since the middle box was last empty.

We found that when the prediction worked reasonably well, the ratio of clicks to characters typed was better than 0.8—i.e., it usually required significantly fewer clicks than an able-bodied person would have needed using a full keyboard. When prediction was poor—for instance when constructing a sentence radically different from any in the database—it required up to twice as many clicks as characters typed.

Download

ELocutor is free, open source software downloadable from *http://holisticit.com/eLocutor/ elocutorv3.htm*. A discussion list is located at *http://groups.yahoo.com/group/radiophony*.

Part of the download is the entire source code. I might warn you, though, that it bears some resemblance to a bowl of spaghetti, for which I bear full responsibility. I hadn't programmed for more than 10 years when I started this project, so my skills were outdated and rusty. I did not have a design, only a few hints now and then on the direction in which it should evolve. The code grew with my understanding of the problem, and the results show it. Very simple programming techniques have been used, as is obvious from the code shown in this chapter.

Future Directions

eLocutor was always intended as a rapid application development (RAD) project,* something that would allow me to show Professor Hawking during our infrequent and short meetings how far the design had progressed. The intention was to rewrite it some time, after the design could be frozen in the shape of a working prototype that people had actually been using and providing feedback on. At that point, I would pick a programming language that worked across platforms, so that Macs or Linux should also be accessible to those severely motor disabled.

However, inspired by what T. V. Raman achieved with Emacspeak (covered in Chapter 31), I am now considering an entirely different kind of project. Emacs is, of course, not just an editor, but a very versatile platform that people have extended over the years to allow you to read mail, handle appointments, browse the Web, execute shell commands, etc. By merely adding on a smart text-to-speech capability and context-sensitive commands, Raman brilliantly made everything that could be accessed through Emacs accessible to the blind.

---

* *http://en.wikipedia.org/wiki/Rapid_application_development*.

So, I'm wondering whether the same can be done for the motor disabled. Advantages of this approach are:

- Designers would no longer have to worry about the mouse, for Emacs allows you to do everything without it.

- eLocutor wouldn't just be an accessible editor, but would rather make all the capabilities of the computer accessible.

- I might also find more support this way among the open source developer community, which seems to be far better on platforms historically associated closely with Emacs use than in the MS Windows world.

I am therefore appealing to readers of this chapter to teach me how to extend Emacs such that the same one-button navigation of a tree becomes possible. Better still would be someone wishing to take up this project with whatever help I might be able to provide.

Another direction to take this software would be to address the enormous problem of children who become disabled in the first years of life, such as those with cerebral palsy and severe autism, who typically do not get an education because they cannot communicate back to the teacher in a normal classroom. If such a child could communicate via software, she might be able to attend normal school.

Here, the challenge for the software writer is even greater. Normally, you assume that a person using a computer is literate. In this case, the child has to be able to use a computer in order to *become* literate. The software we write must appeal to a child enough to entice her to use it as her primary means of communicating with the world, before she can read. What a daunting, yet hugely interesting task! Of course, the software would be great in teaching any child how to use a computer at a very early age, not just disabled kids. Anyone willing to collaborate?

## CHAPTER THIRTY-ONE

Emacspeak: The Complete Audio Desktop

T. V. Raman

A DESKTOP IS A WORKSPACE THAT ONE USES TO ORGANIZE THE TOOLS OF ONE'S TRADE. Graphical desktops provide rich visual interaction for performing day-to-day computing tasks; the goal of the *audio desktop* is to enable similar efficiencies in an eyes-free environment. Thus, the primary goal of an audio desktop is to use the expressiveness of auditory output (both verbal and nonverbal) to enable the end user to perform a full range of computing tasks:

- Communication through the full range of electronic messaging services

- Ready access to local documents on the client and global documents on the Web

- Ability to develop software effectively in an eyes-free environment

The Emacspeak audio desktop was motivated by the following insight: to provide effective auditory renderings of information, one needs to start from the actual information being presented, rather than a visual presentation of that information. This had earlier led me to develop AsTeR, Audio System For Technical Readings (*http://emacspeak.sf.net/raman/aster/ aster-toplevel.html*). The primary motivation then was to apply the lessons learned in the context of aural documents to user interfaces—after all, the document *is* the interface.

The primary goal was not to merely carry the visual interface over to the auditory modality, but rather to create an eyes-free user interface that is both pleasant and productive to use.

Contrast this with the traditional screen-reader approach where GUI widgets such as sliders and tree controls are directly translated to spoken output. Though such direct translation can give the appearance of providing full eyes-free access, the resulting auditory user interface can be inefficient to use.

These prerequisites meant that the environment selected for the audio desktop needed:

- A core set of speech and nonspeech audio output services
- A rich suite of pre-existing applications to speech-enable
- Access to application context to produce contextual feedback

Producing Spoken Output

I started implementing Emacspeak in October 1994. The target environments were a Linux laptop and my office workstation. To produce speech output, I used a DECTalk Express (a hardware speech synthesizer) on the laptop and a software version of the DECTalk on the office workstation.

The most natural way to design the system to leverage both speech options was to first implement a speech server that abstracted away the distinction between the two output solutions. The speech server abstraction has withstood the test of time well; I was able to add support for the IBM ViaVoice engine later, in 1999. Moreover, the simplicity of the client/server API has enabled open source programmers to implement speech servers for other speech engines.

Emacspeak speech servers are implemented in the TCL language. The speech server for the DECTalk Express communicated with the hardware synthesizer over a serial line. As an example, the command to speak a string of text was a proc that took a string argument and wrote it to the serial device. A simplified version of this looks like:

```
proc tts_say  {text} {puts -nonewline  $tts(write) "$text"}
```

The speech server for the software DECTalk implemented an equivalent, simplified tts_say version that looks like:

```
proc say  {text} {_say "$text"}
```

where _say calls the underlying C implementation provided by the DECTalk software.

The net result of this design was to create separate speech servers for each available engine, where each speech server was a simple script that invoked TCL's default read-eval-print loop after loading in the relevant definitions. The client/server API therefore came down to the client (Emacspeak) launching the appropriate speech server, caching this connection, and invoking server commands by issuing appropriate procedure calls over this connection.

Notice that so far I have said nothing explicit about how this client/server connection was opened; this late-binding proved beneficial later when it came to making Emacspeak network-aware. Thus, the initial implementation worked by the Emacspeak client communicating to the speech server using stdio. Later, making this client/server communication go over the network required the addition of a few lines of code that opened a server socket and connected stdin/stdout to the resulting connection.

Thus, designing a clean client/server abstraction, and relying on the power of Unix I/O, has made it trivial to later run Emacspeak on a remote machine and have it connect back to a speech server running on a local client. This enables me to run Emacspeak inside *screen* on my work machine, and access this running session from anywhere in the world. Upon connecting, I have the remote Emacspeak session connect to a speech server on my laptop, the audio equivalent of setting up X to use a remote display.

Speech-Enabling Emacs

The simplicity of the speech server abstraction described above meant that version 0 of the speech server was running within an hour after I started implementing the system. This meant that I could then move on to the more interesting part of the project: producing good quality spoken output. Version 0 of the speech server was by no means perfect; it was improved as I built the Emacspeak speech client.

A Simple First-Cut Implementation

A friend of mine had pointed me at the marvels of Emacs Lisp *advice* a few weeks earlier. Som when I sat down to speech-enable Emacs, *advice* was the natural choice. The first task was to have Emacs automatically speak the line under the cursor whenever the user pressed the up/down arrow keys.

In Emacs, all user actions invoke appropriate Emacs Lisp functions. In standard editing modes, pressing the down arrow invokes function next-line, while pressing the up arrow invokes previous-line. To speech-enable these commands, version 0 of Emacspeak implemented the following rather simple advice fragment:

```
(defadvice next-line (after emacspeak)
  "Speak line after moving."
  (when (interactive-p) (emacspeak-speak-line)))
```

The emacspeak-speak-line function implemented the necessary logic to grab the text of the line under the cursor and send it to the speech server. With the previous definition in place, Emacspeak 0.0 was up and running; it provided the scaffolding for building the actual system.

Iterating on the First-Cut Implementation

The next iteration returned to the speech server to enhance it with a well-defined eventing loop. Rather than simply executing each speech command as it was received, the speech server queued client requests and provided a launch command that caused the server to execute queued requests.

The server used the select system call to check for newly arrived commands after sending each clause to the speech engine. This enabled immediate silencing of speech; with the somewhat naïve implementation described in version 0 of the speech server, the command to stop speech would not take immediate effect since the speech server would first process previously issued speak commands to completion. With the speech queue in place, the client application could now queue up arbitrary amounts of text and still get a high degree of responsiveness when issuing higher-priority commands such as requests to stop speech.

Implementing an event queue inside the speech server also gave the client application finer control over how text was split into chunks before synthesis. This turns out to be crucial for producing good intonation structure. The rules by which text should be split up into clauses varies depending on the nature of the text being spoken. As an example, newline characters in programming languages such as Python are statement delimiters and determine clause boundaries, but newlines do not constitute clause delimiters in English text.

As an example, a clause boundary is inserted after each line when speaking the following Python code:

```
i=1
j=2
```

See the section "Augmenting Emacs to create aural display lists," later in this chapter, for details on how Python code is distinguished and its semantics are transferred to the speech layer.

With the speech server now capable of smart text handling, the Emacspeak client could become more sophisticated with respect to its handling of text. The emacspeak-speak-line function turned into a library of speech-generation functions that implemented the following steps:

1. Parse text to split it into a sequence of clauses.

2. Preprocess text—e.g., handle repeated strings of punctuation marks.

3. Carry out a number of other functions that got added over time.

4. Queue each clause to the speech server, and issue the launch command.

From here on, the rest of Emacspeak was implemented using Emacspeak as the development environment. This has been significant in how the code base has evolved. New features are tested immediately because badly implemented features can render the entire system unusable. Lisp's incremental code development fits naturally with the former; to cover the latter, the Emacspeak code base has evolved to be "bushy"—i.e., most parts of the higher-level system are mutually independent and depend on a small core that is carefully maintained.

A Brief advice Tutorial

Lisp *advice* is key to the Emacspeak implementation, and this chapter would not be complete without a brief overview. The *advice* facility allows one to modify existing functions *without changing the original implementation*. What's more, once a function f has been modified by *advice* m, all calls to function f are affected by *advice*.

advice comes in three flavors:

before
> The advice body is run *before* the original function is invoked.

after
> The advice body is run *after* the original function has completed.

around
> The advice body is run *instead of* the original function. The around advice can call the original function if desired.

All *advice* forms get access to the arguments of the *adviced* function; in addition, around and after get access to the return value computed by the original function. The Lisp implementation achieves this magic by:

1. Caching the original implementation of the function

2. Evaluating the advice form to generate a new function definition

3. Storing this definition as the *adviced* function

Thus, when the *advice* fragment shown in the earlier section "A Simple First-Cut Implementation" is evaluated, Emacs' original next-line function is replaced by a modified version that speaks the current line *after* the original next-line function has completed its work.

Generating Rich Auditory Output

At this point in its evolution, here is what the overall design looked like:

1. Emacs' interactive commands are speech-enabled or *adviced* to produce auditory output.

2. *advice* definitions are collected into modules, one each for every Emacs application being speech-enabled.

3. The *advice* forms forward text to core speech functions.

4. These functions extract the text to be spoken and forward it to the tts-speak function.

5. The tts-speak function produces auditory output by preprocessing its text argument and sending it to the speech server.

6. The speech server handles queued requests to produce perceptible output.

Text is preprocessed by placing the text in a special scratch buffer. Buffers acquire specialized behavior via buffer-specific *syntax tables* that define the *grammar* of buffer contents and buffer-local variables that affect behavior. When text is handed off to the Emacspeak core, all of these buffer-specific settings are propagated to the special scratch buffer where the text is preprocessed. This automatically ensures that text is meaningfully parsed into clauses based on its underlying grammar.

Audio formatting using voice-lock

Emacs uses font-lock to syntactically color text. For creating the visual presentation, Emacs adds a text property called face to text strings; the value of this face property specifies the font, color, and style to be used to display that text. Text strings with face properties can be thought of as a conceptual *visual display list*.

Emacspeak augments these visual display lists with personality text properties whose values specify the auditory properties to use when rendering a given piece of text; this is called voice-lock in Emacspeak. The value of the personality property is an Aural CSS (ACSS) setting that encodes various voice properties—e.g., the pitch of the speaking voice. Notice that such ACSS settings are not specific to any given TTS engine. Emacspeak implements ACSS-to-TTS mappings in engine-specific modules that take care of mapping high-level aural properties—e.g., mapping pitch or pitch-range to engine-specific control codes.

The next few sections describe how Emacspeak augments Emacs to create aural display lists and to process these aural display lists to produce engine-specific output.

Augmenting Emacs to create aural display lists

Emacs modules that implement font-lock call the Emacs built-in function put-text-property to attach the relevant face property. Emacspeak defines an advice fragment that *advices* the put-text-property function to add in the corresponding personality property when it is asked to add a face property. Note that the value of both display properties (face and personality) can be lists; values of these properties are thus designed to *cascade* to create the final (visual or auditory) presentation. This also means that different parts of an application can progressively add display property values.

The put-text-property function has the following signature:

```
(put-text-property START END PROPERTY VALUE &optional OBJECT)
```

The *advice* implementation is:

```
(defadvice put-text-property (after emacspeak-personality  pre act)
  "Used by emacspeak to augment font lock."
  (let ((start (ad-get-arg 0)) ;; Bind  arguments
        (end (ad-get-arg 1 ))
        (prop (ad-get-arg 2)) ;; name of property being added
        (value (ad-get-arg 3 ))
        (object (ad-get-arg 4))
        (voice nil))                          ;; voice it maps to
```

```
(when (and (eq prop 'face)      ;; avoid infinite recursion
           (not (= start end))  ;; non-nil text range
           emacspeak-personality-voiceify-faces)
  (condition-case nil ;; safely look up face mapping
      (progn
        (cond
         ((symbolp value)
          (setq voice (voice-setup-get-voice-for-face value)))
         ((ems-plain-cons-p value)) ;;pass on plain cons
         ( (listp value)
           (setq voice
                 (delq nil
                       (mapcar   #'voice-setup-get-voice-for-face value))))
         (t (message "Got %s" value)))
        (when voice ;; voice  holds list of  personalities
          (funcall emacspeak-personality-voiceify-faces start end voice object)))
    (error nil)))))
```

Here is a brief explanation of this *advice* definition:

Bind arguments

First, the function uses the *advice* built-in ad-get-arg to locally bind a set of lexical variables to the arguments being passed to the *adviced* function.

Personality setter

The mapping of faces to personalities is controlled by user customizable variable emacspeak-personality-voiceify-faces. If non-nil, this variable specifies a function with the following signature:

(emacspeak-personality-put *START END PERSONALITY OBJECT*)

Emacspeak provides different implementations of this function that either append or prepend the new personality value to any existing personality properties.

Guard

Along with checking for a non-nil emacspeak-personality-voiceify-faces, the function performs additional checks to determine whether this advice definition should do anything. The function continues to act if:

- The text range is non-nil.

- The property being added is a face.

The first of these checks is required to avoid edge cases where put-text-property is called with a zero-length text range. The second ensures that we attempt to add the personality property only when the property being added is face. Notice that failure to include this second test would cause infinite recursion because the eventual put-text-property call that adds the personality property also triggers the advice definition.

Get mapping

Next, the function *safely* looks up the voice mapping of the face (or faces) being applied. If applying a single face, the function looks up the corresponding personality mapping; if applying a list of faces, it creates a corresponding list of personalities.

Apply personality

Finally, the function checks that it found a valid voice mapping and, if so, calls `emacspeak-personality-voiceify-faces` with the set of personalities saved in the voice variable.

Audio-formatted output from aural display lists

With the *advice* definitions from the previous section in place, text fragments that are visually styled acquire a corresponding `personality` property that holds an ACSS setting for audio formatting the content. The result is to turn text in Emacs into rich aural display lists. This section describes how the output layer of Emacspeak is enhanced to convert these aural display lists into perceptible spoken output.

The Emacspeak `tts-speak` module handles text preprocessing before finally sending it to the speech server. As described earlier, this preprocessing comprises a number of steps, including:

1. Applying pronunciation rules

2. Processing repeated strings of punctuation characters

3. Splitting text into appropriate clauses based on context

4. Converting the `personality` property into audio formatting codes

This section describes the `tts-format-text-and-speak` function, which handles the conversion of aural display lists into audio-formatted output. First, here is the code for the function `tts-format-text-and-speak`:

```
(defsubst tts-format-text-and-speak (start end )
  "Format and speak text between start and end."
  (when (and emacspeak-use-auditory-icons
             (get-text-property start 'auditory-icon)) ;;queue  icon
    (emacspeak-queue-auditory-icon (get-text-property start 'auditory-icon)))
  (tts-interp-queue (format "%s\n" tts-voice-reset-code))
  (cond
   (voice-lock-mode ;;  audio format only if voice-lock-mode is on
    (let ((last  nil) ;; initialize
          (personality (get-text-property start 'personality )))
      (while (and  (
< start end ) ;; chunk at personality changes
                 (setq last
                       (next-single-property-change  start 'personality
                                                     (current-buffer) end)))
        (if personality ;; audio format chunk
            (tts-speak-using-voice personality (buffer-substring start last ))
          (tts-interp-queue (buffer-substring  start last)))
        (setq start  last ;; prepare for next chunk
              personality (get-text-property last  'personality)))))
   ;; no voice-lock just send the text
   (t (tts-interp-queue (buffer-substring start end  )))))
```

The `tts-format-text-and-speak` function is called one clause at a time, with arguments start and end set to the start and end of the clause. If `voice-lock-mode` is turned on, this function further splits the clause into chunks at each point in the text where there is a change in value of the personality property. Once such a transition point has been determined, `tts-format-text-and-speak` calls the function `tts-speak-using-voice`, passing the personality to use and the text to be spoken. This function, described next, looks up the appropriate device-specific codes before dispatching the audio-formatted output to the speech server:

```
(defsubst tts-speak-using-voice (voice text)
  "Use voice VOICE to speak text TEXT."
  (unless (or (eq 'inaudible voice ) ;; not spoken if voice inaudible
              (and (listp voice) (member 'inaudible voice)))
    (tts-interp-queue
     (format
      "%s%s %s \n"
      (cond
       ((symbolp voice)
        (tts-get-voice-command
         (if (boundp  voice ) (symbol-value voice ) voice)))
       ((listp voice)
        (mapconcat #'(lambda (v)
                       (tts-get-voice-command
                        (if (boundp  v ) (symbol-value v ) v)))
                   voice
                   " "))
       (t        ""))
      text tts-voice-reset-code))))
```

The `tts-speak-using-voice` function returns immediately if the specified voice is inaudible. Here, `inaudible` is a special personality that Emacspeak uses to prevent pieces of text from being spoken. The `inaudible` personality can be used to advantage when selectively hiding portions of text to produce more succinct output.

If the specified voice (or list of voices) is not `inaudible`, the function looks up the speech codes for the voice and queues the result of wrapping the text to be spoken between `voice-code` and `tts-reset-code` to the speech server.

Using Aural CSS (ACSS) for Styling Speech Output

I first formalized audio formatting within AsTeR, where rendering rules were written in a specialized language called Audio Formatting Language (AFL). AFL structured the available parameters in auditory space—e.g., the pitch of the speaking voice—into a multidimensional space, and encapsulated the state of the rendering engine as a point in this multidimensional space.

AFL provided a block-structured language that encapsulated the current rendering state by a lexically scoped variable, and provided operators to move within this structured space. When these notions were later mapped to the declarative world of HTML and CSS, dimensions making up the AFL rendering state became Aural CSS parameters, provided as accessibility measures in CSS2 (*http://www.w3.org/Press/1998/CSS2-REC*).

Though designed for styling HTML (and, in general, XML) markup trees, Aural CSS turned out to be a good abstraction for building Emacspeak's audio formatting layer while keeping the implementation independent of any given TTS engine.

Here is the definition of the data structure that encapsulates ACSS settings:

```
(defstruct acss
   family gain left-volume right-volume
   average-pitch pitch-range stress richness punctuations)
```

Emacspeak provides a collection of predefined *voice overlays* for use within speech extensions. Voice overlays are designed to *cascade* in the spirit of Aural CSS. As an example, here is the ACSS setting that corresponds to voice-monotone:

```
[cl-struct-acss nil nil nil nil nil 0 0 nil all]
```

Notice that most fields of this acss structure are nil—that is, unset. The setting creates a voice overlay that:

1. Sets pitch to 0 to create a flat voice.

2. Sets pitch-range to 0 to create a monotone voice with no inflection.

    This setting is used as the value of the personality property for audio formatting comments in all programming language modes. Because its value is an overlay, it can interact effectively with other aural display properties. As an example, if portions of a comment are displayed in a bold font, those portions can have the voice-bolden personality (another predefined overlay) added; this results in setting the personality property to a list of two values: (voice-bolden voice-monotone). The final effect is for the text to get spoken with a distinctive voice that conveys both aspects of the text: namely, a sequence of words that are emphasized within a comment.

3. Sets punctuations to all so that all punctuation marks are spoken.

Adding Auditory Icons

Rich visual user interfaces contain both text and icons. Similarly, once Emacspeak had the ability to speak intelligently, the next step was to increase the bandwidth of aural communication by augmenting the output with auditory icons.

Auditory icons in Emacspeak are short sound snippets (no more than two seconds in duration) and are used to indicate frequently occurring events in the user interface. As an example, every time the user saves a file, the system plays a confirmatory sound. Similarly, opening or closing an object (anything from a file to a web site) produces a corresponding auditory icon. The set of auditory icons were arrived at iteratively and cover common events such as objects being opened, closed, or deleted. This section describes how these auditory icons are injected into Emacspeak's output stream.

Auditory icons are produced by the following user interactions:

- To cue explicit user actions

- To add additional cues to spoken output

Auditory icons that confirm user actions—e.g., a file being saved successfully—are produced by adding an after *advice* to the various Emacs built-ins. To provide a consistent sound and feel across the Emacspeak desktop, such extensions are attached to code that is called from many places in Emacs.

Here is an example of such an extension, implemented via an *advice* fragment:

```
(defadvice save-buffer (after emacspeak pre act)
  "Produce an auditory icon if possible."
  (when (interactive-p) (emacspeak-auditory-icon 'save-object)
    (or emacspeak-last-message (message "Wrote %s" (buffer-file-name)))))
```

Extensions can also be implemented via an Emacs-provided hook. As explained in the brief *advice* tutorial given earlier, *advice* allows the behavior of existing software to be extended or modified without having to modify the underlying source code. Emacs is itself an extensible system, and well-written Lisp code has a tradition of providing appropriate extension hooks for common use cases. As an example, Emacspeak attaches auditory feedback to Emacs' default prompting mechanism (the Emacs minibuffer) by adding the function `emacspeak-minibuffer-setup-hook` to Emacs' `minibuffer-setup-hook`:

```
(defun emacspeak-minibuffer-setup-hook ()
  "Actions to take when entering the minibuffer."
  (let ((inhibit-field-text-motion t))
    (when emacspeak-minibuffer-enter-auditory-icon
      (emacspeak-auditory-icon 'open-object))
    (tts-with-punctuations 'all (emacspeak-speak-buffer))))
(add-hook 'minibuffer-setup-hook 'emacspeak-minibuffer-setup-hook)
```

This is a good example of using built-in extensibility where available. However, Emacspeak uses *advice* in a lot of cases because the Emacspeak requirement of adding auditory feedback to *all* of Emacs was not originally envisioned when Emacs was implemented. Thus, the Emacspeak implementation demonstrates a powerful technique for *discovering* extension points.

Lack of an *advice*-like feature in a programming language often makes experimentation difficult, especially when it comes to discovering useful extension points. This is because software engineers are faced with the following trade-off:

- Make the system arbitrarily extensible (and arbitrarily complex)

- Guess at some reasonable extension points and hardcode these

Once extension points are implemented, experimenting with new ones requires rewriting existing code, and the resulting inertia often means that over time, such extension points remain mostly undiscovered. Lisp *advice*, and its Java counterpart Aspects, offer software engineers the opportunity to experiment without worrying about adversely affecting an existing body of source code.

Producing Auditory Icons While Speaking Content

In addition to using auditory icons to cue the results of user interaction, Emacspeak uses auditory icons to augment what is being spoken. Examples of such auditory icons include:

- A short icon at the beginning of paragraphs
- The auditory icon mark-object when moving across source lines that have a breakpoint set on them

Auditory icons are implemented by attaching the text property emacspeak-auditory-icon with a value equal to the name of the auditory icon to be played on the relevant text.

As an example, commands to set breakpoints in the Grand Unified Debugger Emacs package (GUD) are *adviced* to add the property emacspeak-auditory-icon to the line containing the breakpoint. When the user moves across such a line, the function tts-format-text-and-speak queues the auditory icon at the right point in the output stream.

The Calendar: Enhancing Spoken Output with Context-Sensitive Semantics

To summarize the story so far, Emacspeak has the ability to:

- Produce auditory output from within the context of an application
- Audio-format output to increase the bandwidth of spoken communication
- Augment spoken output with auditory icons

This section explains some of the enhancements that the design makes possible.

I started implementing Emacspeak in October 1994 as a quick means of developing a speech solution for Linux. It was when I speech-enabled the Emacs Calendar in the first week of November 1994 that I realized that in fact I had created something far better than any other speech-access solution I had used before.

A calendar is a good example of using a specific type of visual layout that is optimized both for the visual medium as well as for the information that is being conveyed. We intuitively think in terms of weeks and months when reasoning about dates; using a tabular layout that organizes dates in a grid with each week appearing on a row by itself matches this perfectly. With this form of layout, the human eye can rapidly move by days, weeks, or months through the calendar and easily answer such questions as "What day is it tomorrow?" and "Am I free on the third Wednesday of next month?"

Notice, however, that simply speaking this two-dimensional layout does not transfer the efficiencies achieved in the visual context to auditory interaction. This is a good example of where the right auditory feedback has to be generated directly from the underlying information being conveyed, rather than from its visual representation. When producing auditory output from visually formatted information, one has to *rediscover* the underlying semantics of the information before speaking it.

In contrast, when producing spoken feedback via *advice* definitions that extend the underlying application, one has full access to the application's runtime context. Thus, rather than *guessing* based on visual layout, one can essentially instruct the underlying application to *speak the right thing!*

The emacspeak-calendar module speech-enables the Emacs Calendar by defining utility functions that speak calendar information and advising all calendar navigation commands to call these functions. Thus, Emacs Calendar produces specialized behavior by binding the arrow keys to calendar navigation commands rather than the default cursor navigation found in regular editing modes. Emacspeak specializes this behavior by advising the calendar-specific commands to speak the relevant information in the context of the calendar.

The net effect is that from an end user's perspective, *things just work*. In regular editing modes, pressing up/down arrows speaks the current line; pressing up/down arrows in the calendar navigates by weeks and speaks the current date.

The emacspeak-calendar-speak-date function, defined in the emacspeak-calendar module, is shown here. Notice that it uses all of the facilities described so far to access and audioformat the relevant contextual information from the calendar:

```
(defsubst emacspeak-calendar-entry-marked-p( )
  (member 'diary (mapcar #'overlay-face (overlays-at (point)))))
(defun emacspeak-calendar-speak-date( )
  "Speak the date under point when called in Calendar Mode. "
  (let ((date (calendar-date-string (calendar-cursor-to-date t))))
    (cond
     ((emacspeak-calendar-entry-marked-p) (tts-speak-using-voice mark-personality
date))
     (t (tts-speak date)))))
```

Emacs marks dates that have a diary entry with a special overlay. In the previous definition, the helper function emacspeak-calendar-entry-marked-p checks this overlay to implement a predicate that can be used to test if a date has a diary entry. The emacspeak-calendar-speak-date function uses this predicate to decide whether the date needs to be rendered in a different voice; dates that have calendar entries are spoken using the mark-personality voice. Notice that the emacspeak-calendar-speak-date function accesses the calendar's runtime context in the call:

```
(calendar-date-string (calendar-cursor-to-date t))
```

The emacspeak-calendar-speak-date function is called from *advice* definitions attached to all calendar navigation functions. Here is the *advice* definition for function calendar-forward-week:

```
(defadvice calendar-forward-week (after emacspeak pre act)
  "Speak the date. "
  (when (interactive-p) (emacspeak-speak-calendar-date )
    (emacspeak-auditory-icon 'large-movement)))
```

This is an after *advice*, because we want the spoken feedback to be produced *after* the original navigation command has done its work.

The body of the *advice* definition first calls the function `emacspeak-calendar-speak-date` to speak the date under the cursor; next, it calls `emacspeak-auditory-icon` to produce a short sound indicating that we have successfully moved.

Painless Access to Online Information

With all the necessary affordances to generate rich auditory output in place, speech-enabling Emacs applications using Emacs Lisp's *advice* facility requires surprisingly small amounts of specialized code. With the TTS layer and the Emacspeak core handling the complex details of producing good quality output, the speech-enabling extensions focus purely on the specialized semantics of individual applications; this leads to simple and consequently *beautiful* code. This section illustrates the concept with a few choice examples taken from Emacspeak's rich suite of information access tools.

Right around the time I started Emacspeak, a far more profound revolution was taking place in the world of computing: the World Wide Web went from being a tool for academic research to a mainstream forum for everyday tasks. This was 1994, when writing a browser was still a comparatively easy task. The complexity that has been progressively added to the Web in the subsequent 12 years often tends to obscure the fact that the Web is still a fundamentally simple design where:

* Content creators publish web resources addressable via URIs.
* URI-addressable content is retrievable via open protocols.
* Retrieved content is in HTML, a well-understood markup language.

Notice that the basic architecture just sketched out says little to nothing about how the content is made available to the end user. The mid-1990s saw the Web move toward increasingly complex visual interaction. The commercial Web with its penchant for flashy visual interaction increasingly moved away from the simple data-oriented interaction that had characterized early web sites. By 1998, I found that the Web had a lot of useful interactive sites; to my dismay, I also found that I was using progressively fewer of these sites because of the time it took to complete tasks when using spoken output.

This led me to create a suite of web-oriented tools within Emacspeak that went back to the basics of web interaction. Emacs was already capable of rendering simple HTML into interactive hypertext documents. As the Web became complex, Emacspeak acquired a collection of interaction wizards built on top of Emacs' HTML rendering capability that progressively factored out the complexity of web interaction to create an auditory interface that allowed the user to quickly and painlessly listen to desired information.

Basic HTML with Emacs W3 and Aural CSS

Emacs W3 is a bare-bones web browser first implemented in the mid-1990s. Emacs W3 implemented CSS (Cascading Style Sheets) early on, and this was the basis of the first Aural CSS implementation, which was released at the time I wrote the Aural CSS draft in February 1996. Emacspeak speech-enables Emacs W3 via the `emacspeak-w3` module, which implements the following extensions:

- An aural `media` section in the default stylesheet for Aural CSS.
- *advice* added to all interactive commands to produce auditory feedback.
- Special patterns to recognize and silence decorative images on web pages.
- Aural rendering of HTML form fields along with the associated `label`, which underlay the design of the `label` element in HTML 4.
- Context-sensitive rendering rules for HTML form controls. As an example, given a group of radio buttons for answering the question:

    Do you accept?

  Emacspeak extends Emacs W3 to produce a spoken message of the form:

    Radio group Do you accept? has Yes pressed.

  and:

    Press this to change radio group Do you accept? from Yes to No.

- A `before` advice defined for the Emacs W3 function `w3-parse-buffer` that applies user-requested XSLT transforms to HTML pages.

The emacspeak-websearch Module for Task-Oriented Search

By 1997, interactive sites on the Web, ranging from Altavista for searching to Yahoo! Maps for online directions, required the user to go through a highly visual process that included:

1. Filling in a set of form fields
2. Submitting the resulting form
3. Spotting the results in the resulting complex HTML page

The first and third of these steps were the ones that took time when using spoken output. I needed to first locate the various form fields on a visually busy page and wade through a lot of complex boilerplate material on result pages before I found the answer.

Notice that from the software design point of view, these steps neatly map into *pre-action* and *post-action* hooks. Because web interaction follows a very simple architecture based on URIs, the pre-action step of prompting the user for the right pieces of input can be factored out of a web site and placed in a small piece of code that runs locally; this obviates the need for the user to open the initial launch page and seek out the various input fields.

Similarly, the post-action step of spotting the actual results amid the rest of the noise on the resulting page can also be delegated to software.

Finally, notice that even though these pre-action and post-action steps are each specific to particular web sites, the overall design pattern is one that can be generalized. This insight led to the `emacspeak-websearch` module, a collection of task-oriented web tools that:

1. Prompted the user

2. Constructed an appropriate URI and pulled the content at that URI

3. Filtered the result before rendering the relevant content via Emacs W3

Here is the `emacspeak-websearch` tool for accessing directions from Yahoo! Maps:

```
(defsubst emacspeak-websearch-yahoo-map-directions-get-locations ()
  "Convenience function for prompting and constructing the route component."
  (concat
   (format "&newaddr=%s"
           (emacspeak-url-encode (read-from-minibuffer "Start Address: ")))
   (format "&newcsz=%s"
           (emacspeak-url-encode (read-from-minibuffer "City/State or Zip:")))
   (format "&newtaddr=%s"
           (emacspeak-url-encode (read-from-minibuffer "Destination Address: ")))
   (format "&newtcsz=%s"
           (emacspeak-url-encode (read-from-minibuffer "City/State or Zip:")))))
(defun emacspeak-websearch-yahoo-map-directions-search (query )
  "Get driving directions from Yahoo."
  (interactive
   (list (emacspeak-websearch-yahoo-map-directions-get-locations)))
  (emacspeak-w3-extract-table-by-match
   "Start"
   (concat emacspeak-websearch-yahoo-maps-uri query))))
```

A brief explanation of the previous code follows:

Pre-action

The `emacspeak-websearch-yahoo-map-directions-get-locations` function prompts the user for the start and end locations. Notice that this function hardwires the names of the query parameters used by Yahoo! Maps. On the surface, this looks like a kluge that is guaranteed to break. In fact, this kluge has not broken since it was first defined in 1997. The reason is obvious: once a web application has published a set of query parameters, those parameters get hardcoded in a number of places, including within a large number of HTML pages on the originating web site. Depending on parameter names may feel brittle to the software architect used to structured, top-down APIs, but the use of such URL parameters to define bottom-up web services leads to the notion of RESTful web APIs.

Retrieve content

The URL for retrieving directions is constructed by concatenating the user input to the *base URI* for Yahoo! Maps.

Post-action

The resulting URI is passed to the function `emacspeak-w3-extract-table-by-match` along with a search pattern `Start` to:

a. Retrieve the content using Emacs W3.

b. Apply an XSLT transform to extract the table containing `Start`.

c. Render this table using Emacs W3's HTML formatter.

Unlike the query parameters, the layout of the results page *does* change about once a year, on average. But keeping this tool current with Yahoo! Maps comes down to maintaining the post-action portion of this utility. In over eight years of use, I have had to modify it about half a dozen times, and given that the underlying platform provides many of the tools for filtering the result page, the actual lines of code that need to be written for each layout change is minimal.

The `emacspeak-w3-extract-table-by-match` function uses an XSLT transformation that filters a document to return tables that contain a specified search pattern. For this example, the function constructs the following XPath expression:

```
(/descendant::table[contains(., Start)])[last()]
```

This effectively picks out the list of tables that contain the string `Start` and returns the last element of that list.

Seven years after this utility was written, Google launched Google Maps to great excitement in February 2005. Many blogs on the Web put Google Maps under the microscope and quickly discovered the query parameters used by that application. I used that to build a corresponding Google Maps tool in Emacspeak that provides similar functionality. The user experience is smoother with the Google Maps tool because the start and end locations can be specified within the same parameter. Here is the code for the Google Maps wizard:

```
(defun emacspeak-websearch-emaps-search (query &optional use-near)
  "Perform EmapSpeak search. Query is  in plain English."
  (interactive
   (list
    (emacspeak-websearch-read-query
     (if current-prefix-arg
         (format "Find what near  %s: "
                 emacspeak-websearch-emapspeak-my-location)
       "EMap Query: "))
     current-prefix-arg))
  (let ((near-p ;; determine query type
         (unless use-near
           (save-match-data (and (string-match "near" query) (match-end 0)))))
        (near nil)
        (uri nil))
    (when near-p ;; determine location from query
      (setq near (substring query near-p))
      (setq emacspeak-websearch-emapspeak-my-location near))
    (setq uri
          (cond
           (use-near
```

```
        (format emacspeak-websearch-google-maps-uri
           (emacspeak-url-encode
              (format "%s near %s" query near))))
        (t (format emacspeak-websearch-google-maps-uri
              (emacspeak-url-encode query)))))
  (add-hook 'emacspeak-w3-post-process-hook 'emacspeak-speak-buffer)
  (add-hook  'emacspeak-w3-post-process-hook
         #'(lambda nil
              (emacspeak-pronounce-add-buffer-local-dictionary-entry
               "&#240;mi" " miles ")))
  (browse-url-of-buffer
   (emacspeak-xslt-xml-url
    (expand-file-name "kml2html.xsl" emacspeak-xslt-directory)
    uri))))
```

A brief explanation of the code follows:

1. Parse the input to decide whether it's a direction or a search query.

2. In case of search queries, cache the user's location for future use.

3. Construct a URI for retrieving results.

4. Browse the results of filtering the contents of the URI through the XSLT filter kml2html, which converts the retrieved content into a simple hypertext document.

5. Set up custom pronunciations in the results to pronounce mi as "miles."

Notice that, as before, most of the code focuses on application-specific tasks. Rich spoken output is produced by creating the results as a well-structured HTML document with the appropriate Aural CSS rules producing an audio-formatted presentation.

The Web Command Line and URL Templates

With more and more services becoming available on the Web, another useful pattern emerged by early 2000: web sites started creating smart client-side interaction via Java-Script. One typical use of such scripts was to construct URLs on the clientside for accessing specific pieces of content based on user input. As examples, Major League Baseball constructs the URL for retrieving scores for a given game by piecing together the date and the names of the home and visiting teams, and NPR creates URLs by piecing together the date with the program code of a given NPR show.

To enable fast access to such services, I added an emacspeak-url-template module in late 2000. This module has become a powerful companion to the emacspeak-websearch module described in the previous section. Together, these modules turn the Emacs minibuffer into a powerful web command line that provides rapid access to web content.

Many web services require the user to specify a date. One can usefully default the date by using the user's calendar to provide the context. Thus, Emacspeak tools for playing an NPR program or retrieving MLB scores default to using the date under the cursor when invoked from within the Emacs calendar buffer.

URL templates in Emacspeak are implemented using the following data structure:

```
(defstruct (emacspeak-url-template (:constructor emacspeak-ut-constructor))
  name                            ;; Human-readable name
  template                        ;; template URL string
  generators;; list of param generator
  post-action                     ;; action to perform after opening
  documentation                   ;; resource  documentation
  fetcher)
```

Users invoke URL templates via the Emacspeak command emacspeak-url-template-fetch command, which prompts for a URL template and:

1. Looks up the named template.

2. Prompts the user by calling the specified generator.

3. Applies the Lisp function format to the template string and the collected arguments to create the final URI.

4. Sets up any *post actions* performed after the content has been rendered.

5. Applies the specified fetcher to render the content.

The use of this structure is best explained with an example. The following is the URL template for playing NPR programs:

```
(emacspeak-url-template-define
 "NPR On Demand"
 "http://www.npr.org/dmg/dmg.php?prgCode=%s&showDate=%s&segNum=%s&mediaPref=RM"
 (list
  #'(lambda () (upcase (read-from-minibuffer "Program code:")))
  #'(lambda ()
      (emacspeak-url-template-collect-date "Date:" "%d-%b-%Y"))
  "Segment:")
 nil; no post actions
 "Play NPR shows on demand.
Program is specified as a program code:
ME            Morning Edition
ATC           All Things Considered
day           Day To Day
newsnotes     News And Notes
totn          Talk Of The Nation
fa            Fresh Air
wesat         Weekend Edition Saturday
wesun         Weekend Edition Sunday
fool          The Motley Fool
Segment is specified as a two digit number --specifying a blank value
plays entire program."
 #'(lambda (url)
     (funcall emacspeak-media-player url 'play-list)
     (emacspeak-w3-browse-xml-url-with-style
      (expand-file-name "smil-anchors.xsl" emacspeak-xslt-directory)
      url)))
```

In this example, the custom `fetcher` performs two actions:

1. Launches a media player to start playing the audio stream.

2. Filters the associated SMIL document via the XSLT file *smil-anchors.xsl*.

The Advent of Feed Readers

When I implemented the `emacspeak-websearch` and `emacspeak-url-template` modules, Emacspeak needed to screen-scrape HTML pages to speak the relevant information. But as the Web grew in complexity, the need to readily get beyond the superficial presentation of pages to the real content took on a wider value than eyes-free access. Even users capable of working with complex visual interfaces found themselves under a serious information overload. This led to the advent of RSS and Atom feeds, and the concomitant arrival of feed reading software.

These developments have had a very positive effect on the Emacspeak code base. During the past few years, the code has become *more beautiful* as I have progressively deleted screen-scraping logic and replaced it with direct content access. As an example, here is the Emacspeak URL template for retrieving the weather for a given city/state:

```
(emacspeak-url-template-define
 "rss weather from wunderground"
 "http://www.wunderground.com/auto/rss_full/%s.xml?units=both"
 (list "State/City e.g.: MA/Boston") nil
 "Pull RSS weather feed for specified state/city."
 'emacspeak-rss-display)
```

And here is the URL template for Google News searches via Atom feeds:

```
(emacspeak-url-template-define
 "Google News Search"
 "http://news.google.com/news?hl=en&ned=tus&q=%s&btnG=Google+Search&output=atom"
 (list "Search news for: ") nil "Search Google news."
 'emacspeak-atom-display )
```

Both of these tools use all of the facilities provided by the `emacspeak-url-template` module and consequently need to do very little on their own. Finally, notice that by relying on standardized feed formats such as RSS and Atom, these templates now have very little in the way of site-specific kluges, in contrast to older tools like the Yahoo! Maps wizard, which hardwired specific patterns from the results page.

Summary

Emacspeak was conceived as a full-fledged, eyes-free user interface to everyday computing tasks. To be *full-fledged*, the system needed to provide direct access to every aspect of computing on desktop workstations. To enable fluent *eyes-free* interaction, the system needed to treat spoken output and the auditory medium as a first-class citizen—i.e., merely reading out information displayed on the screen was not sufficient.

To provide a *complete audio desktop*, the target environment needed to be an interaction framework that was both widely deployed and fully extensible. To be able to do more than just speak the screen, the system needed to build interactive speech capability into the various applications.

Finally, this had to be done without modifying the source code of any of the underlying applications; the project could not afford to fork a suite of applications in the name of adding eyes-free interaction, because I wanted to limit myself to the task of maintaining the speech extensions.

To meet all these design requirements, I picked Emacs as the user interaction environment. As an interaction framework, Emacs had the advantage of having a very large developer community. Unlike other popular interaction frameworks available in 1994 when I began the project, it had the significant advantage of being a free software environment. (Now, 12 years later, Firefox affords similar opportunities.)

The enormous flexibility afforded by Emacs Lisp as an extension language was an essential prerequisite in speech-enabling the various applications. The open source nature of the platform was just as crucial; even though I had made an explicit decision that I would modify no existing code, being able to study how various applications were implemented made speech-enabling them tractable. Finally, the availability of a high-quality *advice* implementation for Emacs Lisp (note that Lisp's *advice* facility was the prime motivator behind Aspect Oriented Programming) made it possible to speech-enable applications authored in Emacs Lisp without modifying the original source code.

Emacspeak is a direct consequence of the matching up of the needs previously outlined and the affordances provided by Emacs as a user interaction environment.

Managing Code Complexity Over Time

The Emacspeak code base has evolved over a period of 12 years. Except for the first six weeks of development, the code base has been developed and maintained using Emacspeak itself. This section summarizes some of the lessons learned with respect to managing code complexity over time.

Throughout its existence, Emacspeak has *always* remained a spare-time project. Looking at the code base across time, I believe this has had a significant impact on how it has evolved. When working on large, complex software systems as a full-time project, one has the luxury of focusing one's entire concentration on the code base for reasonable stretches of time—e.g., 6 to 12 weeks. This results in tightly implemented code that creates *deep* code bases.

Despite one's best intentions, this can also result in code that becomes hard to understand with the passage of time. Large software systems where a single engineer focuses exclusively on the project for a number of years are almost nonexistent; that form of single-minded focus usually leads to rapid burnout!

In contrast, Emacspeak is an example of a large software system that has had a single engineer focused on it over a period of 12 years, but only in his spare time. A consequence of developing the system single-handedly over a number of years is that the code base has tended to be naturally "bushy." Notice the distribution of files and lines of code summarized in Table 31-1.

TABLE 31-1. Summary of Emacspeak codebase

Layer	Files	Lines	Percentage
TTS core	6	3866	6.0
Emacspeak core	16	12174	18.9
Emacspeak extensions	160	48339	75.0
Total	182	64379	99.9

Table 31-1 highlights the following points:

- The TTS core responsible for high-quality speech output is isolated in 6 out of 182 files, and makes up six percent of the code base.

- The Emacspeak core—which provides high-level speech services to Emacspeak extensions, in addition to speech-enabling all basic Emacs functionality—is isolated to 16 files, and makes up about 19 percent of the code base.

- The rest of the system is split across 160 files, which can be independently improved (or broken) without affecting the rest of the system. Many modules, such as emacspeak-url-template, are themselves bushy—i.e., an individual URL template can be modified without affecting any of the other URL templates.

- *advice* reduces code size. The Emacspeak code base, which has approximately 60,000 lines of Lisp code, is a fraction of the size of the underlying system being speech-enabled. A rough count at the end of December 2006 shows that Emacs 22 has over a million lines of Lisp code; in addition, Emacspeak speech-enables a large number of applications not bundled by default with Emacs.

Conclusion

Here is a brief summary of the insights gained from implementing and using Emacspeak:

- Lisp *advice*, and its object-oriented equivalent Aspect Oriented Programming, are very effective means for implementing cross-cutting concerns—e.g., speech-enabling a visual interface.

- *advice* is a powerful means for discovering potential points of extension in a complex software system.

- Focusing on basic web architecture, and relying on a data-oriented web backed by standardized protocols and formats, leads to powerful spoken web access.

- Focusing on the final user experience, as opposed to individual interaction widgets such as sliders and tree controls, leads to a highly efficient, eyes-free environment.

- Visual interaction relies heavily on the human eye's ability to rapidly scan the visual display. Effective eyes-free interaction requires transferring some of this responsibility to the computer because listening to large amounts of information is time-consuming. Thus, search in every form is critical for delivering effective eyes-free interaction, on the continuum from the smallest scale (such as Emacs' incremental search to find the right item in a local document) to the largest (such as a Google search to quickly find the right document on the global Web).

- Visual complexity, which may become merely an irritant for users capable of using complex visual interfaces, is a show-stopper for eyes-free interaction. Conversely, tools that emerge early in an eyes-free environment eventually show up in the mainstream when the nuisance value of complex visual interfaces crosses a certain threshold. Two examples of this from the Emacspeak experience are:

  — RSS and Atom feeds replacing the need for screen-scraping just to retrieve essential information such as the titles of articles.

  — Emacspeak's use of XSLT to filter content in 2000 parallels the advent of Grease-monkey for applying custom client-side JavaScript to web pages in 2005.

Acknowledgments

Emacspeak would not exist without Emacs and the ever-vibrant Emacs developer community that has made it possible to do everything from within Emacs. The Emacspeak implementation would not have been possible without Hans Chalupsky's excellent advice implementation for Emacs Lisp.

Project *libxslt* from the GNOME project has helped breathe fresh life into William Perry's Emacs W3 browser; Emacs W3 was one of the early HTML rendering engines, but the code has not been updated in over eight years. That the W3 code base is still usable and extensible bears testimony to the flexibility and power afforded by Lisp as the implementation language.

## CHAPTER THIRTY-TWO

Code in Motion

Laura Wingerd and Christopher Seiwald

The main point is that every successful piece of software has an
extended life in which it is worked on by a succession of programmers
and designers....

Bjarne Stroustrup

EARLY IN THE PLANNING OF THIS BOOK, **G**REG **W**ILSON ASKED CONTRIBUTORS whether *Beautiful Code*
was an apt title. "Much of what you're going to discuss is software design and architecture,
rather than code *per se*," he wrote us.

But this chapter *is* about the code. It's not about what the code does, nor is it about how
beautifully it does it. Instead, this chapter is about how the code *looks*: specifically, how
certain human-visible traits of coding make serial collaboration possible. It's about the
beauty of "code in motion."

What you're about to read is borrowed largely from Christopher Seiwald's article, "The
Seven Pillars of Pretty Code."* In a nutshell, the Seven Pillars are:

- Being "bookish"
- Making alike look alike
- Overcoming indentation
- Disentangling code blocks

---

* The article is available on the Perforce web site: *http://www.perforce.com/perforce/papers/prettycode.html*.

- Commenting code blocks

- Decluttering

- Blending in with existing style

While these may sound like mere coding conventions, they're more than that. They're the outward manifestations of a coding practice that keeps product evolution in mind.

In this chapter, we'll see how the Seven Pillars have supported a piece of code that has been part of a commercial software system for over 10 years. That piece of code is DiffMerge, a component of the Perforce software configuration management system. DiffMerge's job is to produce a classic three-way merge, comparing two versions of a text file ("leg 1" and "leg 2") to a reference version ("the base"). The output interleaves lines of the input files with placeholders marking the lines that conflict. If you've used Perforce, you've seen DiffMerge at work in the *p4 resolve* command and in Perforce's graphical merge tools.

DiffMerge was originally written in 1996. Despite its simple goal, a three-way text merge function turns out to be fraught with intricacy. It's a melting pot of special cases arising from the idiosyncrasies of user interfaces, character encodings, programming languages, and programmers themselves. ("That's not a conflict." "Yes, it is." "No, it's not!")

Over the years DiffMerge has become a locus of significant development at Perforce Software. So, it's not good enough that DiffMerge is simply a correct piece of code. It has to be a piece of code that "plays nice" with the tools we use for coding, debugging, and change management. And it has to be a piece of code that anticipates being changed.

The road from DiffMerge's first implementation to its present-day form has been uneven, to say the least. It's probably no coincidence that the further we strayed from the Seven Pillars, the rockier the road became. Later in this chapter, we'll reveal some of the potholes (and one major wreck) that beset DiffMerge's 10-year journey.

All's well that ends well, however. Today's DiffMerge, reprinted at *http://www.perforce.com/ beautifulcode*, is stable and accepts enhancements with ease. It is a demonstration of how coding in anticipation of future change can produce a beautiful piece of code in motion.

On Being "Bookish"

"The Seven Pillars of Pretty Code" describes guidelines we use at Perforce Software. The Seven Pillars* aren't the only coding guidelines we use, nor are they applied to all of our development projects. We apply them to components such as DiffMerge where the same code is likely to be active in several concurrently supported releases and modified by many programmers. The effect of the Seven Pillars is to make code more comprehensible to the programmers who read it, in more of the contexts in which they find themselves reading it.

---

* And no, we don't call them "The Seven Pillars" back at the office. In fact, we don't really think of them as separate from our language- or component-specific coding guidelines. But when we strip out the latter, they are what's left.

Take, for example, the Seven Pillars' advice to be "bookish." Book and magazine text is composed in columns, usually in columns far narrower than the page. Why? Because narrowness reduces the back-and-forth scanning our eyes must do as we read—reading is easier when our eyes work less. Reading is also easier when what we've just read and what we're about to read are both within our visual range. Research shows that as our eyes change focus from word to word, our brains can take cues from surrounding, unfocused shapes. The more our brains can glean "advance warning" from shapes within the visual periphery, the better they're able to direct our eyes for maximum comprehension.

Research also seems to show that, when it comes to line lengths of text, there's a difference between reading speed and reading comprehension. Longer lines can be read faster, but shorter lines are easier to comprehend.

Chunked text is also easier to comprehend than a continuous column of text. That's why columns in books and magazines are divided into paragraphs. Paragraphs, verses, lists, sidebars, and footnotes are the "transaction markers" of text, saying to our brains, "Have you grokked everything so far? Good, please go on."

Code is not strictly text, of course, but for the purpose of human readability, the same principles apply. Bookish code—that is, code formatted in book-like columns and chunks—is easier to comprehend.

Bookishness is more than simply keeping lines short. It's the difference between code that looks like this:

```
if( bf->end == bf->Lines() && lf1->end == lf1->Lines() &&
    lf2->end == lf2->Lines() ) return( DD_EOF );
```

and code that looks like this:

```
if( bf->end == bf->Lines() &&
    lf1->end == lf1->Lines() &&
    lf2->end == lf2->Lines() )
        return( DD_EOF );
```

The second of these code snippets is taken from DiffMerge. When we read it, our brains sense the scope of the logic at hand, and our eyes don't have to scan very far from side to side to take it in. (The fact that there's a visual pattern created by the choice of line breaks is also important; we'll get to that in a moment.) Being more bookish, the second snippet is easier to comprehend than the first.

Alike Looking Alike

The DiffMerge snippet in the previous section also illustrates another principle of writing for comprehensibility: code that *is* alike *looks* alike. We see this throughout the DiffMerge code. For example:

```
while( d.diffs == DD_CONF && ( bf->end != bf->Lines() ||
                               lf1->end != lf1->Lines() ||
                               lf2->end != lf2->Lines() ) )
```

The preceding demonstrates how line breaks can create a visual pattern that makes it easier for our brains to recognize a logical pattern. We can tell at a glance that three of the four tests in this while statement are essentially the same.

Here's one more example of alike looking alike. This one illustrates coding that lets our brains do a successful "one of these is not the same" operation:

```
case MS_BASE:                    /* dumping the original */

    if( selbits = selbitTab[ DL_BASE ][ diffDiff ] )
    {
        readFile = bf;
        readFile->SeekLine( bf->start );
        state = MS_LEG1;
        break;
    }

case MS_LEG1:                    /* dumping leg1 */

    if( selbits = selbitTab[ DL_LEG1 ][ diffDiff ] )
    {
        readFile = lf1;
        readFile->SeekLine( lf1->start );
        state = MS_LEG2;
        break;
    }

case MS_LEG2:                    /* dumping leg2 */

    if( selbits = selbitTab[ DL_LEG2 ][ diffDiff ] )
    {
        readFile = lf2;
        readFile->SeekLine( lf2->start );
    }

    state = MS_DIFFDIFF;
    break;
```

Even if you don't know what this code is about, it's clear to see, for example, that readfile and state are set in all three cases, but only in the third case is state set unconditionally. The programmer who wrote this paid attention to making alike look alike; those of us reading it later can see at a glance where the essential logic is.

The Perils of Indentation

We've all been taught to use indentation to show the depth of nesting in logical blocks of code. The deeper the nesting, the farther to the right of the page the nested code appears. Formatting code this way is a good idea, but not because it makes the code any easier to read.

If anything, deeply indented code is harder to read. Important logic is crowded off to the right, submerged to almost footnote-like insignificance by the layers of if-then-else code that surrounds it, while trivial tests applied in outer blocks seem elevated in importance. So, while indentation is useful for showing where blocks begin and end, it doesn't make the code any easier for us to comprehend.

The greater peril is not the indentation, however: it's the nesting. Nested code strains human comprehension, plain and simple. Edward Tufte was not being complimentary when he wrote that "Sometimes [PowerPoint] bullet hierarchies are so complex and intensely nested that they resemble computer code." In *Code Complete* (see "Further Reading," at the end of this chapter), Steve McConnell warns against using nested if statements—not because they're inefficient or ineffective, but because they're hard on human comprehension. "To understand the code, you have to keep the whole set of nested ifs in your mind at once," he says. It's no surprise that research points to nested conditionals as the most bug-prone of all programming constructs. We have a bit of anecdotal evidence for this, as you'll read in the section "DiffMerge's Checkered Past."

So the value of indenting each nesting level is not in making code more comprehensible, but in making the coder more aware of incomprehensibility. "Seven Pillars" advises coders to "overcome indentation"—that is, to code without deep nesting. "This is the most difficult of these practices," admits Seiwald, "as it requires the most artifice and can often influence the implementation of individual functions."

Steve McConnell demonstrates some useful implementations in the "Taming Dangerously Deep Nesting" section of *Code Complete*. DiffMerge makes heavy use of two of them: case statements and decision tables. The end result, as you can see in the DiffMerge source, is that the code itself takes on an outline form that lets us discern the big-picture logic by scanning down the left side of the page. Our brains, conditioned to reading outlines in natural-language text, find this easier to comprehend than the sideways-V form of deeply nested code.

Navigating Code

All Seven Pillars are illustrated in DiffMerge, to one extent or another. For example, the DiffMerge code is constructed of discrete, logical blocks. Each block does a single thing or single kind of thing, and what it does is either self-evident or described in a comment that prefaces the block. Code like this is the result of the Seven Pillars' advice to disentangle and comment code blocks. It's analogous to well-organized expository writing, where definition lists and titled sections help readers navigate densely packed technical information.

The lack of clutter also makes the DiffMerge code easier to navigate. One of DiffMerge's clutter-reducing tricks is to use tiny names for variables that are referenced repeatedly throughout the code. This goes against sage advice to use meaningful and descriptive variable names, to be sure. But there's a point at which overuse of long names creates so much clutter that it only impedes comprehension. Writers know this; it's why we use pronouns, surnames, and acronyms in our prose.

The comments in DiffMerge are also clutter-free. In 10-year-old code, it's easy to end up with as many comments that describe how the code *used* to work—along with additional comments about what changed—as comments that describe the current code. But there isn't really any reason to keep a running history of the program's evolution in the code itself; your source control management system has all that information and offers much better ways to track it. (We'll show examples in the next section.) The programmers working on DiffMerge have done a good job keeping the closets clean, as it were. The same goes for code. In DiffMerge, the old code isn't simply commented out, it's *gone*. The remaining code and comments are uncluttered with the distractions of history.*

The DiffMerge code also makes liberal use of whitespace. In addition to reducing the appearance of clutter, whitespace increases comprehensibility. When bookish chunks and alike patterns are set off by whitespace, they take on visual shapes our brains can recognize. As we read through the code, our brains index these shapes; later, we unconsciously use these shapes to find code we remember having read.

Even though it has been changed repeatedly over the years, by many different programmers, the DiffMerge code is largely consistent in its visual appearance, DiffMerge's contributors have each made an effort to "blend in." That is, each one has subjugated personal style and preferences to make his DiffMerge code look like the rest of DiffMerge's code. Blending in produces a consistency that reduces the work our brains have to do. It effectively amplifies all of the readability tricks we've just discussed.

If you've visited *http://www.perforce.com/beautifulcode*, you will have noticed that the DiffMerge code isn't perfect, even by the Seven Pillars' standards. There are places where it could be more bookish, or where code could blend in more, for example. Sure, we'd like to clean those up, but while we like pretty code, we like clean merges even better. Changes to variable names, whitespace, line breaks, and so forth can be more of an obstacle to merging than logic changes. When we make changes like these in one branch, we increase the risk that merging bug fixes from other branches will *create* bugs. Any benefit to be gained by rewriting DiffMerge's ugly parts has to be weighed against the resources it could take to recover from a bad merge. In the section "DiffMerge's Checkered Past," we'll relate what happens when that scale tips.

The Tools We Use

Certainly we need code to be understandable when we read the source files directly. We also need the code to be understandable when we encounter it in diffs, merges, patches, debuggers, code inspections, compiler messages, and a variety of other contexts and tools. As it turns out, code written with the Seven Pillars in mind is more readable in more of the tools we use to manage code.

---

* One comment in DiffMerge does describe a change: "2-18-97 (seiwald) - translated to C++." This comment remains in the code as a historical curiosity.

For example, DiffMerge code is human-readable even without syntax highlighting. In other words, we don't have to depend on context-sensitive source code editors to read it. It's just as readable when displayed as plain text by debuggers, compilers, and web browsers. Here's a snippet of DiffMerge in *gdb*:

```
Breakpoint 3, DiffMerge::DiffDiff (this=0x80e10c0) at diff/diffmerge.cc:510
510                 Mode initialMode = d.mode;
(gdb) list 505,515
505             DiffGrid d = diffGrid
506                     [ df1->StartLeg() == 0 ][ df1->StartBase() == 0 ]
507                     [ df2->StartLeg() == 0 ][ df2->StartBase() == 0 ]
508                     [ df3->StartL1() == 0 ][ df3->StartL2() == 0 ];
509
510             Mode initialMode = d.mode;
511
512             // Pre-process rules,  typically the outer snake information
513             // contradicts the inner snake, its not perfect, but we use
514             // the length of the snake to determine the best outcome.
515
(gdb) print d
$1 = {mode = CONF, diffs = DD_CONF}
(gdb)
```

When working on code that changes as often as DiffMerge (it has been changed 175 times since it was first written), programmers spend considerable time looking at it in diff and merge tools. What these tools have in common is that they restrict the horizontal view of source files, and they add a certain amount of clutter of their own. Code like DiffMerge's is readable even in these conditions. In command-line diffs, its lines don't wrap. In graphical diff tools, we don't have to fiddle with the horizontal scroll bar to see the bulk of its lines, as Figure 32-1 demonstrates.*

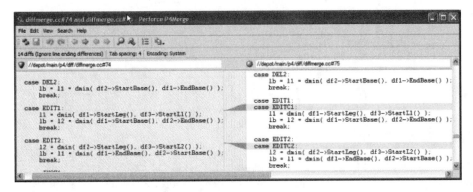

FIGURE 32-1. DiffMerge code viewed in a graphical diff tool

And as Figure 32-2 shows, a margin-hungry annotated history viewer is positively roomy when displaying the bookish DiffMerge code.

---

* This is a screenshot from P4Merge, a graphical tool built on DiffMerge itself.

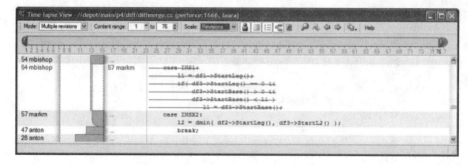

FIGURE 32-2. DiffMerge code in an annotated history viewer

Bookishness not only makes code more readable in merge tools, it makes the code itself easier to merge. For one thing, the scope of an edit is easier to control when logical blocks are set off by whitespace. And for another, having less nested code means having proportionally fewer instances of inverted and leapfrogged block delimiters to sort out.

DiffMerge's Checkered Past

We have a record of every change, branch, and merge involving DiffMerge throughout its 10-year history. And it's an interesting record. Figure 32-3 offers a thumbnail view of changes to the released versions of DiffMerge. It shows that DiffMerge originated in the mainline (the lowest line on the diagram) and has been branched into over 20 releases. Changes to DiffMerge have occured in the mainline, for the most part. But the thumbnail shows peculiar activity in some of the most recent releases.

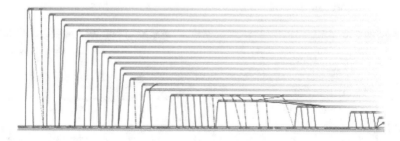

FIGURE 32-3. DiffMerge's release branches

A count of DiffMerge's patches per release branch, seen in Figure 32-4, is even more intriguing. It shows that DiffMerge was rarely patched after it was released—until the 2004.2 release, that is. Then the post-release patch rate soars, only to abate again in the 2006.2 release. Why are releases 2004.2 through 2006.1 so riddled with patches?

Here's the backstory: DiffMerge started out as a serviceable but simple program. In its early life, it did little to discriminate between actual merge conflicts and nonconflicting, adjacent-line changes. In 2004, we enhanced DiffMerge to be smarter about detecting and resolving conflicts. As of the 2004.2 release, DiffMerge was certainly more capable, but it was buggy. We got lots of bug reports in 2004.2 and 2005.1—hence the large number of

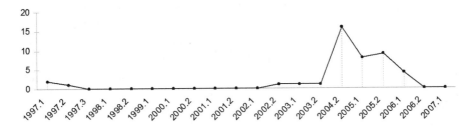

FIGURE 32-4. Number of patches applied to DiffMerge per release

patches. We tried to clean up the code for release 2005.2, but the cleanup resulted in a bug so intractable that we had to restore the 2005.1 version into the 2005.2 release. Then, in 2006, we rewrote the troublesome parts of DiffMerge completely. The rewrite was quite successful, although we did have to tweak it in release 2006.1. Since then, DiffMerge been very stable, and its post-release patch rate is back down to zero.

So, what went wrong when we rewrote DiffMerge in 2004? We believe it was that we had let the code become incomprehensible. Perhaps our code reviews at the time had lost sight of the Seven Pillars, or perhaps we had skipped some reviews entirely. At any rate, although it continued to pass regression testing, DiffMerge sailed into release branches full of bugs we hadn't seen coming on board.

We have no way to measure how readable source code is or how well it conforms to the Seven Pillars. But in retrospect, we see a clue that would have leapt out at us had we been looking for it at the time. Figure 32-5 shows a count of if statements and their successive nesting levels (as inferred from their indentation depths) in each initial branch of Diff-Merge. By the time we branched DiffMerge for 2004.2, apparently, we had doubled the number of if statements in the code. And for the first time, there were ifs nested more three levels deep.

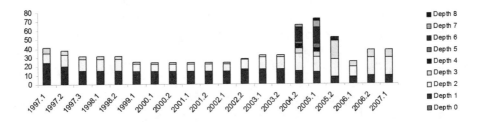

FIGURE 32-5. Number of DiffMerge's if statements at successive indentation depths per release

Correlation is not causation, as they say, and of course there could have been other contributing factors. The design of the enhancements, the test cases, the other coding constructs—even the size of the source code file—any or all of these could have contributed to the higher rate of errors. But given what we know about deeply nested conditionals and comprehensibility, it's hard not to take this glaring correlation at face value.

The 2006 overhaul of DiffMerge was driven by a mandate to overcome indentation. The overhaul replaced deeply nested conditionals with `switch` statements whose case options were values defined in the new `diffGrid` decision table. The table, whose layout was designed to be human-readable, itemized all the conditions we were currently handing *and* gave us placeholders for conditions we might eventually want to handle. Thus, we not only replaced troublesome code, we gave ourselves headroom for future enhancements.

Conclusion

To a programmer working on code in motion, beauty is code that can be modified with a minimum of fuss. You read the code, determine what it does, and change it. Your success depends as much on how well you understood the code to start with as it does on your ability to code. It also depends on how well your code is understood by the *next* programmers to tackle it; if you're never called in to help them out, you've done well.

Were we to trim the narrative from this chapter, all we'd really have left to say is that the success of code in motion depends on how comprehensible it is to the programmers who read it. But this is not news to anyone.

What *is* news is that programmers read code in diffs, patches, merges, compiler errors, and debuggers—not just in syntax-colored text editors—and that they frequently, if unconsciously, infer logic from the visual appearance of code as well as from the code itself. In other words, there's more to comprehending code than meets the eye.

In this chapter, we've examined the effect of using "The Seven Pillars of Pretty Code" as guidelines to make code more comprehensible in more contexts. We've had success with the Seven Pillars. We've used them to write code that can move with the flow of change, and we think that's beautiful.

Acknowledgments

Christopher Seiwald, James Strickland, Jeff Anton, Mark Mears, Caedmon Irias, Leigh Brasington, and Michael Bishop contributed to DiffMerge. Perforce Software holds the copyright to the DiffMerge source code.

Further Reading

Kim, S., *Adaptive Bug Prediction by Analyzing Project History*, Ph.D. Dissertation, Department of Computer Science, University of California Santa Cruz, 2006.

McConnell, S., *Code Complete*, Microsoft Press, 1993.

McMullin, J., Varnhagen, C. K., Heng, P., and Apedoe, X., "Effects of Surrounding Information and Line Length on Text Comprehension from the Web," *Canadian Journal of Learning and Technology*, Vol. 28, No. 1, Winter/hiver, 2002.

O'Brien, M. P., *Software Comprehension - A Review and Direction*, Department of Computer Science and Information Systems, University of Limerick, Ireland, 2003.

Pan, K., *Using Evolution Patterns to Find Duplicated Bugs*, Ph.D. Dissertation, Department of Computer Science, University of California Santa Cruz, 2006.

Reichle, E.D., Rayner, K., and Pollatsek, A., *The E-Z Reader Model of Eye Movement Control in Reading: Comparisons to Other Models*, Behavioral and Brain Sciences, Vol. 26, No. 4, 2003.

Seiwald, C., "The Seven Pillars of Pretty Code," Perforce Software, 2005, *http://www. perforce.com/perforce/papers/prettycode.html.*

Tufte, Edward R., *The Cognitive Style of PowerPoint*, Graphics Press LLC, 2004.

Whitehead, J., and Kim, S., *Predicting Bugs in Code Changes*, Google Tech Talks, 2006.

## CHAPTER THIRTY-THREE

Writing Programs for "The Book"

Brian Hayes

THE MATHEMATICIAN **P**AUL **E**RDÖS OFTEN SPOKE OF *THE BOOK,* a legendary volume (not to be found on the shelves of any earthly library) in which are inscribed the best possible proofs of all mathematical theorems. Perhaps there is also a *Book* for programs and algorithms, listing the best solution to every computational problem. To earn a place in those pages, a program must be more than just correct; it must also be lucid, elegant, concise, even witty.

We all strive to create such gems of algorithmic artistry. And we all struggle, now and then, with a stubborn bit of code that just won't shine, no matter how hard we polish it. Even if the program produces correct results, there's something strained and awkward about it. The logic is a tangle of special cases and exceptions to exceptions; the whole structure seems brittle and fragile. Then, unexpectedly, inspiration strikes, or else a friend from down the hall shows you a new trick, and suddenly you've got one for *The Book.*

In this chapter I tell the story of one such struggle. It's a story with a happy ending, although I'll leave it to readers to decide whether the final program deserves a place in *The Book.* I wouldn't be brash enough even to suggest the possibility except that this is one of those cases where the crucial insight came not from me but from a friend down the hall— or, rather, from a friend across the continent.

The Nonroyal Road

The program I'll be talking about comes from the field of computational geometry, which seems to be peculiarly rich in problems that look simple on first acquaintance but turn out to be real stinkers when you get into the details. What do I mean by computational geometry? It's not the same as computer graphics, although there are close connections. Algorithms in computational geometry live not in the world of pixels but in that idealized ruler-and-compass realm where points are dimensionless, lines have zero thickness, and circles are perfectly round. Getting exact results is often essential in these algorithms, because even the slightest inaccuracy can utterly transform the outcome of a computation. Changing a digit far to the right of the decimal point might turn the world inside out.

Euclid supposedly told a princely student, "There is no royal road to geometry." Among the nonroyal roads, the computational pathway is notably muddy, rutty, and potholed. The difficulties met along the way sometimes have to do with computational efficiency: keeping a program's running time and memory consumption within reasonable bounds. But efficiency is not the main issue with the geometric algorithms that concern me here; instead, the challenges are conceptual and aesthetic. Can we get it right? Can we make it beautiful?

The program presented below in several versions is meant to answer a very elementary question: given three points in the plane, do all of the points lie along the same line? This is such a simple-sounding problem, it ought to have a simple solution as well. A few months ago, when I needed a routine to answer the collinearity question (as a component of a larger program), the task looked so straightforward that I didn't even pause to consult the literature and see how others might have solved it. I don't exactly regret that haste—wrestling with the problem on my own must have taught me something, or at least built some character—but I admit it was not the royal road to the right answer. I wound up repeating the steps of many who went before me. (Maybe that's why the road is so rutted!)

Warning to Parenthophobes

I present the code in Lisp. I'm not going to apologize for my choice of programming language, but neither do I want to turn this chapter into a tract for recruiting Lisp converts. I'll just say that I believe multilingualism is a good thing. If reading the code snippets below teaches you something about an unfamiliar language, the experience will do you no harm. All of the procedures are very short—half a dozen lines or so. Figure 33-1 offers a thumbnail guide to the structure of a Lisp procedure.

Incidentally, the algorithm implemented by the program in the figure is surely in *The Book*. It is Euclid's algorithm for calculating the greatest common divisor of two numbers.

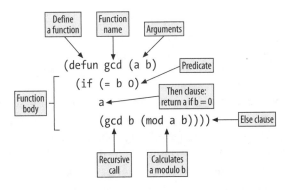

FIGURE 33-1. Bits and pieces of a Lisp procedure definition

Three in a Row

If you were working out a collinearity problem with pencil and paper, how would you go about it? One natural approach is to plot the positions of the three points on graph paper, and then, if the answer isn't obvious by inspection, draw a line through two of the points and see whether the line passes through the third point (see Figure 33-2). If it's a close call, accuracy in placing the points and drawing the line becomes critical.

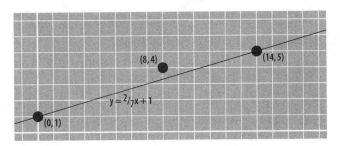

FIGURE 33-2. Three noncollinear points

A computer program can do the same thing, although for the computer nothing is ever "obvious by inspection." To draw a line through two points, the program derives the equation of that line. To see whether the third point lies on the line, the program tests whether or not the coordinates of the point satisfy the equation. (Exercise: For any set of three given points, there are three pairs of points you could choose to connect, in each case leaving a different third point to be tested for collinearity. Some choices may make the task easier than others, in the sense that less precision is needed. Is there some simple criterion for making this decision?)

The equation of a line takes the form $y = mx + b$, where m is the slope and b is the y-intercept, the point (if there is one) where the line crosses the y-axis. So, given three points p, q, and r, you want to find the values of m and b for the line that passes through two of them, and then test the x- and y-coordinates of the third point to see if the same equation holds.

Here's the code:

```
(defun naive-collinear (px py qx qy rx ry)
  (let ((m (slope px py qx qy))
        (b (y-intercept px py qx qy)))
    (= ry (+ (* m rx) b))))
```

The procedure is a predicate: it returns a Boolean value of true or false (in Lisp argot, t or nil). The six arguments are the *x*- and *y*-coordinates of the points *p*, *q*, and *r*. The let form introduces local variables named m and b, binding them to values returned by the procedures slope and y-intercept. I'll return shortly to the definitions of those procedures, but their functions should be apparent from their names. Finally, the last line of the procedure does all the work, posing the question: is the *y*-coordinate of point *r* equal to *m* times the *x*-coordinate of *r*, plus *b*? The answer is returned as the value of the naive-collinear function.

Could it be simpler? Well, we'll see. Does it work? Often. If you were to set the procedure loose on a large collection of points generated at random, it would probably run without error for a very long time. Nevertheless, it's easy to break it. Just try applying it to points with (*x y*) coordinates (0 0), (0 1), and (0 2). These points are surely collinear—they all lie on the *y*-axis—and yet the naive-collinear procedure can't be expected to return a sensible value when given them as arguments.

The root cause of this failure is lurking inside the definition of slope. Mathematically, the slope *m* is $\Delta y/\Delta x$, which the program calculates as follows:

```
(defun slope (px py qx qy)
  (/ (- qy py) (- qx px))))
```

If *p* and *q* happen to have the same *x*-coordinate, then Δx is zero, and $\Delta y/\Delta x$ is undefined. If you insist on trying to calculate the slope, you'll get no further than a divide-by-zero error. There are lots of ways of coping with this annoyance. The method I chose as I first assembled the pieces of this little program was to have slope return a special signal value if px is equal to qx. The Lisp custom is to use the value nil for this purpose:

```
(defun slope (px py qx qy)
  (if (= px qx)
      nil
      (/ (- qy py) (- qx px))))
```

Like the slope, the *y*-intercept of a vertical line is also undefined because the line crosses the *y*-axis either nowhere or (if *x*=0) everywhere. The same nil trick applies:

```
(defun y-intercept (px py qx qy)
  (let ((m (slope px py qx qy)))
    (if (not m)
        nil
        (- py (* m px)))))
```

Now, I also had to re-rig the calling procedure to handle the possibility that the slope m is not a number but a bogus value:

```
(defun less-naive-collinearp (px py qx qy rx ry)
  (let ((m (slope px py qx qy))
        (b (y-intercept px py qx qy)))
    (if (numberp m)
        (= ry (+ (* m rx) b))
        (= px rx))))
```

If *m* is numeric—if the predicate `(numberp m)` returns `t`—then I proceed as before. Otherwise, I know that *p* and *q* share the same *x*-coordinate. It follows that the three points are collinear if *r* also has this same *x* value.

As the program evolved, the need to make special provisions for vertical lines was a continual irritation. It began to look like every procedure I wrote would have some ugly patch bolted on to deal with the possibility that a line is parallel to the *y*-axis. Admittedly, the patch was just an `if` expression, an extra line or two of code, not a major issue of software engineering. Conceptually, though, it seemed a needless complication, and perhaps a sign that I was doing something wrong or making life harder than it had to be. Vertical lines are not fundamentally any different from horizontal ones, or from lines that wander across the plane at any other angle. It's an arbitrary convention to measure slope with respect to the *y*-axis; the universe would look no different if we all adopted a different reference direction.

This observation suggests a way around the problem: rotate the whole coordinate frame. If a set of points are collinear in one frame, they must be collinear in all other frames as well. Tilt the axes by a few degrees one way or the other, and the divide-by-zero impasse disappears. The rotation is not difficult or computationally expensive; it's just a matrix multiplication. On the other hand, taking this approach means I still have to write that `if` expression somewhere, testing to see whether px is equal to qx. What I'd really prefer is to streamline the logic and get rid of the branch point altogether. Shouldn't it be possible to test for collinearity by means of some simple calculation on the coordinates of the points, without any kind of case analysis?

Here's a solution recommended (in a slightly different context) by one web site, which I shall allow to remain anonymous: when Δx is 0, just set $\Delta y / \Delta x$ to 10^{10}, a value "close enough to infinity." As a practical matter, I suspect that this policy might actually work quite well, most of the time. After all, if the input to the program derives in any way from measurements made in the real world, there will be errors far larger than 1 part in 10^{10}. All the same, this is a strategy I did not consider seriously. I may not know what the *Book* version of collinear looks like, but I refuse to believe it has a constant defined as "close enough to infinity."

The Slippery Slope

Instead of drawing a line through two points and seeing whether the third point is on the line, suppose I drew all three lines and checked to see whether they are really the same line. Actually, I would need to draw only two of the lines, because if line $\overline{pq}$ is identical to line $\overline{qr}$, it must also be equal to $\overline{pr}$. Furthermore, it turns out I need to compare only the slopes, not the y-intercepts. (Do you see why?) Judging by eye whether two lines are really coincident or form a narrow scissors angle might not be the most reliable procedure, but in the computational world, it comes down to a simple comparison of two numbers, the m values (see Figure 33-3).

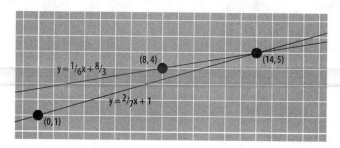

FIGURE 33-3. Testing collinearity by comparing slopes

I wrote a new version of collinear as follows:

```
(defun mm-collinear (px py qx qy rx ry)
  (equalp (slope px py qx qy)
          (slope qx qy rx ry)))
```

What an improvement! This looks much simpler. There's no if expression calling attention to the distinguished status of vertical lines; all sets of points are treated the same way.

I must confess, however, that the simplicity and the apparent uniformity are an illusion, based on some Lisp trickery going on behind the scenes. Note that I compare the slopes not with = but with the generic equality predicate equalp. The procedure works correctly only because equalp happens to do the right thing whether slope returns a number or nil. (That is, the two slopes are considered equal if they are both the same number or if they are both nil.) In a language with a fussier type system, the definition would not be so sweetly concise. It would have to look something like this:

```
(defun typed-mm-collinear (px py qx qy rx ry)
  (let ((pq-slope (slope px py qx qy))
        (qr-slope (slope qx qy rx ry)))
    (or (and (numberp pq-slope)
             (numberp qr-slope)
             (= pq-slope qr-slope))
        (and (not pq-slope)
             (not qr-slope)))))
```

This is not nearly as pretty, although even in this more-explicit form, the logic seems to me less tortured than the "naïve" version. The reasoning is that $\overline{pq}$ and $\overline{qr}$ are the same line if the slopes are both numbers and those numbers are equal, or if both slopes are nil. And, anyway, should one penalize a clever Lisp program just because other languages can't do the same trick?

I would have been willing to call it quits at this point and accept `mm-collinear` as the final version of the program, but for another anomaly that turned up in testing. Both `mm-collinear` and `less-naive-collinear` could successfully discriminate between collinear points and near misses; a case like $p=(0\ 0)$, $q=(1\ 0)$, $r=(1000000\ 1)$ was not a challenge. But both procedures failed on this set of points: $p=(0\ 0)$, $q=(0\ 0)$, $r=(1\ 1)$.

A first question is what *should* happen in this instance. The program is supposed to be testing the collinearity of three points, but here p and q are actually the same point. My own view is that such points are indeed collinear because a single line can be drawn through all of them. I suppose the opposite position is also defensible, on the grounds that a line of *any* slope could be drawn through two coincident points. Unfortunately, the two procedures, as written, do not conform to *either* of these rules. They return nil for the example given above but t for the points $p=(0\ 0)$, $q=(0\ 0)$, and $r=(0\ 1)$. Surely this is pathological behavior by anyone's standards.

I could solve this problem by edict, declaring that the three arguments to the procedure must be distinct points. But then I'd have to write code to catch violations of the rule, raise exceptions, return error values, scold criminals, etc. It's not worth the bother.

The Triangle Inequality

Here's yet another way of rethinking the problem. Observe that if p, q, and r are *not* collinear, they define a triangle (Figure 33-4). It's a property of any triangle that the longest side is shorter than the sum of the smaller sides. If the three points are collinear, however, the triangle collapses on itself, and the longest "side" is exactly equal to the sum of the smaller "sides."

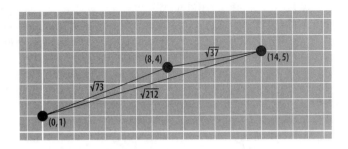

FIGURE 33-4. *Testing collinearity by the triangle inequality*

(For the example shown in this figure, the long side is shorter than the sum of the other two sides by about 0.067.)

The code for this version of the function is not quite so compact as the others, but what's going on inside is simple enough:

```
(defun triangle-collinear (px py qx qy rx ry)
  (let ((pq (distance px py qx qy))
        (pr (distance px py rx ry))
        (qr (distance qx qy rx ry)))
    (let ((sidelist (sort (list pq pr qr) #'>)))
      (= (first sidelist)
         (+ (second sidelist) (third sidelist))))))
```

The idea is to calculate the three side lengths, put them in a list, sort them in descending order of magnitude, and then compare the first (longest) side with the sum of the other two. If and only if these lengths are equal are the points collinear. This approach has a lot to recommend it. The calculation depends only on the geometric relations among the points themselves; it's independent of their position and orientation on the plane. Slopes and intercepts are not even mentioned. As a bonus, this version of the procedure also gives consistent and sensible answers when two or three of the points are coincident: all such point sets are considered collinear.

Unfortunately, there is a heavy price to be paid for this simplicity. Up to this point, all computations have been done with exact arithmetic. If the original coordinates are specified by means of integers or rational numbers, then the slopes and intercepts are calculated without round-off or other error. For example, the line passing through (1 1) and (4 2) has slope $m=1/3$ and y-intercept $b=2/3$ (not decimal approximations such as 0.33 and 0.67). With numbers represented in this way, comparisons are guaranteed to give the mathematically correct answer. But exactness is unattainable in measuring distances. The procedure distance invoked by triangle-collinear is defined like this:

```
(defun distance (px py qx qy)
  (sqrt (+ (square (- qx px))
           (square (- qy py)))))
```

The square root is the culprit, of course. If sqrt returns an irrational result, there's no hope of finding an exact, finite, numeric representation. When distances are calculated with double-precision IEEE floating-point arithmetic, triangle-collinear gives trustworthy answers for points whose coordinates are no larger than about 10^5. Go much beyond that threshold, and the procedure inevitably starts to mistake very skinny triangles for degenerate ones, incorrectly reporting that the vertices are collinear.

There is no quick and easy fix for this failing. Tricks like rotating or scaling the coordinate frame will not help. It's just a bug (or feature?) of our universe: rational points can give rise to irrational distances. Getting exact and reliable results under these circumstances is not quite impossible, but it takes an industrial-strength effort. Where the three points really are collinear, this fact can be proved algebraically without evaluating the square roots. For example, given the collinear points (0 0), (3 3), and (5 5), the distance equation is $sqrt(50) = sqrt(18) + sqrt(8)$, which reduces to $5 \times sqrt(2) = 3 \times sqrt(2) + 2 \times sqrt(2)$. When the points are *not* collinear, numerical evaluation will eventually reveal an inequality, if you calculate enough digits of the roots. But I don't relish the idea of implementing a symbolic algebra system and an adaptive multiprecision arithmetic module just to test trios of points for collinearity. There's gotta be an easier way. In the *Book* version of the algorithm, I expect greater economy of means.

Meandering On

To tell the rest of this story, I need to mention the context in which it took place. Some months ago I was playing with a simple model of river meandering—the formation of those giant horseshoe bends you see in the Lower Mississippi. The model decomposed the smooth curve of the river's course into a chain of short, straight segments. I needed to measure curvature along the river in terms of the bending angles between these segments, and in particular, I wanted to detect regions of zero curvature—hence the collinearity predicate.

Another part of the program gave me even more trouble. As meanders grow and migrate, one loop sometimes runs into the next one, at which point the river takes a shortcut and leaves behind a stranded "oxbow" lake. (You don't want to be standing in the way when this happens on the Mississippi.) To detect such events in the model, I needed to scan for intersections of segments. Again, I was able to get a routine working, but it seemed needlessly complex, with a decision tree sprouting a dozen branches. As in the case of collinearity, vertical segments and coincident points required special handling, and I also had to worry about parallel segments.

For the intersection problem, I eventually spent some time in the library and checked out what the Net had to offer. I learned a lot. That's where I found the tip that 10^{10} is close enough to infinity. And Bernard Chazelle and Herbert Edelsbrunner suggested a subtler way of finessing the singularities and degeneracies I had run into. In a 1992 review article on line-segment intersection algorithms (see the "Further Reading" section at the end of this chapter), they wrote:

> For the ease of exposition, we shall assume that no two endpoints have the same *x*- or *y*-coordinates. This, in particular, applies to the two endpoints of the same segment, and thus rules out the presence of vertical or horizontal segments...Our rationale is that the key ideas of the algorithm are best explained without having to worry about special cases every step of the way. Relaxing the assumptions is very easy (no new ideas are required) but tedious. That's for the theory. Implementing the algorithm so that the program works in all cases, however, is a daunting task. There are also numerical problems that alone would justify writing another paper. Following a venerable tradition, however, we shall try not to worry too much about it.

Perhaps the most important lesson learned from this foray into the literature was that others have also found meaty challenges in this field. It's not just that I'm a code wimp. This was a reassuring discovery; on the other hand, it did nothing to actually solve my problem.

Later, I wrote an item about line-segment intersection algorithms on my weblog at *http://bit-player.org*. This was essentially a plea for help, and help soon came pouring in—more than I could absorb at the time. One reader suggested polar coordinates as a remedy for undefined slopes, and another advocated rewriting the linear equations in parametric form, so that *x*- and *y*-coordinates are given as functions of a new variable *t*. Barry Cipra proposed a somewhat different parametric scheme, and then came up with yet another algorithm, based on the idea of applying an affine transformation to shift one of the segments onto the interval (−1 0),(1 0). David Eppstein advocated removing the problem from Euclidean geometry and solving it on the projective plane, where the presence of "a point at infinity" helps in dealing with singularities. Finally, Jonathan Richard Shewchuk gave me a pointer to his lecture notes, papers, and working code; I'll return to Shewchuk's ideas below.

I was impressed—and slightly abashed—by this flood of thoughtful and creative suggestions. There were several viable candidates for a segment-intersection procedure. Furthermore, I also found an answer to the collinearity problem. Indeed, I believe the solution that was handed to me may well be the *Book* algorithm.

"Duh!"—I Mean "Aha!"

In cartoons, the moment of discovery is depicted as a light bulb turning on in a thought balloon. In my experience, that sudden flash of understanding feels more like being thumped in the back of the head with a two-by-four. When you wake up afterwards, you've learned something, but by then your new insight is so blindingly obvious that you can't quite believe you didn't know it all along. After a few days more, you begin to suspect that maybe you *did* know it; you *must* have known it; you just needed reminding. And when you pass the discovery along to the next person, you'll begin, "As everyone knows...."

That was my reaction on reading Jonathan Shewchuk's "Lecture Notes on Geometric Robustness." He gives a collinearity algorithm that, once I understood it, seemed so natural and sensible that I'm sure it must have been latent within me somewhere. The key idea is to work with the area of a triangle rather than the perimeter, as in triangle-collinear. Clearly, the area of a triangle is zero if and only if the triangle is a degenerate one, with collinear vertices. But measuring a function of the area rather a function of the perimeter has two big advantages. First, it can be done without square roots or other operations that would take us outside the field of rational numbers. Second, it is much less dependent on numerical precision.

Consider a family of isosceles triangles with vertices (0 0), (*x* 1), and (2*x* 0). As *x* increases, the difference between the length of the base and the sum of the lengths of the two legs gets steadily smaller, and so it becomes difficult to distinguish this very shallow triangle from a totally flattened one with vertices (0 0), (*x* 0), and (2*x* 0). The area calculation doesn't suffer from this problem. On the contrary, the area grows steadily as the triangle gets longer (see Figure 33-5). Numerically, even without exact arithmetic, the computation is much more robust.

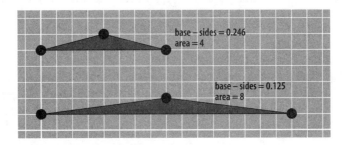

FIGURE 33-5. Testing collinearity by measuring area

How to measure the area? The Euclidean formula 1/2*bh* is not the best answer, and neither is the trigonometric approach. A far better plan is to regard the sides of a triangle as vectors; the two vectors emanating from any one vertex define a parallelogram, whose area is given by the cross product of the vectors. The area of the triangle is just one-half of the area of the parallelogram. Actually, this computation gives the "signed area": the result is positive if the vertices of the triangle are taken in counterclockwise order, and negative if taken in clockwise order. What's most important for present purposes, the signed area is zero if and only if the vertices are collinear.

The vector formula for the area is expressed most succinctly in terms of the determinant of a two-by-two matrix:

$$A = \frac{1}{2} \begin{vmatrix} x_1 - x_3 & y_1 - y_3 \\ x_2 - x_3 & y_2 - y_3 \end{vmatrix} = \frac{1}{2}[(x_1 - x_3)(y_2 - y_3) - (x_2 - x_3)(y_1 - y_3)]$$

Because I'm interested only in the case where the determinant is zero, I can ignore the factor of 1/2 and code the collinearity predicate in this simple form:

```
(defun area-collinear (px py qx qy rx ry)
  (= (* (- px rx) (- qy ry))
     (* (- qx rx) (- py ry))))
```

So, here it is: a simple arithmetical function of the *x*- and *y*-coordinates, requiring four subtractions, two multiplications, and an equality predicate, but nothing else—no ifs, no slopes, no intercepts, no square roots, no hazard of divide-by-zero errors. If executed with exact rational arithmetic, the procedure always produces exact and correct results. Characterizing the behavior with floating-point arithmetic is more difficult, but it is far superior to the version based on comparing distances on the perimeter. Shewchuk provides highly tuned C code that uses floating-point when possible and switches to exact arithmetic when necessary.

Conclusion

My adventures and misadventures searching for the ideal collinearity predicate do not make a story with a tidy moral. In the end, I believe I stumbled upon the correct solution to my specific problem, but the larger question of how best to find such solutions in general remains unsettled.

One lesson that *might* be drawn from my experience is to seek help without delay: somebody out there knows more than you do. You may as well take advantage of the cumulative wisdom of your peers and predecessors. In other words, Google can probably find the algorithm you want, or even the source code, so why waste time reinventing it?

I have mixed feelings about this advice. When an engineer is designing a bridge, I expect her to have a thorough knowledge of how others in the profession have solved similar problems in the past. Yet expertise is not merely skill in finding and applying other people's bright ideas; I want my bridge designer to have solved a few problems on her own as well.

Another issue is how long to keep an ailing program on life support. In this chapter, I have been discussing the tiniest of programs, so it cost very little to rip it up and start over whenever I encountered the slightest unpleasantness. For larger projects, the decision to throw one away is never so easy. And doing so is not necessarily prudent: you are trading known problems for unknown ones.

Finally, there is the question of just how much the quest for "beautiful code" should be allowed to influence the process of programming or software development. The mathematician G. H. Hardy proclaimed, "There is no permanent place in the world for ugly mathematics." Do aesthetic principles carry that much weight in computer science as well? Here's another way of asking the same question: do we have any guarantee that a *Book*-quality program exists for every well-formulated computational problem? Maybe *The Book* has some blank pages.

Further Reading

Avnaim, F., J.-D. Boissonnat, O. Devillers, F. P. Preparata, and M. Yvinec. "Evaluating signs of determinants using single-precision arithmetic." *Algorithmica*, Vol. 17, pp. 111–132, 1997.

Bentley, Jon L., and Thomas A. Ottmann. "Algorithms for reporting and counting geometric intersections." *IEEE Transactions on Computers*, Vol. C-28, pp. 643–647, 1979.

Braden, Bart. "The surveyor's area formula." *The College Mathematics Journal*, Vol. 17, No. 4, pp. 326–337, 1986.

Chazelle, Bernard, and Herbert Edelsbrunner. "An optimal algorithm for intersecting line segments in the plane." *Journal of the Association for Computing Machinery*, Vol. 39, pp. 1–54, 1992.

Forrest, A. R. "Computational geometry and software engineering: Towards a geometric computing environment." In *Techniques for Computer Graphics* (edited by D. F. Rogers and R. A. Earnshaw), pp. 23–37. New York: Springer-Verlag, 1987.

Forrest, A. R. "Computational geometry and uncertainty." In *Uncertainty in Geometric Computations* (edited by Joab Winkler and Mahesan Niranjan), pp. 69–77. Boston: Kluwer Academic Publishers, 2002.

Fortune, Steven, and Christopher J. Van Wyk. "Efficient exact arithmetic for computational geometry." In *Proceedings of the Ninth Annual Symposium on Computational Geometry*, pp. 163–172. New York: Association for Computing Machinery, 1993.

Guibas, Leonidas, and Jorge Stolfi. "Primitives for the manipulation of general subdivisions and the computation of Voronoi diagrams." *ACM Transactions on Graphics*, Vol. 4, No. 2, pp. 74–123, 1985.

Hayes, Brian. "Only connect!" *http://bit-player.org/2006/only-connect*. [Weblog item, posted September 14, 2006.]

Hayes, Brian. "Computing science: Up a lazy river." *American Scientist*, Vol. 94, No. 6, pp. 490–494, 2006. (*http://www.americanscientist.org/AssetDetail/assetid/54078*)

Hoffmann, Christoph M., John E. Hopcroft and Michael S. Karasick. "Towards implementing robust geometric computations." *Proceedings of the Fourth Annual Symposium on Computational Geometry*, pp. 106–117. New York: Association for Computing Machinery, 1988.

O'Rourke, Joseph. *Computational Geometry in C*. Cambridge: Cambridge University Press, 1994.

Preparata, Franco P., and Michael I. Shamos. *Computational Geometry: An Introduction*. New York: Springer-Verlag, 1985.

Qian, Jianbo, and Cao An Wang. "How much precision is needed to compare two sums of square roots of integers?" *Information Processing Letters*, Vol. 100, pp. 194–198, 2006.

Shewchuk, Jonathan Richard. "Adaptive precision floating-point arithmetic and fast robust geometric predicates." *Discrete and Computational Geometry*, Vol. 18, pp. 305–363, 1997. Preprint available at *http://www.cs.cmu.edu/afs/cs/project/quake/public/papers/robust-arithmetic.ps*.

Shewchuk, Jonathan Richard. Lecture notes on geometric robustness. [Version of October 26, 2006.] (*http://www.cs.berkeley.edu/~jrs/meshpapers/robnotes.ps.gz*. See also source code at *http://www.cs.cmu.edu/afs/cs/project/quake/public/code/predicates.c*.)

Afterword

Andy Oram

BEAUTIFUL CODE SURVEYS THE RANGE OF HUMAN INVENTION AND INGENUITY in one area of endeavor: the development of computer systems. The beauty in each chapter comes from the discovery of unique solutions, a discovery springing from the authors' power to look beyond set boundaries, to recognize needs overlooked by others, and to find surprising solutions to troubling problems.

Many of the authors confronted limitations—in the physical environment, in the resources available, or in the very definition of their requirements—that made it hard even to imagine solutions. Others entered domains where solutions already existed, but brought in a new vision and a conviction that something much better could be achieved.

All the authors in this book have drawn lessons from their projects. But we can also draw some broader lessons after making the long and eventful journey through the whole book.

First, there are times when tried and true rules really do work. So, often one encounters difficulties when trying to maintain standards for robustness, readability, or other tenets of good software engineering. In such situations, it is not always necessary to abandon the principles that hold such promise. Sometimes, getting up and taking a walk around the problem can reveal a new facet that allows one to meet the requirements without sacrificing good technique.

On the other hand, some chapters confirm the old cliché that one must know the rules before one can break them. Some of the authors built up decades of experience before taking a different path toward solving one thorny problem—and this experience gave them the confidence to break the rules in a constructive way.

On the other hand, cross-disciplinary studies are also championed by the lessons in this book. Many authors came into new domains and had to fight their way in relative darkness. In these situations, a particularly pure form of creativity and intelligence triumphed.

Finally, we learn from this book that beautiful solutions don't last for all time. New circumstances always require a new look. So, if you read the book and thought, "I can't use these authors' solutions on any of my own projects," don't worry—next time these authors have projects, they will use different solutions, too.

For about two months I worked intensively on this book by helping authors hone their themes and express their points. This immersion in the work of superbly talented inventors proved to be inspiring and even uplifting. It gave me the impulse to try new things, and I hope this book does the same for its readers.

Contributors

JON **B**ENTLEY IS A COMPUTER SCIENTIST AT **A**VAYA **L**ABS **R**ESEARCH. His research interests include programming techniques, algorithm design, and the design of software tools and interfaces. He has written books on programming, and articles on a variety of topics, ranging from the theory of algorithms to software engineering. He received a B.S. from Stanford in 1974, and an M.S. and Ph.D. from the University of North Carolina in 1976, then taught Computer Science at Carnegie Mellon University for six years. He joined Bell Labs Research in 1982, and retired in 2001 to join Avaya. He has been a visiting faculty member at West Point and Princeton, and he has been a member of teams that have shipped software tools, telephone switches, telephones, and web services.

Tim Bray managed the Oxford English Dictionary project at the University of Waterloo in Ontario, Canada in 1987–1989, co-founded Open Text Corporation in 1989, launched one of the first public web search engines in 1995, co-invented XML 1.0 and co-edited "Namespaces in XML" between 1996 and 1999, founded Antarctica Systems in 1999, and served as a Tim Berners-Lee appointee on the W3C Technical Architecture Group in 2002–2004. Currently, he serves as Director of Web Technologies at Sun Microsystems, publishes a popular weblog, and co-chairs the IETF AtomPub Working Group.

Bryan Cantrill is a Distinguished Engineer at Sun Microsystems, where he has spent most of his career working on the Solaris kernel. Most recently he, along with colleagues Mike Shapiro and Adam Leventhal, designed and implemented DTrace, a facility for dynamic instrumentation of production systems that won the *Wall Street Journal*'s top award for innovation in 2006.

Douglas Crockford is a product of our public school system. A registered voter, he owns his own car. He has developed office automation systems. He did research in games and music at Atari. He was Director of Technology at Lucasfilm Ltd. He was Director of New Media at Paramount. He was the founder and CEO of Electric Communities. He was founder and CTO of State Software, where he discovered JSON. He is now an architect at Yahoo! Inc.

Rogerio Atem de Carvalho is a teacher and researcher at the Federal Center for Technological Education of Campos (CEFET Campos), Brazil. He was awarded with the 2006 IFIP Distinguished Academic Leadership Award in Vienna, Austria, for his research on Free/Open Source Enterprise Resources Planning (ERP). His research and consulting interests also include Decision Support Systems and Software Engineering.

Jeff Dean joined Google in 1999 and is currently a Google Fellow in Google's Systems Infrastructure Group. While at Google, he has worked on Google's crawling, indexing, query serving, and advertising systems, implemented several search quality improvements, and built various pieces of Google's distributed computing infrastructure. Prior to joining Google, he was at DEC/Compaq's Western Research Laboratory, where he worked on profiling tools, microprocessor architecture, and information retrieval. He received a Ph.D. from the University of Washington in 1996, working with Craig Chambers on compiler optimization techniques for object-oriented languages. Prior to graduate school, he worked at the World Health Organization's Global Programme on AIDS.

Jack Dongarra received a B.S. in Mathematics from Chicago State University in 1972, and an M.S. in Computer Science from the Illinois Institute of Technology in 1973. He received his Ph.D. in Applied Mathematics from the University of New Mexico in 1980. He worked at the Argonne National Laboratory until 1989, becoming a senior scientist. He now holds an appointment as University Distinguished Professor of Computer Science in the Computer Science Department at the University of Tennessee. He has the position of a Distinguished Research Staff member in the Computer Science and Mathematics Division at Oak Ridge National Laboratory (ORNL), Turing Fellow in the Computer Science and Mathematics Schools at the University of Manchester, and an Adjunct Professor in the Computer Science Department at Rice University. He specializes in numerical algorithms in linear algebra, parallel computing, the use of advanced-computer architectures, programming methodology, and tools for parallel computers. His research includes the development, testing, and documentation of high-quality mathematical software. He has contributed to the design and implementation of the following open source software packages and systems: EISPACK, LINPACK, the BLAS, LAPACK, ScaLAPACK, Netlib, PVM, MPI, NetSolve, Top500, ATLAS, and PAPI. He has published approximately 200 articles, papers, reports, and technical memoranda, and he is co-author of several books. He was awarded the IEEE Sid Fernbach Award in 2004 for his contributions in the application of high-performance computers using innovative approaches. He is a Fellow of the AAAS, ACM, and the IEEE, and a member of the National Academy of Engineering.

R. Kent Dybvig is a professor of Computer Science at Indiana University. He received his Ph.D. in Computer Science from the University of North Carolina in 1987, two years after joining the faculty at Indiana. His research in the design and implementation of programming languages has led to significant contributions involving control operators, syntactic abstraction, program analysis, compiler optimization, register allocation, multithreading, and automatic storage management. In 1984, he created *Chez Scheme* and remains its principal developer. Known for fast compile times and reliability as well as for its ability to run even complex programs with large memory footprints efficiently, *Chez Scheme* has been used to build commercial systems for enterprise integration, web serving, virtual reality, robotic drug testing, circuit layout, and more. It is also used for computer science education at all levels, as well as research in a variety of areas. Dybvig is author of *The Scheme Programming Language*, Third Edition (MIT Press), and is an editor of the forthcoming Revised[6] Report on Scheme.

Michael Feathers is a consultant with Object Mentor. He has been active in the Agile community for the past seven years, balancing his time between working with, training, and coaching various teams around the world. Prior to joining Object Mentor, Michael designed a proprietary programming language and wrote a compiler for it. He also designed a large multiplatform class library and a framework for instrumentation control. Publicly, Michael developed CppUnit, the initial port of JUnit to C++; and FitCpp, a port of FIT for C++. In 2005, Michael wrote the book *Working Effectively with Legacy Code* (Prentice Hall). When he isn't engaged with a team, he spends most of his time investigating ways of altering design over time in large code bases.

Karl Fogel, in 1995, together with Jim Blandy, co-founded Cyclic Software, the first company offering commercial CVS support. In 1997, Karl added support for CVS anonymous read-only repository access, thus allowing easy access to development code in open source projects. In 1999, he wrote *Open Source Development with CVS* (Coriolis). From 2000–2006, he worked for CollabNet, Inc., managing the creation and development of Subversion, an open source version control system written from scratch by CollabNet and a team of open source volunteers. In 2005, he wrote *Producing Open Source Software: How to Run a Successful Free Software Project* (O'Reilly; also online at *http://producingoss.com*). After a brief stint as an Open Source Specialist at Google in 2006, he left to become full-time editor of Question-Copyright.org. He continues to participate in various open source projects, including Subversion and GNU Emacs.

Sanjay Ghemawat is a Google Fellow who works in the Systems Infrastructure Group at Google. He has designed and implemented distributed storage systems, text-indexing systems, performance tools, a data representation language, an RPC system, a malloc implementation, and many other libraries. Prior to joining Google, he was a member of the research staff at DEC Systems Research Center, where he worked on a profiling system and an optimizing compiler for Java, and implemented a Java virtual machine. He received a Ph.D. from MIT in 1995 concerning the implementation of object-oriented databases.

Ashish Gulhati is Chief Developer of Neomailbox, an Internet privacy service, and the developer of Cryptonite, an OpenPGP-compatible secure webmail system. A commercial software developer for more than 15 years, and one of India's first digital rights activists and F/OSS hackers, he has written numerous open source Perl modules, which are available from CPAN. His 1993–1994 articles in *PC Quest* and *DataQuest* magazines were the first in the mainstream Indian computing press to introduce readers to Free Software, GNU/Linux, the Web, and the Internet, many years before the availability of commercial Internet access in India, and formed an important part of the PC Quest Linux Initiative, which resulted in a million Linux CDs being distributed in India since 1995. He is rapidly evolving into a cyborg thanks to an eclectic collection of wearable computers.

Elliotte Rusty Harold is originally from New Orleans, to which he returns periodically in search of a decent bowl of gumbo. However, he currently resides in the Prospect Heights neighborhood of Brooklyn with his wife Beth, dog Shayna, and cats Charm (named after the quark) and Marjorie (named after his mother-in-law). He's an adjunct professor of computer science at Polytechnic University, where he teaches Java, XML, and object-oriented programming. His Cafe au Lait web site (*http://www.cafeaulait.org*) has become one of the most popular independent Java sites on the Internet; his spin-off site, Cafe con Leche (*http://www.cafeconleche.org*), has become one of the most popular XML sites. His books include *Java I/O*, *Java Network Programming*, *XML in a Nutshell* (all O'Reilly), and *XML Bible* (Wiley). He's currently working on the XOM Library for processing XML with Java, the Jaxen XPath engine, and the Amateur media player.

Brian Hayes writes the Computing Science column in *American Scientist* magazine and also has a weblog at *http://bit-player.org*. In the past, he wrote similar columns on mathematics and computer science for *Scientific American*, *Computer Language*, and *The Sciences*. His book *Infrastructure: A Field Guide to the Industrial Landscape* (Norton) was published in 2005.

Jim Kent is a research scientist at the Genome Bioinformatics Group at the University of California Santa Cruz. Jim has been programming professionally since 1983. During the first half of his career, he focused on paint and animation software, authoring among other works the award-winning programs Aegis Animator, Cyber Paint, and Autodesk Animator. In 1996, tired of keeping up with the Windows API treadmill, he decided to pursue his interest in biology, earning a Ph.D. in 2002. As a graduate student, he wrote GigAssembler—a program that produced the first assembly of the human genome—one day ahead of Celera's first genome assembly, helping assure that the bulk of the genome would remain free of patents and other legal entanglements. Jim is an author of 40 scientific papers. His work today is primarily in creating programs, databases, and web sites that help scientists analyze and understand the genome.

Brian Kernighan received his B.Sc. from the University of Toronto in 1964, and a Ph.D. in electrical engineering from Princeton in 1969. He was in the Computing Science Research center at Bell Labs until 2000, and is now in the Computer Science Department at Princeton. He is the author of eight books and a number of technical papers, and holds four patents. His research areas include programming languages, tools, and interfaces that make computers easier to use, often for nonspecialist users. He is also interested in technology education for nontechnical audiences.

Adam Kolawa is the co-founder and CEO of Parasoft, a leading provider of Automated Error Prevention (AEP) software solutions. Kolawa's years of experience with various software development processes has resulted in his unique insight into the high-tech industry and the uncanny ability to successfully identify technology trends. As a result, he has orchestrated the development of several successful commercial software products to meet growing industry needs to improve software quality—often before the trends have been widely accepted. Kolawa, co-author of *Bulletproofing Web Applications* (Hungry Minds), has contributed to and written more than 100 commentary pieces and technical articles for publications such as *The Wall Street Journal*, *CIO*, *Computerworld*, *Dr. Dobb's Journal*, and *IEEE Computer*; he has also authored numerous scientific papers on physics and parallel processing. His recent media engagements include CNN, CNBC, BBC, and NPR. Kolawa holds a Ph.D. in theoretical physics from the California Institute of Technology, and has been granted 10 patents for his recent inventions. In 2001, Kolawa was awarded the Los Angeles Ernst & Young's Entrepreneur of the Year Award in the software category.

Greg Kroah-Hartman is the current Linux kernel maintainer for more driver subsystems than he wants to admit, along with the driver core, *sysfs*, *kobject*, *kref*, and *debugfs* code. He also helped start the linux-hotplug and *udev* projects, and is one half of the kernel stable maintainer team. He works for SuSE Labs/Novell and does various kernel-related things for them. He is the author of the book *Linux Kernel in a Nutshell* (O'Reilly) and the co-author of *Linux Device Drivers*, Third Edition (O'Reilly).

Andrew Kuchling has 11 years of experience as a software developer and is a longtime member of the Python development community. Some of his Python-related work includes writing and maintaining several standard library modules, writing a series of "What's new in Python 2.x" articles and other documentation, planning the 2006 and 2007 PyCon conferences, and acting as a director of the Python Software Foundation. Andrew graduated with a B.Sc. in Computer Science from McGill University in 1995. His web page is at *http://www.amk.ca*.

Piotr Luszczek received his M.Sc. degree from the University of Mining and Metallurgy in Krakow, Poland for work on parallel out-of-core libraries. He earned his doctorate degree for the innovative use of dense matrix computational kernels in sparse direct and iterative numerical linear algebra algorithms. He applied this experience to develop fault-tolerant libraries that used out-of-core techniques. Currently, he is a Research Professor at the University of Tennessee, Knoxville. His work involves standardization of benchmarking of large supercomputer installations. He is an author of self-adapting software libraries that automatically choose the best algorithm to efficiently utilize available hardware and can optimally process the input data. He is also involved in high-performance programming language design and implementation.

Ronald Mak was a senior scientist at the Research Institute for Advanced Computer Science when he was on contract to NASA Ames as the architect and lead developer of the middleware for the Collaborative Information Portal. After the rovers landed on Mars, he provided mission support at JPL and at Ames. He then received an academic appointment with the University of California Santa Cruz, and he was again on contract to NASA, this time to design and develop enterprise software to help return astronauts to the moon. Ron is co-founder and CTO of Willard & Lowe Systems, Inc. (*www.willardlowe.com*), a consulting company that specializes in enterprise information management systems. He has written several books on computer software, and he has degrees in the mathematical sciences and computer science from Stanford University.

Yukihiro "Matz" Matsumoto is a programmer, a Japanese open source evangelist, and the creator of the recently popular Ruby language. He started development of Ruby in 1993, so it's actually as old as Java. Now he works for Network Applied Communication Laboratory, Inc. (NaCl, also known as netlab.jp), which has sponsored Ruby development since 1997. Because his real name is too long to remember and is difficult for non-Japanese speakers to pronounce right, on the Net he uses the nickname Matz.

Arun Mehta is an electrical engineer and computer scientist who has studied and taught in India, the U.S., and Germany. He is one of India's early telecom and cyber-activists, trying to obtain consumer-friendly policies that will help the spread of modern communications in rural areas and among the poor. His current passions include village radio and technology for the disabled. He is a professor and chairman of the Computer Engineering Department of JMIT, Radaur, Haryana, India. His web sites include *http://india-gii.org*, *http://radiophony.com*, and *http://holisticit.com*.

Rafael Manhaes Monnerat is an IT Analyst at CEFET CAMPOS, and an offshore consultant for Nexedi SARL. His interests include Free/Open Source Systems, ERP, and cool programming languages.

Travis E. Oliphant received a B.S. in Electrical and Computer Engineering and Mathematics from Brigham Young University in 1995, and an M.S. in Electrical and Computer Engineering from the same institution in 1996. In 2001, he received a Ph.D. in Biomedical Engineering from the Mayo Graduate School in Rochester, Minnesota. He is a principal author for SciPy and NumPy, which are scientific computing libraries for the Python language. His research interests include micro-scale impedance imaging, MRI reconstruction in inhomogeneous fields, and general biomedical inverse problems. He is currently an Assistant Professor in the Electrical and Computer Engineering Department at Brigham Young University.

Andy Oram is an editor at O'Reilly Media. An employee of the company since 1992, Andy currently specializes in free software and open source technologies. His work for O'Reilly includes the first books ever released by a U.S. publisher on Linux, and the 2001 title *Peer-to-Peer*. His modest programming and system administration skills are mostly self-taught. Andy is also a member of Computer Professionals for Social Responsibility and writes often for the O'Reilly Network (*http://oreillynet.com*) and other publications on policy issues related to the Internet, and on trends affecting technical innovation and its effects on society. His web site is *http://www.praxagora.com/andyo*.

William R. Otte is a Ph.D. student in the Department of Electrical Engineering and Computer Science (EECS) at Vanderbilt University in Tennessee. His research focuses on middleware for distributed real-time and embedded (DRE) systems. He is currently involved in several aspects of developing a Deployment and Configuration Engine (DAnCE) for CORBA Components. This work involves investigation of techniques for runtime planning, and adaptation for component-based applications, as well as specification and enforcement of application quality-of-service and fault-tolerance requirements. Before joining as a graduate student, William worked for a year as a staff engineer at the Institute for Software Integrated Systems after graduating in 2005 with a B.S. in Computer Science from Vanderbilt University.

Andrew Patzer is the Director of the Bioinformatics Program at the Medical College of Wisconsin. Andrew has been a software developer for the past 15 years and has written several articles and books, including *Professional Java Server Programming* (Peer Information, Inc.) and *JSP Examples and Best Practices* (Apress). Andrew's current interest lies in the field of Bioinformatics, using dynamic languages such as Groovy to mine the enormous amounts of available biological data and help perform analysis for scientific researchers.

Charles Petzold is a freelance writer who specializes in Windows application programming. He is the author of *Programming Windows* (Microsoft Press), which in its five editions between 1988 and 1999 taught a generation of programmers about the Windows API. His most recent book is *Applications = Code + Markup: A Guide to the Microsoft Windows Presentation Foundation* (Microsoft Press), and he is also author of a unique exploration into digital technologies entitled *Code: The Hidden Language of Computer Hardware and Software* (Microsoft Press). His web site is *http://www.charlespetzold.com*.

Simon Peyton Jones, M.A., MBCS, C.Eng., graduated from Trinity College Cambridge in 1980. After two years in industry, he spent seven years as a lecturer at University College London, and nine years as a professor at Glasgow University before moving to Microsoft Research in 1998. His main research interest is in functional programming languages, their implementation, and their application. He has led a succession of research projects focused on the design and implementation of production-quality functional-language systems for both uniprocessors and parallel machines. He was a key contributor to the design of the now-standard functional language Haskell, and is the lead designer of the widely used Glasgow Haskell Compiler (GHC). He has written two textbooks about the implementation of functional languages.

T. V. Raman specializes in web technologies and auditory user interfaces. In the early 1990s, he introduced the notion of audio formatting in his Ph.D. thesis entitled

AsTeR: Audio System For Technical Readings, concerning a system that produced high-quality aural renderings of technical documents. Emacspeak is the result of applying these ideas to the broader domain of computer user interfaces. Raman is now a Research Scientist at Google, where he focuses on web applications.

Alberto Savoia is co-founder and CTO of Agitar Software. Before Agitar, he was Senior Director of Engineering at Google; prior to that he was the Director of Software Research at Sun Microsystems Laboratories. Alberto's passion and main body of work and research is in the area of software development technology—in particular, tools and technology to help programmers test and verify their own code during the design and development phase.

Douglas C. Schmidt is a Full Professor in the Electrical Engineering and Computer Science (EECS) Department, Associate Chair of the Computer Science and Engineering program, and a Senior Research Scientist at the Institute for Software Integrated Systems (ISIS) at Vanderbilt University in Tennessee. He is an expert on distributed computing patterns and middleware frameworks and has published more than 350 technical papers and 9 books that cover a range of topics including high-performance communication software systems, parallel processing for high-speed networking protocols, real-time distributed object computing, object-oriented patterns for concurrent and distributed systems, and model-driven development tools. In addition to his academic research, Dr. Schmidt is CTO for PrismTechnologies, and he has over 15 years of experience leading the development of widely used, open source middleware platforms that contain a rich set of components and domain-specific languages that implement key patterns for high-performance distributed systems. Dr. Schmidt received his Ph.D. in Computer Science from the University of California Irvine in 1994.

Christopher Seiwald is the author of Perforce (a software configuration management system), Jam (a build tool), and "The Seven Pillars of Pretty Code" (a paper from which Chapter 32, *Code in Motion*, draws ideas). Prior to founding Perforce, he managed the network development group at Ingres Corporation, where he toiled for years to make asynchronous networking code look palatable. He is currently the CEO of Perforce Software, and still has his hand in coding.

Diomidis Spinellis is an Associate Professor at the Department of Management Science and Technology at the Athens University of Economics and Business, Greece. His research interests include software engineering tools, programming languages, and computer security. He holds an M.Eng. in Software Engineering and a Ph.D. in Computer Science, both from Imperial College London. He has published more than 100 technical papers in the areas of software engineering, information security, and ubiquitous computing. He has also written the two *Open Source Perspective* books: *Code Reading* (Software Development Productivity Award 2004), and *Code Quality* (both Addison-Wesley). He is a member of the IEEE Software editorial board, authoring the regular "Tools of the Trade" column. Diomidis is a FreeBSD committer and the author of a number of open source software packages, libraries, and tools.

Lincoln Stein is an M.D./Ph.D. who works on biological data integration and visualization. After his training at Harvard Medical School, he worked at the Whitehead Institute/MIT Center for Genome Research, where he developed the databases used for the mouse and human genome maps. At Cold Spring Harbor he works on a variety of genome-scale databases including WormBase, the database of the C. elegans genome; Gramene, a comparative genome-mapping database for rice and other monocots; the International HapMap Project Database; and a human biological pathways database called Reactome. Lincoln is also author of the books *How to Set Up and Maintain a Web Site* (Addison-Wesley), *Network Programming in Perl* (Addison-Wesley), *Official Guide to Programming with CGI.pm* (Wiley), and *Writing Apache Modules with Perl and C* (O'Reilly).

Nevin Thompson translated Yukihiro Matsumoto's Chapter 29, *Treating Code As an Essay*, from the Japanese. His clients include Japan's largest television network, as well as Technorati Japan and Creative Commons.

Henry S. Warren, Jr. has had a 45-year career with IBM, spanning from the IBM 704 to the PowerPC. He has worked on various military command and control systems, and on the SETL project under Jack Schwartz at New York University. Since 1973, he has been with IBM's Research Division, focusing on compilers and computer architectures. Hank currently works on the Blue Gene petaflop computer project. He received his Ph.D. in computer science from the Courant Institute at New York University. He is the author of *Hacker's Delight* (Addison-Wesley).

Laura Wingerd formed her early opinions of software configuration management during a decade of wrangling builds and source code for the Sybase and Ingres database products. She joined Perforce Software in its first year and has since acquired quite a bit of SCM expertise from the very Perforce customers she purports to advise. She is the author of *Practical Perforce* (O'Reilly) and a number of SCM-related whitepapers; *The Flow of Change*, a Google Tech Talk, marks her video debut. Laura is currently Vice President of Product Technology at Perforce Software, dividing her time between promoting sound SCM practices and investigating new and better ways to put Perforce to use.

Greg Wilson holds a Ph.D. in Computer Science from the University of Edinburgh and has worked on high-performance scientific computing, data visualization, and computer security. He is now an adjunct professor in Computer Science at the University of Toronto, and a contributing editor with *Dr. Dobb's Journal*.

Andreas Zeller graduated from TU Darmstadt in 1991 and received a Ph.D. in Computer Science in 1997 from TU Braunschweig in Germany. Since 2001, he has been a Computer Science professor at Saarland University in Germany. Zeller researches large programs and their history, and he has developed a number of methods to determine the causes of program failures in open source programs, as well as in industrial contexts at IBM, Microsoft, SAP, and others. His book *Why Programs Fail: A Guide to Systematic Debugging* (Morgan Kaufmann) received the Software Development Magazine productivity award in 2006.

INDEX

Symbols

$ (dollar sign)
  end of line matching in regular
    expressions, 3, 5
  in Perl variable names, 195
% (percent sign), Perl variable names, 195
& (ampersand), && operator in
    JavaScript, 136
( ) (parentheses)
  invoking functions, 144
  type in Haskell, 389
* (asterisk)
  JavaScript operator, 135
  matching zero or more occurrences in
    regular expressions, 3, 4
+ (plus sign)
  JavaScript infix operator, 134
  matching one or more instances in regular
    expressions, 43
. (period)
  . operator in JavaScript, 136
  matching any single character in regular
    expressions, 3

= (equals sign), === (exact-equality
    comparison) operator in
    JavaScript, 135
-> (arrow), indicating object-oriented method
    call in Perl, 195
? (question mark), ?: ternary operator in
    JavaScript, 135
@ (at-sign) in Perl variable names, 195
[ ] (square brackets)
  [ ] operator in JavaScript, 136
  [^ .], matching any character not a space or
    period, 43
  array literals in JavaScript, 144
^ (caret), beginning of line matching in regular
    expressions, 3
{ } (curly braces)
  delimiting code blocks in Ruby, 48
  enclosing function body in JavaScript, 143
  object literals in JavaScript, 145
  statement blocks in JavaScript, 141
| (vertical bar), || operator in JavaScript, 136
' (single quote) transposition operator, 233

Numbers

C

c (character), matching in regular
    expressions, 3
C language
    code for applying a digital filter, 113
    code implementing filesystem layers, 288
    code packing function arguments into a
        single structure, 288
    compilation from specialized high-level
        domain-specific language to, 288
    do-while loop, 4
    early Windows applications, 111
    hexadecimals, 150
    N-dimensional arrays, looping over, 304
    object-oriented model of code in Linux
        driver model, 277
    object-oriented programming and, 8
    operating system (OS) APIs, 429
    Perl interface to libraries, 168
    pointers, 5, 271
        compact code in regular expression
            matcher, 9
    polymorphic object, creating, 221
    population count for 36-bit word, adapting
        to 32-bit word, 151
    population count, counting 1-bits in a word
        x, 148
    PyDict_SetItem( ) function, 300
    Python implementation (see CPython)
    special-purpose syntactic constructs, 407
    structures
        inheriting and manipulating in Linux
            kernel, 272
        PyDictObject, 295
        reference counting, 273–276
    syntactic abstraction mechanism,
        preprocessor macros, 408
C#, 112
    code to implement digital image
        filters, 112
    code written for best performance,
        examining with IL Disassembler, 115
    digital filter algorithm, 116
    image processing code, 114
    indirection in, 290
    Intermediate Language, generating and
        then executing, 118
C++
    cfront preprocessor, compiling C++ code
        into C, 288
    implementation of MapReduce word
        frequency counting example, 382
    inheritance and overloading, 261
    parameterized types, 432

C. elegans genome, 189
caching
    in eLocutor, 486, 495
        SaveReverse subroutine, 495
    namespace URIs after verification, 72
Calendar (Emacs), speech-enabling, 515
calendar-forward-week function, advice
    definition for, 515
callbacks in Bio::Graphics
    usefulness of, 209
    using for each option passed to
        add_track( ), 207
cancellations, handling in Subversion delta
    editor, 25
Cantrill, Bryan, 353–369
capture of a variable reference by a variable
    binding, 408–411
carry-save adder (CSA) circuits, 154–159
cart object (Gene Sorter), 220
cart variables (Gene Sorter)
    avoiding name conflicts, 221
    communication between column filtering
        methods, 224
CAs (Certification Authorities), 164
causalities, 347
CD-ROMs, ISO-9660 filesystem, 279, 281
CERN library, 254
    inner beauty of code, 261–266
        beauty in flow, 265
        brevity and simplicity, 261
        frugality, 262–265
    outer beauty of code, 255–260
Certification Authorities (CAs), 164
CGI scripts
    advantages and disadvantages, 219
    Gene Sorter, 219
    lifetime, 220
    long-term data storage, 220
    short lifetime, advantages of, 221
chain of blocked threads, 356
chaining, 298
    in vector machines, 231
character classes (in regular expressions), 7
children with disabilities, communication in
    classroom via software, 501
choose function (Haskell), 402
CIP (Collaborative Information Portal),
    319–338
    Mars Exploration Rover (MER) mission
        and, 320
        mission needs, 321
    Middleware Monitor Utility, 335
    robustness, 336–337
        dynamic reconfiguration, 337
        hot swapping, 337

F

Factory class (Bio::Graphics::Glyph), 201–205
  dynamic option processing, 207
  make_glyph( ) method, 202
  option( ) method, 202
factory pattern, routing services with, 456–457
familiarity (of beautiful code), 479
FAT-32 filesystem for the USB stick, 279
fault tolerance, MapReduce
      implementation, 379
favorites in eLocutor (frequently used
      words), 496
Feathers, Michael, 75–84
features (genomic), 190
  density of, 191
  handling scale in visual
      representations, 191
feed reading software, 522
ffs (Berkeley Fast Filesystem), 283
fgrep, 2
file readers and file writers (CIP streamer
      service), 326
filesystems, operating systems supporting
      different, 279
  code to access filesystems, 280
  filesystem layers, 285–287
  FreeBSD use of indirection to abstract read
      function arguments, 282–285
Filter class, ApplyFilter( ) method, 116
filterControls method (Gene Sorter
      columns), 224
FilterMethodCS, 116
  optimizing, 117
FilterMethodIL, 119–127
  DynamicMethod instance, invoking, 126
filters, Gene Sorter, 224
finding the definition of a name (JavaScript
      parser), 139
finite automata, regular expressions translated
      into, 45
first-class values, Haskell actions as, 404
FIT (Framework for Integrated Test), 75–84
  challenge of framework design, 78
  classes, 76
    relationships among, 77
  documents serving as tests, 76
  HTML parsing, 80–83
  open framework, 79
  open style of development, benefits of, 83
Fixture class (Java), 77, 79
flex, generating C code implementing high-
      level domain-specific language, 288
flexibility of beautiful code, 481
floating-point arithmetic, IEEE double
      precision, 546

flow in beautiful code, 265
Fogel, Karl, 11–28
for loops
  looping over N-dimensional arrays, 304
  Python iterators as predicates, 305
forkIO function (Haskell), 390, 401
fork-join model of computation, 247
Fortran, 234
  BLAS (Basic Linear Algebra
      Subprograms), 252
  LINPACK package, 235
  required use of Fortran 90 with recursive
      LU, 240
forward web link graph, 376
frameworks
  applied to networked software, 430
  Framework for Integrated Test (see FIT)
  object-oriented, key concepts, 433
free_dicts array (Python), 300
FreeBSD operating system
  high-level I/O abstraction
      independence, 289
  implementation of read system call, 280
    filesystem-independent part, 281
  interface functions and data structures,
      language written in, 287
  read system call, functions to avoid code
      duplication, 290
  supporting different filesystems,
      abstracting read function
      arguments, 282–285
freedom from enforcement from tools
      (flexibility), 481
free-identifier=? predicate, 424
frequently used words in eLocutor, 496
frugality in beautiful code, 262–265
full-text searches, 55
fullword immediate, 152
function arguments abstracted to argument
      pointers, 282–285
function calls, keyword arguments in (Python
      dictionaries), 300
function pointers, used to dispatch a request to
      different functions, 289
functional decomposition of nontrivial
      software, problems created by, 430
functions
  JavaScript, 131, 143
  naming, understanding purpose from the
      name, 226
  reentrant, 227
  reusable, 228
fundamental instructions on RISC and CISC
      computers, 147

G

H

likeliest causes first, examining in
    debugging, 467
linear algebra
    algorithms recast as matrix-matrix
        operations, 231
    core of scientific computing
        calculations, 229
    dense linear systems, decompositional
        approach to solutions, 232
    software for advanced-architecture
        computers, 229
    motivation for development, 230
linear probing, 298
line-segment intersection algorithms, 547
link counting (PageRank), 56
LINPACK, 235–237
    column-oriented algorithms, use of, 235
    implementation of factorization, 235
    resources for further reading, 252
Linux
    desktop environment for secure mail
        system, 168
    native filesystem, 279
Linux kernel, 267–277
    development process, how it works, 277
    devfs, problems with race conditions, 268
    device handling in persistent manner, lack
        of, 268
    devices, physical and virtual portions, 267
    power management for devices, 268
    unified driver and device model, 268
        object reference counting in virtual
            filesystem layer, 273–276
        pointers to struct device, passing
            around, 271
        runtime type checking, lack of, 272
        scaling up to thousands of devices, 276
        small objects loosely joined, 277
        struct device as base class for all
            devices, 268
        sysfs virtual filesystem, 269
LISP
    advice, 505
        extension points, discovery of, 513
        tutorial, 507
    ALGOL-like syntax, attempts at, 130
    macros, 408
    parsing techniques, 130
    procedure definition, 540
list comprehension (Haskell), 400
literals (in JavaScript), 131, 144
    literal symbol in JavaScript parser, 132
load balancing, MapReduce
        implementation, 379
loadable parameters for services, 337
locality, MapReduce implementation, 379

locking, 287
    bank accounts using locks, 386
    handling of locking assertions, 288
    Mutex wrapper facade for acquiring/
        releasing locks, 437
    problems with locks, 387
        error recovery, 388
        lost wakeups and erroneous retries, 388
        no support for modular
            programming, 388
        taking in wrong order, 388
        taking the wrong locks, 388
        taking too few, 387
        taking too many, 387
    Solaris user-level priority inheritance
        bug, 354–368
    strategies for, 432
Log_Handler class, 438
logging
    CIP streamer service, 329–334
    concurrent logging servers,
        implementing, 444–450
    log record formats, 432
    networked logging service (example
        application), 431
    Sawzall language for logs analysis, 382
    sequential logging servers,
        implementing, 439–444
logging server framework, OO design for, 432,
        433–439
    associating concurrency strategy with IPC
        and synchronization, 437
    commonalities, understanding, 434
    key concepts about OO frameworks, 433
    variation, accommodating, 435
Logging_Server abstract base class, 432, 437
    open( ) and request( ) methods, 438
    run( ) method, 439
logical index into an array, translating to
        physical index, 160
logical operators (short-circuiting), in
        JavaScript, 136
longest match, 5
    leftmost longest matching, matchstar
        function, 6
look-ahead computations, 248
lookdict( ) and lookdict_string search
        functions, 300
lookup table
    binary format, 70
        loading, 70
        using to check a name, 71
    Java instance method calls dispatched
        through, 290
lookup type (Gene Sorter columns), 223
loops, escaping in binary search, 54

loose coupling of client applications and middleware services, 324

LU factorization, 230
    error analysis and operation count, 250
    LAPACK SGBTRF routine, 262–265
    LAPACK solution, 238
    multithreaded, 247–250
    recursive, 240–243
    ScaLAPACK solution, 243–245
    simple implementation, 233

Luszczek, Piotr, 229–252

M

m4 macro expander, 408

Mac OS X, development platform for secure mail system, 168

macros
    eLocutor, 499
    offsetof macro, 271
    for syntactic abstraction, types of, 408
    syntax-case macro definition, 411
    (see also syntactic abstraction)

magazines, 356

Mail Daemon (cmaild), Cryptonite, 171
    test suite, 172

mail system (Cryptonite), 162–184
    insights from development process, 162
    mail store, 173
        modifying to use IMAP as backend, 182
        performance bottlenecks with IMAP, 184
        replication, 175, 183
        revamping, 174

Mail::Cclient module (Perl), 184

Mail::Folder module (Perl), 175

Mail::Folder::Shadow module (Perl), 176

Mail::IMAPClient module (Perl), 184

main (I/O action in Haskell), 390

main action (Haskell), 401

Mak, Ronald, 319–338

managed code, 112

mapping (Python), 296

MapReduce, 371–384
    computations easily expressed as MapReduce, 375
    distributed implementation (example), 377–380
        execution overview, 377
    extensions to the model, 380
    programming model, 374
    resources for further reading, 381
    word count program (example)
        C++ implementation, 382

mark-object auditory icon, 514

marks, 413
    appearing in an identifier's wrap, determining associated label, 418

Mars Exploration Rover mission (MER), enterprise system for (see CIP)

match function, 4

matchhere function, 4
    longest matching implementation, 6

matchstar function, 5
    leftmost longest matching, 6

mathematical equations vs. computed solutions, 253

mathematical models, science at the application level, 229

MATLAB, 233

matrix algorithms, 230
    computer architecture effects on, 230
    development with MATLAB, 233
    expressing as vector-vector operations, 231

matrix computations through decomposition, 232

matrix functions built into MATLAB, 233

matrix-matrix operations
    Level-3 BLAS, 230
    linear algebra algorithms recast as, 231
    modularity for performance and transportability, 239

matrix-vector operations
    Level-2 BLAS, 230
    recasting linear algebra algorithms as, 237
    recasting linear algebra in terms of, 231

Matsumoto, Yukihiro, 477–481

mbox files, Cryptonite, 173

Mehta, Arun, 483–501

memory
    check looking at problem size and memory of computer, 265
    conservation of, 258
    content-addressable, 46–49
    usage by binary search, 54
    use of (LAPACK SGBSV routine), 260

memory models for N-dimensional array, 305

menu selection (context-sensitive), in eLocutor long click, 489–491

messenger RNA (mRNA), 218

Meta Classes (ERP5), 343

meta environment (exp procedure), 419

metacharacters (regular expressions), 1, 7

metadata in filesystem layering, 287

method form (syntax-case), 413

Microsoft Intermediate Language (MSIL) (see Intermediate Language)

Microsoft Windows (version 1.0), on-the-fly code generation, 106–112

P

package designs, Java, 66
PageRank, 56
pairs
    key/expression, in JavaScript object
        literals, 145
Panel class (Bio::Graphics), 192, 198
    configuration options, 197
    image_and_map( ) method, 210
    png( ) method, 212
    SVG images, 212
Parallel BLAS (PBLAS), 245–247
    array descriptors, 246
parallel programs, 385
parallel systems with distributed memory, 231
    effects on matrix algorithms, 231
parallelism
    application in web searches, 56
    (see also concurrency)
parallelized word count program
        (example), 372
    with partitioned processors, 373
    with partitioned storage, 372
Params::Validate module (Perl), 179
Parse class (Java), 77, 80–83
    doCells( ) method, 80
    doRows( ) method, 80
    doTables( ) method, 79
    ignore method, 80
    last( ) and more( ) methods, 83
    parsing code, 81
    representation of entire HTML
        document, 82
parser-based digit character verification for
        XML, 66
parsers
    JavaScript, 130–145
        array and object literals, 144
        assignment operators, 137
        constants, 138
        expressions, 134
        functions, 143
        infix operators, 134–136
        precedence, 133
        prefix operators, 136
        scope, 138–140
        statements, 140–143
        tokens, 132
    top-down operator, 129
    XML, checking for correctness in XML
        input, 66
parsing techniques in LISP, 130
partitioned processors for parallelized
        program, 373
partitioned storage for parallelized
        program, 372

partitioning an index based on binary search
        in arrays of postings, 56
partitioning function (MapReduce), 380
partitioning in Quicksort, ideal method, 38
paths
    ERP5, 341
    retracing in eLocutor tree structure, 497
Pattern and Matcher classes (Java), 8
pattern matching
    in regular expressions (see regular
        expressions)
    syntax form in syntax-case, 411
pattern or brush (graphical object), 108
patterns
    applied to networked software, 430
    event-dispatching, 434
    frequently encountered in computer
        programming, 407
    used in OO logging server framework, 432
Patzer, Andrew, 451–462
PBLAS (Parallel BLAS), 245–247
    array descriptors, 246
PCI and USB devices in Linux sysfs, 269
performance
    indirection and, 291
    poor design as root cause of problems, 259
    Python dictionary implementation
        and, 294
    recursion and, 305
    regular expression matcher, 6
    testing for binary search, 101
    XML verifiers, correct design vs., 74
Perl, 50
    alarm function, 171
    anonymous subroutines, 207
    AUTOLOAD feature, 176
    BioPerl, Bio::Graphics module and,
        188–192
    Crypt::PGP5 module, 173
    Cryptonite mail system, 168
    Emacs's cperl mode, 168
    GD library, 211
    GD::SVG module, 212
    prototype-to-production path, DBD::SQLite
        module, 173
    summary of quirkier parts of syntax, 195
    Text::Template module, 173
    Tie interface, used to tie Postgres' large
        objects (BLOBs) to filehandles, 174
Persistence::Database::SQL class, 173
Persistence::Object::Postgres class, 173
Persistence::Object::Simple class, 173
personality text properties (Emacspeak), 508
    converting into audio formatting
        codes, 510
personnel management (MER mission), 322

re-execution (transactions in STM), 394
re-expression and symmetry in
        programming, 34, 37
ref( ) function (Perl), 208
references (variable), capture by a variable
        binding, 408–411
regexps (see regular expressions)
regular expression matcher
    implementation, 3
    reasons for compactness of code, 8
    termination conditions, 6
regular expressions, 1–9, 43–46
    for input validity in Cryptonite mail
        system, 179
    mapping into actions with lex, 288
    notation, 2
    program for printing article-fetch lines
        (example), 43–46
regulatory DNA, 188
regulatory protein bound to specific site of the
        DNA, 206
relational databases
    in eLocutor, 486
        predictor databases, 493
    ERP5, 341
    Gene Sorter and, 223
relationship managers (ERP5), 345
reliability of CIP, 325
    streamer service, 328–336
        logging, 329–334
Replace feature (eLocutor), 494
replication, Cryptonite mail store, 175, 183
Replication::Recall module (Perl), 175
Representational State Transfer (see REST)
representations (syntax-case expansion
        algorithm), 414
reserved words, 139
resources (ERP5), 341
REST (Representational State Transfer),
        452–462
    exchanging data using e-business
        protocols, 457–462
    exposing services to external clients,
        452–455
        defining service interface, 453–455
    routing the service using factory
        pattern, 456–457
restrictions built into code, causing difficult-
        to-find errors, 259
retrieval of data, 230
return statement (JavaScript), 143
reuse of code
    ERP5, 351
    promoted by good design and clear, concise
        code, 261

reusing data to reduce memory traffic, 239
reverse web link graph, constructing with
        MapReduce, 376
revision number, 12
right associative operators (JavaScript), 136
right mouse button as single binary input for
        eLocutor, 487
RISC computers
    with cache hierarchies, 230
        effects on matrix algorithms, 231
    fundamental instructions, 147
    population count
        basic methods, 148
river meandering, model of, 547
RNA sequences, 188
RNA, messenger RNA (mRNA), 218
robustness
    CIP (Collaborative Information
        Portal), 336–337
        dynamic reconfiguration, 337
        hot swapping, 337
    (see also debugging; testing)
Rosettanet e-business protocol, 453
    exchanging requests and responses
        using, 457–462
    web site, 457
RowFixture class (Java), 77
RPG legacy systems, integrating with modern
        client/server software, 460
RSS and Atom feeds, 522
rsync's rolling checksum algorithm, 11
Ruby programming language, 43–49
    array implementation, 52
    beautiful code support
        brevity (Hello World example), 478
        brevity and DRY, 479
        familiarity, 479
        simplicity, 480
    counting article fetches, 47
    delimiting code blocks, 48
    optimizing program that reports most
        popular articles, 49
    stripped-down design, 46
runtime environment (exp procedure), 419

S

same-marks? predicate, 418
Santa Claus problem (concurrent program
        using STM), 396–403
Savoia, Alberto, 85–103
Sawzall language for logs analysis, 382
scalability
    of beautiful code, 259
    CIP, 325
Scalable Vector Graphics (SVG) images, 212

ScaLAPACK
    LU factorization, 243–245
    PBLAS (Parallel BLAS), 245–247
Scheme language
    expanding expressions containing macros
        into expressions in the core
        language, 424
    primitives for converting strings to and
        from symbols, 415
    quasiquote syntax for creating list
        structure, 415
    syntax-case, 411
    transformation of or form into let and
        if, 408
Schmidt, Douglas C., 429–450
scientific method, applied to program
        failures, 466
scope, 138–140
    functions, 143
    new scope for a function or a block, 140
    OO framework, 434
scripting language (MATLAB), 233
scrolling in eLocutor, 498
searches, 41–57
    binary search, 52
        advantages and disadvantages, 54
    content-addressable storage, 46–49
    emacspeak-websearch module for task-
        oriented search, 517–520
    escaping the loop, 54
    optimizing program that reports most
        popular articles, 49
    postings, 55
    ranking results, 56
    regular expressions, 43–46
        using in program that prints article-fetch
            lines, 43–46
    time involved in running and
        programming, 41
    web searches, 56
    weblog data, 42
    writing search algorithm, 50
secure communications, 161–186
    complexity of secure messaging,
        untangling, 163
    Cryptonite mail system, 162–184
    hacking the civilization, 185
    privacy protection for individual
        rights, 185
Seiwald, Christopher, 527–537
self-evaluating? predicate, 417
sequential concurrency models, implemented
        in logging servers, 439–444
serialization, Cryptonite messages, 170
Service class (Cryptonite), 170
Service class (example), 454

service-oriented architecture (see SOA)
services
    exposing to external clients, 452–455
    in multitiered service-oriented
        architecture, 320
Session class (Java), 78
session key, Gene Sorter, 220
sets, computing size for sets represented by bit
        strings, 158
s-expression, 412
    conversion to/from syntax object using
        datum->syntax, 424
    representing a quote form, 421
    representing an if form, 421
SGBSV routine (LAPACK library), 255–260
    implementation details, 261
shadow folder for mailbox messages, 176
shadowed folder for mailbox messages, 176
shards, 56
sharpness filter, 113
shift right immediates instruction, 151
short-circuiting logical operators
        (JavaScript), 136
shortest match, 5
side effects
    in Haskell, 389–391
        being explicit about, 391
    minimizing, 227
sideways sum (see population count)
Simple Object Access Protocol (SOAP), 452
SimpleItem property sheet, 343
simplicity in code, 261
    Ruby programming language, 480
Simplified JavaScript, 130
single binary input for eLocutor, 487
single-binding let forms, transforming with
        exp-let procedure, 422
single-binding letrec-syntax forms, 422
single-chip multi-core machines, 231
skipping bad records (MapReduce), 380
slicing, 304
slopes
    calculating, 542
    comparing to test collinearity, 544–545
    measurement with respect to the
        y-axis, 543
small pieces of code, practicing with, 40
smoke tests, 91
SMP (symmetric multiprocessing)
        machines, 231
SOA (service-oriented architecture)
    loose coupling of services with client
        applications, 324
    three-tiered, CIP implementation, 322
SOAP, using REST over, 452
SOCK_Acceptor type, 443

values
Python dictionaries
different data types in a single
dictionary, 294
searching for, 46
var statement (JavaScript), 141
variabilities in OO framework analysis, 434
variable capture problems, 408–411
solving with hygienic macro
expansion, 409
variable names, Perl, 195
variables
CGI, 220
defining in current block (JavaScript), 141
naming, understanding purpose from the
name, 226
reading/writing a mutable variable, side
effect in Haskell, 390
scope in JavaScript, 138–140
VB (Visual Basic), 485
TreeView control, 488
indexing feature speeding up
retrieval, 492
vector machines, 230
vectorization of linear algebra
algorithms, 237
vector of I/O requests, Unix read system
calls, 289
vectorization and parallelism, algorithmic
approach for exploiting, 230
vector-vector operations
denoted by Level-1, 235
expressing matrix algorithms as, 231
verifiers, XML (see XML verifiers)
version-control system (see Subversion, delta
editor)
vertical line, y-intercept, 542
virtual evaluation stack (in IL), 120
virtual machines, 290
vnode call interface, FreeBSD version 6.1
implementation, 288
vnodeop_desc structure, 286
voice overlays (Emacspeak), 512
voice-lock (Emacspeak), 508
voice-monotone, ACSS setting corresponding
to, 512
vop_generic_args structure (FreeBSD), 286
vop_vector structure (FreeBSD), 280
filesystem layering support, 282
pointer to a bypass function, 284
pointer to vop_vector structure of
underlying filesystem layer, 284
populating bypass and default fields,
filesystem choices resulting from, 284

W

waking up threads in Solaris, 354
Warren, Henry S., Jr., 147–160
web applications, use of Bio::Graphics
output, 191, 210
web link graphs, constructing with
MapReduce, 376
web of trust
key authentication stronger than PKI, 186
key management interface in
Cryptonite, 177
visibility of information in Cryptonite Key
Ring view, 166
web page for this book, xxi
web searches, 55, 56
web services
communication between client applications
and middleware services, 324
use by CIP streamer service for client
requests and responses, 326
Web Services architecture, decision points for
choosing, 452
web site for this book, 382
web.xml file for servlet providing user
interface, 454
web-based genome browsers based on Bio::
Graphics, 211
weblogs, searching, 42
web-oriented tools in Emacspeak, 516–522
basic HTML with Emacs W3 and
ACSS, 517
feed readers, 522
Web command line and URL
templates, 520
websearch module for task-oriented
search, 517–520
webs of trust, 164
well-formedness (XML), 60
Wheeler, David, 290
while loop, 4
while statement (JavaScript), 142
wildcards
in regular expressions, 1
shell, modifying regular expressions to
resemble, 8
window handler (Subversion), 17
Windows Forms code (ImageClip
program), 114
Windows operating systems
native filesystem, 279
threading API, 429
Wingerd, Laura, 527–537
with-syntax form, 413

COLOPHON

The cover image is from *www.clipart.com*. The cover fonts are Akzidenz Grotesk and Orator. The text font is Adobe's Meridien; the heading font is ITC Bailey.

Better than e-books

Buy *Beautiful Code* and access the digital
edition FREE on Safari for 45 days.

Go to www.oreilly.com/go/safarienabled
and type in coupon code XVWGZCB

Search
thousands of
top tech books

Download
whole chapters

Cut and Paste
code examples

Find
answers fast

Search Safari! The premier electronic reference
library for programmers and IT professionals.

Related Titles from O'Reilly

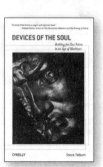

O'REILLY®

Our books are available at most retail and online bookstores.

To order direct: 1-800-998-9938 • order@oreilly.com • www.oreilly.com

Online editions of most O'Reilly titles are available by subscription at safari.oreilly.com

The O'Reilly Advantage

Stay Current and Save Money